Microsoft Windows Server 2008 R2 Administrator's Reference

The Administrator's Essential Reference

Microsoft Windows Server 2008 R2 Administrator's Reference
The Administrator's Essential Reference

Dustin Hannifin

Naomi J. Alpern

Joey Alpern

Aaron Tiensivu, Technical Editor

ELSEVIER

AMSTERDAM • BOSTON • HEIDELBERG • LONDON
NEW YORK • OXFORD • PARIS • SAN DIEGO
SAN FRANCISCO • SINGAPORE • SYDNEY • TOKYO
Syngress is an imprint of Elsevier

SYNGRESS.

Acquiring Editor: Angelina Ward
Project Manager: Paul Gottehrer
Designer: Joanne Blank

Syngress is an imprint of Elsevier
30 Corporate Drive, Suite 400, Burlington, MA 01803, USA

Notices
Knowledge and best practice in this field are constantly changing. As new research and experience broaden our understanding, changes in research methods or professional practices, may become necessary. Practitioners and researchers must always rely on their own experience and knowledge in evaluating and using any information or methods described herein. In using such information or methods they should be mindful of their own safety and the safety of others, including parties for whom they have a professional responsibility.

To the fullest extent of the law, neither the Publisher nor the authors, contributors, or editors, assume any liability for any injury and/or damage to persons or property as a matter of products liability, negligence or otherwise, or from any use or operation of any methods, products, instructions, or ideas contained in the material herein.

Library of Congress Cataloging-in-Publication Data
Application Submitted

British Library Cataloguing-in-Publication Data
A catalogue record for this book is available from the British Library.

ISBN: 978-1-59749-578-3

Printed and bound by CPI Group (UK) Ltd, Croydon, CR0 4YY

Working together to grow
libraries in developing countries

www.elsevier.com | www.bookaid.org | www.sabre.org

ELSEVIER   BOOK AID International   Sabre Foundation

For information on all Syngress publications visit our website at www.syngress.com

This book is dedicated to my grandfathers. Two men who will forever be the greatest of role models.

Contents

About the Author

LEAD AUTHOR

Dustin Hannifin (Microsoft MVP—Office Communications Server) is a systems engineer with expertise in various Microsoft technologies, including SharePoint Server, Office Communications Server, Exchange Server, Active Directory, and System Center Operations Manager. He currently works on projects related to unified communications, collaboration, systems management, and virtualization. Dustin regularly contributes to his blog (www. technotesblog.com) and other technology communities, including leading the Northern Indiana Microsoft User Group and the Microsoft Unified Communications *Virtual* User Group (www.ucvug.org). Dustin holds a bachelor's degree from Tennessee Technological University. Dustin, a Tennessee native, currently resides in South Bend, IN.

CONTRIBUTORS

Joey Alpern currently works as an independent consultant specializing in web development and database component integration. Since the start of his technical career, he has worked in various industries, ranging from the creation of internal systems for technical staffing agencies to dotcom start-ups, with his most recent adventure occurring in the luxury cruise industry. Joey holds a Bachelor of Science in Computer Science from Florida International University. With over 13 years of development and coding experience, he is comfortable with multiple languages, including C++, Java, Visual Basic, .Net, and even Pascal. Additionally, he is Java certified and often prefers working with computers rather than people.

Naomi J. Alpern currently works for Microsoft Consulting Services as a senior consultant specializing in unified communications and IT architecture and planning. Naomi engages face-to-face with Microsoft business customers, assisting them in the successful planning and deployment of Microsoft products. Since the start of her technical career, she has worked in many facets of the technology world, including IT administration, technical training, and, most recently, full-time consulting. Naomi holds a Bachelor of Science in Leisure Services Management from Florida International University. Additionally, she holds many Microsoft certifications, including an MCSE and MCT, as well as other industry certifications such as Citrix Certified Enterprise Administrator, Security+, Network+, and A+. Naomi lives in Charlotte, NC, where she spends her spare time along with her husband, Joey, chasing after their two young sons, Darien, 5, and Justin, 2. On the odd occasion that she runs into some alone time, she enjoys curling up with a cheesy horror or mystery novel for company.

TECHNICAL EDITOR

Aaron Tiensivu has more than 15 years' experience in the IT industry. He is a Microsoft MVP and SME for numerous Microsoft projects, including books, certification exams, and white papers. Aaron likes to keep up-to-date on all the latest products and betas. His current passions are Windows 7 and Server 2008 R2, Exchange 2010, Office Communications Server 2007 R2, and Windows Mobile 6.5 devices. His Microsoft-centric blog has been featured in the *Detroit Free Press* and other various media outlets.

Acknowledgments

This being the first book of mine as a primary author, I feel the need to thank those who helped make this possible for me. I first thank my parents and family for always supporting me and encouraging me to strive for the best, even when they do not understand the work that I am doing. I also thank Gary Byrne for keeping me on track and giving me encouragement when I most needed it. Thanks to all the great folks at Syngress for believing that I would make a decent author. Special thanks to Aaron Tiensivu for making sure that the content was technically correct (and providing some great suggestions along the way). Thanks to Naomi and Joey Alpern for writing two really tough chapters in this book. A big "thank you" to the GCC Tech Ops team (Ed, Jason, and Justin) for always encouraging and inspiring me. You guys rock! Thanks to my manager, John Pozivilko, for understanding those mornings when I walked into work late after spending most of the night writing. I also thank Carolyn Blanding for reviewing every chapter and giving me awesome feedback. Thanks to all of my friends, colleagues, and mentors whom I failed to mention. You inspire me to give it my all every day! I thank my creator and my God, who never ceases to bless me, even when I am so undeserving.

Dustin Hannifin, March 2010

Introduction to Windows Server 2008 R2

The latest release of Microsoft's flagship server operating system, Windows Server 2008 R2, builds upon the core functionality of Windows Server 2008 (R1) providing the most powerful, reliable, and feature-enhanced Microsoft server operating system to date. Windows Server 2008 R2 is arguably as important to the enterprise server as Windows 7 is to the desktop. Whether you are an experienced Windows Administrator or new to the Microsoft server operating system, this book will help you become more versed in managing a Windows Server 2008 R2 server environment.

This chapter will introduce you to Windows Server 2008 R2. It will explain some of the new features, such as PowerShell and BranchCache offered in the operating system. It will also explain the differences between the editions available and help you determine when to deploy each one. This chapter will conclude with the guidance for planning and designing your Windows Server 2008 R2 deployment.

WHAT IS NEW IN WINDOWS SERVER 2008 R2

The R2 release of Windows Server 2008 introduces some new and exciting features. These include not only enhancements to traditional technologies, such as Active Directory and Internet Information Server (IIS), but also newer technologies, such as Hyper-V and PowerShell. In this section, you will be introduced to a few of these new features.

Virtualization (Hyper-V)

If you are an experienced server administrator, you are probably well aware that virtualization is one of the hottest topics in the IT industry. With more green initiatives, increasing power costs, and the demand for administrators to manage more servers, virtualization has gone from an option to a requirement in many organizations. With the release of Windows Server 2008 (R1), it became clear that Microsoft intends to not only compete, but also become a leader in the virtualization market.

With the first release of Windows Server 2008, Microsoft not only gave users a true hypervisor, but also chose to give it to them for free. Windows Server 2008 R2 builds upon Microsoft's virtualization strategy by bringing new features to Hyper-V such as Live Migration, enabling administrators to move virtual machines between two hosts with no downtime or service disruption. Windows Server 2008 R2 also introduces Cluster Shared Volumes (CSVs) for Hyper-V clusters. CSVs allow multiple Hyper-V hosts in a Failover Cluster configuration to simultaneously access the same disk volume. CSVs are at the core of the new Live Migration features in Windows Server 2008 R2 Hyper-V. Hyper-V will be covered in detail in Chapter 7.

BranchCache

BranchCache is a new feature designed to provide a better experience for branch office users. BranchCache in Windows Server 2008 R2 allows servers in branch offices to store a "cached" copy of files and Web sites in the local office for quicker access in that office. BranchCache can be deployed in one of the two modes: hosted BranchCache or distributed BranchCache. Using the hosted method, a cache server is located in the BranchOffice. When a client requests read access to a file from a server across a Wide Area Network (WAN), the file is initially copied across the WAN and opened on the Requesting Client. A copy is also saved in the cache on the hosted cache server in the branch office. The next time someone requests to open the file, it is pulled from the hosted cache server in the branch office instead of the original source across the WAN.

BranchCache can also be deployed in distributed mode. Distributed mode works similar to hosted mode in that it uses a cache in the local office. However, in distributed mode, a server is not needed in the branch office. All cached copies of files are stored on Windows 7 client computers in that office. When a Windows 7 client requests a file, it stores a copy in its local cache. The next time a computer needs to open the file, it pulls it from the cache on one of the peer Windows 7 clients on the local branch office network. BranchCache requires both Windows Server 2008 R2 file servers and Windows 7 clients.

Active Directory

Active Directory has become the cornerstone of Windows Server domains. It is the core of many network environments supporting not only users and computers, but also applications like Microsoft Exchange Server. Active

Directory was first introduced in Windows 2000 Server and has evolved with more reliability and features with each server operating system release. Windows Server 2008 R2 delivers a series of new Active Directory features such as:

■ Recycle Bin—The Recycle Bin allows administrators to restore deleted objects to Active Directory. This feature is welcome to any administrator who has accidentally deleted a user account on a Friday afternoon.

■ Active Directory Administrative Center—Active Directory Administrative Center provides a new way for Windows administrators to perform common tasks within their Active Directory domains. It is a GUI built on top of PowerShell, giving administrators an intuitive and easy-to-use tool to complete daily tasks such as reset passwords, create new user accounts, and manage groups and organizational units.

■ Active Directory PowerShell cmdlets—PowerShell, with the Active Directory cmdlets, provides a rich command line interface to script and automate common Active Directory tasks. Windows Server 2008 R2 contains over 75 cmdlets to perform actions, such as creating new users, resetting passwords, and managing group membership.

■ Active Directory Best Practices Analyzer (BPA)—The Active Directory BPA is a tool to help ensure that your Active Directory deployment is healthy and properly configured. The Active Directory BPA scans your Active Directory deployment and looks for configuration issues or common problems. The Active Directory BPA will then provide a report and recommended remediation steps for the discovered issues. New administrators will find this tool especially helpful to locate misconfigurations or early warning signs within their Active Directory domains.

Internet Information Server 7.5

Windows Server 2008 R1 introduced a fresh, redesigned version of IIS. Windows Server 2008 R2 further enhanced IIS by adding new features like a BPA, a new version of FTP services, and enhanced auditing.

PowerShell

PowerShell is now preinstalled with Microsoft operating systems. PowerShell is a powerful administrative scripting shell written specifically for IT Professionals in charge of managing Windows systems. Windows Server 2008 R2 comes with PowerShell 2.0 as well as a host of cmdlets that can be used to manage various roles and features of the operating system including IIS, Active Directory, and Remote Desktop Services. PowerShell 2.0 now has the added advantage of the ability to send commands remotely instead of having to be logged on to the server to execute cmdlets and scripts.

DirectAccess

DirectAccess is a new remote connectivity feature included as part of the Windows Server 2008 R2 and Windows 7 better together story. DirectAccess allows Windows 7 clients to connect to a Windows Server 2008 R2 network via a secure ipsec connection without the need for traditional VPN (virtual private network) access. This new technology not only allows Windows 7 clients to connect back to the corporate network, but also allows systems on the corporate network to initiate a connection back to the Windows 7 client. This provides a new mechanism for remote management of computers that are rarely physically connected to the company's local area network (LAN). Figure 1.1 depicts a remote client accessing corporate applications via DirectAccess.

File Classification Infrastructure

As part of Windows Server 2008 R2's file and security services, Microsoft has added the File Classification Infrastructure (FCI). FCI is a new service that allows administrators to automatically create classification metadata

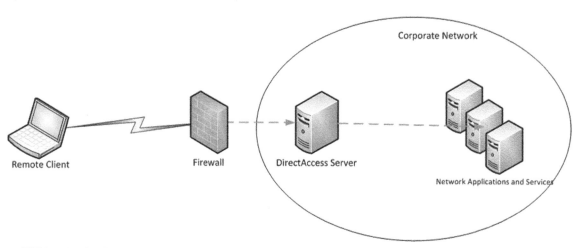

■ **FIGURE 1.1** Windows Server 2008 R2 DirectAccess.

for files based upon the type or the location of the file stored. Retention policies can be created based upon this classification to ensure that actions, such as deletion, are taken on documents that are older than the defined retention period. The FCI provides many new benefits to organizations that have regulatory requirements for managing electronic documents and records. FCI will be covered in more detail in Chapter 10.

Remote Desktop Services

Windows Terminal Services has been renamed to Windows Remote Desktop Services with the release of Windows Server 2008 R2. Remote Desktop Services provides the same functionality as the traditional terminal services did with some new enhancements to provide greater security and a better end-user experience. We will explore Remote Desktop Services in detail in Chapter 8.

WINDOWS SERVER 2008 R2 EDITIONS

Windows Server 2008 R2 is available in six editions. It is important to understand the difference between these editions so that you can determine the edition that best meets your organization's needs. Table 1.1 outlines the key differences between Windows Server 2008 R2 editions.

Table 1.1 Windows Server 2008 R2 Editions

Features	Foundation Edition	Web Server Edition	Standard Edition	Enterprise Edition	Datacenter Edition	Itanium Edition
Active Directory Domain Services	X		X	X	X	
Active Directory Federation Services				X	X	
Network Services [DHCP/DNS]	X	X-DNS only	X	X	X	
Virtualization [Hyper-V]			X	X	X	
File and Print Services	X		X	X	X	
DirectAccess			X	X	X	
BranchCache		X-Web sites only	X	X	X	
Failover Clustering				X	X	X
Hot Add Memory				X	X	X
Hot Add Processors					X	X

Smaller organizations with few servers may only deploy one edition, while some medium or larger organizations may choose to deploy multiple versions to support specific functions. For example, you will need to purchase Windows Server 2008 Enterprise edition if you plan on setting up SQL Server 2008 Clusters. As the network administrator, you will need to evaluate the differences in each edition and know when to install a specific edition.

PLANNING A WINDOWS SERVER 2008 R2 DEPLOYMENT

Proper planning is one of the keys to any successful server infrastructure deployment. Without adequate planning, it is not a question of whether your servers are going to fail; rather, it is about when they will fail? Proper planning and design should address both the technological and business needs of your organization. Planning up front can save you days, weeks, or even months of wasted time when you are in the middle of a server deployment. The approach you take to plan your Windows Server 2008 R2 deployment will depend on many variables specific to your organization. There are, however, a few important steps you need to take to ensure success during your rollout.

Making the business case for Windows Server 2008 R2

Large IT projects, especially network upgrades, rarely take place without business buyin. The single most challenging task of your network upgrade could possibly be getting business and financial backing. You will need to spend time putting together a business case to support your Windows Server 2008 R2 project. This business case will vary depending on your organization's culture and business needs; however, the following are some key features of Windows Server 2008 R2 that will provide a better experience for your end-users as well as save your company in IT costs.

NOTES FROM THE FIELD

Microsoft Solution Accelerators

In addition to the content in this book, you may want to check out Microsoft's Solution Accelerators for deploying Windows Server 2008 R2 features. Solution Accelerators provide guidance and scripts to help you quickly get going with a product or feature. Solution Accelerators can be found on the Microsoft Web site.

Power management

It is no secret that power consumption has recently become a concern for most medium and large organizations. Not only is there an increased demand that corporations take steps to *go green* but also the increased cost of power consumption by servers has become a real concern for many IT departments. Windows Server 2008 R2 includes several technologies to help reduce power consumption. These include virtualization and a new Windows technology known as Core Parking. Core Parking attempts to channel processing requests into as few processor cores as possible and suspends the cores not being used for active processing. Figure 1.2 depicts a processing workload being moved from one core to another, freeing up an entire processor which can then be suspended to save power. Microsoft tests have shown new power management features in Windows Server 2008 R2 that can reduce power consumption of a single server by as much as 10 percent. This reduced power usage can result in saving significant dollars in larger IT organizations.

Server consolidation

Server consolidation is not a new IT concept. Fewer servers mean lower hardware, software, and management costs. Windows Server 2008 R2 Hyper-V allows you to run multiple virtual servers simultaneously on one physical server. Virtualization technology is definitely not a new

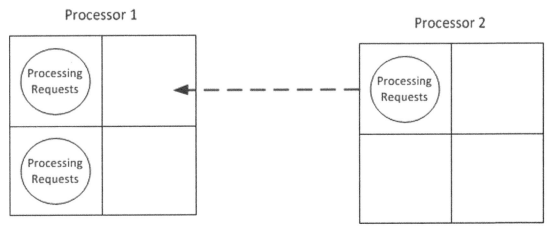

■ **FIGURE 1.2** Windows Server 2008 R2 Core Parking.

concept and several companies now have hypervisors available; however, Microsoft provides Hyper-V free of charge as part of the Windows Server 2008 R2 operating system. If your organization has not yet implemented server virtualization, you should definitely consider making a business case to do so during your Windows Server 2008 R2 deployment. The money your organization can save from server virtualization could easily add up to thousands of dollars per year.

NOTES FROM THE FIELD

Microsoft virtualization ROI calculator

Microsoft has created a free tool to help you determine potential cost savings by deploying virtualization technologies. The Microsoft integrated virtualization Return on Investment (ROI) calculator will help you build a detailed analysis of how your infrastructure can benefit from virtualization. This tool is found online at https://roianalyst.alinean.com/msft/AutoLogin. do?d=307025591178580657.

NOTES FROM THE FIELD

Do not virtualize everything

Virtualization is definitely the hot topic in the IT industry these days. However, not all servers and systems are good virtualization candidates. Typically servers that are already carrying a large workload and consuming most of the hardware's resources are not good candidates to be virtualized. Additionally, Microsoft does not currently support virtualization for some products that require audio/video communications such as Exchange Unified Messaging servers and Office Communications Server 2007 servers performing AV functions.

Improved remote access and branch office experience

Windows Server 2008 R2 includes several new features that help improve the overall end-user experience when using resources on your network. These features may not directly impact on the bottom line of your IT budget, but can make a big impact in the day-to-day tasks performed by your information workers. The DirectAccess feature in Windows Server 2008 R2 can help eliminate headaches of supporting and maintaining VPN remote access services. By implementing DirectAccess, users can make a secure connection to your network without the hassle and overhead of opening a VPN client and connecting back to the network. Additionally Network Access Protection, first introduced in Windows Server 2008 R1

(RTM), has been expanded to cover newer technologies such as DirectAccess. This ensures that as you rollout new remote connectivity features, they will comply with the NAP policies that may have been established using traditional remote access methods.

The BranchCache features can vastly improve the experience for users needing to open files and Web sites across your WAN from branch offices. This improved usability experience can not only make those remote end-users less frustrated by slow WAN links, but also improve their overall productivity. Happier and more productive users are always big pluses to mention when creating a business case for technology deployments.

Create a project plan

A good plan is critical to ensuring that your deployment is successful. If you are performing a simple deployment, this may be as simple as creating a step-by-step task list. Larger and more complex deployments may require more sophisticated project plans or even a dedicated project manager. In either situation, a project plan helps ensure that important steps are not left out and that timelines can be met. Spend some time ensuring that you have a good project plan prior to your rollout. Figure 1.3 depicts what the start of a small project plan might look like.

Document the existing network and server infrastructure

The more information you have about the existing infrastructure, the better. If you have designed your current network, you may already have some or most of this. If you are taking ownership of an existing network, or if you have previously dismissed the sometimes daunting task of

ID	Task Name	Start	Finish	Duration
1	Create Business Case	12/1/2009	12/15/2009	11d
2	Update Existing Documentation	12/7/2009	12/18/2009	10d
3	Create Security Plan and Get Approved	12/21/2009	12/31/2009	9d
4	Create Backup and Recovery Plan	1/11/2010	1/18/2010	6d
5	Create License Plan	1/15/2010	1/21/2010	5d
6	Design Network	2/1/2010	2/10/2010	8d
7	Begin Lab Testing of Design and Plan	2/16/2010	3/1/2010	10d
8	Remediate Lab Test Issues	3/1/2010	3/12/2010	10d
9	Begin Pilot Deployment	3/12/2010	3/18/2010	5d

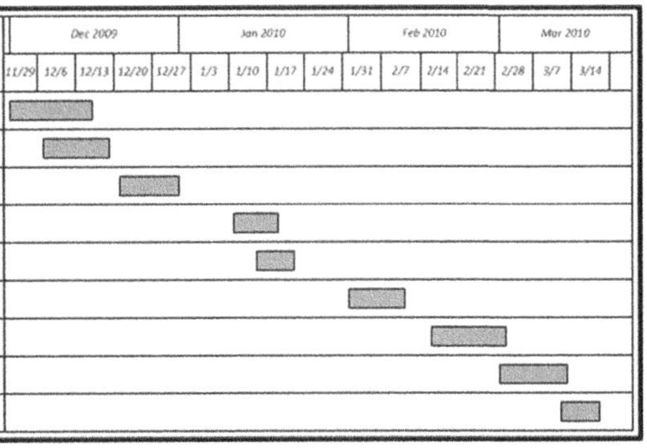

■ **FIGURE 1.3** Windows Server 2008 R2 Simple Project Plan.

creating good documentation, now is the time to do it right. Drawings of servers, switches, and routers help give you a clear high-level picture of your current network. Written documents and spreadsheets can be your best friends when you need to describe more detailed information about a particular system or network. There is no right or wrong tool to document your network. Just make sure that you do it in a way that is easy for you and other administrators to understand.

Security and legal planning

You will need to spend some time ensuring that your deployment plan adequately addresses the security and legal demands of your organization. These requirements will vary from company to company, but all good networks should have a well-thought-out security design. You will want to ensure that you protect your network from would-be intruders both physically and logically. Those who wish to cause harm to your network, or steal your business data may include a random person from the Internet, but could also very well be the disgruntled employee who just happens to have access to the computer room. Depending on the size and complexity of your company, a good security plan for your network may be a time-consuming task to complete. If you have a formal information security or risk department, you should discuss your network design and plans with them.

Your organization may be required to abide by certain federal or state regulations, such as SOX, HIPAA, or GLBA. These regulations usually apply not only to business processes, but also to procedures that determine how data are secured and stored within an organization's computer network. If your organization is regulated by any of these laws, be sure that your network plan follows them. Again if you have a formal information security or risk department, discuss the requirements to comply with any regulatory statutes with them during the planning phase.

Planning for backup and disaster recovery

One of the biggest mistakes network administrators can make is to leave out backup and recovery plans for their networks. Sadly, this occurs more often than not. Backup and recovery planning certainly is not the most exciting task, but it is definitely one of the most important. You can build the most reliable and best performing network on the planet, but it is worthless if you can not recover it in the event of a failure. Build a disaster recovery plan as part of your overall deployment plan. Test this plan before and after your production deployment and continue to test this plan on a regular basis. Having the confidence that you can recover your network in the event of a catastrophic failure is something that will help you sleep better at night.

Planning for licensing and activation

If you are not familiar with Microsoft licensing, this section will introduce you to a few of the basics. The first thing you should understand is that Microsoft does not sell you software per say, but only the rights to use software. When purchasing server operating system licenses, you will need to purchase the following:

- Server Operating System License—This is the license that allows you to install Windows Server 2008 R2. You will need a valid operating system license for each individual installation of Windows Server 2008 on your network. However, there are a couple of exceptions to this rule in the case of virtualization. We will discuss these exceptions later in this section.
- Client Access License (CAL)—You will need to purchase a CAL for each connection to Windows Servers on your network. You can purchase a CAL based upon Per Server or Per Device or User.

Per Server CALs versus Per Device or Per User CALs

- Per Server CALs require that you have a license for each simultaneous connection to a given server. This means that each server maintains a count of open connections. Once the connection limit is reached, the server prevents any new connections. This mode is a cheaper solution if you are deploying only one or two servers on your network.
- Per Device or Per User CALs require that each user or network device, such as a computer workstation, has an allocated license. This licensing model allows each licensed user or device the ability to connect to an unlimited number of Windows servers. This licensing method is best if you plan on deploying a large number of servers on your network.

NOTES FROM THE FIELD

Anonymous connections to Servers

You are not required to purchase licenses for unauthenticated connections to Windows Servers. For example, if you run your company's public Web site on a Windows 2008 R2 server, you only need to purchase an operating system license. You are not required to purchase a CAL for anonymous, unauthenticated users accessing your Web site.

Licensing and virtualization

As stated earlier, there are a couple of exceptions to the requirement that each server installation has a server operating system license. One such exception is virtual machines when running Hyper-V (or other virtualization technology). If you purchase a Windows Server 2008 R2 Enterprise license, you can run up to four Hyper-V virtual machines on that server without purchasing individual licenses for those servers. You may also want to explore purchasing a Windows Server 2008 R2 Datacenter license. A Datacenter license allows you to run an unlimited number of Windows Server 2008 R2 Hyper-V virtual machines on the server with Windows Server 2008 R2 Datacenter installed.

Planning for activation

Windows Server 2008 R2 requires that each server installation go through what is known as an activation process. Product activation is a recent antipiracy technology developed to prevent unlicensed installations of operating systems and applications. Windows Server 2008 R2 product activation requires that each server installation contact an activation server to confirm the validity of the license code used during the installation process. Retail versions of Windows Server 2008 R2 contact Microsoft activation servers over the Internet to activate. Volume license customers have the option of setting up their own activation servers using a service known as Key Management Service (KMS). We will explore KMS in more detail later in this book.

Design your Windows Server 2008 R2 infrastructure

A critical step in your project plan is to design your infrastructure. Just as you documented any existing configurations, you need to design and document the proposed outcome. Whether you have an existing network or you are building one from the ground up, spend ample time designing the end goal. A good design helps you ensure an easy-to-manage and reliable network while poor design can lead to a poor performing infrastructure destined to be plagued with problems. A few days spent designing up-front could save you days of troubleshooting on the back-end. Ensure that your design addresses both the technical and business goals of your organization. A proper design could be the single most important step of your planning process. Use a tool like Visio to draw your design and give you a visual representation of how the network should look after deployment. This drawing should supplement notes and detailed documents to provide a complete design. Keep in mind that you may have to modify your design during the testing phase of your project. You may find network services or issues you failed to address while running through the deployment in your test lab. When you find deficiencies in your design, note them, then go back to your design documentation and update it. Remember that getting this design right before deployment will save you a lot of headaches. Figure 1.4 depicts a design drawing of a small Windows network.

NOTES FROM THE FIELD

Get your design right the first time

The design of your Windows Server 2008 R2 infrastructure is one of the most critical steps in your deployment. If you are struggling with getting the design right, do not be afraid to ask for help. There are many reputable Microsoft Partners with years of experience who can help you with any aspect of your deployment including the design.

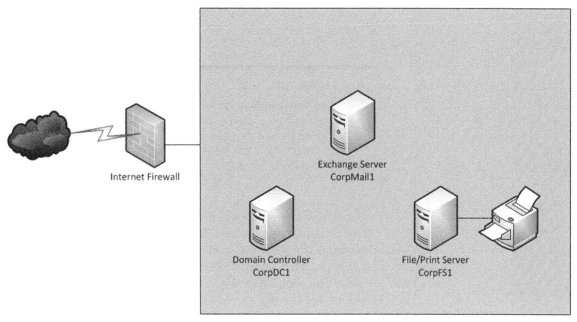

Corporate Network

■ **FIGURE 1.4** An example of a Windows Server 2008 R2 Network.

Test your design and project plan

After you have a good plan in place and have completed a design of what your network should look like, it is time to start testing. This is where you can iron out any kinks or issues you may run into during the rollout. A good test lab is crucial in helping you validate your rollout plan prior to making changes to the production network. The amount and depth of testing required will depend on your current network. If you are building a new network from the ground up, there are fewer configurations to test, while upgrading an existing network may require significant testing against various systems and workstation configurations already connected to your existing network. The following is a list of a few critical items you need to test in-depth before touching your production environment:

- Impact to User Accounts
- Impact to Workstations
- New and Existing Group Policy Objects
- Network Services (DNS, WINS, DHCP)
- Domain and Forest Functional Level Changes
- Domain Controller Replication
- Active Directory Schema Updates
- Impact on WAN Links

NOTES FROM THE FIELD

Upgrading from previous versions of Windows

You can upgrade some previous operating system versions to Windows Server 2008 R2 without the need to perform format the hard drive and perform a clean install. More details on upgrading to Windows Server 2008 R2 can be found in Chapter 2.

After vigorous testing (and remediation of any issues), you will then likely want to begin a pilot deployment as the next phase of your project. A pilot deployment will allow you to test your deployment plan in production, but only upgrade a subset of systems. This lowers your deployment risk. A major disruption would impact only on a subset of systems and users, opposed to your entire network. After a successful pilot, you are ready to begin your full production rollout of Windows Server 2008 R2. The rest of this book will explore everything from installing the operating system to planning for and deploying some of the more complex and feature-rich components of the server operating system.

NOTES FROM THE FIELD

Virtualization and test labs

The evolution of virtualization technology has made setting up test labs much less complicated than in the past. Before virtualization test labs were often costly, as you had to purchase tons of additional hardware to mimic your production network. Today, a few servers and virtualization allow you to set up your entire network in an isolated test environment. Virtualization also allows you to easily snapshot your test network, so that you can roll back your upgrade tests, enabling you to easily run through the tests multiple times and test various options. You should remember, however, that not everything can be tested in a virtualized lab. For example, BIOS that updates your production servers cannot be tested on virtual machines.

SUMMARY

In this chapter, you were introduced to Windows Server 2008 R2 and some of the new and exciting features included in the operating system. You also explored how to properly plan for your Windows Server 2008 R2 deployment, including creating a project plan, designing your infrastructure, and creating the business case. This chapter also addressed some of the key questions that you will need to answer before deploying Windows Server 2008 R2. These include what edition to deploy and what licenses you will need to purchase prior to deployment. Remember that spending ample time in planning can result in fewer and less critical problems during and after your deployment. This is one step you do not want to leave out.

Installing and configuring Windows Server 2008 R2

Properly installing any network operating system (OS) is crucial to ensuring that a server is stable and reliable. It is important to understand the installation process thoroughly prior to deploying Windows Server 2008 R2 into a production network. In this chapter, you will learn about the process to ensure that installation prerequisites are met. You will also explore the Windows Server 2008 R2 installation process and post-installation activities including activation. This chapter will conclude with an introduction to automating installation and a review of administration basics.

PREPARING TO INSTALL WINDOWS SERVER 2008 R2

Prior to installing Windows Server 2008 R2, you need to properly plan your installation and ensure that the prerequisites are met. This planning includes being sure that the server hardware meets the system requirements, determining whether to upgrade an existing OS, and selecting the appropriate Windows Server edition. If performing a custom installation (also known as a clean installation), you will also need to properly size the disk partitions. Spend some time preparing your installation before jumping into it. You will be glad that you did it.

Hardware requirements

Microsoft publishes hardware requirements, also known as system requirements, for every OS it releases. These requirements include the minimum processor speed, memory, and disk space required to install Windows. In almost all cases, you will want to make sure that your hardware exceeds these requirements to provide adequate performance for the services and applications running on the server. The chart in Table 2.1 outlines the minimum hardware requirements to install Windows Server 2008 R2.

Table 2.1 Windows Server 2008 R2 Minimum Hardware Requirements

Hardware	Minimum Requirement
Disk Space	32 GB or more,10 GB or more for Foundation Edition
Processor	1.4 GHz 64 bit
Memory	512 MB
Display	(800 × 600) Capable video adapter and monitor

NOTES FROM THE FIELD

The need for more disk space

You will probably notice that Windows Server 2008 requires significantly more disk space than Windows Server 2003. This is due to the new Windows component store (WinSXS Directory). The component store is where every component of the OS is housed. Even components such as roles and features that are not currently added are in the component store. You will notice that as you add new features and components in Windows Server 2008, you are never prompted for the original installation media. You should also understand that as components are updated via patches and service packs, previous versions are maintained in the component store. This is to ensure reliability of the OS in the event that a service pack or update is uninstalled.

NOTES FROM THE FIELD

Windows Server 2008 R2—64 bit only

Windows Server 2008 R2 is the first Microsoft server OS to support only 64-bit (×64) hardware. This may seem like bad news on the surface; however, it is highly unlikely that you have purchased a new server hardware in the past few years that does not contain 64-bit processors. Newer applications can see markedly increased performance benefits by using more than 3 GB of RAM. By adding more memory, server applications can store more data within fast RAM memory as opposed to having to access information from slow disk drive locations. Today most production grade servers already come preloaded with 4 GB or more of memory. The decision to provide only 64-bit code follows suite with Microsoft's general direction of moving all servers and applications to 64-bit architecture. Other products that support deployment on a 64-bit platform include Exchange Server 2007 and 2010, Office Communications Server 2007 R2, and SharePoint Server 2010.

Preparing the hardware

Prior to installing any OS, you should ensure that your server hardware is optimized. Taking this extra step can ensure a smooth installation process and lessen the likelihood of having to troubleshoot installation errors. Before installing Windows, be sure to complete the following hardware upgrades:

- Install the latest BIOS update
- Update any storage controllers, including storage area network (SAN) host bus adapters (HBA), to the latest firmware release.
- If you plan on using hardware RAID (Redundant Array of Independent Disks), configure it at this time.

Optionally, you may want to power-on the server hardware and let it run for 24 h to perform a "burn in" process. This could reveal issues related to bad hardware components prior to deploying a server to production. This process can also be completed after OS installation.

BEST PRACTICES

Use certified hardware for maximum reliability

For optimal performance and reliability, you should use hardware certified for Windows Server 2008 R2. Certified hardware has been tested to ensure that systems using this hardware remain stable and highly available. Microsoft reports that the main cause of Windows crashes is due to hardware drivers. Using certified hardware will greatly reduce your risk of Blue Screens of Death (BSOD). Microsoft keeps an online list of certified hardware on the Windows Server Catalog Web site at www.windowsservercatalog.com/.

Choosing to upgrade or perform a custom installation

Prior to installing Windows Server 2008 R2, you will need to determine whether to perform a custom installation or upgrade an existing OS. If you are building a new network, or do not currently have servers with a supported upgrade path, then this decision is made for you. You must perform a custom installation. The following provides more details on Upgrades and Custom Installs:

- *Upgrade*—Choosing to upgrade will take you through a process of installing Windows Server 2008 R2, replacing the existing OS, but maintaining data, and user and application settings. As mentioned, the upgrade option is available to you when you have existing Windows

Servers on your network that have a supported upgrade path. Upgrades can be helpful if you have complex applications installed that may require hours to reinstall and configure.

- *Custom (advanced)*—Choosing to perform a custom installation achieves the same result as performing an upgrade except that no data, user settings, or application settings are retained. This is also known as a clean installation. Using this option, along with formatting the OS partition, ensures an optimized fresh installation. This option is required when no existing, upgradable Windows Server OSs are currently installed on the server hardware. This is the most commonly used installation option.

NOTES FROM THE FIELD

Verify hardware requirements before upgrading

Choosing to upgrade does not exclude the necessity for the system to meet minimum hardware requirements. If you choose to upgrade to Windows Server 2008 R2, you will still need to evaluate your server hardware to ensure that it will properly support the new OS and the applications it will host.

Selecting the edition and installation option

Before you can install Windows Server 2008 R2, you will need to know which edition to install and the appropriate installation option to use. You can review the differences between editions in Chapter 1. After selecting your edition, you will need to choose the appropriate installation option. Windows Server 2008 R2 provides you with two options for installation. You can explore these options in more detail in the next section.

Full server installation

This installation option performs a fully featured installation of Windows Server 2008 R2. A full server installation is the same as a traditional Windows Server installation. You may be familiar with this installation option if you have installed previous versions of Windows, such as Windows Server 2003. All of the usual windows components are installed, including the full graphical user interface (GUI) and admin tools. A full server installation can perform any of the functions available in the given edition. This is the best installation option to use when flexibility and full Windows features are needed.

Server core

The server core option provides a very secure, barebones installation of Windows Server 2008 R2. Server core does not include a GUI interface and must be managed via command line or PowerShell locally, or by remote administration tools. This installation option provides a much smaller attack service by installing only the core OS and the components necessary to support the following roles:

- Active Directory Domain Services
- Active Directory Certificate Services
- Active Directory Lightweight Directory Services
- DHCP Server
- DNS Server
- File Server
- Hyper-V
- Print Server
- Media Services
- Web Server

The server core option is a good choice when deploying servers to provide core network services in branch offices. Server core is also a good option where the highest security levels are required.

NOTES FROM THE FIELD

Changing editions postinstallation

Windows Server 2008 R2 introduces a new utility named the Deployment Image Servicing and Management (DISM) tool. This command line utility can be used to upgrade your edition of Windows Server 2008 R2. For example, suppose you install Windows Server 2008 R2 standard edition. After deployment, you decide that you want to configure this server as part of a cluster. Prior to Windows Server 2008 R2, you would have had to completely reinstall the OS and choose the enterprise edition. The DISM tool allows you to upgrade from Foundation to Standard, from Standard to Enterprise, and from Enterprise to Datacenter, using a simple upgrade process and without the need for the original installation media.

INSTALLING WINDOWS SERVER 2008 R2

After you have performed the preinstallation tasks, you are ready to install the OS. In this section, we will go through installing a clean, full server installation of Windows Server 2008 R2. We will be using Enterprise edition in our example; however, this same process also applies to Foundation, Standard, and Datacenter editions. Begin the installation by doing the following:

1. Place the Windows Server DVD into the server's DVD drive and reboot or power on the server.

BEST PRACTICES

Create an installation checklist

You should create a checklist of steps that are required to install and configure Windows Servers for your network. This checklist should contain any special options or configurations that you may have for your network. Keep this checklist updated and follow it to ensure that all the OS installations are standardized. A sample checklist to get you started is provided at the end of this chapter.

---

2. The system should find that the DVD is bootable and begin booting from it. You may be prompted to *Press any key to boot from CD*. If you receive this prompt, simply press a key to confirm that you do want to boot from the installation DVD.
3. The Windows Server 2008 R2 Setup wizard will start.
4. Choose your preferred *Language, Currency,* and *Keyboard* as seen in Figure 2.1, and then click *Next*.
5. You will then be taken to the main installation screen as seen in Figure 2.2. Here you can choose to perform a repair of Windows or start a new installation. Click the *Install Now* option to begin the installation process.
6. Next you will need to select the edition and the option for the Windows Server 2008 R2 installation (see Figure 2.3). In this example, select to install *Windows Server 2008 R2 Enterprise (Full Installation)*. Then click the *Next* button.
7. The next step is to accept the software license agreement and click *Next* to continue the installation.

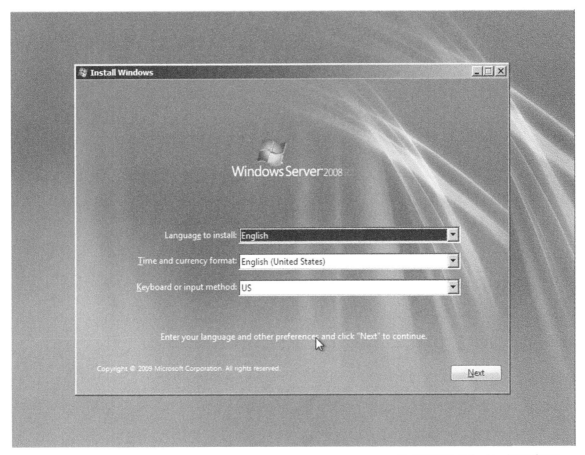

■ **FIGURE 2.1** Preferred Localization Settings.

8. You are now presented with the option to perform either an *Upgrade* or *Custom (advanced)* installation (see Figure 2.4). Since this is a new installation, select the *Custom (advanced)* option to perform a clean installation.
9. Next you will need to choose the drive that you wish to install the OS on. If you do not see any disk drives listed as seen in Figure 2.5, you may need to load a third party storage controller driver. You can do this by selecting the *Load Driver* option. This will allow you to

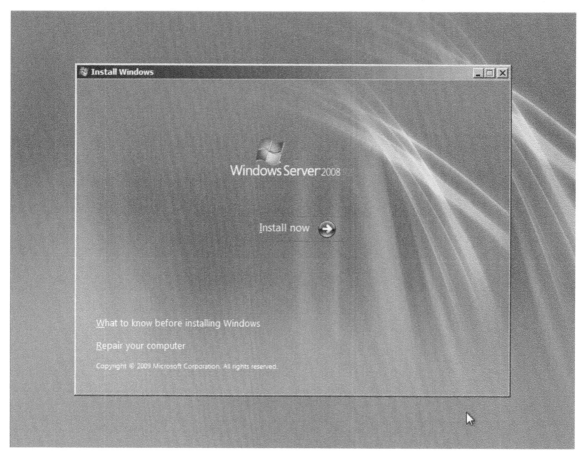

■ **FIGURE 2.2** Main Windows Server 2008 R2
Install Screen.

browse a CD/DVD, USB, or other removable media to locate a driver
for your storage controller. After at least one disk drive appears,
you can select the drive you wish to install Windows on. If there
are multiple partitions on the drive, you can select which partition
you would like to install Windows on. You can also use this screen
to repartition and format drives. In this example, you will notice
that disk drive zero is the only option. After selecting the appropriate
disk drive, click *Next*.

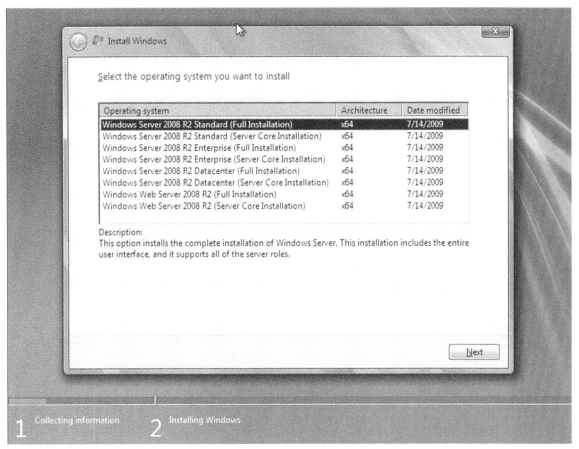

■ **FIGURE 2.3** Selecting a Windows Server 2008 R2 Edition.

10. The installation process will now begin as seen in Figure 2.6. The time to complete the initial installation will depend on several variables including the performance of your server hardware. At this point, Windows Server 2008 R2 will perform the full installation process and automatically reboot. After the installation has been completed, you will be presented the initial log on screen as shown in Figure 2.7.

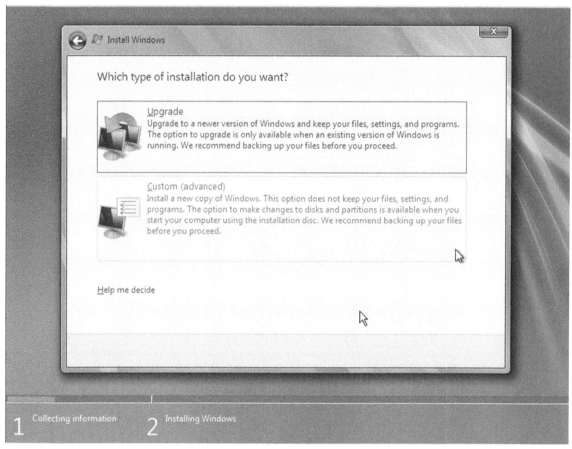

■ **FIGURE 2.4** Choosing to Upgrade or Perform Custom (advanced) Installation.

NOTES FROM THE FIELD

Changes to the Windows installation process

Prior to Windows Server 2008 R1, you were presented with a series of prompts throughout the installation process. When installing Windows Server 2003 R2 and below, you would need to closely watch the installation process as you would need to provide the computer name, network information, and an initial password all during the installation process. These configuration options are all now done when the installation is complete. This means that you can start an installation and perform other tasks without worrying about being prompted to provide configuration information. It is ok. . . go grab a cup of coffee. . . you no longer have to worry about keeping an eye on those server installations.

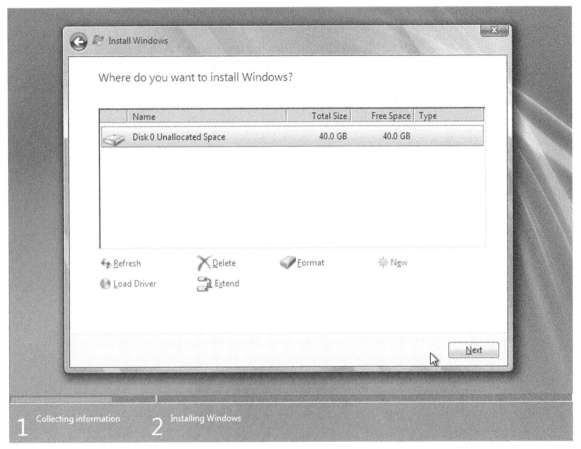

11. Create an initial Administrator password (be sure to use a strong password) and click on *OK*.

This completes the initial installation of Windows Server 2008 R2. You are now ready to perform the postinstallation tasks.

Installing Windows Server 2008 R2—Server Core

Installing Windows Server 2008 R2 Server Core basically follows the same process as installing the full server option. The key differences are revealed only after installation after you log on for the first time. Figure 2.8 shows the console of a server core installation. You can see that there is no windows explorer GUI interface.

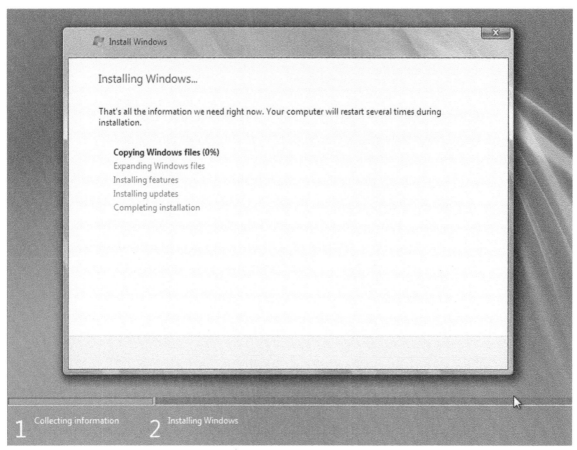

■ **FIGURE 2.6** Windows Server 2008 R2
Installation in Progress.

Upgrading from previous Windows versions

As you learned earlier, there may be occasions when you want to upgrade an existing Windows installation to Windows Server 2008 R2. You will want to ensure that all necessary prerequisites, including hardware system requirements, are met before attempting to upgrade to Windows Server 2008 R2. Additionally, you will want to ensure that the current OS has a supported upgrade path to Windows Server 2008 R2. You will also want to ensure that you have a good backup of the server and any relevant data prior to performing an upgrade installation.

■ **FIGURE 2.7** Windows Server 2008 R2 Initial Logon Screen.

Supported upgrade paths

You should understand that not all Windows Server OSs can be upgraded to Windows Server 2008 R2. If your current OS does not support upgrading, your only option is to perform a custom installation. Figure 2.9 shows the supported upgrade paths to Windows Server 2008 R2.

Upgrading to Windows Server 2008 R2

Upgrading to Windows Server 2008 R2 is very similar to performing a custom installation. However, instead of booting from the media (CD/DVD), an upgrade requires that you begin the installation from within

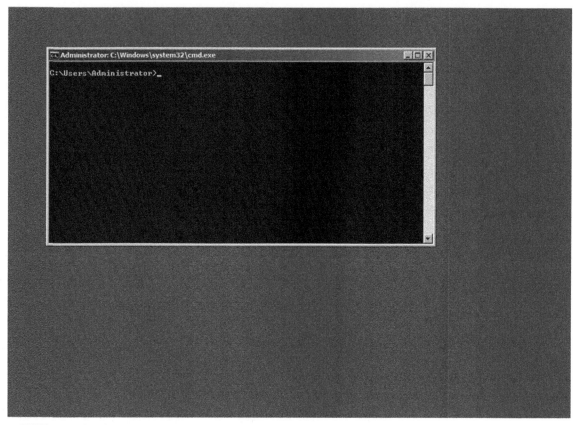

■ **FIGURE 2.8** Windows Server 2008 R2 Server
Core Installation.

the existing OS. To accomplish this, you should boot the existing
version of Windows and then run the setup program from the installation
media. Figure 2.10 shows setup running within Windows Server 2003 R2.

PERFORMING POSTINSTALLATION TASKS

After installing Windows, the real configuration process begins. Postinstallation configuration is where you really define a particular server's
purpose and the services it provides. Just as you have a checklist defined
for installation tasks, you should have a similar checklist defined for standard configuration tasks.

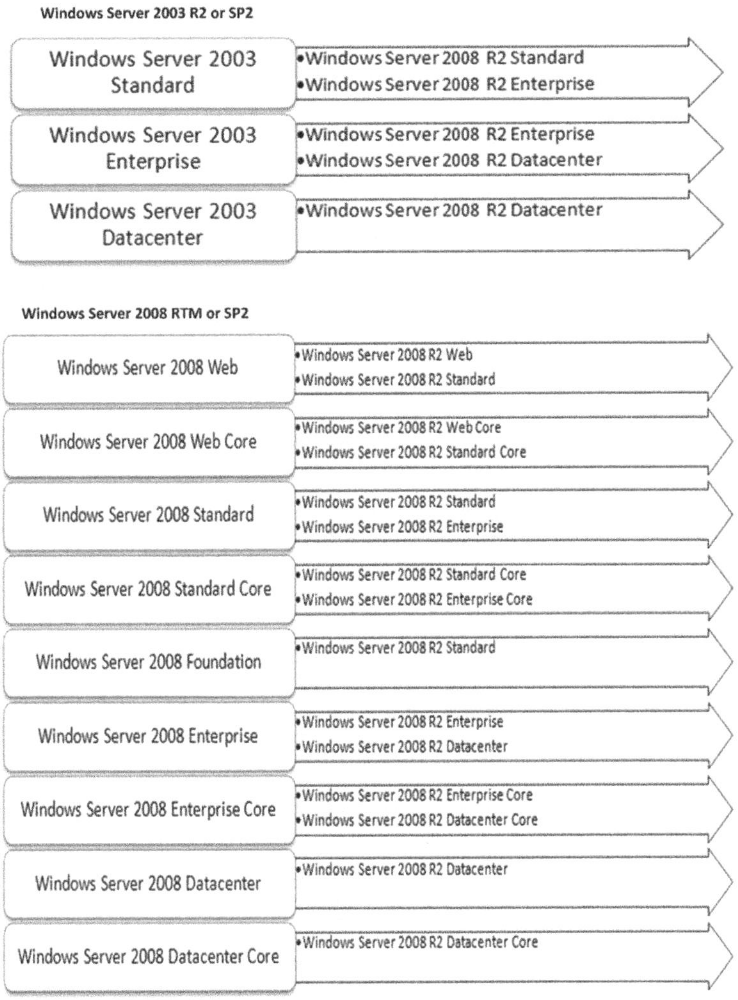

Windows Server 2003 R2 or SP2

Windows Server 2003 Standard	•Windows Server 2008 R2 Standard •Windows Server 2008 R2 Enterprise
Windows Server 2003 Enterprise	•Windows Server 2008 R2 Enterprise •Windows Server 2008 R2 Datacenter
Windows Server 2003 Datacenter	•Windows Server 2008 R2 Datacenter

Windows Server 2008 RTM or SP2

Windows Server 2008 Web	•Windows Server 2008 R2 Web •Windows Server 2008 R2 Standard
Windows Server 2008 Web Core	•Windows Server 2008 R2 Web Core •Windows Server 2008 R2 Standard Core
Windows Server 2008 Standard	•Windows Server 2008 R2 Standard •Windows Server 2008 R2 Enterprise
Windows Server 2008 Standard Core	•Windows Server 2008 R2 Standard Core •Windows Server 2008 R2 Enterprise Core
Windows Server 2008 Foundation	•Windows Server 2008 R2 Standard
Windows Server 2008 Enterprise	•Windows Server 2008 R2 Enterprise •Windows Server 2008 R2 Datacenter
Windows Server 2008 Enterprise Core	•Windows Server 2008 R2 Enterprise Core •Windows Server 2008 R2 Datacenter Core
Windows Server 2008 Datacenter	•Windows Server 2008 R2 Datacenter
Windows Server 2008 Datacenter Core	•Windows Server 2008 R2 Datacenter Core

■ **FIGURE 2.9** Windows Server 2008 R2 Supported Upgrade Paths.

NOTES FROM THE FIELD

Media not required

Starting with Windows Server 2008 R1, you are no longer required to provide the installation media when adding or removing Windows components to the OS. Microsoft has added the necessary files to the system as part of the installation. You can safely remove that DVD after the OS is up and running.

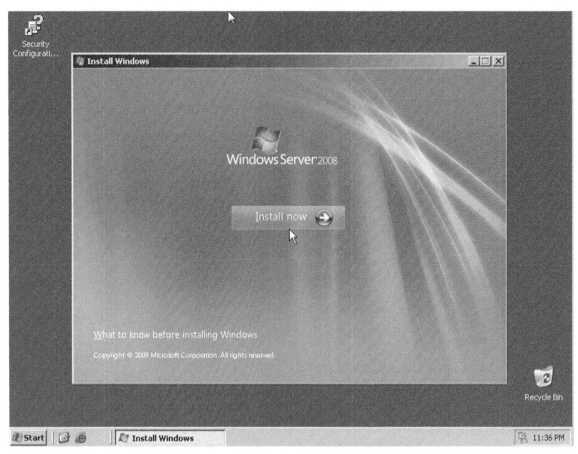

■ **FIGURE 2.10** Windows Server 2008 R2 Setup.

Configuring initial settings

After logging into Windows for the first time, you will be presented with a page that will assist you in performing important initial configuration tasks (see Figure 2.11) such as naming the computer, choosing the time zone, and configuring the IP address. Let us take a look at each of these initial configuration settings:

- *Activate Windows*—Selecting this link will allow you to activate Windows. We will explore activation in more detail later in this chapter.
- *Set Time Zone*—You can use this option to set the appropriate time zone for the physical location of this server.
- *Configure Networking*—Configure Networking will take you to the Network Connections window, where you can manage which network

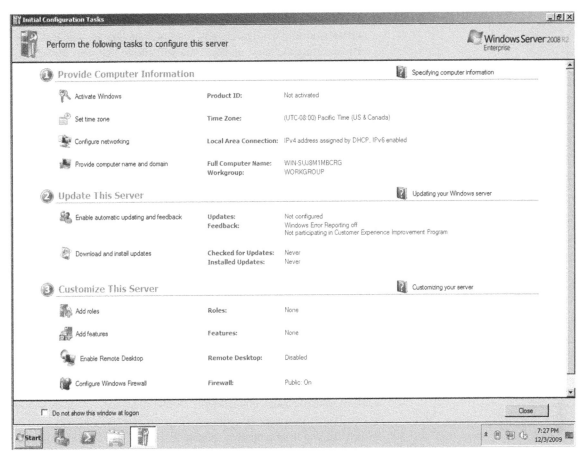

■ **FIGURE 2.11** Initial Configuration Tasks.

adapters are enabled, and which protocols to use, and set the IP configuration for each adapter.

■ *Provide Computer Name and Domain*—You can use this option to name the computer and optionally join it to a Windows domain.

■ *Enable automatic updating and feedback*—This option allows you to enable and configure automatic updates which can be set up to regularly download and installation Windows and other Microsoft updates. You can optionally configure Windows to send error reports to Microsoft anonymously. You can read more about errorreporting in the chapter on monitoring and troubleshooting.

- *Download and install updates*—Use this option to install the latest updates prior to configuring any roles or installing any applications. By installing the latest updates, you will ensure that your server is properly secured prior to production deployment
- *Add Roles*—Select this option to add Windows Server 2008 R2 roles. Roles help define the server's purpose and services that it provides. We will discuss roles in more detail shortly.
- *Add Features*—Add Features allows you to add features such as Windows Backup, or Clustering Services.
- *Enable Remote Desktop*—Use this option to enable Remote Desktop. Remote Desktop allows you to connect to the server's console remotely to administer the system.
- *Configure Windows Firewall*—You can optionally set up any special configurations for the Windows firewall at this time. The Windows firewall is discussed in detail in the security chapter.

Configure networking

The first configuration step that most administrators perform is setting up the network configuration. This can be as simple as assigning a static IP address or as complicated as adding additional network adapters or protocols. By default, the network adapter for your server will be configured to receive a Dynamic Host Configuration Protocol (DHCP) IP address. In most cases, especially, when setting up mission critical servers, you will want to change this setting to a static IP address. If you do choose to use DHCP to assign IP addresses to your servers, you will want to ensure that you have a highly available and reliable DHCP infrastructure. If your servers do not have static IPs or cannot request a DHCP address, they will be inaccessible from the network. Microsoft never recommends DHCP addresses for DNS servers and Active Directory domain controllers. If you want to play it safe, use static IPs for your servers.

NOTES FROM THE FIELD

NIC teaming

These days most servers come from the factory with at least two network adapters that can be configured in what is known as a Network Interface Card (NIC) team. NIC teams allow multiple physical network adapters to appear to the OS as one logical network adapter. In the event that one physical adapter, or the network switch port that it is connected to, fails, the server will fail over to the other adapter with little or no loss of network connectivity.

Naming a computer and joining domains

Each Windows computer on your network will need to be given a name. This name is used to uniquely identify the computer. When naming your computers, be sure to come up with a naming standard that makes sense. You should be able to easily look at a computer's name and know, to some extent, what purpose it serves. For example, you may want to name a Web Server Web1 or a file server NYFS1.

In most situations, you will be joining your Windows Servers to an Active Directory domain. If this is the case, you will want to do this during the initial configuration. Joining a server to a domain offers many advantages over a stand-alone, non-domain joined server. We will explore domains and Active Directory in detail in Chapter 4.

Understanding roles and features

Microsoft began introducing a concept known as "roles" in Windows Server 2003. The idea was to provide an easy way to install components that are necessary to support a specific function. For example, if an administrator wanted to set up an Internet Information Services (IIS) Web Server, to support .Net Web applications, he would historically need to know how to add the IIS components, the ASP.Net components, etc. Microsoft felt that it would be easier for administrators if individual administrator could just select the role such as "Web Application Server," and all necessary components would be installed to support that. The Windows Server 2003 role screen can be seen in Figure 2.12.

Microsoft further evolved the role concept with the release of Windows Server 2008 R1 and now Windows Server 2008 R2 by making the addition of roles as the only way to install components to support a specific function.

Beginning with Windows Server 2008 R1, Microsoft took components that provided additional features, and that were not necessarily required to fulfill a specific role, and grouped them into the "Features" area. Features allow you to add additional functionality, such as backup services to the server. For example, you may want to install the File Server role on a server to provide file sharing capabilities to your organization. You may later decide that you want to make the file server highly available. You would need to add the Fail-Over Cluster feature to provide this additional functionality to the File Server role.

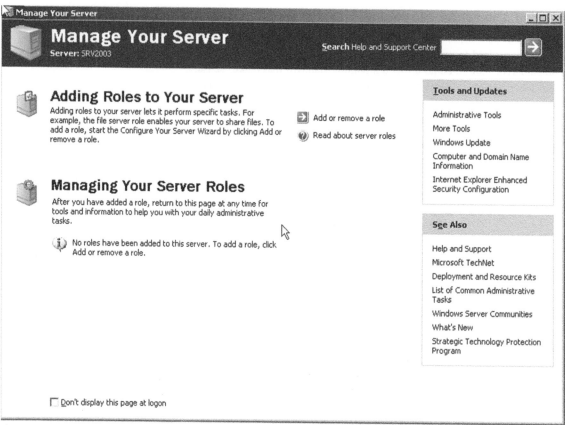

■ **FIGURE 2.12** Windows Server 2003 Role Management.

Windows Server 2008 R2 roles

In this section, we will review each of the roles available in Windows Server 2008 R2. You should understand these roles and the services they provide prior to installing them on your server. Tables 2.2 and 2.3 provide a description of the available server roles and features, respectively.

Installing additional software

In most cases, you will also need to install additional management software, such as antivirus applications, after you get Windows up and running. Be sure that you have tested these applications and services in your lab prior to installing them on production servers. The following are some important applications that you may need to install after the installation of Windows:

Table 2.2 Windows Server 2008 R2 Server Roles

Active Directory Certificate Services	The Active Directory Certificate Services (AD CS) role provides the necessary functionality to support a Public Key Infrastructure (PKI). AD CS can manage certificates for users, computers, or applications.
Active Directory Domain Services	The Active Directory Domain Services (AD DS) role adds the necessary components needed to allow the server to become an Active Directory Domain controller. After installing the AD DS role, you will still need to perform the traditional DCPromo process. We will cover Active Directory Domain Services in detail in the Active Directory Chapter.
Active Directory Federation Services	The Active Directory (AD FS) role adds the necessary components required to support a federated Active Directory configuration. AD FS provides a service known as claims-based authentication allowing organizations to extend authentication for their applications to other Active Directory forests on the same network, or across the Internet.
Active Directory Lightweight Directory Services	The Active Directory Lightweight Directory Services (AD LDS) role adds the necessary components required to support applications that traditionally would use Active Directory Domain Services to store data specific to that application. Applications can be used to store data in AD LDS instead of the production Active Directory domain data store.
Active Directory Rights Management Services	The Active Directory Rights Management Services (AD RMS) role adds the necessary components to support rights management features within applications such as Microsoft Office, SharePoint Server, and Exchange Server. Rights Management depends on PKI services, such as those provided by Active Directory Certificate Services, to add specific rights or limits to documents or email messages. For example, by using AD RMS, you can do things such as prevent others from printing a Microsoft Word document, or forwarding a sensitive email outside the company.
Application Server	The Application Server role adds the necessary components to support ASP.Net Web applications. This role will add things such as .Net Framework and Internet Information Services (IIS) 7.5.
DHCP Server	The DHCP server role adds the necessary components to support Dynamic Host Configuration Protocol (DHCP) IP assignment and configuration on your network. We will explore DHCP in detail in Chapter 3.
DNS Server	The DNS Server role adds the necessary components required to support Domain Naming System (DNS) servers on your network. DNS provides name resolution and is a necessary role required to support Active Directory Domain Services.
Fax Server	The Fax Server role adds the necessary components to support and manage fax services on your network. This includes managing other faxing hardware or faxing software installed on the server.
File Services	The File Services role includes components necessary to support and manage file servers. The File Services role can include components to build a Distributed File System (DFS) name space, support Distributed File System Replication (DFSR), or allow Unix machines to access the file server via Network File System (NFS).
Hyper-V	The Hyper-V role adds virtualization capabilities to the server. The Hyper-V role installs all necessary components to allow the server to support and manage virtual machines using Microsoft Hyper-V.

Continued

Table 2.2 Windows Server 2008 R2 Server Roles *Continued*

Network Policy and Access Services	The Network Policy and Access Services role adds components necessary to support network admission services first introduced in Windows Server 2008 R1. Network Access Protection (NAP) allows you to ensure that network computers meet certain criteria, such as having up-to-date antivirus definitions, before they are allowed to communicate with other systems on your network. The Network Policy and Access Services role also adds traditional network access components such as Routing and Remote Access Services.
Print and Document Services	The Print and Document Services role provides necessary services to support print servers within your organization. This includes sharing, managing, and deploying network printers. This role also supports management of document scanners on your network.
Remote Desktop Services	Remote Desktop Services, formally known as Terminal Services, provides the ability to centrally manage and run network applications on a Remote Desktop server, opposed to on the local PC workstation. The Remote Desktop Services role also includes components that allow access to the applications from outside the network and via a Web interface.
Web Server IIS	The Web Server role adds necessary components to allow the Windows Server to act as an Internet or Intranet Web Server. Internet Information Services (IIS) has been a component of the Windows Server operating system for years. Beginning with Windows Server 2008 R1, and now in R2, IIS is added via the Web Server role.
Windows Deployment Service	Windows Deployment Services provides a way to easily and rapidly deploy Windows operating systems to computers on your network. We will explore Windows Deployment Service in more detail later in this chapter.
Windows Update Services	Windows Server Update Services (WSUS) allows you to centrally manage and control patch management for Windows computers on your network. WSUS can be used to build an internal Windows update infrastructure to ensure that your network computers are updated as patches are released from Microsoft.

Table 2.3 Windows Server 2008 R2 Features

.Net Framework 3.5.1 Features	.Net Framework 3.5.1 features provide the necessary components to support .Net-based applications such as those written in ASP.Net
Background Intelligent Transfer Service (BITS)	The Background Intelligent Transfer Service (BITS) feature is a file transfer technology developed by Microsoft to ensure that large network file transfers are throttled and managed to occur in the background on network client PCs. BITS ensures that processes such as Windows Updates do not take network bandwidth priority over other network application usage.
BitLocker Drive Encryption	The BitLocker Drive Encryption feature provides full disk encryption for the Windows operating system.
BranchCache	The BranchCache feature is new to Windows Server 2008 R2 and Windows 7. The BranchCache feature installs the necessary components to allow the server to cache remote file servers and Web Servers locally. This helps increase performance of opening files and Web sites for users in branch offices.
Connection Manager Administration Kit	The Connection Manager Administration Kit feature allows you to generate profiles for client computers that use Windows remote network services such as VPN and Dial-Up.

Continued

Table 2.3 Windows Server 2008 R2 Features *Continued*

Desktop Experience	The Desktop Experience feature adds the Windows 7 specific features to the Windows Server 2008 R2 operating system installation. This feature is helpful if you use Windows Server 2008 R2 as your primary desktop operating system, or if you use the server as a Remote Desktop server for end users.
DirectAccess Management Console	The DirectAccess Management console allows you to manage and configure DirectAccess components on your network.
Failover Clustering	The Failover Clustering feature provides traditional clustering services to provide high availability to server roles and other cluster aware applications such as Microsoft SQL Server.
Group Policy Management	The Group Policy Management feature installs the management console to manage and support Group Policy Objects on the local server or in an Active Directory domain.
Ink and Handwriting Services	Ink and Handwriting services include handwriting recognition and ink services typically used by tablet PCs. This feature may be helpful if you run Windows Server 2008 R2 as the primary operating system on a tablet PC.
Internet Printing Client	The Internet Printing Client allows the server to connect and print to Internet Printing Protocol (IPP) based printers.
Internet Storage Name Server	The Internet Storage Name Server (iSNS) feature allows the server to support discovery on iSCSI SAN networks.
LPR Port Monitor	The LPR port Monitor feature allows the Windows server to print to Unix-based LDP print services.
Message Queuing	The Message Queuing feature supports Microsoft Message Queuing services used by applications requiring guaranteed message delivery.
Multipath I/O	The Multipath I/O feature allows the Windows operating system to use multiple, redundant paths to access back-end storage systems such as those used on iSCSI networks.
Network Load Balancing	The Network Load Balancing feature provides high availability and scalability services to applications such as Internet Information Server (IIS) Web sites.
Peer Name Resolution Protocol	The Peer Name Resolution Protocol (PNRP) feature allows computers to use a new multicast name resolution technology to locate and communicate with other systems on the network
Quality Windows Audio Video Experience	The Quality Windows Audio Video Experience (qWave) provides QoS services to AV streaming technologies.
Remote Assistance	The Remote Assistance feature allows users of the server to request or offer remote assistance desktop sharing. This allows another person to securely see and control the desktop of the person needing assistance.
Remote Differential Compression	The Remote Differential Compression feature provides compression and difference only transfer capabilities to services such as Distributed File System Replication (DFSR).
Remote Server Administration Tools (RSAT)	The Remote Server Administration Tools (RSAT) provides a series of MMC snap-ins and command line utilities for remotely managing Windows Server 2008 R2.
RPC over HTTP Proxy	The RPC over HTTP proxy feature allows client RPC based communications to be sent over an encrypted HTTP(s) tunnel. Outlook Anywhere capabilities of Microsoft Exchange Server is an example of an application that uses this feature.
Simple TCP/IP Services	The Simple TCP/IP services feature allows the server to support some of the traditional TCP/IP services, such as Daytime, and Quote of the Day.

Continued

Table 2.3 Windows Server 2008 R2 Features *Continued*

SMTP Server	The SMTP Server feature enables Simple Mail Transfer Protocol (SMTP) services on the server. SMTP allows the transfer of email messages between servers.
SNMP Services	The SNMP Services feature provides Simple Network Management Protocol services on the server. This allows the server to respond to remote SNMP requests or accept traps for SNMP-based monitoring applications.
Storage Manager for SANs	The Storage Manager for SANs feature allows administrators to connect to SAN storage systems and manage storage volumes or logical unit numbers (LUNS) within Windows without having to access the storage-specific management application.
Subsystem for UNIX-based Applications	The Subsystem for UNIX-based applications allows you to run applications written for UNIX-based systems on the Windows platform.
Telnet Client	The Telnet Client feature allows you to connect to remote systems via the telnet protocol.
Telnet Server	The Telnet Server feature allows users to connect to the Windows server via the telnet protocol and perform basic command line administration tasks.
TFTP Client	The TFTP client provides a command line client that can connect to and download files from Trivial File Transfer Protocol (TFTP) based servers.
Windows Biometric Framework	The Windows Biometric Framework feature allows you to use biometric devices such as fingerprint readers to log on to the Windows operating system.
Windows Internal Database	The Windows Internal Database provides traditional database services for Active Directory Rights Management, Windows Server Update Services, and Windows System Resource Manager. For these specific services, the Windows Internal Database can be used instead of downloading and installing Microsoft SQL Server.
Windows PowerShell Integrated Scripting Environment	The Windows PowerShell Integrated Scripting Environment feature provides enhancements to PowerShell including a graphical debug environment for PowerShell scripts.
Windows Process Activation Service	The Windows Process Activation Service (WAS) is used by .Net 3.5.1 applications and IIS 7.5. The WAS extends the IIS process model to Windows Communication Foundation (WCF) services.
Windows Server Backup Feature	The Windows Server Backup Feature allows you to perform file-level and full system image based backups of your Windows Server 2008 R2 servers.
Windows Server Migration Tools	The Windows Server Migration Tools include various utilities to help you migrate older operating systems to Windows Server 2008 R2. These tools can also be used to transfer data and settings from one Windows Server 2008 R2 installation to another.
Windows System Resource Manager	The Windows System Resource Manager allows you to manage how CPU and Memory are allocated to applications and services. This allows you to ensure that certain applications receive all resources required to function optimally.
Windows TIFF IFilter	The Windows TIFF Ifilter feature provides Optical Character Recognition (OCR) on TIFF-based images such as those used by Fax services.
WinRM IIS Extension	The Windows Remote Management (WinRM) IIS Extension allows the server to be remotely managed using WS-Management Web services.
WINS Server	The WINS server provides preDNS NETBIOS based name resolution.
Wireless LAN Service	The Wireless LAN service manages autoconfiguration features for the server if it is connected to any Wireless LAN networks.
XPS Viewer	The XPS viewer can be used to open XPS documents.

- Antivirus/AntiMalware Software
- Enterprise Backup Agents
- Server Monitoring Agents
- Configuration and Hardware/Software Inventory Agents

Configuring disk drives

As a Windows administrator, it is important that you understand how to manage and configure disk drives. As described earlier in this chapter, you can initially set up disk drives and partitions during the installation of the OS; however, you may want to add disk drives or provide more advanced disk functionality after installation. We will now take a look at different disk configuration and management features in Windows Server 2008 R2. After the OS is installed, disk drives can be managed via the command prompt using the diskpart utility or the GUI Disk Management MMC found in Server Manager. You can access Disk Management by opening *Server Manager*, by expanding the *Storage* node, and by selecting the *Disk Management* node.

Basic disks versus dynamic disks

Windows Server 2008 R2 disk drives can be set up as Basic Disks, the default, or Dynamic Disks which provide more advanced features, such as the ability to create a RAID set for increased performance and fault tolerance. If you want to perform software-based RAID, opposed to hardware-based RAID, you will need to change the disks that will be part of the RAID array to Dynamic. You can convert a basic disk to dynamic by right clicking on the disk in Disk Management and then choosing the option *Convert to Dynamic* Disk... as seen in Figure 2.13.

NOTES FROM THE FIELD

Hardware RAID and disk drives

Most server hardware vendors recommend that disk drives be set up as basic disks when using hardware-based RAID configurations. Refer to your server hardware documentation prior to changing disk drives to dynamic.

Dynamic disk volumes

Once disks are converted to dynamic, they can be configured to support the following types of volumes:

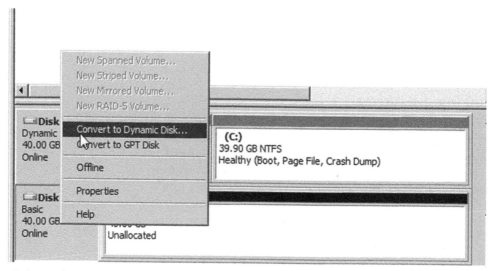

■ **FIGURE** 2.13 Convert Disk Drive to Dynamic.

- *Simple Volume*: A simple volume is the same as a single partition when using basic disks. A simple volume does not provide redundancy.
- *Spanned Volume*: A spanned volume is one that can span multiple physical disk drives that logically appear to the OS as a single drive.
- *Striped Volume*: A striped volume provides software RAID level 0 functionality. RAID level 0 does not provide redundancy in the event of disk failure but does enhance the performance of multiple disks via striping data across two or more disk drives.

NOTES FROM THE FIELD

Disk striping

Disk striping is a technology that has been around for years now. It allows data to be "striped" across multiple disks to enhance disk performance. Instead of one disk read/write head being used to write data, multiple heads from multiple disk drives can be used to write data, thus increasing the performance. Typically, the more disks added to the stripe set, the faster the performance.

- *Mirrored Volume*—A mirrored volume provides software RAID level 1 functionality. Two disk drives are set up as a mirror set, and data that is written to the primary drive is also written to the secondary drive. In the event that the primary disk drive fails, the second disk drive contains the "second copy" of the data and can become the new primary disk drive in the RAID configuration. This technology ensures data fault tolerance and redundancy, but you lose the performance enhancements gained by disk striping.

- *RAID-5 Volume*—A RAID-5 volume provides software-based disk striping with fault tolerance. A RAID-5 volume contains three or more physical disks to create one logical disk drive as seen in Figure 2.14. A RAID-5 volume gives you the performance benefits of a stripped set as seen in striped volumes, while providing disk fault tolerance as seen in mirrored volumes. In RAID-5 volumes, any single disk can fail in the array without any loss of data.

NOTES FROM THE FIELD

Disk hot spares

Some servers provide the ability to add a "hot spare" disk drive. Hot spares provide additional redundancy by providing a standby drive dedicated to replacing a failed drive in a disk array. Traditionally, if a disk drive failed in a disk mirror or RAID-5 array, the administrator would need to immediately replace the failed drive, as failure of a second drive would result in loss of data on the disk array. By using a hot spare, the server will automatically add the standby "spare" drive to the mirror or RAID array and start rebuilding that array.

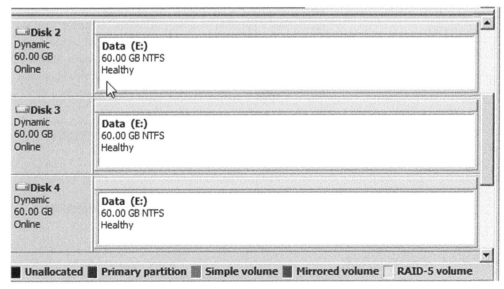

■ **FIGURE 2.14** RAID-5 Volume.

BEST PRACTICES

Backups and disk fault tolerance

Disk drive fault tolerance technologies, such as mirroring and RAID-5, should never be used to replace traditional backups. These technologies are great to ensure that you do not always have to restore data in the event of a single disk failure; however, they do not protect you from multiple disk failures or total server failure. Good backups are always a must whether disk fault tolerance technologies are used or not.

Creating a mirrored volume

Creating a mirrored volume is a fairly easy process. The first step you will need to complete is to add a second physical disk drive to the server. This disk drive will need to be at least of the same size as the first disk in the server. In the following example, we will configure a mirrored disk of the first disk drive which contains our OS installation. To create the mirrored volume, perform the following:

1. Log on to the server and open *Server Manager*, and then expand *Disk Management*.
2. Locate the newly inserted disk. The disk will probably appear as disk 1, as the primary disk is already known as disk 0. Right click on the disk drive and select *Initialize Disk* as seen in Figure 2.15.
3. The *Initialize Disk* window will open. Choose either *MBR* or *GPT* partition tables, and then click *OK*. When formatting disk drives, you must select a partition table format. Windows Server 2008 R2 offers the use of either the legacy Master Boot Record (MBR) or the newer GUID Partition Table (GPT) partition table formats. The newer GPT format offers a few advantages, such as providing redundancy in the partition table to help protect the table from corruption as well as the

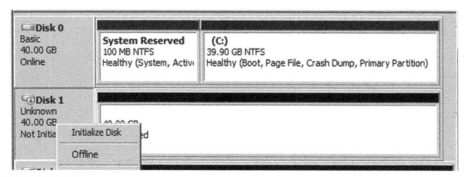

■ **FIGURE 2.15** Initialize Disk Drive.

ability to have partitions larger than 2 Terabytes. For volumes or partitions smaller than 2 terabytes, you can use either MBR or GPT, but for larger volumes you must use the GPT format.

4. Next, you will need to convert both disks to dynamic. Right click on the disk drive and choose *Convert to Dynamic Disk...* as seen in Figure 2.16. You will need to perform this for both the disk drives to be included in the virrored volume.

5. After the disks have been converted to dynamic, you are ready to add the mirror. Right click the original volume on Disk 0 and select *Add Mirror* (see Figure 2.17)

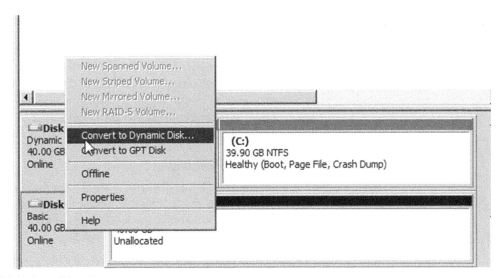

■ **FIGURE 2.16** Convert Disks to Dynamic.

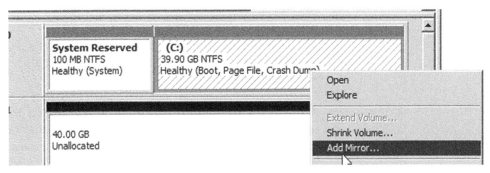

■ **FIGURE 2.17** Add Disk Mirror.

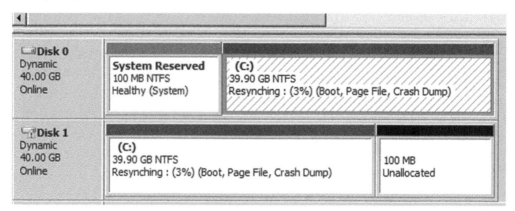

■ **FIGURE 2.18** Newly Established Mirrored Volume.

6. The *Add Mirror* window will appear. Select the disk drive to be used as the mirrored drive and click on the *Add Mirror* button.

7. The mirrored volume has now been established. The mirror will appear in a warning state as seen in Figure 2.18 until the two drives are synchronized. You can see the percentage of completion of the sync process in the disk management console.

Creating a RAID 5 volume

The process of creating a RAID-5 volume is very similar to creating a mirrored volume. This time you will need to ensure that you have at least three disk drives to be included in the RAID array. Once the drives are installed, you are ready to create the RAID-5 volume.

1. Log on to the server, open *Server Manager*, and expand *Disk Management*.

2. You may need to bring the newly installed drives online by right clicking on each drive and choosing the online option.

3. Once the disk drives are online, they can be initialized by right clicking on each drive and choosing *Initialize*.

4. You can now establish a new RAID-5 volume by right clicking on the first drive to be used in the array and choosing *New RAID-5* volume as seen in Figure 2.19.

5. The *New RAID-5 Volume Wizard* will launch. Click *Next* to begin.

6. Add the drives you want to include in the RAID-5 volume, using the *Select Disks* page (see Figure 2.20). Remember that you will need to include three or more disk drives to create a RAID-5 volume. After you have selected the disk drives to use, click on the *Next* button to continue.

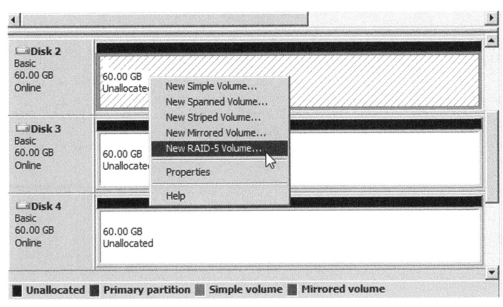

FIGURE 2.19 Create new RAID-5 Volume.

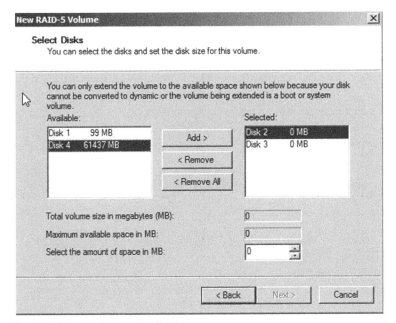

FIGURE 2.20 RAID-5 Volume Drive Selection.

7. Select a drive letter to be used and click *Next*.
8. Choose the option to *Perform a Quick Format* and optionally give the new volume a meaningful label and then click *Next*.
9. At the summary page of the wizard, verify the settings you have selected, and then click on the *Finish* button to create the RAID-5 volume.
10. You will be prompted to convert the drives to dynamic. Click *Yes* to convert the disks to dynamic.
11. You have now established a newly formatted RAID-5 volume as seen in Figure 2.21.

NOTES FROM THE FIELD

Shrinking volumes

Starting with Windows Server 2008 R1, you can shrink volumes to a smaller size if you need to do so. To shrink a volume, right click on the volume and choose shrink. You will be asked to enter the new size, and the volume will be shrunk to that size.

Disk fragmentation

As data is written to a disk over time, it can become fragmented. This means that part of a file could be located in various noncontiguous locations on the disk drive. This decreases the speed with which the read/write heads can access the data, causing slower response times while opening these files. To resolve this issue and ensure that the disk performance is optimal, you should have a regular scheduled disk defragmentation process. Luckily, Windows Server 2008 R2 includes a disk defragmentation

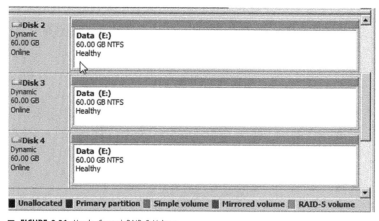

■ **FIGURE 2.21** Newly Created RAID-5 Volume.

utility and automatically schedules it to run on a weekly basis. You can modify the scheduled run time, using the Task Scheduler found in Server Manager.

Enable BitLocker

If you plan on using BitLocker to encrypt the disk drives on your server, you can enable it at this time. This will ensure that the drive is encrypted prior to installing production applications and services. BitLocker will be covered in detail in the security chapter.

Finalizing the configuration

After you complete the setup and configuration of a Windows Server, you should review all configuration changes prior to using the server for production services. Better have someone else review the configuration for you. This will ensure that you have not left out any critical steps, such as assigning the server an IP address or setting up backups.

PRODUCT ACTIVATION AND KEY MANAGEMENT SERVICES

Microsoft OSs are often used by individuals and business organizations that either do not purchase the licenses to use the software or purchase fewer licenses than they really use. To help counter illegal software piracy, Microsoft introduced product activation in retail editions of Windows XP and Windows Server 2003. Microsoft learned that many organizations were not necessarily looking to illegally deploy software, but that they failed to properly manage their license counts or casually reused licenses on multiple computers. Microsoft has continued to include product activation in Windows Vista, Windows 7, Windows Server 2008, and Windows Server 2008 R2. Additionally, Microsoft now requires volume license customers, who previously did not have to activate Windows to activate their installations using Volume License Activation Services. It is important to understand how product activation works, so that you can ensure that Windows Servers on your network are properly licensed.

Understanding Windows Server 2008 R2 product activation

After installing Windows Server 2008 R2, the first option on the initial configuration page is to activate Windows. Product activation is a process where your server installation presents an installation ID to Microsoft activation servers over a secure connection. The activation servers verify the validity of the installation ID. If the ID is determined to be valid, the activation servers send a confirmation ID back to your server and activate the system. You will be reminded regularly with a pop-up notification that you need to activate, until you do so. If you fail to activate Windows within a 30-day grace period, the desktop background will turn black, and you will continue to be reminded to activate. Services and applications will continue to function normally even after the 30-day grace period. Previous versions of Windows would prevent you from logging into the system and certain services would cease to function if you failed to activate Windows within the 30-day grace period. Microsoft chose to remove these limitations in Windows Server 2008. Perform the following steps to activate Windows properly:

1. Click the *Activate Windows* link either on the initial configuration page or inside the *Server Manager*.
2. Enter the product key that came with your license purchase (see Figure 2.22). Then click the *Next* button.
3. Windows will begin trying to activate using the server's internet connection (see Figure 2.23).

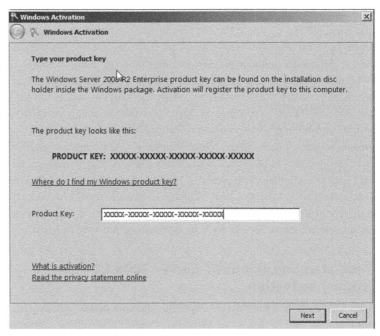

■ **FIGURE 2.22** Windows Server 2008 R2 Product Key.

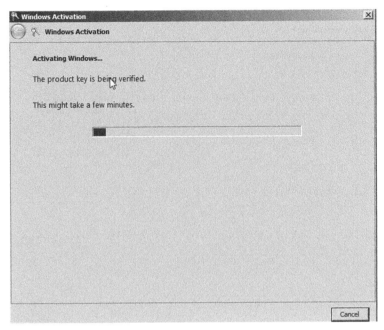

■ **FIGURE 2.23** Windows Server 2008 R2 Activation.

4. If activation is successful, you will see a success screen as seen in Figure 2.24. If the activation fails, you will need to use the option to activate via telephone.

NOTES FROM THE FIELD

Should I activate my lab computers?

If you are setting up temporary lab computers (used for less than 30 days), do not activate them. Keep in mind that you should use this option only if the servers are temporarily set up for a lab or test environment. If you use the server for more than 30 days, or as a permanent lab, you are legally required to purchase a license for that server. Alternatively, you can purchase a TechNet or MSDN subscription which has special license considerations for test lab and development servers.

Overview of Key Management Services

As previously mentioned, Microsoft now requires even volume license customers to activate their installations of Windows. This activation is known as the Volume License Activation. You can probably imagine that this may pose several problems to large enterprises that may deploy

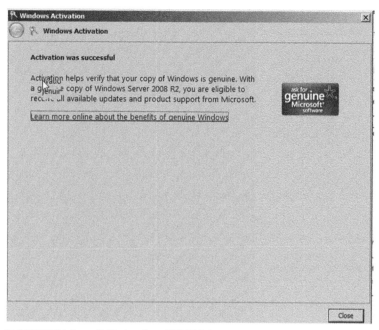

■ **FIGURE 2.24** Successful Windows Server 2008 R2 Activation.

hundreds or thousands of servers and workstations with Windows installed. To help make this process more manageable for volume license customers, Microsoft introduced Key Management Services (KMS). KMS allow you to set up your own activation or KMS servers on your network. These KMS servers securely connect to Microsoft activation servers using an enterprise activation key. The Microsoft activation servers verify whether the key is valid and determines how many licenses are covered with the entered enterprise key. The Microsoft activation servers then return information back to your KMS server, informing it of how many Windows Servers can connect to it for activation. The KMS server then builds a pool of activations. When a server on your network successfully activates using KMS, one activation is removed from the pool and assigned to the server that requested activation. Once all activations have been used, additional servers can no longer use KMS to activate. Activations can, however, be returned to the pool if the servers using them are decommissioned and removed from your network. Servers that use KMS to activate are required to check in, or contact the KMS server at least once in every 180 days. If the server fails to check in with KMS, then the OS will be deactivated. Deactivation will tell the server to act as if it were never activated at all. KMS can be installed on any Windows Server

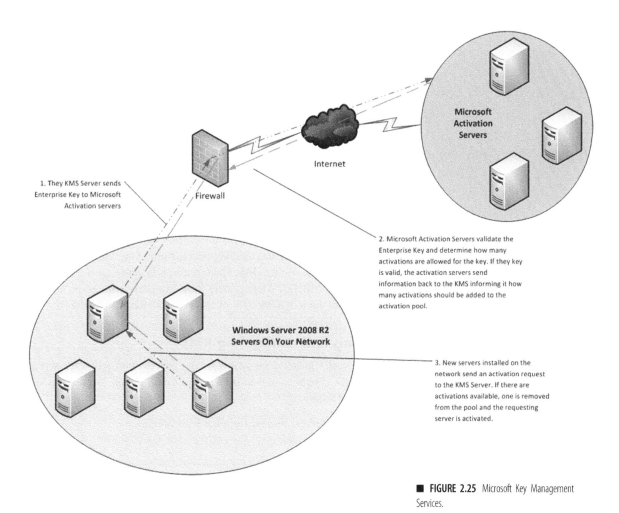

1. They KMS Server sends Enterprise Key to Microsoft Activation servers

Firewall

Internet

Microsoft Activation Servers

2. Microsoft Activation Servers validate the Enterprise Key and determine how many activations are allowed for the key. If they key is valid, the activation servers send information back to the KMS informing it how many activations should be added to the activation pool.

Windows Server 2008 R2 Servers On Your Network

3. New servers installed on the network send an activation request to the KMS Server. If there are activations available, one is removed from the pool and the requesting server is activated.

■ **FIGURE 2.25** Microsoft Key Management Services.

2003, Windows Server 2008, or Windows Server 2008 R2 computer. It can coexist on the same server as other network services. Figure 2.25 depicts how KMS works for volume license customers.

Designing a KMS infrastructure

You should properly plan and design your network to support KMS if you plan on using it for product activation. It is important to provide redundancy for KMS services on your network to ensure that systems can fail-over to another KMS server if your primary server fails. Servers requiring activation depend on the use of DNS Service (SRV) records to locate KMS activation servers on your network. As part of your KMS deployment, you need to ensure that you also have redundant DNS servers on your network.

NOTES FROM THE FIELD

KMS and Windows 7

KMS can also be used to activate Windows 7 workstations on your network. You simply need to enter a Windows 7 Enterprise Activation Key on your KMS servers, and they will begin activating Windows 7 workstations.

After setting up KMS, you will want to ensure that you properly monitor the availability of KMS services on your network. You should see special event log events related to KMS. There is also a System Center Operations Manager (SCOM) 2007 Management Pack available that can be used to monitor KMS via a SCOM 2007 or SCOM 2007 R2 deployment.

Installing and configuring KMS

KMS are easily installed on any Windows Server 2008 R1 or R2 server by running a simple command from a command prompt. To install KMS perform the following:

1. Open a command prompt from the *Start Menu*.
2. Type the command:

```
cscript C:\Windows\System32\slmgr.vbs -ipk <Your
Enterprise KMS Key>
```

Then press *Enter*.

3. Now activate the KMS key by typing:

```
cscript C:\Windows\System32\slmgr.vbs -ato
```

From the same command prompt, then press *Enter*. The KMS Server will activate and create its own SRV records within DNS, assuming that DNS services have been properly established on your network.

NOTES FROM THE FIELD

Minimum number of computers required for KMS

KMS will not begin activating computers until you have reached a minimum threshold of systems on your network. You must establish 25 Windows Vista

---

or Windows 7 workstations or 5 Windows 2008 R1 or R2 servers on your network before KMS begins activating systems. If you do not meet this requirement, you will want to continue activating computers with Microsoft using MAK keys.

AUTOMATING THE INSTALLATION PROCESS

It is likely that you will find yourself installing Windows Server 2008 R2 more than once or twice. Microsoft has done a great job of making the Windows Server 2008 R2 installation fast and administrator friendly; however, as you begin to deploy more servers on your network, you will want to make the deployment process more efficient than inserting the DVD into each server, booting the server, and manually going through the installation process. Microsoft has provided some great tools to help automate the installation process. After the automation features have been set up, Windows can be deployed to tens, hundreds, or thousands of servers with just a few clicks of the mouse.

Overview of Windows Deployment Services

Windows Deployment Services (WDS) is a server role that allows you to easily create and manage standard Windows installations or images and rapidly deploy them to servers and workstations on your network. WDS was first introduced in Windows Server 2008 and Windows Server 2003 Service Pack 2. WDS replaces previous deployment services, such as Remote Installation Services (RIS) for Windows workstations and Automated Deployment Services (ADS) for Windows Servers.

There are several considerations that you must take into account when setting up WDS. WDS requires proper infrastructural components that it depends on already deployed. Before using WDS, you must ensure that the following are set up and configured properly on your network:

- Active Directory Domain Services—The WDS Server must be a member of an existing Active Directory Domain.
- DNS—WDS requires a DNS infrastructure already set up and configured.
- DHCP—In order for WDS to function properly, a DHCP service must be available on your network.
- PreBoot Execution Environment (PXE) Boot capable server—Server that you wish to use WDS to deploy the OS to should support PXE. PXE is the process of booting a computer from its network adapter. Typically, this process involves downloading a boot image from the

networks and loading it into the computer's memory. This feature is available on most of the standard NICs that come with enterprise servers today.

NOTES FROM THE FIELD

WDS and network bandwidth

As you may assume, deploying Windows via WDS requires pushing a significant amount of files over the network. WDS uses multicast technologies to ensure that multiple simultaneous OS deployments do not bring your network to its knees. By using multicast, you can deploy Windows to multiple computers via one multicast network stream.

Installing and configuring WDS

After ensuring that the necessary WDS prerequisites are met, you will be ready to install and configure the WDS server role. To install and configure WDS, perform the following steps:

1. Open *Server Manager* by going to *Start | Administrative Tools | Server Manager*.
2. From the *Roles* node, click on the *Add Roles* link. This will launch the *Add Roles Wizard*. Click *Next* to begin adding the WDS role.
3. Select the *Windows Deployment Services* role as seen in Figure 2.26 then click *Next*.
4. On the *Windows Deployment Services* overview page, click *Next*.
5. Choose to install both the *Deployment Server* and *Transport Server* role services. Then click *Next*.
6. Click the *Install* button on the *Confirm Installation Selections* screen. This will complete the installation of the WDS server role.

Once installation is complete, you can access the WDS server management console via Server Manager as seen in Figure 2.27.

Enable WDS services and adding images

We now need to configure the server for WDS and enable the service. To accomplish this, perform the following:

1. Locate and expand the *Windows Deployment Services* node in *Server Manager*. Then expand the *Servers* sub-node.
2. Right click on the server name and select the *Configure Server* option as seen in Figure 2.28. This will launch the *Windows Deployment Services Configuration Wizard*. Click *Next* to begin WDS configuration.

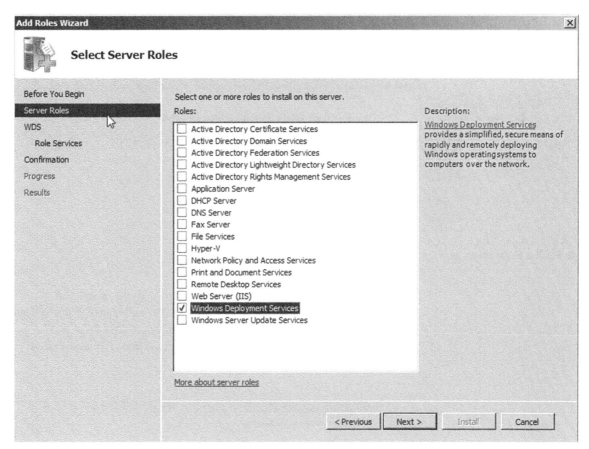

■ **FIGURE 2.26** Select Windows Deployment Services Role.

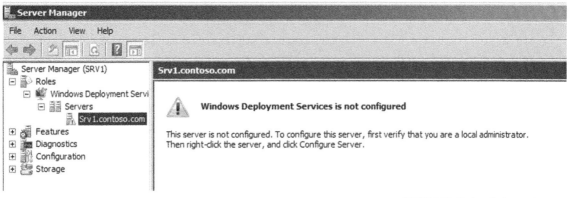

■ **FIGURE 2.27** Windows Deployment Services Management Console.

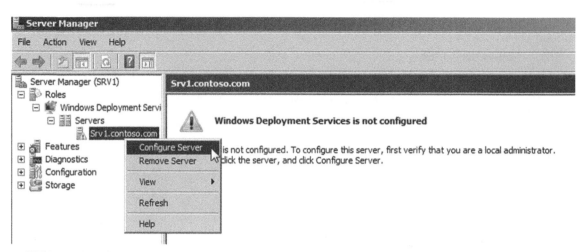

■ **FIGURE 2.28** The Configure Server Option.

3. Choose the location where you wish to store the images and installation files to be deployed via WDS (see Figure 2.29). You need to ensure that this location is large enough to store large files. Microsoft does not recommend using the same drive as the OS to store images. Click *Next* to continue.

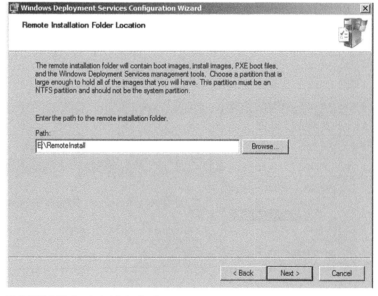

■ **FIGURE 2.29** Remote Installation Location.

4. You now need to select how you want WDS to respond to PXE clients. You have three options to choose from. They are as follows:

❑ *Do not respond to any client computers*—This option will tell WDS not to respond to any PXE requests. This option effectively disables the ability of WDS to respond to PXE boot requests.

❑ *Respond only to known client computers*—This option allows WDS to respond to PXE requests only from computers that have been prestaged with accounts setup in Active Directory prior to contacting the WDS server. A computer is prestaged by using Active Directory Users and Computers to manually create a new computer account. When the computer name is entered during the WDS deployment process, the computer is connected to the prestaged account already set up in Active Directory.

❑ *Respond to all client computers (known and unknown)*—This option instructs WDS to always respond to PXE boot requests. If the checkbox to *Require administrator approval for unknown computers* is checked, then computers that are not prestaged in Active Directory will require an administrator to first approve the PXE boot request before allowing the requesting computer to review a boot image from the WDS server.

5. After selecting a WDS PXE option, click *Next*. The Wizard will then configure and start WDS services. After you are taken to the *Operation Complete*, click on the *Finish* button.

6. If you have left the *Add images* option checked prior to clicking on the *Finish* button, you will be taken to the *Add Images Wizard*. If you have unchecked the box, you can easily add images by right clicking on the *Install Images* or *Boot Images* node and click on the option to add image.

7. To add a boot image, right click on the *Boot Images* folder and choose the *Add Boot Image* option.

8. For our example, we will add the default boot image from the Windows Server 2008 R2 DVD. The boot image is used to provide an initial operating environment to load the OS. The boot image allows the system to boot to a state where the OS can be installed. You must use a boot image anytime you want to load the OS via an image or unattended installation. The image is located in the sources folder on the DVD. Select this file path as seen in Figure 2.30 and then click *Next*.

9. Enter a name for the boot image (the default is Microsoft Windows Setup (×64)) and then click *Next*.

10. Click *Next* again to begin the process of copying the boot image to the WDS server.

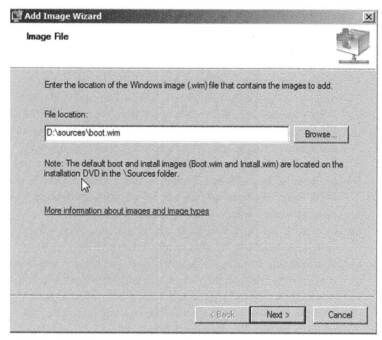

■ **FIGURE 2.30** Windows Deployment Services Boot Image.

11. After receiving confirmation that the operation has been completed successfully, click on the *Finish* button.
12. You should now see the Boot Image listed as shown in Figure 2.31.
13. You can perform the above steps to add the default Windows images to the *Install Images* folder. To add the installation images, choose the installation.wim file instead of the boot.wim.

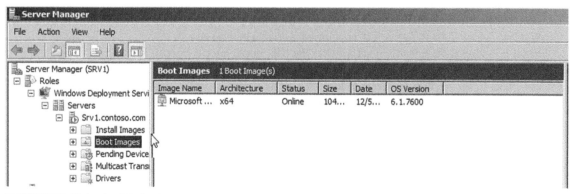

■ **FIGURE 2.31** Windows Installation Boot Image.

You should now have an active WDS server on your network. To test WDS PXE boot a server without Windows installed and see if it boots from the WDS server.

Unattended installation and automated deployment

You can use a combination of unattend.xml files, and the WDS schedule-cast option to fully automate Windows OS deployments. By using the Windows Automated Installation Kit, you can create custom unattend. xml files to customize the installation by performing actions, such as entering the product key, automatically adding specific server roles, and setting the default time zone. You can then use the WDS schedule-cast option to schedule automatic deployment of installation to servers.

NOTES FROM THE FIELD

Virtual machine deployment

You can use WDS to deploy Windows to virtual machines in the same way as you deploy Windows to physical servers; however, most administrators choose to use virtual machine templates for faster deployment. Since virtual machines are really just files, you can simply copy the files to create a new server.

ADMINISTRATION BASICS

Windows Server administration has evolved drastically since the days of Windows NT 4.0. Microsoft continues to make administration tools more efficient and wizard driven to ensure that the configuration tasks can be done quickly and consistently. Although, we will be exploring a lot of administration tools in the later chapters, it is important that you have an understanding of some basic concepts prior to looking at individual utilities.

Microsoft Management Console 101

The Microsoft Management Console (MMC) was introduced with the release of Windows 2000 as the premier tool for managing Windows Servers. The MMC was not only powerful but also very customizable. The concept was simple – A single console that would allow multiple tools known as snap-ins to be added. Administrators could use the out-of-box consoles, or create their own customized consoles. These consoles could be used on the server itself, or remotely from an administrator's workstation. MMC was well received by Windows administrators and continues to be used with the release of Windows Server 2008 R2. In fact,

Server Manager, which will be discussed in the next section, is more or less a Microsoft developed, feature-rich MMC. Let us explore some basic MMC concepts. We will first start by creating a new console with a few snap-ins. To create a new console, perform the following:

1. Create a new console by going to *Start | Run*, and type *MMC* in the run box. Then click on *OK*. This will open a new console with no snap-ins (see Figure 2.32).
2. Now let us add a couple of snap-ins. Go to the *File* menu and choose *Add/Remove Snap-in*. This will open the *Add/Remove Snap-in* selection window.
3. Add *Event View* and *Services* as seen in Figure 2.33. If asked for the computer to connect to choose *Local Computer*, then click on the *OK* button.
4. You will now see the left pane of the console, under the *Console Root*, populated with the snap-ins you selected. You can now manage the selected options by clicking on one of the snap-ins. Click to highlight the *Services* snap-in.

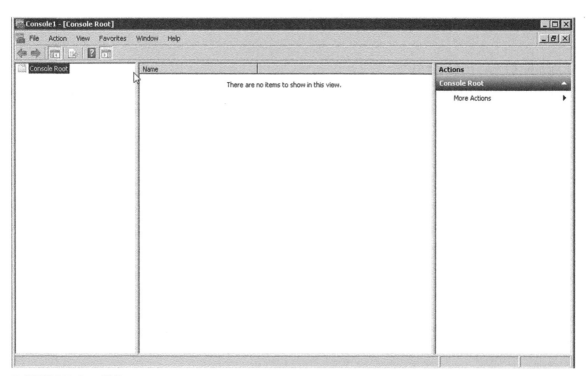

■ **FIGURE 2.32** Empty MMC.

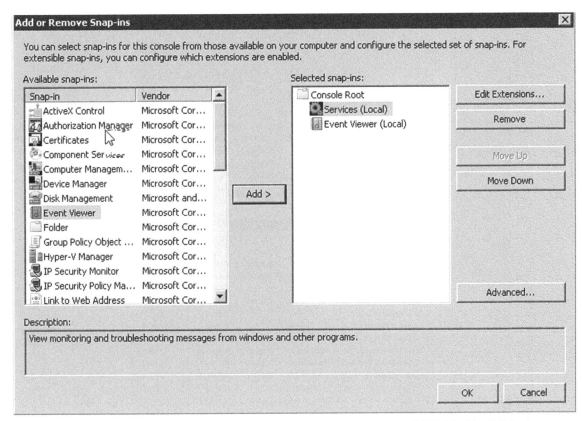

FIGURE 2.33 Select MMC Snap-Ins.

5. The middle-pane will populate with a list of Windows services. The middle pane is used to display the administrative options based on the snap-in that was selected in the left pane (see Figure 2.34).

6. If you click on any service, you will see new options appear in the far right hand pane. This pane is known as the *Actions Pane*. The Actions Pane will usually include common actions that can be performed on the item selected in the middle pane. In our example, you can click on a service such as the *DNS Client* service. Then click on the *More Actions* option in the *Actions Pane*. Choose the option *Restart Service*. This will restart the DNS Service.

7. Now that you have created a custom MMC, you may want to save it for future use. To save the console, simply go to the *File* menu and choose the *Save As. . .* option. Choose a file name and location and

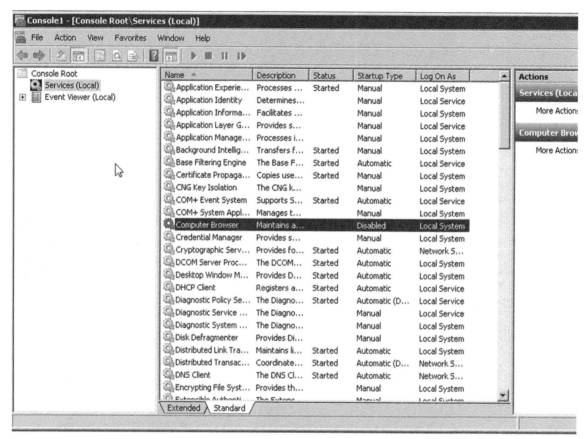

■ **FIGURE 2.34** Windows Services Snap-In.

click on the *Save* button. In future, you can open this console simply by double-clicking it.

You should now have a basic understanding of what the MMC is and how you can use it to administer Windows Servers. We will now take a look at Server Manager.

Overview of Server Manager

If you have administered Windows Servers prior to Windows 2000, you may remember a tool known as the Server Manager. Server Manager was one of the key management tools in the Windows NT 4.0 OS. NT 4.0 Server Manager, as seen in Figure 2.35, was used to set up and manage servers and workstations in a NT 4 domain. This provided a "single pane of glass" view of computers and computer settings on your network.

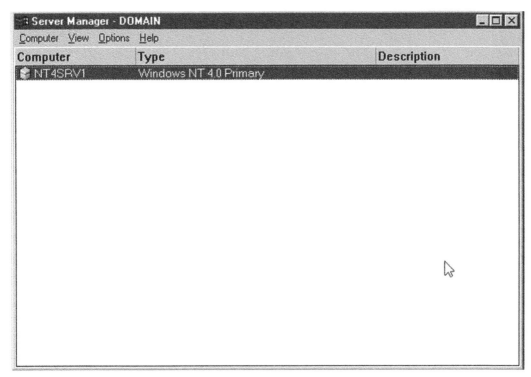

■ **FIGURE 2.35** Windows NT 4.0 Server Manager.

With the release of Windows 2000 server, Microsoft did away with Server Manager and introduced the MMC. MMCs quickly replaced the server manager, as they were more modular and customizable. MMCs also allowed 3rd party software to use the same interface as Windows administrative tools. Many administrators began building their own MMCs to provide the familiar "single pane of glass" management interface that they experienced in Windows NT 4.0.

During the development cycle of Windows Server 2008 R1, Microsoft determined that they could offer the best of the NT world's Server Manager and Windows 2000/2003's MMCs by creating a newly redesigned Server Manager based upon the MMC (see Figure 2.36). Windows Server 2008 and 2008 R2 offer a console built to perform the majority of Windows administrative tasks from a single interface. Server Manager will automatically add the required management snap-ins when new roles or features are added.

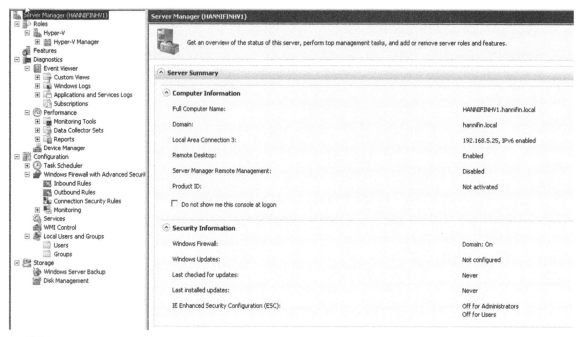

FIGURE 2.36 Windows Server 2008 R2 Server Manager.

Server Manager is by default pinned to the task bar for ease of access and also available via the Start Menu. Make sure that you are comfortable with Server Manager. This will likely be the management tool most often used when managing Windows Server 2008 R2.

Introduction to PowerShell

For years, Unix and Linux administrators have experienced the flexibility of very powerful command shells for administrators. Complex administrative tasks that might have required hours of work using GUI tools could easily be accomplished within minutes, using the powerful command line shell technologies in these OSs.

Over the past few years, Microsoft has been developing and evolving PowerShell to bring the same command line administrative power found in Unix and Linux to the Windows platform. PowerShell is quickly becoming the administrative tool of choice for many administrators. Exchange Server 2007 was the first major product shipped by Microsoft that used PowerShell as the foundation for all administrative functions.

The Exchange 2007 GUI tools actually call underlying PowerShell commands and scripts in the background. This concept was such a success with Exchange administrators that it is quickly becoming the standard administrative framework for most Microsoft products, including Windows Server. Windows Server 2008 R2 comes packed with PowerShell cmdlets for administrating everything from Windows services to Active Directory. If you have not taken the time to learn the PowerShell basics, now is the time to do so. We will cover PowerShell in detail in Chapter 11. Feel free to jump over to this chapter if you want to explore PowerShell right away.

Windows Server 2008 R2 administration tools

As you progress through this book, you will be introduced to various Windows Server 2008 R2 administrative tools. However, there are some key tools you should familiarize yourself with up front. These tools provide administration of some of the most basic, yet most critical aspects of the Windows OS.

Event Viewer

You will explore the Event Viewer in great detail in the chapter on monitoring and troubleshooting. The event viewer provides very detailed logs about errors, warnings, and general information regarding events that occur in the OS or applications hosted on the system. The event viewer is crucial not only for understanding problems when they occur, but also for monitoring changes and security of healthy systems.

Services

The Services console provides you with information regarding all Windows Services and their state. The Services console allows you to start, stop, and restart services installed on the server. Familiarize yourself with the services console. You will use it often.

Local Users and Groups

The Local Users and Groups console allows you to manage users and groups local to the server. Local Users and Groups are used to control who has what level of access to the local computer for which they reside. These should not be confused with Active Directory Users and Groups which will be covered in Chapter 4. Local Users and Groups do not extend beyond the local computer in which they are created. If you plan on deploying an Active Directory domain, you may not spend a lot of time administering local users and groups; nevertheless, it is important that you understand how they can be used to provide or restrict access to a given server.

Storage

The Storage console is the main administrative tool for managing Windows disk drives. Earlier in this chapter, you learned how to use the Storage console to create new volumes to be used by the server. The storage console can also be used to extend and shrink volumes as well as assign or change drive letters assigned to volumes and partitions. The Storage console is also used to initialize and configure newly added disk drives.

Task Scheduler

Windows Server 2008 R2 comes with a built-in task scheduler allowing administrators to create automated jobs or tasks. These jobs can be set up to run based on various criteria, such as scheduled times or when a specific event occurs. These jobs run without requiring administrative input. Jobs can be set up to perform serveral actions including running scripts, displaying message dialogs, or sending email messages. An example of a scheduled task would be a weekly disk defragmentation job that needs to run off hours when an administrator is not available to manually start the job. Scheduled tasks can also be used to perform tasks, such as backups or running command line utilities.

The Task Scheduler management console is located in Server Manager under the Configuration node as seen in Figure 2.37. You will notice that there will already be a list of predefined tasks configured.

To create a new scheduled task, perform the following:

1. Open Server Manager.
2. Expand the Configuration node and right click on Task Scheduler. Then choose the option Create Task.
3. The main task window will be displayed as seen in Figure 2.38. Enter a descriptive name for the task and configure security options for the task. Security options define how the task runs and how it can run when no user is logged on. If the task will need access to resources on other systems, you may need to run it under the context of another user account. If this is required, you can enter the account information by clicking on the Change User or Group button. After configuring information on the General tab, select the Triggers tab.

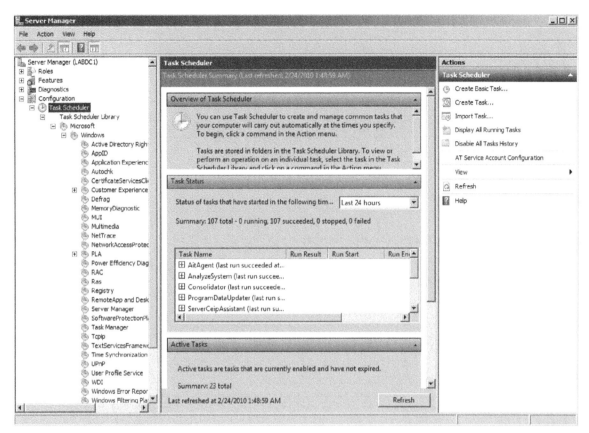

■ **FIGURE 2.37** Windows Server 2008 R2 Task Scheduler.

4. The Triggers section is used to define what events, including scheduled times, trigger the scheduled task to run. As you can see in Figure 2.39, several different triggers can be used to start a scheduled task. You can also select multiple triggers that can be used to kick off a scheduled task. After you define the triggers used to start the task, select the Actions tab.

5. You can now use the Actions tab to define what actions are to be performed in the event that the scheduled task is triggered to run. Like triggers, you can define multiple actions to occur. For example, you could have the task run a batch file to copy files from one server to another and also send an email notifying an administrator that the task ran. After selecting the actions to perform, select the Conditions tab.

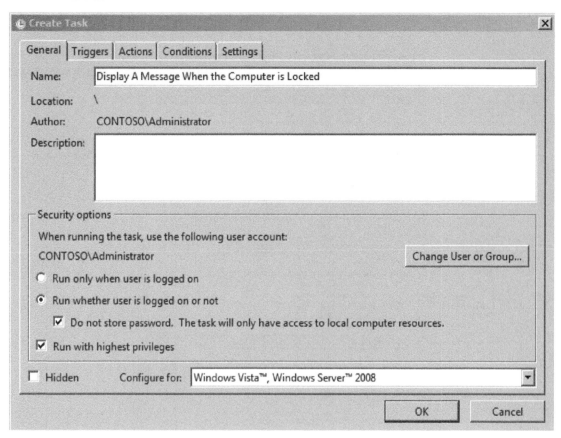

■ **FIGURE 2.38** Create New Scheduled Task.

6. Scheduled tasks can use conditions to ensure that tasks run only under certain circumstances. For example, you may only want a task that makes use of lot of processing power to only start if the computer is idle for 30 minutes. After defining any optional conditions, you may want to tie to the scheduled task, select the Settings tab.

7. Using the settings section, you can define additional settings that should be applied to the scheduled task. For example, you may want the task to stop if it has been running for more than 6 h or you may want the task to rerun if it fails the first time. As you can see from Figure 2.40, there are various additional settings you can tie to a scheduled task. After you have configured any additional settings for the scheduled task, click on OK to create the new task.

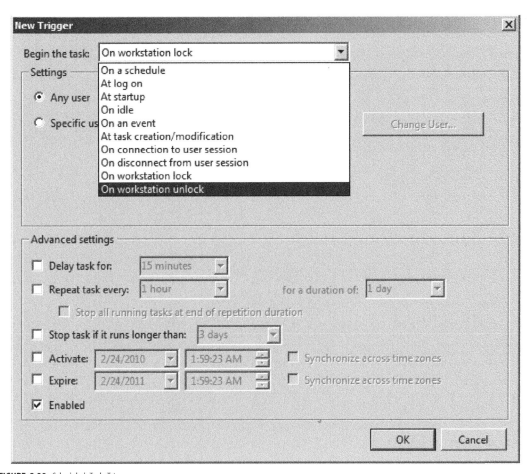

■ **FIGURE 2.39** Scheduled Task Triggers.

After the task is completed, it will be displayed in the Task Scheduler console in Server Manager. If you want to test the task, you can simply right click on the task and choose the *Run* option.

INSTALLATION AND CONFIGURATION CHECKLIST

Here is a sample Windows Installation and Configuration Checklist. You can use this as a template to create your own checklist for server configuration.

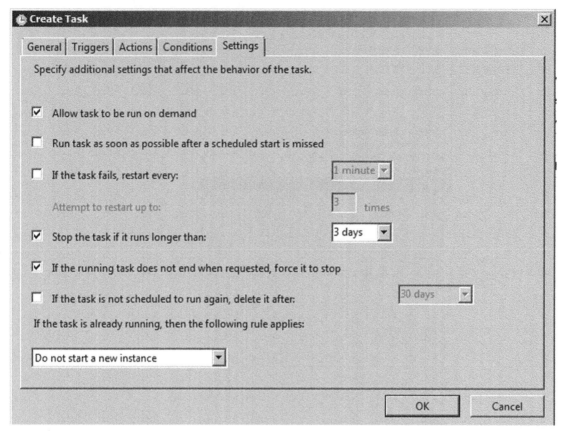

■ **FIGURE 2.40** Additional Scheduled Task Settings.

SUMMARY

In this chapter, you were introduced to the various steps and planning required to install and to configure Windows Server 2008 R2. You learned to choose between a server upgrade and custom, clean installation. You were introduced to Server Core and you might want to consider deploying it as opposed to a full server installation. This chapter covered the new Windows activation process and KMS. You also explored how to automate Windows deployment using WDS. Chapter 2 concluded with an introduction to Windows Server administration and some of the tools that will be covered throughout this book.

3

Windows Server 2008 R2 networking

Organizations large and small depend on computer networks to operate their businesses. Employees require anywhere access to data, while clients and business partners demand enhanced collaboration and real-time communications. The need for fast, dependable, and feature-rich networks has never been greater. As a Windows administrator, you need to have the skills necessary to manage, monitor, and troubleshoot networks. Even if you work in an organization with a separate network team, it is crucial that you understand how networks operate and how Windows relies on the network to ensure availability of critical business services and applications and provides several network features itself.

This chapter covers the networking features available in Windows Server 2008 R2 as well as guidance for planning and setting up a Windows Server 2008 R2 network. You will also learn how to plan and set up services such as Remote Access, Domain Naming System (DNS), and Dynamic Host Configuration Protocol (DHCP). This chapter will conclude with an overview of some common network management and monitoring tools.

OVERVIEW OF WINDOWS SERVER 2008 R2 NETWORKING

Microsoft has enhanced many of the core network features with the release of Windows Server 2008 and 2008 R2. Windows Server 2008 R2 also comes with some newly added features that deliver greater security, reliability, and a better end-user experience.

Network and Sharing Center

The Network and Sharing Center is the new central console to configure and manage network settings in Windows Server 2008 R1, Windows Vista, Windows Server 2008 R2, and Windows 7. It includes options that allow you to manage network adapters, enable or disable file sharing, change network location settings, and troubleshoot connection problems. We will explore the Network and Sharing Center in more detail later in this chapter.

Redesigned TCP/IP Network Stack

Windows Server 2008 R2 includes what Microsoft calls "The Next Generation TCP/IP Stack." During the development of Windows Server 2008, Microsoft chose to completely redesign the TCP/IP stack to improve performance, add new features for IP version 4 (IPv4), and to include support for IP version 6 (IPv6). The redesign includes new features such as:

- *Fail back support for default gateways*—Windows Server 2003 and Windows XP provided the ability to add multiple default gateways for redundancy. If one gateway became unreachable, Windows could fail over to a backup default gateway. Windows Server 2003 and Windows XP did not, however, provide an automatic check of the unreachable gateway to determine when it came back online. An administrator would have to manually fail back the computer to the original gateway. Windows Server 2008 introduces the ability to have the computer perform regular "checks" of a dead or unreachable gateway. Once the gateway becomes reachable again, the computer will fail back to the original gateway automatically.
- *TCP chimney off-load*—As networks have advanced over the years, so has the amount of processing required to manage and maintain network connections. Significant increases in CPU utilization have been seen when performing large data transfers, such as those seen during backups and on iSCSI Storage Area Network (SAN) connections. Typically, this increased utilization is seen on 1-gigabit and 10-gigabit connection speeds. To address this issue, Microsoft developed the ability to off-load all TCP connection processing to a TCP Off-load Engine (TOE) card. TOE cards are special network adapters built specifically to off-load TCP traffic from the computer's main CPU. This allows the TOE card to carry the additional processing load, freeing up the computer's primary CPU for other processing requests.
- *Network Diagnostics Framework*—The Network Diagnostics Framework helps to locate and diagnose network connectivity problems and in many cases it will take the end-user through a series of steps to find the cause of connectivity loss and fix it. It can help resolve several common issues, such as IP address conflicts, dead default gateways, stopped DHCP client services, or disconnected media.

DNS enhancements

Windows Server 2008 now includes new DNS features including IPv6 support and the GlobalNames zone. The GlobalNames zone provides single-label name resolution without the need for a dedicated Windows

Internet Naming System (WINS) deployment. DNS design and deployment will be discussed in detail later in this chapter.

NOTES FROM THE FIELD

The Windows Internet Naming System (WINS)

For those who are unfamiliar with WINS; it was originally developed to support name resolution over Windows networks separated by wide area network (WAN) links. WINS provided name resolution of NETBIOS names before DNS became the primary technology used for computer name resolution. Though not as prevalent, WINS can be seen on a lot of Windows networks today supporting legacy NETBIOS based applications. The new GlobalNames zone is Microsoft's solution to help traditional WINS deployments to move to DNS technologies for name resolution.

Policy-based QoS

Traditionally, Quality of Service (QoS) has been set up to throttle or prioritize traffic between network switches and routers; however, Policy-based QoS in the Windows Server 2008 R2 allows administrators to deploy these features to servers and desktops. This ability opens the door to more enhanced network bandwidth management. Policy-based QoS will be explored in more detail later in this chapter.

SMB 2.0

Server Message Block (SMB) 1.0 was originally developed for sharing files in Windows operating systems. SMB 2.0 was released as part of the Windows Server 2008 R1 and Vista operating systems, and remains in 2008 R2 and Windows 7 today. SMB 2.0 has greatly been enhanced to increase the performance of SMB file traffic. Copying files between two SMB 2.0 capable systems occurs at much greater speeds as those seen using SMB 1.0. Several enhancements to SMB, such as the ability to perform multiple operations at the same time, make it more efficient. SMB 1.0 would perform only one operation and wait for a response before moving to the next. SMB 2.0 can issue two to three operations or more making it more efficient and faster in the eyes of the end-user. An additional benefit to SMB 2.0 is that it also has the ability to sustain a file transfer even if a brief network disconnect occurs. Have you ever been in the middle of a very large file transfer, and suddenly the network connection briefly drops? Do you remember the frustration of having to start the file transfer all over again? SMB 2.0 can automatically maintain the file transfer during that brief connectivity drop and continue copying files after the connectivity is restored. SMB 2.0 is available in Windows

Server 2008, Windows Server 2008 R2, Windows Vista, and Windows 7 operating systems.

You may be wondering, "What happens if I transfer a file between a SMB 2.0 capable system and a SMB 1.0 capable system, such as Windows XP?" In this situation, the file transfer process will use the 1.0 version of SMB providing backward compatibility to the older operating system.

Windows Firewall

Microsoft first included the Windows Firewall in Windows Server 2003 and Windows XP. The Windows Firewall in Windows Server 2003 provides the ability to "lock down" certain ports and applications resulting in a greater level of security not only for applications but also for the server system as a whole. Though the Windows Firewall was a great addition from a security standpoint, it did have a few shortcomings. The firewall was cumbersome to configure at times, especially for less experienced Windows administrators. It also filtered only traffic incoming to the server, so all outbound connections were allowed by default.

Windows Server 2008 R1 and R2 include a new version of the Windows Firewall with a much improved administrative experience. The Windows Firewall has been configured using a console built into the Server Manager interface (see Figure 3.1). The firewall now has the ability to filter both inbound and outbound connections. Additionally, Windows Server 2008 R2 services and some applications will automatically create necessary firewall rules to ensure that they can communicate properly with the network. Additionally, the firewall has APIs which allow application developers to publish their own exception requirements to the firewall during installation of their given application. The firewall can also be changed on a per-network interface, opposed to a particular rule or configuration applying to all interfaces. You will learn about the Windows Firewall in detail in Chapter 10.

IPv6 support

IPv6 is the next generation IP protocol designed to eventually replace IPv4. Windows Server 2008 R2 natively supports both IPv6 and IPv4 out-of-box. Both are installed and enabled by default in Windows Server 2008 R2. As with most technologies, support for IPv4 will continue to be required for several years but in the near future IPv6 may very well become the IP standard. To assist organizations in moving to IPv6, Windows Server 2008 R2 includes several standards-based IPv4 to IPv6 transition technologies such as Teredo, 6to4, and IP-HTTPS, all of which

■ **FIGURE 3.1** Windows Server 2008 R2 Firewall Configuration.

will be covered in more detail later in this book. We will explore IPv6 in a little more detail later in this chapter.

Network awareness

Windows Server 2008 R2 has the ability to sense changes in network connectivity, whether this is connecting and disconnecting on the same network or plugging into a different network altogether. The Network Awareness APIs in Windows Server 2008 R2 allow developers to write applications that can rely on this network state change monitoring and react when changes occur. For example, an application may require a connection to the corporate network for certain features to function properly. Using Network Awareness APIs, the developer could instruct the application to display only those features when it detects that the computer is connected to the corporate LAN.

Network Access Protection

Network Access Protection (NAP), originally released in Windows Server 2008 R1, is a technology that ensures that computers on your network comply with IT health policies. NAP makes sure that client computers have current operating system updates installed, antivirus software running, and custom configurations related to ensuring that the client is compliant with corporate IT policies. NAP restricts the computer's network access until it verifies whether the client is in compliance. If the computer is found not to be in compliance with set policies, the end-user can be offered a way to remediate the problem and then granted full network access.

DirectAccess

DirectAccess is a new feature introduced in Windows Server 2008 R2 and Windows 7. DirectAccess provides end-users with constant, secure connectivity to the corporate network anytime an Internet connection is available and without the need for traditional Virtual Private Network (VPN) client software installed. This connection not only gives end-users easy access to the company network, but also provides systems such as configuration management and software distribution server's access to the PC. This is a Win-Win feature for end-users and IT departments alike. DirectAccess is accomplished by creating a secure tunnel between the Windows 7 workstation and the Windows Server 2008 R2 network. We will be looking at DirectAccess in more detail in Chapter 13 as part of the Windows Server 2008 R2 and Windows 7 "Better Together" story.

Exploring Network and Sharing Center

The Network and Sharing Center is the new central console for managing TCP/IP network connectivity and features, such as Windows File sharing. The new Network and Sharing Center is the "one-stop shop" to view, manage, and troubleshoot your network connectivity in Windows Server 2008 R2.

The Network and Sharing Center can be accessed *via* a few methods. It can be accessed *via* the control panel under the Network and Internet section (see Figure 3.2), by right clicking on a network connection in the system tray or by right clicking on the Network option in the Start menu and choosing properties.

You will notice several options presented when you first open the Network and Sharing Center. In the top middle section of the window, you will see a basic connectivity map as seen in Figure 3.3. The simple map provides a visual representation of network connectivity from the operating system's

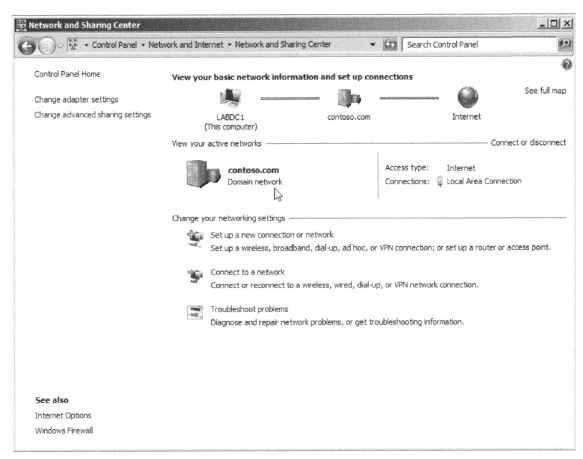

■ **FIGURE 3.2** Network and Sharing Center.

perspective. This includes the ability to access a local network and the Internet. If the server fails to connect to either of these, the map will display the problem area with a red disconnected status. The connectivity map may vary slightly depending on what type of network your computer is connected to.

View your basic network information and set up connections

■ **FIGURE 3.3** Simple Network Map of Domain Joined Computer.

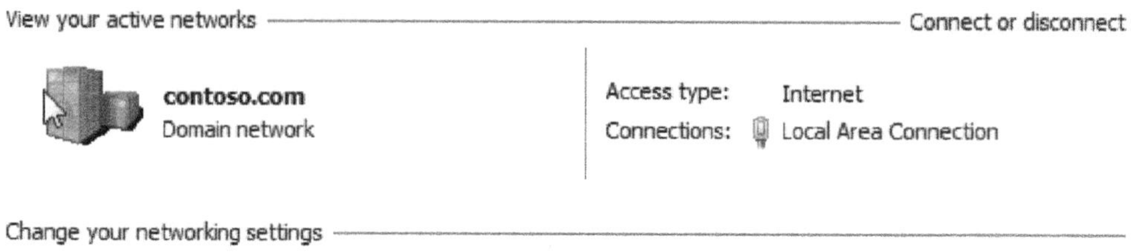

View your active networks ——————————————————————————— Connect or disconnect

contoso.com
Domain network

Access type:	Internet
Connections:	Local Area Connection

Change your networking settings ————————————————————————

■ **FIGURE 3.4** Network Connectivity.

Below the connectivity map, you will see a section that lists the name and type of the network you are connected to along with the media (wired or wireless) providing the connection (see Figure 3.4). By clicking on any connected media type, you can view the status of the connection as well as make configuration changes, such as disabling the network adapter or setting the IP address.

Moving down the window, you will see a section named "Change your network settings" (see Figure 3.5). Here you can change various aspects of your network connection, including setting up a new connection to a remote network *via* VPN or dial-up, connecting to an existing network, or diagnosing current network problems.

The left-hand section of the Network Sharing Center provides links to the following network and configuration settings:

- *Change adapter settings*—This link opens the network connections window. Here you can perform tasks such as disabling/enabling network adapters, and assigning IP addresses and protocols to those adapters.
- *Change advanced sharing settings*—This link takes you to the window that allows you to turn network sharing, network discovery, and public

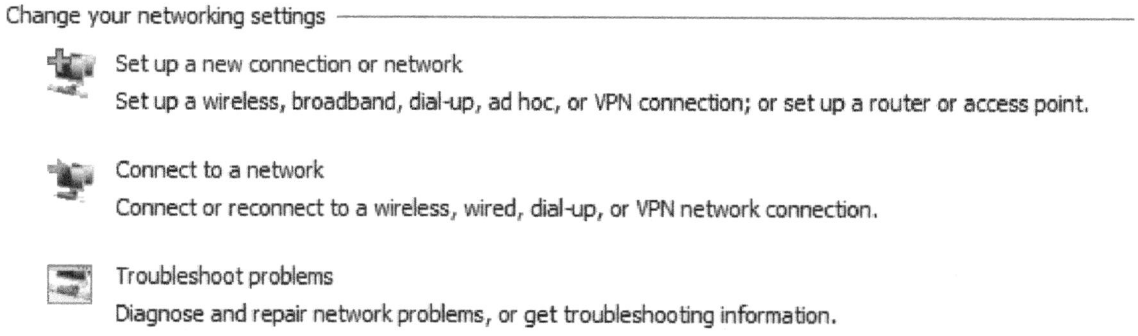

Change your networking settings ——————————————————————————————

 Set up a new connection or network
Set up a wireless, broadband, dial-up, ad hoc, or VPN connection; or set up a router or access point.

 Connect to a network
Connect or reconnect to a wireless, wired, dial-up, or VPN network connection.

 Troubleshoot problems
Diagnose and repair network problems, or get troubleshooting information.

■ **FIGURE 3.5** Change Network Settings.

folder sharing on and off. These settings can be turned on or off for each network profile individually.

NOTES FROM THE FIELD

See Also Links

Throughout the configuration windows in Windows Server 2008 R2, Microsoft has embedded "See Also Links." The links take you to the configuration and management consoles similar to the current console where the links appear.

Network profiles

Windows Server 2008 and Windows Vista introduced a new way to manage network configuration based upon the network that the computer is connected to. For example, you can configure the computer to open Windows Firewall ports for Remote Desktop connectivity while connected to the corporate network and to disable the ports when connected to a public network. Windows Server 2008 R2 includes the following network profile types:

- *Domain*—The domain network profile is used when the computer is connected to the network that hosts the domain that it is a member of. For example, if a computer is a member of the Contoso.com domain, the domain network profile will be used when that computer connects to the network that hosts the Contoso.com domain.
- *Private*—The private network profile is used when connecting the computer to a trusted network that does not host the domain in which the computer is joined. This profile is less restrictive than the public profile and thus should only be used on trusted networks, such as a home network or in situations where the computer is connected to the corporate network, but not joined to a Windows domain.
- *Public*—The public network profile should be used when connecting the computer to a non-trusted network, such as a public Wi-Fi hotspot. This profile is much more restrictive toward other network computers and devices.

You will more than likely not be moving your production servers between various networks on a regular basis. However, it is important that you understand how Network Profiles impact on the operating system's configuration to ensure that proper settings are applied for your given network scenario. For example, if you open a Windows Firewall port for the private profile and the computer is using the domain profile, then the firewall change that you made will have no impact on the computer's current configuration.

PLANNING AND DEPLOYING A TCP/IP NETWORK INFRASTRUCTURE

Window networks depend upon a reliable TCP/IP infrastructure. A properly designed and managed TCP/IP network helps to ensure a successful Windows Server 2008 R2 deployment, while a poorly designed network almost guarantees that problems are going to occur during and after your deployment. Spend time to make sure that your network is healthy before rolling out Windows Server 2008 R2. If you already have a well-managed and reliable IP network, give yourself a pat on the back. This is not always an easy objective to accomplish.

Introduction to TCP/IP

Most of today's networks, including the Internet, rely heavily on the TCP/IP protocol. The TCP/IP protocol stack has been around since the early days of computer networks and remains the *de facto* standard of enterprises today. Before setting up or managing a Windows network, you need to have a good understanding of how TCP/IP works. In this section, we will cover some of the basics of TCP/IP and how they apply to Windows. If you are already an experienced network administrator, now might be a good time to review and refresh your IP knowledge.

IP addresses

IP addresses are unique binary numbers assigned to hosts on an IP network. Think of IP addressing in the same way as you think of the addresses of houses in your neighborhood. Each house requires a unique street address. When someone needs to visit your home, they direct their vehicle to your address. The same applies in the world of TCP/IP networks. Every computer and device attached to the network requires a unique IP address. Data that needs to reach a certain computer on the network is sent to its IP address.

As mentioned, IP addresses are binary numbers; however, most people prefer to read IP addresses in decimal format for ease of use. It is important that you as a network administrator understand this concept to properly troubleshoot and manage IP networks.

IP address classes

IP addresses are distributed into five classes: Class A, Class B, Class C, Class D, and Class E. All IP addresses belong to a class based upon their decimal value of the first octet. Classes A, B, and C are the ones you will see used on corporate networks. Class D IPs are reserved multicast addresses that cannot be assigned to a single computer but used to send and receive multicast traffic. Class E addresses are reserved for use by the Internet Engineering Task Force (IETF). The IP classes and their corresponding range of IP addresses are listed in Table 3.1.

IP subnetting

A subnet mask is another group of dotted decimal numbers, representing a binary number that distinguishes which part of the IP address represents the network. The subnet mask is used to allow computers to determine whether the addresses of other computers they wish to communicate with are on the local network or on a remote network. If the computer resides on a remote network, the communication request is sent to the default gateway. Figure 3.6 explains how subnet masks work.

Table 3.1 IP Address Classes

Class	Range
A	1.0.0.1–127.255.255.255
B	128.0.0.1–191.255.255.255
C	192.0.0.1–223.255.255.255
D	224.0.0.1–239.255.255.255
E	240.0.0.1–255.255.255.255

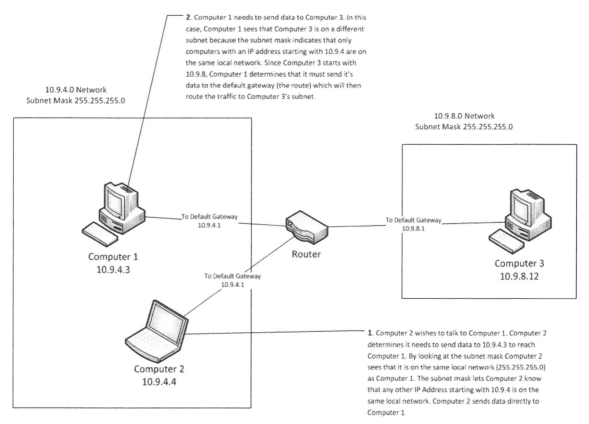

2. Computer 1 needs to send data to Computer 3. In this case, Computer 1 sees that Computer 3 is on a different subnet because the subnet mask indicates that only computers with an IP address starting with 10.9.4 are on the same local network. Since Computer 3 starts with 10.9.8, Computer 1 determines that it must send it's data to the default gateway (the route) which will then route the traffic to Computer 3's subnet.

10.9.4.0 Network
Subnet Mask 255.255.255.0

10.9.8.0 Network
Subnet Mask 255.255.255.0

To Default Gateway
10.9.4.1

To Default Gateway
10.9.8.1

Computer 1
10.9.4.3

Router

Computer 3
10.9.8.12

To Default Gateway
10.9.4.1

Computer 2
10.9.4.4

1. Computer 2 wishes to talk to Computer 1. Computer 2 determines it needs to send data to 10.9.4.3 to reach Computer 1. By looking at the subnet mask Computer 2 sees that it is on the same local network (255.255.255.0) as Computer 1. The subnet mask lets Computer 2 know that any other IP Address starting with 10.9.4 is on the same local network. Computer 2 sends data directly to Computer 1

■ **FIGURE 3.6** How the Subnet Mask Works.

Table 3.2 Standard Subnet Masks

	Subnet Mask	Number of Supported Hosts per Network
Class A	255.0.0.0	Over 16 million
Class B	255.255.0.0	Over 16 thousand
Class C	255.255.255.0	254

The three main IP address classes have default subnet masks. The standard subnet masks for each class, including number of supported hosts on each network are listed in Table 3.2.

The default subnet mask is not practical in most network configurations. For example, let us say that you owned a Class B network of 159.247.0.0. Using the default mask, you could have over 16,000 computers on one nonroutable network segment. What if you had a remote office connected *via* a WAN link? Would you need to acquire another Class B network range for that office? First, this would be a major waste of your IP addresses and second, good luck on getting someone to give you that many. Luckily, you can create custom subnet masks to split up your IP addresses. By simply changing the subnet mask from 255.255.0.0 to 255.255.255.0, you have instantly given yourself 254 unique routable networks that can support 254 hosts each. Creating a custom subnet mask is as simple as adding some binary ones to replace zeros in the mask. But what if you need to support 400 computers in a remote network? What does the mask look like then? This is where it gets a little tricky. You will need to convert the dotted decimal to its binary equivalent and perform a simple calculation. Let us take a look at this process.

1. Decide how many subnets or networks you need to support. This is pretty easy to calculate. Figure out how many networks you have that are separated by a router.
2. Decide how many hosts you need on each network. You need to plan for the number of computers and other IP devices that you will want to support at each network location. Remember that you may need IP addresses for network switches, printers, and other IP-enabled devices on top of the number of computers that you need to support each network. You should plan for growth here as well. Give yourself at least 10% growth room for a given network.
3. Calculate the subnet mask. You now have enough information to calculate the proper custom subnet mask. Perform the following to calculate your subnet mask.

a. Convert the standard subnet mask to binary. If we are using an IP network of 160.240.0.0, then the mask would be 255.255.0.0. The binary conversion is 11111111.11111111.00000000.00000000. Notice that it takes eight binary numbers to make up the number between each decimal. This is why each number between the decimal is referred to as an octet.

b. Add one to the number of networks (subnets) you need. Assume that you need five networks. Add one to it to get six.

c. Convert the decimal number to binary. You can do this manually or the calculator in Windows works great for this. In our example, we convert the decimal number six to binary, which is 110.

d. Calculate the bits required for the mask. This is equal to the bits required to create the binary number. Since 110 is three individual numbers, 3 bits are required.

e. Add the bits to the standard subnet mask resulting in a new binary subnet mask of 11111111.11111111.11100000.00000000. Now convert this binary back to decimal resulting in 255.255.224.0. You now have the subnet mask to use on each network segment.

Now that you have learned how to create a custom subnet mask, you should be aware that you can use a special subnet calculator to perform these steps for you. However, it is important that you understand how subnetting works if you plan on supporting Windows networks.

Public- versus private-IP addresses

IP networks expanded and grew much larger than the original creators of the protocol ever intended. IP blocks or classes were originally developed with a limited number of available addresses. With the emergence of global interconnected networks and the Internet, many organizations found themselves in an IP address shortage crisis. This is where private-IP addresses come into play. Private-IPs constitute a set of three IP address ranges, one from each of the three primary classes that are not routable on the Internet (see Table 3.3). The result of not making them Internet routable is that anyone can use them on their networks. If the private-IP addresses need to connect to the Internet, a Network Address Translator (NAT) device must be used to translate the private-IP to a public-IP. This technology allows organizations to purchase a limited number of public-IP addresses and use private-IP addresses on computers connected to their internal networks. The private-IP addressed computers can then use the NAT device, which is assigned a public-IP, to communicate on the Internet. A simple private-IP addressed network is depicted in Figure 3.7. The use of private-IPs and NAT not only decreases the usage of public-IP

Table 3.3 Private–IP Ranges

	IP Range
Class A	10.0.0.0– 10.255.255.255
Class B	172.16.0.0– 172.31.255.266
Class C	192.168.0.0– 192.168.255.255

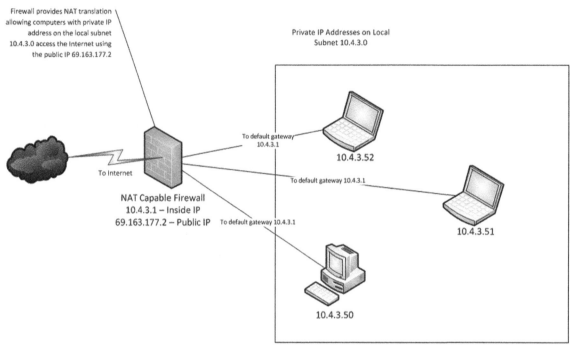

Firewall provides NAT translation allowing computers with private IP address on the local subnet 10.4.3.0 access the Internet using the public IP 69.163.177.2

Private IP Addresses on Local Subnet 10.4.3.0

To default gateway 10.4.3.1

10.4.3.52

To Internet

To default gateway 10.4.3.1

NAT Capable Firewall
10.4.3.1 – Inside IP
69.163.177.2 – Public IP   To default gateway 10.4.3.1

10.4.3.51

10.4.3.50

■ **FIGURE 3.7** A Private-IP Network.

addresses, but also makes networks more secure by hiding computers from the global Internet. Private-IP addressing is a technology that continues to be available in IPv6.

Introduction to IPv6

IPv6 is the next generation IP network protocol developed to replace the aging IPv4. As mentioned earlier, the designers of IPv4 never expected that billions of IP addresses would be needed to support the global networks we have today. Even with the increased use of private-IP ranges and technologies, such as NAT, the number of available public-IP addresses continues to decline. It has become very clear that future IP networks will require a lot more addresses than that are available in IPv4. This is where IPv6 comes in. IPv6 moves from 32-bit (4 octets) IP addresses to 128-bit IP addresses. This increases the number of available addresses to such a large number that every person on earth could have roughly 3961408125713216879677197 5168 addresses. Yes, that is a lot of IP addresses. The intent of the Internet Engineering Task Force (IETF), the governing body of IP networking, was not just to create some insanely large number just to ensure that we do not run out, but for easier management and assignment of IP ranges. IPv6 allows large blocks to be assigned, providing more efficient routing and easier administration of those IP ranges.

Though IPv6 is clearly the future of IP networks, the adoption rate has been very low to date. Major changes to enterprise networks, such as changing IP addresses, are never cheap or quickly implemented. Chances are that IPv6-based networks will emerge and grow over the next few years, but IPv4 will not be going away in the near future.

As a Windows administrator, the important thing to understand is that Windows Server 2008 R2 fully supports IPv6, and can efficiently communicate on both IPv4- and IPv6-based networks.

IPv4 to IPv6 transition technologies

To help organizations move to IPv6, there are several standards-based technologies that have been created to allow IPv6 applications function over an IPv4 network. Windows Server 2008 R2 includes support for some of these technologies, including Teredo, 6to4, IP-HTTPS, and ISATAP. A brief explanation of each is provided below:

- *Teredo*—Teredo is a standards-based protocol that provides IPv6 connections for IPv4-based computers that are behind an IPv4-based NAT. Teredo is a key technology allowing organizations to make IPv6 connections without changing IP addresses of computers on their internal private subnets.
- *6to4*—6to4 is a standards-based protocol that allows computers with public-IPv4 addresses to make IPv6-based connections over the IPv4-based Internet. It is a key technology allowing organizations to begin transitioning to IPv6 while the Internet at large continues to be based on IPv4.
- *IP-HTTPS*—IP-HTTPS is a Microsoft technology that allows Windows 7 and Windows Server 2008 R2 computers behind a firewall to establish IPv6 connectivity over an IPv4 network by creating an IPv4-based tunnel in which IPv6 packets can travel.
- *ISATAP*—ISATAP is a standards-based technology that provides IPv6 connectivity across an IPv4-based internal network.

Designing IP networks

We discussed the necessity of planning for a Windows Server 2008 R2 deployment in Chapter 1. The same requirement applies to building IP-based networks. You need to spend ample time planning prior to building your network infrastructure. Be sure to document your game plan so that you will not forget the critical tasks. Remember that your Windows network is not worth much if your workstations and servers cannot communicate. As part of your design, you need to understand and document what network services and applications you plan to support. You need to know how they communicate, what protocols they use, and how much bandwidth they require. You will also want to consider the following while developing your plan:

- Number of physical locations and logical networks
- Number of networks' devices you plan to support
- Expected growth of your network
- Availability and redundancy requirements
- Bandwidth needs
- Routing options
- Network switch needs
- VLANs
- Network locations that will host servers
- VPNs and Remote Access technologies
- Internet access and firewall locations

These are just a few of the topics that you will need to spend time designing and documenting prior to deployment of an IP infrastructure. The end design should match up with your Windows Server 2008 R2 deployment plan. The IP infrastructure must be designed to support the various requirements of network applications provided by Windows Servers. In the end-user's eyes, if the network is down, so are the services it supports.

Policy-based QoS

QoS features allow administrators to configure certain network protocols and applications to have a higher network bandwidth priority than others. QoS also allows administrators to limit the bandwidth used by lower priority applications. The use of QoS has increased rapidly over the past several years as more organizations have begun using their networks to send more than just email and browse the Web. Today's businesses are using their networks to stream multimedia from and to the Internet, use cloud-based services, and support Voice over IP (VoIP) phone systems. Using these services requires prioritizing some protocols over others. QoS has traditionally been a network feature that could be set up on network routers and layer 3 switches. The network devices are set up to inspect network traffic and give certain protocols a higher priority than others.

The most widely used method of implementing QoS is using differential services code point (DSCP) tagging. DSCP assigns a value between 0 and 63 to data packets. QoS services read this value and give higher numbers, a higher priority on the network.

NOTES FROM THE FIELD

QoS in Windows Server 2003 and Windows XP

Microsoft introduced some basic QoS APIs in Windows XP and Windows Server 2003. This allowed application developers to apply QoS settings to their applications but was limited in features and needed to have code written to support QoS. Additionally, the administrator would need to install the QoS packet scheduler on the Windows Server after Windows installation. It should be noted that to support QoS, the full network path has to trust the QoS values coming from the client. This is typically something implemented on internal networks, but due to an organization's inability to control Internet-based network routers, it is rarely implemented over an Internet connection.

Windows Server 2008 R2 includes the feature Policy-based QoS. Policy-based QoS allows Windows administrators to apply DSCP values to traffic entering or leaving a computer based on application, port number, protocol, or source and destination IP addresses. These QoS polices can be applied to Windows Vista, Windows 7, Windows Server 2008, and Windows Server 2008 R2 computers and users logged onto these operating systems. These policies are deployed *via* traditional group policies. This means that you can apply different QoS policies to different systems based upon their Active Directory (AD) site, OU membership, or the domain they belong to. This makes QoS management very granular and less complicated to administer. Let us set up and see Policy-based QoS in action. Policy-based QoS can be especially helpful in VoIP technology deployments such as Microsoft Office Communications Server 2007 R2.

Creating a Policy-based QoS GPO

In the below exercise, we will create a new Policy-based QoS GPO for traffic destined for port 80 (http). This will give standard Web browsing traffic a higher value leaving the computer over other network traffic. If the network devices support the DSCP value provided by the policy, they will also give the traffic higher priority.

1. In our example, we will use a local computer policy; however, the same policy can be set up in AD. Open the group policy editor:

Start | Run type *gpedit.msc* and click *OK*. The *Local Group Policy Editor* will open as seen in Figure 3.8.

2. Expand the nodes *Computer Configuration | Windows Settings* and *User Configuration | Windows Settings* (see Figure 3.9). You will notice that Policy-based QoS can be applied to the computer or to the user. For our example, we will use a computer-based policy.

3. Right click the *Policy-based QoS* node and choose *Create New Policy*.

4. The *Policy-based QoS Wizard* will launch (see Figure 3.10). Enter a descriptive name in the *Policy Name* field. Then use the *Specify DSCP value* option to set a DSCP value. In our example, we will not be throttling the traffic so leave this option unchecked. Click *Next* to continue.

5. We can assign the DSCP policy to specific applications by choosing the executable, or if this server is set up as a Web application server,

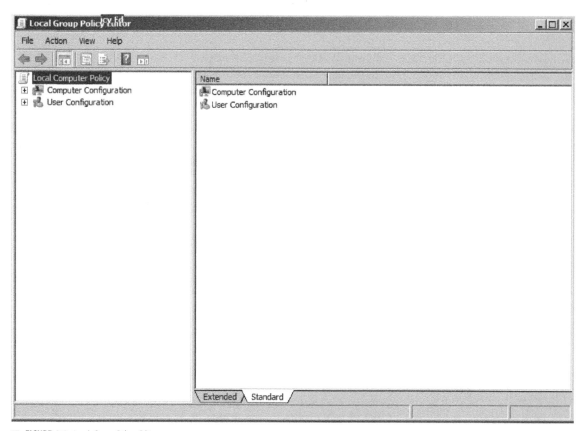

■ **FIGURE 3.8** Local Group Policy Editor.

■ **FIGURE 3.9** Computer and User Policy-Based QoS Options.

we can specify the URL of the application. For our example, we will leave the default of *All Applications* selected (see Figure 3.11). Click *Next* to continue.

6. We can specify that this policy applies only to certain source or destination IP addresses (see Figure 3.12). We will leave both of these options as the default for our example. Click *Next*.

7. We now need to choose the protocol and port number or range that we want the DSCP value to (see Figure 3.13). For our testing purposes, let us choose port 80 (http) as the destination port. This will allow us to easily use a Web browser to test our policy. Click *Finish* to create the policy.

8. You should now see the policy appear under the *Policy-based QoS* node in the *Local Group Policy Editor* window as seen in Figure 3.14.

9. Now let us test our new policy. To perform this test, you will need to download and install Network Monitor. Network Monitor can be downloaded from Microsoft Download Center at http://download. microsoft.com. After installing Network Monitor, open it by going to *Start | All Programs | Network Monitor 3.3*.

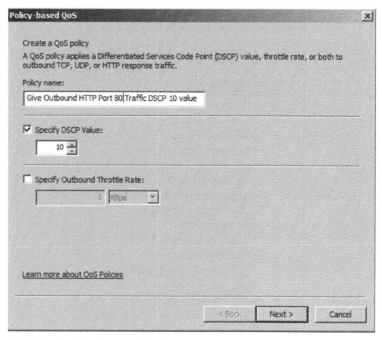

■ **FIGURE 3.10** Policy Name and DSCP Value.

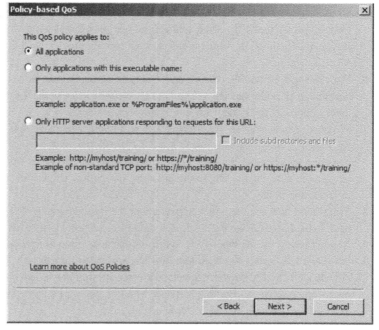

■ **FIGURE 3.11** Policy-Based QoS Applications.

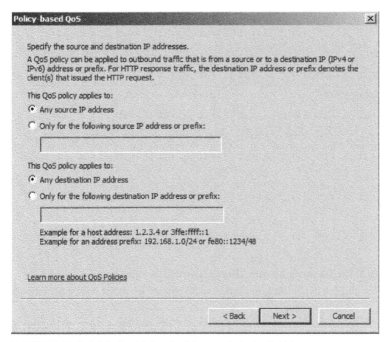

■ **FIGURE 3.12** Limit Policy-Based QoS to Listed Source or Destination IP Addresses.

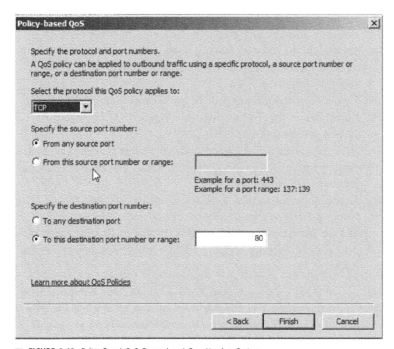

■ **FIGURE 3.13** Policy-Based QoS Protocol and Port Number Options.

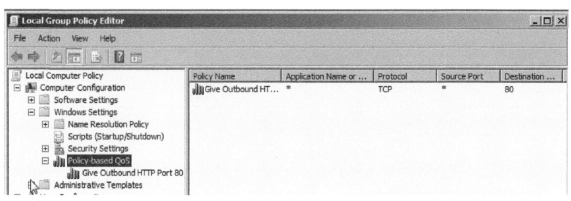

■ **FIGURE 3.14** New Policy-Based QoS Policy.

10. The Network Monitor *Start Page* will be opened as seen in Figure 3.15. Click the link *New Capture Tab* to set up a new network capture session.

11. A new capture tab will be opened. Click the *Start* button at the top of the *Network Monitor* window to start capturing traffic (see Figure 3.16).

12. Now let us create some outbound http traffic. Open Internet Explorer by going to *Start | All Programs | Internet Explorer*.

13. Browse a standard http Web site. Then close *Internet Explorer*.

14. Go back to the *Network Monitor* window and click the *Stop* button. You should see that the utility has captured traffic in the frame summary pane (see Figure 3.17).

15. Expand the *iexplorer.exe* node in the network conversations pane.

16. Locate one of the *IPv4* sessions (see Figure 3.18) and select the session you want to view.

17. After selecting an IPv4 session, notice the list of frames in the frames summary pane as seen in Figure 3.19. Select a frame that contains *DstPort=HTTP(80)*.

18. Expand the *IPv4* section in the frame details pane (see Figure 3.20). Notice the *DifferentiatedServicesField* subnode. You will notice that the frame has been given a DSCP value of 10. This shows that the policy is correctly applying a DSCP value to outbound port 80 traffic.

Test various QoS policies in your test lab during your Windows Server 2008 R2 deployment. You can use them to help ensure that the critical applications receive necessary network bandwidth to perform optimally.

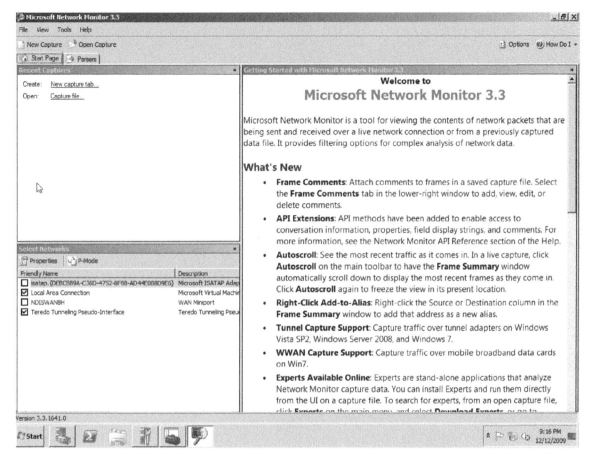

■ **FIGURE 3.15** Network Monitor Start Page.

ROUTING AND REMOTE ACCESS

Windows Server 2008 R2 includes Routing and Remote Access features to provide basic IPv4 and IPv6 routing as well as remote access services, such as VPN and dial-up. These access features allow remote users to connect to the corporate network and access network resources, such as file servers, print servers, and intranet Web sites. VPN and dial-up services can also be used to provide site–site connectivity within the corporate network. Additionally, you can use the routing features in Routing and Remote Access to create a router between two separate subnets. As you learned earlier in this chapter, networks are rarely composed of a single

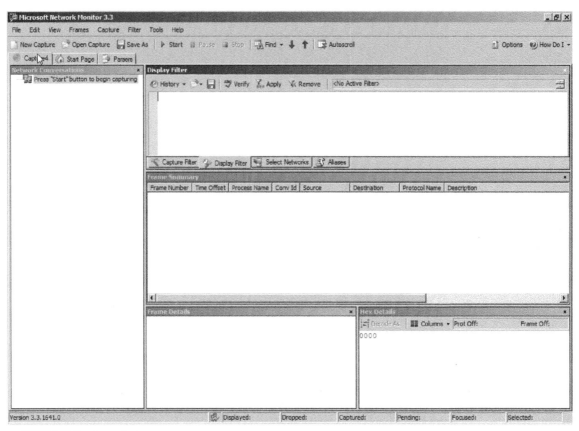

■ **FIGURE 3.16** New Capture Session.

subnet and require a router to send traffic between subnets. Most organizations deploy dedicated router appliances to create this functionality, but Windows Server 2008 R2 Routing and Remote Access can be used to fulfill the same needs to route traffic between two separate logical subnets.

Installing Routing and Remote Access

Routing and Remote Access is installed by adding the Network Policy and Access Services role. To install Routing and Remote Access, perform the following:

1. Open Server Manager by selecting Start | Administrative Tools | Server Manger.

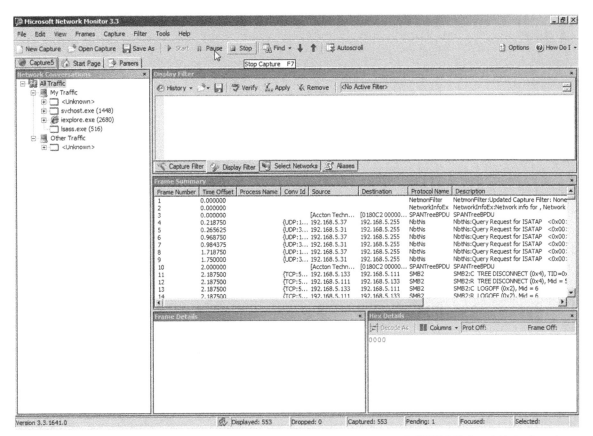

FIGURE 3.17 Network Monitor Captured Traffic.

2. The Server Manager window will open. Select the Roles node, then click the Add Roles link in the middle pane.
3. The Add Roles Wizard will launch. Click Next to continue.
4. Select the Network Policy and Access Services role as seen in Figure 3.21. Then click Next.
5. This will take you to the role summary screen. Click Next to continue.
6. Select the Routing and Remote Access role service (see Figure 3.22). Then click Next.
7. Verify the selection and then click Install. When the installation is complete, click Close.

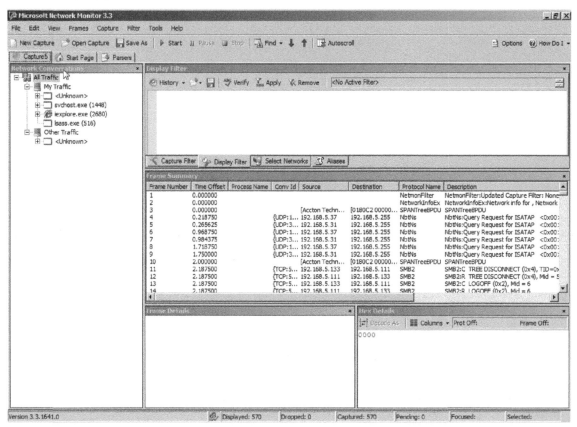

■ **FIGURE 3.18** Selected IPv4 Session frames.

8. You can manage Routing and Remote Access by opening Server Manager and selecting Roles | Network Policy and Access Services | Routing and Remote Access as seen in Figure 3.23.

Configuring Routing and Remote Access to support Remote Access VPN

You can set up Routing and Remote Access to provide remote users access to your network *via* VPN services. The following exercise will take you through configuring Routing and Remote Access to support VPN connectivity. You will need to ensure that your VPN server has two network adapters (NICS) installed prior to configuring Routing and Remote Access to support VPN.

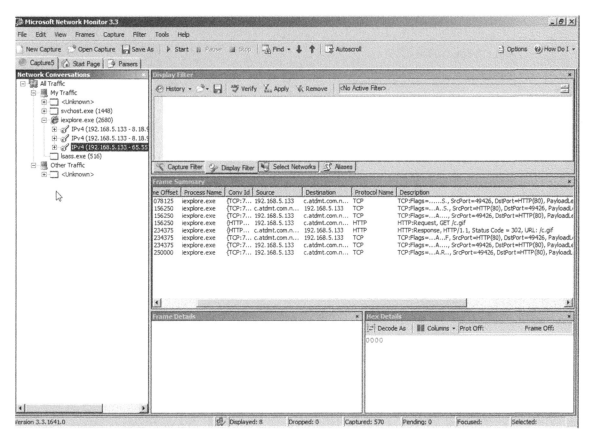

FIGURE 3.19 The Frames Summary Pane.

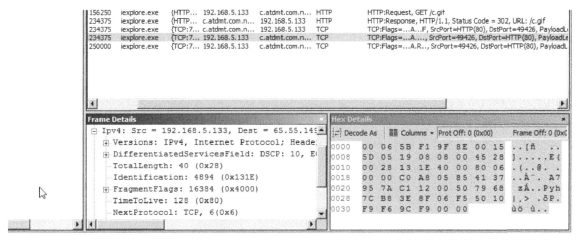

FIGURE 3.20 IPv4 Session Frame Details.

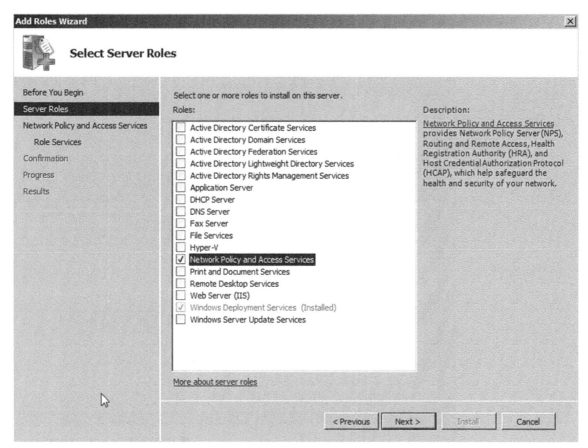

■ **FIGURE 3.21** Add Network Policy and Access
Services Role.

1. Launch Server Manager by opening Start | Administrative Tools |
   Server Manager.
2. Select the Routing and Remote Access node from Roles | Network
   Policy and Access Services | Routing and Remote Access.
3. Right click the Routing and Remote Access node and select the option
   Configure and Enable Routing and Remote Access (see Figure 3.24).
4. The Routing and Remote Access Setup Wizard will launch. Click
   Next to begin configuration.
5. Select the first option—Remote Access (dial-up or VPN). Then click
   Next.
6. Since we will be providing only VPN services, select only the VPN
   option for remote access (see Figure 3.25). Then click Next.

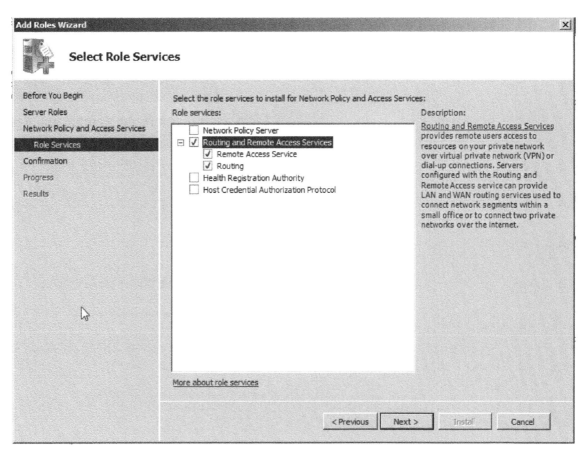

■ **FIGURE 3.22** Routing and Remote Access Role Services.

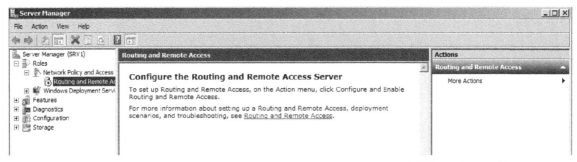

■ **FIGURE 3.23** Routing and Remote Access Management Console.

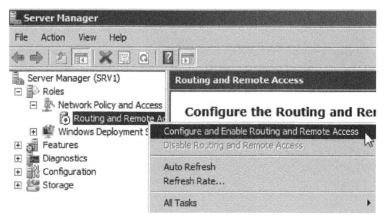

■ **FIGURE 3.24** Configure and Enable Routing and Remote Access.

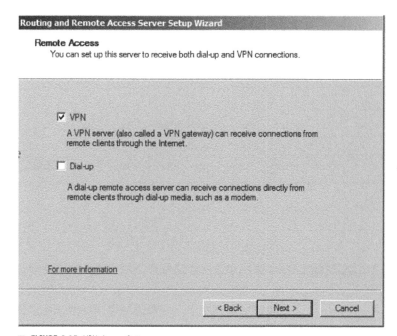

■ **FIGURE 3.25** VPN Access Option.

7. Select a network interface that connects the VPN server to the Internet (see Figure 3.26). Routing and Remote Access will use the Internet-connected adapter to accept incoming VPN connections and use the other adapter to route inbound VPN traffic to the corporate network. Leave the option *Enable security on the selected interface*

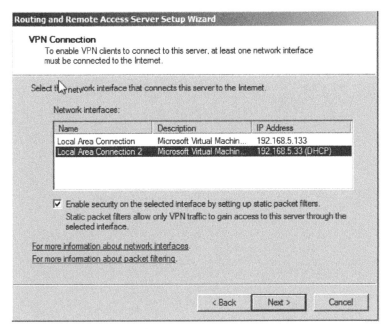

Routing and Remote Access Server Setup Wizard

VPN Connection
To enable VPN clients to connect to this server, at least one network interface must be connected to the Internet.

Select the network interface that connects this server to the Internet.

Network interfaces:

Name	Description	IP Address
Local Area Connection	Microsoft Virtual Machin...	192.168.5.133
Local Area Connection 2	Microsoft Virtual Machin...	192.168.5.33 (DHCP)

☑ Enable security on the selected interface by setting up static packet filters.
Static packet filters allow only VPN traffic to gain access to this server through the selected interface.

For more information about network interfaces.
For more information about packet filtering.

[< Back] [Next >] [Cancel]

■ **FIGURE 3.26** Select Internet Interface.

by setting up static packet filters checked. This will set up packet filters to ensure that only VPN traffic is allowed to communicate to the Internet-facing interface, providing a greater level of security. Click Next to continue.

8. Select how you would like to assign IP addresses to clients connecting to the network via VPN (see Figure 3.27). You can choose to have the computers request an address either from your existing DHCP pools or from a range of specific addresses. For this example, we will use DHCP (DHCP is covered later in this chapter). Then click Next.

9. Select how you want the VPN server to authenticate. Here you can choose whether to have the VPN server authenticate users or send the authentication to a Remote Authentication Dial-in User Service (RADIUS) server. In larger deployments, you may want to use RADIUS. RADIUS can provide a greater level of security and management by handling authentication for VPN connections instead of allowing them to authenticate directly to your AD domain. In our example, we will allow the VPN server to authenticate users (see Figure 3.28). Select the option No, and use Routing and Remote Access to authenticate connection requests. Then click Next.

10. Verify your settings on the summary page, and then click Finish.

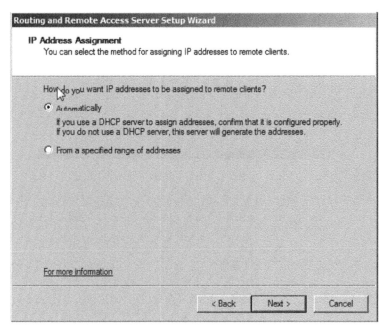

■ **FIGURE 3.27** Automatic IP Assignment.

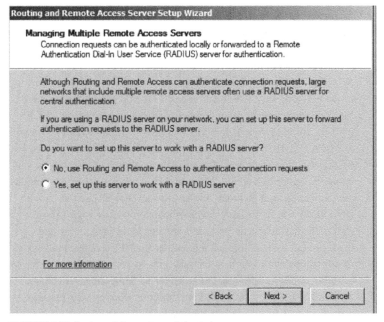

■ **FIGURE 3.28** Routing and Remote Access Authentication.

11. The server is now configured to support VPN connections via Point-to-Point Tunneling Protocol (PPTP), Layer 2 Tunneling Protocol (L2TP), and Secure Socket Tunneling Protocol (SSTP).

NOTES FROM THE FIELD

Consider DirectAccess

Windows Server 2008 R2 continues the tradition of supporting remote dial-up and connectivity services. If you have Windows 7 clients on your network, you may want to consider setting up DirectAccess instead or along with traditional VPN access. DirectAccess provides a secure remote connection back to the corporate network without the need for traditional VPN services. We will discuss DirectAccess in detail in Chapter 13.

PLANNING AND DEPLOYING DNS

DNS is one of the most mission-critical components used by today's Windows networks. DNS name resolution is a process that translates computer names to IP addresses and *vice versa*. In this section, we will explore what DNS is and how it works. It is important to understand how to set up, configure, and manage DNS before deploying a Windows Server 2008 R2 network. If the DNS services break, so does your network. We will then discuss designing and then deploying DNS services. We will finish our DNS discussion by exploring how to administer and troubleshoot Windows Server 2008 R2 DNS services.

Overview of name resolution and DNS

Before setting up and configuring DNS, it is important to understand how name resolution works and why it is needed by Windows networks. Like most other network services covered in this chapter, you need to understand what is going on "under the covers" to really grasp how the service works and why it is important.

DNS at a basic level is performing one main function, resolving names to IP addresses. Earlier in this chapter, you learned that computers use TCP/IP to communicate and that each computer is given a unique IP address. For computer A to talk to computer B, computer A must know the IP address of computer B. IP-based communication poses a small problem to humans. How do you remember all of those IP addresses? Think about having to remember the IP address of your 20 favorite Web sites on the Internet (remember all computers, even Web servers hosting Web sites, require IP address-based communication). Luckily, this is where DNS helps. DNS allows us to remember a name known as a Fully Qualified

Domain Name (FQDN) instead of the IP address of the computer that we are trying to reach. We can reach www.bing.com or www.microsoft.com by simply typing the Web address, also known as the FQDN. DNS then translates this FQDN to an IP address. After DNS translates the name to IP address, your computer connects to that address. So how exactly does all of this work? The example below will take you through the Windows name resolution process.

1. Your computer would like to access the Web site www.bing.com.
2. Your computer's DNS client service sends a name resolution request to the DNS Server whose IP address is listed in the DNS Servers section of the computer's IP configuration. We will refer to this server as the local DNS Server.
3. The local DNS Server receives the request and determines if it should host the domain name being requested. If it does host the domain, then it looks up the DNS record and returns it to the client. If it does not host the domain, the local DNS Server queries a root DNS Server for the IP address of the .com DNS Server.
4. Once the IP of the .com DNS Server is received, the local DNS Server queries the .com DNS Server for the IP address of the bing.com DNS Server.
5. The local DNS Server then queries the bing.com DNS Server for the IP address of www.bing.com.
6. Your client computer then receives the IP address of the www.bing.com server from your local DNS Server. Figure 3.29 illustrates this process.

DNS zones

DNS Servers host zones which in turn host records that resolve a name to an IP address. The zone is the authoritative source for information about the domain name managed by that zone. A DNS zone is typically the same as the domain name being hosted on the DNS Server. For example, if the DNS Server will be hosting the domain syngress.com, then the zone syngress.com must be created on the DNS Server. There are two Primary zone types that can be set up on a DNS Server—Forward Lookup Zones and Reverse Lookup Zones.

- *Forward Lookup Zones*—Forward Lookup Zones allow the DNS Server to resolve queries where the client sends a name to the DNS Server to request the IP address of the requested host.
- *Reverse Lookup Zones*—Reverse DNS zones perform the opposite task as Forward Lookup Zones. They return the fully qualified domain name (FQDN) of a given IP address. For example, a client could send

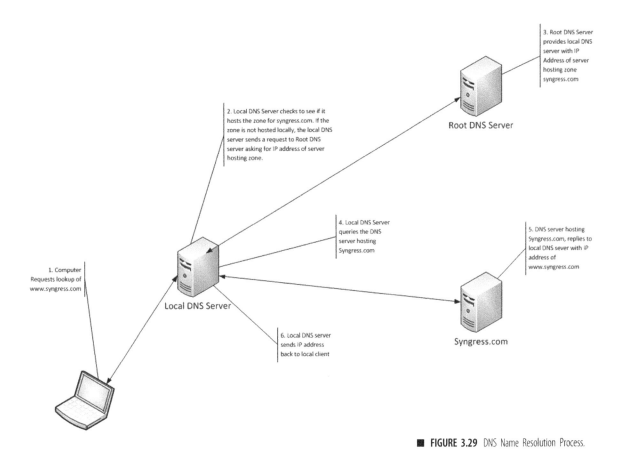

■ FIGURE 3.29 DNS Name Resolution Process.

the IP address of 69.163.177.2 to a DNS Server. If the server hosted a reverse zone that included that IP address, it would return the FQDN for that address, such as www.syngress.com.

In addition to the standard zone types, DNS zones can be further broken down into the following zone types:

- *Primary zone (stored in* AD)—These zones are stored in AD and replicated *via* normal AD replication. This provides an optimized way to replicate the zones within your corporate network. Primary zones stored in AD follow the same multimaster rules as other AD services. This means that you can perform updates on any AD Domain Controller and they will replicate to the other Domain Controllers.
- *Primary zone (standard)*—Standard Primary zones are stored in a flat file on the DNS Server. The Primary zone is considered the master

copy of the zone database file. All updates to the zone must be performed on the Primary zone server.

- *Secondary zone*—Secondary zones are read-only copies of the Primary zones. Secondary zones replicate a copy of the zone from the Primary zone server to provide redundancy. Any updates to the zone must be performed on the Primary zone server.
- *Stub zone*—Stub zones are similar to Secondary zones in that they are read-only copies of the zone database file. Stub zones, however, contain only the Name Server (NS), Start of Authority (SOA), and host (A) records for the Name Servers.

BEST PRACTICES

Create Reverse Lookup Zones

Some applications require the ability to perform Reverse DNS Lookups. As a best practice, you should set up Reverse Lookup Zones for IP subnets on your network.

Global Naming Zones

Before Windows networks relied so heavily on DNS, they used the Windows Internet Naming Service (WINS) to provide name resolution. WINS provides the ability to resolve a NETBIOS name to an IP address. If you support legacy applications that rely on NETBIOS names, it is highly possible that you are still supporting WINS on your network. To help organizations move away from WINS, Microsoft developed Global Naming Zones (GNZs). GNZs, in Windows Server 2008 R2, allow companies to decommission WINS while still supporting NETBIOS names. GNZs require that your domain controllers be at Windows Server 2008 or later. Windows Server 2003 DCs do not support GNZs.

DNS records

DNS records are the data of DNS zones. Records map host names to IP addresses and IP addresses to host names. The most commonly used DNS records are listed below:

- *A (Host) Record*—A records are standard records that map the FQDN of a host to an IP address. For example, the syngress.com zone could contain a host record www that points to the IP address of the Syngress Web site.
- *CNAME (Alias) Record*—CNAME records, also known as aliases, map a host name to an existing A record. For example, a CNAME record could map www.syngress.com to Web server1.syngress.com.

■ *MX (Mail Exchanger) Record*—MX records are used to map a domain name to an A record for mail delivery. MX records also contain a priority to allow failover to secondary mail servers in the event that your primary mail server is unavailable. MX records are crucial to ensure mail flow.

■ *NS (Name Server) Record*—NS records identify all the authoritative DNS servers for a given zone. The primary DNS Server and the secondary DNS Server should have NS records in the zone.

■ *SRV (Service) Record*—SRV records provide autodiscovery of TCP/IP resource on the network. Using SRV records, clients can query the domain for information about a particular service, such as what server it may reside on. SRV records are being used by more and more applications to provide autodiscovery for products such as Exchange Server and Office Communications Server.

■ *PTR (Pointer) Record*—PTR records are Reverse Lookup records that reside in Reverse DNS zones. PTR records perform the opposite function as A records.

Designing a DNS infrastructure

When creating your DNS design documentation, you will want to ensure that the infrastructure is highly available and redundant. As previously mentioned, DNS is one of the most mission-critical services on your network. As you design your DNS infrastructure, you will want to consider the following:

■ Number of physical and logical networks that will need name resolution.
■ Available WAN bandwidth.
■ Number of domains or zones you will need to support.
■ Other non-Windows-based DNS hosts.
■ Where DNS zones will be stored—AD or DNS flat files?
■ Integration with WINS servers.
■ Can GNZs replace WINS?
■ What types of records will be required?
■ How many records will be needed?
■ Will subdomains be required (subdomain.syngress.com)?
■ Will DNS Forwarding be used?
■ Number of clients using DNS for name resolution.

Remember that a good DNS design allows quick name resolution to clients and provides adequate redundancy so that DNS services remain available in the event of a DNS Server failure. As mentioned throughout this book, you will want to test your design thoroughly before deploying to a production network. DNS is no exception. You need to be able to answer questions such as "Does name resolution still work efficiently if a DNS Server fails?" and "Is the DNS response time quick enough to support the number of clients on my network?" Be sure that you adequately document your DNS design. As your network grows, you will want to refer the design and make modifications to support new network segments and increased numbers of clients. Figure 3.30 depicts a design of a small network.

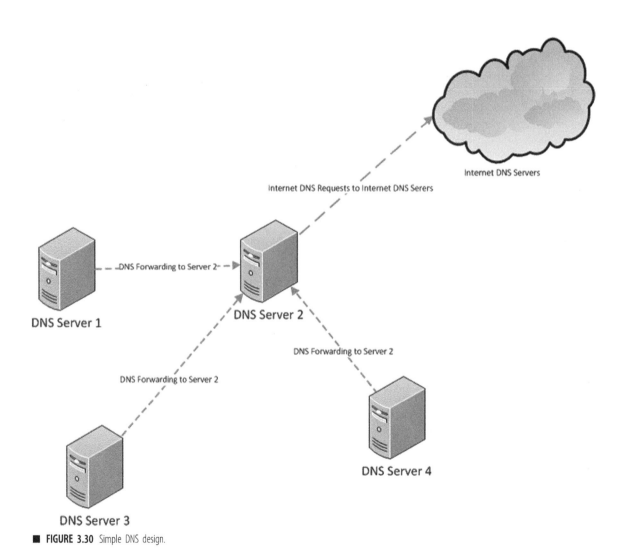

■ **FIGURE 3.30** Simple DNS design.

Deploying DNS

After designing (and testing) your DNS infrastructure, you are ready to begin deployment. How you deploy will depend upon how you plan to configure and support DNS. DNS can be installed just like any other server role, or if you are planning on using DNS on an AD Domain Controller, it is installed using the AD dcpromo process. We will explore using DNS with AD in detail in Chapter 4, so in this chapter we will focus on deploying nonAD integrated DNS Servers.

Installing the DNS Server role

Installing DNS can be done the same way as you would install any other server role. To install DNS perform the following steps:

1. Open Server Manager from Start | Administrative Tools | Server Manager.
2. Click to highlight the Roles node in the left pane. Then click the Add Roles link in the middle pane. This will launch the Add Roles Wizard.
3. Click Next to begin the installation process.
4. Select DNS Server from the list of available roles (see Figure 3.31). Then click Next.
5. The Introduction to DNS Server page will appear. Click Next to continue.
6. Confirm that DNS was selected on the summary page, and then click Install.
7. After DNS installation is completed, you will be taken to an installation results page. Verify that the DNS role was installed successfully, and then click Close.
8. You should now see the DNS role listed under the Roles node in Server Manager as seen in Figure 3.32.

Configuring DNS Servers

After DNS is installed, you will need to configure the service to support name resolution. The primary DNS configuration tool is the DNS console in Server Manager. Let us take a look at DNS Server configuration settings.

You can access the server's DNS properties by expanding the nodes *Roles | DNS Server | DNS*, and then right clicking the listed DNS Server and choosing *Properties* as seen in Figure 3.33.

The properties window will open and you will be presented with a series of configuration tabs as seen in Figure 3.34.

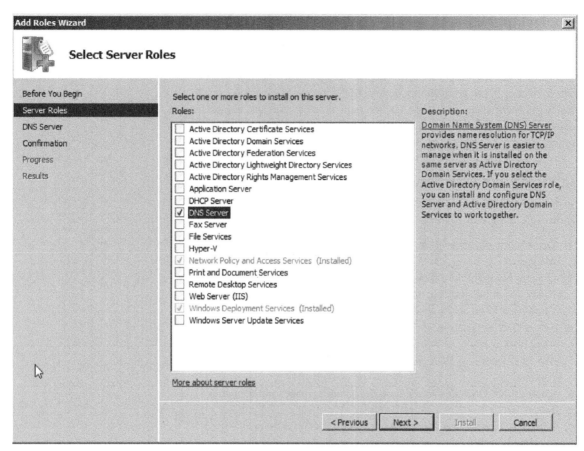

■ **FIGURE 3.31** Select DNS Server role.

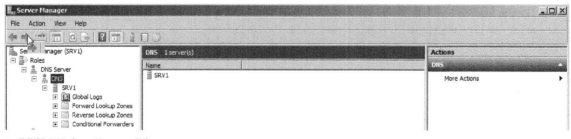

■ **FIGURE 3.32** Server Manager—DNS
Server role.

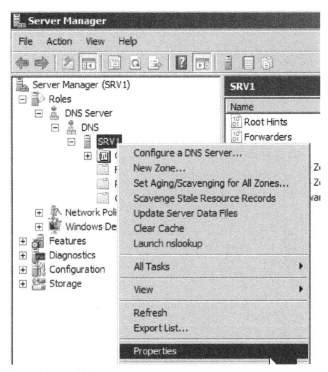

■ **FIGURE 3.33** Opening DNS Properties.

We will now take a look at each of the configuration tabs and explore the options that can be set up. The following configuration tabs are displayed in the DNS properties window:

■ *Interfaces*—The Interfaces tab allows you to select the IP addresses (including IPv6 addresses) that you want to listen for DNS requests on. By default, the option to listen on all interfaces is selected.
■ *Forwarders*—The Forwarders option allows you to specify the DNS Servers that the current DNS Server can forward the requests to, if it cannot resolve the requested query.

BEST PRACTICES

Using DNS forwarders

As a best practice, you should have a set of DNS Servers that use root hints to perform DNS lookups. You should then configure all other DNS Servers on your network to forward Internet-based requests to these servers. Forwarders provide additional security against DNS cache poisoning by limiting which servers pull records from Internet DNS Servers.

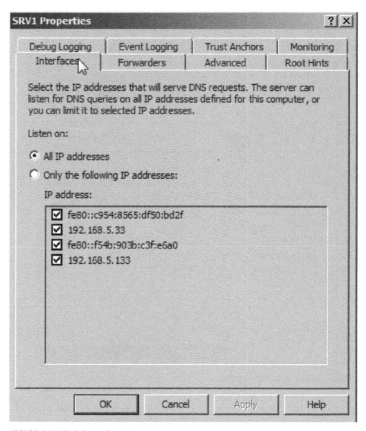

■ FIGURE 3.34 DNS Server Properties.

■ *Advanced*—Most DNS installations will not require you to modify the settings on the Advanced tab; however, there may be occasions where changing these options are necessary.

□ Disable recursion—Disabling recursion will prevent the DNS Server from performing a referral lookup of zones not hosted on this DNS Server. If recursion is disabled and a client queries the DNS Server for a zone that is not hosted on the DNS Server, the query will fail.

□ BIND Secondaries—Enabling this option will allow Windows DNS Servers to perform fast zone transfers to compatible BIND DNS Servers. Fast zone transfers use compression to perform a faster transfer of data from a primary DNS Server to secondary DNS Servers.

□ Fail on load if bad zone data—Enabling this option will instruct the DNS Server to not load the zone if there are errors in the zone files.

- ❏ Enable round robin—This feature, enabled by default, allows DNS to use round robin techniques to send traffic to multiple IP addresses for a single host.
- ❏ Enable netmask ordering—This feature, also enabled by default, ensures that a host IP on the client's local subnet will be returned if multiple IP addresses (host records) are given for a single hostname.
- ❏ Secure cache against pollution—This feature attempts to prevent the local DNS cache from being polluted by discarding records in the cache that could be considered insecure due to the fact that they were received from a DNS Server that is not part of the domain path that the original request was sent to.

- *Root Hints*—The root hints tab lists the root DNS Servers that the server will use to resolve a query if it does not host the zone.
- *Debug Logging*—Debug Logging allows you to create a very detailed log of DNS packets sent and received by the DNS Server. Debug Logging can create very large logs depending on how many packets are captured. It is only recommended that you turn on Debug Logging when troubleshooting DNS problems.
- *Event Logging*—This setting configures what type of DNS events should be written to the DNS Event Log. By default, the *All Events* option is selected.
- *Trust Anchors*—Trust Anchors are part of DNS Security Extensions (DNSSEC). Trust Anchors are used to validate responses from remote DNS Servers.
- *Monitoring*—The Monitoring tab allows you to perform basic or recursive queries against the DNS Server manually or on a scheduled basis.

Setting up DNS zones

Hosting a domain on a DNS Server requires setting up the zone for that domain. To set up a new DNS zone, perform the following:

1. Open Server Manager from Start | Administrative Tools | Server Manager.
2. Select the Forward Lookup Zones node from Roles | DNS Server | DNS | <your DNS Server name> (see Figure 3.35).
3. Right click the Forward Lookup Zones node and select New Zone. The New Zone wizard will launch. Click Next to begin creating a new DNS zone.
4. Select the zone type (see Figure 3.36). If this is the first copy of the zone, you will want to select the Primary zone option. Then click Next.

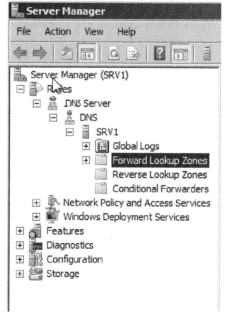

■ **FIGURE 3.35** Forward Lookup Zones.

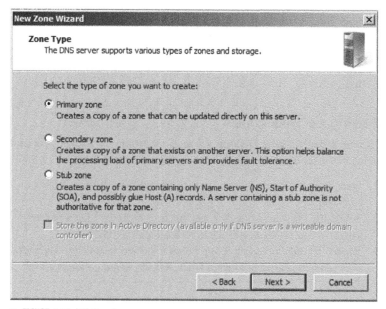

■ **FIGURE 3.36** DNS Zone Type.

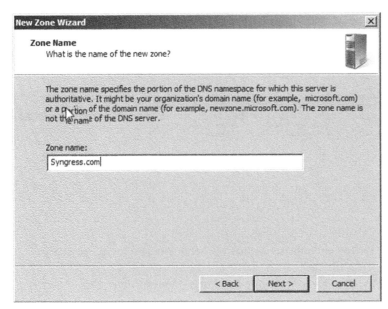

■ FIGURE 3.37 Zone Name.

5. Enter the Zone Name. This is the namespace for which this server will be authoritative. For example, if the server is hosting Syngress.com, enter that into the Zone Name field as seen in Figure 3.37. Then click Next.
6. If this is a new zone, enter a name for the DNS file. If the zone was previously set up on another server, such as a lab, you can use an existing DNS file to prepopulate the zone on this server. Click Next to continue.
7. Select whether you want to allow dynamic updates or not. By default dynamic updates are disabled. Click Next to continue.
8. Verify your settings on the summary page, and then click Finish to create the zone.
9. You will see the zone now listed in Server Manager as seen in Figure 3.38. You can select the zone to see records that belong to the zone in the middle pane. By default every zone creates NS and SOA records.

Replicating DNS zones

After you set up your primary DNS zone, you will then want to replicate the zones to at least one secondary server. To set up DNS replication, perform the following:

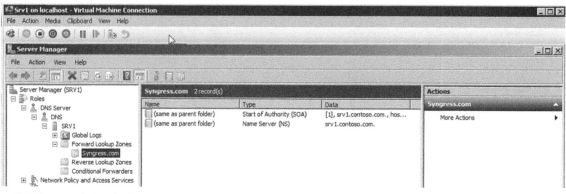

■ **FIGURE 3.38** Newly Created DNS Zone.

1. Log on to the server that will serve as a host to the secondary DNS zone.
2. Open *Server Manager* from *Start | Administrative Tools | Server Manager*.
3. If the DNS Server Role is not installed, you will need to install it.
4. Select the *Forward Lookup Zones* node from *Roles | DNS Server | DNS | <your DNS Server name>*.
5. Right click the *Forward Lookup Zones* node and select *New Zone*. The New Zone wizard will launch. Click *Next* to begin creating a new DNS zone.
6. Select the zone type (see Figure 3.39). Since this will be a Secondary zone, select the *Secondary zone* option. Then click *Next*.
7. Enter the name of the zone (see Figure 3.40). This should be the same name as the Primary zone. In our example, we will use Syngress.com.
8. Enter the IP address of FQDN of the primary DNS Server (see Figure 3.41). Then click *Next*.
9. Click the *Finish* button to complete the set up of the Secondary zone. You now need to allow the Secondary zone to pull information from the primary. To do this, log on to the primary DNS Server.
10. Open *Server Manager* from *Start | Administrative Tools | Server Manager*.
11. Select the *Forward Lookup Zones* node from *Roles | DNS Server | DNS | <your DNS Server name>*
12. Right click the zone you wish to modify. Then click *Properties*. In our case, we will be modifying Syngress.com.
13. Click to select the *Name Servers* tab.
14. Enter the IP address and FQDN of the secondary DNS Server (see Figure 3.42). Then click *OK*.

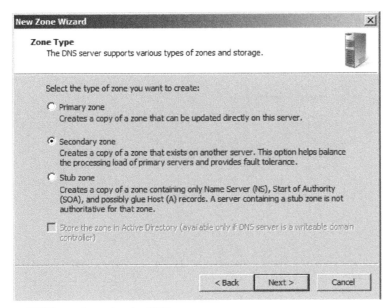

■ **FIGURE 3.39** Creating Secondary DNS Zones.

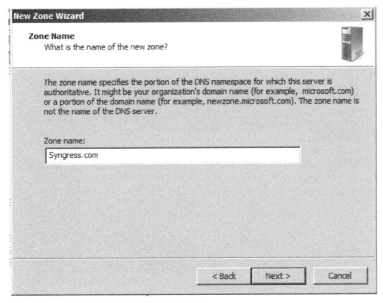

■ **FIGURE 3.40** Secondary Zone Name.

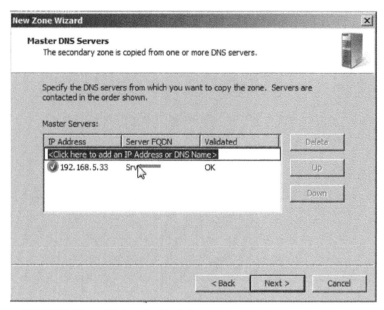

■ **FIGURE 3.41** Primary DNS Server Used for Replication.

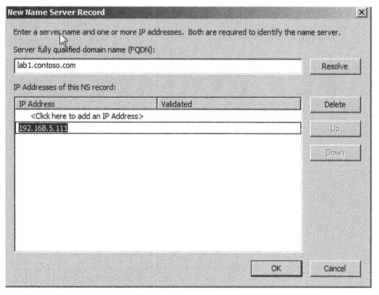

■ **FIGURE 3.42** Adding secondary DNS Server.

15. You should now be able to go back to the secondary DNS Server and see the zone data inside the zone. Any new records created on the primary server should automatically replicate to the secondary server.

Creating DNS records

After DNS zones are set up, configured, and verified, you are ready to start creating records. To create a new DNS record, perform the following:

1. Log on to the server that hosts the primary DNS zone.
2. Open *Server Manager* from *Start | Administrative Tools | Server Manager*.
3. Expand the DNS role and servers. Then expand the *Forward Lookup Zones* node. Right click the zone where you want to create a new record and select *New Host (A or AAAA) Record...*
4. Enter the host name to complete the FQDN, and then enter the IP address that the record should point to (see Figure 3.43).
5. You can now test the new host record. Ensure that your computer is set to use your DNS Server as the primary DNS Server in the TCP/IP settings.
6. Open a command prompt.
7. Type *nslookup* at the command prompt, and then hit *Enter*.

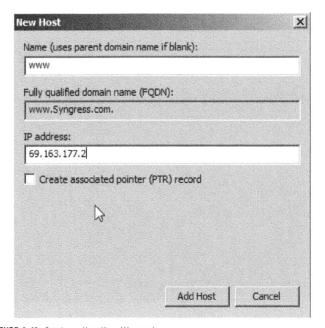

■ **FIGURE 3.43** Creating a New Host (A) record.

8. Type *www.syngress.com.*
9. You should come back with a nonauthoritative reply with the IP address you specified when setting up the record (see Figure 3.44).

Dynamic DNS records

Dynamic DNS (DDNS) allows dynamic creation and updates to DNS records. By allowing DDNS, hosts can automatically update their own records within the DNS zone. Using DDNS raises some obvious security questions. For this reason, it is best practice not to enable DDNS for any zones that are facing the public Internet. You should also consider using Secure Dynamic Updates on your LAN when the DNS zones are AD integrated. We will explore DDNS further in Chapter 4.

DNS and Active Directory

In this chapter, we have primarily covered traditional DNS systems using primary and secondary DNS zones. When using DNS in an AD environment, you have the option to integrate zones into AD instead of using the primary/secondary model. There are some inherit benefits of using AD integrated zones. We will discuss this option in length in Chapter 4.

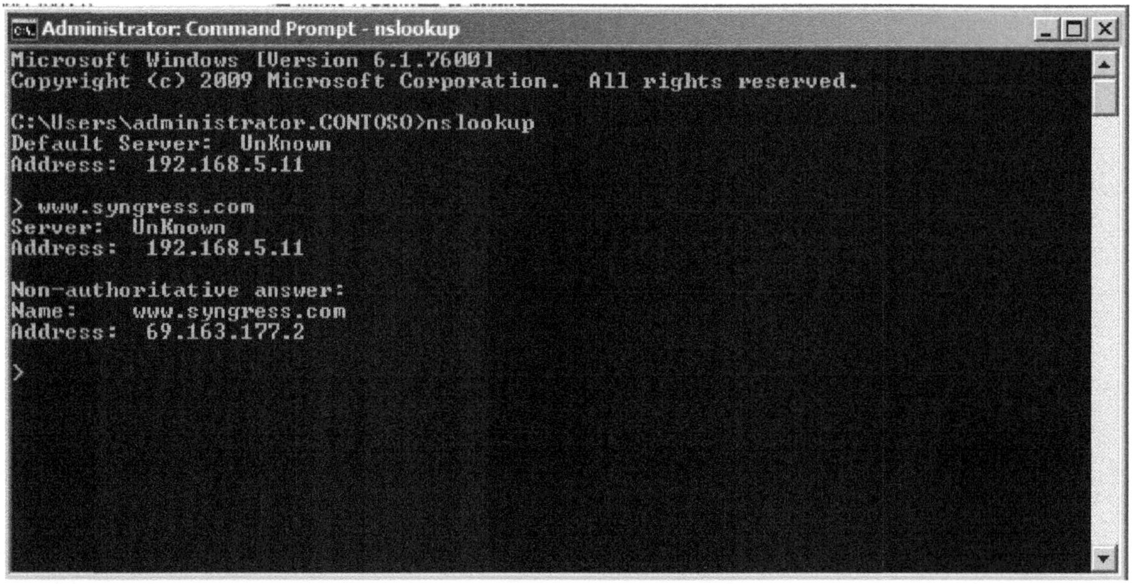

```
Administrator: Command Prompt - nslookup

Microsoft Windows [Version 6.1.7600]
Copyright (c) 2009 Microsoft Corporation.  All rights reserved.

C:\Users\administrator.CONTOSO>nslookup
Default Server:  UnKnown
Address:  192.168.5.11

> www.syngress.com
Server:  UnKnown
Address:  192.168.5.11

Non-authoritative answer:
Name:    www.syngress.com
Address:  69.163.177.2

>
```

■ **FIGURE 3.44** Testing DNS Record with NSLookup.

Securing DNS

Due to the critical nature of DNS services, it is important that you make sure your DNS Servers are as secure as possible. This is especially true for DNS Servers that are connected to the Internet. Consider implementing some of the following to secure your DNS Servers:

- Open only necessary firewall ports required to perform name resolution (53 TCP/UDP).
- Restrict log-on to DNS Servers to DNS admins.
- Turn off recursive lookups if the DNS Servers will be used only for responding to queries for zones they host. If you plan to allow clients to use the DNS Servers for name resolution, you will need to leave this on.
- Do not allow DDNS Updates for non-AD-based zones. Be sure to use only Secure Dynamic Updates for AD-integrated zones.
- Ensure that zone transfers can occur only to authorized secondary servers.

Taking the preceding steps and following other security best practices can help ensure that your DNS Servers remain secure and reliable.

Monitoring and troubleshooting DNS

To ensure that you have reliable DNS services, you need to monitor your DNS Servers and ensure that they perform name resolution properly. In this section, we will take a look at some of the tools provided in Windows to monitor DNS and troubleshoot problems.

Event log and debug logging

You will want to review the DNS event log on a regular basis to ensure that services are online and available. Search the event log for any error events and correct any issues that appear in the event log. You should also keep an eye on warning events. These can point to configuration issues that may not currently be causing an outage, but could do so at a future time.

Debug logging can really help you home in on the root cause of DNS problems (see Figure 3.45) where the solution may not be apparent using other monitoring methods and event logs. You will not want to leave debug logging enabled all the time. Turn it on when you need details on DNS packets sent and received from and to the server. After resolving the problem, be sure to disable debug logging to prevent the hard drive from filling up. The debug log settings can be found in the properties of the DNS Server.

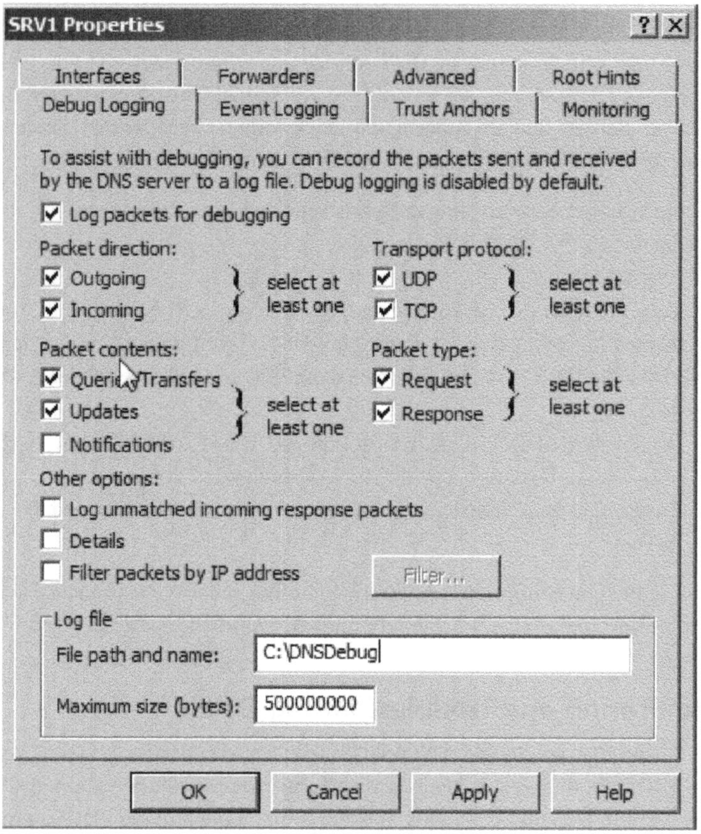

■ **FIGURE 3.45** Debug Logging.

DNS Monitoring tab

You can test basic query functionality of the DNS Server by going to the server properties and selecting the *Monitoring* tab. Here you can manually run both simple and recursive queries against the DNS Server manually and on a scheduled basis.

NSLookup and DNScmd

NSLookup and DNScmd are two very important command line tools that can assist in troubleshooting DNS problems. You should have both of these tools as part of your admin toolkit. Luckily, they are already installed on the server as a part of the operating system.

- NSLookup is a tool used to test queries against DNS Servers. You can run this command line tool from your workstation and point it to a DNS Server that you wish to test. You can then run various queries against the server to see detailed information on the data returned.
- DNScmd is a tool now included as a part of the Windows operating system. DNScmd includes an array of options that allow you to perform DNS administrative actions from the command line. These actions include creating/deleting DNS zones, adding and deleting records, and managing the DNS windows services. Table 3.4 lists some commonly used DNScmd commands.

Viewing cache

If your DNS Server does recursive queries against other DNS Servers, it will begin building a cache of lookups it has performed. The next time the same lookup is requested, the DNS Server simply pulls the query result from the cache. You can view the cache by going to the DNS Server, and then going to the *View* menu and selecting the *Advanced* option. You will see the cache folder appear in the management console. You can open the zone to review records or right click and the option *Clear Cache* to delete all cached copies of the records.

Table 3.4 Common DNScmd Commands

Command	Description	Example
DNScmd/zoneadd *zonename*/primary	Create a new primary DNS zone	DNScmd/zoneadd syngress.com/primary
DNScmd/zoneadd *zonename*/secondary *IP Address of Primary*	Create a new secondary DNS zone	DNScmd/zoneadd syngress.com/secondary 10.1.3.4
DNScmd/zonedelete *zonename*	Delete a DNS zone	DNScmd/zonedelete syngress.com
DNScmd/enumzones	List DNS zones on a server	DNScmd/enumzones
DNScmd/zoneprint *zonename*	List all the DNS records in a zone	DNScmd/zoneprint syngress.com
DNScmd/recordadd *zonename hostname* A *IP Address*	Create a new host (A) record	DNScmd/recordadd syngress.com www A 10.1.3.3
DNScmd/recordadd *zonename* @ MX *priority* **FQDN of mail server**	Create a new mail exchanger (MX) record	DNScmd/recordadd syngress.com @ MX 100 mail.syngress.com

Aging and scavenging

The aging and scavenging process allows DNS to perform basic automated administration by deleting old DNS records that are no longer in use. This feature will be more important for AD-integrated zones but can also be helpful for standard primary/secondary DNS zones.

The aging and scavenging process can be set up on the server level, zone level, or both. Server level settings apply to all the zones on the server. Zone-level settings can be set on individual zones to override the server-level settings. Aging and scavenging are set up either in the server properties or in the zone properties (see Figure 3.46).

After providing your preferred scavenging settings, you have to enable a DNS Server to actually run the scavenge process. To do this, open the server properties window, and then select the *Advanced* tab. Click the option *Enable automatic scavenging of stale records* (see Figure 3.47).

Using the default settings, the scavenge process will run every seven days and will purge records that have not been updated in fourteen days.

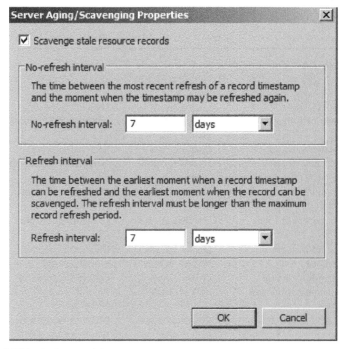

■ **FIGURE 3.46** Server Level Scavenging.

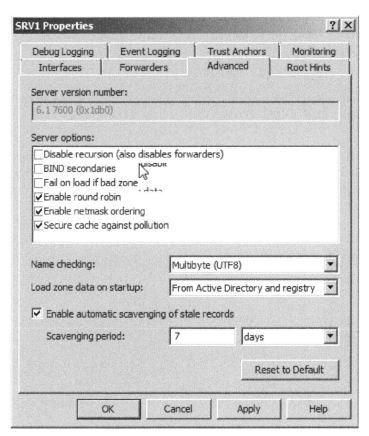

■ **FIGURE 3.47** Enabling a DNS Server to run the scavenge process.

Overview of WINS

The WINS provides name resolution services for NETBIOS names on Windows networks. WINS was originally developed to provide NETBIOS name resolution before Windows networks relied so heavily on DNS. WINS works much like DNS in the sense that DNS maps FQDNs to IP addresses while WINS maps NETBIOS names to IP addresses.

You should probably try to avoid using WINS if you are building a new network. Microsoft is deemphasizing WINS in current operating systems and may decide to remove support in future Windows versions. With that being said, it is possible that at some point you may end up needing to administer an existing network that still uses WINS for legacy applications or operating systems. You should understand how WINS works prior to taking ownership of that network.

NOTES FROM THE FIELD

WINS and IPv6

WINS is considered as a legacy name resolution service; thus it does not support IPv6 addresses. You need to keep this in mind if you have WINS deployed and plan on moving to IPv6. You may want to consider GNZs in DNS instead of WINS.

WINS is deemphasized to the point that it is not considered a role in Windows Server 2008 R2. To set up a WINS server, you will need to install the service from the Features node in Server Manager (see Figure 3.48).

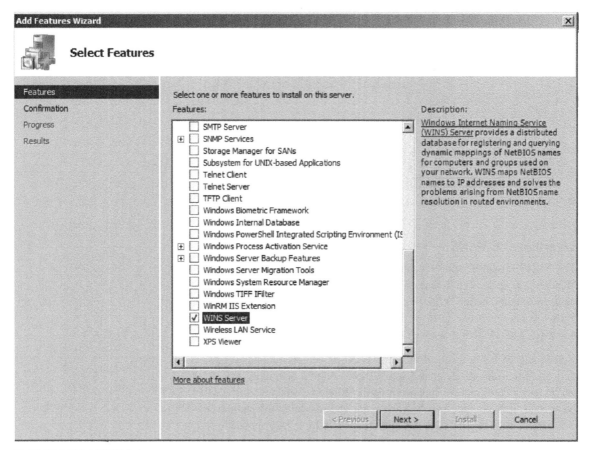

■ **FIGURE 3.48** Install WINS Feature.

Once the WINS feature is installed, it can be used immediately. You can configure clients and servers to register with the WINS server, and they will begin creating records within the WINS database.

When planning for WINS, you may want to consider placing a WINS server on larger network segments to limit the amount of traffic being sent over WAN links. Like DNS, you can place multiple WINS servers on your network that replicate with each other. WINS servers can be set up for push replication, pull replication, or both. During push replication, the server "pushes" changes out to replication partner. During pull replication, a WINS server "pulls" changes from a replication partner.

If mission-critical applications rely on WINS, you should also consider deploying multiple WINS servers for redundancy. Clients can then be pointed to multiple WINS servers for failover in the event that the primary server fails.

PLANNING AND DEPLOYING DHCP

We will round out this chapter covering the DHCP. As you learned earlier in this chapter, every device that communicates on a TCP/IP network must have an IP address. This includes computer workstations, laptops, network printers, routers, and servers. As you can imagine, the number of required IP addresses can add up. Think about managing a network with 5000 computers or even 10,000 computers. How do you assign IP addresses to each computer? This is where DHCP comes in. In this section, we will discuss what DHCP is and how it works. We will also cover installing and configuring DHCP and finish out the section learning how to troubleshoot DHCP.

Overview of DHCP

Most administrators know that managing a large network can be a daunting task at times. Can you imagine how daunting it would be to manually assign IP addresses to every device on your network? DHCP solves this problem by creating "pools" of IP addresses that can be "leased" by computers. DHCP is an industry standard protocol used to assign IP addresses to client computers. So exactly how does this process work? The DHCP process is outlined in the following steps and depicted in Figure 3.49.

1. A client configured to use DHCP for IP assignment sends a broadcast out to the network asking for an IP address.
2. The DHCP server picks up this broadcast and offers the requesting DHCP client an IP address from its pool.

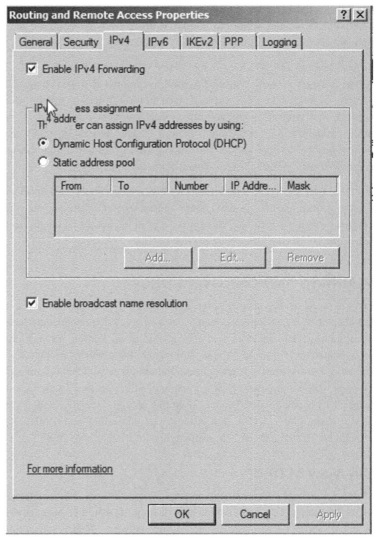

■ **FIGURE 3.49** DHCP IP Assignment Process.

3. The DHCP client sends a request back to the DHCP server basically stating that it truly wants to use the offered IP address.
4. The DHCP server then sends an acknowledgment back to the DHCP client stating that it has accepted the request.
5. On a scheduled basis, based upon a DHCP server setting, the client will renew its lease and send a request to the DHCP server for renewal.

6. If the DHCP server accepts the request, it sends another acknowledgment back to the DHCP client, informing it that it can continue to use the same IP address and resets the lease period. Once the new lease period expires, the client must perform steps 5 and 6 again.

DHCP provides not only IP addresses to clients, but also other configuration information, such as DNS Servers, the default gateway, and subnet mask information. Not only does DHCP prevent you from having to configure all of your devices, but also changes to your network can be made to all DHCP clients simply by making a configuration change on the DHCP server. The new configuration changes are pulled down by clients when they request a new IP address.

BEST PRACTICES

Assigning IP addresses to servers

In most cases, it is best practice to use static IP assignments for servers. Additionally, it is highly recommended that DHCP be never used to assign IP addresses to DNS Servers or AD domain controllers.

Planning for DHCP

Like DNS, DHCP is considered one of the most critical services on Windows network. If DHCP fails, then the client computers do not receive IP addresses and thus they cannot communicate on the IP network. If you want a reliable and highly available IP network, then DHCP failure is not an option. There are several factors to consider when designing your DHCP infrastructure.

- The number of physical and logical network locations requiring automatic IP configuration
- Router placement
- WAN connections and speed
- VLANs
- Availability requirements
- IP configuration options sent to clients

DHCP relay agents

A key point to remember is that DHCP requests are broadcasts that will not traverse most network routers. This means that you must put a DHCP server or DHCP relay agent on each IP segment or subnet. A DHCP relay agent is a component of Routing and Remote Access that simply forwards DHCP requests to another network segment (see Figure 3.50).

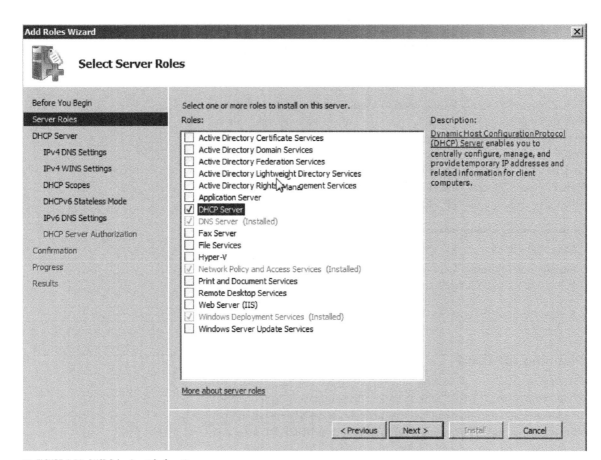

■ **FIGURE 3.50** DHCP Relay Agent Configuration.

NOTES FROM THE FIELD

DHCP forwarding on network routers

Many of today's network routers provide DHCP-forwarding services. If your network routers support DHCP forwarding, you may want to consider using them to forward DHCP requests instead of DHCP relay agents.

Planning for DHCP high availability

When deploying DHCP servers, you will want to ensure that you provide highly available DHCP services. There are a couple of ways to achieve this:

- *Multiple DHCP servers*—This is the most common method used to ensure DHCP availability. In this scenario, you can set up multiple DHCP servers and distribute the active IP addresses across them. For example, DHCP Server 1 might offer IP addresses from 10.1.1.1 to 10.1.1.50 and DHCP Server 2 might offer the IP addresses from 10.1.1.51 to 10.1.1.100. In the event that DHCP Server 1 fails, DHCP Server 2 would still be online and offer addresses to DHCP clients. When setting up multiple DHCP servers, you should consider how you want to split up your IP ranges. Several common practices exist, including the 80/20 split and the 50/50 split. The 80/20 split involves adding 80% of your IP addresses to one DHCP server and 20% to the other server. Using the 50/50 split, you place half of your IP addresses on one DHCP server and the other half on a second DHCP server.
- *DHCP cluster*—Using Windows Clustering Services you can set up a DHCP server on the top of a Windows Cluster. This active/passive availability option will allow a DHCP server to fail over to a secondary node in the cluster if the primary node fails. We will be exploring Windows Clustering in Chapter 9.

You can use the Multiple DHCP server method, the DHCP Cluster method, or a combination of the two to provide high availability to DHCP.

Deploying DHCP

DHCP is installed by adding the DHCP role in Server Manager. The initial set up process will install the DHCP components and will take you through the initial configuration of the DHCP server. To add the DHCP server role, perform the following steps:

1. Open Server Manager from Start | Administrative Tools | Server Manager.
2. Click to highlight the Roles node in the left pane. Then click the Add Roles link in the middle pane. This will launch the Add Roles Wizard.
3. Click Next to begin the installation process.
4. Select DHCP Server from the list of available roles (see Figure 3.51). Then click Next.
5. You will be taken to the DHCP summary page. Click Next to continue.
6. The first configuration option will ask you to provide the domain name and the DNS Servers to provide to each client. These are the DNS Servers that each DHCP client will use for name resolution. Enter the IP address of two DNS Servers on your network, and then click Next.
7. If you are using WINS, you will need to specify the IP addresses of the primary and secondary WINS servers. If WINS is not used, leave

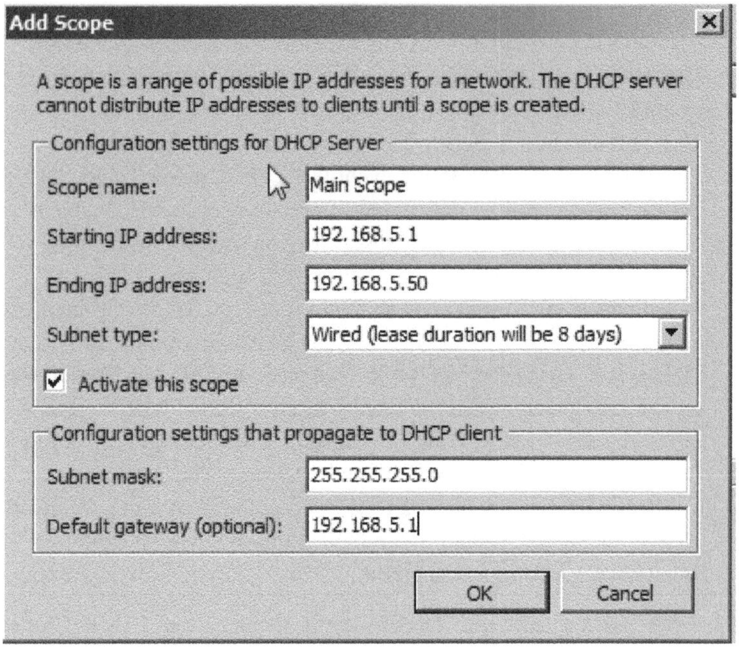

■ **FIGURE 3.51** Select DHCP Server Role.

the option *WINS is not required for applications on this network* selected. Then click Next.

8. You are now ready to set up a DHCP scope. Remember that a scope is the range of IP addresses you want to make available to DHCP clients. Enter the DHCP range as seen in Figure 3.52. At this stage, you can also set the subnet mask and default gateway to be used by DHCP clients. After setting the scope range and options, click OK. Then click Next.

9. If you are using IPv6, you can now add the DHCPv6 configuration information. For our example, we will disable stateless DHCP mode for the server. Then click Next.

10. You will now need to authorize the DHCP server in AD, assuming that you have AD deployed on your network. DHCP authorization ensures that only authorized DHCP servers can offer IP addresses to DHCP clients. Choose or enter credentials that have the ability to authorize DHCP servers (see Figure 3.53), then click Next.

11. You will now see the DHCP install summary screen. Verify whether the settings are correct. Then click Install. This process will now install, perform initial configuration, and authorize DHCP.

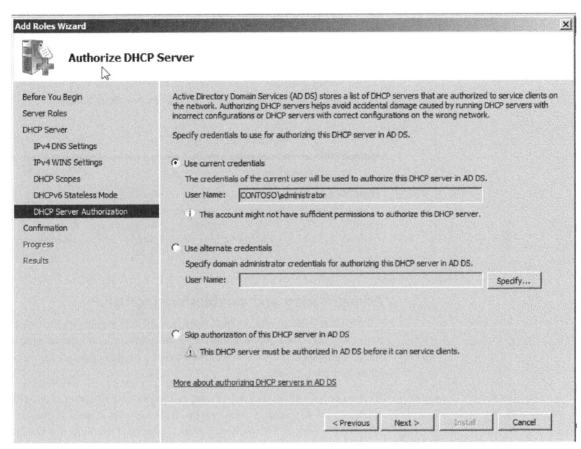

■ **FIGURE 3.52** Creating DHCP Scopes.

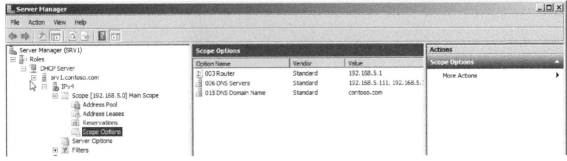

■ **FIGURE 3.53** Authorize DHCP Server.

12. Once the installation is completed, you should see an installation success message. The server should now start to lease IP addresses to DHCP client computers.
13. The DHCP Management console will appear under the Roles node in Server Manager. You can go here to change configuration options, including changing lease settings or adding additional scopes.

NOTES FROM THE FIELD

DHCP advanced options for devices

Some devices like Voice over IP Phones require custom options to be set for the DHCP scope. These custom options can be added to DHCP easily but you will need to get the full list of options from your hardware provider.

Administering and troubleshooting DHCP

After DHCP is set up and running, there is very little ongoing maintenance required. There are a few administrative concepts that you need to understand thoroughly. These include reservations, exclusions, and the new allow and deny filters.

If you need to add additional IP ranges to your DHCP server, you will simply need to create a new scope. This can be done by opening the DHCP node in Server Manager, and then right clicking the DHCP server. You should select the option *Create new scope*. This will launch the wizard to create a new scope. Enter the necessary configuration information similar to what you did during the initial installation of the role.

Additionally, you can add what is known as an exclusion range to an existing scope. An exclusion range is just a range of IP addresses to exclude from the range being offered to clients. This can be helpful if you have a range of IP addresses that you temporarily do not want to be used on the server, or if you need to reserve certain ranges for network devices, printers, *etc*.

DHCP Filters is a new feature available in Windows Server 2008 R2. DHCP filters permit you to specifically allow or deny specific network adapter hardware addresses. The deny option can be very useful if you have a rogue computer that you want to ensure does not get an IP address on your network.

NETWORK MONITORING AND TROUBLESHOOTING UTILITIES

To properly manage and monitor your Windows network, you need to become familiar with the tools required to manage, monitor, and trouble-shoot problems. Let us take a look at some of the basic network utilities.

- Ping—This is one of the most basic, yet most useful tool you will use when troubleshooting server problems. The ping utility does just that it pings a given server name or IP address to see if the host is responding on the network. If a server fails to respond to a ping, it may be off-line.
- PathPing—PathPing provides a more in-depth ping test that not only tests to see if the host is alive, but also displays the IP paths that the ping has gone through, such as network routers. PathPing also gathers statistics related to the ping test.
- NSLookup—NSLookup is a key DNS name resolution testing utility. The NSLookup command allows you to send queries to DNS Servers to ensure that they respond and provide the correct result to the query.
- Network Monitor (netmon)—Network Monitor allows you to capture network traffic and packets on your network and analyze them. Network Monitor is a great utility to understand which servers talk to each other and what protocols and ports they use to do so.

Using ping, PathPing, and NSLookup

Ping, PathPing, and NSLookup are great tools to assist with testing and troubleshooting Windows networks. Brief examples of using each are provided below.

As mentioned, Ping can be used to see if an IP address is "alive" on the network. The ping utility will also return the time it took the ICMP ping packet to reach the target IP and receive a reply. To perform a simple ping, open a command prompt and issue the command Ping IP Address or Hostname. For example, Ping 192.168.4.1 or Ping server1 PathPing commands are issued in the same format but provide more in-depth analysis of the path being taken by the ping.

The NSLookup utility can help you test name resolution using DNS. To perform a simple DNS query test using NSLookup, simply open a command prompt and enter the command NSLookup FQDN of host, for example, NSLookup www.syngress.com. You can additionally move to a NSLookup console by simply entering NSLookup at a command prompt. From there you can perform a query by entering a hostname. You can also change DNS Servers for queries by entering the command `server DNS Server FQDN`, for example, `server ns1.syngress.com`.

Overview of Network Monitor

Microsoft originally included a slimmed-down version of the Network Monitor as part of the operating system. As an administrator, you could add the component and use the lightweight Network Monitor version. The fully featured version of Network Monitor was included as part of System Management Server (SMS). Recently Microsoft released a fully functional Network Monitor that was made available free from the Microsoft Download Center Web site. Network Monitor 3.3 can be downloaded *via* this link:

www.microsoft.com/downloads/details.aspx?displaylang=en&FamilyID= 983b941d-06cb-4658-b7f6-3088333d062f

After installing Network Monitor, it can be launched from a desktop shortcut or *via* the Start menu. Upon launching, the main Network Monitor window will open as seen in Figure 3.54. This is where you can start a new packet capture process and select the network adapters to include in the capture.

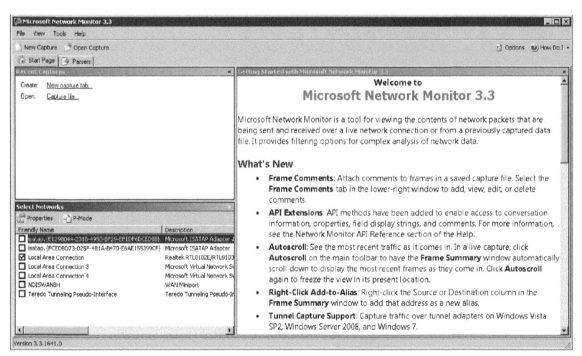

■ **FIGURE 3.54** Microsoft Network Monitor.

To begin a new network capture, click the *Capture* button opening a new capture tab. Then click the *Start* button. You will immediately see packet information displayed in real-time as traffic flows to and from the selected network interfaces. After you have finished capturing traffic, click the *Stop* button. When troubleshooting, typically, you will start the capture just prior to a specific error appearing, and then stopping the capture after the error occurs.

After you have captured network data, you can view frame details of captured packets by selecting a frame in the frame summary pane. The details will be displayed in frame details (see Figure 3.55). Here you can dissect exactly what information was inside the frame. You can optionally limit information displayed in the frame summary pane by selecting the specific application you want to view from the left pane.

If you want to further limit the types of traffic displayed in the frame summary pane, you can create filters. A filter is a way to view only specific traffic based upon criteria defined in the filter. For example, if you want to view only URL traffic for syngress.com, you could apply the http URL filter as seen in Figure 3.56.

The Network Monitor can be a very valuable tool when troubleshooting issues that are related to network connectivity. Using Network Monitor, you

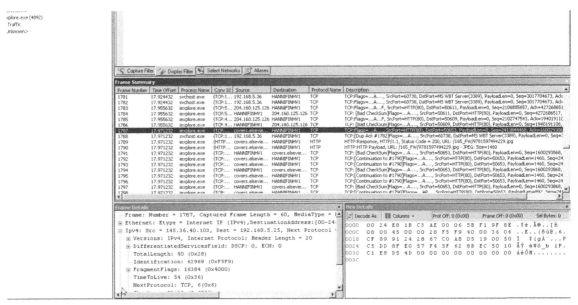

■ **FIGURE 3.55** Frame Details from Captured Packets.

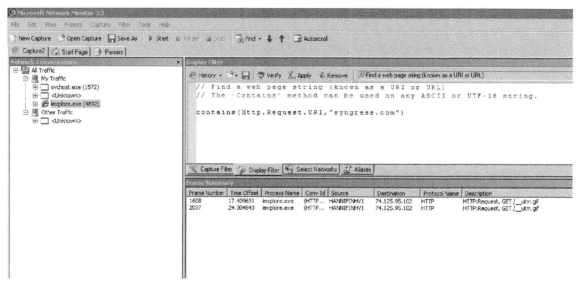

■ **FIGURE 3.56** Using a Network Monitor Display Filter.

can view in-depth details about where servers are attempting to communicate and what type of traffic is being sent over particular network interfaces.

SUMMARY

In this chapter, we covered what you need to understand to design and implement Windows Server 2008 R2 networking services. We explored IP networking basics and core Windows networking services such as DHCP, DNS, and Remote Access. We discussed how these technologies can be implemented on your network and the features they bring to your Windows Server 2008 R2 deployment. This chapter discussed the processes to design and implement these services, using Windows Server 2008 R2. This chapter concluded with an introduction to a few network management and monitoring utilities such as Ping, PathPing, NSLookup, and Network Monitor.

Chapter 4

Feature focus: Active Directory

Active Directory (AD) is at the core of most Windows networks. Their security, reliability, and access depend on a stable and properly administered AD infrastructure. AD is Microsoft's version of a network directory service. Think of a network directory service like a phone book. Phone books contain data about people, phone numbers, and addresses. If you want to find a business's phone number, you search the directory (phone book). The same concept applies to Windows networks. AD contains information about users, groups, computers, network locations, and application configurations. On top of that, AD provides tons of security controls and processes to ensure that only authorized people have access to protected data.

In this chapter, you will learn how to properly plan for an Active Directory Domain Services (AD DS) deployment. You will then explore how to install, configure, and administer an AD domain, including how to manage users, groups, and Group Policy Objects (GPOs). This chapter will also cover new features such as the AD Recycle Bin and Offline Domain Join. This chapter will conclude with a brief overview of other AD services and how to troubleshoot AD.

WHAT IS NEW IN ACTIVE DIRECTORY?

AD was first introduced with the release of Windows 2000 Server. Most of the core functionalities have remained the same through Windows Server 2003, Windows Server 2008, and now Windows Server 2008 R2. However, with each release, Microsoft has made some performance improvements and added new features. In this section, we will take a look at some of the new AD features in Windows Server 2008 R2.

Active Directory Recycle Bin

AD now includes an undelete option known as the Recycle Bin. The AD Recycle Bin acts a lot like the Windows recycle bin we are all very familiar with. The AD Recycle Bin stores objects for 180 days (by default) after they are deleted from AD. This allows for easy full fidelity recovery of deleted AD objects using PowerShell commands. The one main requirement to use this feature is that your AD forest is in Windows Server 2008 R2 native mode, and all domain controllers (DCs) in the domain need to be running Windows Server 2008 R2. Let us take a closer look at the AD Recycle Bin.

BEST PRACTICES

Never test new features in production

Never try out new features in a production environment. You should *always* test them in a lab environment and fully understand them before using them in your production environment. Just because a new feature exists, it does not mean it should or can be used in your specific deployment. Do your homework and try it out in a lab first.

---

1. First verify that the AD forest is in Windows Server 2008 R2 Native mode. You can verify this by opening *Active Directory Domains and Trusts* from *Start | Administrative Tools*.
2. To verify the forest functional level, right-click the root node in the management console and choose the option *Raise Forest Functional Level* (see Figure 4.1).
3. The Raise Forest Functional Level window will pop up. The window will display the current forest functional level as seen in Figure 4.2. If the forest is not in Windows Server 2008 R2 native mode, it will need to be raised prior to attempting to use the AD Recycle Bin. Please note that you need to understand the consequences of raising your forest functional level which will be discussed in full detail later in this chapter.
4. After verifying that your forest is in Windows Server 2008 R2 native mode, you will need to enable the recycle bin. This is done by running a PowerShell cmdlet.
5. AD PowerShell can be accessed from *Start | Administrative Tools | Active Directory Module for PowerShell*.
6. Enter the following command to enable the recycle bin (see Figure 4.3): `enable-adoptionalfeature "Recycle Bin Feature" -Scope ForestorConfigurationSet -Target contoso.com`
7. When prompted, choose *[Y] Yes* to enable the recycle bin on the Target.
8. Now that the recycle bin is enabled, we will test the recycle bin by deleting an organizational unit (OU) named My User OU. To do this, open *Active Directory Users and Computers (ADUC)*. Create a new

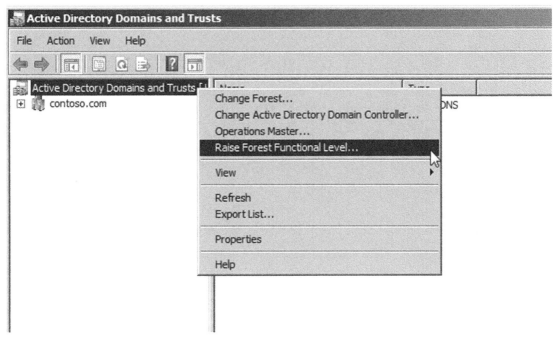

■ **FIGURE 4.1** Raise Forest Functional Level.

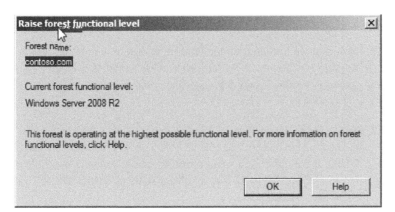

■ **FIGURE 4.2** Current forest functional level.

OU named My User OU. When creating the OU, be sure to uncheck the box saying *Protect Container from Accidental Deletion*. We will discuss deletion protection later in this chapter. In our example, you will need to ensure that this box is unchecked so that we can delete the object.

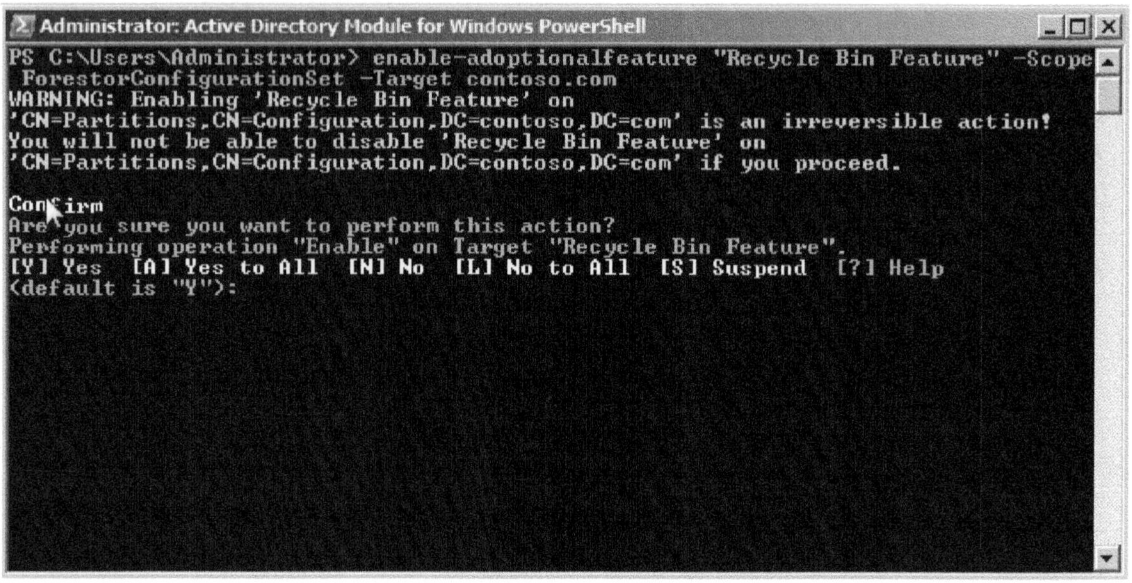

FIGURE 4.3 Enable Active Directory Recycle Bin.

9. After creating the OU, delete it by right-clicking on the *My User OU* and choosing *Delete*. Click *Yes* to verify you do indeed want to delete this object (see Figure 4.4).

10. Now that we have deleted the OU, let us restore it from the AD Recycle Bin. Return to PowerShell with AD cmdlets loaded.

11. At the PowerShell, promptly enter the command: Get-ADObject -SearchBase "CN=Deleted Objects,DC=test,DC=local" -ldapFilter "(objectClass=*)" -includeDeletedObjects.

12. This will list the contents of the recycle bin. Notice the ObjectGUID on each of the objects (see Figure 4.5). You will want to note the GUID of the object you want to restore. In our example, we will restore the My User OU with an objectGUID of de167a00–2457 –4fb0–9ccc-465a3523332f2.

13. To restore the object, enter the command Restore-ADObject -identity de167a00-2457-4fb0-9ccc-465a3523332f2 (see Figure 4.6).

14. You can refresh your view of ADUC, and the My User OU will instantly reappear.

We used a simple example of how you can quickly recover a deleted object. It is important to understand that this tool could be used to easily

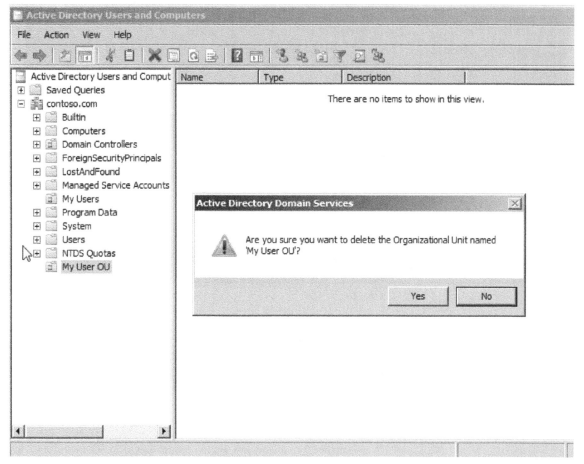

restore accidental deletion of not only simple OUs but also entire OU structures that could contain thousands of users, groups, or computers.

Offline Domain Join

Offline Domain Join is a new feature in Windows Server 2008 R2 and Windows 7 that allows you to join a computer to an AD domain without having connectivity to a DC. The Offline Domain Join is a three-step process described subsequently:

1. The *djoin* command line tool is run on a Windows 7 or Windows Server 2008 R2 computer that is joined to the domain. The djoin/ provision option is used to provision a computer account for the

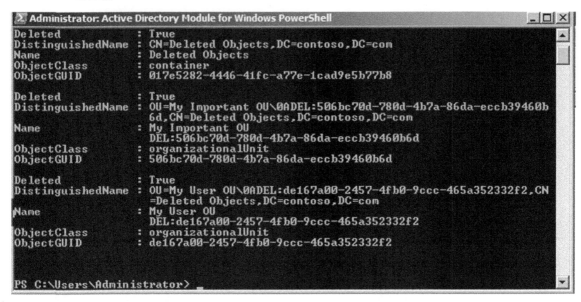

FIGURE 4.5 Deleted Active Directory Objects.

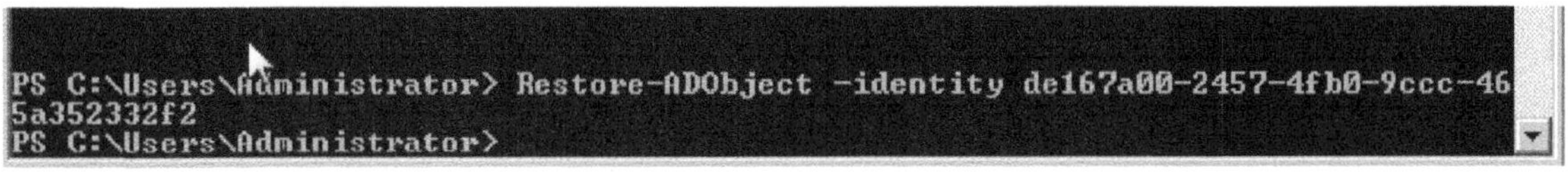

```
PS C:\Users\Administrator> Restore-ADObject -identity de167a00-2457-4fb0-9ccc-46
5a352332f2
PS C:\Users\Administrator>
```

FIGURE 4.6 Restore Active Directory Object.

computer for which you want to perform an Offline Domain Join. This generates a file to be used by the computer that will be joining the domain.

2. The file is copied to the computer that will be joining the domain via Offline Domain Join. The *djoin* command is run with the/requestODJ parameter. This will copy the Offline Domain Join file to the Windows directory and instruct the computer to join the domain on boot.

3. Boot the computer when connected to the network hosting the AD domain. The domain join process will automatically join the computer to the domain.

The Offline Domain Join process can be very useful when you are automatically deploying a large number of computers, or if you want to give someone the ability to join a computer to the domain, without them needing special privileges in AD. The following tasks will walk you through the process to perform an Offline Domain Join.

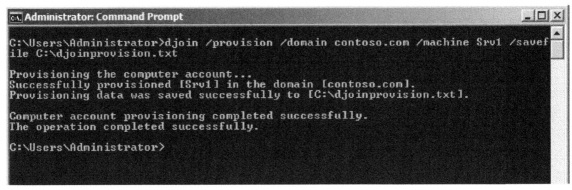

In this process, we will be using two computers. LABDC1 will be the DC hosting the contoso.com domain. Srv1 will join the LABDC1 domain using the Offline Domain Join process.

1. Log on to the domain controller (LABDC1).
2. Open a command prompt and enter the command `djoin/provision/ domain contoso.com/machine Srv1/SaveFile C:\djoinprovision. txt` (see Figure 4.7). This command is telling the computer to run the djoin provisioning process for the contoso.com domain. Create a djoin file for the server Srv1 and save it as C:\djoinprovision.txt. After running the command, you should receive confirmation that the offline domain join file was created successfully.
3. You now need to copy the file to the computer you want to join to the domain. You can use any method you prefer to copy the file. We just need to have it on the machine that we want to join to the domain.
4. Log on to the server we want to join to the domain (Srv1). Check the computer properties to ensure that the computer is a member of a workgroup and not joined to the domain (see Figure 4.8).

Computer name, domain, and workgroup settings ————————————————

Computer name:	SRV1	🖫Change settings
Full computer name:	SRV1	
Computer description:		
Workgroup:	WORKGROUP	

Windows activation ——————————————————————————————

■ **FIGURE 4.8** Computer properties.

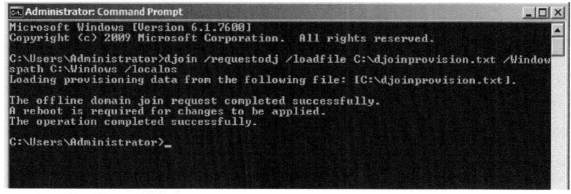

■ **FIGURE 4.9** Perform offline Domain Join process.

5. Open a command prompt and run the command `djoin/requestODJ/loadfile C:\djoinprovision.txt/Windowspath C:\Windows` (see Figure 4.9). This command is telling the computer that on next boot, it should join the domain using the information provided in the file C:\djoinprovision.txt. You should see a success message and a notice stating you must reboot the computer for it to complete the offline domain join process.

6. You can now power down or reboot the computer as you normally do after joining a computer to a domain. At this point, the computer is joined to the domain and needs to reboot for changes to take effect on the local machine.

7. Log on to the computer and view computer properties to verify that it was indeed joined to the domain (see Figure 4.10).

Active Directory module for PowerShell

Windows Server 2008 R2 is the first Microsoft server OS to include PowerShell as part of the standard OS installation. To go along with the

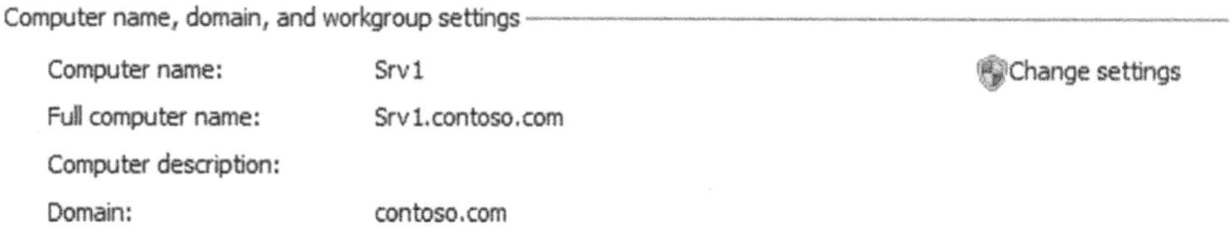

Computer name, domain, and workgroup settings ─────────────────────────────

Computer name: Srv1   🛡️Change settings

Full computer name: Srv1.contoso.com

Computer description:

Domain: contoso.com

■ **FIGURE 4.10** Computer joined to domain.

built-in PowerShell functionality, Windows Server 2008 R2 includes a series of cmdlets to administer AD via PowerShell. Using the AD Module for PowerShell, you can use PowerShell to administer user, computers, groups, domains, and DCs. You can learn more about using PowerShell to administer Windows and AD in Chapter 11.

Active Directory Best Practices Analyzer

AD now includes a best practices analyzer (BPA). BPAs for other Microsoft products have been around for several years. The most popular of these is the Exchange Server BPA. BPAs do exactly as their name implies. The BPA will scan your servers and analyze software configurations. It will then compare those configurations to a list of best practices provided by the Microsoft product group responsible for that particular piece of software. As an AD administrator, you should not only run the AD BPA after deploying AD, but on a regular basis postinstallation or when significant configuration changes have been made to your environment. Let us explore the AD BPA in more detail.

1. The AD BPA is automatically installed with the AD DS role. You can access the BPA by selecting the AD node in Server Manager, then scrolling down to the BPA as seen in Figure 4.11.
2. To run the BPA, click the *Scan this Role* link. This will start a scan of the AD DS on the server.
3. After the scan completes, the results of the scan will be displayed inside the BPA window. You can immediately see any noncompliant configuration settings or warnings under the noncompliant tab. You

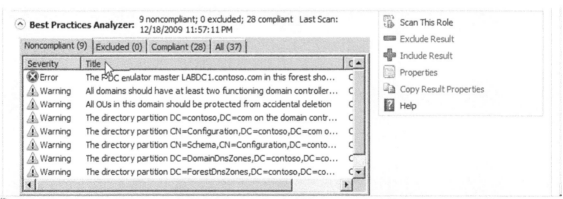

■ **FIGURE 4.11** Active Directory best practices analyzer.

can also click on any alert to see the full details of the issue and how to resolve it (see Figure 4.12).

4. You can click the *Compliant* tab if you want to see the rules that were run in which the system was in compliance with best practices configurations.

5. The BPA can be rerun at any time from Server Manager. Run this tool and remediate any issues on a regular basis to ensure that your AD domain remains highly reliable and healthy.

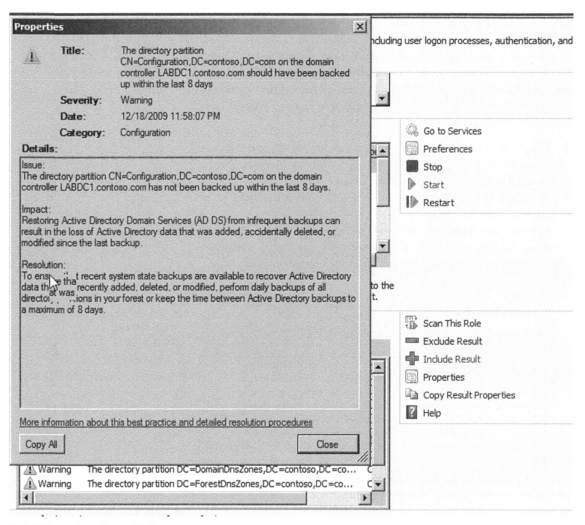

Properties ✕

⚠ **Title:** The directory partition CN=Configuration,DC=contoso,DC=com on the domain controller LABDC1.contoso.com should have been backed up within the last 8 days

Severity: Warning

Date: 12/18/2009 11:58:07 PM

Category: Configuration

Details:

Issue:
The directory partition CN=Configuration,DC=contoso,DC=com on the domain controller LABDC1.contoso.com has not been backed up within the last 8 days.

Impact:
Restoring Active Directory Domain Services (AD DS) from infrequent backups can result in the loss of Active Directory data that was added, accidentally deleted, or modified since the last backup.

Resolution:
To ensure that recent system state backups are available to recover Active Directory data that was recently added, deleted, or modified, perform daily backups of all directory partitions in your forest or keep the time between Active Directory backups to a maximum of 8 days.

More information about this best practice and detailed resolution procedures

[Copy All]   [Close]

⚠ Warning   The directory partition DC=DomainDnsZones,DC=contoso,DC=co...
⚠ Warning   The directory partition DC=ForestDnsZones,DC=contoso,DC=co...

including user logon processes, authentication, and

⚙ Go to Services
▦ Preferences
■ Stop
▷ Start
Ⅱ▷ Restart

🔳 Scan This Role
▬ Exclude Result
➕ Include Result
▦ Properties
▥ Copy Result Properties
❓ Help

■ **FIGURE 4.12** Active Directory BPA Warning.

NOTES FROM THE FIELD

Active Directory BPA and previous OS versions

The AD BPA can be run against DCs running the previous version of Windows Server to check for misconfigurations on those OSs as well.

Active Directory Web Services

Windows Server 2008 R2 AD includes Web services that provide remote management capabilities for AD. The Active Directory Web Services are primarily built to allow administrators to remotely administer AD using PowerShell. This allows you to send PowerShell commands to a remote DC from your local PC or other management server. Additionally, the Active Directory Web Services provide a way for developers to write applications that use the Web services to interact with AD.

Active Directory Administrative Center

The new Active Directory Administrative Center (ADAC) provides a way for administrators to perform regular management tasks via an easy-to-use interface built on top of PowerShell. This means that as an administrator you can use the GUI interface to perform a task and the GUI then makes a call to a PowerShell script or cmdlet to complete the requested task. Most of the same functions you perform in ADUC can be performed in the new ADAC-rich GUI interface. Whether you are a new or seasoned Windows administrator, you will want to check out the new AD Admin Center.

Managed service accounts

Many applications and network services require the use of service accounts. These accounts are typically dedicated to a specific application and have passwords set to never expire. This ensures no accidental service disruption due to the expiring of a password. This, however, poses a security problem, especially for organizations which must comply with various government regulations. Microsoft has addressed this issue with a new feature known as Managed Service Accounts. Managed service accounts allows AD to automatically manage the passwords and Service Principal Names (SPNs). AD will automatically manage and change the password on a regular basis and ensure that the service using the account gets the password update. A managed service account is not created using the ADUC console but via the New-ADServiceAccount PowerShell cmdlet.

NOTES FROM THE FIELD

AD BPA and previous versions of Active Directory
The AD BPA can be pointed at other DCs besides the one it is installed on. This allows you to run a best practice check against other Windows 2008 R2 DCs or even downlevel DCs running Windows Server 2008 R1 and Windows Server 2003.

PLANNING FOR ACTIVE DIRECTORY

Whether you are upgrading an existing AD infrastructure or building a new one from the ground up, it is important to properly plan your deployment. For our discussion, we will focus on new deployments, however, we will note some specifics you should be aware of when upgrading your domain to Windows Server 2008 R2 AD.

Active Directory basics

Before jumping into your design, it is important that you have a basic understanding of the architecture and how AD works behind the scenes. It is important to remember that AD is not only a security service for your network but also a database containing configuration information about your network. For example, Exchange Server 2007 and 2010 store critical configuration data in AD. This ensures that critical application data can be highly available and protected by geographic resilience.

Active Directory domain controllers

A DC is a server with the AD DS role installed and has been designated as a DC by running the dcpromo process discussed later in this chapter. All DCs contain a copy of the AD database.

The Active Directory data store

The AD database is saved in a file on every DC in the domain. The AD database is stored in the NTDS.DIT file located in the NTDS folder of the system root, usually C:\Windows. AD uses a concept known as multimaster replication to ensure that the data store is consistent on all DCs. This process is known as replication.

There is no single master copy of the AD data store, thus, each DC (except for Read-Only domain controllers (RODCs)) can read and write to the data store. The replication process ensures that all DCs have the newest copies of any changes made to AD. Multimaster replication allows administrators to make changes on any DC in the domain and be confident that those changes will replicate to all other DCs.

Active Directory partitions

AD is broken down into three partitions that must be replicated to all DCs:

- *Domain partition*—The domain partition includes data related to the AD domain. It includes objects such as users, groups, computers, and printers.
- *Schema partition*—The schema partition contains the attributes and classes that make up the AD schema. These attributes define what type of data is stored in AD and how that data is linked to other AD objects. For example, the schema contains a first name field that is used to store the first name for every user account in the domain. Think of the AD schema like the fields in a database table.
- *Configuration partition*—The configuration partition includes information about the configuration of AD such as domain and forest settings.

NOTES FROM THE FIELD

Extending the Active Directory schema

The AD schema is extensible, which means new classes and attributes can be added by performing an AD schema extension. Various applications, including Microsoft Exchange Server and Office Communications Server, require extending the AD schema before they can be installed on your network. Typically, you can identify a schema extension file by an ldf extension at the end of the name. Ldf files typically contain all of the schema changes for a given update.

BEST PRACTICES

Planning to extend the Active Directory schema

It is very rare that the process to extend the AD schema fails. However, it is important to understand that schema extensions are irreversible. New additions to the schema cannot be deleted but only disabled. Though this is usually a low-risk process, you should always test schema extensions in a lab prior to deploying them in production.

Planning for Active Directory forest and domains

During the early stages of your AD planning, you need to consider how many forests and domains will be needed to support your network. To properly plan your forests and domains, you need a clear understanding of each of them and how they apply to an AD deployment.

- *Domains*—A domain is the base foundation of an AD hierarchy. AD domains contain objects such as users, computers, groups, and printers. One or more domains make up an AD deployment.
- *Trees*—A tree is composed of one or more domains arranged in a hierarchical fashion. Trees are made up of a parent domain and one or more child domains. The child domains share a contiguous namespace with the parent domain. This means the child domains are named by prepending a domain name to the fully qualified domain name (FQDN) of the parent. For example, a parent domain name may be fabrikam.com. The child domain would then be called northamerica.fabrikam.com.
- *Forests*—A forest is a collection of one or more trees. Forests use different FQDNs. Forests maintain their own security but provide interaction between all domains in the organization. All domains in a forest have a two-way, transitive trust.

Active Directory trust relationships

Trust relationships allow administrators in one AD domain assign permissions to users and groups in another domain and vice versa. For example, a trust relationship could be established between contoso.com and frabrikam.com. If a two-way trust is established, then administrators in contoso.com could give users from frabrikam.com access to resources in the contoso.com domain. Trust relationships come in the following types:

- *Forest trust*—A forest trust is a trust relationship established between two separate forests. This allows all domains in a forest to trust all domains in another forest. Forest trusts are transitive which means if domain A trusts domain B, and domain B trusts domain C, then domain A automatically trusts domain C.
- *Shortcut trust*—A shortcut trust is a manually created trust between two domains. This is also transitive. A shortcut trust can be useful when dealing with complex trees from multiple forests. Shortcut trusts can be set up between child domains (see Figure 4.13) to improve log-on performance between the two domains.
- *External trust*—An external trust is a traditional trust relationship meaning, a trust relationship can be setup between domain A and domain B but does not automatically include domain C in the trust relationship. External trusts can be one-way or two-way.
- *Realm trust*—A realm trust can be set up to provide a transitive or nontransitive trust between a Windows Server 2008 R2 domain and another Kerberos v5 compliant realm such as UNIX or Linux environments. This trust can be one-way or two-way.

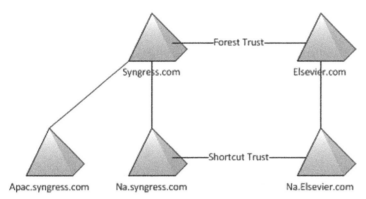

■ **FIGURE 4.13** Shortcut trust between two child domains.

There may be situations where multiple domains will be required due to security or ownership requirements. One example of this is during acquisitions of other companies. Your company may acquire another company that already has an AD domain. In situations like this, you may need to build a trust relationship to allow users from your domain to have access to data in the acquired domain and vice versa.

You may also consider the usage of a resource forest. This is when you deploy an application, such as Microsoft Exchange Server, into its own domain (see Figure 4.14). This allows for better segregation of permissions as Microsoft Exchange exists in one domain, while the Exchange users reside in another. This provides a security boundary for administrators.

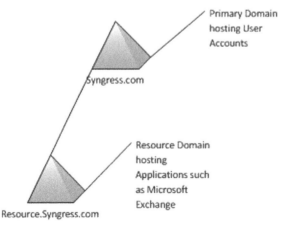

■ **FIGURE 4.14** Exchange Server deployed in a resource domain.

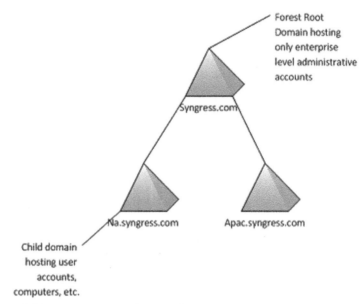

■ **FIGURE 4.15** Active Directory with an empty forest root.

Another scenario where multiple domains may be required is if you want to create what is known as an empty forest root. An empty forest root provides an additional layer of security, as all forest level accounts are stored only in the forest root, while all other users, computers, and various other objects are stored in the child domain(s). Figure 4.15 depicts an empty forest root deployment.

The specifics of how many domains and forests you deploy will vary between organizations. If you have a somewhat simple environment with a single group which needs to own the AD domain, you may want to consider sticking with a single domain. This provides less complexity than multiple domains and a single domain has been shown to easily support up to a million objects (users, computers, etc). If you administer a more complex environment where more security boundaries need to be implemented or there is more political concern around who can manage what, you may need to look at deploying multiple domains. Be sure to thoroughly plan this prior to deploying AD.

Active Directory and DNS

There are some special DNS considerations that need to be taken into account when planning for AD. You need to understand these options when building your AD design.

Active Directory domain name

The AD domain name that you choose will also be a DNS FQDN. This means that this domain name will have a zone on each of the AD DNS servers. As best practice, if you want to use an Internet compliant name such as Syngress.com, you will want to purchase this domain name to ensure that it is not used by someone else. You may also want to consider using a nonstandard domain name such as Syngress.local.

If you choose to use an Internet standard FQDN for your domain name, you will need to consider whether you want to use the same domain name for your internal and external namespace or use a separate domain name for internal and external namespaces. Using the same domain name means your Internet presence and your internal AD domain will share the same FQDN from a DNS perspective. Important things to note when using this option are:

- Public and private DNS namespace is the same.
- The shared single domain name makes access less complicated for users. For example, they can log on to their computers using their e-mail address as their username.
- Extra precaution must be made to ensure that no internal resources are accidentally published to the Internet. This is a major security concern when using this method.
- You will need to maintain both DNS zones (internal and external) separately.

If you choose to use separate domain names for internal and external namespaces, you will want to consider the following points:

- The difference between external and internal resources is easy to understand for end users.
- DNS is managed separately for each domain.
- Users will need to understand that the internal domain is used for internal resources only.
- This can provide a greater level of security by not allowing an overlap between your internal and external domain names.

NOTES FROM THE FIELD

Active Directory domain rename

At some point, due to organizational change or internal business decisions, it may be necessary to change the name of your AD domain. Microsoft provides a process and tools to rename your AD domain in the postdeployment phase. This process is somewhat complex and is not recommended unless absolutely necessary. The more preferred method to undergo a domain rename is to create a new AD domain and migrate to the new domain. In some cases, it may not even be supported to migrate to a new domain, for example, if Microsoft Exchange server has been deployed in the domain.

Planning for domain controllers

As part of your AD deployment, you will need to plan for DC placement. You will need to know how many DCs to deploy and in what locations they need to be deployed. You should consider how many DCs are needed to provide ample redundancy and which physical locations need DCs installed locally. You may want to consider deploying multiple DCs in larger offices to prevent authentication traffic over your Wide Area Network (WAN) in the event that one DC fails.

BEST PRACTICES

Physical security of Domain Controllers

It is critical that you provide physical security to DCs. It may be tempting to set up a DC in an empty cube or other insecure location in remote office locations. This is a bad idea. Remember, every DC stores the AD database that includes the keys to your network, including administrator passwords. Make sure you always keep DCs in secure locations behind a locked door. If there are physical security concerns in a remote location, you should consider deploying RODCs which do not store passwords for administrative accounts locally. RODCs will be discussed in more detail in Chapter 10.

Planning for Active Directory sites and replication

You will need to consider sites and replication strategies as part of your AD deployment. As described earlier in this chapter, AD is a multimaster database, meaning every DC has a local copy of the database and the ability to make changes to it. To ensure that all copies of the database remain consistent, AD uses replication between all DCs. To help ensure reliable and efficient replication between DCs separated by WAN links, AD uses sites and site links. Sites also ensure that authentication traffic from computers is sent to a DC on the local network before attempting to use a DC in a remote location. In the simplest terms, a site is defined as a network where servers are connected by a 10 MB or greater link. Sites can be further defined as subnets assigned to a single physical location. For example, the New York, Boston, and Nashville locations could be defined as AD sites. When users authenticate with the network, the authentication process attempts to use a DC in the same site as the computer the user is logging into. This prevents authentication traffic from randomly hitting various DCs across the network which could possibly saturate your WAN links.

AD uses replication connections between DCs to replicate changes to the AD database. The Knowledge Consistency Checker (KCC) will automatically create replication connections between DCs within a site. This ensures that reliable and efficient replication takes place between DCs within a subnet. Replication between DCs in a local site always occurs every 5 min. This is known as intrasite replication as it occurs between DCs in the same site.

Replication between two separate sites is known as intersite replication. Intersite replication is set up manually and is accomplished by creating site links. Each site can have one or more site links configured to replicate with other sites. When planning your replication strategy, you should consider using multiple site links between sites if possible. This allows AD to continue to replicate in the event of one site failing. Each site link can be set up with an associated cost. In scenarios where multiple site links are used between sites, the lower cost-site link is used when available. If the lower cost-site link fails, then the higher cost-site link will be used. For example, a site link can be set up between the Boston and New York offices. A second site link could then be set up between Boston and Nashville at a higher cost. The Boston DC will use the site link to the New York office for replication during normal conditions. However, if the network link between Boston and New York fails, Boston will replicate to the Nashville site to ensure that replication continues. Figure 4.16 depicts the aforementioned scenario of a hub-and-spoke replication strategy with a redundant hub site.

Global Catalog servers

Global Catalog (GC) servers are DCs assigned to host additional information about the forest. A typical DC contains details about the domain in which it resides, however, GC servers contain additional information about every domain in the forest. GCs are especially important to properly plan when deploying multiple AD domains. GCs are designated using the AD Sites and Services console as seen in Figure 4.17. Some applications, such as Microsoft Exchange server, rely on connectivity to GCs opposed to normal DCs. You will want to ensure that you have adequate redundancy for GCs when planning your AD deployment.

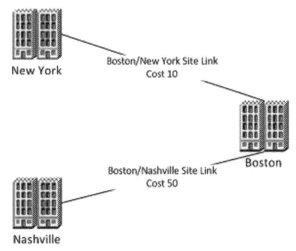

FIGURE 4.16 Active Directory replication topology.

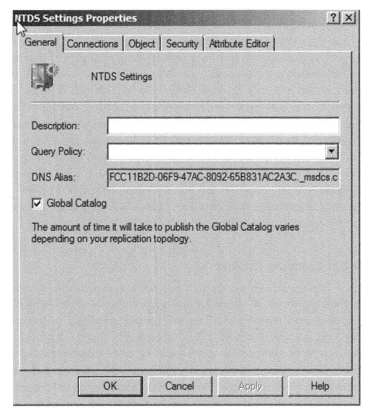

FIGURE 4.17 Global Catalog configuration.

Planning for operations masters

AD includes a group of roles known as the Flexible Single Master Operations (FSMO) roles. Each FSMO role is assigned to a single DC to perform a specific function with the forest or domain. Consider the following points when planning for FSMO roles in your deployment:

- *PDC emulator*—The PDC emulator simulates legacy Windows NT systems that require the use of a PDC. The PDC also handles urgent replication tasks that fall out of the normal scope of AD replication. For example, when a user account is locked out due to failed log-on attempts, the lockout should instantly be replicated to all DCs in the domain. The PDC emulator ensures that all DCs immediately get the lockout update. The PDC emulator exists on one DC in each domain.
- *Relative ID (RID) Master*—The RID Master hands out RIDs all DCs in the domain. RIDs are used by DCs to create a unique ID for each object created in AD. The RID Master provides each DCs a pool of RID numbers to be used for new objects. When a DCs pool of RIDs gets low, the RID Master allocates more RIDs to that DC. The RID Master resides on one DC within each domain. If the RID Master is offline for a significant amount of time, you may find yourself without the ability to add new computers or users to your domain.
- *Infrastructure Master*—One DC in each domain acts as the Infrastructure Master. The Infrastructure Master maintains user and group membership references. When group changes are made, the Infrastructure Master ensures that these changes get replicated throughout the domain.
- *Schema Master*—This is a forest wide role meaning it exists on only one DC in the entire forest. The Schema Master role controls all updates to the AD schema. In the event that the schema needs to be modified such as deploying Exchange 2007 or 2010, the schema updates must occur on the Schema Master.
- *Domain Naming Master*—The Domain Naming Master is also a forest wide role. This role manages the addition or removal of domains within the forest. If the Domain Naming Master is offline, you will find yourself not having the ability to add additional domains to the forest.

Planning for domain and forest functional levels

Windows domains can exist at various forest and domain functional levels. Functional levels determine the compatibility and features that can be used in the domain or forest. For example, each release of Windows Server

Table 4.1 Active Directory Domain and Forest Functional Levels

	Domain Controller OS Supported
Windows 2000 Native	Windows 2000 Server Windows Server 2003 Windows Server 2003 R2 Windows Server 2008 Windows Server 2008 R2
Windows 2003	Windows Server 2003 Windows Server 2003 R2 Windows Server 2008 Windows Server 2008 R2
Windows 2008	Windows Server 2008 Windows Server 2008 R2
Windows 2008 R2	Windows Server 2008 R2

typically includes replication improvements, however, to take advantage of those improvements, the domain must be at that release's functional level. To support a specific functional level it is required that all DCs in the domain or forest be running specific releases of the OS. Domain and Forest functional levels and their required DC OSs are listed in Table 4.1:

NOTES FROM THE FIELD

Forest and functional levels and rollback

In most cases, raising the domain or forest functional level is a one-way street. This means that once you raise the functional level to support new features, you cannot roll back. One exception to this rule is that rollback from Windows Server 2008 R2 to Windows Server 2008 is supported if the recycle bin feature has not been enabled.

INSTALLING AND CONFIGURING ACTIVE DIRECTORY DOMAIN SERVICES

We will now walk through installing and configuring AD DS for a new domain. This process involves adding the AD DS role and then running the dcpromo process. After installing AD, we will explore postinstallation steps. To install AD domain services, perform the following tasks:

1. Log on to the server with an account with local administrator rights.
2. Open *Server Manager and* then click on the *Roles* node in the left pane; then click the *Add Roles* link. This will launch the *Add Roles Wizard.* Click *Next.*

3. Select the *Active Directory Domain Services* option. You will be prompted to add *.Net Framework 3.5.1 Features.* Click *Add Required Features*; then click *Next* to continue. You will be taken to the AD introduction page. Click *Next* to continue.

4. Confirm that you do want to install AD DS and then click *Install.* After the install completes, you should see a success confirmation page. Verify whether the install was successful, then click *Close.*

Now that the AD role has been installed, you need to perform the dcpromo process which will promote the server to a DC. Go to *Start | Run.* Type *dcpromo* in the run box as seen in Figure 4.18 and then click *OK.* This will launch the AD DS Wizard.

5. At the *Active Directory Domain Services* page (see Figure 4.19), click *Next* to begin.

6. You will be taken to the OS compatibility page. Click *Next* to continue.

7. You must now choose whether this DC will be part of an existing forest or used to establish a new forest (see Figure 4.20). For our example, choose *Create a new domain in a new forest* since we are creating a new forest and domain. Click *Next.*

8. You now need to enter the FQDN for the new domain. Enter it into the text box as seen in Figure 4.21, then click *Next.* The wizard will then verify that the chosen domain does not already exist on the network.

9. You now need to select the *Forest Functional Level* to use for the new forest being deployed. If you are building a new domain that will only use Windows Server 2008 R2 DCs, you can select the Windows Server 2008 R2 functional level (see Figure 4.22). Then click *Next.*

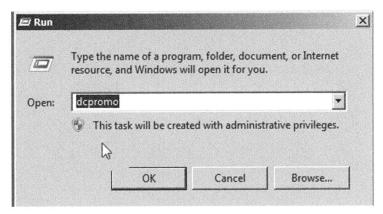

■ **FIGURE 4.18** dcpromo command.

FIGURE 4.19 Active Directory Domain Services Wizard.

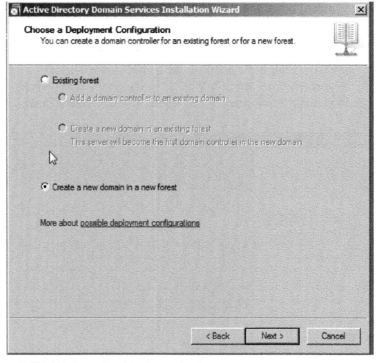

FIGURE 4.20 Create a New Active Directory domain.

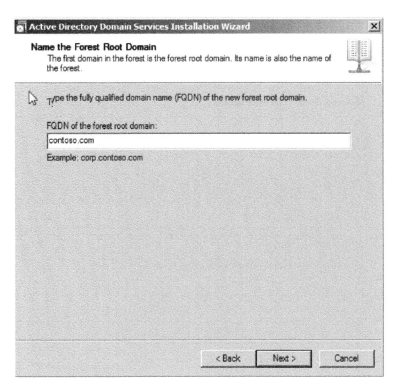

■ FIGURE 4.21 New domain name.

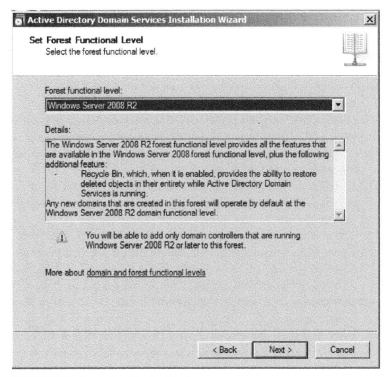

■ FIGURE 4.22 Choosing Forest Functional Level.

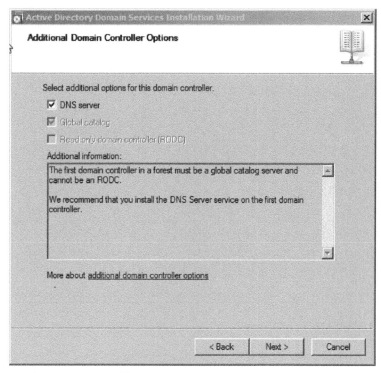

■ **FIGURE 4.23** Select DNS, global catalog, and Read-Only DC options.

10. You can now select whether you want to include DNS as part of the install as well as set the option to designate it as a GC (see Figure 4.23). Since this is the first DC in a new domain, it is required to be a GC. If you were adding a DC to an existing domain, you could optionally check the option to make this an RODC. Ensure that the option for *DNS* is selected, then click *Next*.

11. If you receive a warning like the one in Figure 4.24, click *Yes* to continue. This warning is notifying you that you should ensure you own the domain you are using for AD.

12. You now need to select the drive and path to install AD files (see Figure 4.25). In most simple installations, you can accept the defaults; however, you may choose to install the AD Database, Log Files, and SYSVOL folder on different disk drive spindles providing better performance. After selecting the paths to install AD files, click *Next* to continue.

13. In the next step, you need to create a Directory Services Restore Mode password. This password is used to access the system when

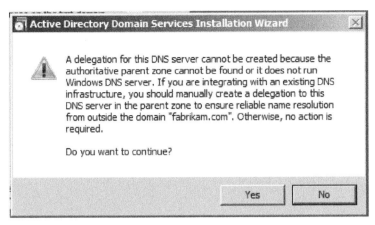

■ FIGURE 4.24 Active Directory DNS zone warning.

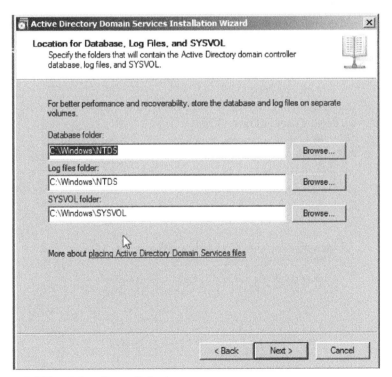

■ FIGURE 4.25 Active Directory File locations.

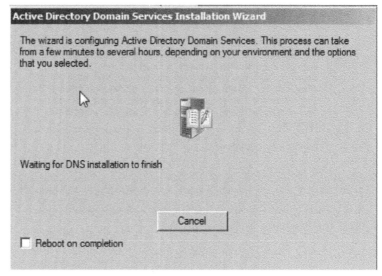

■ FIGURE 4.26 Active Directory dcpromo in progress.

you boot it into Active Directory Services Restore mode. Be sure to use a strong password and keep it somewhere safe. You will be required to create a Directory Services Restore Mode password for each DC you install. Click *Next* to continue.

14. Verify the AD options on the summary page, then click *Next* to start the dcpromo process.

15. During dcpromo, you can monitor the process from the wizard window as seen in Figure 4.26.

16. After the dcpromo process completes, you will be taken to the Completing the AD DS Installation Wizard page. Click *Finish* to complete the wizard.

17. For the dcpromo process to complete, the server needs to be rebooted. Click *Restart Now* at the restart prompt as seen in Figure 4.27.

■ FIGURE 4.27 Restart after dcpromo.

When the server restarts, it will restart as a DC in the new domain. Log on to the server with the same credentials used for the administrator account when the server was in a workgroup. The local administrator will have now been promoted to the domain administrator account.

If you open Server Manager, you should now see the AD DS and DNS roles listed under the Roles node. By expanding the AD DS node, you will see two subnodes named ADUC and AD Sites and Services (see Figure 4.28).

After initial installation, you should run the BPA as described earlier in this chapter. By running the BPA, you can clear up any additional configuration tasks that are necessary and ensure that no major problems are found with your fresh installation. The initial run of the BPA will flag a few issues that should be corrected immediately. These include:

- *The PDC emulator in this forest should synchronize with a valid time source*—As a best practice, you should synchronize your PDC emulator with an Internet time server. The BPA will give you the command `w32tm/config/computer:<name of your DC>/ manualpeerlist.time.windows.com/syncfromflags:manual/ update`
- *The domain has only one functioning domain controller*—You should immediately deploy a second DC for redundancy. With only one DC deployed, a DC failure would cause your entire domain to be offline. To add a second DC, perform the following tasks:

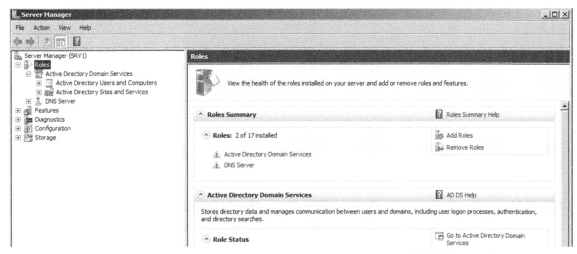

■ **FIGURE 4.28** Active Directory Role.

1. Set up a new Windows Server 2008 R2 server.
2. Set a static IP address and set the first DC as the primary DNS server.
3. Install the AD DS role and run dcpromo.
4. When prompted, select the option *Add domain controller to an existing domain*.
5. Select the existing domain name.

This will promote the DC into the existing domain. You should then be able to log on to the new DC as the domain administrator account setup when promoting the first DC. You can perform the aforementioned steps for each additional DC you want to add to the domain.

- *The directory partition has not been backed up*—You should set up backups as soon as possible after performing the dcpromo process. To backup AD, backup the system state on the server.

After correcting the aforementioned initial issues, run the BPA again to ensure they were properly corrected. Once you have resolved BPA issues, you should have a reliable and supportable Active Directory Domain.

The task you will need to complete is setting up your initial AD site. Even if you currently have only one site, you should define the subnets to properly set up AD's site configuration.

ACTIVE DIRECTORY ADMINISTRATION BASICS

As an AD administrator, you will want to become very familiar with the tools used to manage and maintain AD. The primary tools you will use to manage AD are:

- Active Directory Users and Computers
- Active Directory Sites and Services
- Active Directory Domains and Trusts
- Active Directory Administrative Center
- AD Module for PowerShell

Some of the aforementioned tools are accessible via the standard Server Manager interface, while the Active Directory Domains and Trusts, ADAC, and AD Module for PowerShell are accessed via their respective interfaces.

Active Directory Users and Computers

ADUC is the standard console for managing users, computers, and OUs in AD (see Figure 4.29). ADUC can be accessed via Server Manager or via the Administrative Tools folder from the Start Menu.

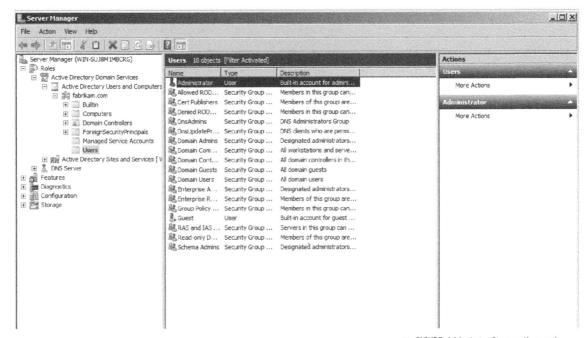

■ **FIGURE 4.29** Active Directory Users and Computers.

ADUC can also be used to raise the domain functional level. To raise the level, right-click on the domain name and choose the option *Raise Domain Functional Level*. Additionally, you can use ADUC to RID, PDC emulator, and Infrastructure FSMO roles to another server. This is done by logging onto the DC you wish to transfer one or more of the roles to. Then, open the ADUC console. Right-click on the domain and select the *Operations Masters* option. Select the appropriate tab for the FSMO role you wish to transfer and click *Change* (see Figure 4.30).

Active Directory Sites and Services

AD Sites and Services is the standard console for setting up and managing AD Sites (see Figure 4.31). Using the AD Sites and Services console, you can create and manage sites, subnets, site links, and site-link bridges. The AD Sites and Services console can be accessed via Server Manager or the Administrative Tools folder from the Start Menu.

The AD Sites and Services console also allows you to manage intersite transports. This setting allows you to configure AD site links to use IP for the site link (default) or set SMTP as the site link. SMTP should only

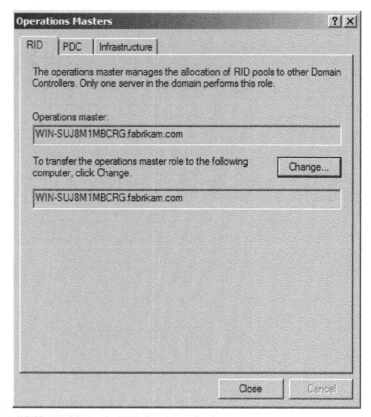

■ **FIGURE 4.30** Selecting the FSMO role to be transferred.

be used for slow and unreliable WAN links. You will use this tool to establish site links anytime you set up a new remote subnet that will contain a DC.

Active Directory Domains and Trusts

The Active Directory Domains and Trusts console is used to manually create trust relationships between domains and to raise the forest functional level. The Active Directory Domains and Trusts console is accessed from the Administrative Tools folder in the Start Menu (see Figure 4.32).

To raise the forest functional level, right-click on the domain name in the console and select the option *Raise Forest Functional Level*. The Domains and Trusts console can also be used to transfer the Domain Naming Service FSMO role to another DC. This is accomplished by opening the Domains and Trusts console on the DC that you want to transfer the role to.

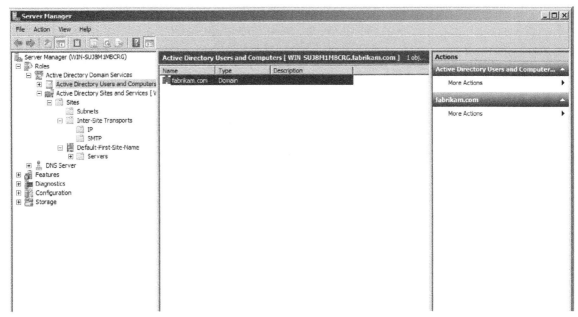

■ **FIGURE 4.31** Active Directory Sites and Services.

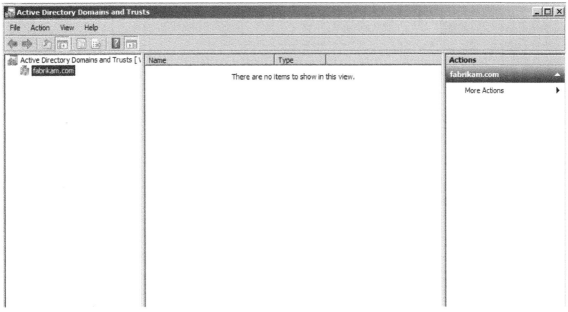

■ **FIGURE 4.32** Active Directory Domains and Trusts.

Then, right-click on the root node of *Active Directory Domains and Trusts* and choose the option *Operations Masters*. Click the *Change* button to transfer the FSMO role to this DC.

Active Directory Administrative Center

As previously mentioned, the ADAC is a new tool introduced in Windows Server 2008 R2. The ADAC (see Figure 4.33) is a new, easy-to-use, GUI tool written on top of PowerShell. ADAC provides enhanced features such as the ability to manage multiple domains from a single pane of glass, a comprehensive search, and an integrated password reset tool. You may choose to use this tool over ADUC for many of the common day-to-day administration tasks for AD, such as resetting passwords or creating new user accounts. ADAC is accessed from the Administrative Tools folder in the Start Menu.

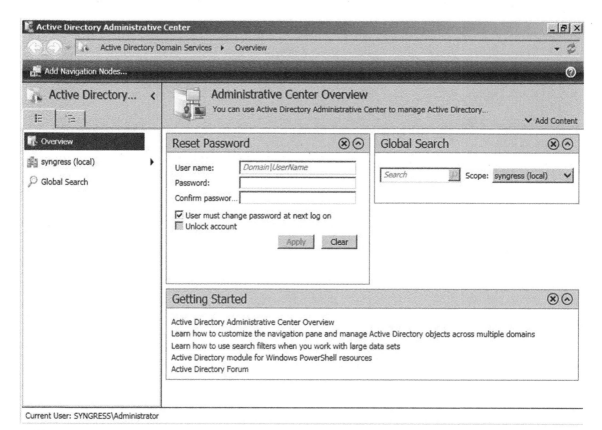

■ **FIGURE 4.33** Active Directory Administrative Center.

Active Directory Module for PowerShell

The AD Module for PowerShell allows you to perform many of the core AD tasks from the PowerShell command line. By using PowerShell, you can easily automate common tasks or save scripts for future use. PowerShell also allows you to more easily update hundreds or thousands of accounts with a few simple commands. The following types of tasks can be performed within PowerShell with the AD Module loaded:

- User and Computer Account Administration
- Create and Administer Groups
- Create and Administer Managed Service Accounts
- Create and Administer Organizational Units
- Create and Administer Password Policies
- Manage the Forest or Domain
- Manage Domain Controllers
- Search for and Modify Objects in the Domain

Whether you are a "command line junkie" or new to PowerShell, the new module for AD could easily become one of your primary administrative tools. It could end up saving your hours of time by automating updates and streamlining the process to update mass numbers of objects. You can access the AD Module for PowerShell from the Administrative Tools folder in the Start Menu. The AD Module for PowerShell will be covered in-depth in Chapter 11.

ADMINISTERING USER AND COMPUTERS

Managing users and computers is one of the day-to-day duties that will be performed on a regular basis. User and computer account objects in AD represent the true users and computers on your network. Both are used in unique ways to manage and secure your domain.

User accounts

User accounts are assigned to people who need to access your network. User accounts allow end users to log on to individual servers or the AD domain. As a best practice, every user should be assigned his or her own user account.

Local user accounts

Local user accounts are created on individual computers and give users access only to the computer in which they are created. Local user accounts do not provide access to any AD domain resources. If you deploy an AD domain, local user accounts should only be used sparsely as they must be managed and maintained on every individual computer they are created on. Local user accounts are good to use for providing temporary access to a server by someone who may not have a regular domain user account, or some application service accounts may require that you set them up as local use accounts.

Domain user accounts

Domain user accounts are created on a DC in the AD domain and provide access to domain resources. These resources can include servers, file shares, printers, Web sites, and AD settings. Domain user accounts are stored in the AD database, thus get replicated to all DCs in the domain. Domain User accounts are usually the preferred method for providing access to your Windows network.

Account usernames, passwords, and security policies

User accounts provide people access to your network. Giving someone a user account is like giving them a key to open certain doors within your organization. Behind those doors resides your company's data. To protect your organization's data, you need to ensure that the user's "keys" are not stolen or compromised. Each user account is assigned a username and password. The username and password combination is used to verify that the user is really who he says he is.

Usernames

Usernames are typically well known within an organization and not considered part of the "key." Usernames are used to simply identify the user who is using his key. You will want to come up with a standard naming convention for all users on your network. This provides consistency and helps keep user accounts manageable. Some examples of naming conventions are:

- Firstname.lastname—John.Doe
- First initial of first name + last name—Jdoe
- Lastname + first initial of first name—Doej

You may want to consider naming the username the same as the user's e-mail alias. This can help ensure that users do not forget their username. The naming convention you use should make sense for your organization. Usernames should be easy for users to remember.

Passwords

A password (key) is assigned to each user account. The passwords ensure that only authorized users are accessing the network. For network access to be granted, each user must identify himself with his username and then enter a password that only the user assigned to the account knows. This combination validates that the person accessing the network to ensure they are truly who they say they are.

After log-on is complete, the user is granted access to resources in which his key allows him to access. If the user does not have access to a particular resource such as a file share, he will receive an access denied error when trying to access the resource.

User account properties

In addition to the username and password properties, domain user accounts include additional properties such as office location, office phone number, and e-mail address. These fields can be referenced (and populated) by various applications, including Microsoft Exchange Server, Office Communications Server, and SharePoint Server. Some of the additional user account properties are:

- First Name
- Last Name
- Initials
- Display Name
- Description
- Office
- Telephone Number
- E-mail
- Web page
- Physical Address Information (Street, City, State, Country)
- Organization Information (Job Title, Department, Company, Manager, Direct Reports)

The following exercise will walk you through setting up a user account in AD:

1. Log on to a DC and open *Server Manager*.
2. Expand the nodes *Roles | Active Directory Domain Services | Active Directory Users and Computers | <your domain>*.
3. Right-click on the *User's* container. Then, select the option *New → User*. The New Object User wizard will launch.

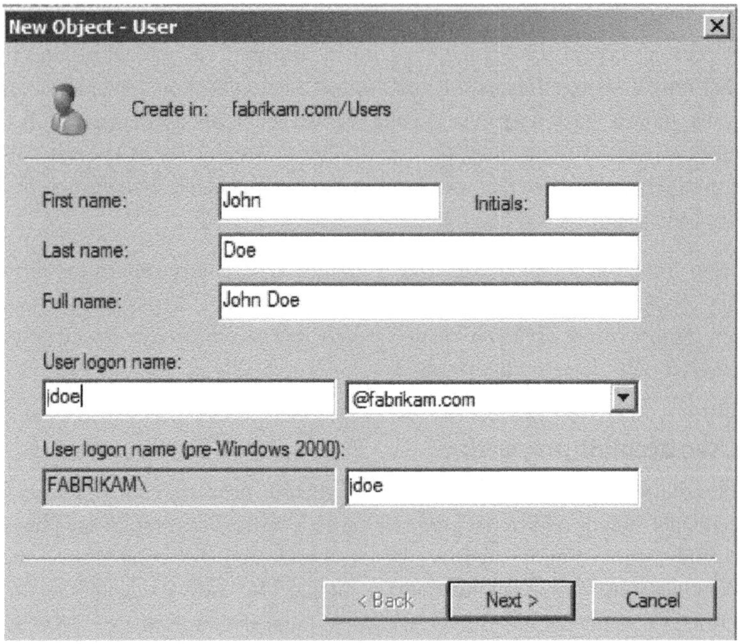

■ **FIGURE 4.34** Create New User Account Wizard.

4. Type *John* and *Doe* in the *First name* and *Last name* fields, respectively. Type *jdoe* in the *User logon name* text box as seen in Figure 4.34. Then, click *Next*.
5. Enter and confirm a password for the user. In our example, we will use *Pass@word1*. Leave the box selected for *User must change password at the next logon*. This will force John Doe to change his password the first time he logs on to the network. The following password options are available when creating user accounts:
   ❏ *User must change password at next logon*—This setting forces the user to change his password during the first logon.
   ❏ *User cannot change password*—This prevents the user from changing his password.
   ❏ *Password never expires*—This exempts the user from any account policies that might force password changes after *x* number of days.
   ❏ *Account is disabled*—This disables the user account. It cannot be logged onto until it is enabled again.
6. Click *Next* to continue.
7. Verify the account settings and click *Finish* to create the user account.

BEST PRACTICES

Use a management server or local workstation for admin tasks

As a best practice, you should not perform day-to-day account management operations on a DC. Instead, you should set up a management server or a workstation with the administrative tools installed. You can then run the tools and connect to a DC remotely when creating new accounts. This provides a great level of security by limiting, who can actually log on to a DC.

Built-in user accounts

AD creates two default user accounts during installation. The Administrator and Guest accounts are created during the dcpromo process. The Administrator is the first and primary administrator to the domain. The Administrator account has full permissions to everything within the domain. The Guest account is disabled by default. The Guest account is a low-privileged account with limited permissions in the domain. It can be used to provide temporary access to network resources; however, as a best practice, you may want to create a limited user account instead. As mentioned earlier, each user should have a unique account on your domain, including people who need only temporary access.

Account security policies

User account security policies help ensure that user accounts are protected and properly secured. Using account security policies, you can set the following account policies for AD accounts:

- Password Policy
- Account Lockout Policy
- Kerberos Policy

The password policy allows you to configure requirements for user passwords. The password policy options are defined in Table 4.2.

NOTES FROM THE FIELD

Multiple password policies

Windows Server 2008 R1 first introduced the ability to have multiple password policies in a single domain. This allows you to set up different password requirements assigned to different groups of users. For example, you can have a more strict password policy assigned to administrative-level accounts.

Table 4.2 Active Directory Domain Password Policy

Policy	Description	Default Setting
Enforce password history	By enabling this policy, users cannot use any of the previously remembered passwords. For example, using the default setting of 24, the user cannot use any of the previous 24 passwords when setting a new password	24 Passwords remembered
Maximum password age	By enabling this setting, passwords expire every x number of days. The number of days configured here define how often the users will be forced to change their passwords	42 days
Minimum password age	By enabling this setting, passwords require to remain the same for x number of days. For example, the default setting of 1 day requires that a user keep the same password for at least 1 day	1 day
Minimum password length	By enabling this setting, users must include at least x number of characters in their passwords. The longer the password the more secure it is. However, the longer the password the harder it is to remember. You should find a happy medium for your network. Most security best practices recommend at least 8 characters, though some organizations are asking users to begin using passphrases opposed to passwords. This can increase the character count dramatically, thus increasing account security	Seven characters
Password must meet complexity requirements	By enabling this setting, users must create passwords that are considered complex. Complex passwords require that the password use characters from three of the following four sets of characters: • Upper Case • Lower Case • Number • Special Characters such as #, @, ! Complex passwords cannot contain part or all of the user's full name or username	Enabled
Store passwords using reversible encryption	This setting essentially stores passwords in a plain text format. This is to provide backwards compatibility with some legacy applications but is not recommended.	Disabled

In addition to the password policy, you can set an account lockout policy. The account lockout policy "locks" the user's account after a defined number of failed password attempts. The account lockout prevents the user from logging onto the network for a period of time even if the correct password is entered. You should set an account lockout policy to help thwart off those who may attempt to compromise user accounts by brute force methods of guessing username and password combinations. The account lockout policy contains the following settings:

- *Account lockout duration*—This is the amount of time the account will remain locked out. This is commonly set to 20 or 30 min. An administrator can manually unlock the account at any time after it has been locked.
- *Account lockout threshold*—This is the number of invalid log-on attempts allowed before the account is locked out. After the defined threshold is reached, the account then becomes locked until the account lockout duration passes or an administrator manually unlocks the account.
- *Reset account lockout counter after*—This setting defines the number of minutes that must pass before the lockout counter will set itself to zero after an invalid log-on attempt has been detected.

The third account policy is the Kerberos Policy. This policy allows you to define Kerberos authentication settings. Kerberos authentication is discussed in Chapter 11. The Kerberos policy has the following definable settings:

- *Enforce user logon restrictions*—By enabling this setting, the Kerberos Key Distribution Center (KDC) will validate each ticket request against the user account rights policy.
- *Maximum lifetime for a service ticket*—This setting defines how long a service ticket is valid. After the ticket expires, the user account will be rejected by the resource and will have to request a new ticket from the KDC.
- *Maximum lifetime for a user ticket*—This setting defines the maximum age in minutes that the user ticket or ticket granting ticket (TGT) is valid.
- *Maximum lifetime for user ticket renewal*—This setting defines the number of days that a TGT can be renewed for continued use.
- *Maximum tolerance for computer clock synchronization*—Kerberos is time-sensitive protocol. This is a security feature to ensure that expired tickets cannot be used because of computer clocks being set incorrectly. This setting allows you to set the maximum amount of time difference Kerberos will allow between the domain and computers joined to the domain.

The account policies are set using the Group Policy Management console located in Server Manager. To manage the account policies, you need to edit the default domain group policy. Perform the following tasks to modify account policies:

1. Open *Server Manager*.
2. Expand the nodes *Features | Group Policy Management | Forest: <your forest name> | Domains | <your domain name>*.

3. Right-click the *Default Domain Policy* and choose the *Edit* option.

4. Expand the nodes *Computer Configuration | Policies | Windows Settings | Security Settings | Account Policies*.

5. Select the policy you want to modify. After making changes, close the *Group Policy Management Editor*. Changes will be automatically saved.

Administering computer accounts

Just like users, computers also have accounts in AD and are automatically created when a computer joins the domain. Typically, the administrative burden for computer accounts is much less than users. Computer accounts do contain properties that can be populated such as information regarding who manages the system, its physical location, and delegation settings.

BEST PRACTICES

Cleanup old computer accounts

Most organizations are disciplined about disabling and remove user accounts for users who no longer need access to the network. However, many companies fail to disable and remove old computer accounts from the AD. As a best practice, you need to implement process to disable and remove old computer accounts from your AD domain. This not only tightens security but also helps keep stale computer accounts from sitting around in your domain.

ADMINISTERING GROUPS AND ORGANIZATIONAL UNITS

Groups and Organizational Units allow administrators to better organize user and computer accounts within their respective domains. This section will describe aspects of planning and managing Groups and Organizational Units within your AD domains.

Administering groups

Groups were developed to provide a more simplified approach to organizing users and providing access to network resources. In this section, we will discuss the various types and options available for AD groups and how to implement them in your deployment.

Group types

AD uses two primary group types—Security Groups and Distribution Groups. These two group types provide very different features within your AD deployment:

- *Distribution Groups*—Distribution Groups are used solely for the purpose of nonsecurity-related functions such as sending e-mail to many people at the same time. Distribution Groups are used heavily by Exchange server and more recently, Office Communications Server.
- *Security Groups*—These groups are used to organize and assign permissions to users and computers. Security Groups can also provide the same functionality as a distribution group.

Group scopes

Group scopes determine whether membership and permissions can apply to only a single domain, a domain tree, or an entire forest. Three group scopes exist to provide access at different levels within your organization. Table 4.3 provides details on the three group scopes available in Windows Server 2008 R2 AD.

Nesting groups

In addition to including users and computers within groups, you can also make group members of other groups. This is known as group nesting. Nesting can be beneficial when used in moderation, however, creating multiple levels of nesting can not only increase the complexity of your group management but also add additional load to your servers. Table 4.4 provides information about which groups can be nested into others.

Table 4.3 Active Directory Group Scopes

Group Scope	Membership	Resource Permissions
Domain local group	Users or computers from any domain	Permissions assigned to resources in the local domain only.
Global group	Users or computer from local domain only	Permissions assigned to resources in any domain
Universal group	Users and computers from any domain	Permissions assigned to resources in any domain

Table 4.4 Active Directory Group Nesting

Group Scope	Groups that can be Nested Inside this Scope
Domain Local	Universal Global Domain local
Global	Global
Universal	Global Universal

Planning for groups

Before setting up groups in AD, you should properly plan and document how you want to use groups within your organization. Just like user accounts, you need a consistent naming convention and usage strategy. One of the more common group strategies involves creating domain local groups related to various resources such as file shares, printers, and internal applications. Then, global groups are created for various workgroups such as marketing, finance, and IT. Users are then assigned to the global groups. To give a specific workgroup permission to a resource, you simply add the global group to the local group. If a resource spans multiple domains, you may want to consider the usage of universal groups. As a best practice, use universal groups only when necessary as they create additional replication traffic across the forest when changes are made. Figure 4.35 depicts what a typical group configuration might look like.

Administering Organizational Units

OUs, like groups, are a way of organizing users, computers, and groups within AD. Unlike groups, OUs are not used to assign permissions to resources but only to organize and manage AD objects. In many ways, OUs are to AD as folders are to file systems. Additionally, OUs provide the ability to apply GPOs and to delegate administrative control over limited numbers of users, groups, and computers.

Planning for Organizational Units

When planning your OU hierarchy, you need to consider the best approach for organizing your users, groups, and computers. Some companies create OU structures based upon geography, others by business unit, and yet others by some other structure within their companies. The way you set up OUs really depends on your organization and how you plan on using the OUs. Things to consider when planning your OU structure are as follows:

- How do you want to manage users? By location? Business unit?
- Will separate administrators be responsible for specific business units or geographic locations?

Accounting Share —Modify Access To— Accounting Modify Access Group —Member Of— Accounting Team Group —Member Of— John Accountant

■ **FIGURE 4.35** Active Directory Groups.

- Do specific business units or geographic locations need similar desktop configurations?
- Try to prevent nesting OUs too deep. The deeper the OU structure, the more complexity you will be adding to your deployment.

Creating and managing Organizational Units

OUs are created within the ADUC console. To create a new OU, perform the following tasks:

1. Log on to a DC and Open *Server Manager*.
2. Expand the nodes *Roles | Active Directory Domain Services | Active Directory Users and Computers*.
3. Right-click on the domain name (e.g., contoso.com) and select the option *New → Organizational Unit*. The *New Object—Organizational Unit* window will appear.
4. Give the OU a meaningful name and ensure that the option to *Protect container from accidental deletion* is selected (see Figure 4.36). This option prevents you from accidentally deleting OUs which may contain hundreds or thousands of users, computers, and groups. As a best practice, always choose to protect the OU when creating it.

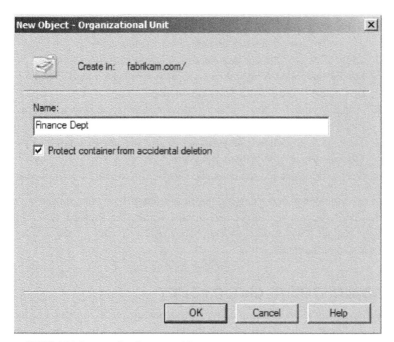

■ **FIGURE 4.36** Creating a New Organizational Unit.

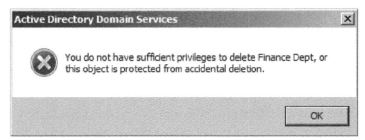

■ **FIGURE 4.37** Error deleting protected Organizational Unit.

5. Click *OK* to create the OU.
6. The OU should now be displayed under the domain in ADUC. If you attempt to delete the OU, you will receive an error message, as seen in Figure 4.37, informing you that the OU is protected. To delete the OU, you will need to open the OU properties by right-clicking on it and then disabling the protection option selected during creation.

Additionally, you can delegate the administrative functions of an OU to other users such as administrators who may be responsible for a specific business unit. Perform the following tasks to delegate permissions to an OU:

1. Log on to a DC and open *Server Manager*.
2. Expand the nodes *Roles | Active Directory Domain Services | Active Directory Users and Computers | <your domain name>*.
3. Right-click the OU that you want to delegate permissions to and choose the option *Delegate Control*. This will launch the Delegation of Control Wizard. Click *Next* to continue.
4. Add the administrator(s) whom you want to delegate permissions to (see Figure 4.38); Then click *Next*.
5. Select the permissions that you want to give the administrator over the OU (see Figure 4.39); then click *Next*.
6. Verify the delegation summary and click *Finish* to delegate permissions.

In the aforementioned example, the financeadmin1 account should have the ability to manage users and groups within the Finance OU. The financeadmin1 will *not* have rights to manage users and groups in other OUs within the domain.

ADMINISTERING GROUP POLICY

Group Policy is widely used in Windows networks of all sizes to manage various user and computer policies. In this section, we will explore Group Policy and how to properly deploy it within an AD domain.

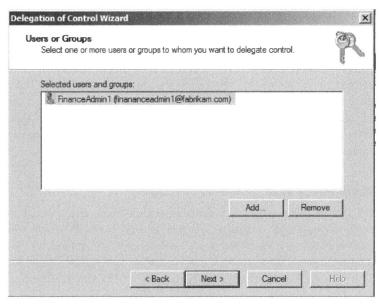

■ FIGURE 4.38 Delegating Control over an Organizational Unit.

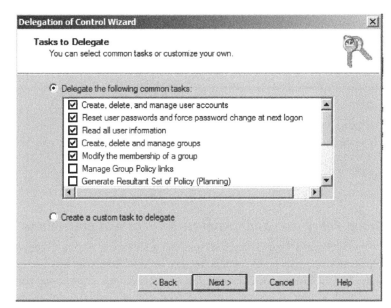

■ FIGURE 4.39 Select Permissions to Delegate.

Overview of Group Policy

Group Policy was first introduced in Windows Server 2000 AD and was widely adopted as the standard method to manage user and computer configurations for Windows networks. Group Policy allows administrators to set and enforce settings on users and computers within the domain. These settings include security settings, restricting access to specific parts of the OS, and deploying software. At the core of the Group Policy is GPOs. GPOs contain the settings you wish to apply to computers or users and are applied locally or to sites, domains, or OUs within AD.

Group Policy links and security filtering

GPOs can be linked to AD sites, domains, or OUs. They can also be set up locally on individual computers. As you develop your GPOs, you will need to understand what objects you wish to apply the settings to. For example, if you want to prevent access to the Windows control panel for all users in the HR department, you could apply a GPO with those settings to the OU containing all the users in HR. Maybe you want to configure a specific Internet Explorer homepage for every user in the New York location. You could create a GPO with the IE settings defined and apply it to the New York AD site.

In addition to linking GPOs, you can also filter them based upon security. A user or computer must have read and apply permissions to a GPO before it applies to him. You can limit which users or computers can apply a specific GPO by adding or removing them to the GPO permissions as seen in Figure 4.40.

NOTES FROM THE FIELD

GPOs apply to users and computers only

GPOs apply to users and computers only. They do not apply to groups. Groups can be used to security-filter GPOs but you cannot apply a GPO to an AD group.

Group Policy user and Computer Settings and preferences

Every GPO has a User Settings section and a Computer Settings section which means it can apply settings to user objects, computer objects, or both. As you expand each section, you will see various settings that can be applied to user or computer objects. You can configure the following groups of settings within a GPO:

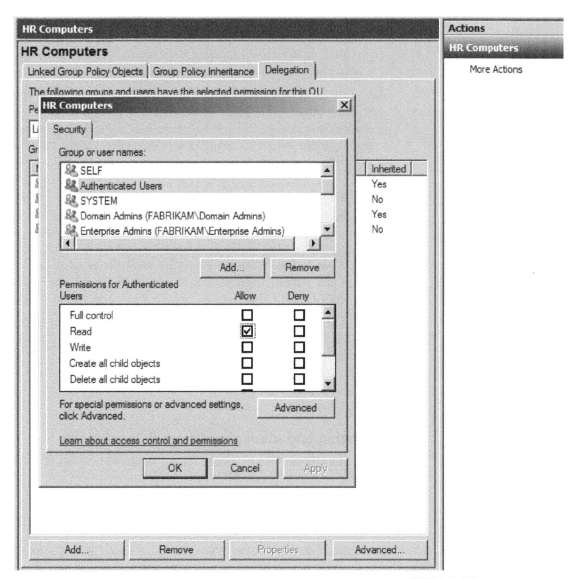

- *Software Settings*—Software Settings allow you to use GPOs to deploy applications such as Microsoft Office.
- *Windows Settings*—Windows Settings allow you to configure basic windows settings such as startup and shutdown scripts, folder redirection, and Public Key Policies.

- *Administrative Templates*—Administrative Templates allow registry keys to be modified on systems applying the policy. This allows administrators to configure detailed settings for Windows and other applications, including Microsoft Office.

Group Policy Preferences were first introduced in Windows Server 2008 R1. Group Policy Preferences allow for even more granular control of various Windows settings. Group Policy Preferences additionally have better targeting techniques such as applying the GPO to only specific OSs, specific hardware specs, or IP address ranges.

Group Policy processing order

It is important that you understand how Group Policy is applied and the processing order is used to apply GPOs. As mentioned earlier, GPOs can be set up on the local computer or applied to AD Sites, Domains, and OUs. When multiple GPOs are configured, the order in which they are applied to a user or computer is important. In the event of a conflict, the next policy applied will override the one that was applied before it. GPOs are applied in the following order:

1. Local Policies created on the computer
2. GPOs applied to AD Sites
3. GPOs applied to Active Directory Domains
4. GPOs applied to AD OUs
5. GPOs applied to AD child OUs

Creating and managing Group Policy Objects

GPOs are created using the Group Policy Management console in Server Manager. To create a new GPO, perform the following tasks:

1. Log on to a DC and open *Server Manager*.
2. Expand the nodes *Features | Group Policy Management | <your forest name> | Domains | <your domain name>*.
3. Right-click an OU where you want to create a new GPO and select the option *Create a GPO in this domain and link it here*. Optionally, you could right-click on the Domain itself if you wanted to assign the GPO to the entire domain.
4. Enter a name that describes the use of this policy. For example, *HR Computer Policy*. The new policy will appear under the OU you selected to apply it to (see Figure 4.41).
5. Right-click on the newly created policy and select *Edit*.
6. The GPO management editor window will open. Here, you can configure specific settings for users and computers. In our example,

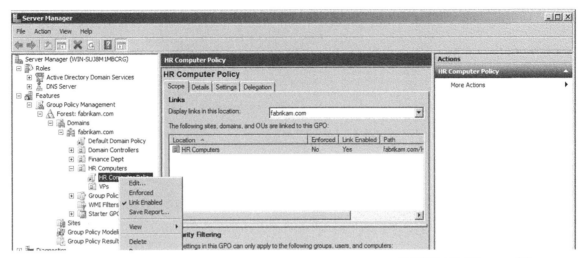

■ **FIGURE 4.41** Editing a new GPO.

we will configure the HR GPO to turn on branch cache as seen in Figure 4.42. After editing the setting, close the GPO management editor window.

7. The new GPO will now apply to all computers in the HR OU as seen in Figure 4.43.

We will now assume that we have a VPs OU that we want to be sure they do not get the new settings. To prevent them from having the GPO applied, we need to block inheritance. By blocking inheritance, we tell the OU to not apply any parent GPOs. To block inheritance to the VPs child OU, right-click the OU and select the option *Block Inheritance*. You should now notice that a blue exclamation appears over the OU as seen in Figure 4.44.

Troubleshooting Group Policy

Group Policy can be one of the toughest technologies to troubleshoot in an AD deployment. Luckily, Microsoft has provided some good tools to assist with troubleshooting issues.

GPUDATE and GPRESULT

GPUDATE and GPRESULT are two command-line utilities you can run from a machine to perform a group policy update or display the results of the currently applied GPOs.

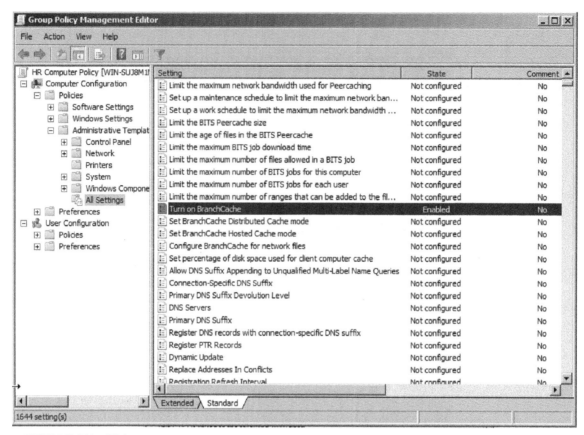

- GPUPDATE can be used to update the current computer's Group Policy Settings. By issuing the/force parameter, GPUDATE will force a fresh push of policies down to the specific user and computer.
- GPRESULT can be used to display currently applied GPOs and those that have been filtered out due to security settings or other configurations. If you do not see changes taking effect after creating a new GPO, run GPRESULT from the machine or user the policy is applied to. If it does not show up as applied, then you need to troubleshoot possible security misconfigurations on the GPO.

Resultant Set of Policies and modeling tools

The Resultant Set of Policies (RSOP) can be used to help iron out GPO conflicts. The RSOP will take a specific user and computer choice and will provide a report of what policies will be applied if the selected user logs

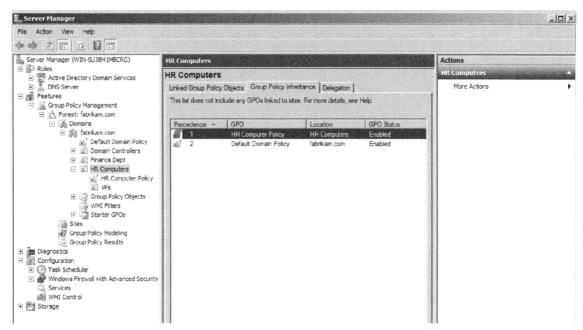

■ **FIGURE 4.43** Newly created and applied GPO.

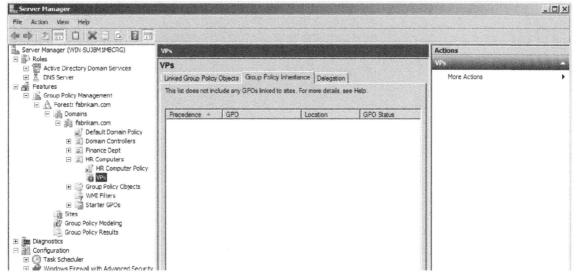

■ **FIGURE 4.44** Organizational Unit Blocking Inheritance.

on to the selected computer. RSOP can be very powerful in verifying your GPO configuration as well as troubleshooting issues.

The Modeling tool is helpful when you are still planning your GPOs. The modeling tool allows you to walk through "whatif" scenarios for deploying Group Policy. This tool is very useful when blocking inheritance and enforcing GPOs.

OTHER ACTIVE DIRECTORY SERVICES

Windows Server 2008 R2 includes additional AD services beyond the traditional Active Directory Domain Servers. These enhancements extend AD to provide additional functionality and services to Windows networks.

ACTIVE DIRECTORY CERTIFICATE SERVICES

Most organizations must deal with the reality of security threats both outside and within their company. To help provide a higher level of security, many companies have started deploying their own internal public key infrastructure (PKI). PKIs allow you to deploy certificates to users, computers, network devices, and applications. These certificates can then be used to encrypt data and verify the identity of network objects. The most common form of PKI you are probably familiar with is Secure Sockets Layer (SSL)-based Web sites. Typically when you place an order from a well-known shopping site, you will be connected via a secure session using SSL based upon PKI technologies. Several Microsoft products themselves are starting to rely on PKI to function properly or provide enhanced feature sets. Both Exchange Server and Office Communications server rely on certificates as part of their core functionality. Active Directory Certificate Services is a Windows solution for deploying a PKI on your network. Active Directory Certificate Services requires adequate planning to ensure that the core PKI is secure and well managed. Though an overall PKI deployment is outside the scope of this book, it is important that you understand Windows Server 2008 R2 helps simplify deployment by making Active Directory Certificate Services a standard role. To set up Active Directory Certificate Services, you simply add the role using Server Manager.

Planning for Active Directory Certificate Services

Microsoft continues to evolve its core PKI solution with each release of Windows Server to allow organizations of all sizes to deploy their own internal certificate services providing support for secure Web sites, smartcard logons, and encrypted data transfers between servers. Though deploying an Active Directory Certificate Services-based PKI is somewhat easy to set up, adequate planning still needs to take place prior to setting up your own deployment. Before you create a deployment plan, you should have a good understanding of a few basic certificate services concepts. Some of these key concepts are defined below:

- *Certificate*—Certificates are at the core of a PKI deployment. Certificates are used to encrypt and decrypt data, verify the identity of the source, and ensure that the data was not tampered with while moving from point A to point B. Certificates are issued to users, computers, or network devices by Certificate Authorities (CAs). CAs not only issue certificates but manage their lifecycle, including the renewal process, as each certificate has a defined expiration date and must be renewed to continue to function properly. Figure 4.45 shows an example of a certificate used to secure an IIS Web site allowing for https-based, SSL-based connections.
- *Root certificate authority*—In most PKI deployments, the root certificate authority (CA) is the first CA in a multilevel hierarchy. Typically, the Root CA only issues certificates for intermediate CAs or issuing and policy CAs depending on the number of levels in the hierarchy. Root CAs are typically taken offline after the subordinate CAs have been set up.
- *Intermediate certificate authority*—Intermediate CAs are typically used in larger multilevel deployments with more than two levels in the hierarchy. Intermediate CAs are a subordinate CA of the Root CA and issues certificates used to set up issuing and policy CAs.
- *Policy certificate authority*—Policy CAs are used to enforce security policies for deploying certificates as defined by the organization.
- *Issuing certificate authority*—Issuing CAs are the actual CAs used to issue certificates to computers, users, and network devices. The issuing CAs are usually subordinate of intermediate or policy CAs.
- *Enterprise certificate authority*—An enterprise CA integrates with AD and uses AD to store CA configuration data. The use of AD implies that to deploy an enterprise CA, the CA must be a member of an AD domain. Additionally, certificates are automatically issued when a user or computer requesting a certificate has permissions to issue new certificates.
- *Stand-alone certificate authority*—A stand-alone certificate authority does not integrate with AD and uses flat files to store configuration information. A stand-alone CA does not require AD and can be deployed in environments with or without an AD domain. Any

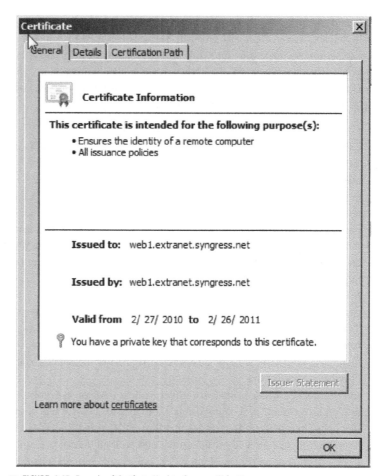

■ **FIGURE 4.45** Example of Certificate Used to Secure a Web site.

certificate requested must be manually issued using the certificate management console. A stand-alone CA is often used as a Root CA as it can be easily taken offline without worrying about domain membership issues or the need to talk to AD.

■ *Certificate revocation lists (CRLs) and online certificate status protocol (OCSP)*—CRLs and the OCSP are the methods used to determine if a certificate has been revoked by a CA. A certificate administrator may need to revoke a certificate if a system is no longer in use or if the certificate has been compromised. CRLs or OSCP are used to inform connecting clients or servers that a certificate has been revoked. OSCP was first introduced in Windows Server 2008 R1 (RTM) as an alternate method to determine if a certificate has been revoked. The use of CRLs require that the CA generate a new CRL list and clients to download the CRL list from a CRL distribution point on a regular basis. Using OSCP is more of a real-time request for the revoke list as the client requests the list from a CA.

When planning your PKI deployment, you will need to consider various decision points during the design process. For example, will the PKI be supporting multiple domains or a single domain?. You will also need to know what type of hierarchy to deploy and the number of levels to include. Additionally, you will need to ensure that your Active Directory Schema is updated to the Windows Server 2008 schema level to support the new features in Windows Server 2008 R2 Active Directory Certificate Services.

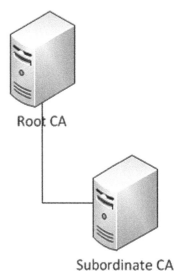

Planning your Certificate Authority hierarchy

As a best practice, larger organizations will want to deploy multiple levels of CAs for manageability and security purposes. Additionally, the Root CA is typically used to create intermediate CAs and is then taken offline for security purposes. Figure 4.46 depicts a two-level hierarchy. The Root CA that is used strictly for creating a second CA acts as a policy-and certificate-issuing CA.

■ FIGURE 4.46 Two-level Certificate Authority hierarchy.

Planning for Certificate Revocation List distribution points

As part of your design, you need to properly plan for CRL distribution points. By default, each Enterprise CA will publish the CRL to AD and inform clients that the CRL can be accessed using an LDAP URL. The disadvantage of using the default is that as the CRL is published to AD, it must be replicated to all DCs in the domain before you can be sure that all clients can see the updated CRL. As you are aware, AD replication happens on a scheduled basis thus, it could take some time for CRL changes to fully replicate throughout your network. If you need CRL changes to be available sooner, you can create http-based distribution points which can be managed by the CA. If CRL changes are infrequent on your network, you may be ok with using the default LDAP URL.

Other planning decisions you need to consider are:

- Will clients outside the corporate firewall need to use internal PKI protected systems? If so, the certificate chain must be viewable from the outside world.
- Who will manage the PKI? There are special security groups created within AD for Enterprise CA deployments. Some organizations may

leave the administration to the AD admins, while others may have dedicated security departments that manage the PKI.

■ You will want to monitor your PKI to ensure that it remains healthy. This can be accomplished by reviewing the logs on a regular basis. Additionally, there is a System Center Operations Manager (SCOM) 2007 R2 Management Pack available to allow SCOM to monitor your PKI deployment.

Be sure you spend ample time planning and testing your design in a lab before implementing a PKI on your production network. A simple PKI can be somewhat easy to implement but a bad deployment could cause major headaches and possible security issues.

Deploying Active Directory Certificate Services

Now that we have explored the planning process for an Active Directory Certificate Services-based PKI, we will walk through the process to install and set up a two-level or two-tier PKI deployment. In our exercise, we will be using a server named RootCA which will be deployed as a standalone CA used for our Root CA. We will be using a secondary server named SyngressCA which will be a policy and issuing subordinate CA. The SyngressCA will be an Enterprise CA installation.

First, we need to set up and install our Root CA. To set up the Root CA, log on to the RootCA server and perform the following tasks:

1. Open *Server Manager*.
2. Select the *Roles* node and then click the *Add Role* link in the middle pane which will launch the Add Roles Wizard.
3. Click *Next* to begin the wizard.
4. Select the *Active Directory Certificate Services* role as seen in Figure 4.47, then click *Next*.
5. On the introduction page, click *Next* to continue.
6. Be sure that only the *Certificate Authority* role service is selected (see Figure 4.48), then click *Next*.
7. You will notice that since the computer is not a member of an AD domain, it can only be a Standalone CA (see Figure 4.49). Ensure that the *Standalone CA* is selected, then click *Next*.
8. Select the *Root CA* option for the CA type (see Figure 4.50), then click *Next*.
9. You now need to create a new private key for the CA. If you happen to restore a CA from backup, you would want to select the option *Use existing private key*. This would ensure that the certificate chain remains intact and all issued certificates would remain valid in the

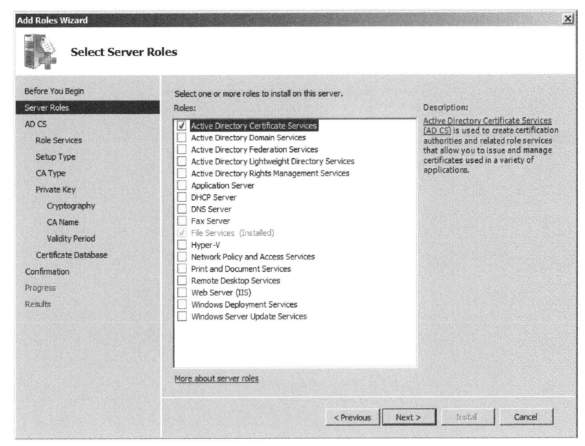

■ **FIGURE 4.47** Active Directory Certificate Services Role.

event of the need to restore the CA. Since we are setting up a new CA, choose the option *Create a new private key and* then click *Next*.

10. You now need to select a cryptography service and hash algorithm (see Figure 4.51) to use for signing certificates. The stronger the encryption level, the more secure the key is, however, this also adds additional load on the CPU of the server. In most cases, the default selections should be sufficient. For high-security environments, you may want to increase the key character length and algorithms used. Then click *Next* to continue.

11. You now need to provide a meaningful name and description for the CA. In our example, we will name the CA "SyngressRootCA." After entering a name for the CA, click *Next* to continue.

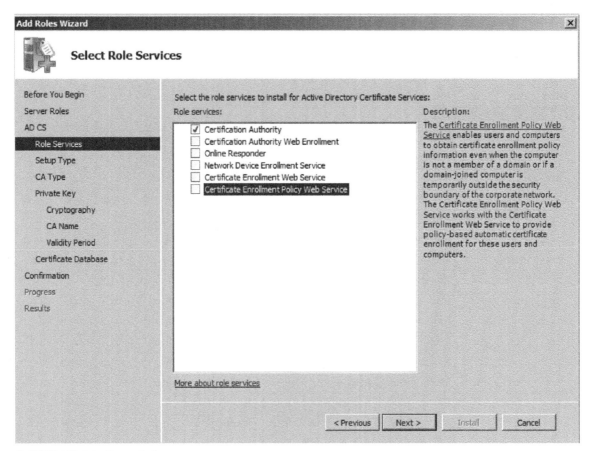

■ **FIGURE 4.48** Active Directory Certificate
Services Role Services Selection.

12. Select the number of years that you want certificates issued from
this CA to be valid (see Figure 4.52). Since the Root CA is only issuing
certificates for other CAs, this period can be longer than certificates
being issued from issuing CAs. In our example, we selected 10 years.
After selecting the validity period, click *Next* to continue.

13. You now need to select the location to store CA and certificate
configuration information. Remember that standalone CAs do not
store the information in AD but to the file system on the local server.
As a best practice, you will want to ensure that this data is on a
reliable and redundant disk subsystem such as a mirrored disk drive.
After selecting the path to store configuration information, click *Next*
to continue.

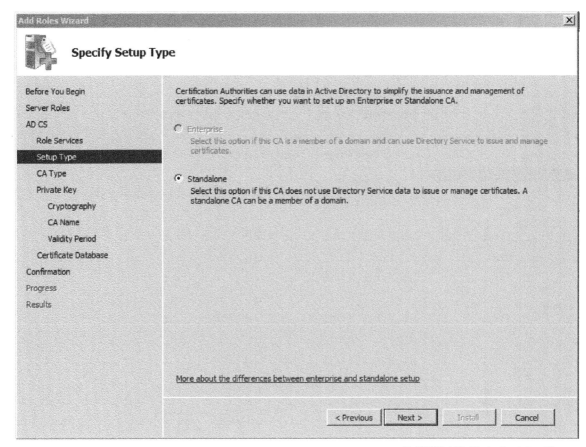

■ **FIGURE 4.49** Selecting Stand alone CA.

14. Confirm the settings on the confirmation page, then click *Install*.

15. After the install completes successfully, click *Close* to close the Add Roles Wizard.

You have now successfully installed your Root CA. The next step is to set up the issuing subordinate CA named SyngressCA. On this server, we will be setting up an Enterprise CA. You will want to ensure it is part of the domain before you begin installation. To set up the CA, log on to the server SyngressCA and perform the following tasks:

1. Open *Server Manager*.

2. Select the *Roles* node and click the *Add Roles* link in the middle pane. This will launch the Add Roles Wizard.

3. Click *Next* to continue.

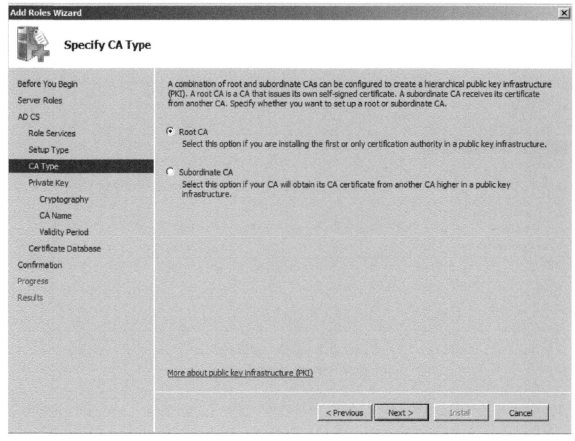

4. Select the *Active Directory Certificate Services* role and then click *Next*.
5. On the Introduction page, click *Next*.
6. For this CA, select all of the Role Services except Network Device Enrollment Service and Certificate Enrollment Web Server as those cannot be installed at the same time as the CA (see Figure 4.53). If prompted to add any required role services, such as IIS, choose to add those. Then click *Next* to continue.
7. This time you want to select the option to install an *Enterprise CA*. Notice that the Enterprise CA option is not grayed out as the server is a member of an AD domain. After selecting to install an *Enteprise CA*, click *Next* to continue.

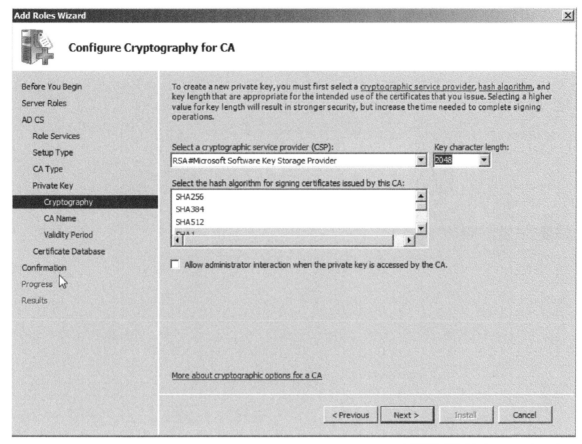

FIGURE 4.51 Selecting cryptography service and hash algorithm.

8. You now want to select the option to set up this server as a *Subordinate CA* as seen in Figure 4.54; then click *Next*.

9. Since this is a new CA, select the option *Create a new private key* and click *Next* to continue.

10. Select the cryptography and hash methods to use. In this exercise, accept the defaults and click *Next* to continue.

11. Enter a meaningful name for your CA. This is how the CA will be referred in certificates and by computers. In our example, we name this CA SyngressCA as seen in Figure 4.55, then click *Next*.

12. We now need to select the parent CA from which we want to be issued a certificate. However, the parent CA (RootCA) is not a member of the domain and thus cannot be selected. To request a certificate, we

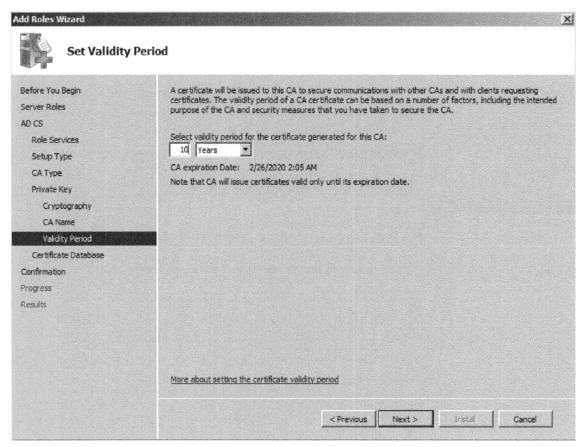

FIGURE 4.52 Select Certificate Validity Period.

need to choose the option to *Save the request to file and manually send it later to a parent CA* (see Figure 4.56); then click *Next*.

13. Select the location to save the certificate database, then click *Next*. Remember you may want to put the CA database files on disk drives that have RAID redundancy.

14. You now need to select the authentication type. This is how clients will authenticate when sending Web requests to the server. In our example, we will use *Windows Authentication*. After selecting authentication type, click *Next*.

15. Verify settings on the confirmation page, then click *Install*.

16. After installation successfully finishes, click *Close* to close the Add Roles Wizard.

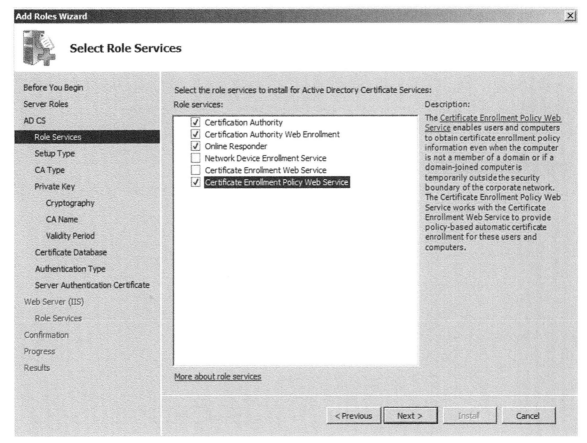

■ **FIGURE 4.53** Certificate Authority Role Services.

You have completed the process to install the CA role on each server. The next step is to configure the RootCAs CRLs publishing and complete the certificate request from the issuing child CA. Perform the following procedures to accomplish these tasks:

First, we will create a CRL distribution point. Since the Root CA will be taken offline, we will publish the CRL to a folder on the local C: drive of the Root CA. We can then copy the CRL to removable media such as a USB drive.

1. Log on to the Root CA (RootCA).
2. Create a new folder at the root of C:\named CRL.
3. Open *Server Manager*.

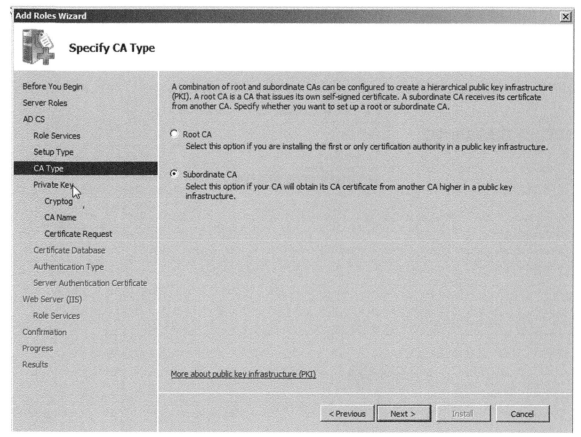

■ **FIGURE 4.54** Select the subordinate CA install option.

4. Expand the node *Roles | Active Directory Certificate Services*.
5. Right-click on the Root CA node (SyngressRootCA) and choose *Properties*.
6. Select the *Extensions* tab.
7. Make sure the *CRL Distribution Point* is selected from the drop-down menu, then click *Add*.
8. In the location text box, enter the path *C:\CRL*, then select each of the following options from the drop-down menu, and choose *Insert*:
   a. <CAName>
   b. <CRLNameSuffix>
   c. <DeltaCRLAllowed>

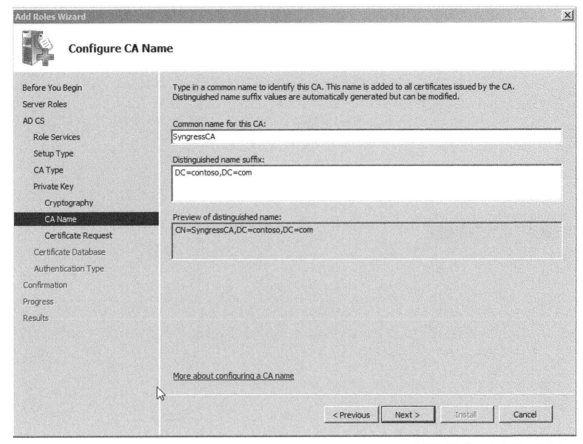

At the end of the string at.*crl.*, these options will create a full location string
of C:\CRL\<CAName><CLRNameSuffix><DeltaCRLAllowed>.crl
(see Figure 4.57). By including these variables, the CRL file will be named
using the name of the CA and include options to allow delta CRLs. Click
OK to save the CRL location.

9. Select the options to *Publish CRLs to this location* and to *Publish
   Delta CRLs to this location* (see Figure 4.58); then click *OK*.
10. When prompted to restart Active Directory Certificate Services, click *Yes*.
11. Expand the CA node in Server Manager and right-click the *Revoked
    Certificates* node and choose *All Tasks | Publish*.
12. When prompted to publish a new CRL (see Figure 4.59), click *OK*.

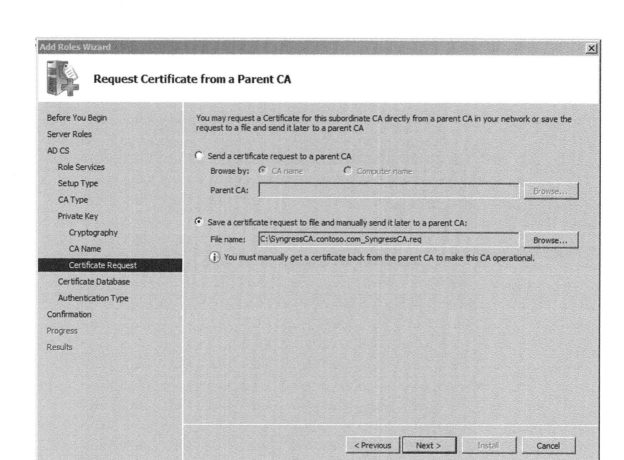

■ **FIGURE 4.56** Request Certificate from Parent CA.

You should now be able to browse the path C:\CRL and see the newly published CRL as seen in Figure 4.60.

Now that you have created the CRL, you need to copy it to the subordinate CA (SyngressCA). After copying the file to the subordinate CA, we need to import it into the certificate store. Perform the following tasks to import the CRL:

1. Open a new MMC console by opening a run prompt from *Start | Run*. Enter *mmc* in the run box and click *OK*.
2. Add the Certificates snap-in by going to *File | Add/Remove Snap-in. . . .*
3. Add the *Certificates* snap-in and choose *Computer Account*, then click *OK*.
4. Right-click the *Person* certificate store and choose *All Tasks | Import*.
5. Click *Next* to begin the Import Wizard.

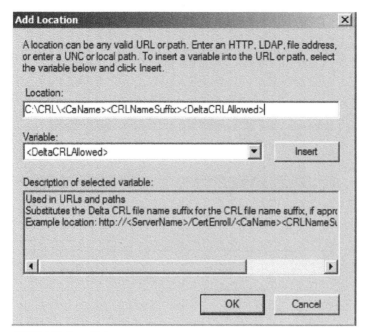

■ **FIGURE 4.57** Create CRL Location.

6. Enter the path to the CRL file copied to the subordinate CA (see Figure 4.61), then click *Next*.

7. Accept the setting to place certificate in the Personal store and then click *Next*. Then click *Finish* to import the CRL.

8. Now that the CRL is imported to the subordinate CA, we are ready to issue a certificate from the Root CA to the subordinate CA creating a certificate chain between the two. To issue the certificate, perform the following tasks: Copy the request file that was created while adding the Active Directory Certificate Services role to the subordinate CA to the Root CA.

9. On the Root CA (RootCA), open *Server Manager*.

10. Expand the node *Roles | Active Directory Certificate Services*.

11. Right-click on the Root CA and choose *All Tasks | Submit New Request*.

12. Browse to the request file you copied over and click *OK*.

13. You should now see the certificate request in the Pending Requests section (see Figure 4.62). Right-click the certificate request and choose *All Tasks | Issue*.

14. You should now be able to click on the *Issued Certificates* node and see the certificate.

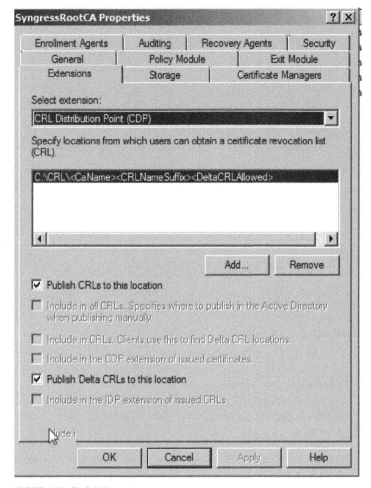

■ **FIGURE 4.58** CRL Publishing options.

15. Double-click the certificate to open it, then select the *Details* tab.
16. Click the *Copy to File* button which will launch the Certificate Export Wizard. Click *Next* to begin. Now that the certificate has been issued, we need to copy it back to the subordinate CA and import it.
17. Select the option *Cryptographic Message Syntax Standard - PKCS #7 Certificates*. Then, select the checkbox to *include all certificates in the certificate path if possible*. Then click *Next*.
18. Select a location and name to save the exported certificate. This is the location you need to copy the file from to be copied onto the subordinate CA. After selecting a path and file name, click *Next*. Click *Finish* to complete the wizard.

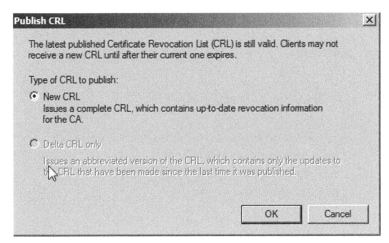

■ **FIGURE 4.59** Publishing New CRL.

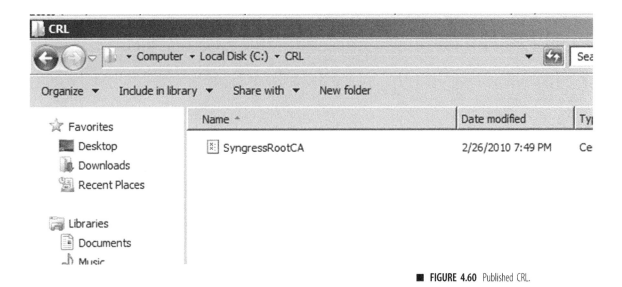

■ **FIGURE 4.60** Published CRL.

Now that you have issued and exported the certificate, copy the file to the subordinate CA (SyngressCA) and perform the following tasks to import the issued certificate.

1. Open *Server Manager* on the subordinate CA.
2. Expand the node *Roles | Active Directory Certificate Services*.
3. Right-click the subordinate CA node (SyngressCA) and choose *All Tasks | Install CA Certificate*.

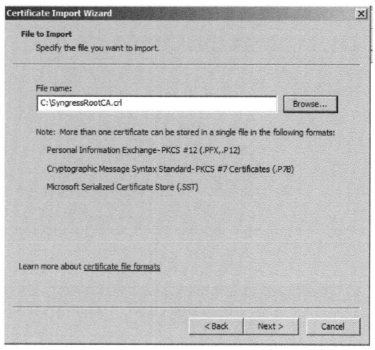

■ FIGURE 4.61 Path to CRL.

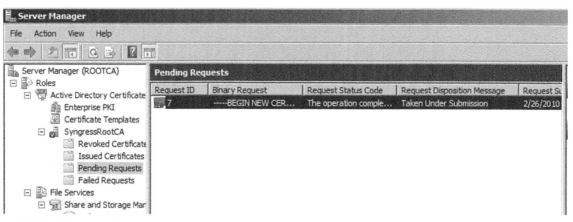

■ FIGURE 4.62 Pending Certificate Request.

4. Browse to the location of the issued certificate that was copied from the Root CA and select that certificate.

5. You should now be able to start the subordinate CA by right-clicking on the CA and choosing *All Tasks | Start Service*.

After the service starts, the CA can now begin to issue certificate requests as needed.

ACTIVE DIRECTORY FEDERATION SERVICES

Organizations in today's global market have found themselves needing to extend their applications beyond the corporate LAN. Many organizations find themselves needing to securely provide clients, vendors, and business partners access to their internal applications or extranets. Additionally, organizations looking at cloud services to host applications are finding it necessary to provide a secure single-sign onto these environments. These needs create a lot of questions around security and account management. Microsoft created Active Directory Federation services (ADFS) as a solution to this issue. ADFS was first introduced with the release of Windows Server 2003 R2 and has been further improved in Windows Server 2008. ADFS uses what is known as claims-based authentication to provide a mechanism to authenticate across network boundaries. The claims-based authentication is done by passing tokens between ADFS servers in separate AD domains. The ADFS servers are set up to act as account and resource servers which can authenticate users based upon a claims token that is passed between ADFS servers and presented to the claims aware application. ADFS is still considered an early technology, but if you have applications where single sign-on is required across networks, you should consider deploying ADFS. By using ADFS, you can allow users in other organizations or other nontrusted forests in your organization to access claims aware applications on your network. The two primary scenarios where ADFS is used today are:

■ Extranet applications—It is common for businesses to deploy an application such as SharePoint server in an extranet or perimeter network. The problem created by doing this is that most perimeter networks do not have direct access to the internal AD environment. This means internal users need a second account and password to log on to the perimeter application. This means that more account management burden on IT departments and internal employees have another set of credentials to remember. By deploying ADFS, you can enable claims-based authentication in the extranet SharePoint deployment which allows internal users to log on using their internal AD accounts.

- Business-to-business (B2B) extranet applications—You may also want to consider using ADFS for extranet applications that are heavily used by business partners, clients, or vendors. In the B2B scenario, you use claims-based authentication to allow users from business partners to log on to the extranet application using the AD accounts from their own internal domain. This not only provides a single-sign-on (SSO) experience to the end users from the business partner, but puts the burden of account management back on the business partner's IT department. In the B2B scenario, you still control which users from the business partner have access to the application, you just allow the other organization to maintain and manage the accounts used to log on. This also helps ensure that employees who no longer work for the business partner have their access properly removed from your application.

ADFS will continue to evolve with future releases of Windows. More focus will be given around enhancing claims-based authentication for cloud-based services allowing your corporate users to log on to a cloud service using the same credentials they would use to access resources on your LAN.

Planning for Active Directory Federation Services

Prior to deploying ADFS, you should properly plan your environment and ensure that the business requirements will be met by your proposed solution. For example, if you want to provide SSO for an extranet application in your permiter network, you will need to ensure that your design includes an AD forest and ADFS servers in the permiter network. You will also need to ensure that the applications support claims-based authentication using ADFS. After you document business requirements, you can begin designing your deployment. Figure 4.63 depicts an ADFS deployment with an application installed in the perimeter network. ADFS in this design is providing SSO for corporate users with existing user accounts in an internal AD forest.

ADFS has several prerequisites that must be met prior to deployment. The prerequisites are:

- PKI—ADFS requires certificates to secure communications between two environments. Self-signed certificates can be used for testing and lab purposes but should not be used in production deployments.
- Windows Server 2008 R2 Enterprise—ADFS servers require Windows Server 2008 R2 Enterprise edition or greater.

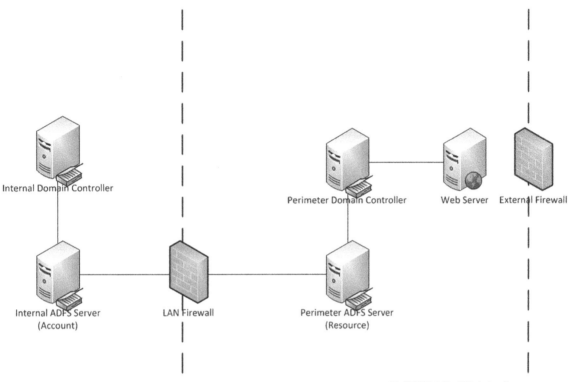

Internal Domain Controller

Perimeter Domain Controller   Web Server   External Firewall

Internal ADFS Server   LAN Firewall   Perimeter ADFS Server
(Account)   (Resource)

■ **FIGURE 4.63** ADFS design diagram.

- AD Domains—ADFS requires that an AD domain exists on both the account and resource side.
- FS Web Agent installed on application server—The Web server hosting the application will need the federation services Web agent installed.

Other factors that you must consider as part of your planning process are:

- Are there redundancy and high availability requirements?
- Will the ADFS deployment involve several AD domains?
- Do you have a PKI deployed to support certificate requirements of ADFS?
- Who will manage access using ADFS?

Be sure that you can answer the aforementioned questions as part of your design and planning process. As with all features in this book, be sure you spend ample time testing your design in a lab environment before making changes to your production environment.

Deploying Active Directory Federation Services

Deploying ADFS can vary depending on what your solution requires. In this section, we will discuss the general steps to setting up ADFS to support an extranet SSO configuration for an organization's employees. Users will have accounts in the internal AD forest, while the application will reside in a forest in the perimeter network. In this example, we will set up ADFS roles on existing DCs that reside in separate AD forests. Note that in production deployments, it is highly recommended not to colocate ADFS roles on DCs. An extranet forest is set up in the perimeter network to support a Web-based application, while company employees have accounts in an internal AD forest and need SSO capabilities to the extranet application. Figure 4.64 depicts the deployment we will be using in this example.

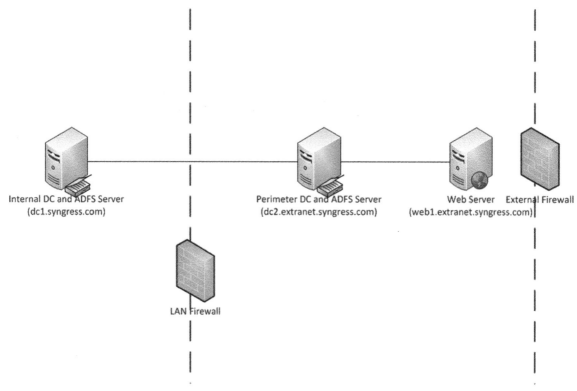

Internal DC and ADFS Server
(dc1.syngress.com)

Perimeter DC and ADFS Server
(dc2.extranet.syngress.com)

Web Server   External Firewall
(web1.extranet.syngress.com)

LAN Firewall

■ **FIGURE 4.64** Example of ADFS deployment.

NOTES FROM THE FIELD
Both SharePoint Server 2007 and SharePoint Server 2010 are claims aware applications thus support ADFS for authentication. To set up SharePoint 2007 with ADFS, see the Microsoft Tech Net article found here: http://technet.microsoft.com/en-us/library/cc772498(WS.10).aspx.

To set up ADFS, we will need to complete the following tasks:

- Set up the ADFS role for the internal and external AD forests.
- Install Web agent for claims aware Web application.
- Configure ADFS Certificates.
- Complete ADFS Server Configuration.

In the following sections, we will walk through the process to complete each of the aforementioned tasks to deploy ADFS.

Set up the ADFS role for the internal and external Active Directory forests

The first task we need to complete is to install the ADFS role on each of our ADFS servers. The ADFS servers will need to be able to communicate over port 443 (https) between each other. In our example, we will be installing the ADFS role on our existing DCs. Keep in mind that this is not recommended for production deployments for security and management purposes. To install ADFS on each of the DCs, perform the following tasks:

1. Open *Server Manager*.
2. Select the *Roles* node and then click the *Add Roles* link in the middle pane.
3. Select the *Active Directory Federation Services* role and then click *Next*.
4. On the Introduction page, click *Next*.
5. Select the *Federation Service* on the Add Role Services page (see Figure 4.65), then click *Next*. If prompted, choose to *Add Required Role Services*.
6. We now need to choose a server authentication certificate. In a production deployment, you will want to request a certificate from an internal CA or 3rd party certificate provider. For our example, we will choose to use a self-signed certificate. Note that using a self-signed certificate will require that all clients import the certificate to their certificate trust list. Select the option to create a self-signed certificate (see Figure 4.66) and then click *Next*.

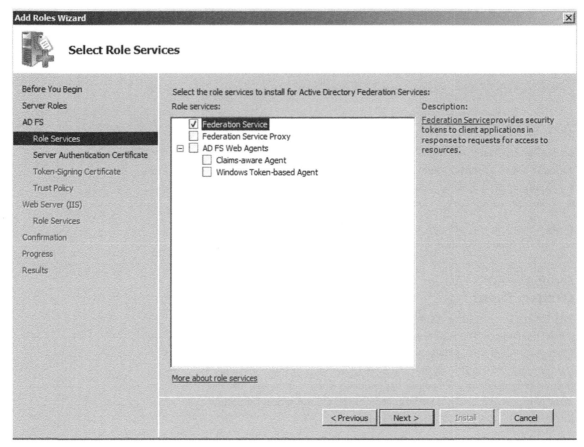

■ **FIGURE 4.65** ADFS Role Services.

7. You now need to select the token-signing certificate. This is the certificate that the ADFS server will use to sign tokens to allow clients and servers to verify the identity of a token. Again, in a production scenario, you will want to use a certificate issued by a CA, however, for this example, we will again choose to use a self-signed certificate. Select the self-signed certificate option and then click *Next*.

8. You now must select whether to create a new trust policy or using an existing policy. Since this is a new deployment of ADFS you will need to select the option to *Create a new trust policy*. The trust policy defines how other ADFS servers can authenticate or access resources in the environment. The trust policy is what

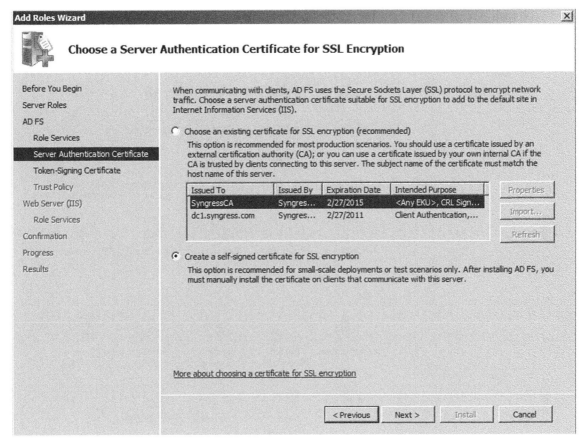

■ **FIGURE 4.66** Service Authentication Certificate selection.

restricts or allows communications over ADFS. After selecting to create a new policy, click *Next*.

9. You will notice that IIS is one of the required roles added for the installation of ADFS. Click *Next* though the IIS section accepting the default role services.

10. Click *Install* on the confirmation page.

11. After the installation completes, click *Close*.

Remember you will need to add the ADFS role to both of the ADFS services using the aforementioned steps. After adding the ADFS role to both servers, you will need to configure each server to require SSL communications and accept client certificates. Again you will need to perform the following tasks on both of the ADFS servers:

Default Web Site Home

■ **FIGURE 4.67** Default Web site configuration options.

1. Open *Server Manager*.
2. Select the node *Roles | Web Server (IIS) | Internet Information Services (IIS) Manager*.
3. Select the *Default Website* node and then open the *SSL Settings* option as seen in Figure 4.67.
4. Select the options to *Require SSL* and *Accept* client certificates (see Figure 4.68). Then click *Apply*.

After configuring SSL settings, you will need to install the ADFS Web agent on the ADFS application server and configure certificate settings so that the Web server will trust the server authentication certificate from the extranet ADFS server (dc2.extranet.syngress.net).

■ **FIGURE 4.68** Default Web site SSL settings.

Install Web agent for claims aware Web application

The next task we need to complete when setting up ADFS is to configure our Web application to support claims-based authentication. This is done by adding the ADFS Web agent. The Web agent comes in two forms:

- *Claims-Aware Agent*—The claims-aware agent is used for applications that support claims-based authentication natively. If your Web application has been developed to support claims authentication, you should install this agent.
- *Windows Token-based Agent*—The Windows token agent is used to support applications that are not natively capable of supporting claims-based authentication. Using the Windows token-based agent, traditional Windows-based authentication Web sites can be set up to work with ADFS. If you are using a Windows token agent, you will want to set up the ADFS server prior to installing the Web agent as you will be asked to specify the name of the ADFS server when adding the Web agent role service.

To install the Web agent, perform the following tasks:

1. Log on to the Web application server and open *Server Manager*.
2. Select the *Roles* node, then click the *Add Roles* link in the middle pane.

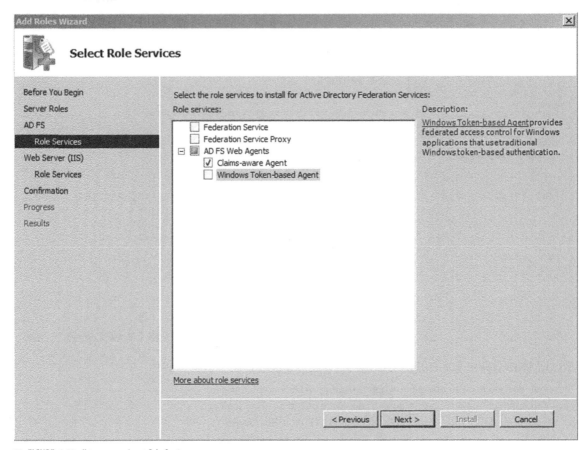

■ **FIGURE 4.69** Claims-aware Agent Role Service.

3. Click *Next* to begin.
4. Select the *Active Directory Federation Services* role and click *Next*.
5. On the Introduction page, click *Next*.
6. Select the *Claims-aware Agent* (see Figure 4.69), then click *Next*.
7. On the Confirmation page, click *Install* to install the Web agent.
8. After the installation completes, click *Close*.

Configure ADFS certificates

Now that we have installed all of the ADFS components, we need to ensure that all proper components trust the correct certificate chains or single certificates since we have used self-signed certificates in this example deployment. Some of the following steps would be unnecessary in a production deployment where a trust CA was used. Complete the following steps to complete the certificate setup process for ADFS.

The first step is to create a self-signed server authentication certificate for the Web application server (web1.extranet.syngress.net). If you remember, the server authentication certificates for both ADFS servers were created when adding the role to each of those servers. To create the server authentication certificate for the Web server, perform the following tasks:

1. Open *Server Manager*.
2. Select the node *Roles | Web Server (IIS) | Internet Information Services (IIS) Manager*.
3. In the middle pane, select the Web server node (WEB1) and then open the *Server Certificates* option (see Figure 4.70).
4. In the right Actions pane, click the link to *Create Self-Signed Certificate* (see Figure 4.71).
5. In the dialog box requesting a friendly name, enter *web1 self signed*, then click *OK*.
6. Select the *Default Website* (or Web site hosting your claims aware application) in the middle pane of the IIS Management console.
7. Click the *Bindings* link in the right Action pane.
8. Click *Add* to create a new binding in the Site Bindings window.
9. Select a type of *https* and select the self-signed certificate you just created (see Figure 4.72), then click *OK*.
10. Open the SSL settings of the Web site and choose the options to *Require SSL* and to *Accept* client certificates.

We now need to export the server authentication certificate and the token-signing certificate from the ADFS server in the extranet so that it can be imported to the trusted certificates store on the Web server. Additionally, we need to export the token-signing certificate from the ADFS server on the internal LAN (dc1.syngress.com). This certificate will be used while configuring the ADFS servers.

To export the token-signing certificate from the internal LAN ADFS server (dc1.syngress.com), perform the following tasks:

1. Log on to the internal ADFS server (dc1.syngress.com).
2. Open *Server Manager*.
3. Expand the node *Roles | Active Directory Federation Services*.
4. Right-click on the *Federation Service* node and choose *Properties*.
5. From the *General* tab, click the *View* button from the Token-signing Certificate section of the window (see Figure 4.73).
6. Select the *Details* tab from the Certificate window and click *Copy to file* (see Figure 4.74).
7. Click *Next* to begin the Certificate Export Wizard.

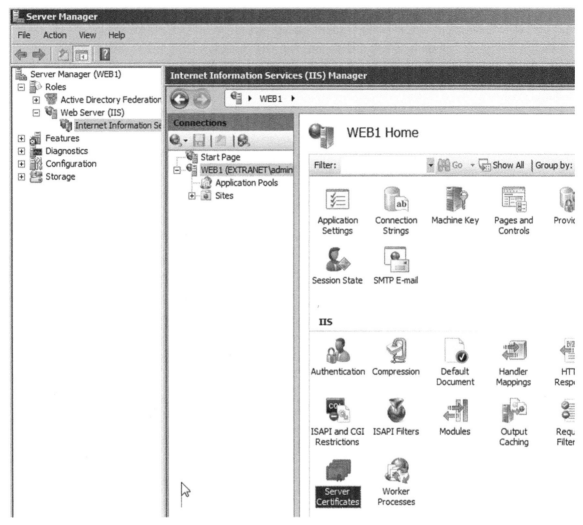

■ **FIGURE 4.70** Web Server Configuration options.

8. Select the *No, do not export the private key* option and click *Next*.
9. Accept the default export format of *DER encoded binary X.509 (.CER)*, then click *Next*.
10. Enter a path and filename to export the certificate, then click *Next*.
11. Click *Finish* to export the certificate. You should receive a confirmation dialog informing you that the export was successful.

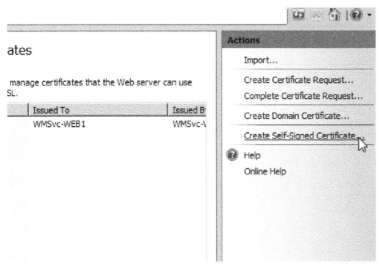

■ **FIGURE 4.71** Create a new Self-Signed Certificate.

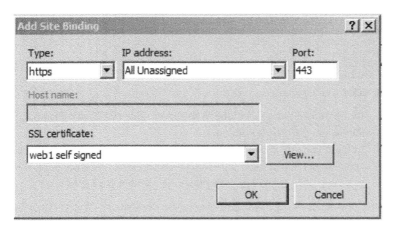

■ **FIGURE 4.72** Add SSL Binding to Web application.

Copy the certificate file to the extranet ADFS server (dc2.extranet. syngress.net) for use during ADFS setup.

To export the server authentication certificate from the extranet ADFS server, perform the following tasks:

1. Log on to the extranet ADFS server (dc2.extranet.syngress.net) and open *Server Manager*.
2. Select the node *Roles | Web Server (IIS) | Internet Information Services (IIS) Manager*.

FIGURE 4.73 Federation Service properties.

3. In the middle pane, select the Web server node (DC2) and then open the *Server Certificates* option.
4. In the middle pane, right-click the dc2.extranet.syngress.net certificate and choose *Export*. Enter a patch to save the certificate and a password to protect the private key (see Figure 4.75), then click *OK*.

You now need to copy the certificate to the Web server (Web1). We will then import the certificate to the computer's trusted certificate store. After copying the certificate to the Web server, perform the following tasks:

1. Open a new mmc console by clicking *Start | Run* and typing *mmc* and then clicking the *OK* button.
2. You now need to add the certificates snap-in by clicking *File | Add/ Remove Snap-in*.
3. Select the *Certificates* snap-in and choose *Add*. When prompted for the type of account to manage certificates, select *Computer Account* and then click *Next*.
4. Select *Local Computer* for the computer to manage, then click *Finish*.
5. Click *OK* to close the add/remove snap-ins window.

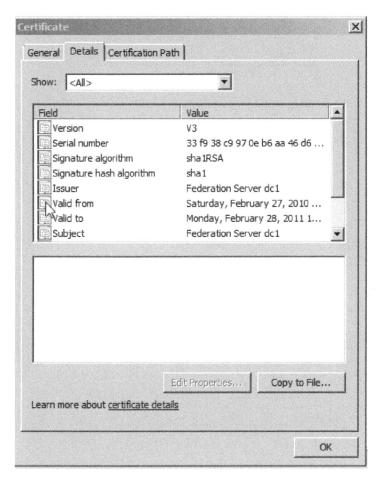

■ **FIGURE 4.74** Certificate properties.

6. Expand the *Certificates* node, then right-click on the *Trusted Root Certificate Authorities* node and choose *All Tasks | Import*.
7. Click *Next* to start the Certificate Import Wizard.
8. Enter the path and file name of the exported server certificate from the extranet ADFS server (dc2.extranet.syngress.net) as seen in Figure 4.76; then click *Next*.
9. Enter the password you previously assigned to protect the certificate's private key, then click *Next*.
10. Ensure that the import location *Trusted Root Certificate Authorities* is selected and click *Next*.
11. Click *Finish* to import the certificate. You should receive a confirmation dialog box that the import was successful.

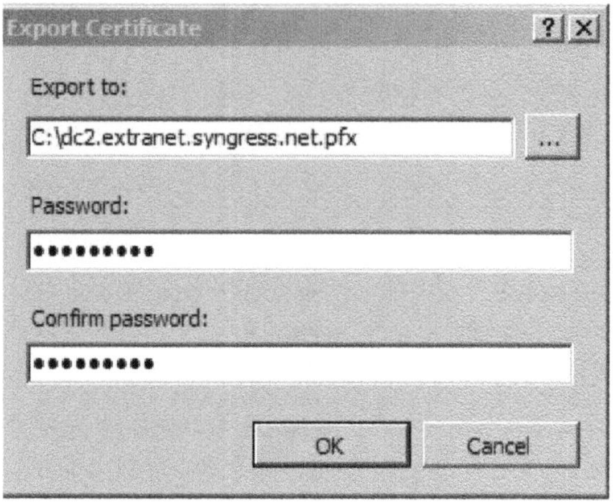

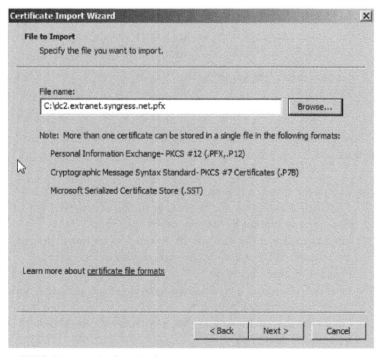

FIGURE 4.75 Exporting a Server Certificate.

FIGURE 4.76 Import Certificate Wizard.

Complete ADFS server configuration

We now need to complete the configuration of the ADFS servers and assign permissions. In this section, we will configure a trust policy for each ADFS server, set up group claims to provide access to the application, and configure connectivity to each AD forest from the respective ADFS server. During the configuration, we will refer to the internal ADFS server as the account federation server because users on this side of the federated trust will be accessing resources in the extranet. We will refer to the extranet federation server as the resource federation server because users will access the Web application on this side of the federated trust.

We first need to configure the account federation server (dc1.syngress. com). This will involve configuring the trust policy, exporting the trust policy so it can later be imported on the resource federation server, and connect the ADFS server to the internal AD forest by creating an account store. To configure the account federation server, perform the following tasks:

1. Log on to the account federation server (dc1.syngress.com) and open *Server Manager*.
2. Expand the nodes *Roles | Active Directory Federation Services | Federation Service*.
3. Right-click the *Trust Policy* node and select *Properties*.
4. We now need to create the federation URI that will be used to uniquely identify this service. In the *Federation Service URI* text box, type *urn: federation:syngress* (see Figure 4.77). Note that the URI is case sensitive.
5. The federation service endpoint URL should already be prepopulated with a URL that points to the ADFS server. If this is correctly pointed to the ADFS server, accept the default URL and then click the *Display Name* tab.
6. Enter a meaningful name to identify this trust policy, for example, *Account Domain (Syngress.com)*, then click *OK*.

You now need to export the trust policy so that it can later be imported on the resource federation server. To export the trust policy from the account ADFS server, perform the following tasks:

1. Open *Server Manager*.
2. Expand the nodes *Roles | Active Directory Federation Services | Federation Service*.
3. Right-click on the *Trust Policy* node and select the option *Export Basic Partner Policy*.

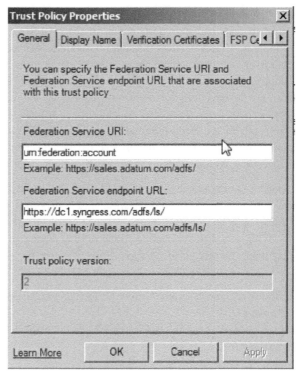

■ FIGURE 4.77 Trust policy properties.

4. In the Export Basic Partner Policy dialog box, browse to the path and enter a file name for the policy to be exported, for example, *C:\dc1.syngress.com_trustpolicy.xml*, then click *OK*.
5. Copy the trust policy file to the resource federation server.

You now need to create a group claim on the account federation server. This group claim will be used to provide access to the claims application via the resource federation server. To create the group claim, perform the following tasks on the account ADFS server (dc1.syngress.com):

1. Open *Server Manager*.
2. Expand the nodes *Roles | Active Directory Federation Services | Federation Service | Trust Policy | My Organization*.
3. Right-click the *Organization Claims* node and select *New | Organization Claim*.
4. Enter a name for the claim, for example, *Syngress Claim*, then click *OK*.

We now need to connect the account ADFS server (dc1.syngress.com) with the internal AD domain. This is done by creating an Account Store on the ADFS server. To create an account store, perform the following tasks on dc1.syngress.com:

1. Open *Server Manager*.
2. Expand the nodes *Roles | Active Directory Federation Services | Federation Service | Trust Policy | My Organziation*.
3. Right-click on the *Account Store* node and choose *New | Account Store*. This will launch the Add Account Store Wizard.
4. Click *Next* to begin.
5. Choose the option *Active Directory Domain Services* and click *Next*.
6. Ensure that the option to *Enable this account store* is selected and click *Next*.
7. Click *Finish* to create the account store.

We now need to map an AD global group to the group claim that we previously created. This group is how you will provide users access to the application in the extranet. Any user added to the group mapped to the group claim will be given SSO access to the extranet Web application. To create the group-to-group claim mapping, perform the following tasks on the account federation server (dc1.syngress.com):

1. Open *Server Manager*.
2. Expand the nodes *Roles | Active Directory Federation Services | Federation Service | Trust Policy | My Organziation | Account Stores*.
3. Right-click *Active Directory* and select *New | Group Claim Extraction*.
4. Click *Add* to add an AD global group and then select the claim to map the group to (see Figure 4.78), for example, the *Syngress Claim* set up previously. Then click *OK*.

We have now successfully set up the account ADFS server and now need to configure the resource ADFS server (dc2.extranet.syngress.net). To configure the resource federation server, perform the following tasks:

1. Log on to the server *dc2.extranet.syngress.net*.
2. Open *Server Manager*.
3. Expand the nodes *Roles | Active Directory Federation Services | Federation Service*.
4. Right-click on the *Trust Policy* node and select *Properties*.
5. On the *General* tab, enter a federation service URI in the text box. For example, *urn:federation:resource*. Remember the URI is case sensitive.

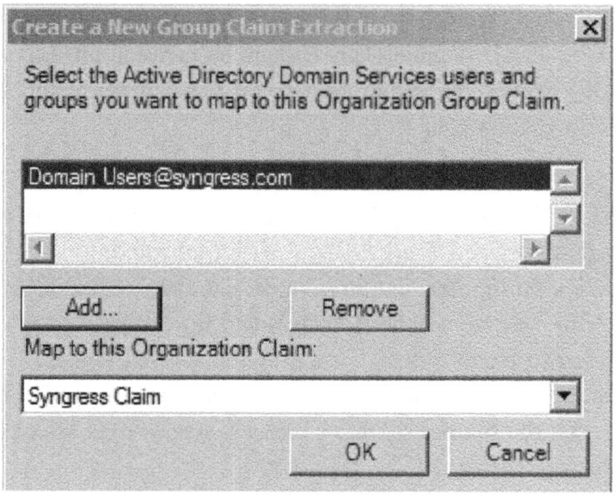

FIGURE 4.78 New Group Claim Extraction.

6. Verify whether the Federation service endpoint URL is pointed to the ADFS server (*https://dc2.extranet.syngress.net/adfs/ls*) as seen in Figure 4.79. Then click the *Display Name* tab.
7. Enter a meaningful name for the trust policy, for example, *Resource Domain Policy (Syngress Extranet)*, then click *OK*.

This will configure the resource trust policy. You should now export this policy using the same steps you used to export the policy for the account federation server. After exporting the policy, copy it to the account federation server (dc1.syngress.com).

We now need to create a group claim for the resource side. To create the group claim, perform the following tasks:

1. Open *Server Manager*.
2. Expand the nodes *Roles | Active Directory Federation Services | Federation Service | Trust Policy | My Organization*.
3. Right-click the *Organization Claims* node and select *New | Organization Claim*.
4. Enter a meaningful name for the claim, for example, *Extranet Claim*, then click *OK*.

After creating the group claim, we need to add the AD account store. Follow the same steps as you did for the account federation server to add the extranet domain account store. After adding the account store, you will need to add the claims-aware Web application to the extranet ADFS server. To do this, perform the following tasks:

■ **FIGURE 4.79** Trust Policy properties.

1. Open *Server Manager*.
2. Expand the nodes *Roles | Active Directory Federation Services | Federation Service | Trust Policy | My Organization*.
3. Right-click on *Applications* and select *New | Application*. This will launch the *Add Application Wizard*. Click *Next* to begin.
4. Select the option *Claims-aware application* and then click *Next*.
5. Enter a descriptive name and the secure URL for the Web application (see Figure 4.80), then click *Next*.
6. Select the type of identity claim that you want to use with the application. In most cases, you will want to use the User Principal Name (UPN) option. Select the *UPN* option and then click *Next*.
7. Ensure that *Enable this application* is selected, then click *Next*.
8. Click *Finish* to complete the Add Application Wizard.
9. You now need to enable the claim for the application. Select the newly created application (*Extranet Application)* under the applications node.
10. Right-click the *Extranet Claim* and choose *Enable* (see Figure 4.81).

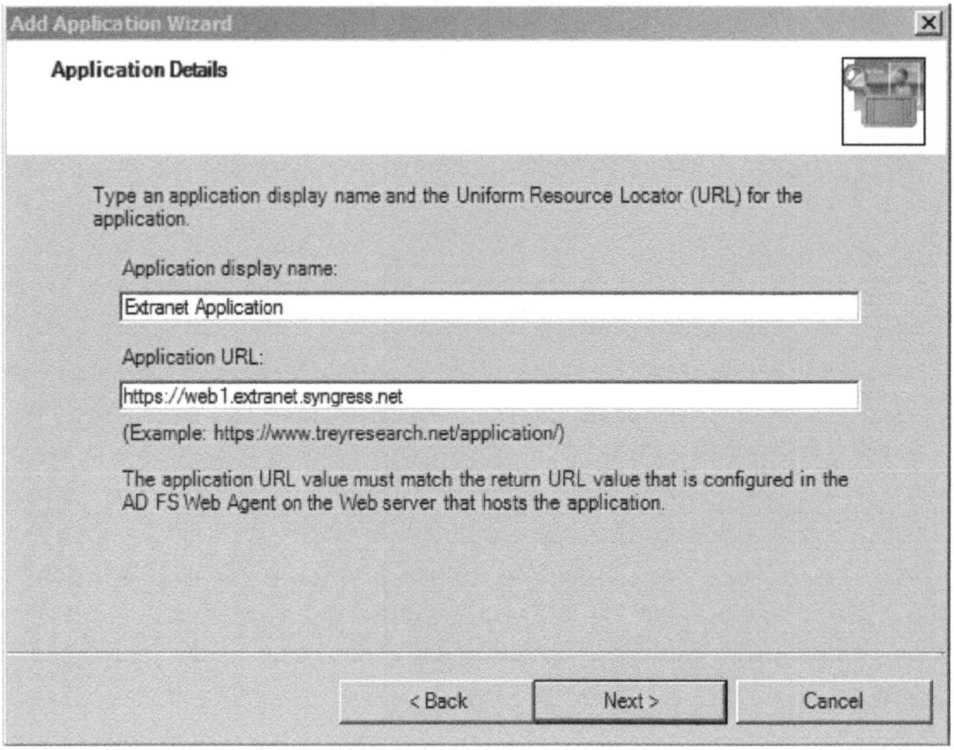

■ **FIGURE 4.80** Application Details.

We are now ready to import the trust policy from one ADFS server to the other. You should have already exported each trust policy and copied it to the other server. On the account ADFS server, we will be importing the trust policy for a new resource partner and on the resource ADFS server, we will be importing the trust policy for a new account partner. To import the trust policy on the account ADFS server (dc1.syngress.com), perform the following tasks:

1. Open *Server Manager*.
2. Expand the nodes *Roles | Active Directory Federation Services | Federation Service | Trust Policy | Partner Organizations*.
3. Right-click the *Resource Partners* node and select *New | Resource Partner*. This will launch the *Add Resource Partner Wizard*. Click *Next* to begin.
4. Select the *Yes* option that you do have a *Resource Partner Policy file*.
5. Browse to the policy file that you copied from the resource ADFS server (see Figure 4.82), then click *Next*.

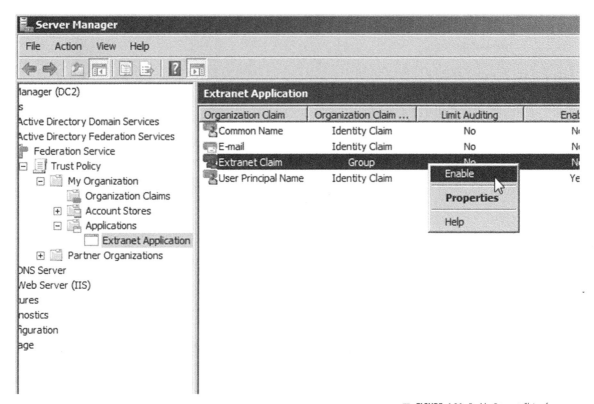

■ **FIGURE 4.81** Enable Extranet Claim for Extranet Application.

6. Verify the resource partner details and click *Next*.
7. Choose the option *Federated Web SSO*. If there were an AD trust relationship setup between the two forests, you would choose the option *Federated Web SSO with Forest Trust*. Since there is no preestablished trust relationship, choose the *Federated Web SSO* option, then click *Next*.
8. Verify that the *UPN Claim* and *Email Claim* options are selected and then click *Next*.
9. Select the option to *replace all UPN suffixes with following* and then enter the internal domain name, *syngress.com*. Then click *Next*.
10. Select the option to *replace all email suffixes with the following* and then enter the internal domain name, *syngress.com*. Then click *Next*.
11. Verify whether the option to *Enable this resource partner* is selected and then click *Next*.
12. Click *Finish* to complete the import of the trust policy.

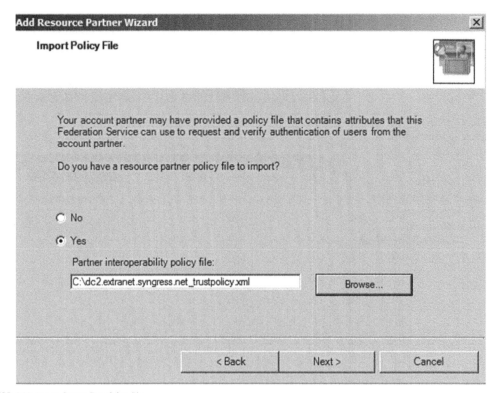

■ **FIGURE 4.82** Import Partner Trust Policy File.

You now need to add the trust policy for the account ADFS server to the resource ADFS server (dc2.extranet.syngress.net). To import the policy, log on to the server dc2.extranet.syngress.net and perform the following tasks:

1. Open *Server Manager*.
2. Expand the nodes *Roles | Active Directory Federation Services | Federation Service | Trust Policy | Partner Organizations*.
3. Right-click on the *Account Partners* node and select *New | Account Partner*. This will launch the Add Account Partner Wizard. Click *Next* to begin.
4. Click *Yes* that you do have an *Account Partner Policy File*.
5. Browse to the trust policy file that was exported from the account partner (see Figure 4.83), then click *Next*.
6. Verify whether the partner details point to the account partner, dc1.syngress.com, then click *Next*.

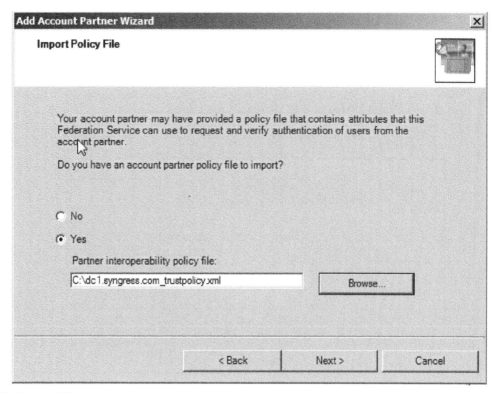

■ **FIGURE 4.83** Import Policy File.

7. Ensure that the option to *Use the verification certificate in the policy file* is selected and then click *Next*.
8. Select the *Federated Web SSO* option, then click *Next*.
9. Ensure that the options to use *UPN claim* and *Email claim* are selected, then click *Next*.
10. Add the domain *syngress.com* to the accepted *UPN suffixes* (see Figure 4.84), then click *Next*.
11. Add the domain *syngress.com* to the accepted *Email suffixes*, then click *Next*.
12. Ensure that the option to *Enable this account partner* is selected, then click *Next*.
13. Click *Finish* to complete the *Add Account Partner Wizard*.

We now simply need to link the two claim mappings, *Syngress Claim* and *Extranet Claim*. This is done by logging onto the resource ADFS server (dc2.extranet.syngress.net) and performing the following tasks:

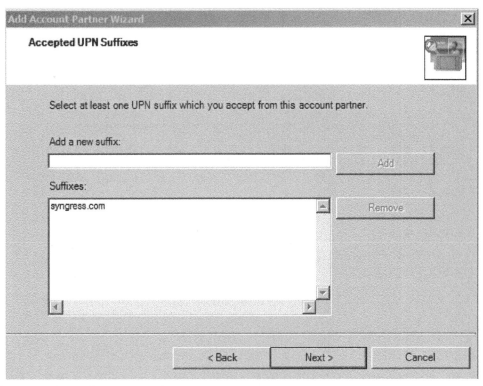

FIGURE 4.84 Accepted UPN Suffixes.

1. Open *Server Manager*.
2. Expand the nodes *Roles | Active Directory Federation Services | Federation Service | Trust Policy | Partner Organizations | Account Partners*.
3. Right-click the new account partner you just set up and select the option *New | Incoming Group Claim Mapping* (see Figure 4.85).
4. Enter the name of the group claim that was set up on the account federation server *(Syngress Claim)* in the Incoming Group claim name field and select *Extranet Claim* from the Organization Group Claim down-down list (see Figure 4.86). Then click *OK*.

Finally, we need to map the Extranet Claim to a global group in the extranet AD forest. You will then configure your application to allow this group access. To map the extranet claim to a resource group, perform the following tasks:

1. Open *Server Manager*.
2. Expand the nodes *Roles | Active Directory Federation Services | Federation Service | Trust Policy | My Organization*.

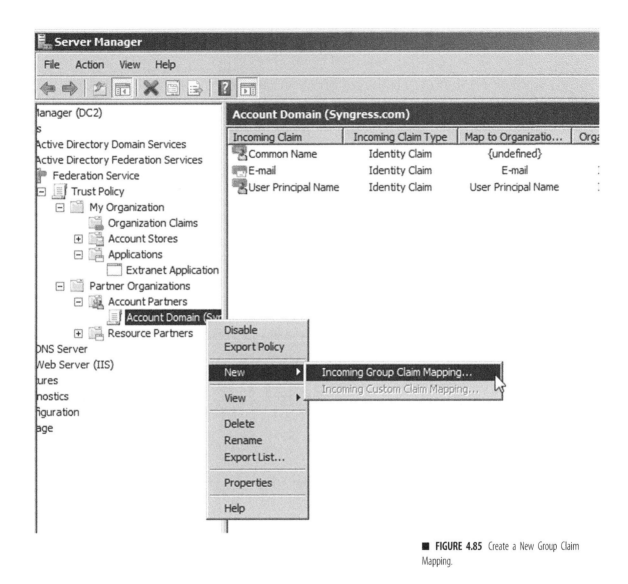

■ **FIGURE 4.85** Create a New Group Claim Mapping.

3. Select the node *Organization Claims* and right-click the *Extranet Claim* in the middle pane and select *Properties*.
4. Select the *Resource Group* tab in the Group Claim Properties window.
5. Select the option *Map this claim to the following resource group* and then browse to the resource group you want to add (see Figure 4.87). Then click *OK*.

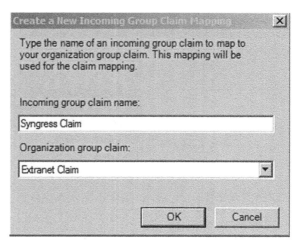

■ **FIGURE 4.86** Group Claim Mapping settings.

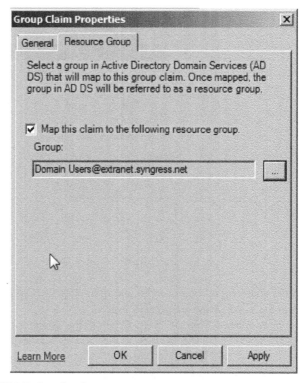

■ **FIGURE 4.87** Group Claim Properties.

You should now be able to provide domain users in the syngress.com domain access to the extranet application by simply providing the domain users' global group in the extranet.syngress.net domain access to the application.

ACTIVE DIRECTORY LIGHTWEIGHT DIRECTORY SERVICES

Active Directory Lightweight Directory Services (AD LDS), formerly known as Active Directory Application Mode (ADAM), provide a subset of full AD features to directory-enabled applications. AD has become the directory service of choice for many organizations. Many applications are now written to access AD for user information. There may be instances where it is not feasible or you may not want specific applications connecting to your production AD forest (especially those requiring significant schema updates). As an alternate solution, you may be able to use AD LDS. AD LDS can also be used as an account store, when user accounts need to reside in a separate database from your production AD domain.

Installing and configuring Active Directory Lightweight Directory Services

In this section, we will walk through installing AD LDS and configuring the ADAMSync to synchronize the AD LDS instance with an AD domain.

To install the AD LDS role, perform the following tasks:

1. Open *Server Manager*.
2. Select the *Roles* node, then click the *Add Roles* link in the middle pane. This will launch the Add Roles Wizard.
3. Click *Next* to begin.
4. Select the *Active Directory Lightweight Directory Services* role as seen in Figure 4.88. If prompted, click the button to *Add Required Components*. Click *Next* to continue.
5. Click *Next* on the Introduction page.
6. Click *Install*.
7. After the installation completes, click *Close*.

After installing the role for AD LDS, you will need to set up the service. This can be done via the AD LDS management console in Server Manager. To open the AD LDS console, expand the roles node within Server Manager and select the AD LDS console. To set up the AD LDS service, perform the following tasks:

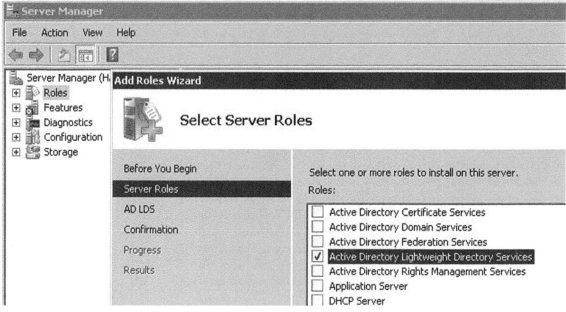

■ **FIGURE 4.88** AD LDS Server Role.

1. Click the *Setup AD LDS* link inside of the AD LDS management console (see Figure 4.89). This will launch the AD LDS Setup Wizard. Click *Next* to continue.
2. Since this is the first AD LDS instance in your organization, select the option *A unique instance* and then click *Next*. This will create a brand new instance of the AD LDS service.
3. Enter a name and description for the new AD LDS instance, then click *Next*.
4. Enter the port numbers to use for LDAP and Secure LDAP connections. In our example, we will be using 50000 and 50001, respectively (see Figure 4.90).
5. Optionally, you can now create an Application partition. We will go ahead and create an application partition. Select the option *Yes, create an application directory partition*. Then enter the distinguished name of the partition (CN=Application, DC=Contoso, DC=com). Then click *Next*. The application partition is a special directory partition for storing application-specific settings that may use the directory service.
6. Specify the location to store the AD LDS data files and then click *Next*.

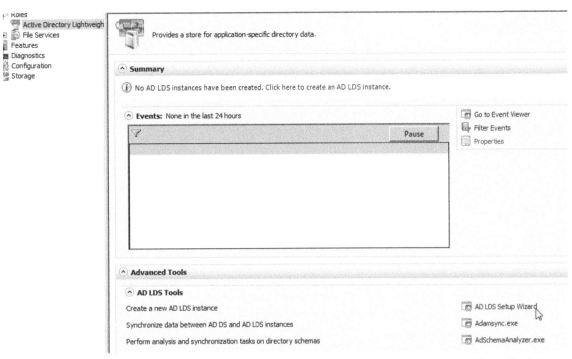

■ **FIGURE 4.89** AD LDS Setup Wizard Link.

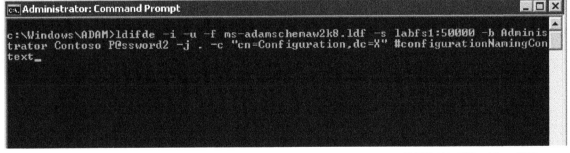

■ **FIGURE 4.90** LDAP and Secure LDAP port numbers for AD LDS.

7. Now specify the account that you want to use to run the AD LDS service. If the service will need to access other resources on the network, you will need to run it under an account with appropriate permissions to those resources.

8. Select the account that you want to give initial administrative access to the AD LDS instance and then click *Next*.

9. Select any optional schema extensions that you want applied to the AD LDS instance. Your selection here will vary depending on how the instance will be used. For example, if you plan on syncing with an AD domain, you will need to install the *MS-AdamSyncMetadata.LDF*. After selecting the optional LDF files to import, click *Next*.

10. Verify your settings and click *Next* to continue. After the setup completes, click *Finish*.

The AD LDS service is now installed. The next step we want to do is extend the AD LDS schema and set up syncing with the AD domain. To complete these tasks, perform the following procedures:

1. Open a command prompt and change to the directory C:\Windows\Adam

2. To import the Windows Server 2008 schema, run the command ldifde -i -u -f ms-adamschemaw2k8.ldf—s server:port—b username domain password -j. -c "cn=Configuration,dc=X" #configurationNamingContext (see Figure 4.91).

3. Next, we need to modify the XML configuration file that will be used to set up the sync. Browse to the directory C:\Windows\Adam and locate the file MS-AdamSyncConf.xml and make a copy of the file naming the new file AdamSync.xml.

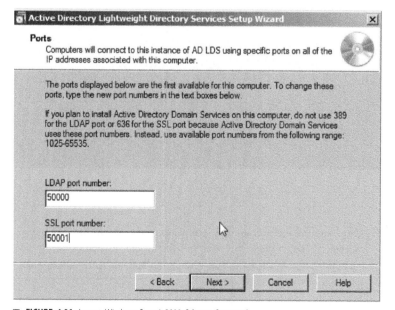

■ **FIGURE 4.91** Import Windows Serve4 2008 Schema Command.

4. Open the new file AdamSync.xml in Notepad.
5. Update all of the fields that point to the Fabrikam domain with the
   contextual information pointing to yours. Change the <target-DN>
   field to CN=Application, DC=contoso, DC=com. This will tell
   everything to sync to the new partition we set up while adding the role.
   Your AdamSync.xml file should look similar to Figure 4.92. After
   updating the file, save and close it.

```
AdamSync - Notepad
File   Edit   Format   View   Help
<?xml version="1.0"?>
<doc>
 <configuration>
  <description>sample Adamsync configuration file</description>
  <security-mode>object</security-mode>
  <source-ad-name>contoso.com</source-ad-name>
  <source-ad-partition>dc=contoso,dc=com</source-ad-partition>
  <source-ad-account></source-ad-account>
  <account-domain></account-domain>
  <target-dn>CN=Application,DC=Contoso,DC=Com</target-dn>
  <query>
   <base-dn>dc=Contoso,dc=com</base-dn>
   <object-filter>(objectClass=*)</object-filter>
   <attributes>
    <include></include>
    <exclude>extensionName</exclude>
    <exclude>displayNamePrintable</exclude>
    <exclude>flags</exclude>
    <exclude>isPrivelegeHolder</exclude>
    <exclude>msCom-UserLink</exclude>
    <exclude>msCom-PartitionSetLink</exclude>
    <exclude>reports</exclude>
    <exclude>serviceprincipalname</exclude>
    <exclude>accountExpires</exclude>
    <exclude>adminCount</exclude>
    <exclude>primarygroupid</exclude>
    <exclude>userAccountControl</exclude>
    <exclude>codePage</exclude>
    <exclude>countryCode</exclude>
    <exclude>logonhours</exclude>
    <exclude>lockoutTime</exclude>
   </attributes>
  </query>
  <schedule>
   <aging>
```

■ **FIGURE 4.92** AdamSync.xml.

6. At the command prompt, enter the command adamsync/i servername: portname configxmlfile. For example, enter adamsync/I labfs1:50000 adamsync.xml. This will install the configuration in the XML file.
7. You are now ready to sync the AD LDS instance with the AD domain. To do this, enter the command adamsync/sync server:port dn of partition. For exadamsync/sync labfs1:50000 "CN=Application, DC=Contoso, DC=Com"

This completes the process to set up the sync between AD and AD LDS. If you wanted the sync to occur on a regular basis, you could save the command in a batch file and set up a scheduled task to run the sync on a regular basis.

ACTIVE DIRECTORY RIGHTS MANAGEMENT SERVICES

Rights Management has become a growing demand in some organizations, especially those that are heavily regulated. Active Directory Rights Management Services (AD RMS) allow users to add additional security and protection features to items such as Microsoft Office documents and email messages. AD RMS allows you to restrict things such as the ability to forward email messages outside the company, or prevent users opening a document from printing it. If you have a need to provide more strict controls over company documents, you may want to explore AD RMS more in-depth.

COMMONLY USED ACTIVE DIRECTORY POWERSHELL COMMANDS

Table 4.5 lists some of the most commonly used AD PowerShell Commands.

SUMMARY

This chapter covered the various aspects of deploying and managing AD DS. In this chapter, we explored the new features in Windows Server 2008 R2. We then looked at planning an AD deployment. We then walked through the process of installing a new AD DS server. After installing AD DS, we covered the various administrative efforts you need to consider when managing AD domains. This included administering users, computers, and groups and organizing them using OUs. We also covered how group policy can be used in your deployment to centrally manage

Table 4.5 Active Directory PowerShell Commands

PowerShell Command	Description
Add-ADGroupMember	Add one or more users and a group
Add-ADPrincipalGroupMembership	Add a user to one or more groups
Enable-ADAccount	Enable an account
Disable-ADAccount	Disable an account
Get-ADComputer	Get an Active Directory Computer or computers
Get-ADDefaultDomainPasswordPolicy	Get the domain's password policy
Get-ADDomain	Get an Active Directory Domain
Get-ADDomainController	Get one or more domain controllers
Get-ADForest	Get an Active Directory Forest
Get-ADGroup	Get an Active Directory group or groups
Get-ADGroupMember	Get users who are members of an Active Directory group
Get-ADOrganizationalUnit	Get Active Directory Organization Units
Get-ADPrincipalGroupMembership	Get groups that have a specific member
Get-ADUser	Get Active Directory Users
Move-ADDirectoryServer	Move a domain controller to a new Active Directory site
Move-ADDirectoryServerOperationMasterRole	Move Operating Master Roles
Move-ADObject	Move objects within the domain
New-ADComputer	Create a new Active Directory Computer Account
New-ADFineGrainedPasswordPolicy	Create a new fine grained password policy
New-ADGroup	Create a new group
New-ADOrganizationalUnit	Create a new OU
New-ADUser	Create a new user account
Remove-ADComputer	Delete a computer account
Remove-ADGroup	Delete an Active Directory group
Remove-ADGroupMember	Remove a user from an Active Directory group
Remove-ADOrganizationalUnit	Delete an Active Directory OU
Remove-ADPrincipalGroupMembership	Remove a user from one or more Active Directory groups
Restore-ADObject	Restore an object in Active Directory
Search-ADAccount	Search for Active Directory user and computer accounts
Set-ADAccountExpiration	Set an Active Directory user account to expire
Set-ADAccountPassword	Reset a user's password
Set-ADComputer	Modify an Active Directory Computer Account
Set-ADDefaultDomainPasswordPolicy	Change the domain password policy
Set-ADDomainMode	Raise the domain functional level
Set-ADGroup	Change an Active Directory Group
Set-ADOrganizationalUnit	Change an Active Directory OU
Set-ADUser	Change an Active Directory User
Unlock-ADAccount	Unlock an Active Directory User Account

user and computer settings to ensure consistency across computer configurations within your domain environment. We further explored other AD services such as Active Directory Certificate Services, Active Directory Federation Services, Active Directory Lightweight Directory Services, and Active Directory Rights Management Services. To conclude this chapter, we explored a few of the most commonly used Active Directory PowerShell cmdlets.

Windows Server 2008 R2 file and print services

Windows Server 2008 R2 includes a rich set of features to provide network file and print services. In this chapter, we will explore the different aspects of managing and administering Windows Server 2008 R2 file and print services. We will cover setting up and managing traditional file shares along with enhanced file sharing using distributed file system (DFS) and network file system (NFS) features. We will also take a look at file server management features such as reporting, quotas, and file screening. This chapter will also cover administering print services to centrally manage network printers. The chapter will conclude with an overview of network scanner management and workflow.

OVERVIEW OF FILE AND PRINT SERVICES

File and print services have been a core component of the Windows operating system since the early days of Windows. The fundamental ability to connect to a central computer to access and share files remains a requirement in most organizations today. Windows Server 2008 R2 provides traditional file-sharing features while giving both users and administrators additional features to enhance the usability and management of file servers. Microsoft has also taken steps to provide better integration with other operating systems, such as Linux, by including NFS services in Windows Server.

In addition to file-sharing services, most organizations require the ability to centrally manage and control printers on the network. Very few organizations have the ability, or need, to provide all users with their own printers. Windows Server 2008 R2 print services allow you to set up shared printers that can be used by multiple users within the organization. Windows Server 2008 R2 print services allow administrators to share and control access to network printers as well as deploy printers to users via Group Policy.

NOTE

Details on making file and print servers highly available will be discussed in Chapter 9.

ADMINISTERING FILE SHARES

As a Windows administrator, you should understand the various aspects of creating, securing, and managing Windows file services. Basic file-sharing services and advanced file server features such as DFS, Quotas, and Branch Cache all require the addition of the File Services role. In this section, we will take a look at the basics of file sharing.

Creating shared folders

Before you can share files and folders from a Windows Server, you need to enable the service. This is done via the Network Sharing Center. To enable file sharing, perform the following:

1. Open Network and Sharing Center from *Start | Control Panel* then click on the *Network and Internet* link. Then open *Network and Sharing Center*.
2. Click the *Advanced sharing settings* link in the left pane.
3. You should now see the options to enable file and printer sharing and to enable public folder sharing (see Figure 5.1). Public folder sharing, as the name implies, sets up public share folders that anyone on the network can access. In our exercise, we will enable only file and printer sharing. We will enable file sharing by selecting the option *Turn on file and printer sharing*. Then click *Save Changes*. By turning on the file and printer sharing, the file server role is automatically added to the server. In our example, we will not enable public folder sharing.

NOTES FROM THE FIELD

Public folder sharing

Be careful when you enable public folder sharing, as it does not restrict access to the public share folders. By default the Everyone group is given read/write access to the public share folders. In many organizations, this is not a best practice for file servers and you may want to ensure that this feature remains disabled.

---

4. Now that we have enabled file and printer sharing we can set up a new shared folder. To do this, right click on a folder you wish to share, and then click *Properties*.

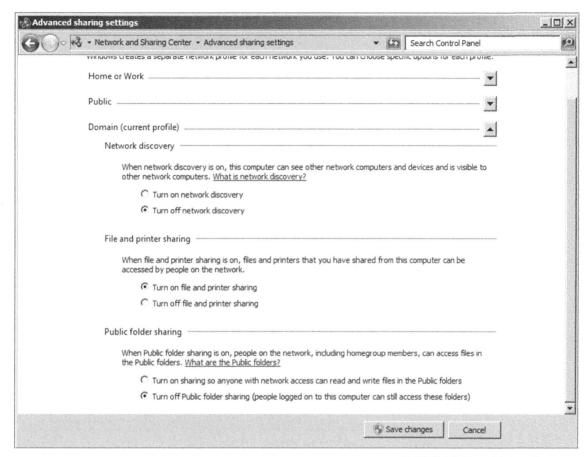

■ FIGURE 5.1 Advanced sharing settings.

5. Click the *Sharing* tab as seen in Figure 5.2.
6. Click the *Share* button.
7. You must now select whom you want to have access to the shared folder and what level of access they should have. For our example, we will give Domain Users read access to the ClientData shared folder as seen in Figure 5.3.
8. Click the *Share* button when you have added all groups or users who should have access to the shared folder. Then click *Done* in the confirmation window.

You can now see the shared folder by browsing the UNC path of the server as seen in Figure 5.4.

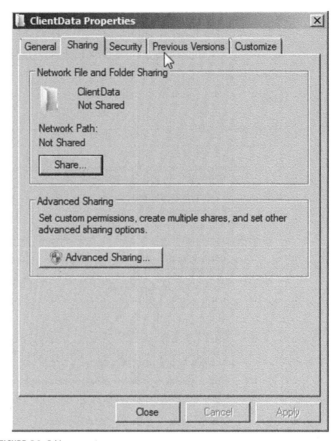

■ **FIGURE 5.2** Folder properties.

Securing shared folders

Windows uses two types of permissions to secure shared folders. These are shared folder permissions and file/folder permissions:

■ Shared folder permissions—Shared folder permissions are applied to the shared folder only and not to the contents it contains. This means that you cannot use shared folder permissions to provide a different level of security to subfolders or files within the share. Furthermore, shared folder permissions are effective only when accessing the shared folder from the network. If someone tries to access the folder by logging on to the computer in which it is shared, shared folder permissions do not limit access. In most cases, it is recommended that the use of share permissions be limited and file permissions be used to restrict access to share folders and the files they contain.

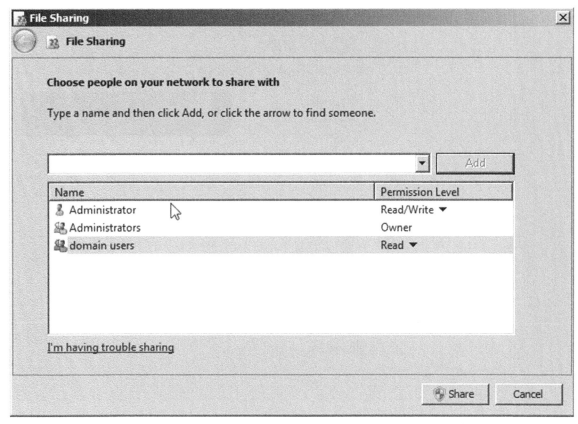

■ **FIGURE 5.3** Share access.

- File/folder permissions—File/folder permissions use NTFS security to limit access to files and folders on a computer. They are similar to shared folder permissions in that you can assign access to local or domain users and groups; however, file/folder permissions provide better security and more granularity when assigning access. For example, with file/folder permissions you can give domain users access to client data share, but limit access to a file within that share to only people in the accounting department. In most cases, file/folder permissions are the preferred method for managing access to network file shares and the files and folders they contain.

When both shared folder and file/folder permissions are used, the most restrictive applies. For example, if John is given Full Control using shared folder permissions and is given Read-Only using file/folder permissions, his effective permissions are Read-Only. You should also understand that

■ **FIGURE 5.4** New shared folder.

every time a deny permission is set, it trumps any other permissions. For example, let us assume that John is a member of the accounting group. John's account is given Full Control permission to the ClientData shared folder. The accounting group is denied read permissions to the ClientData shared folder. Since John's account is a member of the accounting group, his effective permissions deny him access to the ClientData shared folder even though his individual account has rights to this folder. When multiple file/folder permissions are used, the effective rights are a combination of the user and group rights unless an explicit deny is used. For example, assume that John is a member of the accounting group. John is given read access to the ClientData shared folder. The accounting group is given modify rights to the shared folder. John's effective permissions to the ClientData shared folder are modify.

Now that you have an understanding of permissions, we will take a look at the permissions setup on the shared folder we created in the previous section.

1. Right click on the shared folder and select *Properties*.
2. Click on the *Sharing* tab. Then click the *Advanced Sharing* button (see Figure 5.5).
3. Click the *Permissions* button. This will display the shared folder permissions as seen in Figure 5.6. Notice that by default, the Everyone group is assigned Full Control access at the shared folder level. This does not necessarily mean that everyone has access to this share folder. You will see that file/folder permissions restrict who can access the

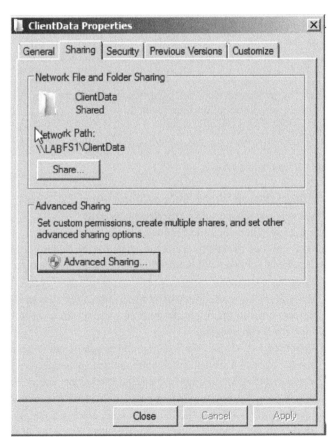

■ **FIGURE 5.5** Sharing configuration tab.

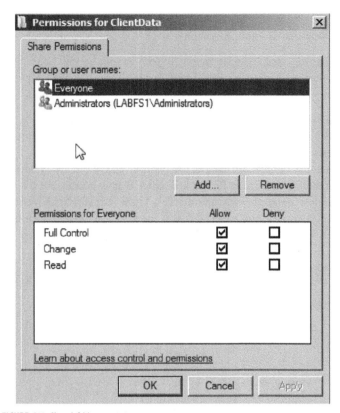

■ **FIGURE 5.6** Shared folder permissions.

share folder. Remember that the most restrictive of file/folder permissions and shared folder permissions is used.

4. Click *Cancel*. Then click the *Security* tab.
5. You will now see the file/folder permissions for the folder (shared) as seen in Figure 5.7. You will notice that three groups and one user have access in our example:
   ❑ *SYSTEM*—This is the group used by the operating system to perform tasks to the folder. In most cases, you will want to leave this permission assigned.
   ❑ *Administrator*—This is the local computer administrator account.
   ❑ *Domain Users*—This is the domain group that we assigned read access to during initial setup of the share. Notice that access was set up using file/folder permissions opposed to shared folder permissions.
   ❑ *Administrators*—This is the local computer administrators group. By default the administrators group is granted access to all shared folders unless explicitly removed or denied access.

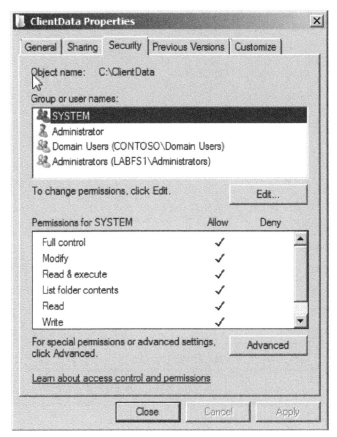

■ **FIGURE 5.7** Folder Security permissions.

6. From the security tab you can add, remove, or change access rights to the shared folder. For example, let us give domain users modify rights to the ClientData shared folder. This will give them the ability to not only read files but also add and change files within the shared folder. To give domain users modify rights, click on the *Edit* button. Then select the *Domain Users* group. Next select the *Allow* checkbox as seen in Figure 5.8. Click the *OK* button. Users within the domain users group now have modify access to the ClientData folder.

As you can see, file/folder permissions provide the ability to give access to files and folders in a very granular fashion. File/folder permissions have six main access levels. They are defined in Table 5.1.

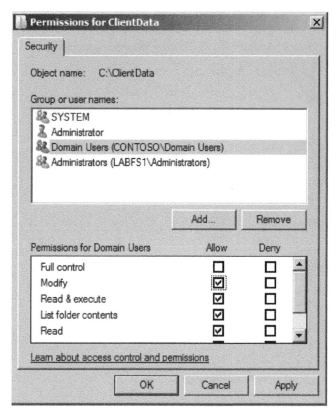

■ **FIGURE** 5.8 Updating folder permissions.

Table 5.1 Standard Permissions

Permission	Access
Full Control	This is the highest level of access to a file or folder. Full control gives the user full access to the file or folder allowing him to make any changes including changing permissions and taking ownership.
Modify	Modify permission gives the user the ability to make changes to existing files or create new files. This is typically the permission used to give users read/write access to a folder/file.
Read & Execute	Read & Execute access gives the user the ability to read files and folder contents and execute applications from a folder. This is the permission typically used to give a user read-only access to a folder.
List folder contents	List folder contents does just that. It gives the user the ability to only list the contents of a folder. This right does not give the user the ability to open files within the folder.
Read	Read access gives the user the ability to read files and folder contents. This access is automatically added when Read & Execute is selected.
Write	Write access gives the user the ability to write new files and folders, but not necessarily the ability to read them.

In most cases, standard permissions can be used to provide the level of access required by users. However, there may be occasions where more granular access settings may be required. In those cases, you can use Special Permissions to set user access. Special permissions can be accessed by selecting the *Advanced* button from the Security tab. Then click *Change Permissions*. Select the user or group whose permissions you wish to change, then click *Edit*. The special permissions window will appear as seen in Figure 5.9. Here, you can set special permissions for the selected file or folder. Special access permissions are defined in Table 5.2.

Special permissions give you the ability to maintain very granular control over file and folder access. You should always properly document permissions on network-shared folders.

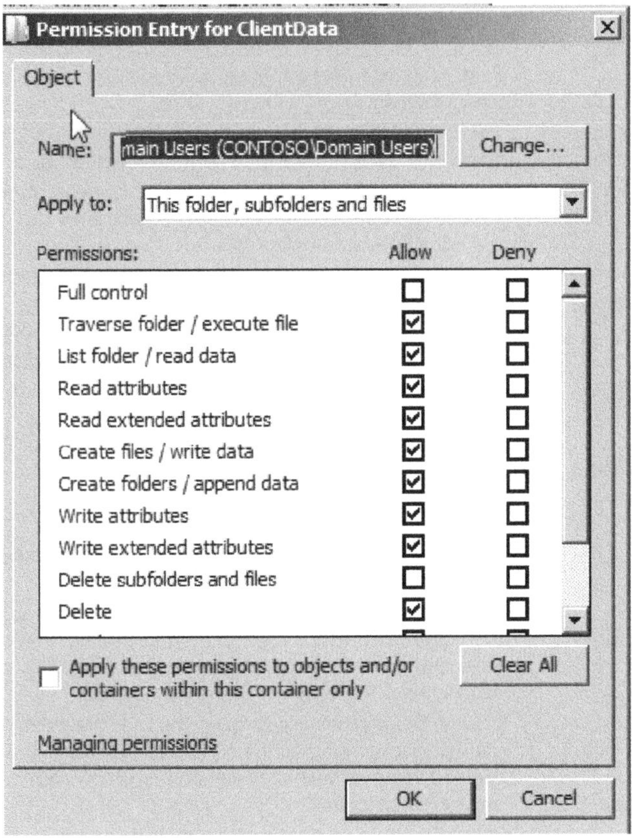

■ **FIGURE 5.9** Special access permissions.

Table 5.2 File/Folder Special Permissions

Permission	Access
Traverse folder/execute file	Traverse folder allows you to move through a folder to access a subfolder. For example, if you do not have access to the ClientData share, but do have access to a subfolder named invoices in the ClientData share, the traverse folder permission gives you the ability to move through the ClientData folder to access the invoices subfolder. Execute file permission gives the user the ability to execute files.
List folder/read data	List folder gives the user the ability to view files and folders within a folder. Read Data gives the user the ability to open a file with read-only access.
Read attributes	Read attributes give the user the ability to view the attributes of a file or folder. For example, with this permission a user could look at the properties of a file or folder to see if it was hidden or classified as a system file.
Read extended attributes	The read extended attributes permission gives the user the ability to view metadata fields related to a file or folder. For example, Microsoft Word documents include an author field. Read extended attributes gives the user the ability to view this field.
Create files/write data	Create files allows the user to create files within a folder. Write data allows the user to overwrite existing data.
Create folders/append data	Create folders gives the user the ability to create new subfolders within the folder. Append data gives the user the right to add new data to a file.
Write attributes	Write attributes gives the user the ability to change the attributes of a file or folder. For example with Write attributes rights, a use can make a file or folder hidden.
Write extended attributes	Write extended attributes gives the user the ability to make changes to metadata fields such as the author field in Word documents.
Delete subfolders and files	This permission gives the user the ability to delete subfolders and files in the current folder, even if the user does not have explicit delete permissions on the subfolders or files.
Delete	The Delete permission gives the user the ability to delete the current file or folder.
Read permissions	Read permissions access gives the user the ability to view the current permissions set on the selected file or folder. Read permissions does not give the user the ability to actually read the contents of the file or folder.
Change permissions	Change permissions access gives the user the ability to manage access rights to the current file or folder. The user can add, remove, or change any of the current permissions on the file or folder.
Take ownership	Take ownership gives the user the ability to take ownership of a file or folder.

> **NOTE**
> As best practice, you should limit assigning permissions to users directly. Use groups whenever possible when assigning permissions to files and folders.

Permissions inheritance

Inheritance is another important aspect of user access for files and folders. Unless specified otherwise, folders and files inherit the permissions of their parent folder. For example, if you create a new folder named invoices in the ClientData shared folder, it will automatically assume the same permissions as the ClientData folder.

There may be occasions where you need to prevent permissions inheritance on specific files or folders. To remove inherited permissions, perform the following:

1. Right click on the subfolder or file within the parent folder and select *Properties*.
2. Select the *Security* tab. Then click the *Advanced* button.
3. Click *Change Permissions*. This will display the Advanced Security Settings window as seen in Figure 5.10.
4. Notice that the option *Include inheritable permissions from this objects parent* is selected. To remove permission inheritance, deselect the checkbox.
5. A Windows Security dialog will appear as seen in Figure 5.11. By choosing the *Add* option, the existing inherited permissions will be copied to the permissions list for the folder or file. Use this option if you want to simply modify the existing permissions that were being inherited from the parent. By choosing the *Remove* option, the existing permissions will be removed from the object and you will need to add new permissions to the object.

You may also find yourself needing to force permission inheritance on all objects within a folder. Selecting the option *Replace all child object permissions with inheritable permissions from this object* will force all files and subfolders to inherit permissions from the current folder. This is a great way to quickly reset all permissions of child objects to match the parent.

Access-based enumeration

Starting with Windows Server 2003, Microsoft made it possible to prevent users from seeing files they do not have access to. Prior to that, all files in

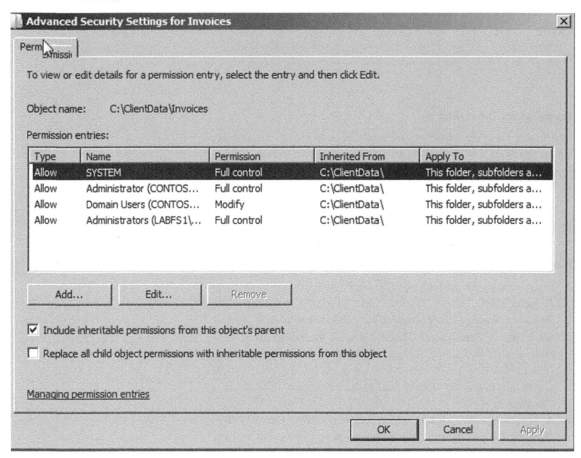

■ **FIGURE 5.10** Advanced Security Settings.

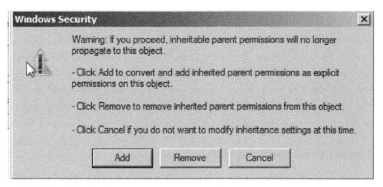

■ **FIGURE 5.11** Windows Security Warning.

a shared folder were visible to a user even if he did not have access to them. Access-based enumeration (ABE) allows a user to see only the files he or she has access to. For example, an administrator may create a new shared folder giving members of the accounting group modify access. The accounting manager may create a new excel spreadsheet and save it in this shared folder. She may then restrict access to this file to herself. If ABE is turned on, all the other members of the accounting group will not be able to see the file, since they do not have access. ABE can be turned on per shared folder. To turn on ABE, perform the following:

1. Open *Server Manager*.
2. Expand the nodes *Roles | File Services*.
3. Select the *Share and Storage Management* node.
4. In the middle pane, double-click the shared folder that you want to enable ABE on opening the shared folder properties window.
5. Click the *Advanced* button in the properties window.
6. Select the option to *Enable ABE* and then click *OK*.

Publishing shared folders to Active Directory

Active Directory includes the ability to publish your shared folders to the directory service. This allows users to easily find network shares without needing to know the server or share name of the shared folder. Users can simply search Active Directory for the shared folder they wish to access and Active Directory will connect them to the correct server and shared folder name. To publish a shared folder to Active Directory, perform the following:

1. Open Active Directory users and computers (ADUC).
2. Right click the OU that you wish to publish the shared folder to, then select *New | Shared Folder* (see Figure 5.12).
3. Enter a name for the published share and the UNC path to the share location (see Figure 5.13). Then click *OK*.
4. You can now search for the shared folder using Active Directory (see Figure 5.14).

ADMINISTERING DISTRIBUTED FILE SYSTEM SERVICES

DFS was first introduced in Windows 2000 as a way to provide centralized access to network share folders located on different file servers throughout the network. Instead of accessing a server and share, users simply access the DFS access point which connects them to the

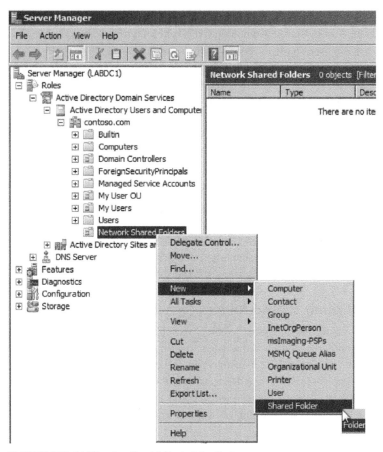

■ **FIGURE 5.12** Publishing New Shared Folder to Active Directory.

correct shared folder. Additionally, DFS can provide shared folder redundancy by having several replicated copies of a single shared folder. DFS Replication (DFSR) was first introduced as a feature in Windows Server 2003 R2 and DFSR provides the ability to replicate a single shared folder between different file servers to provide redundancy and centralized management of shared folders. Both DFS technologies exist in Windows Server 2008 R2 as role services for the file server role. Using a combination of DFS Namespaces and DFSR, you can provide a more manageable, centralized, and highly available file-sharing infrastructure. Figure 5.15 depicts what a typical DFS share might look like. In this section, we will explore the aspects of creating, configuring, and administering DFS Namespaces and DFSR.

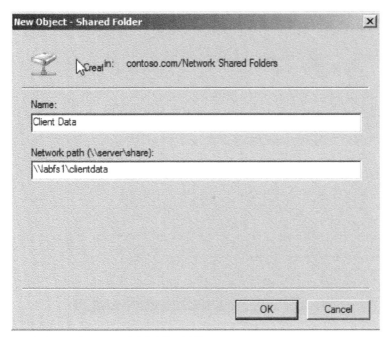

■ **FIGURE 5.13** Creating New Published Shared Folder.

NOTES FROM THE FIELD

DFS compatible applications
Some applications are not compatible with DFS. You will want to verify with
the software vendor to ensure that you can run an application that may
access files from a DFS share.

Configuring and administering DFS Namespaces

DFS Namespaces are used to publish shared folders under a single directory structure. Before setting up a new DFS Namespace, we need to add
the DFS Namespace role service. If the server that you plan to set up
DFS on already has shared folders, you will not need to add the file
services role but only the DFS Namespace role service. Windows Server
2008 R2 supports two namespace types:

- Domain-based namespace—A domain-based namespace stores the
  DFS configuration in Active Directory providing redundancy and high
  availability to the DFS tree. This effectively removes the DFS root
  server as a single point of failure. If the domain functional level is at

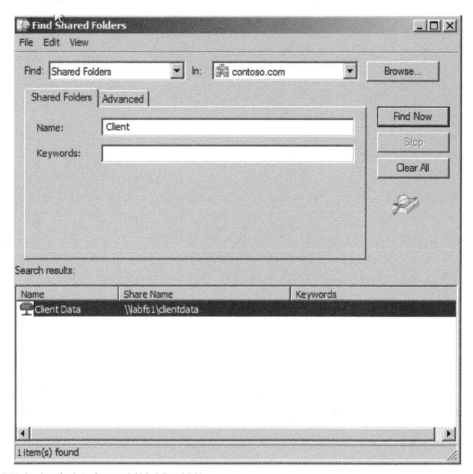

■ **FIGURE 5.14** Searching for Active Directory Published Shared Folder.

least Windows Server 2008 and the forest functional level is at least Windows Server 2003, then Windows 2008 DFS mode can be used for domain-based Namespaces providing additional features such as ABE and increased scalability.

■ Stand-alone namespace—A stand-alone namespace stores DFS configuration on the local computer. High availability and redundancy can be achieved by using Windows cluster features.

To add the DFS Namespace role service, perform the following:

1. Open Server Manager and select the node *Roles | File Services.*
2. In the middle pane click the link *Add Role Services.*

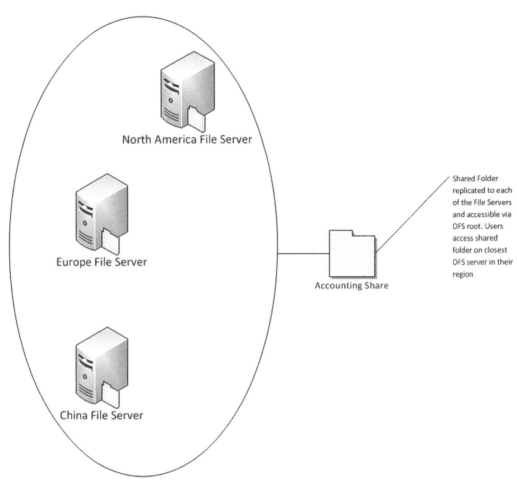

North America File Server

Europe File Server

China File Server

Accounting Share

Shared Folder
replicated to each
of the File Servers
and accessible via
DFS root. Users
access shared
folder on closest
DFS server in their
region

■ **FIGURE 5.15** Example DFS Namespace deployment.

3. Select the *DFS Namespaces* option as seen in Figure 5.16. Then click *Next*.
4. You can now choose to create a new DFS Namespace or create the namespace later. For this exercise, select the option *Create namespace later using the DFS Management snap-in in Server Manager*. Then click *Next*.
5. Click *Install* to install the DFS Namespace role service.

Once the DFS Namespace role service has been installed, DFS Namespaces can be created and managed from Server Manager by selecting the node *Roles | File Services | DFS Management | DFS Namespaces*. To create a new DFS Namespace, perform the following:

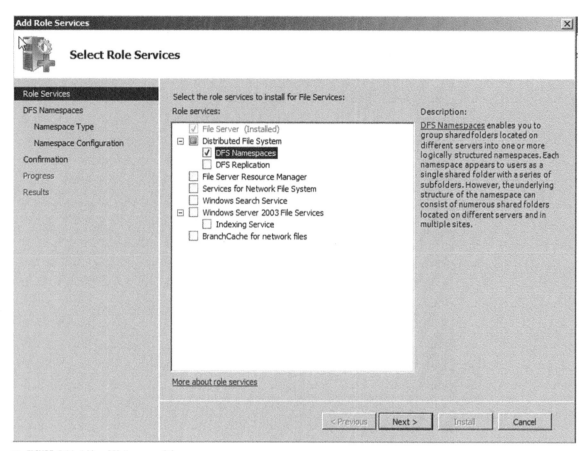

■ **FIGURE 5.16** Adding DFS Namespace Role Service.

1. Right click on the *DFS Namespaces* node and select the option *New Namespace* (see Figure 5.17). This will launch the New Namespace Wizard.
2. Select the server that will host the DFS Namespace (see Figure 5.18). This can be a Windows cluster (discussed in Chapter 9) to provide high availability. Then click *Next* to continue.
3. Enter a name for the Namespace (see Figure 5.19). This is the name by which the namespace will be referred to by clients. Additionally, you can set permissions on the DFS root by clicking the *Edit Settings* button. In most cases, the default option of *All users have read-only permissions* will be sufficient as this access is for DFS only and not the target shared folder within the tree. Click *Next* to continue.

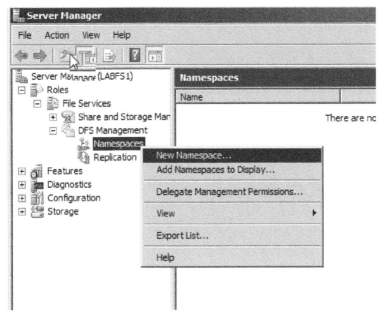

■ **FIGURE 5.17** Creating New DFS Namespace.

4. We now need to select the DFS Namespace type. In our example, we will use a domain-based namespace. Select the option *Domain-based namespace*, and select the option *Enabled Windows Server 2008 mode* (see Figure 5.20). Then click *Next*.

5. Verify the configuration settings and then click *Create*. You should receive a confirmation that the namespace was created successfully.

The namespace will now appear in Server Manager under the Namespaces node as seen in Figure 5.21. Notice that DFS Namespaces are accessed using the Active Directory domains FQDN and namespace name (\\contoso.com\Data).

You can now create folder targets underneath the namespace. These folder targets will link to shared folders on file servers across your corporate network. To create a new target folder underneath the namespace, perform the following:

1. Right click on the namespace and select the option *New Folder*.

2. Enter a name for the new folder (see Figure 5.22). Then click *Add*.

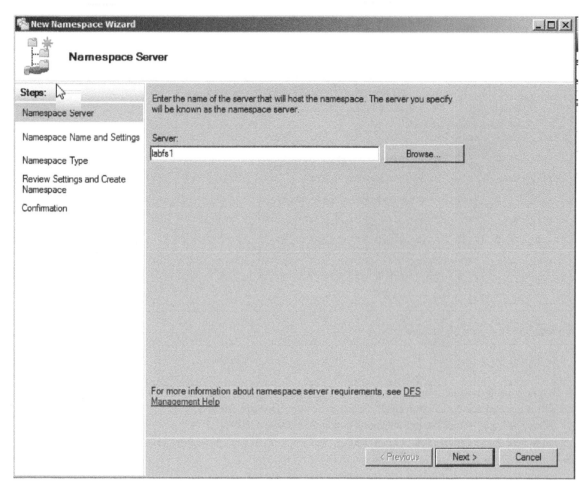

■ **FIGURE 5.18** DFS Namespace host.

3. Enter the UNC path to the shared folder you wish to add to the DFS Namespace (see Figure 5.23). If there are multiple redundant file shares, you can add each share to the folder targets list. After adding all targets, click *OK*.
4. Click *OK* again to create the folder under the DFS root.

You have now added a target folder that links users to the shared folder ClientData on the server labfs1. This shared folder can be accessed by simply browsing the DFS root and selecting the ClientData folder. This folder will refer the client to the ClientData folder on the appropriate file server. In this case, the server would be labfs1. You can create links to

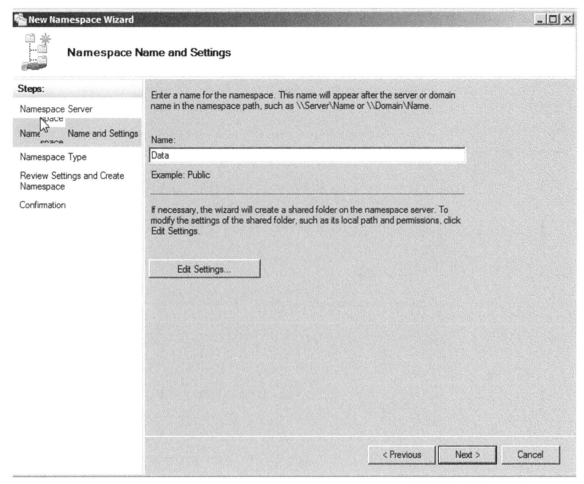

■ **FIGURE 5.19** DFS Namespace Name.

other shared folders on various servers on your network. They can then be accessed via the DFS root\\domain FQDN\DFS Root Name.

Configuring and administering DFS Replication

DFSR is a feature Microsoft developed to provide reliable replication between multiple DFS and standard shared folders. By using DFSR, you can have multiple copies of the same shared folder spread across different servers within your organization. Users can then connect to DFS root, which will then link them to the copy of the shared folder that is closest to them on the network. If the user makes any updates to files within the

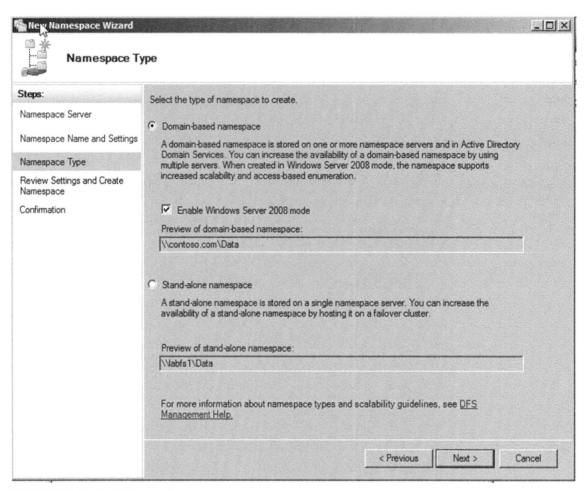

■ **FIGURE 5.20** Selecting DFS Namespace Type.

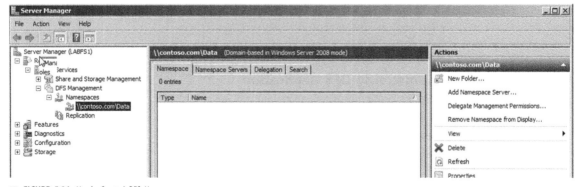

■ **FIGURE 5.21** Newly Created DFS Namespace.

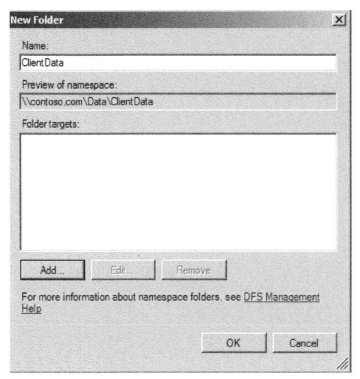

■ **FIGURE 5.22** Naming A DFS Folder.

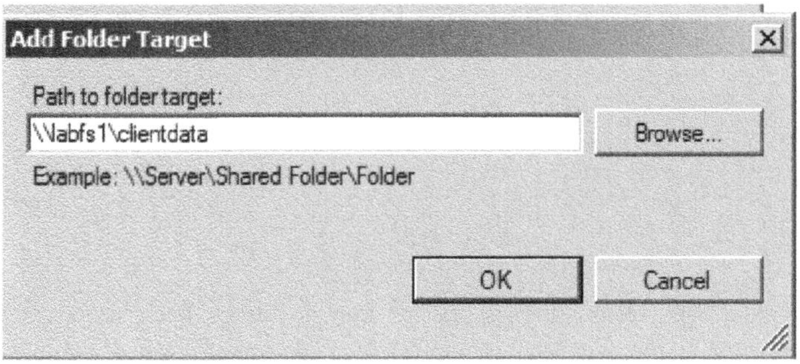

■ **FIGURE 5.23** Adding DFS Target Folder.

shared folder, DFSR will replicate those changes to all copies of the shared folder as depicted in Figure 5.24.

DFSR does not necessarily require DFS Namespaces. It can also be used with standard shared folders. For example, you could configure DFSR to

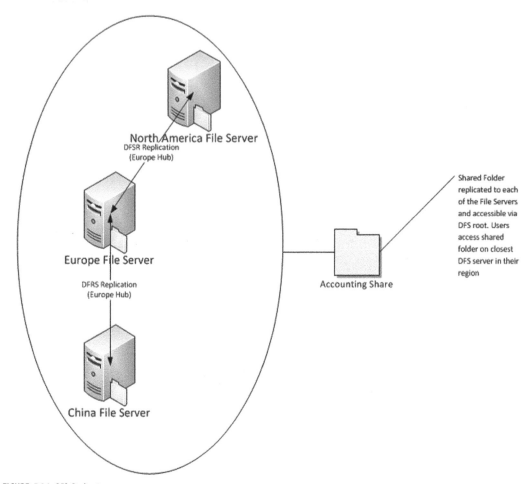

North America File Server
DFSR Replication
(Europe Hub)

Shared Folder
replicated to each
of the File Servers
and accessible via
DFS root. Users
access shared
folder on closest
DFS server in their
region

Europe File Server

DFRS Replication
(Europe Hub)

Accounting Share

China File Server

■ **FIGURE 5.24** DFS Replication.

replicate data from file servers in branch offices back to a central datacenter. In the event that a branch office file server crashed, you would have a second copy of the data in your primary datacenter. DFSR uses advanced algorithms to compress data and replicate only changes to files making it very efficient for wide area networks (WANs). In the following exercise, we will add the DFSR role services and set up DFSR to create a replica of the ClientData share being published in the DFS Namespace.

1. Open Server Manager and select the node *Roles | File services*.
2. In the middle pane, click the link *Add Role Services*.

3. Select the option *DFS Replication* as seen in Figure 5.25. Then click *Next*.

4. Click *Install*.

DFSR should now be installed. Next, we will set up a new shared folder target to replicate the existing ClientData folder to.

1. Log on to the server that will host the second copy of the data and create a new shared folder named ClientData.

2. Log on to the DFS Root host server and open Server Manager and select the node *Roles | File Services | File Services | DFS Management | Namespaces | contoso.com\Data | ClientData*.

3. Right click the selected *ClientData* node and choose the option *Add folder target* as seen in Figure 5.26.

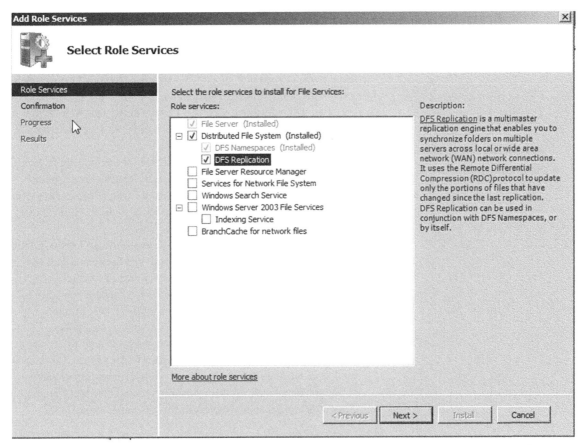

■ **FIGURE 5.25** DFS Replication Role Service.

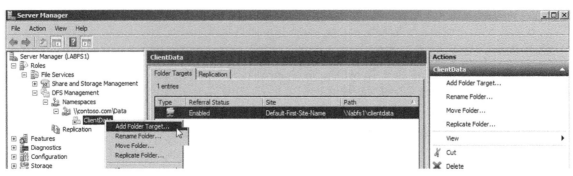

■ **FIGURE 5.26** Adding a Second Target Folder for DFS Namespace Shared Folder.

4. Enter the UNC Path to the second target folder. Then click *OK*.
5. You will be prompted to set up replication to keep the target folders synchronized. Click *Yes* to enable replication between the two folders. This will launch the Replicate Folder Wizard.
6. The first step is to name the replication group and enter the replicated folder name as seen in Figure 5.27. Verify whether this information is correct, and then click *Next* to continue.
7. The wizard should display the two shared folders that were set up in the DFS Namespace (see Figure 5.28). Verify whether these are correct, and then click *Next* to continue.
8. You now need to select the primary member of the replication group. This is the initial data source to be used to replicate to the other folder. In our example, the initial ClientData shared folder was set up on labfs1 so we will choose this as our initial source. After choosing the primary member, click *Next* to continue.
9. Next you will need to select the topology to use for replication. DFSR supports two primary topology types, Hub and Spoke and Full Mesh:
   ❑ *Hub and Spoke*—Hub and Spoke requires at least three member servers and should primarily be used when data are published to a master share (hub), and then replicated to spokes. In this topology, the hub share will always overwrite the spokes.
   ❑ *Full Mesh*—A fully meshed topology means that all folder targets are able to replicate changes to all other folder targets. This means that updates to files can be made on any member server and have them replicated to all other member servers. Full Mesh requires two or more member servers in the replication group.

In our example, we will be using Full Mesh as we only have two member servers. We also want either member server to be able to replicate updates

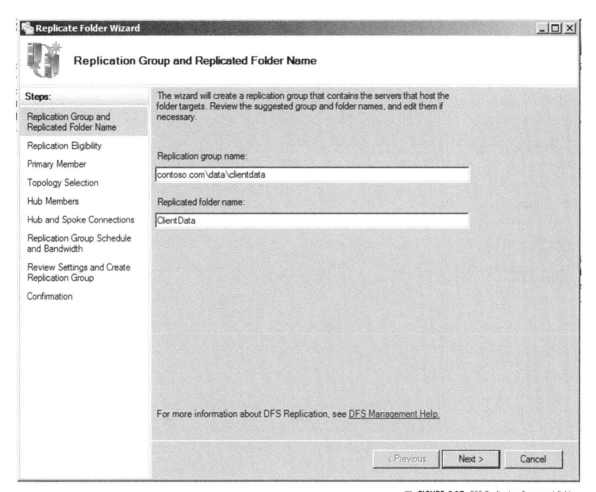

■ **FIGURE 5.27** DFS Replication Group and Folder.

to the other member server. Select Full Mesh (see Figure 5.29) and then
click *Next*.

10. The next step is to select any bandwidth limits or schedules for
    replication to occur. You can use these features to limit the usage of
    WAN links for replication traffic. In our example, we will not be
    limiting bandwidth and replication should occur continuously. Click
    Next to continue.

11. Verify whether the replication settings are correct on the summary
    page, and then click *Create* to set up DFSR. You should see a success
    confirmation page after replication has been set up. Click *Close* to
    close the wizard.

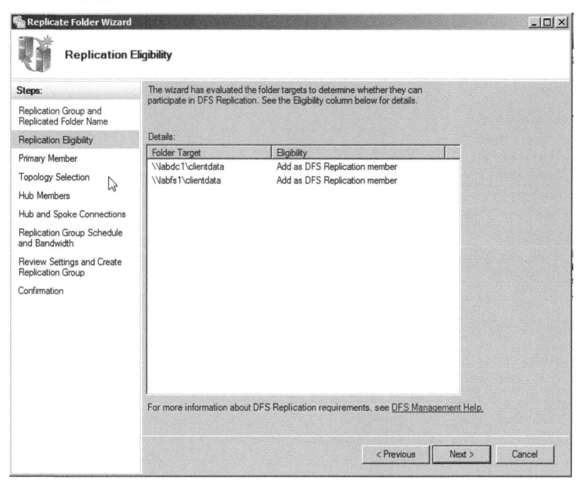

■ **FIGURE 5.28** DFS Replication Eligibility.

Replication should now begin between the two folders. Depending on the amount of data in the initial source server (labfs1), it may take a while for all data to be replicated to the secondary DFS shared folder. You can verify whether replication is occurring by logging onto the second server and browsing the shared folder. You should see that files from the primary server appear in this folder as replication occurs. After initial replication, you should be able to create a file on either shared folder and it should replicate to the other.

Users accessing the DFS root should now be directed to the server which can most efficiently provide access to the chosen shared folder. If either of

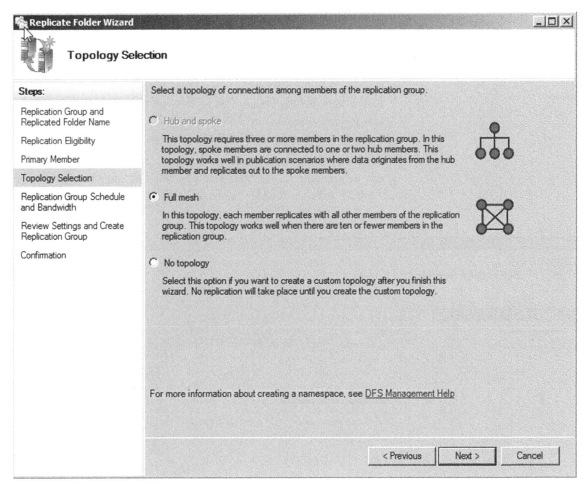

the DFS members fails, the target folder, ClientData, should remain online and accessible by sending users to the server still online.

NOTES FROM THE FIELD

DFS save conflicts

If multiple people are accessing the same file from different DFS access points and the file is saved by all of them, which version is saved? To handle conflicts, the last write wins, meaning that the version of the file that was last saved is the one that will be replicated to all copies of the file.

FILE SERVER RESOURCE MANAGER

In this section, we will discuss how the File Server Resource manager (FSRM) can be used to provide additional features such as quotas, file screens, reporting, and file classification services to your Windows file servers. The File Server Resource Monitor first appeared in Windows Server 2003 and has been carried on to Windows Server 2008 R2 adding new features along the way. FSRM is an additional role service for the File Server role and can be installed via Server Manager as seen in Figure 5.30.

After the role service has been installed, the FSRM management console can be accessed via the Start Menu by selecting *Start | Administrative Tools | File Server Resource Manager*. As seen in Figure 5.31, the FSRM console is organized into five main sections:

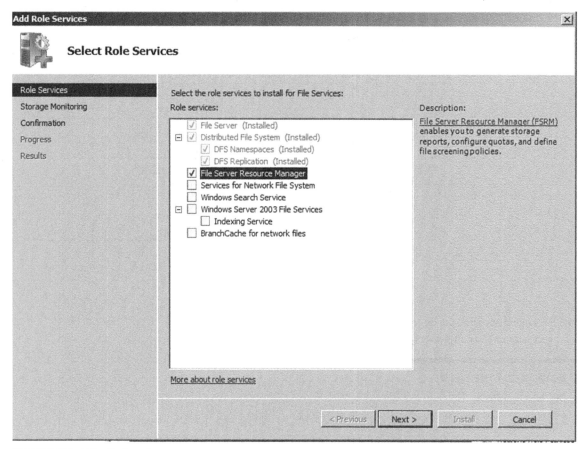

■ **FIGURE 5.30** Adding File Server Resource Manager Role Service.

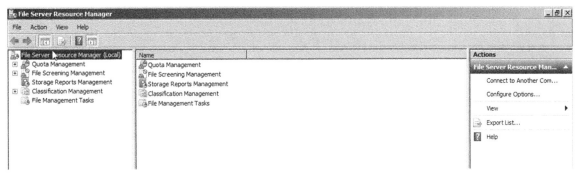

■ **FIGURE 5.31** The FSRM Console.

- Quota Management
- File screening management
- Storage reports management
- Classification management
- File management tasks

Quota management

Quota management allows administrators to allot soft and hard quotas on folders within a volume. By using quotas, each user is restricted to consuming a limited amount of disk space for a given folder. This limit can be soft, meaning that the user is only warned that they are exceeding their quota but will still be allowed to save the file or the limit can be a hard quota, meaning that the user is not allowed to save additional data to the folder once he has reached his quota limit. Additionally, FSRM can e-mail users and administrators informing them that they have exceeded their quotas. For example, you might want to set a 200-MB quota on the client data folder. You can use FSRM to create a new quota on the path C:\ClientData and use the predefined template 200 MB limit Reports to Users. This template will limit each user to saving a maximum of 200 MB to the ClientData shared folder and e-mail them warnings at 85%, 95%, and 100% quota usage levels as seen in Figure 5.32.

NOTES FROM THE FIELD

Quota e-mail notifications

FSRM uses the E-mail Address field from Active Directory user accounts to send users e-mail alerts regarding their quota usage. If you do not populate this field with each user's correct e-mail address, they will not receive quota notifications.

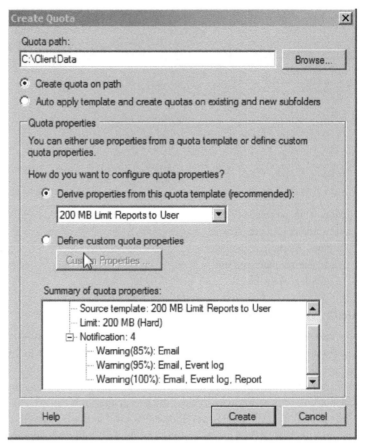

■ **FIGURE 5.32** Creating Quotas.

File screening management

File screens allow administrators to restrict the types of files saved to folders. For example, you may wish to prevent users from saving personal music files such as MP3s to shared folders (see Figure 5.33). File screens look at the file extension to determine whether the file is allowed to be stored in a specific folder. Like quotas, FSRM can send e-mail notifications to users if they attempt to violate a file screen policy. FSRM file screening management comes with a few predefined templates with common file extensions. You can also create your own customized templates to meet your own needs. File screens can be set up in active or passive mode. Active mode will prevent the restricted file types from being saved to the folder, while passive mode only monitors restricted file types.

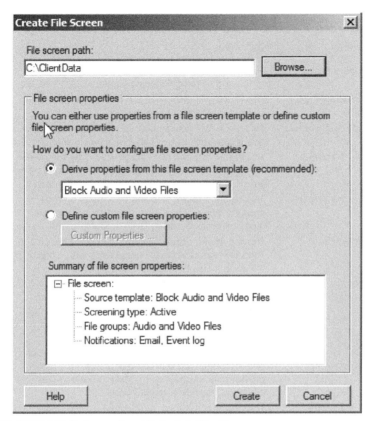

■ **FIGURE 5.33** File Screen to Prevent Storing Audio/Video Files.

Storage reports

FSRM provides some basic storage reporting for Windows file servers. These reports can be run *ad hoc* or set to run on a scheduled basis. Additionally the reports can automatically be e-mailed to administrators when they are generated. FSRM provides nine report types. They are defined in Table 5.3.

Classification management

Classification management is a new feature in Windows Server 2008 R2 that can be used to classify files based upon rules or folders in which they are stored. Using classification management, you can provide better records management for files on your network. We will explore classification management in more detail in Chapter 10.

Table 5.3 File Server Resource Manager Storage Reports

Report	Definition
Duplicate files	This report will display all the files in the volume or folder that have duplicate copies.
File screening audit	This report will display all the files that violate a file screen for a folder or volume.
Files by file group	This report will display files and file counts by their group type such as text files, office files, image files, etc.
Files by owner	This report displays files created/saved by the owner. This allows administrators to easily identify users who are saving large amounts of data on the file server.
Files by property	This report displays files and file counts by their property values. This helps identify specific property types that may be using large amounts of disk space.
Large files	This report will display files that are considered large. The minimum size file is configurable with 5 MB being the default size to include in the report.
Least recently accessed files	This report will display the files in the folder or volume that have gone the longest period without being accessed. This report provides administrators a good way to review files that have not been accessed for a long period of time.
Most recently accessed files	This report will display files that have gone the shortest period of time without being accessed. This report provides administrators the ability to review files that are being used on a regular basis.
Quota usage	This report will display quotas that exceed a specified disk space usage level. This report includes a list of all users who have saved files in the folder or volume and how much of their allocated quota they have used.

File management tasks

File management tasks is a new feature introduced with the release of Windows Server 2008 R2. Using file management tasks, administrators can set up scheduled operations to scan volumes and folders on file servers and review specific file properties. Based upon rules defined for the properties, the scheduled task can then move the file to a folder where it can be archived, or custom command can be performed on the file. A great example of using a file management task would be to move any files not accessed in the last 180 days to an archive folder. An administrator could then back up the archive folder and delete the files from the server. This is known as a file expiration task. Additionally, the file expiration task can e-mail a notification to the owner of files that are about to be moved to the archive folder.

SERVICES FOR NETWORK FILE SYSTEM

Services for NFS provides file-sharing features for UNIX-based clients. Using services for NFS, you can create shared folders that are accessible from UNIX clients requiring the NFS protocol. Services for NFS is added as an additional role service to the file server role. After adding the role service, you will see a new NFS sharing tab added to folder properties as seen in Figure 5.34. From this tab you can create a shared folder as a NFS share and assign permission to UNIX clients.

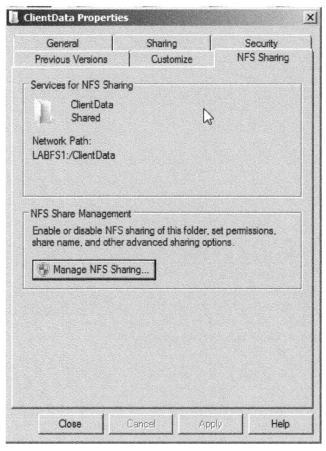

■ **FIGURE 5.34** NFS Sharing Properties.

WINDOWS SEARCH SERVICE

The Windows Search Service is a file server role service that provides indexing of common files on Windows computers. By installing the Windows Search Service, clients can search more quickly for files, using an index that is stored on the file server. You can modify the content being indexed via the Indexing Options control panel as seen in Figure 5.35

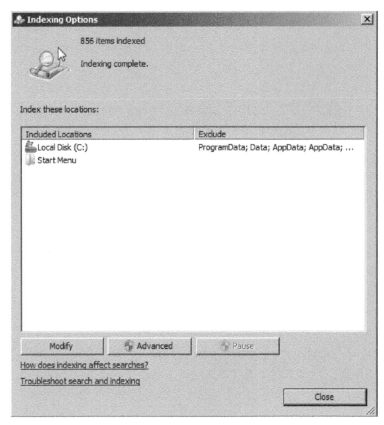

■ **FIGURE 5.35** Windows Search Service Indexing Options.

For legacy support, the Windows Server 2003 indexing service can be used on Windows Server 2008 R2 servers. This service is not recommended unless a specific application requires the service to be installed. The Windows Server 2003 indexing service can be added as a role service.

BRANCH CACHE FOR NETWORK FILES

Branch Cache is a new feature in Windows Server 2008 R2 that allows branch offices to cache files from file servers and intranet Web sites locally to a branch office. With branch cache enabled, the first time a file is accessed it is copied across the WAN and opened on the local computer. A cached copy is then saved on a server designated as the local cache or another client computer. The next time a computer tries to access the remote file, it is accessed via the branch office cache location. Branch cache requires Windows Server 2008 R2 servers and Windows 7 clients. We will explore branch cache in detail in Chapter 13.

ADMINISTERING PRINT AND DOCUMENT SERVICES

As a Windows administrator you will probably be charged with setting up and managing print services on your network. In most cases, you will have various printers scattered across your network. By deploying Windows print and document services, you can centrally manage network printers as well as network scanners. In this section, we will explore installing and configuring print and document services in Windows Server 2008 R2.

Installing print services

Installing print services for Windows Server 2008 R2 is done by adding the Print and Document Services role. This role is added using Server

Manager. Print services includes four primary role services (see Figure 5.36):

- Print Server
- LPD Service
- Internet Printing
- Distributed Scan Server

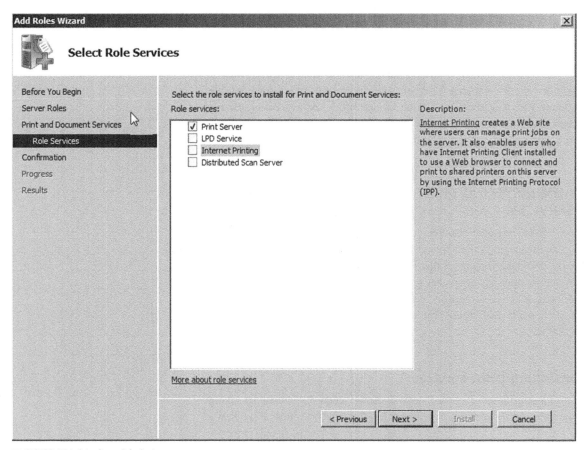

■ **FIGURE 5.36** Print Server Role Services.

Administering a print server

The print server role service adds all components necessary to set up, share, and manage network printers. After installing this role, you will notice that the Print Management console will be added to Server Manager and can be accessed from the node *Roles | Print and Document Services | Print Management* (see Figure 5.37).

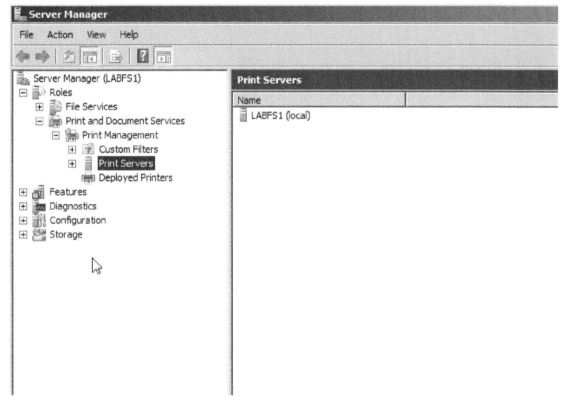

■ **FIGURE** 5.37 Print Management Console.

Installing a network printer on print server

Using the print management console, you can manage all your network printers from one central console. One of the first steps you will want to perform is to install network printers on your print server. This can be done by performing the following steps within the print management console:

1. Select the *Printers* node under *Print Management | Print Servers | your print server name* (see Figure 5.38).

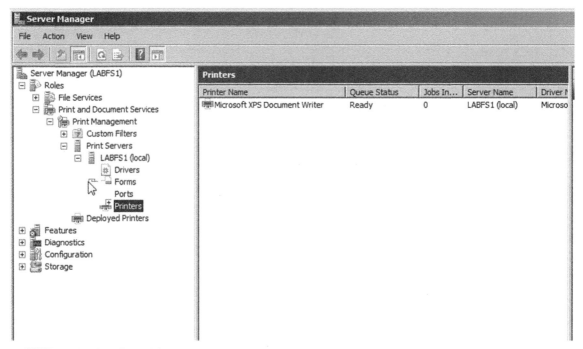

■ **FIGURE** 5.38 Print Server Printers Node.

2. Right click the *Printers* node and select the option *Add Printer...*
3. You can choose how to locate the printer you want to install including searching the network, using an existing port, or creating a new port. In this exercise, we will choose the option to search the network (see Figure 5.39). Then click *Next*.

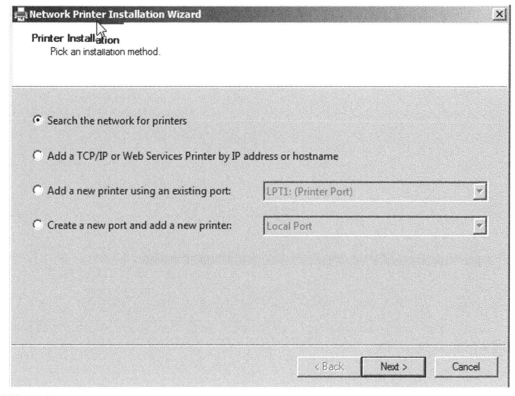

■ **FIGURE 5.39** Printer port options.

4. The printer installation wizard will begin searching the local network for printers. After the search is complete, any network printers found are listed in the wizard as seen in Figure 5.40.

5. Select the printer you want to install, and then click *Next*. The wizard will attempt to add a port for the selected printer.

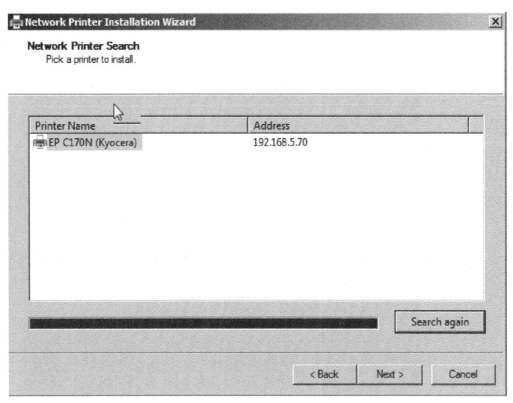

■ **FIGURE 5.40** Searching for Network Printers.

6. You will next need to give the printer a name and share name (see Figure 5.41). Additionally, you can list location and comments to make it easier for users to find the printer. For example, by using the notation HQ/2nd/Processing Room, users can search for a printer based on its location. When searching Active Directory for printers, a user could enter the search HQ/2nd/* to list all printers on the second floor in the HQ building.

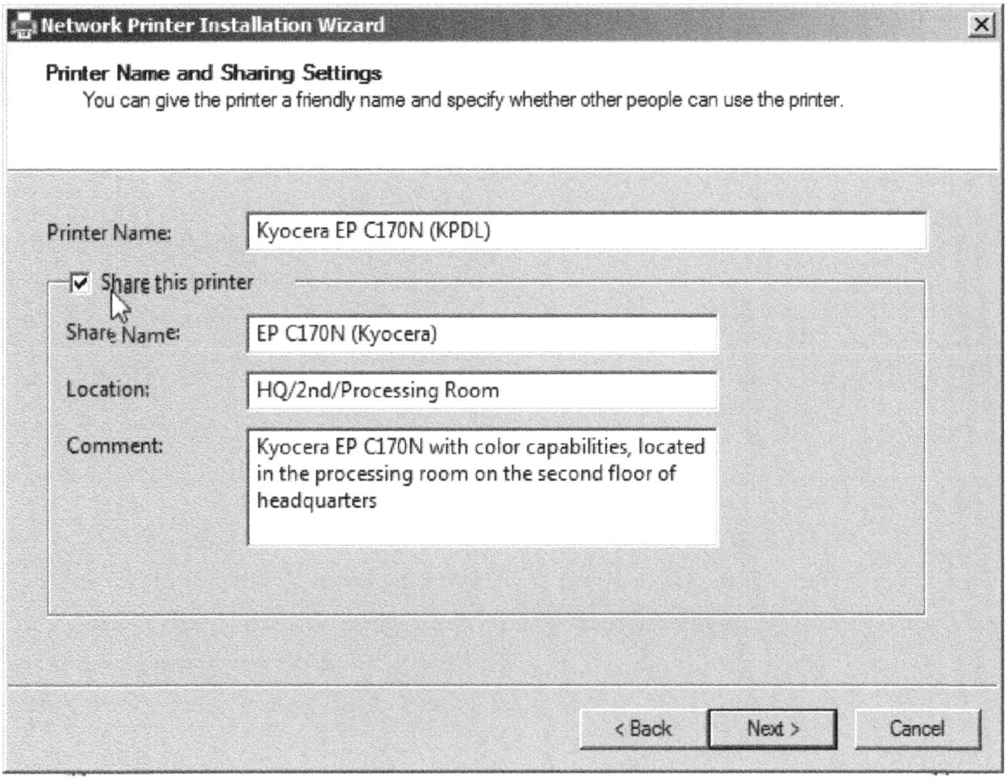

■ **FIGURE 5.41** Creating Printer Share.

7. After entering relevant printer information, click *Next* to continue. Then click *Next* again to install the printer driver. When the installation is complete you will receive a confirmation page. Click *Finish* to close the wizard.

Once the printer has been created, you can make the printer more accessible and easier to find by publishing it to Active Directory. To do this, locate the printer in the printer management console and choose properties. Then click the *Sharing* tab and select the option *List in Directory* as seen in Figure 5.42. Then click *OK*.

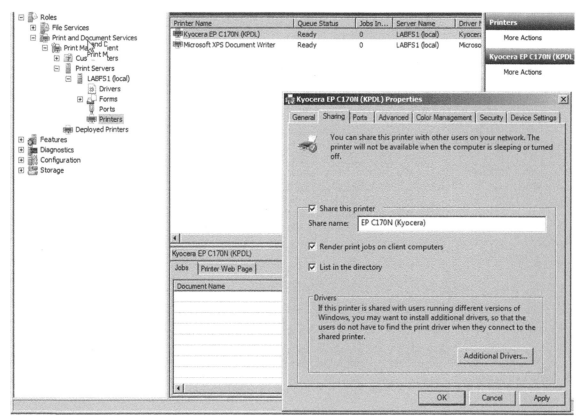

■ **FIGURE 5.42** Publishing Shared Printer to Active Directory.

You can now access this printer from a Windows client by entering the UNC path to the printer share (\\Server Name\Printer Share) or by searching Active Directory as seen in Figure 5.43.

Deploying printers using Group Policy

Additionally, you can push shared printers out to users via Group Policy. To deploy a printer via Group Policy, perform the following:

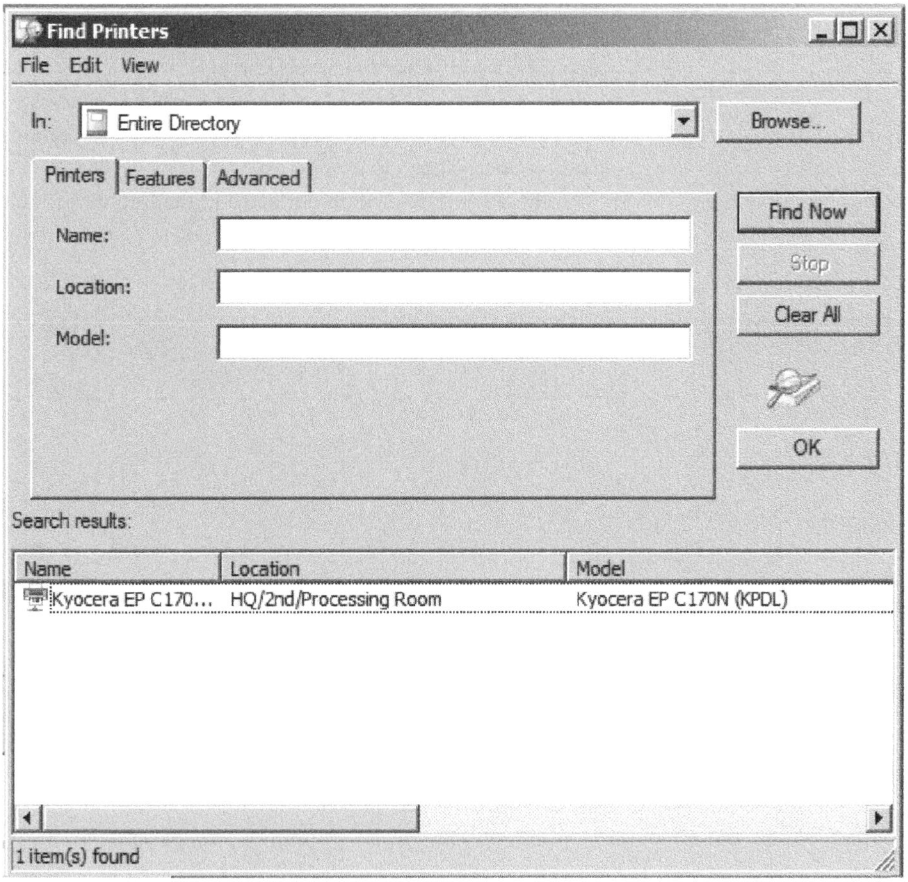

■ **FIGURE 5.43** Searching Active Directory for Published Printer.

1. Locate the printer in the printer management console. Then right click the printer you want to deploy and choose the option *Deploy with Group Policy*. This will open the Deploy with Group Policy window.
2. Click the *Browse* button to select the GPO you want to use to deploy the selected printer (see Figure 5.44). If you want to use a new GPO specifically for deploying printers, you will need to create the GPO prior to using the *deploy with group policy* option within the print management console.
3. Next you need to select whether you want the printer to be deployed to computers or users. By selecting computers, the printer will be deployed to any user who logs on to computers to which this policy is applied. If you select users, the printer will be deployed to users to whom the policy is applied, no matter which computer they log on to. If you want to deploy the printer to both users and computers, select both options. Then click *Add*.
4. You should now see the printer listed in the Deploy with Group Policy windows as seen in Figure 5.45. Click *OK* to complete the GPO setup.

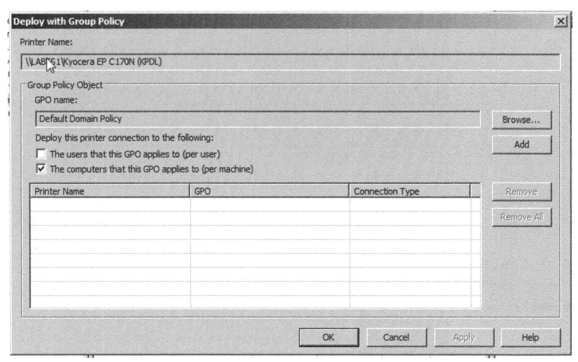

■ **FIGURE 5.44** Deploy with Group Policy Options.

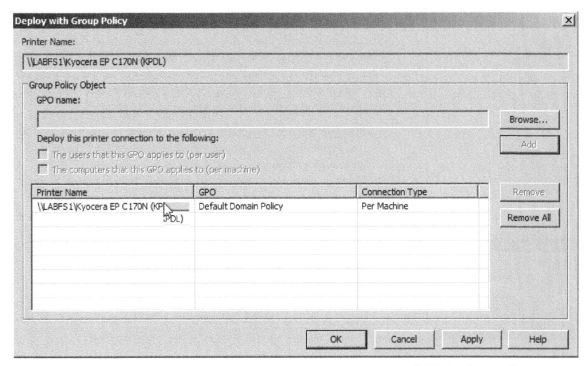

■ **FIGURE 5.45** Selecting a GPO.

You can now log on to a computer that the policy is applied to and you should see the printer installed and ready to use.

Line Printer Daemon service

The Line Printer Daemon (LPD) role service can be added to provide printer support for UNIX-based computers. By installing the LPD service, you can share printers in which UNIX-based computers can connect using their native printing protocol.

Internet Printing

The Internet Printing role service installs services to support the Internet Printing Protocol (IPP) and a Web site where administrators can manage printers installed on the print server. In most cases, you will probably not want to allow your network printers to be accessible via the Internet; however, by using Internet Printing you can provide an easy-to-use interface for new admins or users to manage print queues and connect to shared printers.

Distributed scan server

The distributed scan server role service provides network scan management using Windows Server 2008 R2. Using scan management, you can administer network scanners on your network as well as process and route scanned documents. When adding the distributed scan server role service, there are several options that will need to be configured:

1. First you will need to specify a service account for the service to run (see Figure 5.46). This account needs to be an Active Directory domain user account.
2. Next you will need to specify the temporary folder location to store scanned files while they are being processed by the scan server.

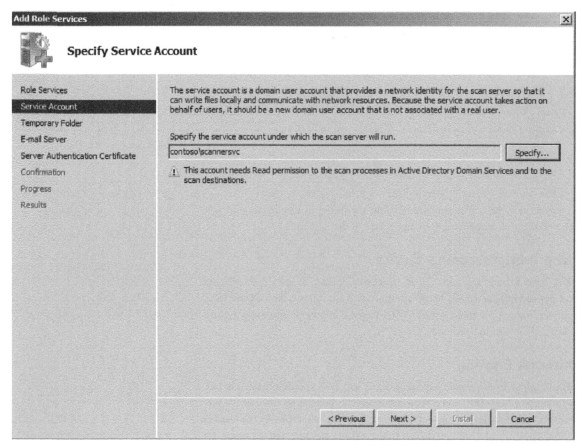

■ **FIGURE 5.46** Scan Management Service Account.

3. You also need to specify an SMTP mail server for relaying notifications from the scan service (see Figure 5.47).
4. Next you will need to specify a certificate to use to provide SSL encryption between the scan server and clients. For testing purposes, you can choose to use a self-signed certificate; however, for production deployments you should use a certificate from an authorized certificate authority.

After you have configured those options, the role service installation will be complete. You will then be required to restart the server before using scan management.

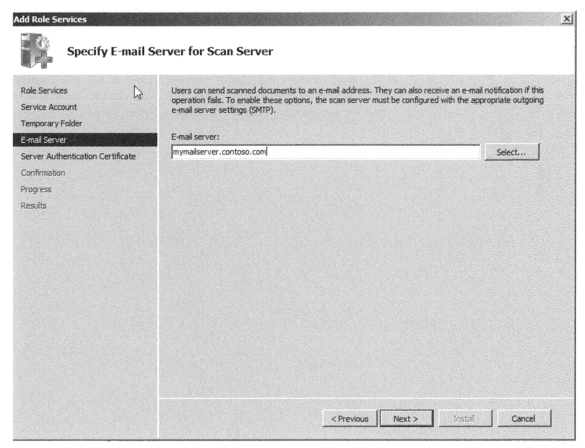

■ **FIGURE 5.47** Scan Management Outgoing SMTP Server.

Once the server reboots, you can access the scan management console via Server Manager. You can configure scan management to accept scanned files from network scanners and route them to network shared folders, SharePoint sites, or e-mail. Use of scan management services in Windows Server 2008 R2 allows you to centrally manage scanning processes and workflows for network scanners.

SUMMARY

This chapter covered file, print, and document services available in Windows Server 2008 R2. In this chapter, we explored the basics of Windows file sharing and how to set up, manage, and secure shared folders on your network. We also discussed using DFS services to provide easy access and high availability to shared folders. This chapter also covered the use of quotas, file screens, storage reports, and file management tasks. We then explored the additional features provided by the Windows Search Service and NFS services.

The second part of this chapter covered setting up and administering Windows Server 2008 R2 print. We concluded this chapter by discussing the new scan services available in Windows Server 2008 R2.

Chapter 6

Internet Information Services 7.5 feature focus

Internet Information Services (IIS) was first included as an optional add-on to Windows NT 3.5.1. With subsequent releases of the Windows Server network operating system, IIS continued to evolve as a core feature of the OS. With the release of Windows Server 2008 R2, Microsoft has further enhanced IIS, providing the most feature rich and secure Web server to date.

In this chapter, we will explore the various components that make up IIS 7.5 and what features are offered by the Web server. We will explore how to plan for and deploy IIS 7.5 Web servers. We will also learn how to administer IIS 7.5 Web sites. We will conclude this chapter with an introduction to administering File Transfer Protocol (FTP) services in IIS 75.

OVERVIEW OF INTERNET INFORMATION SERVICES 7.5

IIS is one of the most widely deployed Web servers in the world. IIS is used by thousands of organizations to serve Web sites on intranets, extranets, and the Internet. IIS not only provides support for hosting basic Web sites but also advanced Web applications using technologies such as ASP.NET and PHP. IIS additionally provides the following features:

- Support for running multiple Web sites on a single host
- A common administrative interface using Server Manager and PowerShell
- Support for SSL-based Web sites using certificates from internal and public PKIs
- Delegation of permissions giving Web developers limited access to servers hosting Web applications
- Modular installation providing a greater level of security and reduced attack surface
- Rich media services allowing organizations to provide streaming media via the Web.

> **NOTES FROM THE FIELD**
>
> **IIS.NET**
> Microsoft has a large community Web site dedicated to IIS. This Web site contains sample scripts and other tools to further enhance IIS as well as whitepapers and how-to's. The Web site can be accessed at http://www.iis. net.

Microsoft has included the following features in IIS 7.5 to further enhance the Windows Web server:

- Request Filtering Module
- Best Practices Analyzer (BPA)
- PowerShell Module
- Support for Managed Service Accounts

Request Filtering Module

The Request Filtering Module is introduced as an add-on extension for IIS 7.0 to allow administrators to block Web requests that are deemed harmful. Request filtering provides additional security to IIS by limiting the types of requests and commands that can be sent to IIS via the Web browser. IIS 7.5 now includes the module as a standard part of the Web server role.

Best Practices Analyzer

IIS 7.5 now includes a BPA. You should run the BPA after initial configuration and on a regular basis thereafter to ensure that your IIS deployment is healthy and optimally configured. We will look at the IIS BPA in greater detail later in this chapter.

PowerShell Module

As with most roles in Windows Server 2008 R2, IIS 7.5 includes a PowerShell Module allowing administrators to perform most administrative functions from the PowerShell command line. Administrators can use PowerShell to quickly perform IIS administrative tasks as well as automate the configuration of IIS for fast and standardized deployment of IIS Web servers.

Support for managed service accounts

You learned in Chapter 4 that Windows Server 2008 R2 Active Directory allows administrators to create managed service accounts. Managed service accounts allow administrators to change the password of a service account without having to update each service using that particular account. IIS 7.5 application pools provide support for managed service accounts. For example, an IIS application pool could be running under the account IIS_Service. For security purposes, an administrator needs to change the password on this account. The administrator simply has to change the password of the Active Directory account. Once the password has been changed, the IIS application pool will automatically update the password field to reflect the new password without administrator interaction.

PLANNING TO DEPLOY IIS 7.5 WEB SERVERS

Prior to installing IIS 7.5, you will want to properly plan for the deployment. There are several important items you will need to take into consideration. These include:

- *Web technology used*—Will the Web server support applications based upon ASP.NET, PHP, or some other development platform?
- *Security requirements*—Will your Web sites and applications use SSL? If so, will you need public or private certificates? What types of authentication methods are required for your applications?
- *Resource requirements*—How much memory and CPU will the Web application require? How much disk space will be used by the application files? How much network bandwidth will be needed to ensure acceptable performance for users? Is the application compatible with 64 bit hardware?
- *Server configuration*—Do you want to use a full server install or core install? What types of logging need to be enabled for the Web site or application? Who will manage the Web server and will they do so by logging onto the server or via remote management tools?
- *Backup and disaster recovery*—In the event of a Web server failure, how will you recover the system? Does your deployment require high availability and load balancing?

You will want to spend ample time planning your IIS deployment to ensure that it can properly support Web sites and applications that will be supported by the Web servers within your organization. Be sure to document the configuration and use standards when configuring IIS. After you complete your deployment, be sure to run the BPA to verify your configuration.

INSTALLING AND CONFIGURING IIS 7.5

IIS 7.5 is installed using the same process as installing other roles in Windows Server 2008 R2. In this exercise, we will explore the process to install IIS 7.5:

1. Open Server Manager and select the *Roles* node. Then click the *Add Roles* link in the middle pane. This will launch the Add Roles Wizard. Click *Next* to continue.
2. Select the *Web Server (IIS)* role as seen in Figure 6.1. Then click *Next*.
3. This will take you to the IIS summary page. Click *Next*.
4. You now must select the role services you wish to use. Starting with IIS 7.0, Windows only installs the components that are required to provide the requested functionality. This provides a reduced attack surface for IIS making it more secure overall. For the purposes of this exercise and other exercises in this chapter, we will select all role services. When installing your production deployment, you should select only the role services required to support your Web sites and

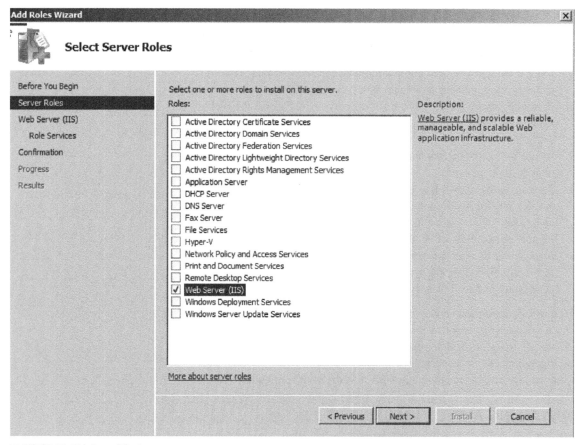

■ FIGURE 6.1 Web Server (IIS) role.

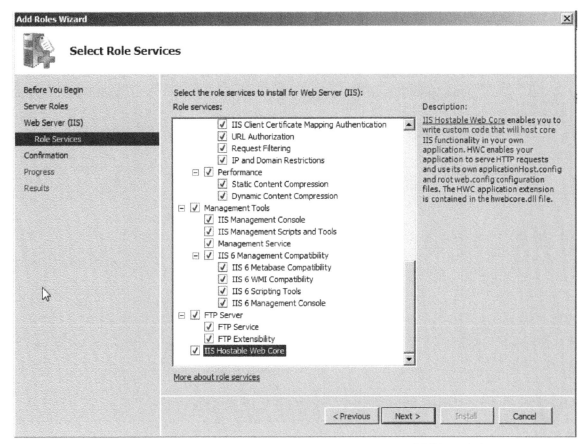

■ **FIGURE 6.2** IIS role services.

applications. After selecting the role services (see Figure 6.2), click *Next* to continue.

5. Verify your selections on the summary page, then click *Install*. This will install the IIS role and the role services you selected in step 4. You can later add or remove role services by selecting the add role services or remove role services links, respectively.

6. When installation is completed, click *Close* to close the Add Roles Wizard.

The IIS 7.5 role has now been added to the Windows Server 2008 R2 server. You can access the IIS management console from within Server Manager by selecting the node *Roles / Web Server (IIS) / Internet Information Services (IIS) Manager* as seen in Figure 6.3.

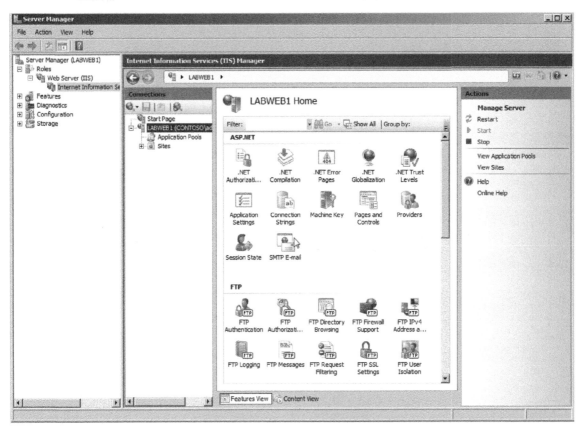

■ **FIGURE 6.3** IIS manager.

NOTES FROM THE FIELD

IIS 6.0 Manager

While installing IIS role services, you may notice that the IIS 6.0 Manager is listed. This is available as a role service to support applications that require IIS 6.0 services. For example, some applications such as Microsoft Exchange 2007 were released prior to IIS 7.0 and 7.5 thus require IIS 6.0 components to function properly. To support these types of applications, install the IIS 6.0 role services.

After you have installed IIS, there are a few postconfiguration steps you may want to perform immediately. For example, IIS logs are saved in the directory %SystemDrive%\InetPub\logs\LogFiles by default. However, using this default directory could allow IIS logs to fill up the operating system drive if left unchecked over time, causing the OS to become unstable. To help remediate this risk, you can move the log files to a separate drive or partition. To configure the log file location, perform the following:

1. Open Server Manager and select the node *Roles | Web Server (IIS) | Internet Information Services (IIS) Manager*.
2. In the middle pane, select the Web server as seen in Figure 6.4.
3. In the features view, scroll down until you see the Logging option as seen in Figure 6.5. Double-click the Logging option to open the logging configuration window.
4. Change the directory to the new location you would like the logs to be stored (see Figure 6.6), then click *Apply*.

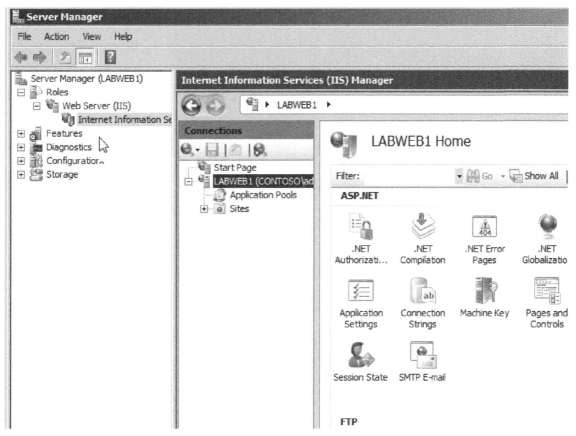

■ **FIGURE 6.4** IIS Web Server.

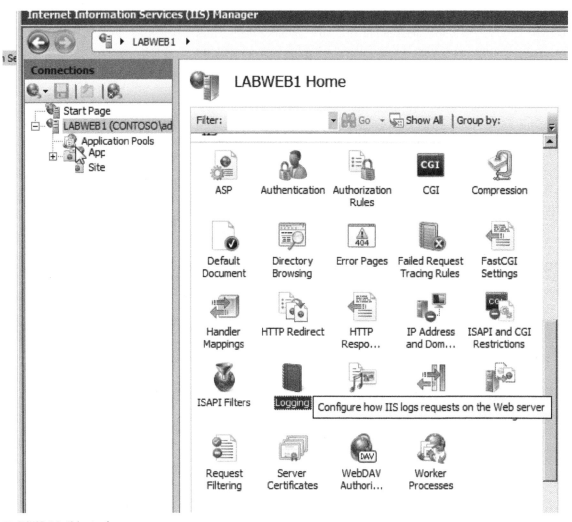

■ **FIGURE 6.5** IIS logging features.

NOTES FROM THE FIELD

IIS Logs

Depending on Web site traffic, IIS Logs can become very large consuming a lot of space on Web servers. You may want to write a script or bat file to regularly purge old IIS logs from the server.

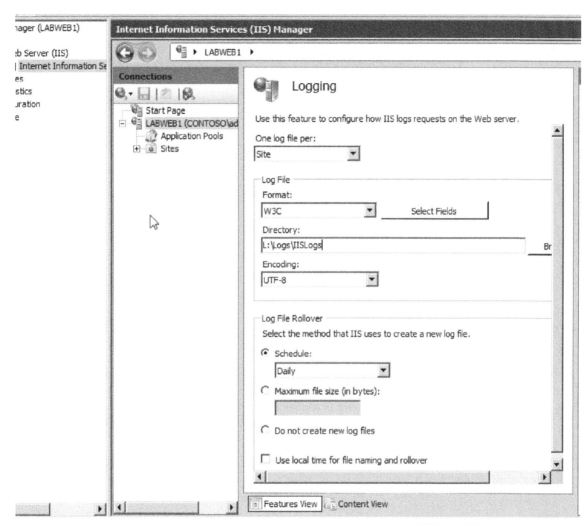

■ **FIGURE 6.6** IIS log directory.

Another task you may want to perform after installing IIS is to run the BPA. The BPA can be accessed from Server Manager by performing the following:

1. Open Server Manager and select the node *Roles / Web Server (IIS)*
2. Scroll down the middle pane until you see the BPA as seen in Figure 6.7.
3. Click the *Scan Role* link to begin the BPA scan process.

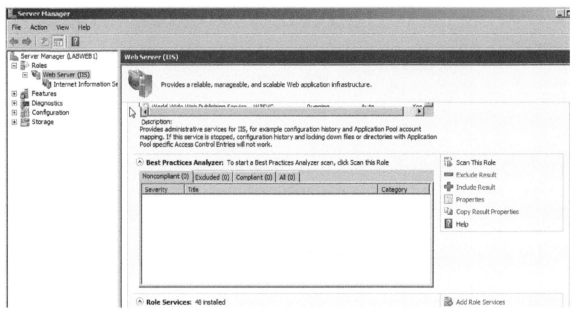

■ FIGURE 6.7 IIS best practices analyzer.

4. The results will be listed as seen in Figure 6.8. If any settings are noncompliant, review the warning and remediation steps to bring the server into compliance. After resolving the issue, rescan the system. You may also want to run the BPA when you set up and configure new Web sites.

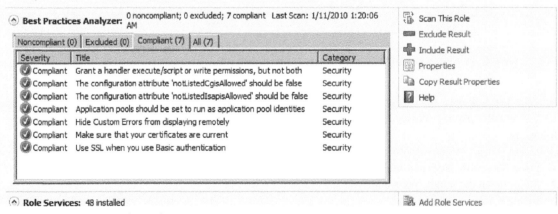

■ FIGURE 6.8 IIS best practices analyzer results.

ADMINISTERING IIS 7.5 WEB SITES

After installing IIS, you are ready to set up and manage new Web sites. In this section, we will walk through setting up and configuring a new Web site using IIS Manager within Server Manager. Before creating new Web sites, you need to have a basic understanding of Web sites and application pools and how they relate to one another.

IIS Web sites

IIS Web sites serve up files used by the Web application or site. IIS Web sites manage all of the security and configuration settings for each site including authentication methods allows, which types of files can be served via the sites, error handling, and the directory where the Web site files are located.

Application pools

Application pools help isolate Web sites so that issues that may occur on one site do not bring down other sites running on the same server. Application pools can also be used to restart a Web site if it begins to consume too many resources on the server, again preventing a single site from interfering with the performance of other sites on the same server. Additionally, application pools allow administrators to set specific sites to run as a defined identity or user account. This gives the application a security context in which it can connect to and access other resources on the network if necessary.

Each IIS Web site runs in an application pool. An application pool can contain one or more IIS Web sites. If an application pool stops or restarts, the IIS Web site is also offline during the time the application pool is stopped.

During the installation of the Web Server role, DefaultAppPool, and Classic.Net AppPools are created along with a Default Web site.

Creating Web sites

To create a new Web site within IIS, perform the following tasks:

1. Open Server Manager and select the node *Roles / Web Server (IIS) / Internet Information Services (IIS) Manager*.
2. In the middle pane, expand the Web server name and right-click the *Sites* node and choose the option *Add Website* as seen in Figure 6.9.

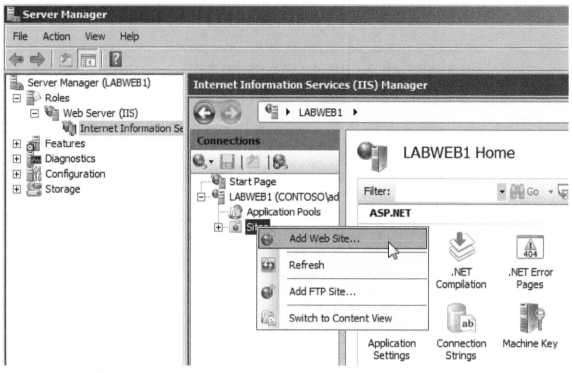

■ **FIGURE 6.9** Adding a Web site.

3. Enter the required site information (see Figure 6.10) including:
   - Site name—This is the name of the site. This should be a name that easily describes the site, for example, "BillingApplication".
   - Application pool—Choose the application pool for this site to run under. By default, a new application pool will be created for the new site.
   - Physical path—Enter the path on the server where the Web site files are located.
   - Binding information—Choose the binding settings such as IP address and protocols used. You can also enter a host header in this section. IIS Web sites can use host headers allowing you to bind more than one Web site to a single IP address. Without the use of host headers, each Web site would require a dedicated IP address.
4. After entering the Web site configuration information, click *OK*.
5. You should now see the new site listed under the sites node in IIS Manager.

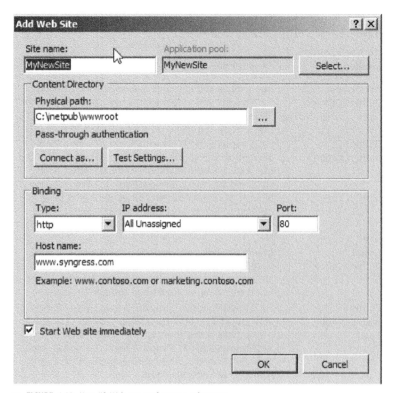

■ FIGURE 6.10 New IIS Web site configuration information.

Any settings for the Web site can now be managed using the IIS Manager in Server Manager. Some of the more common settings that may need to be configured are:

- Authentication—You may need to set the authentication method used by the Web site. IIS can use Anonymous Authentication, Basic Authentication, Digest Authentication, Forms Authentication, and Windows Authentication. IIS can use any one or all of these authentication methods. The IIS Authentication methods are defined in Table 6.1.

- Default document—Web sites have a default document or page that is accessed when accessing the site. To prevent users from having to know the name of this page, the Web site will automatically direct users to the defined default document when they access the Web site URL.

Table 6.1 IIS Authentication Methods

Authentication Method	Description
Anonymous authentication	Anonymous authentication allows anyone to access the Web site without entering a username or password. This authentication method is commonly used for public Web sites where everyone should have access.
Basic authentication	Basic authentication presents the user with a logon dialog box asking for a username and password. If the user enters a valid username and password combination, he is given access to the Web site. It is highly recommended that SSL be used with Basic Authentication as Basic Authentication sends the username and password across the network in clear text.
Digest authentication	Digest authentication provides a much greater level of security than Basic Authentication. Digest authentication can also be used to authenticate users when accessing an application through firewalls.
Forms authentication	Forms authentication provides a very user-friendly authentication method providing the end user with a Web page-based form to enter his credentials. Applications such as Microsoft Exchange Server 2007 and 2010 provide forms-based authentication to the Outlook Web Access feature.
Windows authentication	Windows authentication is used on internal Windows domain environments. Windows authentication uses the Windows domain to authenticate users. This authentication type is heavily used on only intranet Web sites.

- HTTP redirect—The HTTP Redirect option can be used to direct users hitting the Web site to another URL. This is helpful when a Web site has been moved and you want to redirect the users to the new location.

ADMINISTERING THE IIS 7.5 FTP PUBLISHING SERVICE

IIS includes FTP services to allow users to remotely upload files to Web sites they manage. FTP is commonly seen in Web-hosting environments where multiple Web sites are shared on a single Web server. Each Web site owner can then be given access to upload and manage files for his respective Web site by using FTP Publishing Services. To provide FTP access to a Web site, perform the following tasks:

1. Open Server Manager and select the node *Roles / Web Server (IIS) / Internet Information Services (IIS) Manager*.
2. In the middle pane, right-click the Web site you want to add FTP Service to and select the *Add FTP Publishing* option (see Figure 6.11).

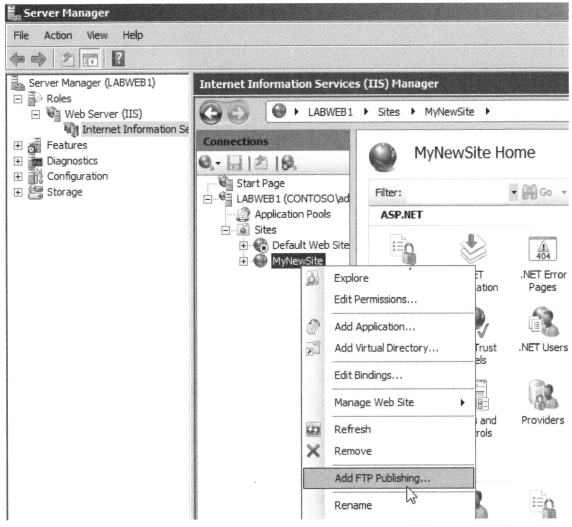

■ **FIGURE 6.11** Add FTP Publishing to Web site.

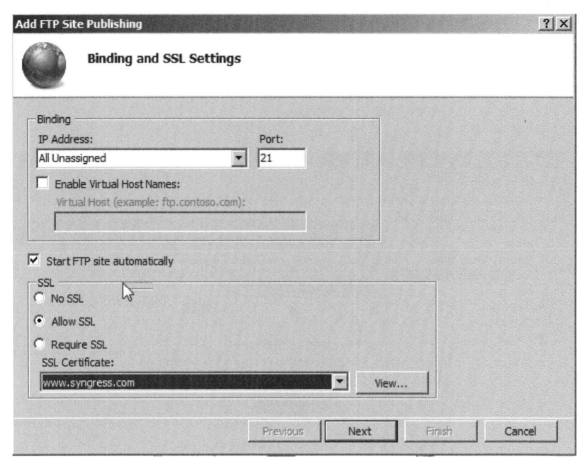

■ **FIGURE 6.12** FTP binding options.

3. If you want to bind FTP to a specific IP address and port number, change those in the bindings section. You can optionally allow or enforce SSL-based Secure FTP as seen in Figure 6.12. Then click *Next*.

4. Configure the authentication and authorization settings by setting an authentication type, entering users or groups allowed to access the Web site, and configuring what level of permissions they have on the site (see Figure 6.13). Then click *Finish*.

You now have enabled FTP services on the selected site. Users can connect to the Web site via an FTP client and upload or change files. Only users in the local group are allowed access and they are only given access to the Web site specified.

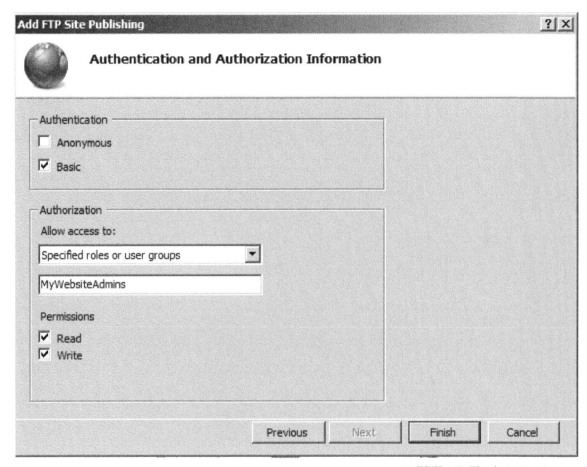

■ **FIGURE 6.13** FTP authentication and authorization settings.

SUMMARY

In this chapter, we were introduced to the new version of IIS included with Windows Server 2008 R2. We discussed the process of planning for an IIS 7.5 deployment and then walked through the various aspects of installing, configuring, and administering IIS 7.5 Web sites. We concluded this chapter by introducing FTP Publishing Services and setting up FTP Publishing Services for a specified IIS Web site.

Hyper-V feature focus

In this chapter, we will discuss the Hyper-V virtualization role in Windows Server 2008 R2. We will explore Microsoft's approach to server virtualization compared to other vendors. We will also discuss planning and deploying Hyper-V, using Windows Server 2008 R2. This chapter will also cover Hyper-V features such as Live Migration and snapshots and how they can be used in your deployment. We will conclude this chapter with an introduction to Microsoft Virtual Machine Manager (VMM).

INTRODUCTION TO VIRTUALIZATION AND HYPER-V

Virtualization technologies have been around the computing world for years; however, the technology has only become a key component to the ever-growing datacenter in the past few years. In recent years, organizations began noticing that the advancement of server CPUs and memory was outpacing operating systems. Many companies found themselves deploying servers where CPU and memory utilization was less than 20% on a regular basis. This is where server virtualization comes in. Server virtualization is a technology that provides the ability to run multiple, isolated operating systems on a single piece of server hardware allowing a much higher level of resource utilization.

Many IT organizations are finding their datacenters with less available power to deploy new server hardware, more expensive network connections, and increased cost in administering hundreds or thousands of servers. As an IT administrator, you have to face the fact that deploying hardware is not cheap. This has sparked the demand for server virtualization technologies. So much that some organizations choose to make virtual machines (VMs) the first option when deploying new systems. Today you can find server virtualization solutions supporting a wide array of systems in development, quality assurance, and production environments. If you have not considered server virtualization, you may want to take a deeper look. Figure 7.1 depicts how a hypervisor works to host VMs.

Physical Server

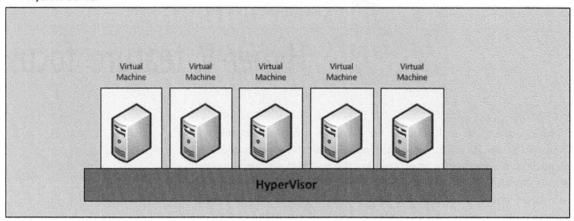

■ **FIGURE 7.1** Server virtualization.

NOTES FROM THE FIELD

Microsoft Hyper-V Server 2008 R2

Microsoft Hyper-V Server 2008 R2 is a free product from Microsoft providing a Hyper-V only version of Windows Server 2008 R2. Hyper-V Server 2008 R2 has all typical Windows features, including the GUI interface, disabled except those required to support Hyper-V in a stand-alone or fail-over cluster configuration.

Microsoft openly expressed that it was committed to being a leader in the server virtualization market with the release of its first true bare-metal type 1 hypervisor in Windows Server 2008 R1. Microsoft further expressed this commitment by evolving Hyper-V by adding new features such as Live Migration with the Windows Server 2008 R2 release. With the addition of new features, and a price tag lower than competitive virtualization technologies, adoption of Hyper-V is seeing a steady increase with each version.

Before deploying Hyper-V, you may find it helpful to understand some of the basics of the hypervisor's architecture. Hyper-V's architecture involves a parent partition that manages the virtualization layer including the VMs running on the server. Hyper-V also installs the device drivers in each guest operating system opposed to the hypervisor. This allows the hypervisor to remain small and optimized for performance. The Hyper-V architecture is depicted in Figure 7.2.

Physical Server

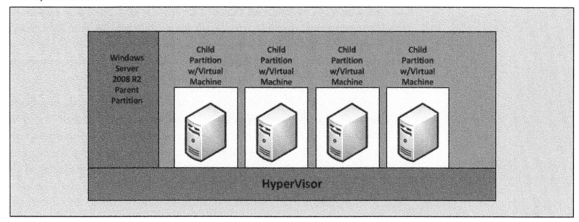

■ **FIGURE 7.2** Hyper-V architecture.

> **NOTES FROM THE FIELD**
>
> **Hyper-V for disaster recovery**
> Many organizations use server virtualization technologies to support their disaster recovery plans. Using Hyper-V allows administrators to quickly and easily bring up new servers on demand. Additionally, VM disks are also stored as VHD files on the host. This allows easy backup of the entire VM.

HYPER-V CHANGES

Windows Server 2008 R2 includes several new enhancements to Hyper-V virtualization services. These enhancements include Live Migration, hot adding and removal of virtual disks, new processor features, and support for jumbo frames on VMs.

Live Migration

Windows Server 2008 R2 includes a much welcomed feature to enhance the process of moving VMs from one Hyper-V host to another. Windows Server 2008 R1 includes a feature known as Quick Migration, which suspends VMs and quickly transfers them to another host. This process does however cause a brief outage to any VMs being moved. When using Quick Migration to move a VM, some applications on that VM may time-out and need to be restarted because of their sensitivity to network or machine disruptions.

Live Migration allows Hyper-V to overcome these limitations when moving VMs by removing the need for them to be temporarily suspended thus removing downtime for applications running on the VMs being moved. Live Migration uses a process to transfer memory pages from the current host to the destination host and then simply transfers ownership of the VM's virtual disks to the destination host.

Live Migration allows administrators to easily, on the fly, add new hosts to a Hyper-V cluster instantly increasing resources needed for VM workloads. Live Migration can also be used to allow administrators to service hosts during normal business hours without impacting on business services and applications. For example, an administrator might want to add additional memory to a Hyper-V host. He could use Live Migration to move any active VMs from the host to another host in the cluster. He could then turn off the host to add additional memory. After adding memory, the administrator could use Live Migration to move the VM workloads back to the host.

Live Migration requires that Hyper-V be deployed on a Windows Server 2008 R2 fail-over cluster. Additionally, Live Migration requires a dedicated network adapter on each Hyper-V host for migration traffic. It is also recommended that processors on all hosts are from the same manufacturer and of the same processor family. This ensures that all processor features can be used.

NOTES FROM THE FIELD

Live Migration and Hyper-V processor compatibility mode

Though it is recommended that all hosts in a Hyper-V cluster have the same processors, Windows Server 2008 R2 Hyper-V includes a new feature known as processor compatibility mode. Processor compatibility mode allows you to include computers with various processor types in a Hyper-V cluster. Processor compatibility mode turns off features of newer processors so that all processors in the cluster use the same features as the processor with the least number of features. This allows you to add older hosts to Hyper-V clusters, but will also cause newer hosts to run with a reduced set of processor features.

Processor enhancements

Windows Server 2008 R2 Hyper-V includes several new processor enhancements including support for 64 processor cores per physical host. Hyper-V can also take advantage of Windows Server 2008 R2 Core

Parking features. Hyper-V moves VM CPU loads to the fewest required number of processor cores, allowing Windows to suspend the cores not being used. As workloads require more CPU resources, the cores are no longer suspended and Hyper-V moves VM workloads to those cores.

Storage enhancements

Windows Server 2008 R2 Hyper-V adds new storage features that allow administrators to easily add and remove VM storage. Hyper-V now allows administrators to add or remove virtual and physical storage hot while the VM is still running. This feature allows administrators to easily reconfigure VM storage without requiring downtime. For example, assume that a production SQL server needs additional storage space for more databases. As the administrator, you can add a new virtual disk drive to store new databases without taking the server offline.

Network enhancements

Hyper-V takes advantage of some of the new networking technologies in Windows Server 2008 R2 including TCP offload, also known as VM Chimney, and jumbo frames. These technologies provide better performance of VMs needing to access data on iSCSI SANs.

PLANNING FOR HYPER-V

Prior to deploying Hyper-V, you will want to ensure that you properly plan for features, licensing, capacity, and installation options. In this section, we will take a look at how to properly plan for Hyper-V in your organization.

Licensing considerations

Hyper-V has several licensing considerations that you need to take into account prior to deployment within your company. As a rule of thumb, you will need an operating system license for each guest VM hosted on the Hyper-V host. There are however several exceptions to this requirement.

- *Windows Server 2008 R2 standard edition*—A standard edition license permits you to run one virtual instance of the operating system on top of the physical operating system. This means that by purchasing one standard edition license, you can install Windows on the physical Hyper-V host, and run one Windows Server 2008 R2 VM on that host without paying additional licensing fees. You will need to purchase a server license for each additional VM with Windows Server 2008 R2 installed.

- *Windows Server 2008 R2 enterprise edition*—Similar to the standard edition, you can purchase one enterprise edition license and install up to four VMs running Windows Server 2008 R2 without purchasing additional licenses.
- *Windows Server 2008 R2 datacenter edition*—A datacenter license allows you to install and run unlimited Windows Server 2008 R2 VMs on the Hyper-V host. It should be noted that unlike standard and enterprise editions, datacenter edition licenses are sold by the processor socket.

The free Hyper-V Server 2008 R2 version does not include any usage rights, meaning that you will need to purchase a license for each VM on that host running Windows.

Hyper-V system requirements and capacity planning

Prior to installing the role, you will need to ensure that your server hardware meets Hyper-V system requirements. Basic requirements are the same as the Windows Server 2008 R2 operating system; however, Hyper-V additionally requires your system to have the following features:

- *Hardware-assisted virtualization*—Both the processor and BIOS must support virtualization. Intel refers to this feature as INTEL VT, while AMD refers to the technology as AMD-V. You will want to ensure that these features are supported and turned on in the system BIOS.
- *Data execution prevention (DEP)*—DEP is a security technology available in most modern systems. You will want to ensure that this is also enabled in the BIOS.

After ensuring that the initial system requirements are met, you will want to properly plan for resource capacity of your Hyper-V hosts. This can be one of the most challenging aspects of planning. VMs require processor, memory, and disk space just like any other server. Your hosts will need to have enough resources to ensure that each VM can use its required resources when necessary. If you have existing physical servers that you plan on virtualizing, it may be helpful to capture performance data for a few weeks prior to moving the server to a VM. By capturing and reviewing performance data, you can better determine how much processing and memory power are required for a given server.

NOTES FROM THE FIELD

Capturing performance data

There are several ways in which you can capture performance data from a server, including using the built-in performance monitor in Windows. However, if you are using System Center Operations Manager (SCOM) 2007 to monitor your server environment, you probably already have that data captured. You can review SCOM reports to see CPU, memory, and disk performance.

If you happen to begin deploying VMs on a host with inadequate resources, you may find yourself in a situation where VMs experience poor performance or will not even start because of lack of capacity. Hyper-V does not support overcommitting memory, which means that if sufficient memory is not available, Hyper-V will not let you start the VM.

NOTES FROM THE FIELD

Virtual machine sprawl

As organizations adopt server virtualization technologies, administrators often find themselves dealing with *virtual machine sprawl*. They find that it is so easy to deploy new VMs they end up deploying VMs for testing, development, and even production that are never used, never documented, and never decommissioned. This proliferation of servers can quickly become a management nightmare. Be sure that you create standard policies and procedures for deploying VMs so that you do not end up with more systems than you can manage.

As you plan for Hyper-V capacity, be sure to leave yourself some room for growth on your Hyper-V hosts. This will ensure that you can easily add new VMs without worrying about insufficient resources.

Planning for features

As part of your Hyper-V planning process, you will need to determine which features you need to support in your deployment. These features will impact on which host operating systems you need to use and what additional hardware may be required. For example, if you want to support Live Migration, you will need to deploy Hyper-V in a fail-over cluster configuration, and this means that you cannot use standard edition as your host operating system (remember from Chapter 2 that standard edition does not support fail-over clustering). Be sure that you verify feature

Table 7.1 Hyper-V Versions and Features Supported

Server Edition	Features Supported
Hyper-V Server 2008 R2	Failover Clustering, Live Migration, 1 TB of memory, eight processors
Windows Server 2008 R2 standard	GUI interface, ability to host additional server roles
Windows Server 2008 R2 enterprise	Failover Clustering, Live Migration, 2 TB of memory, eight processors, GUI interface, ability to host additional server roles
Windows Server 2008 R2 datacenter	Failover Clustering, Live Migration, 2 TB of memory, 64 processors, GUI interface, ability to host additional server roles

requirements before deploying your Hyper-V hosts. Select the Hyper-V version that best meets your needs. Table 7.1 lists some of the key features of Hyper-V and the operating system version required to support them.

INSTALLING AND ADMINISTERING HYPER-V

Now that you have an understanding of how to plan your Hyper-V deployment, let us install and setup the Hyper-V role. To install Hyper-V, perform the following:

1. Open *Server Manager* and select the *Roles* node. Then click the link *Add Roles* in the middle pane. This will launch the Add Roles Wizard. Click *Next* to continue.
2. Select the *Hyper-V* role as seen in Figure 7.3. Then click *Next*.
3. Click *Next* on the Hyper-V summary page.
4. Select a network adapter to use for the first virtual network (see Figure 7.4). Virtual networks provide networking services to VMs. We will discuss virtual networks in more detail later in this chapter. After selecting the adapter to use for the virtual network. Click *Next*.
5. Verify that the Hyper-V role is shown on the summary page. Then click *Install*.
6. When the installation is complete, you should see a success notification page. A warning message should be displayed informing you that the server needs to reboot to complete the installation. Click *Close*. When prompted to restart (see Figure 7.5) click *Yes*.
7. After the server reboots, logon to Windows. The Resume Configuration Wizard should finish the installation of Hyper-V (see Figure 7.6). Click *Close* when the wizard is complete.

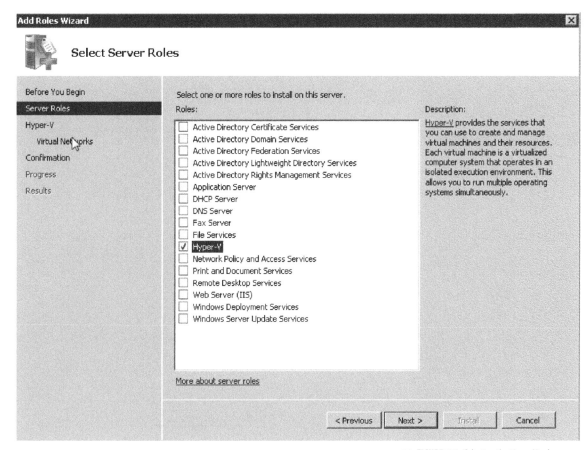

The Hyper-V role is now added to the server and can be accessed via Server Manager. Using Server Manager, you can manage your Hyper-V deployment and update settings.

Administering virtual networks

At some point, you may need to add additional virtual networks or make changes to existing networks. As mentioned earlier, virtual networks provide networking services to VMs. Hyper-V supports the following virtual network types in which VMs can connect:

- *External*—An external virtual network uses the physical computer's network adapter to bridge the virtual network with the physical network. This gives VMs network access just as if they were a physical computer plugged into a network switch.

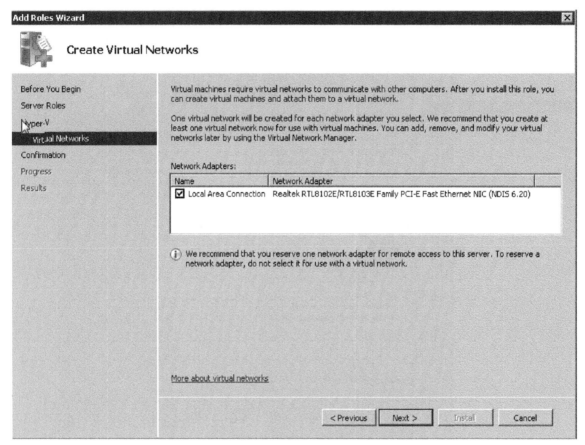

■ FIGURE 7.4 Selecting a virtual machine network.

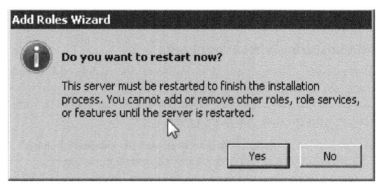

■ FIGURE 7.5 Hyper-V reboot prompt.

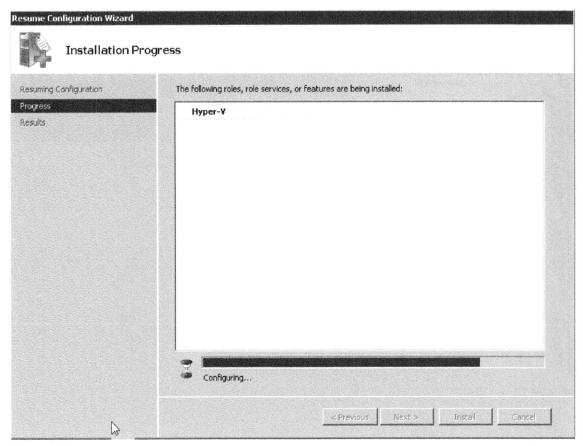

- *Internal*—An internal virtual network isolates VMs so that they can only talk to other VMs on the Hyper-V server, and the Hyper-V server itself. Using this setting prevents VMs from communicating with the physical network.
- *Private*—A private virtual network isolates the VMs so that they can only communicate with each other. Using this network prevents them from communicating with the Hyper-V host or physical network.

You can manage virtual network settings by performing the following:

1. Open *Server Manager* and select the node *Roles | Hyper-V | Hyper-V Manager | <YourServerName>*.
2. Right click the server name (see Figure 7.7) and choose the *Virtual Network Manager* option.

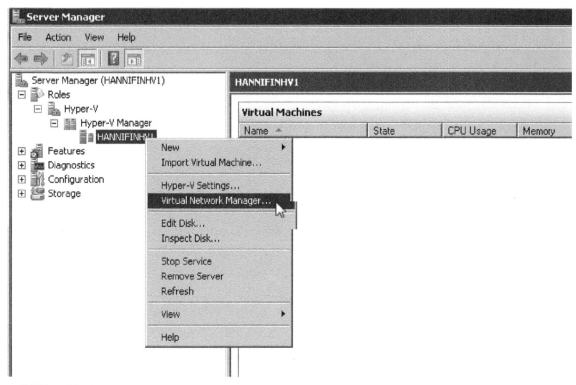

■ **FIGURE 7.7** Hyper-V manager.

3. The *Virtual Network Manager* window will open (see Figure 7.8). Here you can add or remove virtual networks as well as make configuration changes to existing ones.

You can use Virtual Network Manager, as seen in Figure 7.9, to configure the following settings for existing virtual networks:

■ *Name and notes*—You can enter a meaningful name and notes related to the Virtual Network connection. The virtual network name should be something that helps you easily identify that particular network.

■ *Connection type*—Here you can change the connection type to any of the three supported network types.

■ *Enable VLAN identification*—If you use VLAN tagging on your network, you can have Hyper-V's virtual network tag traffic so it knows which VLAN it should be part of.

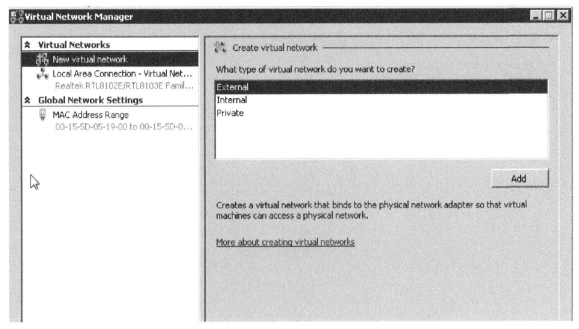

■ **FIGURE 7.8** Virtual network manager.

NOTES FROM THE FIELD

Virtual Network MAC address range

You can use Virtual Network Manager to manage the range of MAC addresses that Hyper-V will assign to VMs. In most cases, you will not need to change this range. If you do however change the range of hardware addresses, be sure that they do not conflict with existing MACs on your network.

Administering Hyper-V host settings

In addition to managing network settings, you may want to change some of the host configuration settings. You can access the Hyper-V settings by performing the following:

1. Open *Server Manager* and select the node *Roles | Hyper-V | Hyper-V Manager | <your hyper-v server name>*.
2. Right click the server name and select the *Hyper-V Settings* option as seen in Figure 7.10.

The Hyper-V settings window will open (see Figure 7.11). Here, you can change the following settings as necessary:

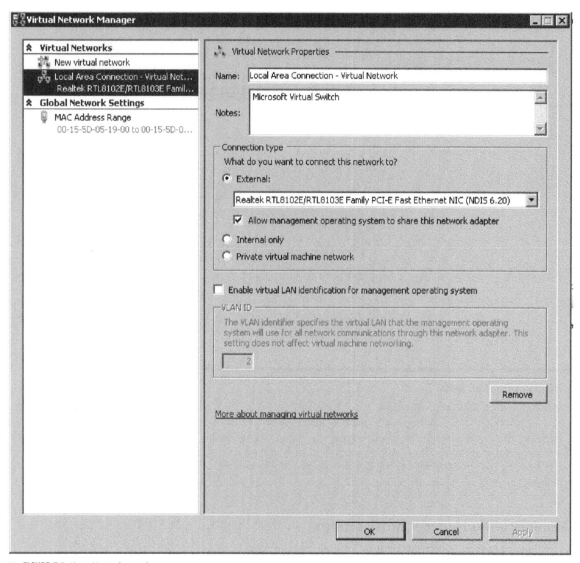

- *Virtual hard disks*—You can change the default directory where virtual disk drives are stored. These are the VHD files where all the data for a VM are stored.
- *Virtual machines*—You can change the default directory where the VM configuration file is stored. This file is used to host all the configuration data related to a VM.

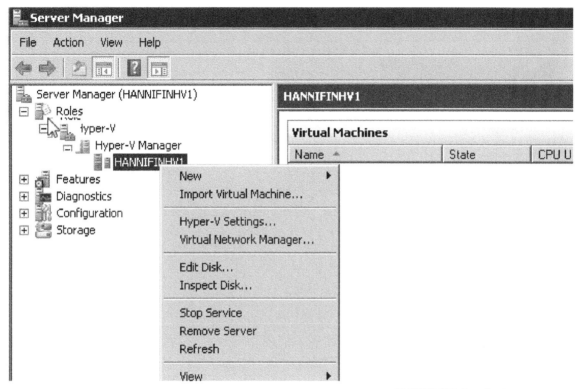

■ **FIGURE 7.10** Hyper-V settings.

■ *Keyboard*—You can use the Keyboard setting to select whether special keyboard combinations will be sent to the VM or the physical host.

■ *Mouse Release Key*—You can use the Mouse Release Key setting to change the key combination that will release the mouse from the active VM window. The use of this combination is necessary only when the VM integration tools are not installed.

■ *User credentials*—This setting allows you to configure Hyper-V to pass the current users credentials to the VM when attempting to access the computer through the Hyper-V Manager console.

■ *Delete saved credentials*—If a set of credentials have been saved when accessing a VM, you can delete the saved credentials from this setting.

■ *Reset check boxes*—Many of Hyper-V's notification dialogs give the administrator the option to never see the notification again. By resetting check boxes, all notification dialogs will be enabled.

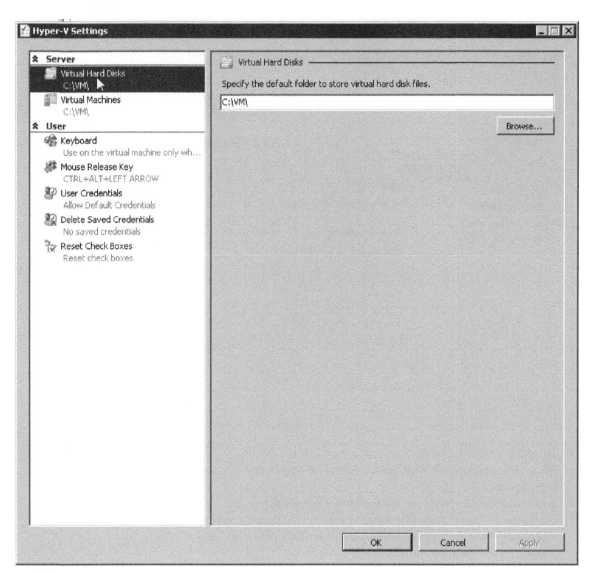

■ **FIGURE 7.11** Hyper-V settings.

CREATING AND ADMINISTERING HYPER-V VIRTUAL MACHINES

In this section, we will discuss creating and managing VMs deployed to a Hyper-V server. This involves creating a new VM, configuring VM settings, and installing an operating system.

Virtual machine files

Before creating new VMs, you will want to have a basic understanding of what makes up a VM on the Hyper-V host. The following are the basic files used by a VM:

- *Virtual machine configuration file*—The VM configuration file is an XML file that stores all the configuration information related to the VM. This file contains information such as amount of memory used, CPU configuration, virtual disk drive configuration, and the virtual network used by the VM.
- *Virtual machine disks (VHD)*—The VHD files make up the actual disk drives used by the VM. All the data, including the operating system and applications, are stored within the VHD files.
- *Snapshot files*—When you take a snapshot of a VM, snapshot files are used to track all changes to the VM. This gives you the ability to roll back to the point where the snapshot was taken.

Virtual machine disk types

When creating new virtual disks for VMs, you will be asked to choose a disk type. The three different VM disk types are:

- *Fixed size*—Fixed-sized disks allocate all space required for the disk upon creation. This means that a 40 GB VHD will use 40 GB of physical disk space from the start. This option should be used when the disk will be used with a VM running applications with heavy disk I/O. Fixed size provides the best performance.
- *Dynamically expanding*—Dynamically expanding disks allocate only a small portion of the maximum disk size upon creation. As more virtual disk space is used, the disk drive will expand in increments. For example, you may create a dynamically expanding disk with a maximum size of 120 GB. Upon creation, you will notice that the VHD consumes only a small amount of physical disk space (less than 1 GB). As data are added to the dynamic disk, the disk will expand as needed until the max disk size is reached. The dynamic expansion uses much less disk space initially but does not perform as well as Fixed-size disks because of the resources required to expand as data are added.
- *Differencing*—A Differencing disk is based upon a parent Fixed of Dynamic disk. The differencing disk keeps track of differences made to a disk so that changes can easily be reversed.

Creating and configuring a virtual machine

In this section, we will look at the process of creating and managing VMs. We will be using the Hyper-V Manager from within Server Manager to perform all administrative functions. To create a new VM, perform the following:

1. Open *Server Manager* and select the node *Roles | Hyper-V | Hyper-V Manager | <your hyper-v server name>*.
2. Right click the server name and select the option *New | Virtual Machine* as seen in Figure 7.12. This will launch the New Virtual Machine Wizard. Click *Next* to begin.
3. The first step is to enter a name for the server (see Figure 7.13). This is how the VM will be displayed within Hyper-V Manager. If you want to change the default location to store the VM configuration files, you can do that here. Then click *Next*.
4. Enter the amount of memory you want to allocate to the VM (see Figure 7.14). You will want to ensure that you give the VM enough memory to support the guest operating system and applications

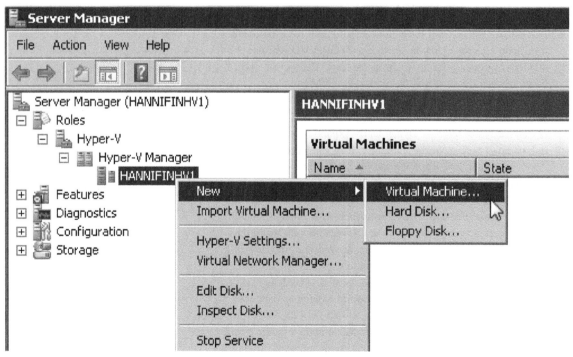

■ **FIGURE 7.12** Create a new virtual machine.

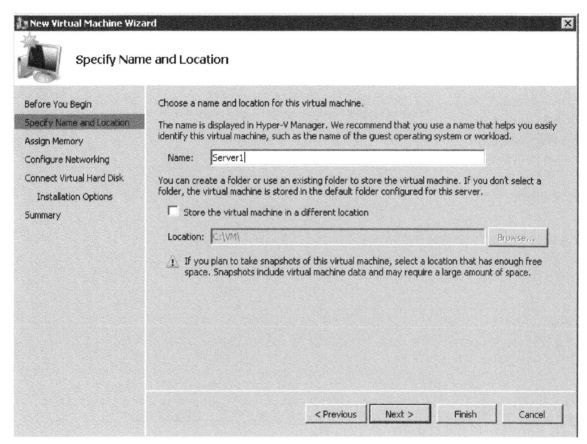

running within the VM. When the VM is started, that amount of memory will be unavailable to other VMs and applications running on the Hyper-V host. After the VM is turned off, that memory will become usable memory by the host operating system. After selecting the amount of memory to dedicate to the VM, click *Next*.

5. Select the virtual network that you want the VM to be connected to (see Figure 7.15). Then click *Next*.

6. Select whether you want to connect an existing VHD disk drive to the VM or create a new disk drive (see Figure 7.16). If you have an existing VHD, you can connect it here; otherwise, choose the option to *Create a new virtual disk drive*. Select the maximum size for the disk drive, and then click *Next*. By default, a new disk selected here will be dynamic.

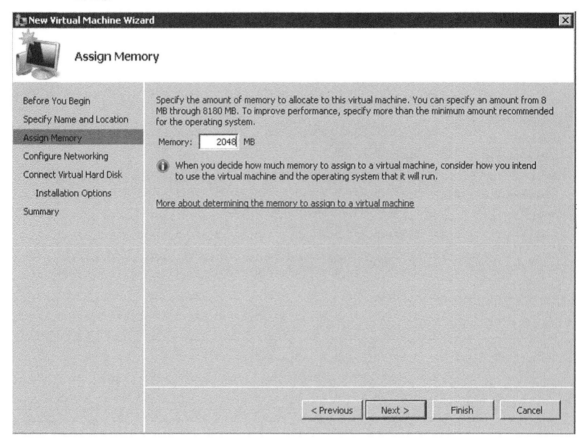

Specify the amount of memory to allocate to this virtual machine. You can specify an amount from 8 MB through 8180 MB. To improve performance, specify more than the minimum amount recommended for the operating system.

Memory: 2048 MB

ⓘ When you decide how much memory to assign to a virtual machine, consider how you intend to use the virtual machine and the operating system that it will run.

More about determining the memory to assign to a virtual machine

■ **FIGURE 7.14** Configure virtual machine memory.

7. Now select how you want to install the guest operating system. Choose one of the following options:

   ❑ *Install an operating system later*—Selecting this option will configure the VM to not configure boot options and allow you to manually install an operating system. Select this option if you are not sure how you plan to install the OS.

   ❑ *Install an operating system from a boot CD/DVD ROM*—Selecting this option will configure the VM to boot off of a CD or DVD in the host computer's optical drive, or from an ISO file located on the host computer. This will allow you to install an operating system from the CD/DVD media provided by the manufacturer or an ISO image downloaded to the host computer.

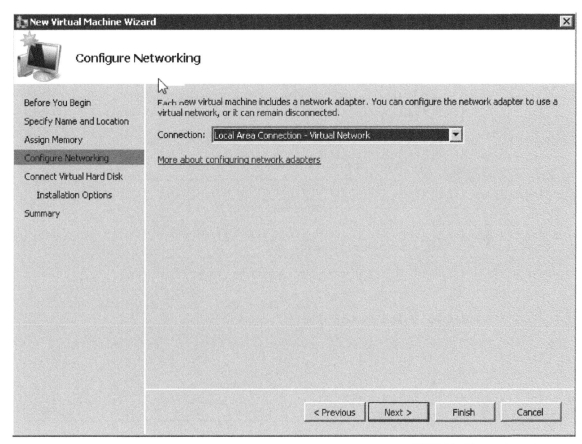

■ **FIGURE 7.15** Select virtual network.

- ❑ *Install an operating system from a boot floppy disk*—Selecting this option will configure the VM to boot off of a virtual floppy disk saved in a file on the host computer.
- ❑ *Install an operating system from a network-based installation server*—Selecting this option will configure the VM to PXE boot from the network allowing you to install the operating system via a network-based install.

After selecting how you want to install the operating system click *Next*.

8. Verify the VM settings and click *Finish* to create the VM.

The VM will be created and can be accessed from the Hyper-V host within Hyper-V Manager as seen in Figure 7.17.

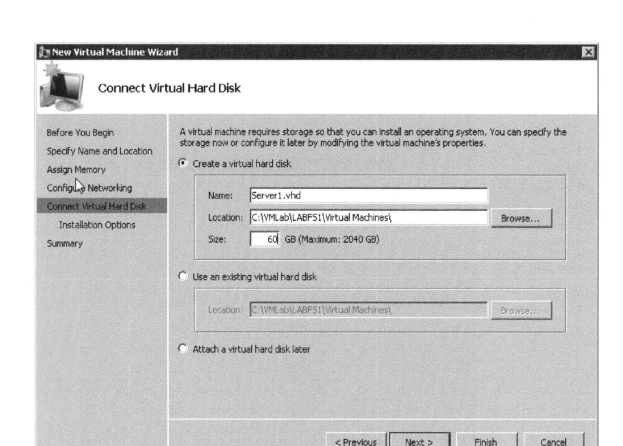

■ **FIGURE 7.16** Configure virtual disk drive options.

Supported virtual machine operating systems

Prior to installing a guest operating system on a VM, you should be aware of those that are supported. Hyper-V supports the following guest operating systems:

- Windows Server 2008 R2
- Windows Server 2008 ($\times$86 and $\times$64)
- Windows Server 2003 R2 ($\times$86 and $\times$64)
- Windows Server 2003 ($\times$86 and $\times$64)
- Windows 2000 Server
- Windows 7 ($\times$86 and $\times$64)
- Windows Vista ($\times$86 and $\times$64)
- Windows XP ($\times$86 and $\times$64)

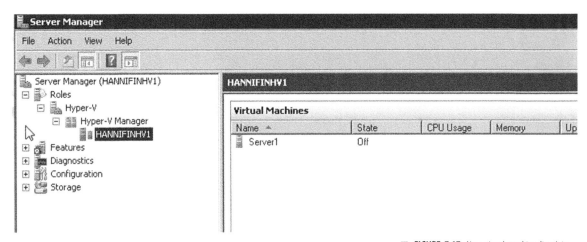

■ **FIGURE** 7.17 New virtual machine listed in Hyper-V manager.

- SuSE Linux Enterprise Server 10
- SuSE Linux Enterprise Server 11
- RedHat Enterprise Linux 5.2
- Redhat Enterprise Linux 5.3

NOTES FROM THE FIELD

Hyper-V unsupported operating systems

That an operating system is not supported by Hyper-V does not mean that it will not run on a Hyper-V VM. Supported guest operating systems are those that have been verified by Microsoft to function properly on Hyper-V and have configurations officially supported by Microsoft professional support services.

Installing the guest operating system

If you have selected an installation option when creating a VM, then you can begin the operating system installation process simply by powering on the VM. To start the VM, locate the server within Hyper-V Manager. Right click the VM and select *Start* (see Figure 7.18).

After starting the VM, you can open the console by double-clicking the VM within Hyper-V Server Manager. This will allow you to see the VM boot. After the VM boots from the installation media, you can begin the operating system installation process just like a physical computer (see Figure 7.19).

After installing the guest operating system, you will want to install the Hyper-V integration services. Integration services provide a way for

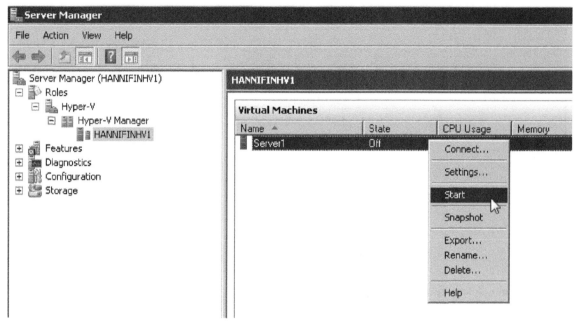

■ **FIGURE 7.18** Starting a virtual machine.

the VM to communicate with this Hyper-V host, allowing the VM to synchronize with the host, providing the host with the ability to interact with VM VSS Services, providing heartbeat capabilities between the Hyper-V host and the VM, and allowing the host to send a clean shutdown command to the VM. Additionally the integration services installation will install enhanced network adapter, display, and mouse drivers on some operating systems. To install integration services, perform the following:

1. When the guest operating system installation is complete, logon to the VM.
2. From the Virtual Machine Connection window, select the menu option *Action | Insert Integration Services Setup Disk* (see Figure 7.20).

NOTES FROM THE FIELD

Windows Server 2008 R2 and integration services

Windows Server 2008 R2 guest VMs will already have the integration services installed as part of the operating system. You will not need to install the integration services a second time.

---

3. Complete the setup wizard to install integration servers and reboot when prompted.

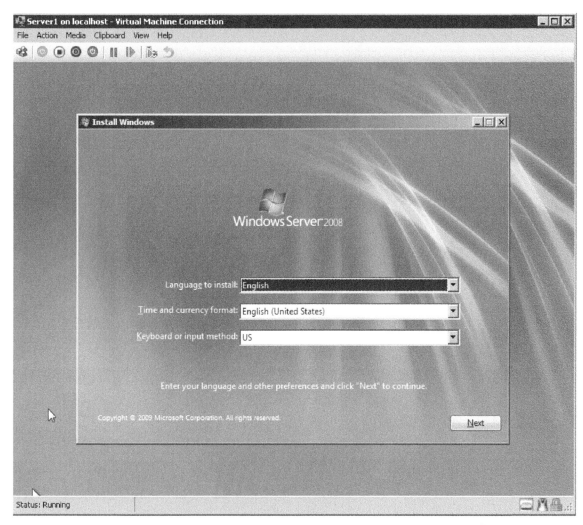

■ **FIGURE 7.19** Installing guest operating system.

Updating virtual machine settings

After creating a VM, you may, at some point, want to modify settings. For example, you may need to add additional memory or processors to support a new application being installed on the VM. VM settings can be accessed by performing the following:

1. Right click on the VM within Hyper-V Manager and select *Settings* (see Figure 7.21).
2. The VM settings window will open as seen in Figure 7.22. Here you can modify the various configuration options for the VM.

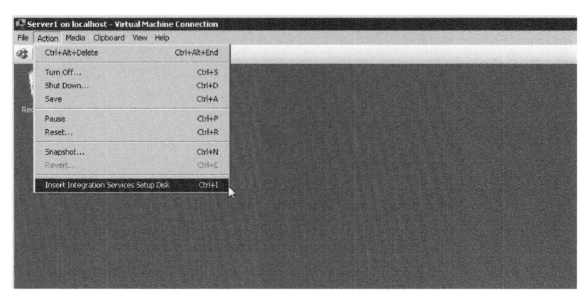

■ FIGURE 7.20 Insert integration services setup disk.

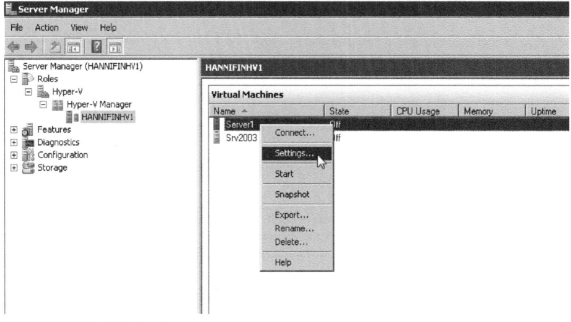

■ FIGURE 7.21 Opening virtual machine settings.

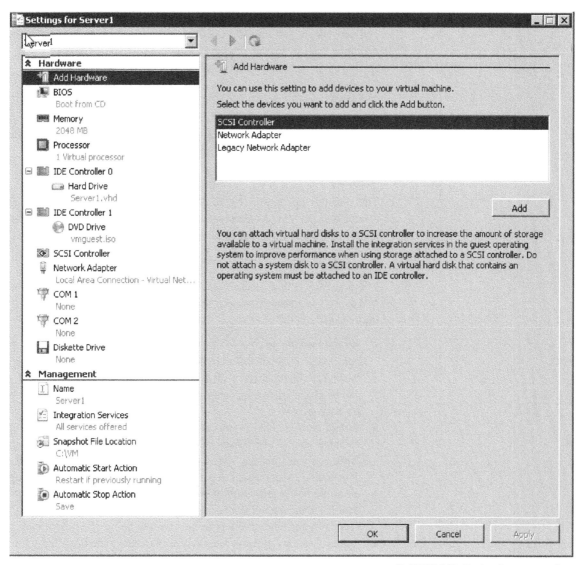

■ **FIGURE 7.22** Virtual machine settings window.

The following options can be configured for a VM.

Add hardware

The Add Hardware option can be used to add new hardware to the VM. Using the Add Hardware option, you can add SCSI controllers for additional disk drives, additional network adapters, or a legacy network adapter to support a network-based installation of operating systems, general network support for older operating systems, and network support for operating systems that do not have integration services installed.

BIOS

The BIOS option can be used to set boot order of VM devices. Typically this setting is used to boot from the correct location when installing a guest operating system. For example, if you are installing the OS from a CD, you should select the CD as the first boot device.

Memory

The memory option can be used to increase the amount of memory allocated to the VM. As mentioned previously, you may need to increase memory to support new applications or increased workloads on the VM.

Processor

The processor option can be used to add or remove processors from the VM as well as manage processor resources. You can configure the following resource options:

- *Virtual machine reserve*—This setting reserves the specified percentage of resources to this VM. This will ensure that the specified percentage of resources is always available to the VM. This setting can be useful when you want to guarantee that resources are available for a given VM.
- *Virtual machine limit*—You can use this setting to limit the processor resources that can be consumed by this VM. For example, by entering 20%, you will limit the VM to using only 20% of the physical CPU. This setting is very useful to prevent a rogue machine from consuming all of the host's processing power. This setting can be used to ensure that development and test servers do not interfere with production servers by maxing out the processors on the host.
- *Relative weight*—Relative weight is used to determine this VMs importance related to other VMs on the host. In the event of two machines requesting processing, the one with the higher weight is given priority over the other. You can use this setting to ensure that mission critical VMs are given a processor priority higher than that of other VMs.

IDE disk controllers

Each VM is configured with two IDE disk controllers. The operating system must be installed on a disk drive attached to an IDE controller. You can select the IDE controllers to add additional disk drives and DVD drives.

SCSI controllers

SCSI controllers can be used to add disk drives that do not contain the operating system. For best performance, SCSI controllers should be used for secondary storage when the integration services are not installed. However, when the integration services are installed, SCSI or IDE controllers can be used.

NOTES FROM THE FIELD

Hot-add disk drives

Windows Server 2008 R2 Hyper-V allows administrators to add or remove disk drives to VMs without turning off the VM. Only SCSI controllers support hot-add and remove features. You cannot hot-add or remove a disk drive to or from an IDE controller.

Network adapters

You can select any listed network adapter to configure the settings for that adapter. These include MAC address, VLAN tagging, and which virtual network the adapter is connected to.

Comm Ports

Each VM includes the option to connect to physical Com Ports via a named pipe connection. This setting can be useful if you need to give the VM access to Com Port options such as modems.

Diskette Drive

The Diskette Drive option can be used to give the VM access to a virtual floppy image. This can be used to install some operating systems or load drivers that might be available on a virtual floppy disk file.

Name

You can use the Name setting to rename the label for the VM. Note that this does not change the computer name within the operating system. This option only changes the label for how the machine is referenced within Hyper-V Manager.

Integration services

The Integration Services setting allows you to disable or enable individual services offered by Integration Services. For example, you can use this setting to disable synchronization between the VM and the Hyper-V host.

Snapshot file location

This setting allows you to change the path to where snapshot files are stored for this VM. You may want to change this if you need additional disk space for snapshots that is not available using the default path.

Automatic start and stop actions

These settings allow you to configure how you want the VM to act when the physical host boots or shuts down. For example, you can use this setting to configure the VM to perform a clean shut down every time a shutdown command is sent to the physical host.

HIGH AVAILABILITY, LIVE MIGRATION, AND SNAPSHOTS

Windows Server 2008 R2 fail-over clustering options can be used to provide high availability services to a Hyper-V host. By creating a fail-over cluster, you can ensure that all VMs running on a Hyper-V host remain online in the event a host failure. Fail-over clustering is also a requirement for Live Migration.

Live Migration

Windows Server 2008 R2 includes a much welcomed feature to enhance the process of moving VMs from one Hyper-V host to another. Windows Server 2008 R1 included a feature known as Quick Migration, which suspended VMs and quickly transferred them to another host. This process did however cause a brief outage to any VMs being moved. When using Quick Migration to move a VM, some applications on that VM might time-out and need to be restarted because of their sensitivity to network or machine disruptions.

Live Migration allows Hyper-V to overcome the limitations found in Quick Migration when moving VMs by removing the need for them to be temporarily suspended. This removes the requirement for brief downtime for applications running on the VMs being moved. Live Migration uses a process to transfer memory pages from the current host to the destination host and then simply transfers ownership of the VM's virtual disks to the destination host. The Live Migration process is depicted in Figure 7.23.

Live Migration allows administrators to easily, on the fly, add new hosts to a Hyper-V cluster instantly increasing resources used by VM workloads. Live Migration can also be used to allow administrators to

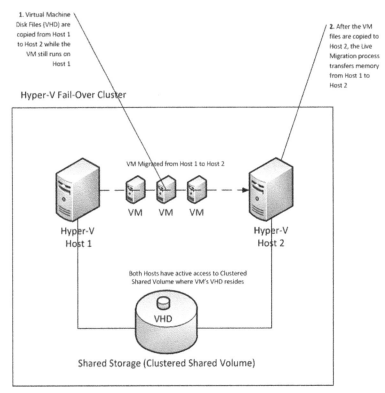

1. Virtual Machine Disk Files (VHD) are copied from Host 1 to Host 2 while the VM still runs on Host 1

2. After the VM files are copied to Host 2, the Live Migration process transfers memory from Host 1 to Host 2

Hyper-V Fail-Over Cluster

VM Migrated from Host 1 to Host 2

VM   VM   VM

Hyper-V
Host 1

Hyper-V
Host 2

Both Hosts have active access to Clustered
Shared Volume where VM's VHD resides

VHD

Shared Storage (Clustered Shared Volume)

■ **FIGURE 7.23** Hyper-V Live Migration process.

service hosts during normal business hours without impacting on business services and applications. For example, an administrator might want to add additional memory to a Hyper-V host. He could use Live Migration to move any active VMs from the host to another host in the cluster. He could then turn off the host to add additional memory. After adding memory, the administrator could use Live Migration to move the VM workloads back to the host.

Configuring Hyper-V to support Live Migration

Live Migration requires that Hyper-V be deployed on a Windows Server 2008 R2 fail-over cluster. Additionally, Live Migration requires a dedicated network adapter on each Hyper-V host for migration traffic. It is also recommended that processors on all hosts are from the same manufacturer and of the same processor family. This ensures that all processor features can be used.

NOTES FROM THE FIELD

Live Migration and Hyper-V processor compatibility mode

Though it is recommended that all hosts in a Hyper-V cluster have the same processors, Windows Server 2008 R2 Hyper-V includes a new feature known as processor compatibility mode. Processor compatibility mode allows you to include computers with various processor types in a Hyper-V cluster. Processor compatibility mode turns off features of newer processors so that all processors in the cluster use the same features as the processor with the least number of features. This allows you to add older hosts to Hyper-V clusters, but will also cause newer hosts to run with a reduced set of processor features.

We will now go through the process of setting up Hyper-V to support Live Migration. We will assume that Hyper-V is already set up on a Windows Server 2008 R2 fail-over cluster. The actual process of setting up a fail-over cluster is covered in Chapter 9. Perform the following exercise to complete setup and configure a Hyper-V cluster with Live Migration capabilities.

Snapshots

Snapshots allow an administrator to create a point-in-time capture of a VM. This includes the configuration, power, and disk states of the VM. Snapshots are very valuable in several situations such as development and test environments. For example, a developer could create a snapshot of a test VM prior to installing a newly developed application. After creating the snapshot, the developer could install the application and verify the process. To perform the same process, the developer could simply revert to the snapshot instead of uninstalling the application. By reverting the snapshot the machine will be returned to the exact state that it was in at the time the snapshot was taken. Snapshots can also be used prior to performing a "risky" procedure to a VM. For example, you could take a snapshot prior to installing a new service pack. If the service pack installation failed or had adverse effects, the machine could be reverted to the state prior to installing the hotfix.

BEST PRACTICES

Best practices for snapshots of production servers

Creating snapshots of servers causes a decrease in server performance. For this reason, you should only snapshot production servers during off peak hours or a maintenance period. You do not want to run a production workload on a snapshotted VM for an extended period of time. If a snapshot remains for an extended period of time, it can grow to a level that may require several hours to remove. This is because removing a snapshot forces all the changes to be committed back to the original disk behind the scenes. Additionally reverting back to a snapshot may cause unwanted effects such as the VM losing connectivity with the domain. This is because computer accounts change their Active Directory password on a regular basis. If the password has been changed and the machine has been reverted back to a previous snapshot, it will also revert the password to the one that was used at the time the snapshot was taken creating a mismatch between the computer and the computer account in Active Directory.

Microsoft does not recommend taking snapshots of Active Directory domain controllers. Reverting to a previous snapshot of a DC could cause unwanted effects on your domain and could possibly cause versioning issues with the Active Directory database.

INTRODUCTION TO SYSTEM CENTER VIRTUAL MACHINE MANAGER 2008 R2

If you are responsible for a medium-sized to a large virtualized enterprise, then at some point you will likely realize that the management of multiple virtual host machines can be very cumbersome and time-consuming when using the standard console for each machine. VMM simplifies their management by consolidating everything you need into one console. In fact, you can manage your Hyper-V, Virtual Server, and even VMware ESX hosts all via VMM.

If you are already using SCOM, you can use the data it collects via its monitoring capabilities to further advantage. Performance and Resource Optimization (PRO) leverages it and recommends actions to be taken to improve the performance of your VMs. You can even configure it to automatically make certain adjustments on your behalf in order to maintain the level of performance your customers require.

VMM not only consolidates the functionality built into Hyper-V but also adds to it. With VMM performing, physical-to-virtual (P2V) migrations is greatly simplified and can be done without service interruption. VMM will also convert your VMware machines to VHDs, using a similar technique called virtual-to-virtual transfers.

For development and testing environments, VMM provides a self-service Web portal you can configure to delegate VM provisioning while maintaining management control of the VMs.

By implementing a centralized library for the storage VM components, you can leverage these building blocks to quickly stand up new VMs as demand dictates.

You can also create scripts to increase your level of automation, because VMM is built on Windows PowerShell. The various wizards included in VMM are typically just a pretty interface to generate a PowerShell script. VMM provides the functionality to view the code behind these scripts to help expand your knowledge of the scripting language.

While this chapter can provide you only with a high-level synopsis of what VMM can do to help you with managing your enterprise, it will help to illustrate how easy it can be to leverage and exploit to your advantage.

System requirements for system center virtual machine manager

Before designing your VMM architecture, you should decide whether you want to implement VMM on a single server or share the load of VMM's multiple components across separate servers. As a rule of thumb, if you need to support twenty or fewer VM hosts, you can use a smaller single processor server. If you suspect that you will eventually have a greater number, up to 150 or more servers, then consider a multiple processor server. If you will be supporting groups of VM hosts in diverse locations, you might want to use a multiple-server approach. For a complete list of hardware requirements and software prerequisites for either deployment option, visit the TechNet Web site at http://www.microsoft.com/systemcenter/virtualmachinemanager/en/us/system-requirements.aspx#Server.

SUMMARY

In this chapter, we covered a brief introduction to server virtualization technology and the new features in Windows Server 2008 R2 Hyper-V. We then discussed planning for a Hyper-V deployment. This chapter also covered the various aspects of planning for a Hyper-V deployment. We then explored installing and configuring the Hyper-V role. We next discussed creating and configuring VMs and installing a guest operating system. We concluded this chapter with an overview of Live Migration and snapshots as well as an introduction to System Center Virtual Machine Manager.

Windows Server 2008 R2 Remote Desktop Services

In this chapter, we will explore Windows Server 2008 R2 Remote Desktop Services, formerly known as Terminal Services. This chapter will cover the new features in Remote Desktop Services, including the new names for services. We will also review planning for a Remote Desktop Services deployment. We will then cover the process of installing and configuring the various roles that make up Remote Desktop Services.

OVERVIEW OF REMOTE DESKTOP SERVICES

Remote Desktop Services is another key component of Microsoft's virtualization strategy. While Hyper-V delivers server virtualization, Remote Desktop Services delivers presentation virtualization and virtual desktop infrastructure (VDI) technologies. Remote Desktop Services provides server-hosted access to Windows-based applications and desktops. This removes the need for applications to be installed and run locally on individual workstations. Remote Desktop Services allows organizations to centrally manage and control access to applications as well as allows access from low-end PCs or thin clients.

Remote Desktop Services, which was first introduced as Terminal Services in Windows NT 4.0, allows organizations to provide better management of applications and access in unique situations where a user might not have access to a corporate PC. For example, many organizations, such as hospitals, may deploy thin clients in patient rooms. These machines are light weight, inexpensive, and easy to maintain. Remote Desktop Services can provide doctors and nurses with access to important applications or even fully featured Windows-based desktops from these thin clients. Since all the application processing is done centrally on a server, the thin clients need very little resources to provide adequate computing power to the end user. There are several situations where Terminal Services make sense such as providing access to applications from branch offices with slow connectivity, or give users secure access to corporate applications from their home PCs. The rest of this chapter will provide you with guidance so that you can determine how Remote Desktop Services would best fit into your organization.

WHAT IS NEW IN REMOTE DESKTOP SERVICES

With the release of Windows Server 2008 R2, Terminal Services has been renamed Remote Desktop Services. If you have experience administering Terminal Server in previous operating systems, you should be aware of the new Windows Server 2008 R2 names of various Terminal Server technologies. Table 8.1 lists the old versus new name for common Remote Desktop Services and admin tools.

Along with a new name, Microsoft has also added several new features to further enhance Remote Desktop Services. In this section we will explore some of the feature changes to the various components of Remote Desktop Services.

Remote Desktop Session Host

The Remote Desktop Session Host role includes several new features to provide a better administration experience as well as increased security for Remote Desktop Services deployments. Changes to Remote Desktop Session Host include:

- *Client experience configuration*—You can now centrally manage Remote Desktop audio/video redirection and Windows Aero

Table 8.1 Remote Desktop Services Name Changes

Windows Server 2008 and Prior Name	Windows Server 2008 R2 Name
Terminal Services	Remote Desktop Services
Terminal Services Manager	Remote Desktop Services Manager
Terminal Server	Remote Desktop Session Host
Terminal Services Configuration	Remote Desktop Session Host Configuration
Terminal Services Licensing	Remote Desktop Licensing
Terminal Services Licensing Manager	Remote Desktop Licensing Manager
Terminal Services Gateway	Remote Desktop Gateway
Terminal Services Gateway Manager	Remote Desktop Gateway Manager
Terminal Services Session Broker	Remote Desktop Connection Broker
Terminal Services RemoteApp Manager	RemoteApp Manager
Terminal Services Web Access	Remote Desktop Web Access

interface options for Remote Desktop clients. These client experience features can be configured when adding the Remote Desktop Session Host role.

- *Roaming user profile cache management*—Larger Remote Desktop Services deployments may have hundreds or even thousands of users logging into Remote Desktop Servers. It is common to see cached copies of profiles using a lot of storage space on Remote Desktop Servers. To help control the disk space usage of cached profiles, a GPO can be applied to Remote Desktop Servers placing a quota on the amount of disk space that can be used by cached profiles. If the quota is reached, the server will delete profiles of users with the oldest last logon until the profile cache falls below the quota.

- *Remote Desktop IP Virtualization*—Remote Desktop IP Virtualization allows administrators to create a pool of IP addresses allowing each Remote Desktop Session to have a unique IP address. This feature is useful for applications that may require each instance to have a unique IP or when troubleshooting and you need to track the IP of a particular session on a Remote Desktop Server.

- *Enhanced CPU scheduling*—Remote Desktop Services now includes a processor scheduling feature known as Fair Share Scheduling. This feature distributes CPU resources evenly across each Remote Desktop Session, ensuring that one user session does not impact on the performance of another user's session. This scheduling is done automatically by the Remote Desktop Server and does not require configuration.

Remote Desktop Virtualization Host

The Remote Desktop Virtualization Host is a new role included in Windows Server 2008 R2 Remote Desktop Services and provides a fully featured VDI solution for Windows. Remote Desktop Virtualization Host allows administrators to set up pools of Hyper-V virtual machines that can be logged onto by users. Users can be assigned unique machines or assigned the next available machine in the pool. This gives users fully featured desktop computers accessible via a remote connection.

RemoteApp and Desktop Connection

Windows Server 2008 R2 further extends the features of RemoteApp to VDI-based virtual desktops. Windows Server 2008 R1 allows administrators to use RemoteApp to make access to Terminal Services-based applications seamless to end users. Users can launch an application shortcut from their local computer or terminal, and that application appears to launch locally instead of displaying a Remote Desktop Session to the Terminal Server.

Windows Server 2008 R2 in conjunction with Windows 7 publishes available RemoteApp applications and Desktop Virtualization Host-based VMs to the Start Menu of Windows 7 clients. This allows end users to easily access applications and virtual desktops they have access to by simply opening them from the Start Menu on their local computer.

Remote Desktop Connection Broker

The Remote Desktop Connection Broker in Windows Server 2008 R2 now extends the broker capabilities to virtual desktops in a Remote Desktop Virtualization Host. As with the previous versions of the sessions broker, the Remote Desktop Connection Broker provides load balancing and ensures users reconnect to existing sessions after a disconnect. The Remote Desktop Connection Broker connects users to the new RemoteApp and Desktop Connection feature.

Remote Desktop Gateway

The Remote Desktop Gateway feature includes several new enhancements over the previous Terminal Services Gateway. The new Remote Desktop Gateway includes the following new features:

- Gateway level idle and session timeouts
- Logon and system messages
- Pluggable authentication
- Network access protection (NAP) remediation

Gateway level idle and session timeouts

This feature allows administrators to configure idle and session timeouts on the gateway itself. By setting these timeouts, administrators can ensure that unused sessions are disconnected and active users are forced to periodically reconnect.

Logon and system messages

Administrators can now configure special message windows to be displayed to users when connecting to a Remote Desktop Services Gateway. System messages can be used to provide active users with important notifications such as information regarding system outages. The logon message can be used to provide users with important notifications every time they logon. These can be useful to advertise new applications or services available via the gateway.

Pluggable authentication

Pluggable authentication allows developers to write custom authentication modules for Remote Desktop Gateways. This can be used to further enhance Remote Desktop Gateway services by providing such features as Two-Token authentication.

Network access protection remediation

NAP remediation features allow computers connecting via a Remote Desktop Gateway to remediate any noncompliant security settings prior to connecting to the network. This ensures that even computers connecting via Remote Desktop Gateways comply with corporate NAP policies.

Remote Desktop Web Access

Remote Desktop Web Access was known, as in Windows Server 2008 R1, as Terminal Server Web Access providing users with a portal to view and connect to available RemoteApp-based applications within a Web browser. The new Remote Desktop Web Access feature includes the following enhancements over Terminal Service Web Access:

- Security-trimmed RemoteApp filtering
- Forms-based authentication (FBA)
- Public and private computer options
- Single sign-on

Security-trimmed RemoteApp filtering

Windows Server 2008 R1 Terminal Services Web Access displays any RemoteApp Web applications available on the system to all end users. This allows users to see RemoteApps even if they do not have access to them. Windows Server 2008 R2 Remote Desktop Web Access now security trims the interface so that users see only RemoteApp shortcuts they have access to.

Forms-based authentication

Remote Desktop Web Access now offers the ability to provide FBA. This provides a more user friendly logon page which users may be used to from other applications such as Outlook Web Access (OWA) in Microsoft Exchange.

Public and private computer options

Users can now specify what type of computer they are connecting from when logging into Remote Desktop Web Access. This provides more strict security settings when logging in from a public computer such as a kiosk.

Single sign-on

When using Terminal Server Web Access in Windows Server 2008 R1, users were prompted twice to logon to RemoteApps via the Web interface. They were prompted once to access the Web access server and a second time when launching the application. Remote Desktop Web Access provides single sign-on so that users need to logon only initially to the Web access site. Credentials are then passed to the RemoteApp automatically.

Remote Desktop Client Experience

Several new features have been added to further enhance the Remote Desktop experience for Windows 7 client computers. Windows 7 clients connecting to a Windows Server 2008 R2 server gain these additional features:

- *Multiple monitor support*—Remote Desktop Services now supports multiple monitors for Windows 7 clients. This allows RemoteApps to take advantage of multiple monitors in the same manner as if they were running as applications on the local computer.
- *A/V playback*—Remote Desktop Services now redirects Windows Media Player-based A/V content to the client computer where it is played locally using the memory and CPU of the client computer to view the content locally.
- Windows 7 Aero—Remote Desktop Services support Windows 7 Aero features when the connecting client is a Windows 7 computer.

Remote Desktop Services PowerShell module and Best Practices Analyzer

Remote Desktop Services now comes with more management features and options including a PowerShell module and Best Practices Analyzer (BPA). Using PowerShell, administrators can perform most Remote Desktop Services administration via a PowerShell command prompt.

The BPA helps administrators verify that their Remote Desktop Services configuration is following best practices and that there are no misconfigurations that could negatively impact on the deployment.

PLANNING TO DEPLOY REMOTE DESKTOP SERVICES

Prior to installing Remote Desktop Services, you should properly plan your deployment. You should consider the following:

- What Remote Desktop Services are needed?
- Are the applications you want to use over Remote Desktop Services compatible?

- Is access from outside the corporate firewall required?
- What infrastructure is required to support Remote Desktop Services?
- How many concurrent sessions do you need to support?
- Do you want to provide Web-based access to RemoteApps?
- Will you be using PCs, ThinClients, or a combination of both as clients for Remote Desktop Services?
- What are the availability requirements of Remote Desktop Services?
- Will Users need access to applications offline?
- Will users have access to RemoteApps only or access to full desktops?

These are just a few of the questions that need to be answered before deploying Remote Desktop Services. For example, if you need access to Remote Desktop applications from the Internet, you will want to deploy the Remote Desktop Gateway. If users need the ability to run an application while "disconnected" from the corporate network, and the Internet, then Remote Desktop Services is not the solution for that application. After reading through the following section on installing and configuring Remote Desktop Services, you should be in a better position to answer some of these questions for your deployment planning.

NOTES FROM THE FIELD

Remote Desktop Services and application licensing

Before deploying an application as a RemoteApp, you should make sure the software license allows installation on a Remote Desktop Server. Some software vendors prohibit the installation of their software on a shared application server, using technologies like RemoteApp.

INSTALLING AND CONFIGURING REMOTE DESKTOP SERVICES

In this section we will take a look at installing and configuring various components of Remote Desktop Services. We will discuss what features each provides and go through the actual setup process of these services. As with other roles you have learned about in this book, Remote Desktop Services is added as a standard Windows role using Server Manager. Let us take a look at installing Remote Desktop Role Services.

Installing and configuring Remote Desktop Session Host

The Remote Desktop Session Host is what you might consider the traditional Remote Desktop Services (or Terminal Services) role. The Remote Desktop Session Host provides presentation virtualization by remotely displaying server-hosted applications or desktops to PCs and thin clients. By using RemoteApp capabilities, users can access a server-hosted application in a seamless window making the application appear to be running on the local PC (see Figure 8.1).

To connect to a Remote Desktop Session Host, clients use the Remote Desktop Client which comes preinstalled on Windows XP, Windows Vista, and Windows 7.

To install the Remote Desktop Session Host, perform the following:

1. Open *Server Manager*. Then select the *Roles* node in the left pane.
2. Click the *Add Roles* link in the middle pane to launch the Add Roles Wizard.
3. Select the *Remote Desktop Services* role. Then click *Next*.
4. Click *Next* on the Remote Desktop Services Introduction page.

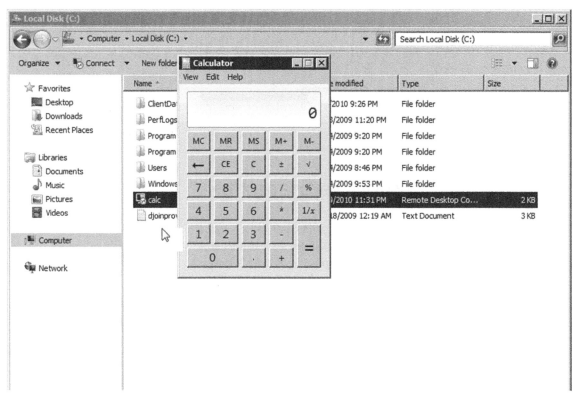

■ **FIGURE 8.1** Remote Desktop Services RemoteApp.

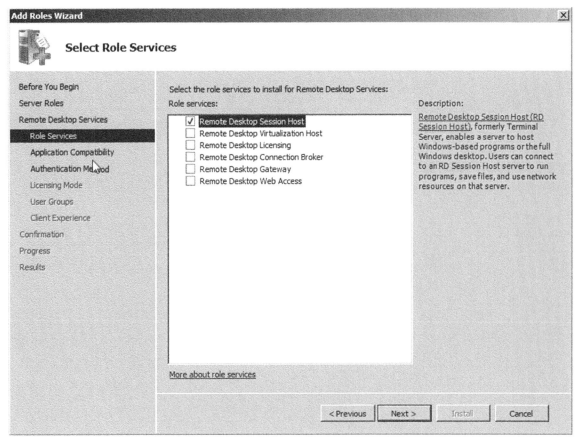

FIGURE 8.2 Remote Desktop Session Host role service.

5. Select the *Remote Desktop Session Host* role service as seen in Figure 8.2. Then click *Next*.
6. Notice the warning message about application installation. If you have already installed applications on this server, you may need to reinstall them after installing Remote Desktop Services. This is because adding the Remote Desktop Session Host changes the server configuration to support applications in a multiuser manner. After reading the warning and verifying that you have not installed any applications, click *Next* to continue.
7. Next you must determine whether you want to enable Network Level Authentication (see Figure 8.3). Network authentication enhances security of Remote Desktop Sessions by performing user authentication prior to completing the full connection process.

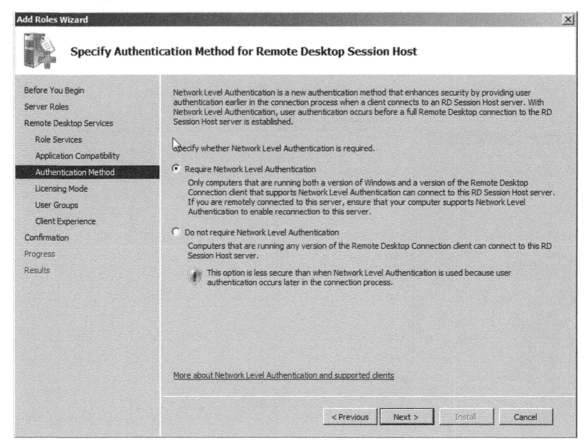

■ FIGURE 8.3 Remote Desktop Session Host Network Level Authentication.

Network Level Authentication requires that the client operating system and the version of Remote Desktop Client support Network Level Authentication. Windows XP Service Pack 3, Windows Vista, and Windows 7 all support Network Level Authentication. In this exercise, we will choose to use Network Level Authentication. Then click *Next*.

8. In the next step, you will need to select your licensing mode for Remote Desktop Session Host. Just as with the operating system, each connection to the Remote Desktop Session Host requires a Remote Desktop Client Access License (CAL). You can choose one of three licensing options for Remote Desktop Session Host:

   ❑ *Configure later*—Choosing this option will allow you to skip choosing a license mode at this time and select the mode you want to use after adding the role.

❏ *Per device*—Using this option, each device such as computers or thin-clients will require a CAL to connect to the server. You may want to use this option when you have computers or thin-clients that are shared by multiple users. This allows you to have an unlimited number of users and buy CALs only for each device connecting to the Remote Desktop Server.

❏ *Per user*—You use this option, when each user needs access to Remote Desktop Services. This is a better licensing option when you have a limited number of users who access Remote Desktop Services. This allows a user to connect from multiple computers, thin-clients, or other devices using only a single CAL.

In this exercise choose the *Per device* option. Then click *Next*.

9. The next step is to select who should be able to use Remote Desktop Session Host services on this server. To control access, Windows uses a Remote Desktop Users local computer group. You can choose to add additional users or groups to this local group now (see Figure 8.4), or later. For now let us accept the default group of Administrators. Then click *Next*.

10. In the next step, if you want to enable enhanced Client Experience settings you can choose to do so (see Figure 8.5). These settings improve the user experience by redirecting audio and video from the server back to the client machine as well as redirecting audio recording from the client back to the application running on the server. You can also optionally enable Aero features by enabling the *Desktop Composition* option. The Remote Desktop clients will need to be running a Windows 7-based operating system to support these enhanced features. In this exercise, we will enable all options. Then click *Next*.

11. Verify settings on the Confirm Installation Settings page, and then click *Install*.

12. After the installation is completed, you will be prompted to restart the server. Select *Yes* to reboot. After the server restarts, logon where the installation will be complete. Click the *Close* button in the *Resume Installation Wizard* to complete the installation.

You will now see the Remote Desktop Services role in Server Manager (see Figure 8.6). You can use the consoles under this role to manage the Remote Desktop Session Host.

The Remote Session Host has three main configuration consoles. They are

■ RemoteApp Manager
■ RD Session Host Configuration
■ Remote Desktop Services Manager

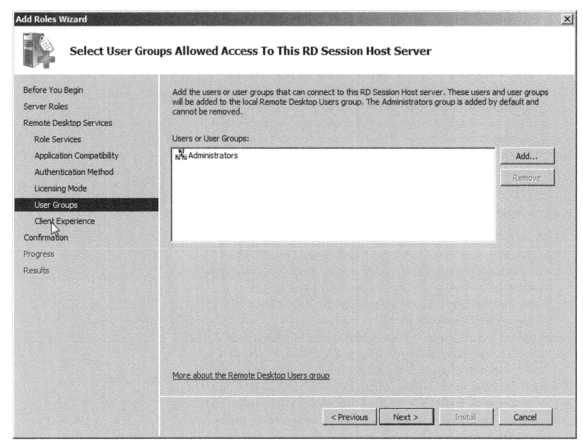

■ **FIGURE 8.4** Remote Desktop Session Host user access.

RemoteApp Manager

RemoteApp Manager is used to create and manage applications installed on the server that will serve as a RemoteApp. To set up a RemoteApp perform the following:

1. Open *Server Manager* and expand the nodes *Roles | Remote Desktop Services*.
2. Right click the *RemoteApp Manager* node and select the option *Add RemoteApp Programs* (see Figure 8.7). This will launch the *RemoteApp Wizard*. Click *Next* to begin.
3. Select a program you wish to make available via RemoteApp services or click *Browse* to locate a program to use (see Figure 8.8). In this exercise, we will choose the Calculator application.

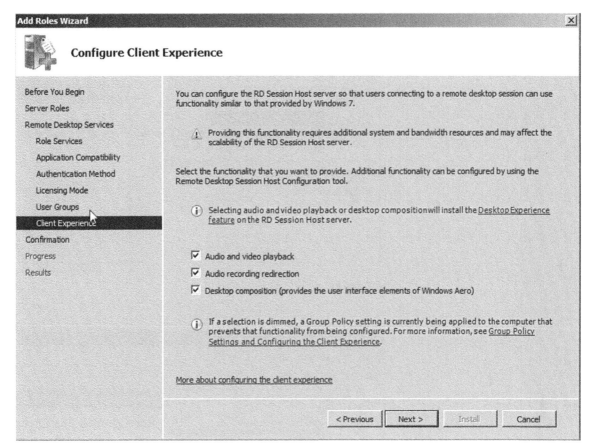

■ **FIGURE 8.5** Enhanced Client Experience settings.

4. You can set advanced options for the application by clicking the *Properties* button. In the *Properties* window, you can set advanced settings like parameters to pass to the application at launch or limiting access to the application to specific users or groups as seen in Figure 8.9. In our example, we will accept the default to allow all authenticated users access to the application. Click *OK* to close the Properties window and then click *Next* in the RemoteApp Wizard.

5. Review the settings on the summary page, and then click *Finish*. This completes the setup of the RemoteApp.

You can now connect to the RemoteApp from another computer. To do so, you will need to connect to the RemoteApp via the Web interface (discussed later in this section) or a custom remote desktop file. In this

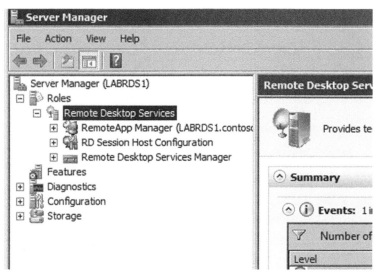

■ **FIGURE 8.6** Remote Desktop Services role.

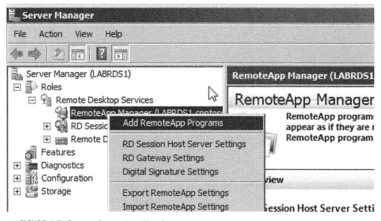

■ **FIGURE 8.7** Opening RemoteApp Wizard.

exercise, we will create a custom remote desktop file to use. You can use the RemoteApp Manager console to create a custom RDP file that can be distributed to users to provide connectivity. To create the custom RDP file, perform the following:

1. Locate the program in *RemoteApp Manager* (see Figure 8.10). Right click the program and choose *Create RDP File*. This will launch the RemoteApp Wizard. Click *Next* to begin.

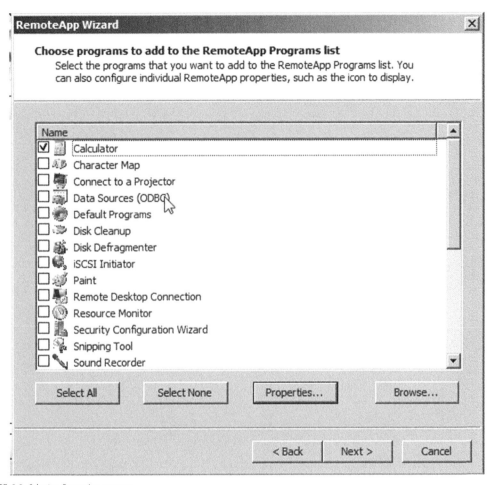

RemoteApp Wizard

Choose programs to add to the RemoteApp Programs list

Select the programs that you want to add to the RemoteApp Programs list. You can also configure individual RemoteApp properties, such as the icon to display.

Name
☑ Calculator
☐ Character Map
☐ Connect to a Projector
☐ Data Sources (ODBC)
☐ Default Programs
☐ Disk Cleanup
☐ Disk Defragmenter
☐ iSCSI Initiator
☐ Paint
☐ Remote Desktop Connection
☐ Resource Monitor
☐ Security Configuration Wizard
☐ Snipping Tool
☐ Sound Recorder

Select All   Select None   Properties...   Browse...

< Back   Next >   Cancel

■ **FIGURE 8.8** Selecting RemoteApp program.

2. Enter a path to save the RDP file, and optionally change any configuration settings such as host, gateway, and certificates. Then click *Next* (see Figure 8.11)
3. Verify the settings on the Review Settings page. Then click *Finish*.

A new remote desktop configuration file should be saved to the path you specified. You could now distribute this file to other users or computers within your organization. To access the RemoteApp, users just double-click the custom configuration file and logon with their Active Directory credentials. If they have been authorized to access the application, it should launch and appear as if it were running locally on their workstations as seen in Figure 8.12.

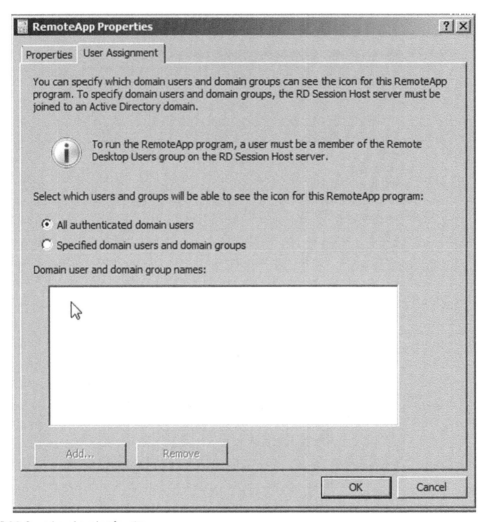

Remote Desktop Session Host Configuration

The Remote Desktop Session Host Configuration console is used to set up and configure connections to the Remote Desktop Server. A default connection is already set up during the installation of the role service. You can modify this connection or create new ones. In the following exercise, we will review the Remote Desktop Session Host connection settings:

1. Select the node *Roles | Remote Desktop Services | RD Session Host Configuration*.

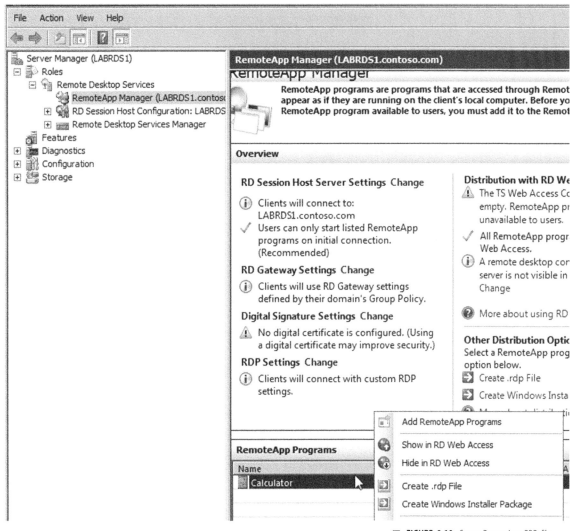

File   Action   View   Help

Server Manager (LABRDS1)
Roles
 Remote Desktop Services
  RemoteApp Manager (LABRDS1.contoso...
  RD Session Host Configuration: LABRDS
  Remote Desktop Services Manager
 Features
 Diagnostics
 Configuration
 Storage

RemoteApp Manager (LABRDS1.contoso.com)

RemoteApp Manager

RemoteApp programs are programs that are accessed through Remot
appear as if they are running on the client's local computer. Before yo
RemoteApp program available to users, you must add it to the Remot

Overview

RD Session Host Server Settings Change

ⓘ Clients will connect to:
   LABRDS1.contoso.com
✓ Users can only start listed RemoteApp
   programs on initial connection.
   (Recommended)

RD Gateway Settings Change

ⓘ Clients will use RD Gateway settings
   defined by their domain's Group Policy.

Digital Signature Settings Change

⚠ No digital certificate is configured. (Using
   a digital certificate may improve security.)

RDP Settings Change

ⓘ Clients will connect with custom RDP
   settings.

Distribution with RD We

⚠ The TS Web Access Co
   empty. RemoteApp pr
   unavailable to users.

✓ All RemoteApp progr
   Web Access.

ⓘ A remote desktop cor
   server is not visible in
   Change

ⓦ More about using RD

Other Distribution Optic
Select a RemoteApp prog
option below.
▣ Create .rdp File
▣ Create Windows Insta

▣ Add RemoteApp Programs
🌐 Show in RD Web Access
🌐 Hide in RD Web Access
▣ Create .rdp File
▣ Create Windows Installer Package

RemoteApp Programs

Name
Calculator

■ **FIGURE 8.10** Create RemoteApp RDP file.

2. Locate and right click on the *RDP-Tcp* connection in the middle pane
   (see Figure 8.13). Then select the *Properties* option.
3. This will open the RDP-Tcp Properties window. The following can be
   configured from the connection properties:
   ❑ *General*—From the General tab, you can configure most of the
     connection's security settings such as encryption level used and
     what level of authentication to accept. Additionally, you can also
     assign a certificate to the connection to provide encrypted
     connectivity to the server.

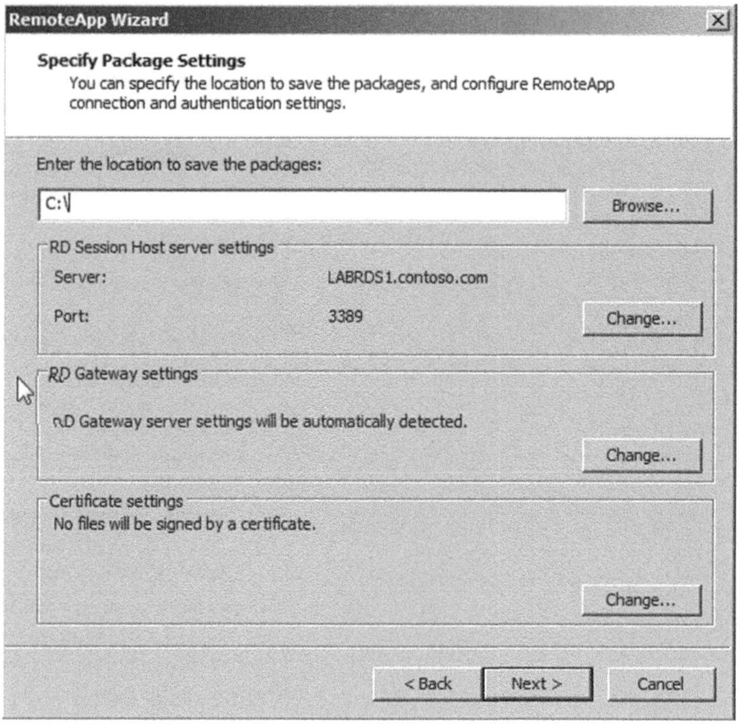

■ **FIGURE 8.11** RemoteApp settings.

- ❏ *Log on settings*—You can use this tab to configure how you want new sessions to logon to the host. You can choose to user information provided by the client, or auto-logon using a specified account. In most cases, you will want to choose the option *Use client-provided logon information.*
- ❏ *Sessions*—The Sessions tab allows you to override session and idle timeouts set per individual users. If you choose to use these settings, they will apply even to the user using this connection.
- ❏ *Environment*—The Environment tab allows you to configure an application to launch upon logon to a Remote Desktop Session. This can be used when providing users with access to full desktop via RemoteApp.
- ❏ *Security*—The Security tab can be used to provide users and groups with access to the Remote Desktop Session Host services. As a best practice, it is recommended that users and groups be added to the local Remote Desktop Users group as opposed to using the Security tab.

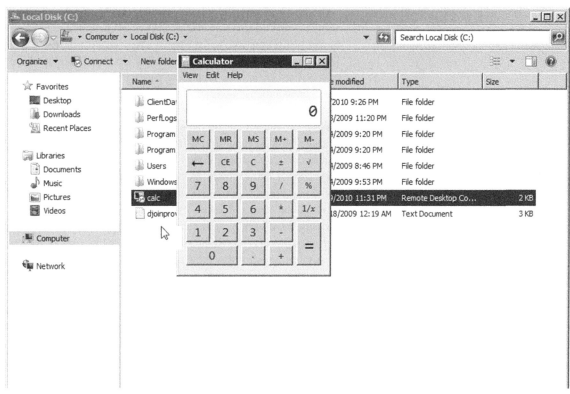

■ **FIGURE 8.12** Windows Calculator running as a RemoteApp.

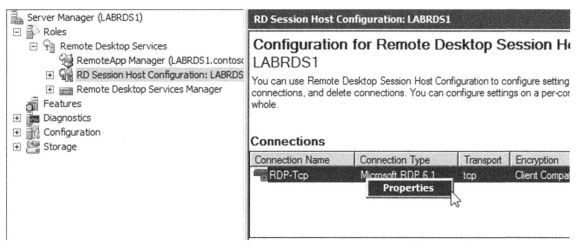

■ **FIGURE 8.13** RDP connection properties.

❑ *Network Adapter*—The Network Adapter tab can be used to specify where to use a dedicated adapter for Remote Desktop Session Host connectivity or share a single adapter for Remote Desktop and other network services. The Network Adapter tab can also be used to limit the number of concurrent users connecting via the connection.

❑ *Client settings*—The Client Settings tab can be used to enable or disable certain settings on the client connecting to the Remote Desktop Session Host server. These include color depth for connections or disabling remote drive and printer redirection (see Figure 8.14). For example, by disabling remote drive redirection, you could prevent users from copying files off of the server. If left enabled, the Remote Desktop Session Host will attempt to map a network drive back to your computer's local drives.

❑ *Remote Control*—The Remote Control tab can be used to override per-user settings for Remote Control. The Remote Control option allows you to view and share a Remote Desktop Session with another user. For example, Bob and Jay both could open a remote desktop connected to the host and be logged into a desktop. Bob could then open the Remote Desktop tools to locate Jay's session. Once he found the session, he could request that Jay allow him to remote view his session.

The Licensing Diagnosis node (see Figure 8.15) can be used to troubleshoot licensing issues and verify that you have configured licensing for the Remote Desktop Server.

Remote Desktop Services Manager

The Remote Desktop Services Manager is used to review and manage remote desktop connections to the server. Using this console, you can force users to logoff the system and to end processes that may be consuming unnecessary resources.

Installing and configuring Remote Desktop Licensing

The Remote Desktop Licensing services role is used to manage and renew Remote Desktop Services CALs. A server with the Remote Desktop Licensing services role is required so that Remote Desktop Session Host servers can properly license themselves and manage how many people are connected. A single Remote Desktop Licensing services host can provide licensing for multiple Remote Desktop Sessions Host servers.

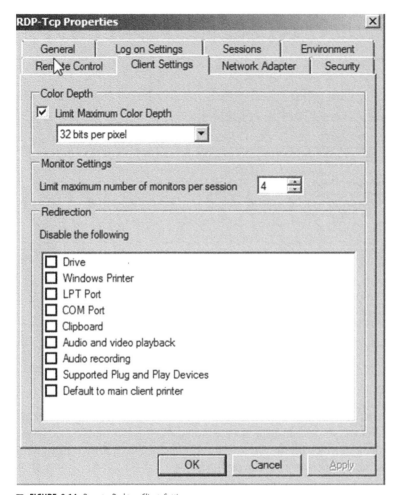

■ **FIGURE 8.14** Remote Desktop Client Settings.

To install Remote Desktop Licensing services, perform the following:

1. Open *Server Manager* and select the *Roles* node. Then click the *Add Role Services* link. This will launch the Add Role Services wizard.
2. Select the *Remote Desktop Licensing* role service. Then click *Next*.
3. If you are already running previous versions of Terminal Services, you can turn on the discovery scope so that previous servers can locate the licensing server. If you are using only Windows Server 2008 R2 Remote Desktop Servers, then do not configure this option. Click *Next* to continue.
4. Verify your settings and click *Install*.
5. When the installation is complete, click *Close*.

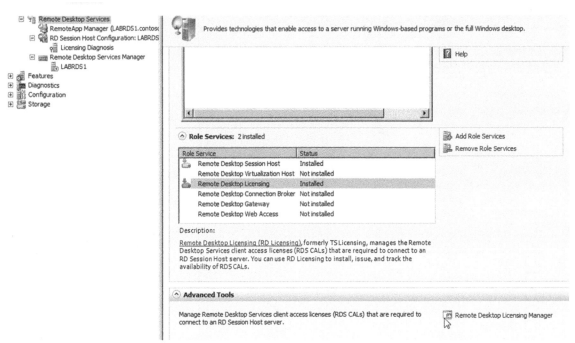

FIGURE 8.15 Launching Remote Desktop Services License Manager.

After completing the installation of the Remote Desktop Licensing services, you can manage licenses using the Remote Desktop Licensing Manager which can be accessed by clicking the link under advanced tools in Server Manager (see Figure 8.15).

Using Licensing Manager (see Figure 8.16), administrators can easily add and activate Remote Desktop licenses. After purchasing licenses, you will need to use the Licensing Manager to add them to the license server.

Installing and configuring Remote Desktop Web Access

Remote Desktop Web Access creates a Web-based portal with links to RemoteApps. Deploying Remote Desktop Web Access, in most cases, can remove the administrative burden of having to create and manage custom RDP connection files. Users simply locate and access RemoteApps by logging into the Remote Desktop Web Access portal. Within the portal, they will see shortcut links to the RemoteApps that they have access to.

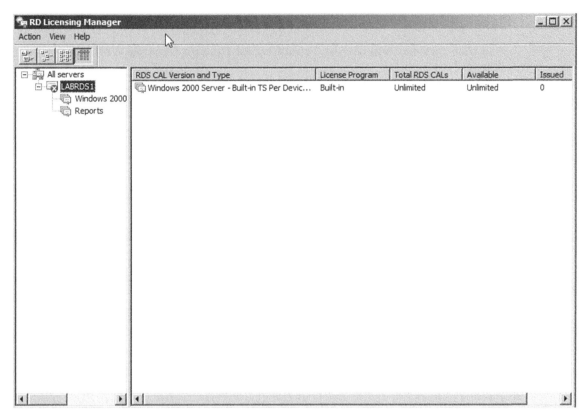

■ FIGURE 8.16 Remote Desktop License Manager.

To install and configure Remote Desktop Web Access perform the following:

1. Open *Server Manager*.
2. Select the *Roles* node. Then click the *Add Role Services* link under the Remote Desktop Services role.
3. Select the *Remote Desktop Web Access* option. You may be prompted to add the Internet Information Services (IIS) Role, as it is a prerequisite for Remote Desktop Web Access. If presented with a prompt to install other role services as seen in Figure 8.17, click *Add Required Role Services*. Then click *Next*.
4. If IIS is not installed, you will need to select options for installing IIS. In this exercise, use the default selections, and then click *Next*.
5. Click *Install* at the confirmation page. When the installation is complete, click *Close*.

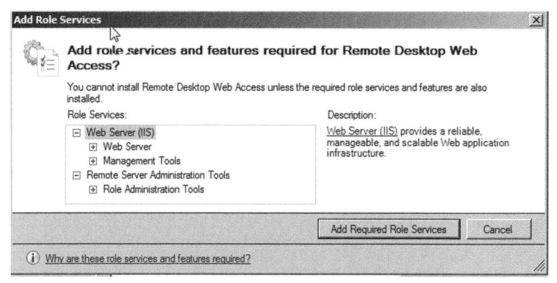

■ **FIGURE 8.17** Adding IIS Role services.

After the wizard completes the installation you should notice that IIS has been added to the server and the Remote Desktop Web Access portal has been set up under the Default Web site as seen in Figure 8.18. The site can be accessed via the URL https://servername/RDWeb.

NOTES FROM THE FIELD

Remote Desktop Web Access SSL certificate

The Remote Desktop Web Access Web site uses a self-signed certificate by default. For production deployments, you should request a certificate from an enterprise PKI or a public certificate provider.

You can easily display a RemoteApp to the Web site from the RemoteApp Manager console. Simply right click the program and select the option *Show in RD Web Access* (see Figure 8.19).

The RemoteApp should now be visible on the Remote Desktop Web Access site. To access the RemoteApp, perform the steps below:

1. Browse the URL of the Remote Desktop Web Access Web site (https://servername/RDWeb). Ignore any certificate warnings. These are due to the certificate being self-signed.
2. At the logon prompt, enter your Active Directory username and password. Be sure to use the format domain\username in the username field (Contoso\John). Then click *Logon*.

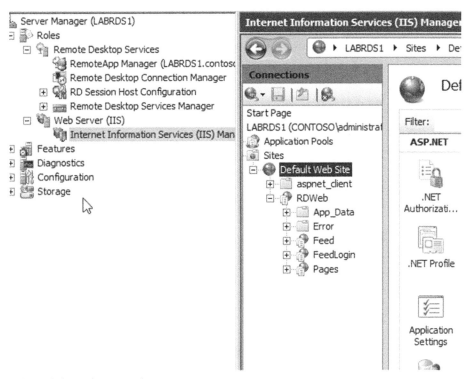

■ FIGURE 8.18 Remote Desktop Web Access portal.

3. After you logon, you will be taken to the RemoteApp Programs page as seen in Figure 8.20. Here you will see RemoteApps that you have access to.
4. To launch a RemoteApp, click the icon. This will start the connection process as seen in Figure 8.21.
5. Shortly after the connection process starts, the application show appears.

As mentioned earlier in this chapter, the Remote Desktop Web Access interface is security trimmed, meaning that users will see only applications to which they have been provided access via Remote Desktop Session Host.

Installing and configuring Remote Desktop Gateway

The Remote Desktop Gateway provides the ability to securely connect to Remote Desktop applications from outside your corporate firewall without the need for a VPN connection. A Remote Desktop Gateway creates a SSL tunnel between the client computer and the gateway server. The Remote Desktop Session is then created within this tunnel. Figure 8.22 depicts a typical Remote Desktop Gateway deployment.

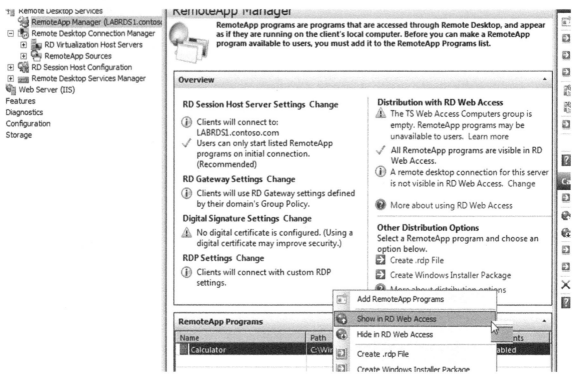

■ **FIGURE 8.19** Adding a RemoteApp in Remote Desktop Web Access.

NOTES FROM THE FIELD

Remote Desktop Gateway firewall ports

The Remote Desktop Gateway will need port 443 opened inbound on your Internet firewall to allow connections from outside. Port 443 is the default port used for SSL services.

In the following exercise, we will go through the process of installing and configuring a Remote Desktop Gateway. For this exercise, we will be configuring a dedicated server for the Remote Desktop Gateway services.

1. Open *Server Manager* on the server you wish to set up as the Remote Desktop Gateway.
2. Select the *Roles* node. Then click the *Add Role* link. The Add Roles wizard will launch. Click *Next* to continue.
3. Select the *Remote Desktop Services* role. Then click *Next*.

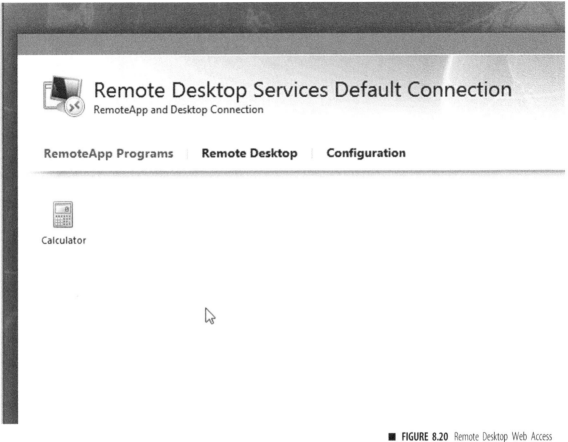

■ **FIGURE 8.20** Remote Desktop Web Access programs.

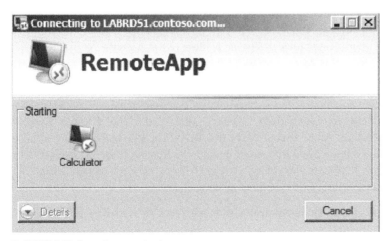

■ **FIGURE 8.21** RemoteApp connection in progress.

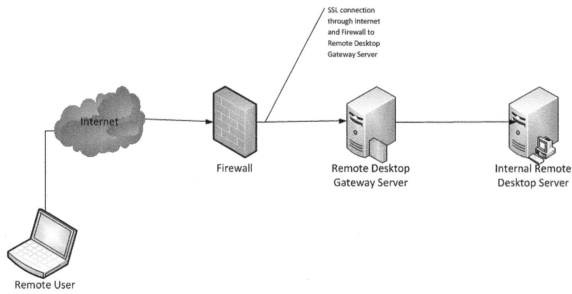

SSL connection
through Internet
and Firewall to
Remote Desktop
Gateway Server

Internet

Firewall

Remote Desktop
Gateway Server

Internal Remote
Desktop Server

Remote User

■ **FIGURE 8.22** Example of a Remote Desktop
Gateway deployment.

4. At the Introduction to Remote Desktop Services page, click *Next*.
5. Select the *Remote Desktop Gateway* on the role services selection page.
6. When prompted, select the option *Add Required Role Services* (see Figure 8.23). This will add other roles required to support the Remote Desktop Gateway role service. This includes IIS components and the RPC/HTTP proxy feature. Click *Next* to continue.
7. You now need to select a certificate that will be used to provide SSL encryption for RDP connections. For a production deployment, this certificate should be requested from an internal PKI or a public certificate provider. For the purpose of this exercise, let us choose the option to create a self-signed certificate (see Figure 8.24). Click *Next* to continue.

The next step of the wizard requires that you create a Remote Desktop Connection Authorization Policy (RD CAP) and Remote Desktop Resource Authorization Policy (RD RAP). The RD CAP determines which users are allowed to connect through the Remote Desktop Gateway. The RD RAP specifies which systems remote users can access when connecting through the Remote Desktop Gateway.

8. Select the option to create authorization policies *Now*. Then click *Next*.

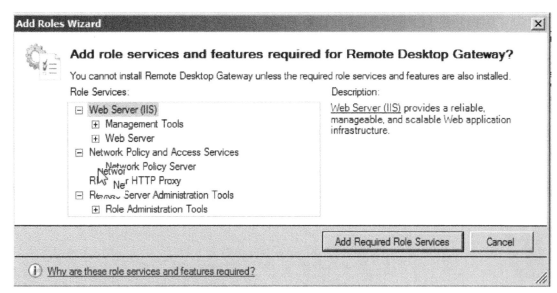

■ FIGURE 8.23 Remote Desktop Gateway Required Role Services.

9. Add the groups that will be associated with both the RD RAP and RD CAP policies (see Figure 8.25). In this exercise, let us use the *Administrators* group. After adding groups that you want to associate with authorization policies, click *Next*.

10. Enter a name for the RD CAP policy. In this exercise, we will use the default *TS_CAP_01*.

11. Select the authentication methods you want to support. For our example, we will use the *Password* method. After selecting the authentication policy, click *Next* to continue.

12. Enter a name for the RD RAP policy (see Figure 8.26). We will use the default name *TS_RAP_01*.

13. You can now limit which computers users can connect to through the gateway by specifying a computer group within Active Directory. As best practice, you should create an Active Directory group and place computers that you want to allow gateway access to in that group. In our exercise, we will select the option *Allow users to connect to any computer on the network*. After selecting what users can connect to, click *Next* to continue.

Limiting Which Computers Users Can Access Through Gateway

14. On the Network Policy and Access Services page, click *Next*.

15. Ensure that the *Network Policy Server* option is selected, and then click *Next*. This is an additional component that is required to support the Remote Desktop Gateway.

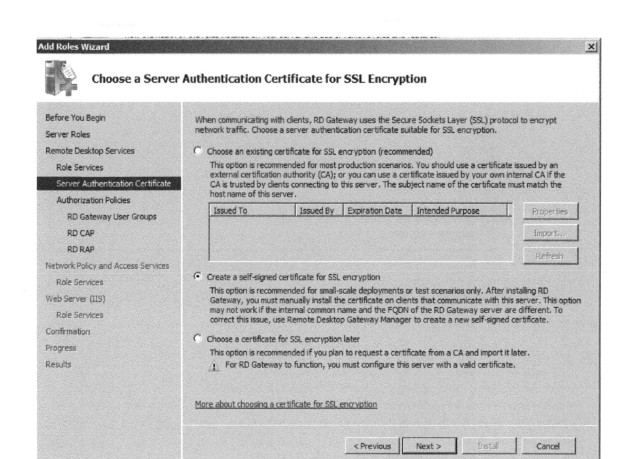

■ FIGURE 8.24 Selecting Remote Desktop Gateway SSL certificate.

16. Click *Next* on the IIS overview page.
17. Accept the currently selected IIS role services by click *Next*. Again these role services are required to support the Remote Desktop Gateway.
18. Verify your installation settings on the summary page. Then click *Install*.
19. When the installation is complete, click *Close*.

This completes the basic setup of the Remote Desktop Gateway. You can now configure a Remote Desktop client to connect to a server using the gateway. You can configure the Remote Desktop client to use the gateway by modifying the *Connect From Anywhere* settings on the advanced tab (see Figure 8.27).

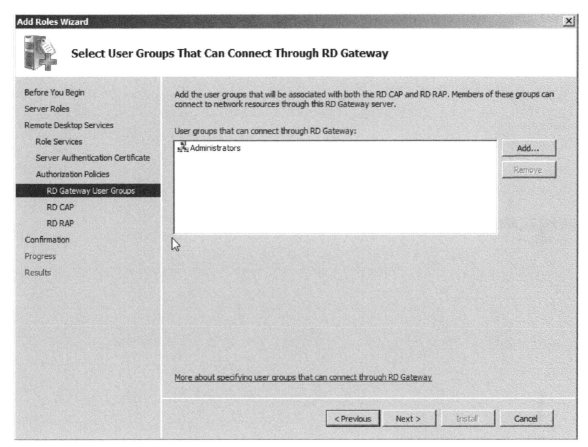

■ **FIGURE 8.25** Selecting groups authorized to use Remote Desktop Gateway services.

NOTES FROM THE FIELD

Remote Desktop Gateway self-signed certificate

If you use the self-signed certificate for the Remote Desktop Gateway, you will need to manually add the certificate to the trusted certificates store on any clients connecting through the gateway. If a client does not trust the self-signed certificate, the connection will fail.

The Remote Desktop Gateway server is a great way to provide business partners or home users with access to secure remote sessions without the need for VPN. The use of the Remote Desktop Gateway also allows you to limit access to specific users and then can limit which computers those

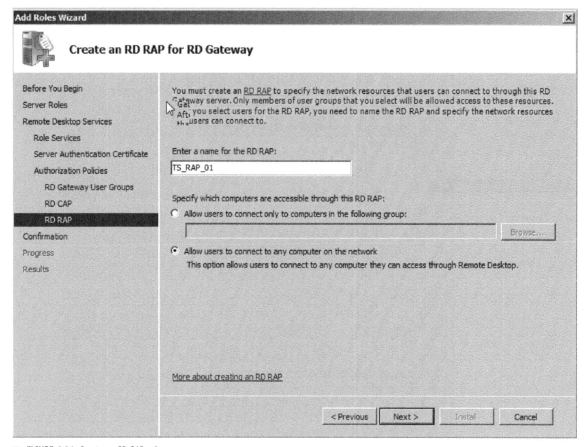

users can connect to. Additionally, the Remote Desktop Gateway can be integrated with NAP to ensure that the connecting computers comply with corporate security policies.

Overview of Remote Desktop Virtualization Host

Using Remote Desktop Virtualization Host role services, you can deploy a fully featured VDI within your organization. A VDI allows you to provide computer workstation capabilities to your users, while maintaining the workstation, a virtual computer, inside the datacenter. This provides greater security, better manageability, and easier troubleshooting for end-user computer problems. For example, if a user's "virtual" workstation crashes, that user can quickly be assigned a new workstation and be

■ FIGURE 8.27 Remote Desktop client Gateway settings.

up and running within minutes opposed to hours it may take to rebuild a physical computer.

A Windows Server 2008 R2 VDI uses a combination of Hyper-V and Remote Desktop Services to provide users with a pool of virtual machines, meaning that each user remotely connects and logs onto the next available machine in a group. As a second option, the VDI deployment can provide some or all users with a dedicated virtual machine, meaning that the user would connect to the same VM each time they logged on. Figure 8.28 depicts what a small VDI deployment might look like.

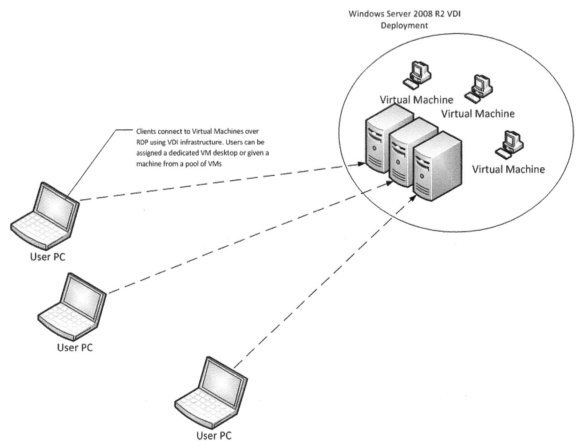

Windows Server 2008 R2 VDI Deployment

Virtual Machine

Virtual Machine

Virtual Machine

Clients connect to Virtual Machines over RDP using VDI infrastructure. Users can be assigned a dedicated VM desktop or given a machine from a pool of VMs

User PC

User PC

User PC

■ **FIGURE 8.28** Windows Server 2008 R2 VDI.

Planning for a VDI deployment

Prior to deploying a VDI using Remote Desktop Services and Hyper-V, you should spend time properly planning your deployment. You first need to determine whether you will be using a pool of VMs or whether each user will have his or her own dedicated VM. You may also decide whether you need a hybrid deployment to support both pools and dedicated VMs.

As part of the planning process, you will also need to properly size your hardware to support the number of VMs required for your user base. You will want to ensure that the VMs are not starved for computing resources that could impact on your end-user's ability to use the system.

You may also need to consider the mobility of your company's workforce. Since a VDI solution stores the workstations, along with their associated data, on servers in the datacenter, VDI may not be a good fit for organizations that have a highly mobile workforce.

Additionally, you will need to consider the requirements for deploying VDI using Hyper-V and Remote Desktop Services. To deploy virtual desktop pools, your Active Directory domain must be Windows Server 2008 functional level or higher. If you wish to support dedicated personal virtual machines, your domain functional level will need to be Windows Server 2008 R2. You also need to ensure that Hyper-V is installed prior to installing the Remote Desktop Virtualization Host role service.

Installing and configuring Remote Desktop Virtualization Host, Connection Broker, and Session Host for VDI

In this exercise, we will go through the process of deploying a simple VDI, using Windows Server 2008 R2. We will be supporting dedicated virtual machines for our end users. Microsoft refers dedicated VMs as personal virtual desktops. Before you begin setting up VDI services, review Figure 8.29, which explains servers required as part of the deployment and how users connect to virtual desktops using the solution.

In this exercise, we will be performing the following:

■ Set up Remote Desktop Virtualization Host Services
■ Install Remote Desktop Connection Broker
■ Install Remote Desktop Session Host and Web Access
■ Configure the Remote Desktop Connection Broker, Desktop Session Host, and Web Access
■ Test Connectivity to A Dedicated Windows 7 Virtual Machine

Set up Remote Desktop Virtualization Host Services

The first step we need to perform is to set up the proper role services on the server that will host the VMs. We will be adding the Remote Desktop Virtualization Host role service. By installing this role service, Hyper-V will be installed as a required component. Prior to installing Remote Desktop Virtualization Host, you will need to ensure that your server hardware supports Hyper-V.

1. Open *Server Manager* and select the *Roles* node. Then click the *Add Roles* link. This will launch the Add Roles wizard. Click *Next* to continue.
2. Select the *Remote Desktop Services* role. Then click *Next*.

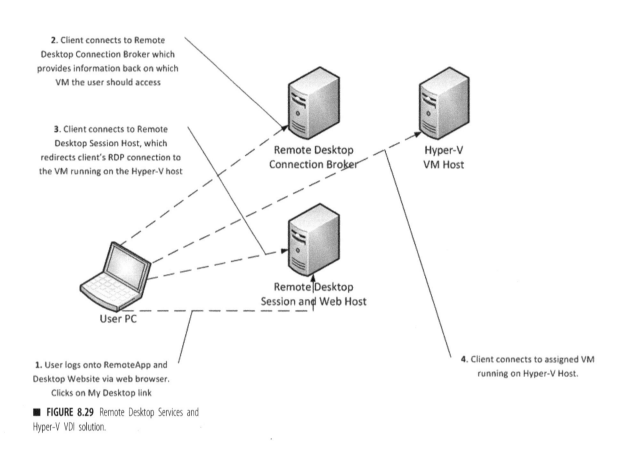

2. Client connects to Remote Desktop Connection Broker which provides information back on which VM the user should access

3. Client connects to Remote Desktop Session Host, which redirects client's RDP connection to the VM running on the Hyper-V host

Remote Desktop Connection Broker

Hyper-V VM Host

Remote Desktop Session and Web Host

User PC

1. User logs onto RemoteApp and Desktop Website via web browser. Clicks on My Desktop link

4. Client connects to assigned VM running on Hyper-V Host.

■ **FIGURE 8.29** Remote Desktop Services and Hyper-V VDI solution.

3. On the Remote Desktop Services Introduction page, click *Next* to continue.

4. Select the *Remote Desktop Virtualization Host* option as seen in Figure 8.30. You will be prompted to add the Hyper-V role services. Click *Add Required Role Services*. Then click *Next*.

5. Click *Next* at the Hyper-V introduction page.

6. Select the network adapter to use for the virtual network (see Figure 8.31). Then click *Next*.

7. On the verify settings page, click *Install*. Then click *Close*.

8. At the restart prompt, click *Yes* to restart the computer.

9. After the computer restarts, the Resume Configuration Wizard will complete the installation of Desktop Virtualization Host with Hyper-V. After the wizard completes the installation, click *Close*.

10. Next you will need to create a new virtual machine for each desktop you want to provide to users. If using dedicated desktops, each user will need his or her own VM. If using pools, you will need enough

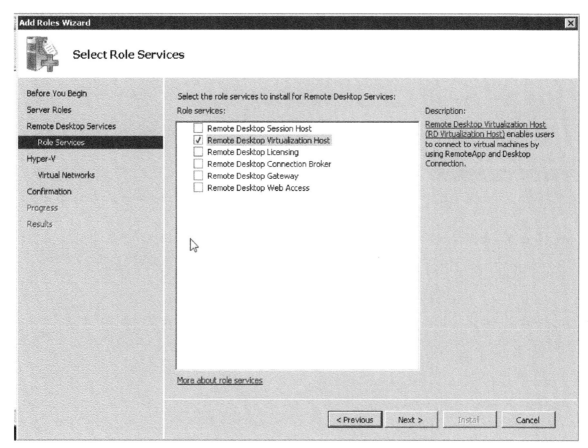

■ **FIGURE 8.30** Remote Desktop Virtualization Host Role Service.

VMs to support the maximum number of concurrent users. See Chapter 7 for details on installing a guest operating system on a VM. For Virtualization Host Services to work properly, the VM needs to be labeled in the Hyper-V interface using a fully qualified domain name, for example, win7vm.syngress.com.

Install Remote Desktop Session Broker

Now that the Virtualization Host is set up, we need to install and configure the Remote Desktop Connection Broker. The Connection Broker manages the process of connecting the client workstation to the virtual machine running on Hyper-V. To install the Connection Broker, logon to the connection broker server and perform the following:

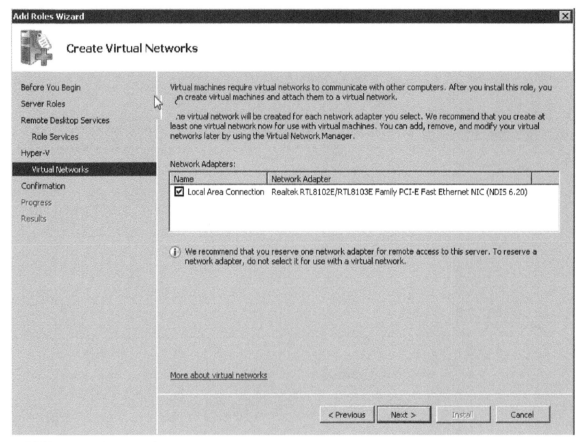

■ FIGURE 8.31 Select Hyper-V network adapter.

1. Open *Server Manager*.
2. Select the *Roles* node. Then click the *Add Roles* link launching the Add Roles Wizard. Click *Next*.
3. Select the *Remote Desktop Services* role. Then click *Next*.
4. Click *Next* on the Remote Desktop Services Introduction page.
5. Select the *Remote Desktop Connection Broker* and then click *Next*.
6. Verify the install selections, and then click *Install*.
7. When the installation is complete, click *Close*.

Install Remote Desktop Session Host and Web Access

The next step is to install the Remote Desktop Session Host and the Web Access role services. Logon to the server that will be providing these services and perform the following:

1. Open *Server Manager*.
2. Select the *Roles* node. Then click the *Add Roles* link launching the Add Roles Wizard. Click *Next*.
3. Select the *Remote Desktop Services* role. Then click *Next*.
4. Click *Next* on the Remote Desktop Services Introduction page.
5. Select the *Remote Desktop Session Host* and *Remote Desktop Web Access* role options. If prompted, click *Add Required Role Services*. This will add Web access prerequisites including IIS. Click *Next* to continue.
6. Click *Next* on the *Application Compatibility Page*.
7. You now need to select the network authentication for support. If you are running older clients, you may need to choose *Do not require Network Level Authentication*; however, if you are using a newer operating system such as Windows 7 with a newer version of the Remote Desktop client, choosing *Require Network Level Authentication* will provide a greater level of security. In this exercise, we will choose *Require Network Level Authentication*. After choosing the authentication level, click *Next* to continue.
8. You now need to select the licensing that you plan to use for your Remote Desktop deployment. In this exercise, we will select the option *Configure later* (see earlier discussion in this chapter on Remote Desktop licensing). After selecting the licensing option, click *Next* to continue.
9. You now need to select the initial groups that you want to provide Remote Desktop services to as seen in Figure 8.32. (Note, this can be changed post install). After selecting the initial groups that you want to provide access to, click *Next* to continue.
10. Optionally, select any enhanced options you want to allow over Remote Desktop, including Audio/Video playback (see Figure 8.33). Then click *Next*.
11. Click *Next* on the IIS Introduction page.
12. Accept the default IIS role services and click *Next*.
13. Verify your selections on the Confirmation page and then click *Install*.
14. After the installation finishes, you will be prompted to restart the server. Click *Yes* to reboot.
15. After the server comes back online, logon to complete the install process. Click *Close* when the installation is complete.

Configure the Remote Desktop Connection Broker, Desktop Session Host, and Web Access

Now that all components are installed, we are ready to configure them to complete the VDI setup. Again we assume that you have already set up one or more virtual machines that will be dedicated to users. Remember

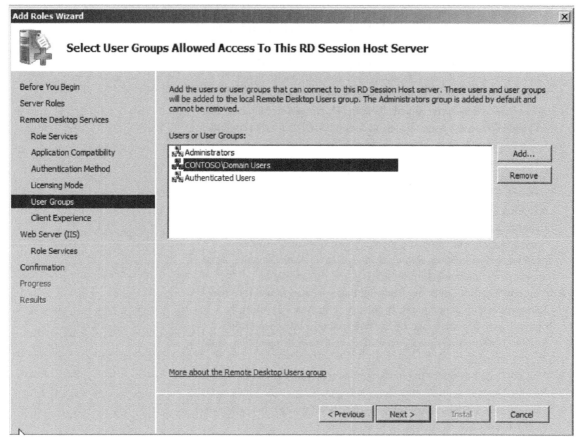

■ **FIGURE 8.32** Remote Desktop access.

that the label name within Hyper-V needs to be a fully qualified domain name (see Figure 8.34). Additionally, the VM must have Remote Desktop turned on.

To configure server components, first logon to the Remote Desktop Connection Broker and perform the following:

1. Open *Server Manager*.
2. Expand the nodes *Roles | Remote Desktop Services | Remote Desktop Connection Manager | RD Virtualization Host Servers*.
3. Select the node *Personal Virtual Desktops* (see Figure 8.35).
4. Click the *Configure* link in the middle pane to launch the *Configure Virtual Desktops Wizard* which will take you through setting up the broker to support virtual desktops.
5. Click *Next* to begin the wizard.

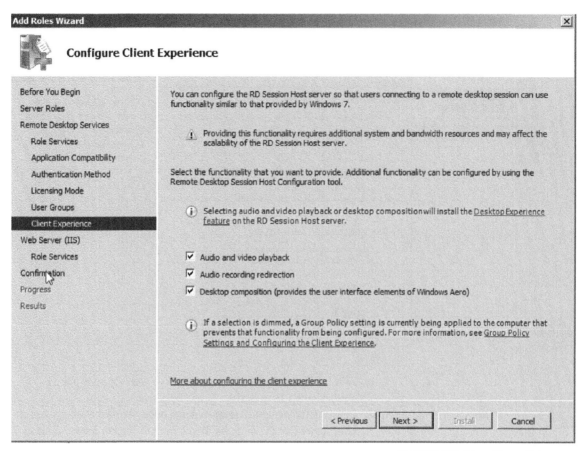

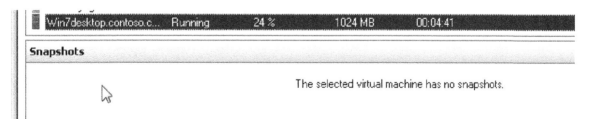

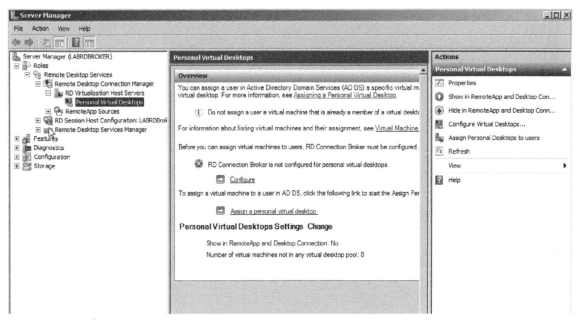

■ FIGURE 8.35 Personal Virtual Desktops configuration node.

6. Add the hostname of the Hyper-V server you set up as the Virtualization Host Server. Then click *Next*.

7. Enter the fully qualified domain name of the Remote Desktop Session Host server (see Figure 8.36). If you need to support remote desktop clients earlier than 6.1, you will need to specify an alternative FQDN for the same session host. This can be accomplished by creating a new host (A) DNS record, and pointing it to the same Remote Desktop Session Host server. This FQDN is used purely to provide an alternative name that older clients will use to connect. Notice the option at the bottom of the page to not autoconfigure the session host. In most cases, you will want to leave this option unchecked, which will allow the wizard to automatically configure the session host server for redirection. After entering the FQDN of the Remote Desktop Session Host, click *Next*. The wizard will attempt to connect to the session host. If successful, it will configure the session host for redirect support.

8. You now must specify the FQDN of the Remote Desktop Web Host server. In our exercise, this is the same server as the Remote Desktop Session Host. Enter the FQDN of the Remote Desktop Web Host, and click *Next*.

9. Verify your configuration on the confirmation page. Then click *Apply*.

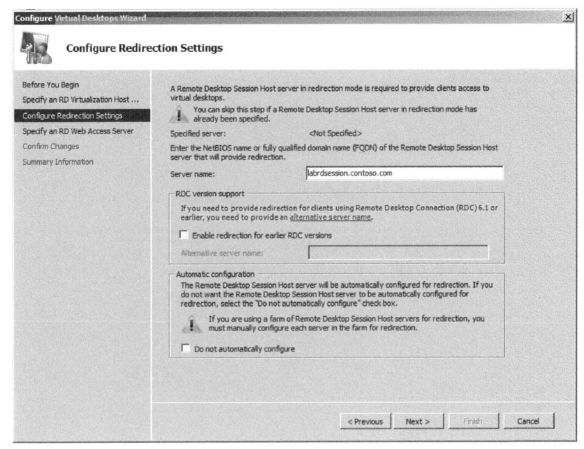

10. Click *Finish* to close the *Configure Virtual Desktops Wizard*. Notice that the option to *Assign Personal Virtual Desktop* is select. This will launch the *Assign Personal Virtual Desktop Wizard*. Using this wizard, we will assign a user to his desktop. Every time a user logs onto a Personal Virtual Desktop session, they will access the assigned VM.

11. Select the user and the VM that you want to assign the user to (see Figure 8.37), and then click *Next*.

12. Click *Assign* to complete the *Assign Personal Virtual Desktop Wizard*.

13. Verify that the assignment was successful, and then deselect the option to *Assign Another Virtual Machine to Another User*. If selected, this would allow you to assign more users to move VMs. Click *Finish* to complete the assignment.

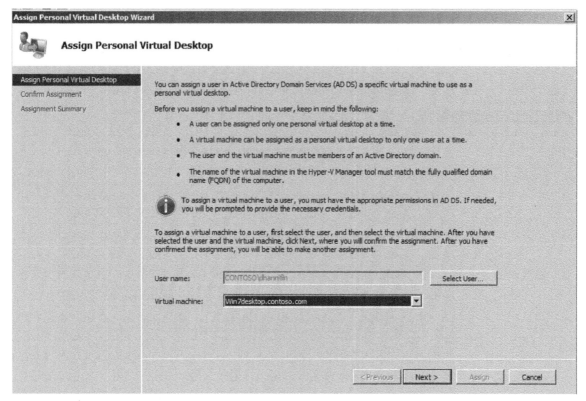

■ FIGURE 8.37 Selecting the user and the VM to assign to the user.

Now that you have assigned a user to a VM, you need to configure the Remote Desktop Web Host to use the broker server. To configure the host, perform the following:

1. Logon to the *RemoteApp and Desktop Connection* Web site by accessing the URL *https://<RemoteDesktopWebHostServerName>/ RDWeb* (see Figure 8.38).
2. Ignore any certificate warnings. For a production deployment, you will want to assign a trusted certificate to the RD Web site.
3. Enter credentials with administrative access to the site and click the *Sign-in* button.
4. Click the *Configuration* tab.
5. On the *Configuration* page, change the *Select Source Server to Use* option to *An RD Connection Broker Server*. Then enter the FQDN of the connection broker. Click *OK* to save the configuration changes. After the settings are saved, click *Sign-out*.

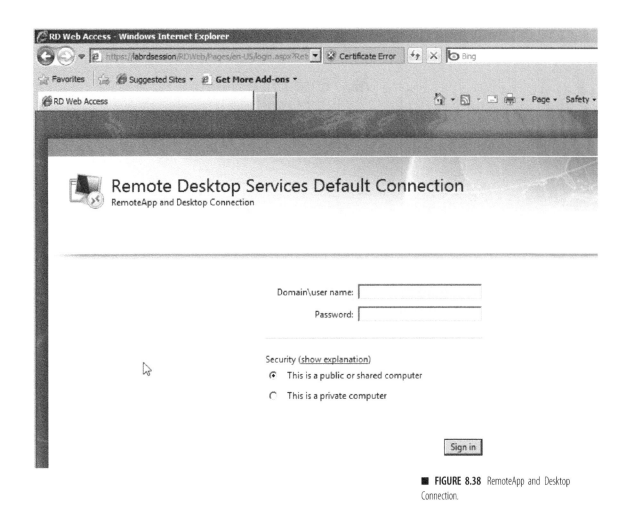

■ **FIGURE** 8.38 RemoteApp and Desktop Connection.

Test connectivity to Virtual Machine

Now that the VDI configuration is complete, we are ready to test our configuration. To test the configuration, simply logon to the RemoteApp and Desktop Connection Web site as the user you previously assigned to the VM. After logging on, click the *My Desktop* icon as seen in Figure 8.39.

You will now be connected to the virtual machine via Remote Desktop. Every time the user logs onto Remote Desktop Web Host and clicks on the *My Desktop* link, he will be logged onto his assigned VM.

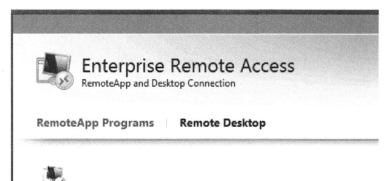

■ **FIGURE 8.39** My Desktop.

SUMMARY

In this chapter, we explored the newly renamed Remote Desktop Services and the new features offered by Windows Server 2008 R2. This chapter first provided an introduction to new features available in Windows Server 2008 R2. We then discussed planning and deploying traditional Remote Desktop Services features as well as new services such the Remote Desktop Gateway. This chapter concluded with an introduction and guidance to VDI using Hyper-V and Remote Desktop Services.

Windows Server 2008 R2 high-availability and recovery features

In this chapter, we will discuss high-availability (HA) and recovery features available in Windows Server 2008 R2. This chapter will begin by providing an overview of planning for HA and disaster recovery as well as new features available in Windows Server 2008 R2. We will discuss how you can use HA options to provide system redundancy ensuring that critical business applications remain online in the event of a failure of the primary server. Additionally, we will discuss how Windows Network Load Balancing (NLB) features can be used to provide HA and resource balancing for front-end applications and web servers. This chapter will also take you through a sample exercise of setting up and managing HA features. This chapter will conclude with a discussion of planning and ensuring that you have reliable backups of your Windows servers.

INTRODUCTION TO HIGH AVAILABILITY

Many large organizations rely heavily on computer systems for mission critical business processes. In fact, some companies rely on these systems so much that a single hour of downtime for a critical system can end up costing a company thousands of dollars. Most administrators are well aware of all the things that can cause downtime to a server, including hardware failures, operating system issues, and regular maintenance. Microsoft has developed and continued to evolve HA solutions over the years to meet the needs of organizations that require very high uptimes even in the event of a server failure.

NOTES FROM THE FIELD

High availability versus disaster recovery

It is important to understand the differences between HA and disaster recovery when administering a Windows network. Though the two are very

---

different, their purposes can overlap in some instances. Traditionally, HA is used to ensure that an application remains online in the event of server failure. Disaster recovery is usually defined as a process used to recover a business process including systems in the event that the system has been completely lost or in the worst-case scenario, the geographic location that hosted the business process and supporting systems has been destroyed or taken offline by a natural disaster such as fire, flood, hurricane, or tornado. With that understanding, there are situations where overlap occurs. For example, a Windows Server 2008 R2 geo-cluster, discussed later in this chapter, provides not only HA services, but disaster recovery as well.

Windows Server 2008 R2 offers several features to ensure that applications and network services can sustain a failure of a primary server without the application or service experiencing significant downtime. The two primary Windows features that offer HA are

- Failover Clusters
- Network Load Balancing Clusters

Let us take a look at both of these features to understand their differences and how they can be used to provide HA to applications and services on your network.

Failover Clusters

Failover Clusters provide HA by implementing a "failover" process from a primary server (active) to a standby server (passive). Each server in the cluster is referred to as a node. Using the active/passive technology reserves one or more servers that sit idle in the event of a failure on the active server. In the event of a failure of the active node, a passive node will become active and carry on all activities the previous active node performed. Failover Clusters are typically used for back-end applications such as Microsoft Exchange Server or SQL Server. Figure 9.1 depicts a typical Windows Server 2008 R2 two-node Failover Cluster.

Network Load Balancing Clusters

NLB is the second type of HA service offered by Windows Server 2008 R2. Load balancing clusters can offer HA features to traditional front-end services such as IIS-based Web sites. NLB Clusters work in a very similar fashion as hardware-based network load balancers in that they distribute traffic between multiple servers that are members of the cluster. In the event that a server fails, NLB will direct traffic only to online servers, skipping the failed server. NLB Clusters not only provide HA services but

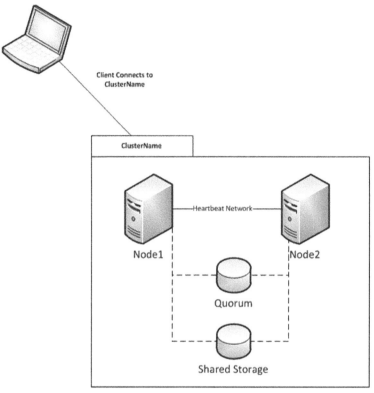

■ **FIGURE 9.1** Two-node Failover Cluster.

also balance traffic between all servers in the cluster ensuring that the load is evenly distributed. This also provides an easy way to scale front-end systems. For example, you might have two web servers in a NLB Cluster. Suppose the load on those servers becomes heavy and the Web site performance decreases dramatically. You notice that load is using all of the CPU resources on both web servers. You could simply add a third node to the cluster providing additional resources. The network traffic would then be distributed across three servers opposed to two. Figure 9.2 depicts a typical network load balanced cluster.

BEST PRACTICES

Change management
Even with HA and recovery technologies, you should always follow good change management processes when making changes to any, and especially mission critical systems. Be sure that you document any

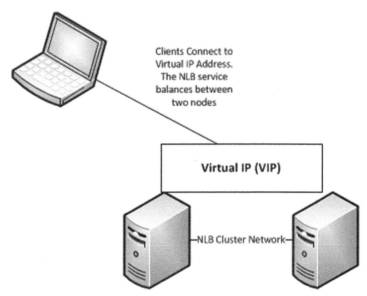

Clients Connect to
Virtual IP Address.
The NLB service
balances between
two nodes

Virtual IP (VIP)

NLB Cluster Network

■ **FIGURE 9.2** Three-node Network Load-Balanced Cluster.

configuration changes to production systems, and if your organization
requires, get proper approval before making changes. Even with HA
technologies, misconfigurations can easily bring business services offline
and cause helpdesk phones to start ringing.

NEW HIGH-AVAILABILITY AND RECOVERY FEATURES

Windows Server 2008 R2 includes several features to further enhance HA
and backup services. These include new features such as PowerShell
support for clustering and the ability to backup individual files and folders
with Windows Backup.

Failover Cluster PowerShell support

Failover Clusters can now be set up and administered using PowerShell
2.0. This includes not only the new cmdlets for Failover Clustering but
also the ability to remotely send commands to cluster services via
PowerShell 2.0. With the added support for PowerShell, the cluster.exe
command line utility is being deemphasized and may not be available in
future releases of Windows.

Cluster-Shared Volumes

Failover Clustering supports the use of Cluster-Shared Volumes (CSVs). These are volumes that can be accessed by multiple nodes of the cluster at the same time. This brings new benefits to Hyper-V deployments by providing Live Migration and reduced number of LUNs required. Live Migration allows you to move virtual machines between two hosts in a Failover Cluster with no downtime. CSV make this process possible.

Since previous versions of Windows could only have one host actively accessing the LUN, a failover would cause all VMs stored on a LUN to failover. Prior to Windows Server 2008 R2, Microsoft recommended that each VM in a Failover Cluster be assigned its own LUN to ensure that a single VM could fail over. For many deployments, this resulted in a lot of LUNs being assigned to each Hyper-V Host. Windows Server 2008 R2 removes this restriction using CSV allowing both hosts to access the volume at the same time, enabling a single VM on a LUN to fail over without requiring over VMs on that same LUN to do the same.

Improved Cluster Validation

Windows Server 2008 introduced the Cluster Validation Wizard. By using this wizard, administrators could easily verify and set up a cluster ensuring that it was in a supported configuration. If the cluster passed the validation wizard, it was considered to be in a correct configuration. Windows Server 2008 R2 adds additional tests to further ensure that a cluster can be validated using the Cluster Validation Wizard.

Support for additional cluster aware services

The Remote Desktop Connection Broker and DFS Replication (DFSR) can both be configured on a Failover Cluster to provide HA and redundancy to these services.

Ability to backup individual files and folders

Windows Server 2008 R1 (RTM) backup did not have the ability to select individual files and folders to be backed up. This was a feature offered in previous versions of Windows such as Windows Server 2003. Windows Server 2008 R1, however, provided the ability to backup only a full volume. Windows Server 2008 R2 has brought back the feature to allow administrators to selectively choose which files and folders to include in a backup set.

PLANNING FOR HIGH AVAILABILITY

Deploying HA features on your network requires adequate planning and testing prior to production use of the solution. One of the first planning steps you should perform is to determine what the expected uptime requirements are for the system. You may find out that the actual business need for the system does not even require HA features. This all depends on how long it takes to restore the system and how long the organization can work without the system being online. This needs to be reviewed from a business standpoint and should have buy-in from those in charge of the business process that is supported by a particular system. Additionally, you will need to determine whether the particular system is supported using Windows Server 2008 R2 HA features. For example, Microsoft SQL Server is a cluster aware application, and therefore can be supported using Failover Clustering features. IIS web servers can be configured using NLB features. A third-party database server may not be cluster aware, and therefore you may not be able to provide an HA solution for that application using Windows Server 2008 R2 Failover Clustering. There are Generic Application and Generic Service options for setting up applications and services that are not cluster aware. These, however, provide only basic Failover Clustering features. This allows you to set up HA services for the following standard Microsoft applications and services are cluster-aware meaning that they can be deployed on a Windows Server 2008 R2 Failover Cluster to provide HA:

- Microsoft SQL Server
- Microsoft Exchange Server
- DHCP Server
- File Server
- DFS Server
- Distributed Transaction Coordinator
- iSNS Server
- Message Queuing
- Print Server
- Remote Desktop Connection Broker
- Hyper-V Host
- WINS

After you have determined that HA features are required and that they can be supported by Windows Server 2008 R2 Failover Clustering or NLB, you can begin planning your HA solution.

Understanding how Failover Clustering works

As you previously learned, Windows Failover Clusters provide HA by deploying multiple servers in a cluster. The cluster hides the fact that multiple servers are deployed meaning that client computers see all servers in the cluster as a single server. Each server in the cluster is referred to as a node. Windows clustering uses an active/passive concept to support HA services. This means that active nodes are online and performing all processing requested by the installed application. In the event that the active node fails, the cluster fails-over to the passive node when then becomes active. The new active node continues to handle processing of the application.

Cluster nodes use heartbeat and quorum to determine which node is online and active and to initiate a failover in the event of a node failure. The heartbeat is used to determine whether nodes of the cluster are online. Each node communicates over the heartbeat network continuously to determine whether the other nodes are online. If an active node fails to return a heartbeat request, the cluster will fail over to a passive node. Quorum is used to ensure that the cluster can continue to function and nodes can recover in the event of failure. The quorum also helps ensure that clusters do not experience "split brain" which is where an active and passive node both believe they should be the active node. For a node in an active/passive cluster to become active, it must be able to communicate with the quorum. If a node cannot communicate with the quorum, it cannot become active. Windows Server 2008 R2 allows you to use a quorum disk or a file share, known as a file share witness. Failover Clusters can use any of the following quorum configurations:

- Node Majority—This quorum setting is used when there are an odd number of nodes in the cluster. This ensures that a cluster can tolerate failure of half of the nodes (rounded up) minus one.
- Node and Disk Majority—This quorum setting should be used for clusters with an even number of nodes. Using this setting, the cluster can tolerate failure of half of the nodes (rounded up) if the quorum disk remains online. If the quorum disk goes offline, the cluster can tolerate half of the nodes (rounded up) minus one. For example, if a four-node cluster can remain online if two nodes fail and the disk quorum remains online or if one node fails and the quorum disk fails.
- Node and File Share Majority—This quorum setting is used for clusters that require special configuration using a file share instead of a

quorum disk. For example, Exchange Server 2007 Continuous Cluster Replication (CCR) uses a file share witness.

■ No Majority-Disk Only—This setting is not recommended but using this quorum setting allows the cluster to tolerate failure of all nodes as long as the quorum disk remains online.

We will explore setting up quorum later in this chapter when we discuss administering Failover Clusters.

Planning for a Failover Cluster

When planning to implement a Failover Cluster, you need to answer the following preliminary questions:

■ How many node (server) failures should be tolerated? Windows Server 2008 R2 Failover Clusters can be configured with multiple nodes. For example, you could provide an active node with two passive nodes. In the event that the active node failed, one of the passive nodes would become active. In the event that the second node failed, the other passive node would then become active. This allows a Failover Cluster to support failure of multiple nodes.

■ Does the cluster need to support geographic resiliency? With the release of Windows Server 2008 R1, Failover Clusters now have the ability to span a wide area network. Using a geo-cluster, you can have an active node in one datacenter and the failover node in a datacenter in another geographic location. In the event of complete datacenter loss, the cluster could fail over the node in the second datacenter. Figure 9.3 depicts a Windows Server 2008 R2 geo-cluster.

■ Can the application sustain the brief time required to fail over to another node in the cluster? Failover Clusters require a very brief period of time to fail over in the event of a node going offline. You will want to ensure that your system, including front-end applications, can support this very brief outage. For example, you may deploy SQL server on a Failover Cluster. During the failover process, there will be a very brief period of time where the front-end application cannot talk to the SQL back-end. You need to verify whether the application can easily reconnect after the brief outage occurs. This outage is usually just a few seconds.

■ How will you be notified in the event of a node failure? The beauty of Failover Clustering is that the application remains online when a server fails. However, what if you as the administrator are not aware that a failure has occurred. The application is still online after all; thus,

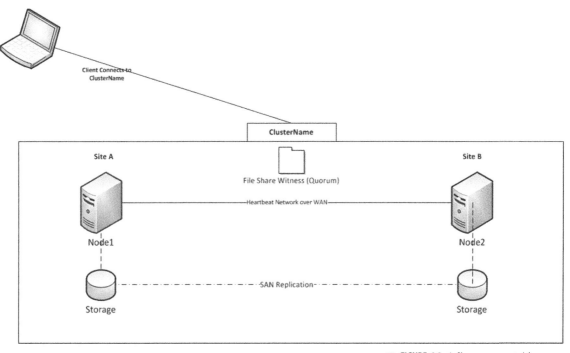

helpdesk phone lines probably are not ringing. This does not negate the fact that you need to know that a node has gone down and the cluster has failed-over. You need to be able to troubleshoot and resolve the issue that caused the failover to begin with. You also need to restore failover capabilities; otherwise, a second node failure could cause a service outage depending on how many failover nodes are available.

INSTALLING AND ADMINISTERING FAILOVER CLUSTERING

We will now take a look at the process of installing, configuring, and managing a Windows Server 2008 R2 Failover Cluster. This section will

- Help you ensure that cluster prerequisites are met.
- Take you through installing cluster features.
- Take you through connecting cluster nodes to shared storage to be used by the cluster.

- Validate the configuration and create a new cluster, using cluster management tools in Server Manager.
- Explore the process of administering a Failover Cluster, including manually performing a failover.
- Discuss testing the cluster by causing a service disruption on the active node.

Failover Clustering prerequisites

Before we set up a failover cluster, we need to ensure that our servers meet the necessary prerequisites. These include server hardware, software, and networking.

Server hardware requirements

When choosing servers to use in your failover cluster, you need to verify that the hardware meets requirements for use in Windows clusters. The most important requirement is that server hardware, including all components, must be certified for Windows Server 2008 R2. Certified hardware must be strenuous tests by Microsoft hardware labs. This hardware can be easily identified by the logo "Certified for Windows Server 2008 R2." Additionally, you can find a full list of certified hardware on the Windows Server Catalog Web site at http://www.windowsservercatalog.com.

NOTES FROM THE FIELD

Best practices

As best practice, Microsoft recommends not only that hardware be certified, but also that all servers in a Failover Cluster be the same brand and model, and have the same configuration. Using the exact same server configuration for each nodes ensures that all nodes follow a standard and that the cluster can support the greatest level of availability.

Network requirements

Clustered servers will require multiple network adapters for configuration. You will need at least one adapter for the primary Windows network, and a second adapter for cluster heartbeat communications. The heartbeat network allows cluster nodes to communicate with each other and verify availability (see Figure 9.4). Typically, this is a dedicated and isolated network. If a passive cluster node cannot communicate with the active node over the heartbeat network, it assumes that the active node is offline and initiates a failover.

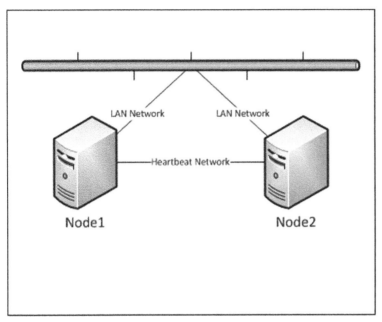

■ **FIGURE 9.4** Cluster Heartbeat Network.

If you will be using an iSCSI SAN as the shared storage medium, you will need at least one adapter or host bus adapter (HBA) to connect the server to the iSCSI network. Preferably, you should have two adapters or HBAs to provide redundancy for the connection to the iSCSI SAN.

NOTES FROM THE FIELD

NIC teaming

For additional redundancy to your HA solution, you may want to deploy NIC teaming. Many servers provide the ability to combine two physical network adapters so that they appear to the operating system as one adapter. In the event that a network adapter or switch port fails, the other adapter will continue to provide connectivity to the network. The operating system will still see the network adapter in a connected state. NIC teaming is not supported for iSCSI network connections.

Additional network requirements include:

- All cluster nodes must be members of the same Active Directory Domain.
- DNS must be used for name resolution by cluster nodes.

You will want to be sure that you have enough IP addresses reserved for all adapters used by a cluster node (local network, heartbeat, iSCSI). You may want to reserve a block of IP addresses for use by Windows Failover Clusters.

Operating system requirements

You will need to be sure to deploy a supported edition of Windows Server 2008 R2 to set up a Failover Cluster. The Failover Clustering features are available only in Enterprise, Datacenter, and Itanium editions of Windows Server 2008 R2. One exception to this is that Windows Server 2008 R2 Hyper-V server edition can participate in a Hyper-V Failover Cluster. All servers in a cluster should run the same operating system edition and be at the same service pack and patch level.

Storage requirements

Storage planning is another important aspect that must be considered for Windows Server 2008 R2 Failover Clusters. The main requirement is that the cluster use shared storage. This means that each node in the cluster has access to the same LUN with the exception of geo-clusters where the storage is replicated using storage replication technologies. You will additionally want to ensure that the shared storage is configured as basic disks opposed to dynamic and it is recommended that all partitions are formatted using NTFS. If you plan on using a quorum disk or CSVs, you will need to ensure that those are formatted as NTFS.

Prior to setting up storage for your cluster, be sure that the SAN or other shared storage is compatible with Windows Server 2008 R2 Failover Clusters. You will need to confirm this with your storage vendor.

After verifying whether all of the prerequisites are met, you will want to install the base operating system on all servers, join them to the Active Directory domain, and ensure that they are physically cabled to the correct networks and power sources. After performing the basic setup, you will be ready to start setting up the cluster.

Adding Failover Clustering feature

After verifying that your hardware and software meet the prerequisites required for a Windows Failover Cluster, you are ready to begin setting up the cluster. The first step is to add the Failover Cluster features to each cluster node. This is done via performing the following steps in Server Manager:

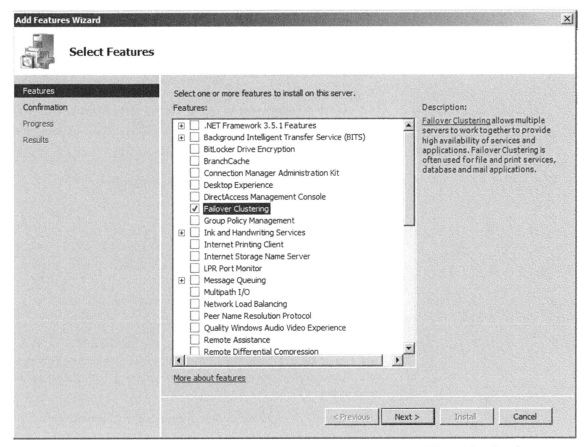

■ **FIGURE 9.5** Failover Cluster feature.

1. Select the *Features* node in *Server Manager*. Then click the *Add Features* link in the middle pane. This will launch the Add Features Wizard.
2. Select the *Failover Clustering* feature as seen in Figure 9.5. Then click *Next*.
3. Click *Install* to install the feature.
4. Verify that installation was successful and then click *Close*.
5. Verify that the Failover Cluster Manager now appears in Server Manager as seen in Figure 9.6.

Configuring server networks

After adding the Failover Clustering feature, you will be ready to set up networking. This includes the heartbeat network and if necessary, iSCSI

■ **FIGURE 9.6** Failover Cluster Manager.

networks. As best practice, the iSCSI, LAN, and Heartbeat networks should be separate subnets and physical networks or VLANs. Your network adapter configuration for each cluster node may look similar to the one depicted in Figure 9.7.

In our example, we will use the following subnet configurations:

192.168.5.0/24—Local Area Network
172.16.0.0/24—iSCSI Network
10.1.1.0/24—Cluster Heartbeat Network

Assign IP addresses to the respective network adapters for each of these networks and verify connectivity. Just as you added the Failover Clustering feature, you will need to configure network settings on each cluster node.

Connecting cluster nodes to shared storage

After setting up networking, you are ready to connect your servers to their respective storage. In our example, we are using an iSCSI SAN for shared storage. During setup, you will want to limit LUN access to

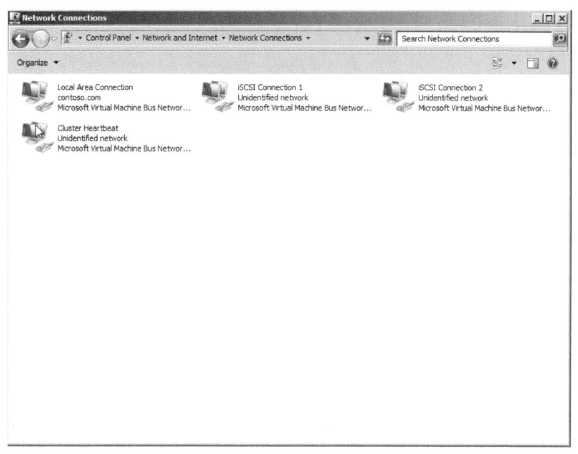

the primary node only. If two nodes concurrently access a LUN prior to completing the cluster setup, the LUN could become corrupted. This can be accomplished by ensuring that all the disks stay "offline" on the passive node. If using an iSCSI SAN, you may want to use multipathing. Multipathing enables the server to use load-balance and failover between two separate network connections. This provides improved performance and redundancy for iSCSI connections. If you plan on using multipathing, you need to install the Multipath IO feature. To add multipath support, perform the following:

1. Open *Server Manager* and select the *Features* node.
2. Click the *Add Features* link in the middle pane launching the *Add Features Wizard*.
3. Select the *Multipath I/O* option as seen in Figure 9.8. Then click *Next*.
4. Click *Install* on the Confirmation page.
5. When installation is complete, click *Close*.
6. Add this feature to each node in the cluster.

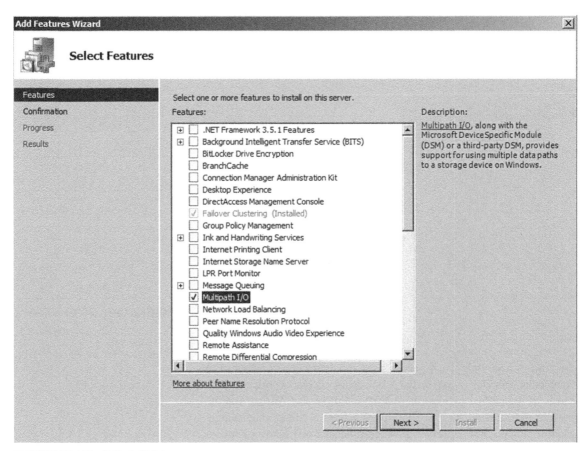

■ **FIGURE 9.8** Adding Multipath I/O features.

After you have installed multipathing support, perform the following steps to connect each node to the iSCSI SAN, using the Microsoft iSCSI Initiator:

1. Open the *iSCSI Initiator* from *Start | All Programs | Administrative Tools | iSCSI Initiator.*
2. Select the *Discovery Tab.*
3. Click *Discover Portal* and enter the IP address of the iSCSI SAN (see Figure 9.9). Then click *OK.*
4. Select the *Targets* tab. You should now see the assigned iSCSI storage listed in Discovered Targets (see Figure 9.10).
5. Select one of the volumes you want to connect, and then click *Connect.*
6. In the *Connect to Target* window, select the *Enable multi-path* option as seen in Figure 9.11. Then click *Advanced.*

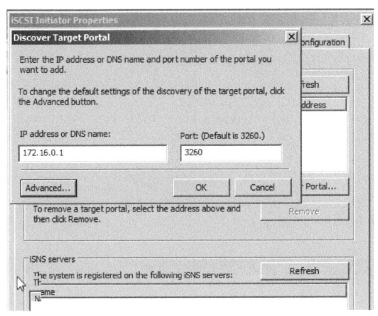

■ **FIGURE 9.9** Add iSCSI Portal to Discover.

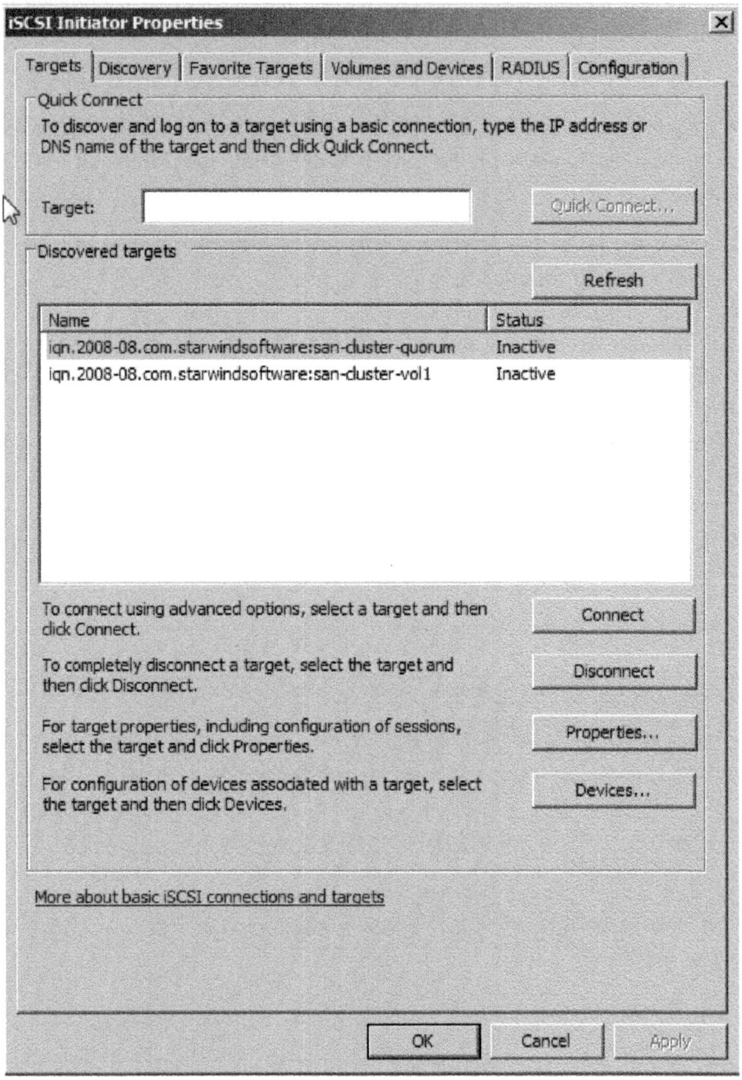

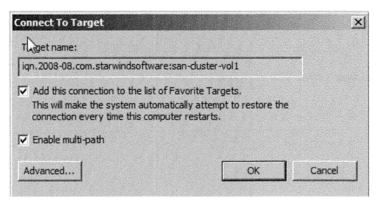

FIGURE 9.10 iSCSI Targets.

FIGURE 9.11 Connect to iSCSI Target.

7. Configure the following iSCSI advanced options (see Figure 9.12):

- ❑ *Local Adapter*—Select the *Microsoft iSCSI Initiator.*
- ❑ *Initiator IP*—Select the IP address assigned to the first iSCSI network adapter.
- ❑ *Target Portal IP*—Select the IP Address of the iSCSI SAN.

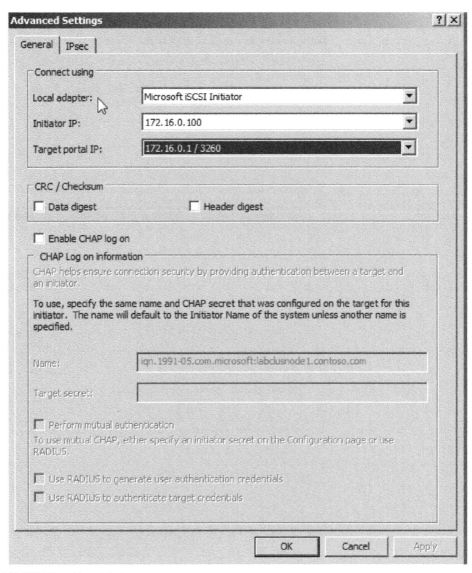

■ **FIGURE 9.12** iSCSI Initiator Advanced Settings.

Optionally you can configure CHAP authentication if required to secure connectivity to your iSCSI SAN. After configuring the initiator advanced settings, click *OK*. Then click *OK* to close the Connect to Target window.

You should now see the volume connected as seen in Figure 9.13. You should now perform steps 5 through 7 again for the same volume, except this time selecting the second initiator IP in step 7. This will connect both

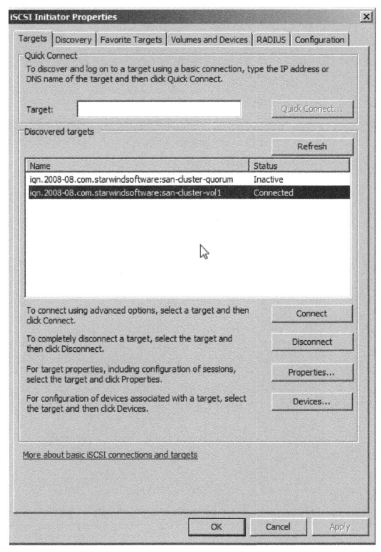

■ **FIGURE 9.13** Connected iSCSI Target.

the iSCSI adapters to the volume. You will need to repeat this process to connect each volume to the active node of the cluster and then connect the passive node to each volume of the cluster.

After connecting to each volume, you can verify whether they are connected by opening *Disk Management* in Server Manager (see Figure 9.14).

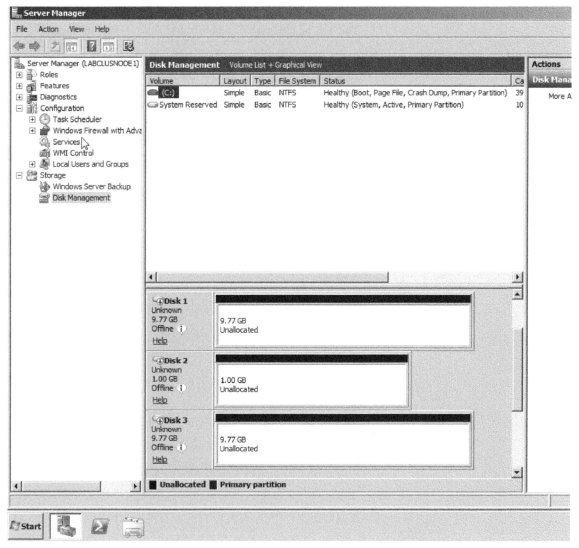

Notice that since you have multiple connections (each iSCSI network adapter) opened to each target, the disks are listed twice in Disk Management. This is due to the fact that you have not yet enabled multipath on the server. To enable multipath, perform the following:

1. Open the *MPIO* control panel (*Start | Control Panel | MPIO*).
2. Select the *Discover Multi-Paths* tab.
3. Select the *Add support for iSCSI devices* option. Then click *Add* (see Figure 9.15).
4. You will be prompted to reboot; click *Yes* to reboot the server.

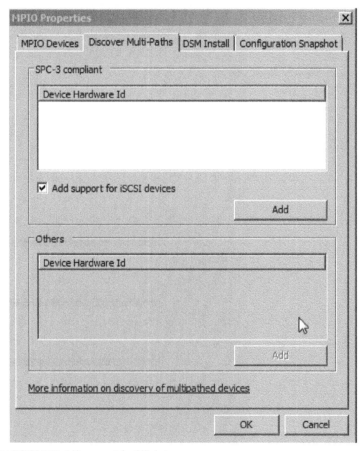

■ **FIGURE 9.15** Adding support for iSCSI devices.

After the server reboots, multipath will be enabled. You can verify this by opening Disk Management in Server Manager. You should now see each SAN disk listed only once. You will again need to perform this on each node of the cluster.

After each node can see all disks, you will need to logon to the active node and bring one of the disk drives online and create a new volume. This can be done via Disk Management in Server Manager. Perform the following steps to bring the disk that will be used for quorum online and create a new volume:

1. Open *Server Manager*.
2. Select the node *Storage | Disk Management*.
3. Right click the disk that you want to bring online and select the *Online* option (see Figure 9.16).

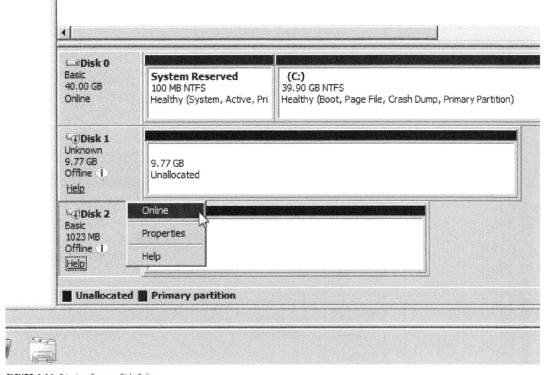

■ **FIGURE 9.16** Bringing Quorum Disk Online.

4. Right click the same disk and choose *Initialize*.

5. Right click the *unallocated space* and choose *Create Simple Volume* (see Figure 9.17).

6. Complete the *New Simple Volume Wizard* to create a new volume. Format the volume as NTFS, use the drive letter of Q, and label the volume quorum.

The disk should now be ready to be used for cluster quorum settings. You are now ready to validate your cluster configuration.

Verifying cluster configuration using the Cluster Validation Wizard

The Cluster Validation Wizard will perform a series of rigorous tests to ensure that you storage, nodes, and network are configured properly to

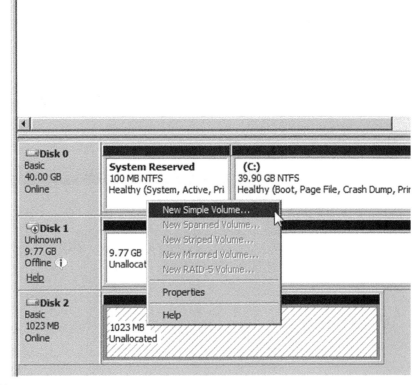

■ **FIGURE 9.17** Creating a New Simple Volume for Quorum.

support a Windows Server 2008 R2 failover cluster. Using this wizard, you can validate that your nodes are ready to be used to create a new cluster. You can also run this wizard against an existing cluster to validate that it is properly configured. To validate your configuration, perform the following on either node of the cluster:

1. Open *Server Manager*.
2. Select the node *Features | Failover Cluster Manager*.
3. Click the *Validate Configuration* link in the middle pane (see Figure 9.18). This will launch the Validate a Configuration Wizard.
4. Click *Next* to begin.
5. Select all nodes that will participate in the cluster configuration. This can be done by typing their FQDN or by browsing for them, using the Browse button (see Figure 9.19). After selecting all nodes to be used by the cluster, click *Next*.
6. Select the option to *Run All Tests*. Then click *Next*.

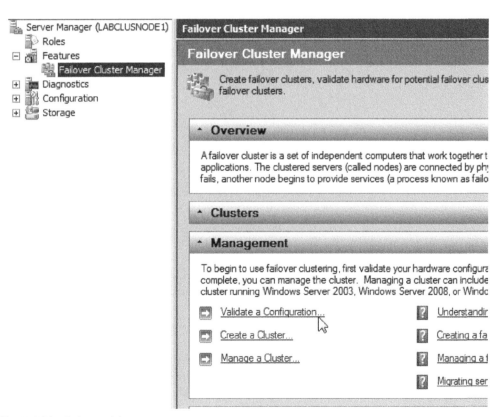

■ **FIGURE 9.18** Validate Configuration link.

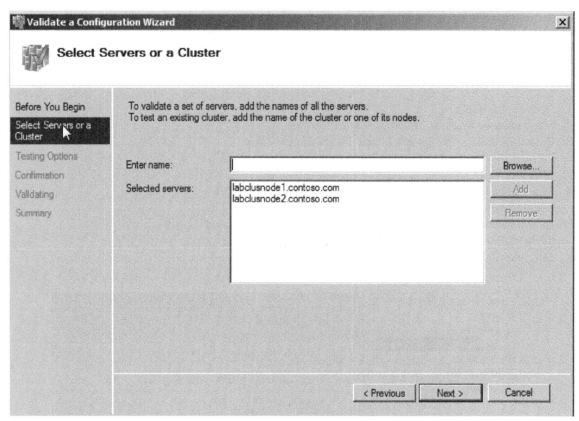

■ **FIGURE 9.19** Select Cluster nodes.

7. Verify that the correct nodes are selected on the Confirmation page. Then click *Next* to begin the validation process.
8. You will see a series of tests begin to run as seen in Figure 9.20. It may take several minutes for all the tests to be completed. When the validation process is complete, click *View Report* to view the results of the validation tests.
9. Review the report for any warnings or errors (see Figure 9.21). You will need to correct any errors before creating a cluster. Warnings may require an issue to be resolved in some cases and in others they can be safely ignored. For example, if using iSCSI storage, the report will list a network warning for the iSCSI network adapters, stating that they are on the same subnet.

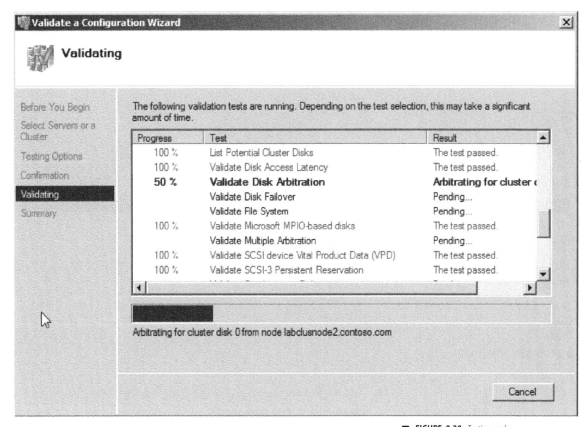

FIGURE 9.20 Testing nodes.

After reviewing the validation report, you can close it and click *Finish* to close the wizard. If you need to correct any errors and warnings, you will need to run the Validation Wizard again after correcting the errors. After verifying whether your configuration is cluster ready, you can create a new Failover Cluster.

Creating a new Failover Cluster

To create a new Failover Cluster, perform the following steps:

1. Open *Server Manager*.
2. Select the node *Features | Failover Cluster Manager*.
3. Click the *Create A Cluster* link in the middle pane. This will launch the *Create Cluster Wizard*.
4. Click *Next* to begin.

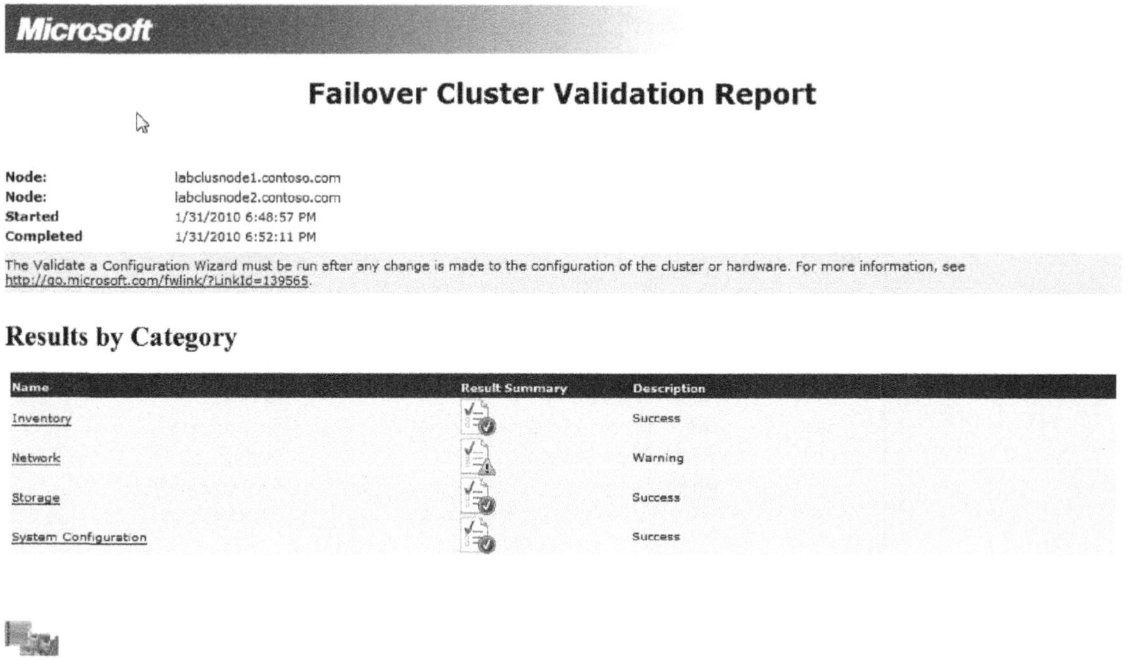

Microsoft

Failover Cluster Validation Report

Node:	labclusnode1.contoso.com
Node:	labclusnode2.contoso.com
Started	1/31/2010 6:48:57 PM
Completed	1/31/2010 6:52:11 PM

The Validate a Configuration Wizard must be run after any change is made to the configuration of the cluster or hardware. For more information, see http://go.microsoft.com/fwlink/?LinkId=139565.

Results by Category

Name	Result Summary	Description
Inventory		Success
Network		Warning
Storage		Success
System Configuration		Success

■ **FIGURE 9.21** Validation Wizard Report.

5. Add the servers that you want to become nodes in the cluster (see Figure 9.22). Then click *Next*.
6. Enter the name and IP address to be used for the cluster (see Figure 9.23). The name you choose is the name that will be used to administer the cluster. After entering the cluster name and IP address, click *Next*.
7. Verify the settings on the Confirmation page, and then click *Next*. The wizard will create the new cluster.
8. Verify that the cluster was created successfully, and then click *Finish*.

You should now see the new cluster displayed in the Failover Cluster Manager node as seen in Figure 9.24.

Add primary storage to cluster

Now that we have successfully created our cluster with a quorum disk, we need to bring the primary disk to be used for file shares online. To do this, perform the following:

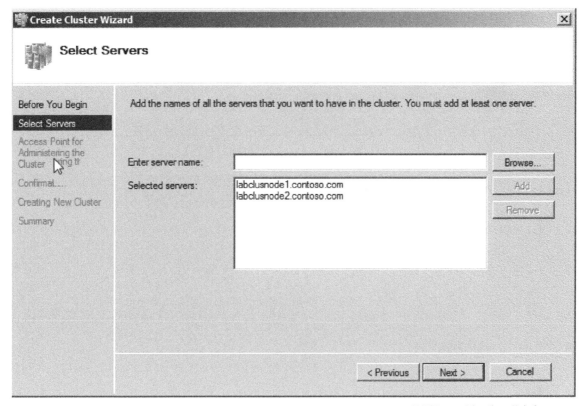

■ **FIGURE 9.22** Select Cluster Node Servers.

1. Open *Server Manager* and select the *Disk Management* console.
2. Bring the disk online and initialize it. Then create a new simple volume.
3. After creating a new usable volume, expand the cluster node and select *Storage* as seen in Figure 9.25. You will notice that the quorum disk is already online.
4. Right click the *Storage* node and select *Add Disk*.
5. Select the newly created disk in the Add Disks to Cluster window and click *OK*.

You should now see the newly added disk appear in the Storage node as seen in Figure 9.26.

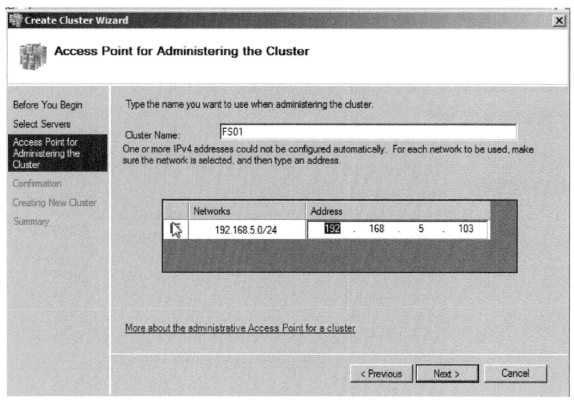

FIGURE 9.23 Selecting Cluster Name and IP Address.

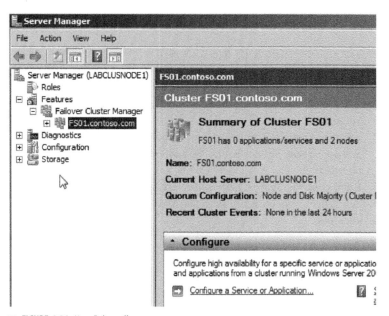

FIGURE 9.24 New Failover Cluster.

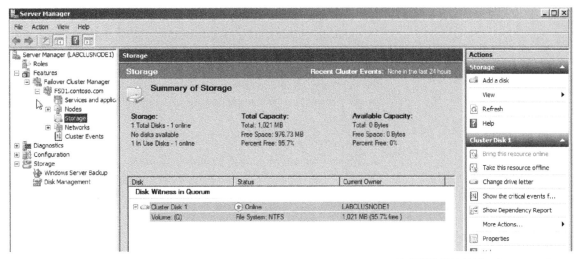

■ **FIGURE 9.25** Add New Storage to a Cluster.

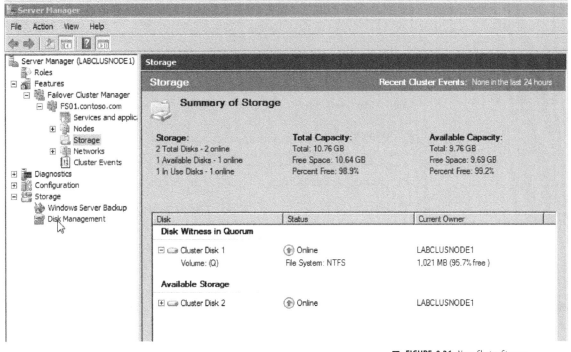

■ **FIGURE 9.26** New Cluster Storage.

Configure service or application

Now that the cluster is set up, you are ready to set up the service or application you wish to support on the cluster. In our example, we will be using the cluster to provide HA to a windows file server. You now need to add the File Services role to each node of the cluster. After adding the appropriate services, perform the following to set up the cluster as a clustered file server:

1. Open *Server Manager.*
2. Expand the node *Features | Failover Cluster.*
3. Select the cluster and click the *Configure Service or Application* link in the middle pane (see Figure 9.27). This will launch the HA Wizard.
4. Click *Next* to begin.

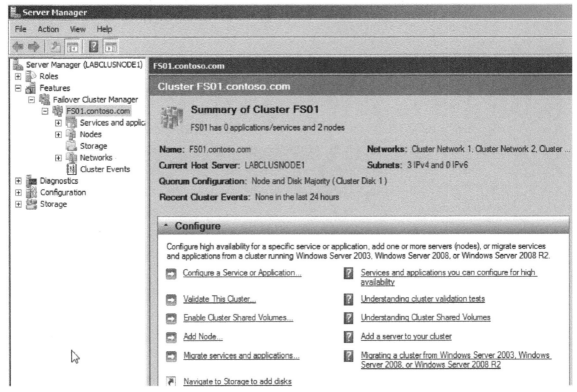

■ **FIGURE 9.27** Configure Service or Application for Failover Clustering.

5. Select the service or application you want to make highly available. In our example, select the *File Server* option as seen in Figure 9.28. Then click *Next*.

6. Enter a name and IP address that clients will use to connect to the cluster (see Figure 9.29). Clients do not connect to individual server names but the name of the cluster itself. This is required as part of the clustering service. If clients connected to the name of the server nodes, they would lose connectivity if a node failed. If connected to the cluster name, the cluster will automatically fail the connection over to the second node. After entering the cluster name and IP address, click *Next*.

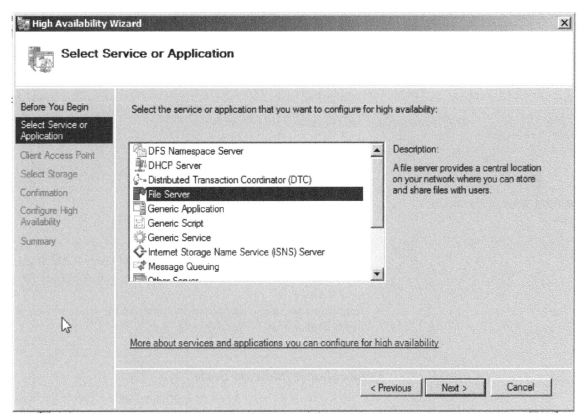

■ **FIGURE 9.28** Select Service or Application to be supported by cluster.

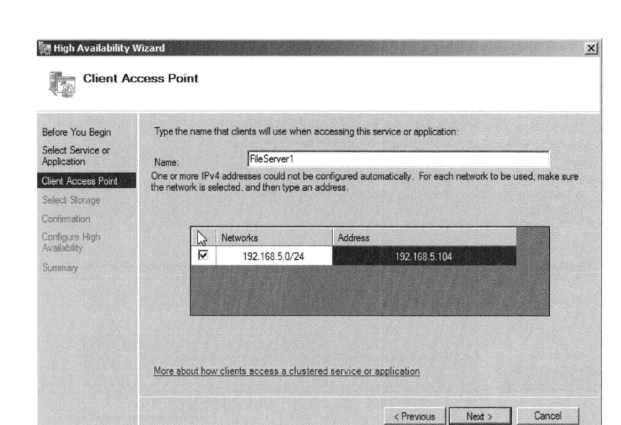

■ **FIGURE 9.29** Enter Cluster Name and IP
Address.

7. Select the disk that will hold the file shares (see Figure 9.30). This is the disk drive and data that will be made highly available. Click *Next* to continue.
8. Confirm settings and click *Next* to configure the file server services as highly available.
9. Click *Finish* on the success page.

Create shared folder on cluster

The file server cluster should now be configured and accessible to clients using the cluster name established for client connectivity. You are now

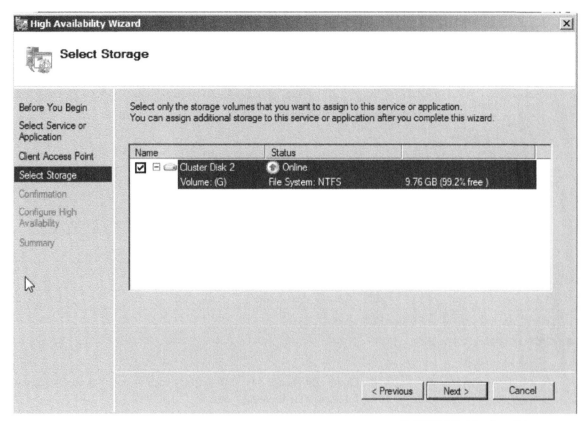

■ **FIGURE 9.30** Select Cluster Disk.

ready to create a new file share for clients to access. Perform the following to create a new file share on the cluster:

1. Open *Server Manager*.
2. Expand the *Features | Failover Cluster* node.
3. Expand the cluster node | *Services and Applications*.
4. Right click on the cluster name and select *Add Shared Folder* as seen in Figure 9.31.
5. Select the location to create the new share, and then click *Next*.
6. Set Permissions on the Share then click *Next*.
7. Enter a share name (see Figure 9.32). Then click *Next*.

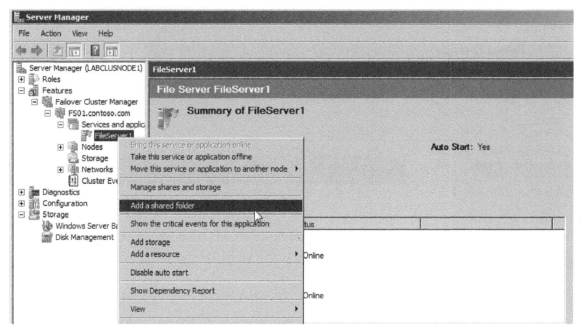

■ **FIGURE 9.31** Add shared folder to cluster.

8. Optionally change any SMB settings such as enabling Access-Based Enumeration. Then click *Next*.
9. Optionally set share permissions, and then click *Next*.
10. If you want to publish the share to a DFS namespace, enter that information now. Then click *Next*.
11. Verify settings for the new clustered file share, and then click *Create*.
12. Verify that the process has been completed successfully, and then click *Close*.

You have now successfully completed setup of a shared folder on the clustered file server. Before placing data on the cluster, you should test moving the cluster from one node to another, and test a failover of the cluster by shutting down the active node.

Testing Failover of Cluster

To failover the cluster, perform the following:

1. Open *Server Manager*.
2. Expand the node *Features | Failover Cluster*.

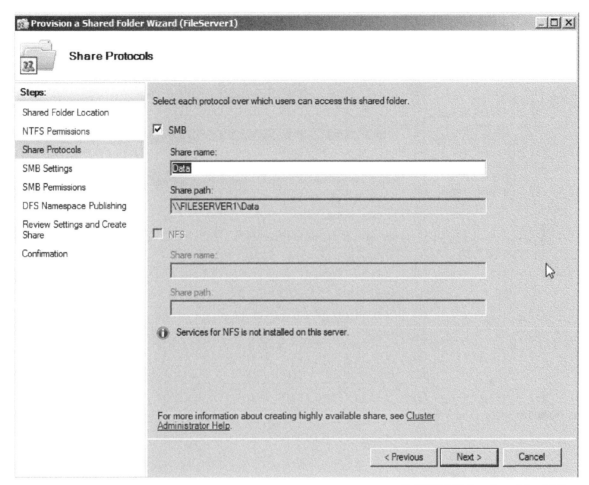

FIGURE 9.32 Name Clustered Shared Folder.

3. Expand the cluster node and select *Services and applications.*
4. In the middle pane, right click the service and select the option *Move this service or application to another node.* Choose the node you want to become the active node (see Figure 9.33).
5. If prompted, confirm that you want to move the cluster to the other node. The move process will begin and the cluster status will move to pending. After the cluster moves to the other node, you should see that node as active.

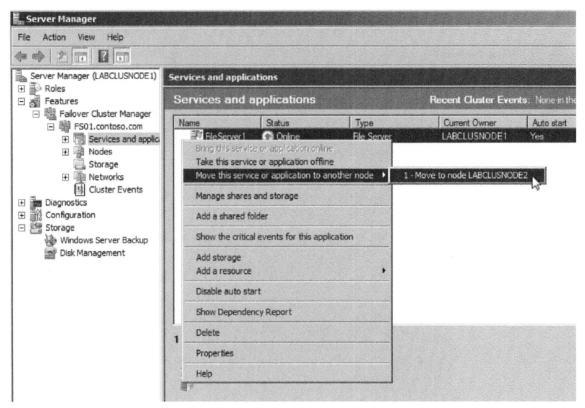

■ **FIGURE 9.33** Move service to another cluster node.

If you want to test the failover of the cluster, simply shut down the active host. After a few seconds, you should see the cluster automatically failover to the passive node.

After testing failover, you should run the validation wizard one final time to verify whether the cluster is production ready and is in a supported configuration.

> **NOTES ON HYPER-V**
> When building a Failover Cluster for Hyper-V, you can add the Hyper-V role after creating the Failover Cluster. At that point, you can enable clustered shared volumes and enable Live Migration. This will allow you to move running virtual machines from one host to another.

Administering a Failover Cluster

After you set up a new cluster, you will need to make sure that you are familiar with the management interface and understand how to perform basic cluster administration tasks. You also need to have an understanding of how to monitor the health of your cluster as well as how to perform regular maintenance. Each cluster has four primary areas for administration and monitoring:

- Services and Applications
- Nodes
- Storage
- Networks
- Cluster Events

Services and applications

This section is used to manage the application or service supported by the cluster. For example, this node can be used to create new shared folders on a file server cluster. You can also use the Services and Applications node to manually failover the cluster in the event that you want to test failover capabilities or perform maintenance on the primary node. Additionally, the Services and Applications node allows you to run a dependency report which will graphically display all dependencies in the cluster as seen in Figure 9.34.

BEST PRACTICES

Applying updates and patching cluster nodes

As best practice, you should apply service packs and updates to a passive node of the cluster first. After applying the updates, move the cluster to the passive node, and then apply updates to the nodes that were previously active.

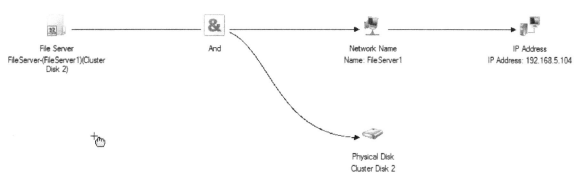

■ **FIGURE 9.34** Cluster dependency report.

Nodes

The Nodes section allows you to manage existing cluster nodes as well as add new ones. By adding new nodes, you can provide additional availability to the cluster; however, if you change the number of nodes, you may need to change the quorum setting. You can also use the Nodes section to evict nodes form the cluster. In the event that a node fails, you may need to use the evict option to remove it from the cluster.

Storage

The Storage section is used to add and remove storage to and from the cluster. If new disks are configured, they should be added to the cluster, using the Add Disk option. You can also use the Storage section to simulate a failure of the quorum disk. This is helpful in testing what types of failures your cluster can tolerate, without going offline.

NOTES FROM THE FIELD

Cluster shared volumes for Hyper-V

If you are using the cluster to host Hyper-V virtual machines, and you want to provide Live Migration services, you will need to enable CSV by right clicking on the cluster node and selecting the option to *Enable Cluster Shared Volumes*. You should *only* select this option if the cluster will be supporting Hyper-V fail-over and Live Migration.

Networks

The Networks section allows you to administer the network settings for the cluster. These settings include specifying which networks can be used for cluster communications and which can be used for client connectivity (see Figure 9.35). For example, you may want to ensure that the cluster cannot perform node-to-node communications through the iSCSI network.

Cluster Events

The Cluster Events section can be used to monitor Windows events related to the failover cluster. This includes configuration warnings and critical errors such as failover events (see Figure 9.36). These events should be reviewed on a regular basis either manually or by monitoring tools such

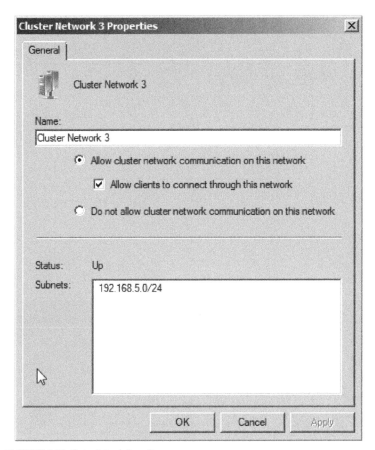

■ **FIGURE 9.35** Cluster Network Properties.

as Microsoft System Center Operations Manager 2007. Error events in this log typically represent a degradation in the health of the cluster.

Using PowerShell to manage Failover Clusters

You can use PowerShell to perform many common administrative tasks for Failover Clusters. This provides an easy way to manage a cluster from the command line and also to automate tasks using scripts. It is recommended that you use PowerShell over the cluster.exe command line tool as cluster.exe is being deemphasized and may not be available in future versions of Windows. Let us take a look at a couple of PowerShell commands that can be used to help manage a cluster.

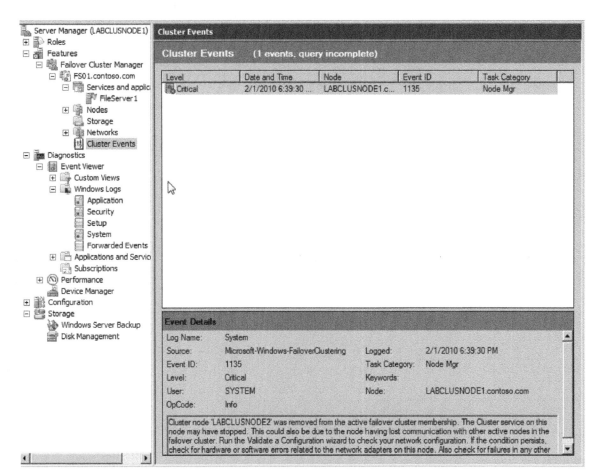

■ **FIGURE 9.36** Cluster Event Log.

Move-ClusterGroup—This command can be used to manually fail the cluster over to a passive node. For example:

`Move-ClusterGroup -name FileServer1` will manually move the file server to any available passive node.

You could also issue the command `Move-ClusterGroup -name FileServer1 -node ClusNode2` to specify which passive node to fail the cluster over to. This command could be helpful if you have an automatically schedule patch install for clustered servers. You could create a PowerShell script that will manually failover the cluster and schedule it to run after the passive node has been patched.

Test-Cluster—This command can be used to run the validation wizard from the command line. This command can be used to regularly automate running the validation test. For example, you could create a PowerShell script that issues the following command:

`Test-Cluster -ReportName Z:\ClusterValidationReport.mht`. This would run the validation wizard and save the report on the Z: drive which could easily be a shared folder on a network server.

INSTALLING AND ADMINISTERING NETWORK LOAD BALANCING

As previously mentioned, NLB is a technology used to provide HA and balance traffic between two front-end application servers such as IIS Web sites. Windows Server 2008 R2 NLB is depicted in Figure 9.37.

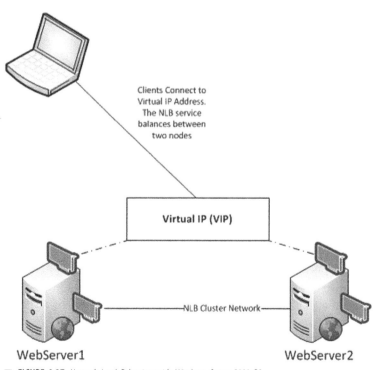

■ **FIGURE 9.37** Network Load Balancing with Windows Server 2008 R2.

Network Load Balancing prerequisites

Prior to installing NLB, you will need to add the feature from Server Manager. You will also need to ensure that you have a dedicated Virtual IP (VIP) address. The VIP is what clients use to connect to the NLB cluster. Additionally, if you plan to use unicast mode, you will need a second dedicated network adapter for load balancing.

Adding Network Load Balancing feature

The first step to setting up NLB is to add the feature from Server Manager. You will need to perform this on each server you want to add to the NLB cluster. To add NLB to the server, perform the following:

1. Open *Server Manager*.
2. Select the *Features* node.
3. In the middle pane, click the *Add Features* link. The Add Features Wizard will launch.
4. Select the *Network Load Balancing* (see Figure 9.38) feature, and then click *Next*.
5. Click *Install*.
6. When installation is complete, click *Close* to complete the feature installation process.

Creating a Network Load Balancing cluster

After installing the NLB feature on each server that will become a cluster node, you are ready to create a new cluster. Perform the following to create a new NLB cluster:

1. Open the *Network Load Balancing Manager* from *Start | All Programs | Administrative Tools | Network Load Balancing Manager*.
2. Right click *Network Load Balancing Clusters* and select *Create New Cluster* (see Figure 9.39).
3. Enter the hostname of the cluster node you wish to configure. Then click *Connect* (see Figure 9.40).
4. Select the interface that you want to use for the NLB cluster. Remember that this has to be a dedicated network adapter if you plan on using unicast mode. Select the interface you want to use, and then click *Next*.
5. Select the IP address that you want to dedicate for cluster traffic. You also need to select the host priority (see Figure 9.41). The lower numbered node is the first to receive traffic. Then click *Next*.

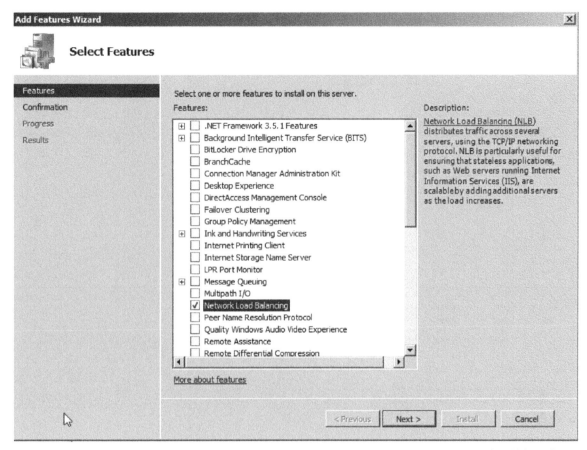

■ **FIGURE 9.38** Network Load Balancing feature.

6. Enter the cluster VIP address (see Figure 9.42). This is the address that clients will use to connect to the cluster. This IP will be shared among all nodes of the cluster. Then click *Next*.

7. You now need to configure the cluster operation mode (see Figure 9.43). You can use one of the following modes:
   ❑ Unicast
   ❑ Multicast
   ❑ IGMP Multicast

In addition to selecting the cluster operation mode, you can optionally enter a FQDN that will be used to refer to the cluster IP. Click *Next* to continue.

8. You now need to configure the NLB ports range, protocols, and filtering mode (see Figure 9.44):

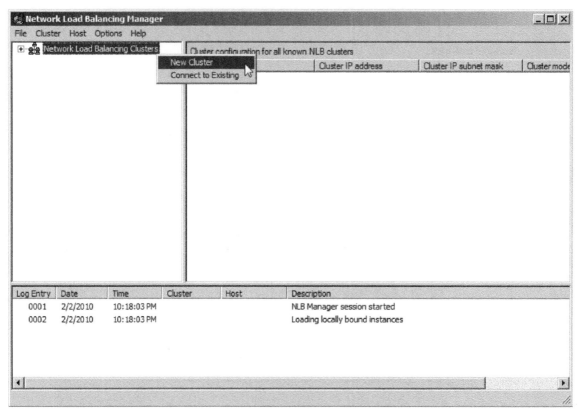

■ **FIGURE 9.39** Network Load Balancing
Manager.

❏ *Ports Range*—This is the range of ports that will be load balanced.
You should limit this range to the ports used by the application
being load balanced. For example, if you are load balancing an IIS
Web site, you will more than likely want to use ports 80 and 443.

❏ *Protocols*—Similar to port range, you need to select the protocols
(TCP or UDP) used by the application being load balanced.

❏ *Filtering Mode*—Filtering mode is used to help configure
"stickyness." Many applications may require that once a session is
initiated to a host the client must continue to use the same host to
complete certain transactions. For example, an ecommerce site
could host a checkout process. The application may require that
you remain on the same host to perform the checkout. To help
ensure that this session "sticks" to the same host, you can use
filtering. By choosing Multiple host and setting affinity to single,

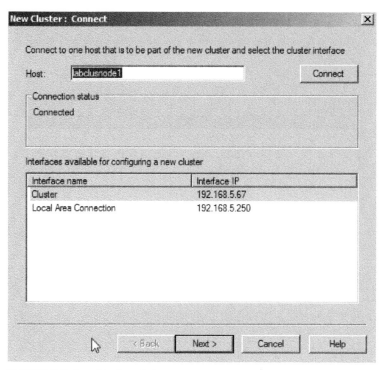

■ **FIGURE 9.40** Connect to Cluster Host.

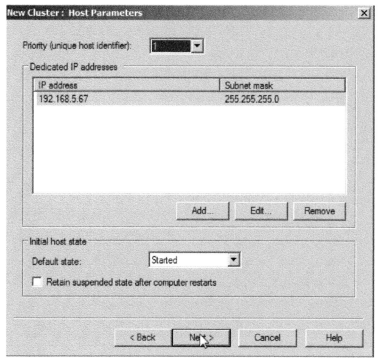

■ **FIGURE 9.41** Host Parameters.

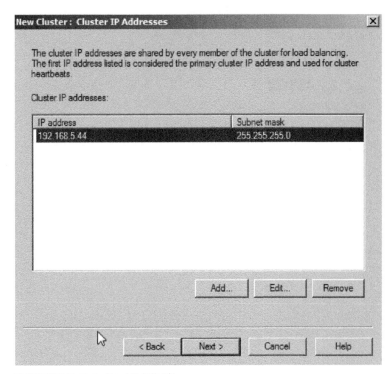

■ **FIGURE 9.42** Cluster Virtual IP (VIP) Address.

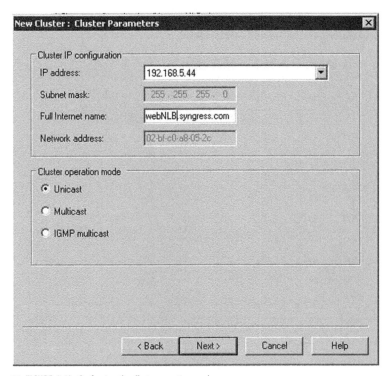

■ **FIGURE 9.43** Configuring the Cluster operation mode.

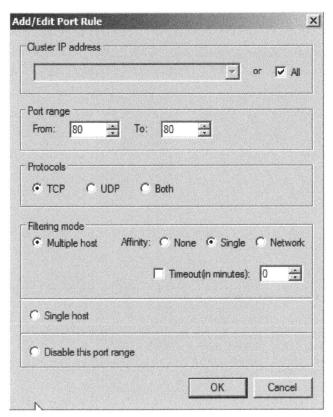

■ FIGURE 9.44 Configuring the NLB Ports range, Protocols, and Filtering mode.

NLB will ensure that as long as the client comes from the same IP address, it will remain on the same node for the duration of the session. By setting affinity to Network, NLB will ensure that the client's network, subnetted to a class C, will continue the session on the same host. This is useful if the clients are NAT'd behind firewall with multiple public IP addresses.

After configuring port rules and filtering, click *Finish* to complete the setup of the NLB cluster. You will see several configuration steps taking place in the Network Load Balancer Manager. When the configuration is complete, you should see a newly set up NLB cluster similar to Figure 9.45.

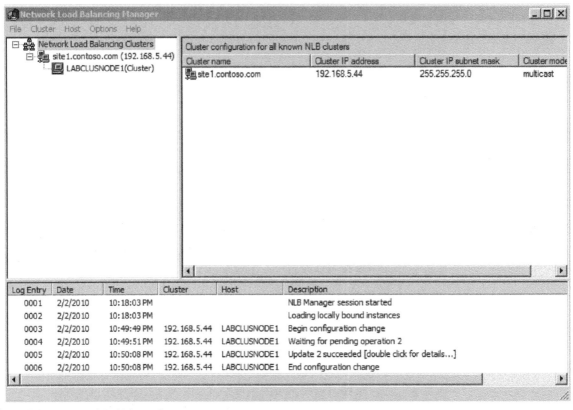

■ **FIGURE 9.45** Network Load Balancing Cluster.

Adding an additional node to the NLB cluster

After initial setup, you will need to add the rest of the nodes to the cluster. To add additional nodes, perform the following within Network Load Balancer Manager:

1. Right click the cluster and select the option to *Add Host to Cluster*.
2. Enter the server name of the host you wish to add as a node and click *Connect*.
3. Select the interface you wish to use for the cluster, and then click *Next*.
4. Select the priority of the new node, and then select the IP address to be used for cluster traffic. Then click *Next*.
5. Verify that the port and affinity configuration matches that of the other node. These options should be grayed out. Then click *Finish*.

The Network Load Balancer Manger should perform a few configuration steps and then add the second node to the cluster.

You can now test the cluster by accessing the NLB cluster IP address. If you want to verify NLB functionality and that failover is working properly, you can shut down one of the nodes. You should still be able to access the application or Web site on the cluster IP address.

PLANNING FOR BACKUPS AND DISASTER RECOVERY

One of the most important and overlooked functions of administering a Windows network is planning for and implementing good backup and recovery solutions. Typically, administrators learn to implement good recovery processes and practices only after they have survived a disaster situation where they lost data that was critical to the company. If you want to be a good administrator, plan for worst case scenarios and hope for the best.

Disaster recovery planning

In most organizations, planning for disaster encompasses a lot more than just the IT department. How a company defines a disaster varies from one organization to another. A small business may consider a disaster the complete loss of the office building. A larger organization could consider the loss of a critical system as a disaster. It really depends on your recovery needs and how dependent your organization is on the systems that support it. The actual process of planning for big disaster will require involvement from various aspects of the company and will involve planning outside of the formal IT organization. For example, if the company loses an entire building because of fire, plans will need to be put into action that cover logistics around facilities, communications, emergency services, IT, etc. Do not make your disaster recovery an "IT Thing," but make it a business thing. Work with various business units to determine which systems are critical to business processes and ensure that you have a good plan in place for those first. Work with the owner of each business application and determine a realistic option for the following:

- Recovery Point Objective (RPO)—The RPO is the longest acceptable data loss expressed in time. For example, can your organization function if the given system loses the last 24 h of data?
- Recovery Time Objective (RTO)—The RTO is the acceptable amount of downtime permitted for a given system. For example,

it may only be acceptable that the organization have an email outage of 4 h in the event of a disaster. This means that email must be backed up with messages flowing within 4 h of the disaster.

As you build your disaster plan, document and test it. You do not want to guess at critical decisions in the time of crisis.

As you begin to build your disaster recovery plan, consider the various technologies that can be used to provide recovery from a disaster. These can include clustering technologies, offsite replication services, or traditional backups. For example, you might want to consider supporting a critical file server via a geo-cluster for automated failover in the event of a disaster. On the other hand, you may only want to perform tape backups of your print server as it may not be deemed critical. Again you need to thoroughly document each system and what technologies you can use for disaster recovery. Document the recovery process in such a way that another person could perform the recovery in the event that you are unable to do so.

After determining the method to use for recovery, implement and test it on a regular basis. Without regular testing, there is no guarantee that your recovery process will work as you expect in the time of a real disaster.

As part of your disaster recovery planning, you will need to plan for and implement a good backup strategy. Even with a good disaster recovery plan, you will find yourself needing to backup data, using traditional backup methods for data retention and worst case scenarios (disaster recovery failure).

Backups

Creating a good backup strategy could very well be one of the toughest aspects of your job as an administrator. This strategy should be an evolving process that is modified as necessary to support systems supporting your organization's business functions. You will again want to have an understanding from the business perspective as to how important a given application is to your organization. It may be determined that a SQL server must be backed up every 4 h, yet an application server may need only a weekly backup.

Depending on the size of your organization and the number of servers you manage, you may need to consider an enterprise backup solution opposed to using the built-in Windows Server Backup. Microsoft offers its own version of an enterprise solution as part of the System Center suite of products. System Center Data Protection Manager (DPM) can be used to backup Windows servers as well as applications such as SQL, Exchange, and SharePoint servers. For more information on DPM, visit http://www. microsoft.com/SystemCenter

Some common strategies used for backups include disk-based backup solutions also known as Disk-to-Disk-to-Tape (D2D2T). These solutions involve backing up data to disk drives allowing for quick recoveries. After a defined period of time, the backup is then moved from disk to tape where it can be taken offsite for long-term retention. Backups tend to be performed using one or a combination of several of the following backup types:

- Full backup—This backup type creates a backup of all selected files and folders. When a full backup is complete, the data is marked as being backed up.
- Incremental backup—An incremental backup on backs up changes since the last time a backup was completed. For example, if a backup was completed yesterday, and four files change during the day, an incremental backup will only backup those four files. A recovery would require restoring the full backup, and the incremental. If multiple incrementals are run in between full backups, all incremental backup sets will be required in addition to the full backup when restoring data.
- Differential backup—A differential backup performs backups of only those files that have changed since the last full backup. Similar to an incremental backup, a differential only backs up changes; however, it backs up all changes since the last full. For example, if a full backup is run on Monday, and differentials are run on Tuesday, Wednesday, and Thursday, each differential will backup all changes that took place after Monday.
- Synthetic full—A synthetic full backup creates a full backup from the most recent full backup plus subsequent incremental and/or differential backups. The resulting synthetic full backup is identical to what would have been created from a full backup without the need to transfer data from the client computer to the backup media. Synthetic full backups can greatly enhance restore processes, especially if a given full backup cycle contains many incremental backup sets.
- Transaction log backup—Transaction log backups are used to rapidly backup logs used by transactional-based systems such as database servers. Since transaction logs are small, they can be backed up rapidly allowing of point-in-time copies of the data taken on a regular basis.

For example, a full database backup can be taken at night with transaction log backups taken every 6 h. If the SQL server failed, the data could be restored to the point in time where the transaction log was backed up in the last 6 h.

■ Real-time data protection (RDP)—RDP constantly monitors the data for changes and backs up all changes as they are made. This provides for a restore of data within minutes of the time it was lost.

BEST PRACTICES

Store backup data offsite

As best practice, you should regularly store backup data in an offsite location. In the event of a disaster in which the primary datacenter is destroyed, you may need access to off-site backups.

Just as you did with other disaster recovery processes, you will want to test your restoring capabilities on a regular basis. Whether backups are part of a disaster recovery strategy for a system, or only used for long-term data retention and work case scenarios, they need to be documented, monitored, and tested.

INSTALLING AND ADMINISTERING WINDOWS BACKUP

Windows Server 2008 R2 provides a fairly feature-rich backup solution for backing up individual servers. Windows Server Backup is a feature that can be added to a Windows Server 2008 R2 server to be used to perform backups of the local system only. It cannot backup data from remote servers.

Installing Windows Server Backup

To add Windows Backup to a server, perform the following:

1. Open *Server Manager*.
2. Select the *Features* node and click the link to *Add Features*.
3. Select the *Windows Server Backup Features* option (see Figure 9.46). If you would like the capabilities to manage the backup software using PowerShell, select the *Command-line Tools* option.
4. Click *Next*.

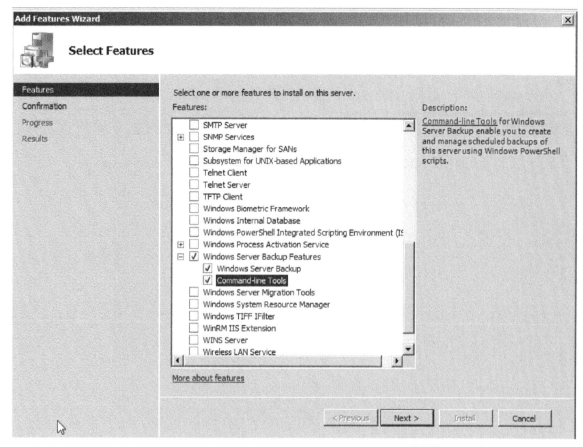

■ **FIGURE 9.46** Windows Backup Feature.

5. Click *Install* to install the backup features.
6. When the installation is complete, click *Close* to end the wizard.
7. You can now launch Windows Server Backup by opening *Start |
   All Programs | Accessories | System Tools | Windows
   Server Backup*.

The main backup window will open as seen in Figure 9.47.

Creating and managing backup jobs

We will start by creating a new scheduled backup job that will backup
the data on our server, using the bare meta recovery option which will

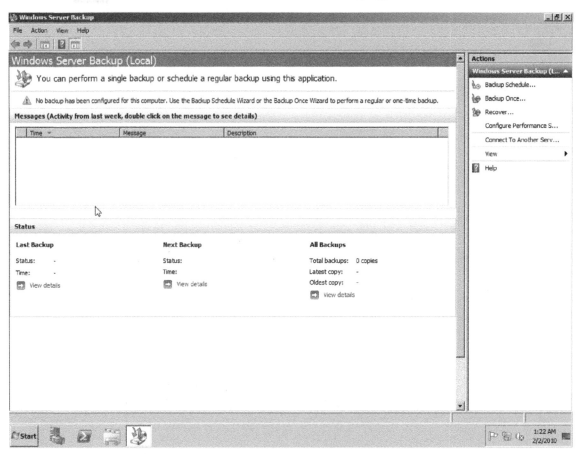

■ **FIGURE 9.47** Windows Server Backup.

backup all data on the server including the operating system configuration. To create a new backup job, perform the following:

1. Open Windows Server backup from *Start | All Programs | Accessories | System Tools | Windows Server Backup*.
2. In the *Actions Pane*, click the *Backup Schedule* link. This will launch the Backup Schedule Wizard.
3. Click *Next* to begin.
4. Choose the backup type you want to perform. A full backup will back up all data on all drives as well as system state. The custom backup will allow you to select what items you want to backup. For this exercise, choose the *Custom* option. Then click *Next*.

5. On the Select Items for Backup page, click *Add Items*.
6. Select the *Bare Metal Recovery* option (see Figure 9.48). This will backup all data and allow you to perform a bare metal restore of the server. A bare metal recovery allows you to completely recover the full operating system and configuration, along with data, to a new server in the event that the primary server fails. Click *OK*. Then click *Next*.
7. The next step is to determine when and how often to backup the data. After selecting the times and how often to backup the data, click *Next* to continue.
8. You now must select where you want to save your backups. Data can be backed up to one of the following locations:
   ❏ *Back up to a hard disk that is dedicated for backups*—Using this option will store backups to a hard disk connected to the server.

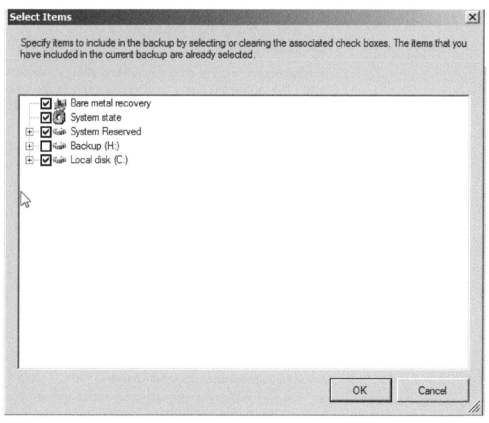

■ **FIGURE 9.48** Back up selections to perform bare metal recovery.

Windows Server Backup will format the disk and it can be used only to store backups. This method will allow you to save multiple copies of backups and backup and restore processes take less time than if using a volume or shared network folder to save backups. You should be aware that by using this method, if the server fails and the disk drive becomes unusable, both the primary system and the backups are lost.

❑ *Back up to a volume*—This option is similar to the back up to hard disk method except you are not required to dedicate the disk drive to backups only. Be aware that using this method will however decrease the performance of any other activity on the volume while backups are running.

❑ *Back up to a shared network folder*—Using this option, you can save backups to a network shared folder. This allows you to save backups on another server. In the event that the primary server fails, the backup data will be located on a disk drive on another server. Backing up to a network shared folder limits you to saving only on backup. Each backup process will overwrite the previous backup.

For this exercise, we will choose to backup data to a network shared folder. When performing a bare metal restore, we will refer to this same network location for the restored data. Select *Back up to a shared network folder* and then click *Next*.

9. Enter the UNC network path where you want to save the backup. For example, \\BackupServer\BackupData and then click *Next*. If prompted for username and password, enter credentials that have access to read and write to the shared folder.

10. Verify the backup settings, and then click *Finish* to schedule the backup job.

The backup job should run at the scheduled time and perform a full backup of the system allowing restore of data and/or full restore to a new server. Let us go through the process of performing a bare metal restore on a new server. Before we begin the process, you will need a Windows Server 2008 R2 DVD on hand to boot the new server from. Perform the following to steps to complete a bare metal restore of a server:

1. Boot the server from the Windows Server 2008 R2 DVD.

2. On the initial screen click *Next* to begin.

3. Click the link *Repair your computer* (see Figure 9.49)

4. Select the option to *Restore your computer using a system image that you created earlier*. Then click *Next*.

■ **FIGURE 9.49** Repair Computer in Windows Setup.

5. When prompted that Windows cannot find a system image on this computer (see Figure 9.50), click *Cancel*. This will allow you to select a location where the backup is stored.
6. Click *Next* to select a system image.
7. You now need to select the network location for your image. This will require connecting the server to the network. Click the *Advanced* button and then click *Search for a system image on the network*.
8. When prompted, enter the UNC path to the network shared folder (see Figure 9.51)
9. Enter the username and password for an account that has access to the shared folder.
10. Select the backup image listed (see Figure 9.52). Then click *Next*.

■ FIGURE 9.50 Cannot locate image.

■ FIGURE 9.51 Select Backup Path.

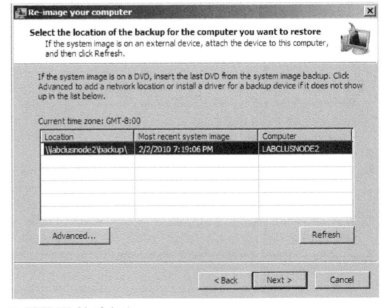

■ FIGURE 9.52 Select Backup Image.

11. Select the backup set you want to restore. Then click *Next*.
12. You can additionally set other restore options such as install drivers or exclude specific disks from the restore. Click *Next* to continue.
13. Verify the restore settings, and then click *Finish* to begin the restore process. If prompted to overwrite existing drives, you will need to click *Yes* to allow the backup to overwrite data on the disks. Keep in mind that any data on the existing disks will be destroyed.

When the restore is complete, the server will automatically reboot. After the new server completes the startup process, it should be in the same state as the original server at the time of backup.

SUMMARY

In this chapter, we explored the various HA and recovery options available in Windows Server 2008 R2. We discussed setting up and managing Windows Failover Clusters for back-end systems such as SQL servers and implementing NLB for front-end servers such as IIS web servers. We discussed the need for a good disaster recovery plan and how you can begin your planning process. We concluded this chapter with a discussion on the importance of backups and explored how to set up and administer Windows Server Backup.

Securing Windows Server 2008 R2

One of the key concerns in most IT shops today is security. With the release of Windows Server 2008 R2, Microsoft introduces a variety of new features, as well as the enhancement of some existing favorites, which will give you the ability to enrich security in your environment. Common administrative concerns include securing your systems, preventing and alerting for security breaches, maintaining an audit trail, and handling administrative errors and system access challenges. You can begin to address many of these concerns natively with Windows Server 2008 R2.

For example, let us assume that a large percentage of the user workforce in your environment is mobile. Laptops are hauled between home offices, remote offices, satellite locations, and main facilities every day by users across the enterprise. A typical concern in such a portable environment revolves around the data content stores on the workstations that are being moved about every day. If a user's laptop were to be stolen or lost, the nature of the data on the device must be considered. If the data represented highly sensitive or confidential information about the company, and the data were to fall into the wrong hands, the resulting impact to the company may be devastating.

By taking certain precautions as an administrator, you can help to safeguard company assets and possibly even protect trade secrets. In this instance, the implementation of encryption technologies such as BitLocker or Encrypted File System may have helped to protect the data from being compromised on the stolen laptop. Even if the laptop were to fall into the wrong hands, with encryption technologies in place, the attacker would require user-specific information to gain access to the files.

All of the features discussed in this chapter, when implemented properly, will contribute to the enhancements of your environmental security in different ways. All of them utilize the native feature set present in Windows Server 2008 R2, and each function within a distinct security niche. As we go through this chapter, you will be discovering many new features that Microsoft has introduced with Windows Server 2008 R2, which focus on all aspects of Windows systems and environments.

APPLOCKER

AppLocker is a new feature that allows administrators to focus on client-side software restrictions. It is not so much new feature functionality, as it is an expansion and improvement on a previously existing feature set. In earlier iterations of Windows Server, an Active Directory (AD)-based Group Policy configuration set called Software Restriction Policies granted administrators the capability to control Windows XP workstations and regulate the software that was allowed to execute.

Being able to prevent applications from running grants an administrator a centralized control over software execution in the environment. This control mechanism may be used in countless ways across many different environments and scenarios. For example, in some environments, drastic workstation restrictions may be appropriate, especially where users are known for installing unauthorized applications on company systems. Whereas in other environments denying settings for particular ActiveX controls or specific software applications may be all that is required. Regardless of the user-based restrictions, the ability to control software may be a handy feature in any environment where rouge software exists.

Software Restriction Policy settings allow administrators to control software executions by file extension as well as through trusted publisher lists. By being able to indicate which publishers are trusted allows administrators to enforce consistent trust lists across the enterprise, extending into digitally signed applications.

With the introduction of Windows Server 2008 R2, the feature set known as Software Restriction Policies was revised to become the now named AppLocker. AppLocker provides the same conceptual feature set as Software Restriction Policies; however, it extends the capabilities by allowing for more intricate specifications and additional robust features. A key point to be aware of with AppLocker is that it is only applicable to Windows 2008 R2 servers and Windows 7 clients. To allow the administration of other Windows clients, Windows 2008 R2 AD has retained the original Software Restriction Policies. Since they exist in tandem, environments with multiple client operating systems existing in parallel will have to work with both sets of policies to attempt to enforce software restrictions across varied platforms. You can see both the Software Restriction Polices and the AppLocker sections side by side within a policy (see Figure 10.1). Something to keep in mind is that if both AppLocker and Software Restriction Policies exist within the same Group Policy, only then will the AppLocker settings be used. You must create separate Group

■ **FIGURE 10.1** Software Restriction Policies and AppLocker Policy Settings.

Policy Objects (GPOs) for AppLocker and Software Restriction Policies. In the following sections, we will focus on AppLocker in more detail.

Enabling AppLocker

For AppLocker policies to be applied to a machine, the first point to be aware of is that there is a local service that must be running on each client machine. AppLocker relies on the *Application Identity* service, and by default on Windows 7 machines, the *Application Identity* service is stopped and set to manual startup. For AppLocker to be able to enforce the configuration settings, you must modify the startup type to Automatic and then start the service.

Once you have gotten the service started, you are half-way there. Before AppLocker will impact a machine, the enforcement mode for the computer must be configured. The enforcement mode is configured through policy settings. AppLocker policy settings are available in the Local Computer Policy as well as from AD GPOs under the Application Control Policies section and can be configured from either policy type. In this section, AppLocker will be discussed as if it is being enforced through the

AD GPOs. The AppLocker section of a GPO is made up of rules that have three enforcement modes:

- Not Configured
- Enforce Rules
- Audit Only

Each of these settings allows the administrator different control over the workstations impacted by the GPOs. *Not Configured* is the default setting, and simply indicates that the rules within this GPO are allowed to be merged with other GPOs; but if conflicting settings exist, then an *Enforce Rules* will override the setting on the *Not Configured* policy. Keep in mind that if rules have been created within this GPO, they will still be enforced on workstations. When the enforcement mode is set to *Not Configured,* it does not negate the existence of the rules.

The next possible setting is *Enforce Rules*. Just as the setting name implies, by configuring this within the GPO, all of the rules within that GPO are enforced on the affected workstations. Rules can be enforced irrespective of the fact whether users are logged on interactively or not. By setting a rule set to *Enforce Rules*, these rules will override other GPOs that have their enforcement mode set to *Not Configured*.

The final choice for enforcement mode configuration is *Audit Only*. Again, as the name implies, this is an audit mode and it does not enforce any rules onto the workstations. This audit mode is very useful for testing new policies to ensure that they perform the desired effect before they are deployed. When *Audit Only* is selected for a policy, and a user on a workstation attempts to run a program identified by a rule in the AppLocker settings, the result of the attempt is logged in the AppLocker event log within Event Viewer. As the system administrator, the log will provide value information for you to collect and review which will allow you to determine if the policy is ready to be toggle to *Not Configured* or *Enforce Rules*, or if some adjustments are required first. Figure 10.2 displays the three enforcement modes available within a GPO for AppLocker. Now that you understand how to enforce AppLocker rules on workstation machines, the next thing that you need to understand is what is controllable through AppLocker. In the next section, we will take a look at the "configuration of AppLocker" rules.

Configuring AppLocker

The first step in configuring AppLocker involves figuring out what applications it is that you want to control. Depending on the environment, the need to restrict applications can come from very different places. In

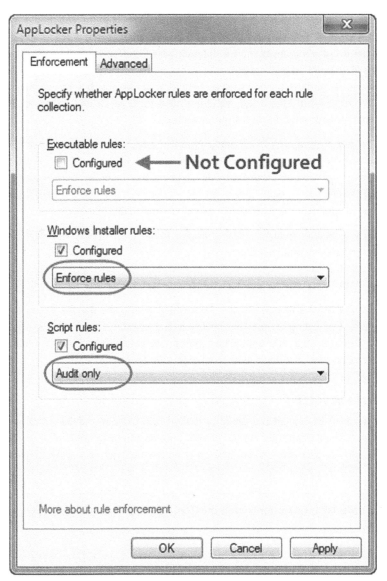

■ FIGURE 10.2 AppLocker Enforcement Modes.

some environments, restrictions may be driven by security concerns where the security group within an organization defines the guidelines for the organization, and sets forth what is considered acceptable to execute. In another organization, the acceptable applications type may be driven by the legal department or from within an application group. The same types of applications may have different implications in varied environments.

Performance is another key factor that may drive your application restriction settings. For instance, if there is a limited amount of bandwidth available to your organization for Internet-based traffic, you may want to restrict superfluous Internet-bound applications to keep bandwidth usage down. Regardless of the rationale behind your choices, before you begin to restrict with AppLocker, you first need to have an understanding of what you are required to restrict or allow.

Ok, now that you have your application list in hand, you can just about get started. You have your GPO created, you have decided on an *Enforce Rules* strategy for your enforcement mode, and now you are on to configuring the applications you want to impact. To do this, you need to create an AppLocker rule. AppLocker rules are broken down into four main collections:

- Executable Rules
- Windows Installer Rules
- Script Rules
- DLLs

Each of these collection types is associated with particular file extension types. Depending on the file extension that you are targeting, you need to configure the rule within the appropriate collection. Table 10.1 lists the collections and their associated extension types:

Default rules

Microsoft has included a group of default rules for each of the collection types. The default rules are not present until an administrator evokes them. To do so, you must right-click on a collection type and select *Create*

Table 10.1 Collection Types and Their Corresponding Extensions

Collection	Associated Extensions
Executable	.exe
	.com
Scripts	.ps1
	.bat
	.cmd
	.vbs
	.js
Windows Installer	.msi
	.msp
DLL	.dll
	.ocx

Default Rules from the menu. This will cause the system to automatically create three preconfigured Allow rules.

The default rules are partially meant to protect the administrator from accidentally locking themselves out by configuring overly restrictive settings. The other major function of default rules is to allow users to execute applications that exist in Windows default folder locations. Depending on the collection, the default rules will vary slightly, but in general, they all serve these same purposes. It is recommended to configure the default rules when working with AppLocker. Once added, the default rules will be visible from the details pane and can be edited as required.

The following tasks are a representation of the default rules broken down by collection:

1. Executable:
   - Allow members of the local Administrator's group to run all applications.
   - Allow members of the Everyone group to run applications that are located in the Windows folder.
   - Allow members of the Everyone group to run applications that are located in the Program Files folder.
2. Windows Installer:
   - Allow members of the local Administrator's group to run all Windows Installer files.
   - Allow members of the Everyone group to run digitally signed Windows Installer files.
   - Allow members of the Everyone group to run all Windows Installer files located in the Windows\Installer folder.
3. Script:
   - Allow members of the local Administrator's group to run all scripts.
   - Allow members of the Everyone group to run scripts located in the Program Files folder.
   - Allow members of the Everyone group to run scripts located in the Windows folder.
4. DLL:
   - Allow members of the local Administrator's group to run all DLLs.
   - Allow members of the Everyone group to run DLLs located in the Program Files folder.
   - Allow members of the Everyone group to run DLLs located in the Windows folder.

Custom rules

As an administrator, one of the best capabilities that can be granted is the ability to customize feature sets. AppLocker is no exception, and if you find yourself staring at the default rules and not seeing where they really fit into your plans for application restriction, do not worry, the capability to customize is present just for you.

When building a customized rule with AppLocker, the first step involves determining which collection is the most appropriate for your new rule. This will be driven by the file extension type that you are trying to control. The collections and their associated file extensions are listed earlier in this section.

So, once you have determined which collection is the most appropriate for your rule, the next preparation step before you can begin configuring rules is to logon to a machine that has your targeted applications installed on it. The reason this is required is that during the creation of the rule, the AppLocker wizard will request information about your application. You must be able to browse to and select the application as it would be installed on client machines. By having the application locally available, this allows you to configure the settings exactly as it would be on client workstations.

Ok, let us finally get down to it. To begin creating your rule, you must right-click on the collection name and select *Create New Rule...* (see Figure 10.3). This will trigger the rules wizard which will walk you through the remainder of the process of rule creation.

The process of custom rule creation is similar across the collections. The first thing you must select is whether this will be an Allow or a Deny rule and which user or group it will apply to. The preferred configuration choice is Allow, and then you will have the ability to configure exceptions to the Allow. Deny rules may also be chosen, but have the chance to be circumvented and are not the best choice of deterrent.

■ **FIGURE 10.3** Creating a New AppLocker Rule.

The next wizard screen asks you to select a condition. A condition specifies the mechanism that the system will use to identify the application in order to enforce restrictions. There are three different conditions that can be utilized to identify your application. The three conditions which are displayed in Figure 10.4 are Publisher, Path, and File hash.

Publisher condition

By selecting the Publisher condition, you will be required to browse to an application file so that the information about the Publisher as well as about the application itself can be retrieved. Publisher is the best selection choice

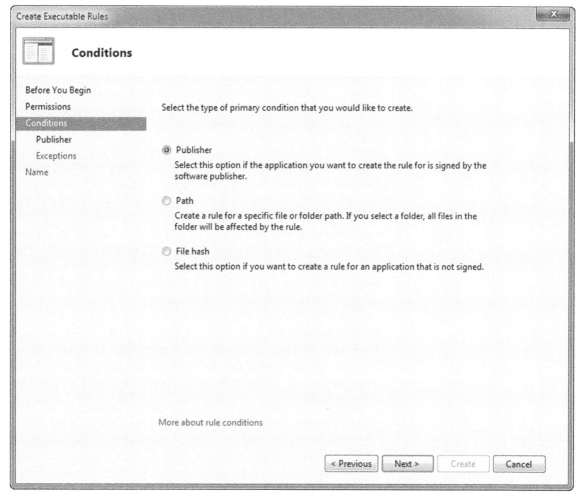

■ **FIGURE 10.4** Conditions.

whenever possible to assure consistency. When an application that has been identified via Publisher is managed by AppLocker, it will always be correctly identified across workstations regardless of the installation directory.

You can also use the Publisher condition to create rules that are more generic and impact multiple applications instead of a single named application. For instance, let us assume that I would like all applications from a particular vendor to be allowed to run on the kiosk machines in my environment. The applications from the vendor are various, and the version information changes frequently. Creating individual rules for each of the applications and then keeping them up to date as changes occur would be a heavy administrative task.

To begin your configuration, you create a GPO and apply it to the kiosk machines OU. Next, you need to create your AppLocker rule. In this case, instead of specifying each individual application with a different rule, you should utilize the Publisher condition to create a single rule that is scoped to the vendor level. To do this, you will still need to have the information of an application to be used as a sampling that has been digitally signed from the vendor you are trying to configure.

Begin the *Create New Rule...* wizard and once you arrive on the conditions screen, select Publisher and browse to the sample application. Once all of the application information has populated on the screen, you can then use the slider shown in Figure 10.5 to adjust the rule to a broader scope. By moving the slider up, it removes the application-specific information from the rule, such as File Version and File Name. You can even go so far up as to remove Product Name, which would leave only the Publisher name of the vendor in the screen, as displayed in Figure 10.5. This would effectively create an AppLocker rule that targets a specific vendor instead of an application created by the vendor.

Path condition

There are times when selecting the Publisher condition is just not possible. If vendors do not digitally sign their applications, then the Publisher condition cannot be utilized. Another viable choice when this is the case is the Path condition.

The Path condition requires you to browse to the location of the executable and select it. The policy will recall the executable file information as well as the path to the executable. Both local paths and network paths may be specified. AppLocker marches to the beat of its own tune, in that path, variables may be specifics; however, the path variables are unique to

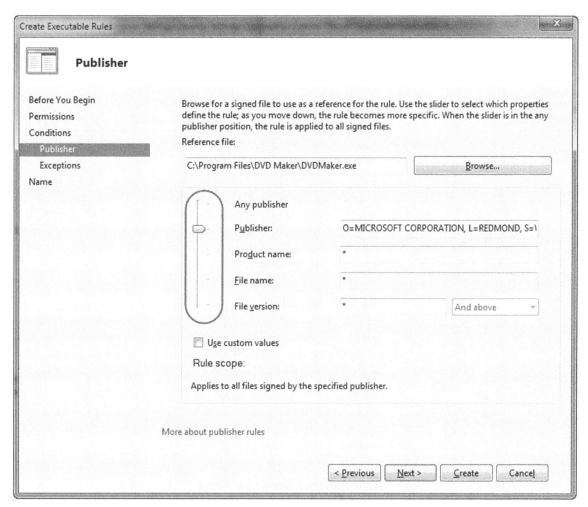

■ **FIGURE 10.5** Publisher Condition.

AppLocker. The path variables used by AppLocker do not follow the standardized Windows environmental variables, and even though some of the values are indeed the same, others are quite different. Table 10.2 displays a comparison between some of the AppLocker path variables and the Windows environmental variables.

When the path option is utilized with an Allow policy, the executable in the selected path will be allowed to run, but executable files in other directory paths, even with the same executable name, will be denied. An example of how Allow behaves is as follows: You configure an Allow rule for

Table 10.2 AppLocker and Windows Environmental Variables

Windows Path	AppLocker Variable	Windows Environmental Variable
Windows	%WINDIR%	%SystemRoot%
System32	%SYSTEM32%	%SystemDirectory%
Windows installation directory	%OSDRIVE%	%SystemDrive%
Program Files	%PROGRAMFILES%	%ProgramFiles% and %ProgramFiles(x86)%

an application named BearToast. The application's executable file, BTst. exe, is located in the C:\Program Files\BToast directory. Configuring this rule only allows applications with that designation executable name within that specific directory to run. Any applications of the same flavor in other directories will be denied.

File hash condition

For applications that are not digitally signed and have varying paths, File hash is an option that may be used. When you are selecting File hash with an application executable, a computation is performed to generate a unique File hash that will be used to identify the applications.

One thing to be aware of is that the File hash will only pertain to that exact version of the application. If different versions of the application exist in the environment, you must create a rule for each that you wish to effect.

Automatically Generate Rules

The final rule creation method available to administrators to create rules within AppLocker is called *Automatically Generate Rules*. Instead of individually creating rules for applications, the *Automatically Generate Rules* allow the administrator to select at the folder level.

All of the applications which reside in the selected folder will automatically be configured within the rule set. You can indicate which conditions should be used to identify the different applications. Publisher conditions are preferred and in the case that a file is not digitally signed, you may indicate an alternative method on the Rule Preferences screen, displayed in Figure 10.6. This is a fast and easy way to create multiple rules in one fell swoop. Also be aware that this method can only be used to create Allow rules.

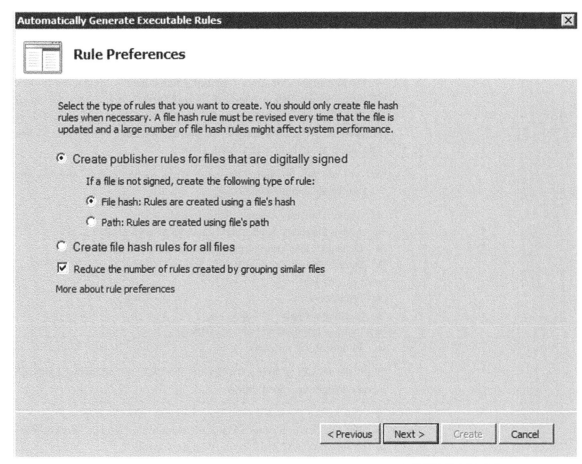

Automatically Generate Executable Rules ☒

Rule Preferences

Select the type of rules that you want to create. You should only create file hash rules when necessary. A file hash rule must be revised every time that the file is updated and a large number of file hash rules might affect system performance.

● Create publisher rules for files that are digitally signed

    If a file is not signed, create the following type of rule:

      ● File hash: Rules are created using a file's hash

      ○ Path: Rules are created using file's path

○ Create file hash rules for all files

☑ Reduce the number of rules created by grouping similar files

More about rule preferences

         [< Previous] [Next >] [Create] [Cancel]

■ **FIGURE 10.6** Rule Preferences.

SERVER CORE

Server Core is a Windows Server installation model that Microsoft introduced with Windows 2008. The basic principle of Server Core revolves around the concept of minimizing the attack surface area. By taking the time to remove unnecessary feature sets and roles and to additionally lock down the ones that are required, you limit an attacker's capability to exploit a particular system.

With Server Core, you are deploying a Windows system in a nearly GUI-less configuration. Essentially, all of the management and tools and actions that you perform on a day-to-day basis must be executed through either local command prompt-based administrative methods or remotely.

In all installations of Windows Server, you have the capability to install server roles and server features. The distinction between the two is that when you install a server role, you are installing a software set that defines what specific function a server will perform in the environment, whereas a server feature is normally a supporting functionality. In addition to most GUI components being removed from a Server Core installation, many of the roles and features available within Windows Server have been stripped as well. By reducing the installation footprint to bare bones, you additionally reduce the attack surface.

Server Core was first introduced with Windows Server 2008 and was limited to the following server roles:

- Active Directory Domain Services (AD DS)
- Active Directory Lightweight Directory Services (AD LDS)
- Dynamic Host Configuration Protocol (DHCP) Server
- Domain Name Services (DNS) Server
- File Services
- Print Services
- Streaming Media Services
- Internet Information Services (IIS)
- Windows Virtualization

With the release of Windows Server 2008 R2, the following additional server roles have joined the list:

- The Active Directory Certificate Services (AD CS) role
- The File Server Resource Manager component of the File Services role
- A subset of ASP.NET in the Web Server role

In addition to server roles, Windows Server has the capability to run additional optional features. The following list of optional features is available with Windows Server 2008:

- Failover Clustering
- Network Load Balancing
- Subsystem for UNIX-based applications
- Windows Server Backup
- Multipath IO
- Removable Storage
- BitLocker Drive Encryption
- Simple Network Management Protocol (SNMP)
- Windows Internet Name Service (WINS)
- Telnet client
- QWAVE

With the release of Windows Server 2008 R2, the following optional features have been added to the list:

- Subset of .NET Framework 2.0
- Subset of .NET Framework 3.0 and 3.5
- Windows Communication Framework (WCF)
- Windows Workflow Framework (WF)
- LINQ
- Windows PowerShell
- Server Manager cmdlets
- Best Practices Analyzer (BPA) cmdlets
- WoW64
- 32-bit support for the Input Method Editor

The Removable Storage feature that was available in Windows Server 2008 has had support removed for Windows Server 2008 R2. Additionally, you now have the capability to connect to a Windows Server 2008 R2 Core installation with Server Manager. This allows the administrator the capability of remote administration from a familiar interface.

An additional fact to be aware of is that Windows Server 208 R2 no longer prompts for a product key during installation. This is true for Windows Server 2008 R2 full installation as well as for Server Core installations. This means that before activation can be successfully accomplished, a product key must be configured from the command prompt for server core. To input a product key, use the following command on the server core machine:

slmgr.vbs/ipk <product key>

Once the key has been entered, you must also activate the server. This can also be accomplished by utilizing the slmgr.vbs command, as shown in Figure 10.7

BITLOCKER

BitLocker is a drive-level encryption feature that Microsoft first made available with Windows Server 2008 and Windows Vista. Microsoft has revised and improved upon particular characteristics of BitLocker with Windows Server 2008 R2 and Windows 7. BitLocker is now more robust and its usage has been simplified to improve on the administrative and user experiences. In this section, we will discuss how you can continue to use BitLocker to enhance the physical security of your device better than before.

■ **FIGURE 10.7** Activating Server Core.

By using BitLocker to encrypt your system at the partition level, all of your files and folders, including all the Windows system files, remain protected. If your laptop were to be stolen, the attacker would be hard-pressed to gain access to the data on the drive by brute force. Since the entire partition has been secured, many of the methods used by the attackers to bypass Windows system security are rendered useless. The only way to successfully access BitLocker-secured data on the drive is to provide the BitLocker prestartup authentication password or the recovery key. Since the BitLocker password is a fundamental piece of the puzzle in unlocking your encrypted partition, is it important to stress to end users the importance of utilizing long and complex passwords.

Preparing for BitLocker

One of the most challenging parts of preparing a machine for BitLocker with Windows 2008 and Windows Vista involved creating the correct number and size partitions on the disk. It sounds like no big deal, but this is a common stumbling block in deploying BitLocker.

Often times, the administrator will prestage a workstation with two partitions, including one that is at least 1.5 GB in size and is to be used as the system volume and is to remain unencrypted. It will store boot files as well as the Windows Pre-Execution environment that are required for prestartup authentication. Often, by the time the administrator has gotten back around to walking through a BitLocker configuration session with the user, there are good chances that the user has modified the system in some way so that BitLocker cannot be enabled.

Microsoft has heard the administrator's voice regarding this function, and with the release of Window Server 2008 R2, has done away with the requirement for an additional partition. Now, a single partition can be configured and the additional system partition will be automatically prepped and created by BitLocker. The system partition is created when BitLocker is activated and it does not have a drive letter, so it will not display in Windows Explorer. By default, there will still be two partitions built, but the space required for the system partition in Windows 7 is only 100 MB as compared to the 1.5 GB with Windows Vista.

This greatly reduces much of the administrator's overhead involved with preconfiguring hard drives in preparation for BitLocker deployments.

Something else to be aware of is that with Windows 7, BitLocker now supports the usage of Smart Cards for drive encryption and decryption. With many organizations moving to two-factor authentication for their user base, extending BitLocker to support Smart Cards reduces the learning curve for users. Instead of being required to understanding multiple methods of access and authentication, Smart Card authentication can be extended across multiple usages.

Drive encryption targets

With the release of Windows Server 2008 R2 and Windows 7, Microsoft has extended what drive types BitLocker can encrypt. Viable drive choices now include operating system drives, fixed data drives, and removable data drives. By choosing to utilize BitLocker on their removable media, end users can further protect valuable company data assets even when they are on the go.

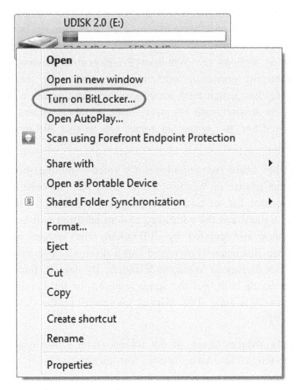

■ **FIGURE 10.8** Enabling BitLocker on a Removable Device.

To enable BitLocker on removable media, the user simply needs to right-click the drive letter and select *Turn on BitLocker,* as depicted in Figure 10.8. The user will have to select a password to access the device, and then will be prompted to print or document the recovery key for the drive. As long as the user can provide the password information, any Windows 7 client can be used to access the encrypted removable media once it has been enabled for BitLocker. Only 64 MB of space is used on the device to enable BitLocker.

Managing BitLocker

To allow uniform security settings across the board in an organization, administrators can utilize Group Policy to control and enforce BitLocker settings. With the release of Windows Server 2008 R2, Microsoft has expanded on the already existing BitLocker GPO configuration options. Administrators now have more granular control over when BitLocker must be utilized and can even force usage on removable drives. Also, drive decryption mechanisms can be specified and settings such as password length and complexity can be enforced via GPO. Finally, administrators can even specify a data recovery agent, allowing for an often much-needed fail safe that can be used to recover BitLocker-protected drives when users misplace or forget their passwords.

Figure 10.9 displays the BitLocker GPO content which is located under *Computer Configuration\Policies\Administrative Templates\Windows Components\BitLocker Drive Encryption*. It is important to develop a BitLocker policy early in the deployment of Windows 7 machines into your environment. Many of the BitLocker settings are enforced when BitLocker is enabled and not when the drives are in use. So, for instance, if you decide to use GPOs to enforce complex passwords for removable devices, any devices already encrypted will be allowed to be decrypted utilizing the mechanism already on the drive. Any new devices being enabled for BitLocker after the policy is in effect will be encrypted following the policy settings.

Being able to distinguish between removable drives and fixed data drives is a new GPO setting that can be used to control Windows 7 installs.

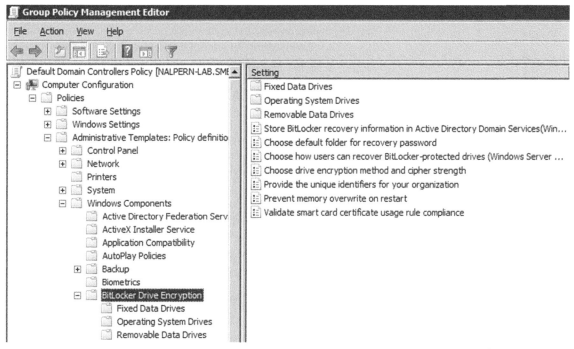

■ **FIGURE 10.9** BitLocker Group Policy Settings.

Having separate sections within the GPO for each drive type gives you the flexibility to meet the security needs of your organization. While some organizations do not allow removable drives at all due to security concerns, the organizations that do allow them can now lock them down much more effectively by requiring that they be BitLocker-enabled before data may be saved onto them.

One of the most exciting new features is specific to recovery. In the Windows 2008/Windows Vista iteration of BitLocker, users were tasked with creating a password and keeping their recovery key safe. They could store it in a share or on a USB drive, or even print it. Regardless of their choice, they were still in charge of keeping it safe. The problem with this as we all know, is that some users are not good at keeping things safe.

So let us say a user were to forget their password and additionally lose track of their recovery key. Without either piece of information, their BitLocker-encrypted drive would potentially become inaccessible, making for one upset user. The one saving grace is that if you are an alert administrator and have realized the potential harm that a user could bring upon them with BitLocker, you may have thought to configure policies to store recovery keys in AD.

If you choose to venture down this path, be warned, because configuring AD to store recovery information for BitLocker-encrypted drives is no small feat. Depending on your AD version, you may require a schema extension. If you have deployed the Windows 2008 schema, you are covered, but if you are running something earlier, such as Windows 2003 SP1 or SP 2, you must perform an import to make the appropriate attributes available. Additionally, there are quite a few scripts to collect and execute in your environment to set permissions and complete preparations.

The obvious benefit in going through all the preparation work is that by storing user recovery keys in AD, you are able to administratively intervene and rescue the user from plight by retrieving their recovery key from AD. In effect, this would allow them to gain access to their drive, decrypt it, and then start the process again by establishing a new password and recovery key. So, the question you probably have is, "So what's wrong with that?" And the answer at the end of the day is, nothing really, but with Windows 2008 R2, Microsoft has made recovery a simpler and less painful process by allowing for the use of a recovery agent.

Enabling a BitLocker recovery agent

With the release of Windows 2008 R2 and Windows 7, you now have the ability to configure the usage of a recovery agent with BitLocker. The concept of a recovery agent is not new and has been in use with EFS technologies for a long time; however, extending it to BitLocker and being able to manipulate it through GPO settings give administrators an edge, sometimes a much-needed edge. If users misplace their password and recovery key, administrators can now use their smart card certificates and public keys to recover the drive instead of having to dig through AD to ferret out a specific user's recovery key. Multiple recovery agents may be specified so that administrators can share the recovery responsibility.

Additionally, the process required to enable a recovery agent is simpler and requires less administrative effort. In the next sections, we will cover each of the steps in the process of enabling a recovery agent in more detail. The high-level steps to enable a BitLocker recovery agent are as follows:

- Step 1: Obtain a certificate appropriate for use as a recovery agent
- Step 2: Configure the recovery agent certificate as part of the Public Key Policies
- Step 3: Configure an identification field for your organization
- Step 4: Configure the appropriate GPO to enable a BitLocker recovery agent for the specific drives

Step 1: Obtain a certificate appropriate for use as a recovery agent

Certificates are in use in more organizations today than ever before. The reinforced need for security in corporations today has made smart card-based certificate usage as a part of two-factor authentication more commonplace. Since certificates have different usages in an organization, you must understand that in the context of BitLocker, we are specifically referring to certificates issued to a user or an administrator that have the capability for data encryption usage. For the certificate issued to be acceptable for BitLocker usage, it is recommended to utilize a certificate with one of the following properties:

- The default object identifier for BitLocker (1.3.6.1.4.1.311.67.1.1)
- The *anyExtendedKeyUsage* identifier (2.5.29.37.0)
- An Encrypting File System (EFS) certificate

Once you have either identified the existing certificates or generated new certificates for the designated BitLocker recovery agents, you are ready to move to the next step.

Step 2: Configure the recovery agent certificate as part of the public key policies

You must now specify the recovery agent certificates within an AD GPO. To do so, open the GPO for editing and browse to the following path:

*Computer Configuration\Policies\Windows Settings\Security Settings\
Public Key Policies\BitLocker Drive Encryption*

Right-click on *BitLocker Drive Encryption* and select *Add Data Recovery
Agents . . . .* The wizard will ask you to select each of the certificates for
use as BitLocker recovery agents. You may select from either the AD, if
you have published certificates for the administrators, or a browse to a.
cer file from a local or shared file path.

Step 3: Configure an identification field for your organization

All drives that are to be enabled for data recovery through the BitLocker
recovery agent feature must be configured with an identification field.
The identification field is populated when BitLocker is activated.
If you have configured the AD GPO value before BitLocker is enabled
on a given drive, then the identification value will be populated based
on the policy. Be aware that if a drive has already been encrypted
with BitLocker before you have configured the organizational identification field via GPO, then you must manually associate the identification field with that drive before the recovery agent can be used.
The *manage-bde* command line tool can be used to manually configure
the value. Another option is to disable and then reenable BitLocker on
the drive.

The identification field can be any value of 260 characters or less, and the
policy for configuring it is called *Provide the unique identifiers for your
organization*, as shown in Figure 10.10, and is located within the following path within Group Policy:

*Computer   Configuration\Policies\Administrative   Templates\Windows
Components\BitLocker Drive Encryption*

Step 4: Configure the appropriate GPO to enable a BitLocker recovery agent for the specific drives

The final step in configuring the BitLocker recovery agent is to configure
the Group Policy setting to enable it for the desired drive types. You can
choose to enable the recovery agent across all drive types, or selectively
enable between fixed data drives, operating system drives, and removable
data drives. The policy name is the same across the three drive types bar-
ring the mention of the drive type name: *Choose how BitLocker-protected
<insert drive type here> drives can be recovered*. Figure 10.11 displays
the policy for the system drive type.

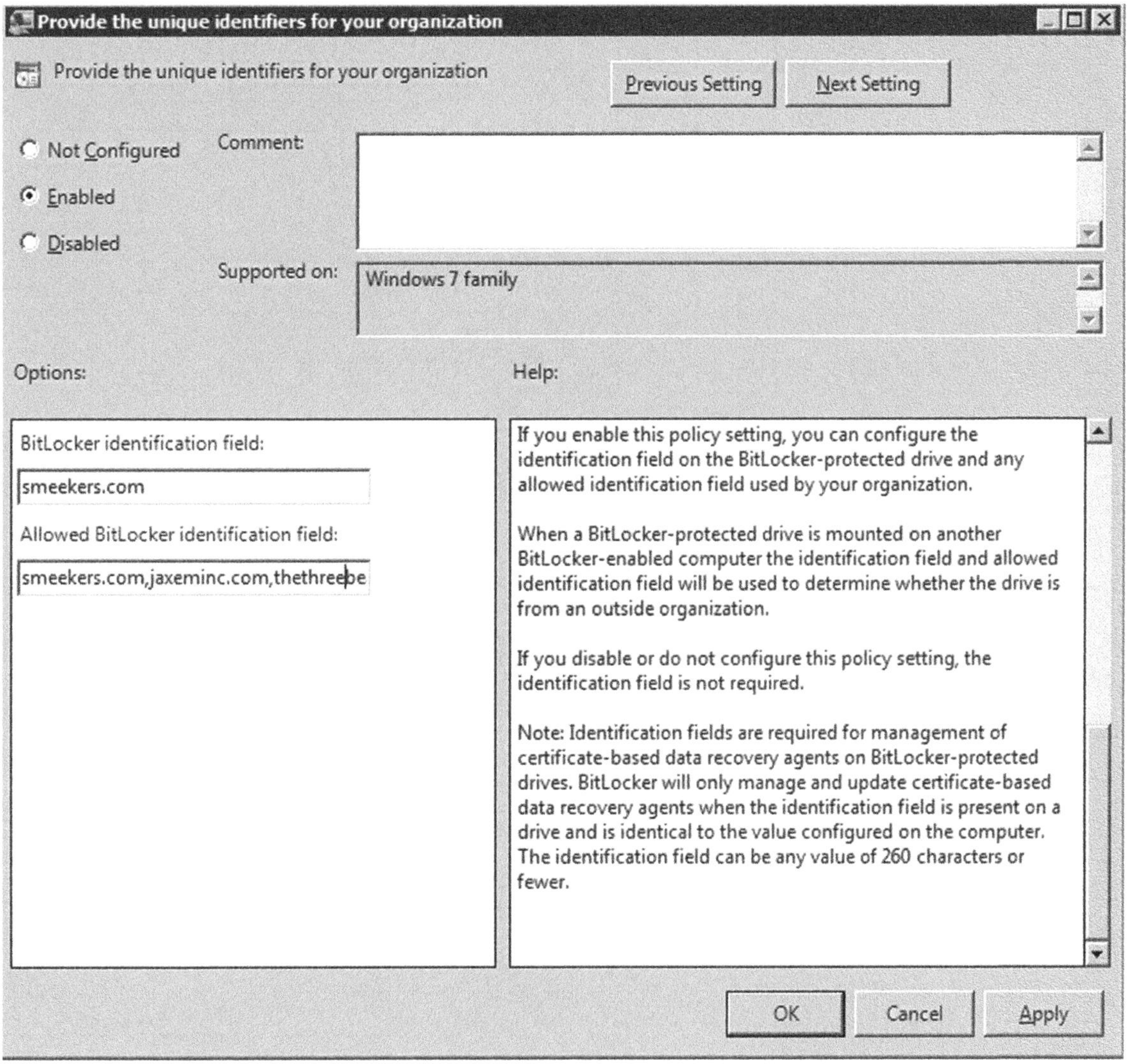

Provide the unique identifiers for your organization

Provide the unique identifiers for your organization

Previous Setting   Next Setting

○ Not Configured   Comment:

◉ Enabled

○ Disabled

Supported on: Windows 7 family

Options: Help:

BitLocker identification field:

smeekers.com

Allowed BitLocker identification field:

smeekers.com,jaxeminc.com,thethreebe

If you enable this policy setting, you can configure the identification field on the BitLocker-protected drive and any allowed identification field used by your organization.

When a BitLocker-protected drive is mounted on another BitLocker-enabled computer the identification field and allowed identification field will be used to determine whether the drive is from an outside organization.

If you disable or do not configure this policy setting, the identification field is not required.

Note: Identification fields are required for management of certificate-based data recovery agents on BitLocker-protected drives. BitLocker will only manage and update certificate-based data recovery agents when the identification field is present on a drive and is identical to the value configured on the computer. The identification field can be any value of 260 characters or fewer.

OK   Cancel   Apply

■ **FIGURE 10.10** Configuring an Identification Field in Group Policy.

SECURITY CONFIGURATION WIZARD

The Security Configuration Wizard (SCW) is a handy tool that was released as a part of the tool suite for Windows 2003 SP1. Its purpose is to allow you to create role-based security policies that can then be applied to any server in your organization. It allows for the repeatable

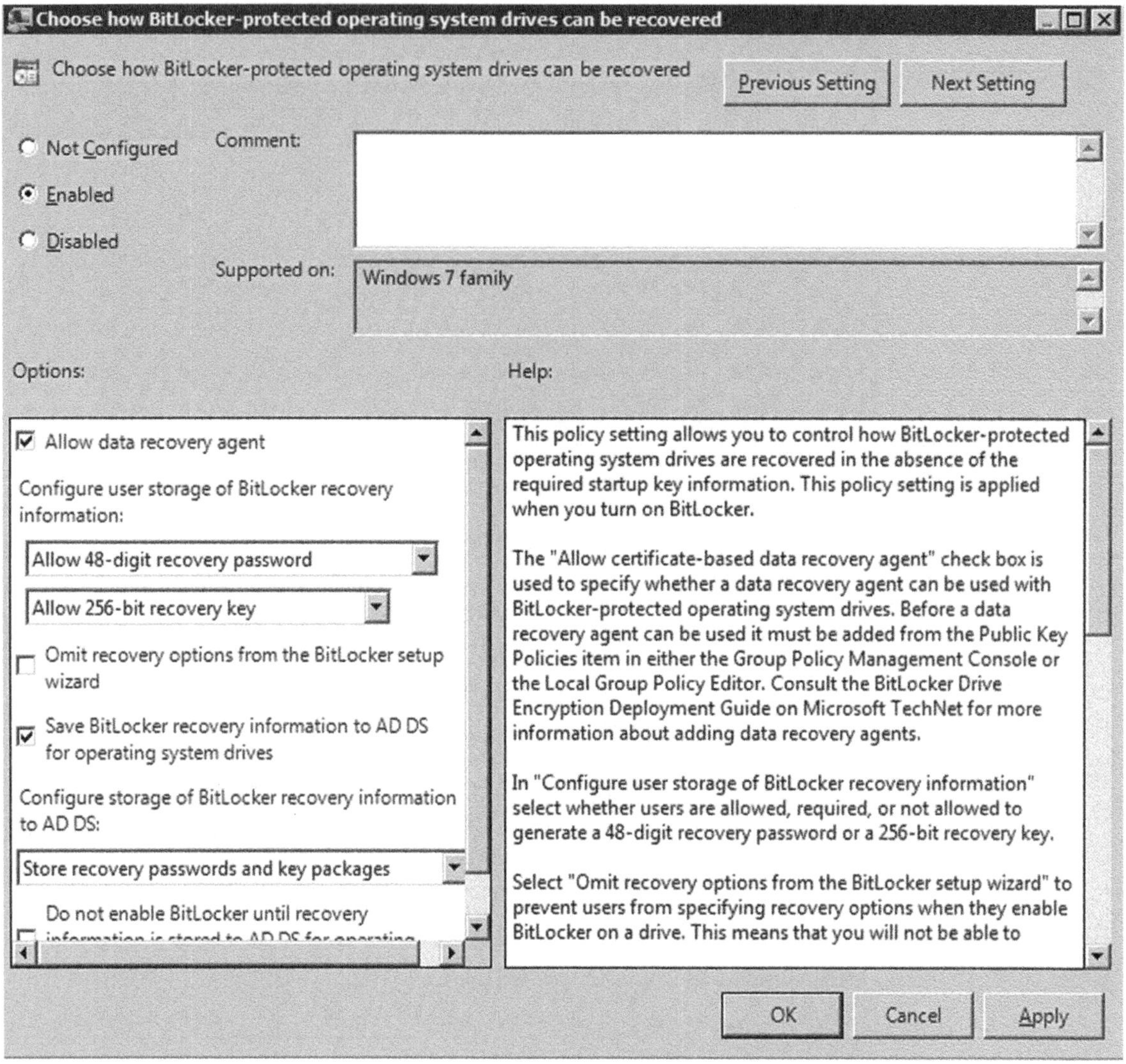

FIGURE 10.11 Enabling the BitLocker Recovery Agent on System Drives.

configuration of security settings across multiple servers in an organization while maintaining consistency and reduction of administrative overhead; basically, all the characteristics administrators look for in a tool!

SCW comes in two flavors, the first is a GUI-based wizard-driven tool, while the second is a command prompt tool called scwcmd. One thing to keep in mind with both of these tools is that they do not perform any configuration changes related to installation and can only manipulate what already exists on the system. They are analysis tools that will examine the current state of your system and report on the findings. They will perform certain configuration-related actions on the local system, such as editing Windows Firewall settings and unused disabling services, but no new software installations can be performed with these tools. It is recommended that before you run the SCW you determine what applications will exist on the server for the particular role you are trying to secure. Then install and run those applications on the server where you are running SCW. This will ensure that SCW takes into consideration any ports and services required for those local applications when creating the security file.

So, the first thing SCW will do when executed is that it will prompt you for what action you are trying to perform. The choices vary between creating a new policy, editing an existing policy, applying a policy, and rolling back the last applied policy. These options are shown in Figure 10.12. Previously, rolling back was a task performed with the command line Scwcmd tool. With Windows Server R2, it is an available GUI-based option.

When selecting to create a new policy, the wizard will walk through analyzing your local system. It will allow you to review its findings of locally installed roles and features, and add or remove as appropriate. Part of the display will include a list of services that would be impacted if the new security policy were to be deployed to the local server. It will also allow you to select if you would like to evaluate and configure additional system settings such as network settings, registry settings, and auditing settings.

Once you complete the configuration settings, the last screen in the wizard will allow you to save your new security configuration file. However, before doing so, you will have the option to add Security Templates into the file if you would like. To save the file, you must choose a name and a file path. The file extension will be .xml. Once you have saved your new security file, you will be prompted to apply it to the local machine, but be aware that applying the file through the wizard imports the settings into the Local Computer Security Policy. These settings are always overridden by domain-based policies; however, it is a great idea to apply the policy locally anyway. Why? Well, by applying the policy to the local machine, you will be able to test to see if the computer has been impacted in the desired fashion. If there are problems with the machine after the policy has been applied, you then use the wizard to rollback the policy and then edit your .xml file to make the appropriate adjustments.

Once you are ready to deploy your policy on a larger scale, it is recommended to utilize Group Policy to target the appropriate machines. The Scwcmd

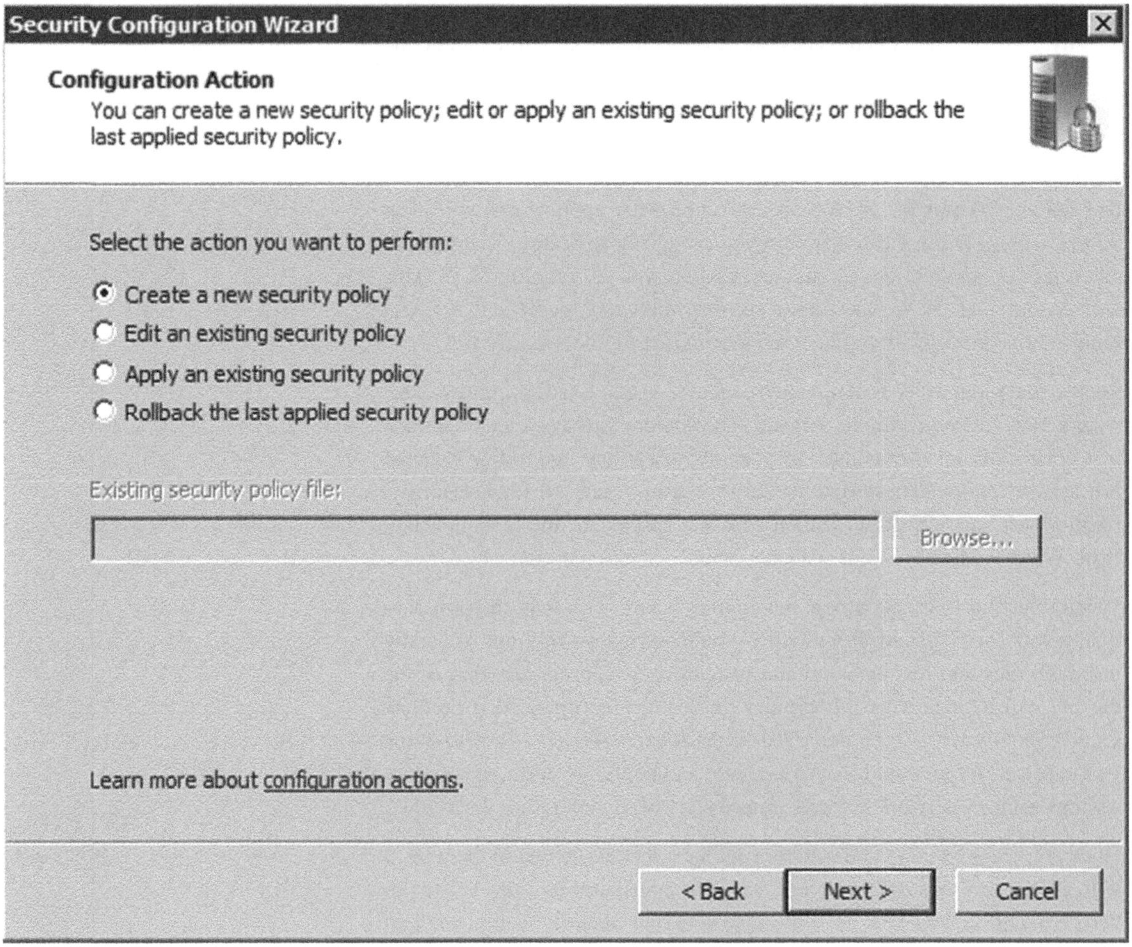

FIGURE 10.12 Security Configuration Wizard Configuration Options.

command line tool will allow you to convert an SCW .xml security file to a GPO by issuing the *scwcmd transform* command. This will allow you to utilize the security file within AD and deploy it to multiple servers of the same role simultaneously. Before rolling out a new SCW security file through Group Policy, it is highly recommended that you test thoroughly.

BEST PRACTICE ANALYZER

When companies develop software, they typically have created use-case scenarios that customers are intended to follow for deployment. Whether the software is targeted at the health care market and is used to print patient bar codes, or is written to be used in construction and is intended to track work streams and dependencies, each piece of software is design to be deployed and utilized in a particular way. Some infrastructure services, such as AD and DNS, must be built and maintained to enable many other products to function properly. To help facilitate best practice installations of key server roles, Microsoft has developed the BPA.

The BPA tool can be utilized from the Server Manager tool, or BPA actions can be initiated through PowerShell. The toolset is installed by default on Windows Server 2008 R2, and its function is to perform analysis actions. It is designed to determine if there are any existing configuration issues such as port blockages that may cause issues and common administrative problems with Windows Server roles.

Since the tool functions on a role basis, it can be found within Server Manager under the corresponding role that you wish to scan. See Figure 10.13 for a sample view. Currently, scan support is offered for only some of the

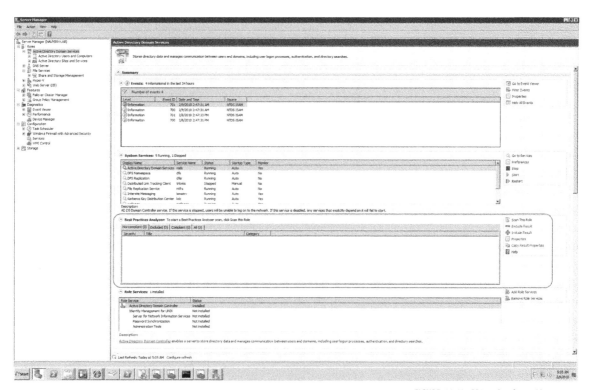

■ **FIGURE 10.13** BPA within Server Manager.

server roles in existence, but additional roles will be made available and released through the use of Windows Update. Support currently exists for the following Windows Server 2008 R2 Roles:

- Active Directory Domain Services
- Active Directory Certificate Services
- Dynamic Host Configuration Protocol
- Domain Name System
- Internet Information Services
- Remote Desktop Services
- Network Policy and Access Services

When the BPA is run on a particular role, the first step in the analysis is to go through and examine the local configuration of the role. The settings and status are compared against best practices across eight different categories. The categories each contain a subset of rules that the scanned system is to be compared against. The eight categories and their descriptions are as follows:

- BPA Prerequisites—Indication that a rule could not be applied. Results in this category do not indicate noncompliance, but instead indicate that compliance could not be validated since a prerequisite was not in place.
- Security—Indication of the risk of exposure to threats, loss of data, theft of data
- Performance—Indication if the role is able to process and respond within expected performance thresholds
- Configuration—Indication of problems with identity-related settings
- Policy—Indication of problems with Group Policy and Registry settings
- Operation—Indication of failure to perform designated function
- Predeployment—Indication of whether best practice rules are satisfied before the role is used in the production
- Postdeployment—Applied after all services have started and the role is running in production

The system will evaluate compliance against the category rules and group the results into one of the three compliance ratings:

- Noncompliant—the role does not meet the best practices conditions set forth in a rule
- Warning—the role does meet the best practices conditions set forth in a rule, but configuration changes may still be needed to remain compliant
- Compliant—the role meets the best practices conditions set forth in a rule

The output of running a scan with the BPA is displayed in Figure 10.14 and as you can see, it is sectioned off into the Good, the Bad, and the Excluded. Any rule that scans as compliance will be displayed in the Compliant tab, any rule that scans as noncompliant will be displayed in the Noncompliant tab, and any rule that you have chosen to Exclude shows in the Excluded tab. Warnings are grouped in with the noncompliance items and exclusions are identified by the administrator.

Exclusions are administrator-configured and may shift over time for different roles. For instance, the first time you run the BPA, the noncompliance list may show a warning stating that all OUs should be set to be protected from accidental deletion. The first few times you might think it is pretty cool that the tool is looking out for you that way, but by the time you have run the BPA for the third or fourth time, you will probably tire of looking at the warning message, hence, the exclusions. By selecting the warning message and clicking the *Exclude Result* option, the warning will move to the Excluded tab and will continue to appear there each time that you run the BPA from then on. If you change your mind in the future and would like to include the warning message into the normal noncompliant view once again, you can do so by selecting the Excluded tab, highlighting the message, and selecting *Include Result* from the actions pane. See Figure 10.14 for a sample of BPA output.

BPA from PowerShell

A key discernment between running the BPA from the Server Manager console and using PowerShell cmdlets is that PowerShell enables you to run scans of multiple roles simultaneously. With the GUI rendition of BPA, you are limited to selecting a single role at a time, executing the BPA, and then examining the results. If a server has multiple roles installed, this can be a tedious and time-consuming process. The solution is the utilize PowerShell.

Before you can actually use PowerShell for BPA though, you must go through the steps of importing the correct modules. BPA requires that

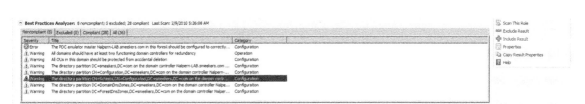

■ **FIGURE 10.14** BPA GUI-Based Output.

you impact both the Server Manager module as well as the Best Practices module. To import the modules, open PowerShell on your server and input the following commands:

> *Import-Module ServerManager*
> *Import-Module BestPractices*

At this point, you are ready to execute the BPA, but to discover what roles are installed on the server that you can run the BPA against, you should execute a *Get-WindowsFeature* command. Sample output is displayed in Figure 10.15.

From here, it is a matter of objective. You can now see which roles are on the server to which BPA applies, and the next step is to decide which ones you would like to run the BPA against. The easier choice is to follow the same format as the Get-WindowsFeature and use the filter to perform the BPA scan against all installed roles. The syntax for this command would be as follows:

> *Get-WindowsFeature | Where {$_.BestPracticesModelId -ne $null} | Invoke-BPAModel*

Figure 10.16 displays the command execution results. One of the first things you will notice after running *Invoke* is that the output results display

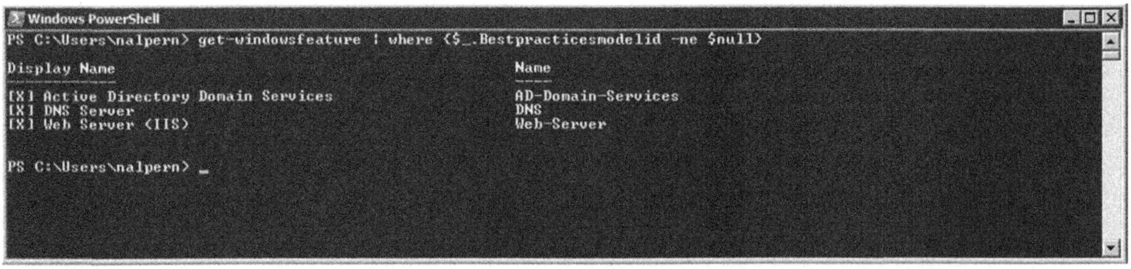

■ **FIGURE 10.15** Get-WindowsFeature Output.

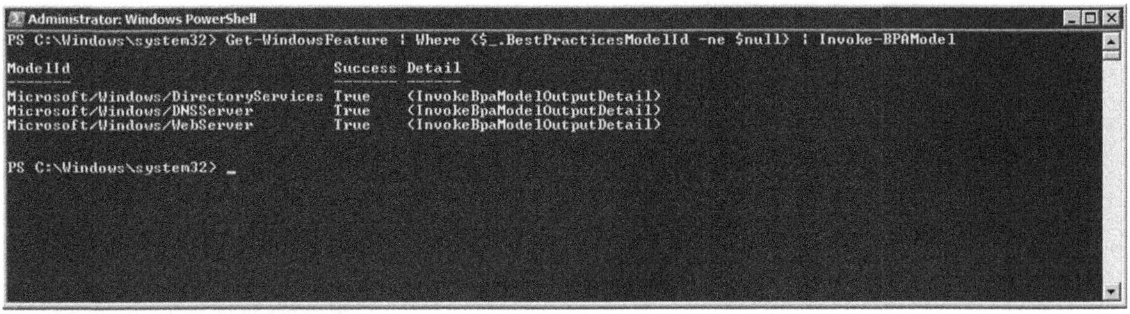

■ **FIGURE 10.16** BPA PowerShell Execution.

whether the run was successful or not, but what they do not show are the actual results. To see the results of the scan, you will need to utilize the *Get-BPAResult* cmdlet.

AUDITING

Security is on the forefront of many administrators' minds today. Understanding who is doing what with your mission critical services can help to identify loopholes in security and assist administrators in battening down the hatches. Today, auditing is more of a requirement than a "nice to have" in many environments, especially those under regulatory compliance restrictions. By taking advantage of Windows-based auditing, you can be better equipped to deal with the requests for data put forth by other groups inside your organization such as Legal and Security.

Being able to natively audit within Windows operating systems is a feature that has existed almost since the dawn of time, back to Windows NT 4.0. Although auditing has evolved with the progression of Microsoft operating systems to become more robust and configurable, the largest change in Windows auditing occurred rather recently—when Microsoft introduced Granular Audit Policies (GAPs) with Windows Server 2008 and Windows Vista.

Traditionally, with Windows 2000 and Windows 2003, auditing policies were broken down into nine distinct categories:

- Audit Account Logon Events
- Audit Account Management
- Audit Directory Services Access
- Audit Object Access
- Audit Logon Events
- Audit Policy Change
- Audit Privilege Use
- Audit Process Tracking
- Audit System Events

Each of these categories contained settings that allowed the administrator to configure what was to be collected as part of an audit trail and recorded in the Event Viewer Security log. Central configuration of the auditing categories was available as a part of AD Group Policy. Essentially, once an administrator created an audit policy in AD within a GPO and linked the GPO to the appropriate places, the machines impacted would understand that they needed to track the policy-designated settings.

The part of Audit Object Access that could never be specified for the machine through Group Policies was the indicator of which users and resources should be tracked specifically. In actuality, by configuring the policy within AD to enable object access auditing, an administrator was only half done with the configuration.

The second step in configuring object access auditing has always involved enabling auditing at the resource level. So, to have a particular resource begin to generate an audit trail, the administrator would have to touch each resource individually to specify that it should audit, and additionally for which users auditing should be tracked. So, for instance, if a file server had 500 shares configured, the probability of requiring an audit trail for any confidential shares is high, but most likely the administrator would not require an access audit trail for all 500 shares. By configuring auditing at the resource level, the administrator would have to physically select each share where auditing was required and enable auditing by configuring the System Access Control List (SACL) for the share. Each and every resource in an environment retains its own SACL which is used to identify the accounts or groups that should be tracked as part of the auditing process.

Now let us examine some of the changes introduced with Windows 2008 and Windows Vista. Microsoft took the nine base categories and evolved them to create GAP. GAP expanded on the original categories and to create a total of 50 categories that could be toggled on and off. This sounds like a really great thing, right? More flexibility, more granular settings, more robust, generally what appears to be an administrator's dream. Well, in some ways yes, while in other ways no.

One of the limitations of GAP in Windows 2008 and Windows Vista is that it cannot be configured with Group Policy. Instead, GAP can only be configured via the command line tool auditpol.exe. Since GAP is applied by executing a tool on the local machine, the end result is that the auditing settings exist within the Local Computer Security Policy on the machine. For computers in a workgroup to configure normally, there is no issue with this, but if a machine is domain-joined, there is the chance for conflict.

If a Group Policy is configured within AD that utilizes the traditional auditing categories, and the policy is applied to the machine on which you have run auditpol.exe to configure GAP, the local settings may be overridden. In order to prevent this, it is recommended to apply a registry change to all machines with GAP configured that will force the machine to ignore Group Policy-based auditing settings.

So as you can see, with Windows 2008 and Windows Vista, auditing capabilities were improved, but unfortunately, the administrative and management of the settings did not follow suit; instead, they were associated with increased administrative overhead and maintenance. For many corporate environments, the end result of the auditing changes released with Windows 2008 and Windows Vista was a pile of frustrated administrators. However, there is light at the end of the tunnel. With the release of Windows 2008 R2, Microsoft has taken to auditing those last few steps to make it robust as well as centrally manageable, ultimately bringing Windows auditing up to a new level of functionality and maturity.

The largest change in auditing with Windows Server 2008 R2 is the capability to administrate and deploy the GAPs from within Group Policy. Instead of relying on auditpol.exe and being forced to create and run scripts to apply granular auditing setting to systems, administrators now have the advantage of utilizing a familiar toolset to enforce GAP. As you can see in Figure 10.17, all of the expanded categories available for auditing within GAP are now exposed and enforceable through GPOs.

Be aware that Group Policy-based enforcement of GAP only applies to Windows 7 and Windows 2008 R2 machines. Even though Windows 2008 and Windows Vista machines support GAP, they must still have separate policies created and applied through the use of auditpol.exe.

Another significant change in auditing for Windows Server 2008 R2 revolves around auditing object access. When you enable object access on a machine in Windows Server 2008 R2, there are no SACLs to create or set on each individual resource. Instead, by utilizing Group Policy settings to enforce audit settings, you have the ability to utilize the Global Audit object policy to identify which users and what level of auditing is configured on the machine SACLs. The Global Audit policy has two choices that can be configured: File System Properties and Registry Properties. Configuring File system Properties is displayed in Figure 10.18. By default, once targeted by a Global Audit policy, all resources will have their SACL configured and enabled for object access auditing. If by chance, the local SACL and the Global SACL are defined on a particular resource, the two lists are combined and the SACLs from both locations will be used for auditing.

The final notable change for object access auditing in Windows Server 2008 R2 is that the messages recorded to the event logs now contain more detail. This is referred to by Microsoft as "Reason for access" reporting. Instead of merely stating that an allow or deny has occurred, now the event will additionally state why the event occurred. An example of an

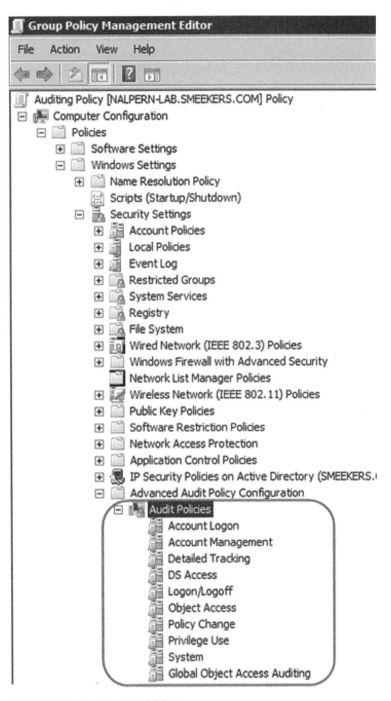

■ **FIGURE 10.17** Group Policy-Based GAP Settings.

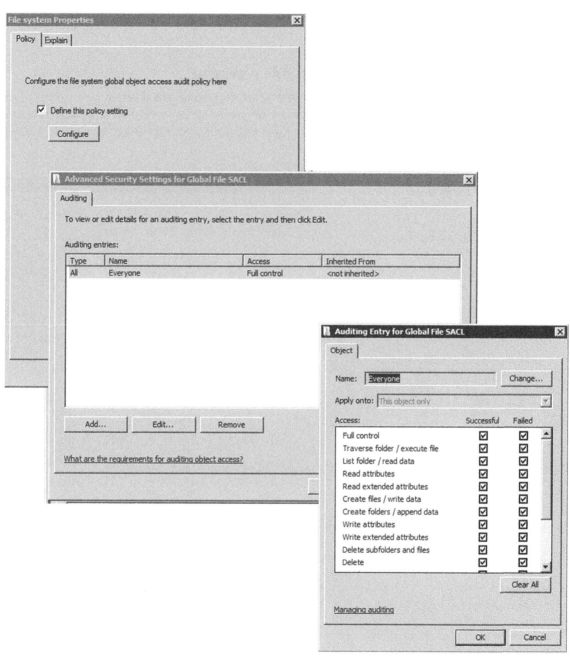

■ FIGURE 10.18 Configuring File System Properties.

Event Viewer message as a result of object access auditing is shown in Figure 10.19.

ENCRYPTING FILE SYSTEM

The situation often arises where confidential or sensitive content in an organization needs to be protected. Many ways exist to protect data in corporate enterprises, but one of the challenges facing administrators is not

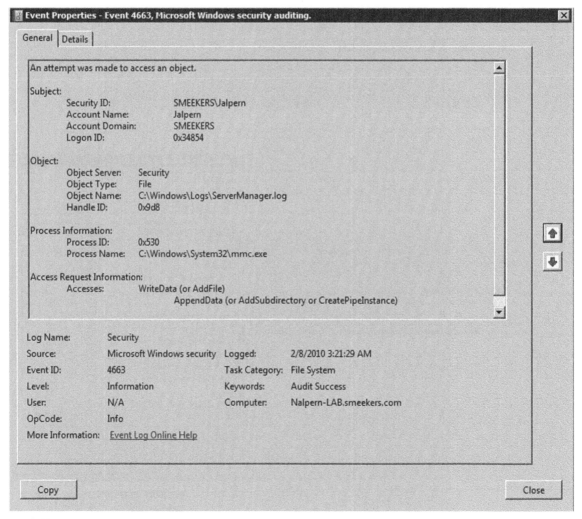

■ **FIGURE 10.19** Audit Message in Event log.

always how to protect content, but more often what data to protect. Administrators rely on end users to identify content that should be protected based on either company policy, or the user's recognition of the sensitivity of particular data.

Often, the data content is not only important, but may also be of a confidential nature. One way to enable users to protect data that they know is confidential is to train them on the usage of EFS. EFS is a file encryption technology that allows end users to store data content on NTFS volumes in encrypted format. EFS is a user-specific technology, meaning that once a file has been encrypted while a user is logged in with a particular username, only that logged-on username can be used to read or decrypt the file.

Enabling EFS is as easy as checking a box. Each file and folder on an NTFS volume has an attribute that is used to enable encryption. See Figure 10.20 for an example of this attribute at the folder level. Once you have enabled a folder for EFS, all files placed into that folder will automatically be encrypted. EFS is a not a new technology, but Microsoft has enhanced some aspects of it with the release of Windows Server 2008 R2.

■ **FIGURE 10.20** Enabling EFS at the Folder Level.

One of the key areas of change for EFS revolves around the introduction of support for new algorithms, as we will discuss in the next section.

EFS keys and algorithms

EFS utilizes both symmetric and asymmetric key technology to encrypt and secure data on NTFS volumes. A symmetric key is a single key which can quickly be used to encrypt or decrypt larger amounts of data. Symmetric keys are often used to encrypt content because of the speed advantage they have over key pairs. EFS utilizes symmetric keys to secure data content.

Asymmetric key pairs are a complimentary pair of keys. One of the keys is used to encrypt while the other to decrypt. Asymmetric keys are slower when dealing with large amounts of data, and so, are not used in EFS to secure data, but are instead used to secure the symmetric key. So, ultimately, it is a combination of keys that are used by EFS to secure a user's data in the file system; a single key to encrypt the data content and a key pair to secure the single key.

In earlier iterations of EFS, Microsoft has employed industry standard encryption algorithms such as Triple DES (3DES) and Data Encryption Standard X (DESX). As encryption standards have developed and improved, Microsoft has continued to update EFS to support the newer protocols, as was evident with the release of Windows XP SP1. From Windows XP SP1, forward EFS began utilizing Advanced Encryption Standard (AES) as its primary encryption mechanism.

The newest version of EFS, included with Windows Server 2008 R2 and Windows 7, has followed in the same footsteps as the preceding versions and has been improved to reflect the algorithm standards that exist today. The following represent the algorithms supported by the Windows Server 2008 R2 iteration of EFS:

- Advanced Encryption Standard
- Secure Hash Algorithm (SHA)
- Elliptic Curve Cryptography (ECC)
- Smart card-based encryption

A critical addition to the preceding list is the new support for ECC. Many environments today are required to comply with stricter regulatory requirements. The addition of ECC allows for these high-security environments to comply with Suite B encryption requirements as set forth by the National Security Agency. Today, Suite B compliance is utilized by United States government agencies to protect classified information.

EFS and policy enforcement

With additional compliance regulations existing in many environments today, administrators often need a mechanism to control the enforcement of certain security policies. In Windows 7 and Windows Server 2008 R2, you have the capability to control the way EFS behaves in the Local Computer Policy on the machine. Utilizing the Local Computer Policy, you have the ability to enforce ECC as well as configure other settings such as if Smart Cards are required for EFS usage. Since Local Computer Policy settings are administrated individually on each computer, it makes it very difficult to use these settings in a larger environment.

The most common way to enforce policy onto large groups of machines in an AD environment is by utilizing Group Policy. In order to address EFS policy enforcement on a broader scale, Microsoft has incorporated settings into Group Policy to allow the capability to control and enforce settings centrally for new EFS components. You will file EFS settings within a Group Policy under *Computer Configuration | Policies | Windows Settings | Security Settings | Public Key Policies | Encrypting File System.*

In Suite B compliance environments, the usage of RSA encryption algorithms is not allowed and only ECC may be used for EFS. Group Policy has three ECC pertinent settings, Allow, Require, and Don't Allow, which are displayed in Figure 10.21.

The Allow setting simply allows the use of ECC, but does not enforce it. This means that both RSA and ECC are available when this setting has been configured. If you are in an environment that requires Suite B compliance, Allow is not an appropriate setting. Instead, you would want to select the second radio button for Require. Require prevents the use of RSA and enforces that ECC be the only protocol in use with EFS. The final setting of Don't Allow blocks the usage of ECC, thus all EFS key sets will be generated utilizing RSA.

Cipher.exe

Cipher.exe is a command that has existed for some time, and essentially embodies a command prompt version of the file system GUI exposure of EFS, but with a little more dynamism. Since administrators are often looking for a faster and more manageable way to perform mundane or repetitive tasks, Cipher.exe fits well into an administrator's toolbox.

Cipher.exe can help to reduce the administrative burden associated with EFS by allowing bulk EFS actions to be performed against the file system. It has the capability to target files and folders and force encryption or

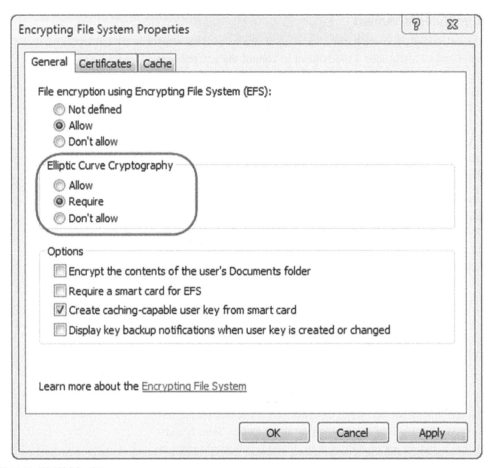

decryption throughout directory structures. Instead of having to move files into a designated folder manually for them to be encrypted, Cipher.exe allows targeting for encryption via the command prompt. Additionally, it can also be used to assist with other EFS administrative tasks such as key management tasks. One such task includes the generation of new user keys, another includes updating encrypted files with new user encryption keys.

With Cipher.exe, two switches exist that allow the administrator to request new EFS keys: /K and /R. /K will allow an administrator to create a new certificate and key, while /R allows an administrator to generate a new recovery certificate and key.

Since Windows 2008 R2 has introduced the capability to generate keys based on the ECC algorithm, Microsoft has enabled the specification of the ECC protocol and key length with the new */ECC:length* switch. The new ECC switch can be used in conjunction with the /K and /R switches to allow the administrator to impact key generation in two ways: first, ECC keys will be generated, and second, the key length for the ECC keys can be specified. The options for the ECC key length include 256, 384, and 521 key lengths. ECC keys can only be used with self-signed certificates.

FILE CLASSIFICATION INFRASTRUCTURE

Imagine opening a door within your company's workspace and seeing a room of pile upon pile of file folders stacked ceiling high and stuffed full with loose pages of information. Some of the file folders may contain related data files while others contain disparate information. Some data is considered pertinent to the company and needs to be kept for many years. Other data may be outdated or stale and in need of purging.

The ceiling-stacked piles stretch the length of the room, and as you continue down the hallway, you notice that the files are distributed ceiling high throughout many rooms. This seems like fiction, but in most IT environments, dealing with file servers in the environment depicts a daily task in an administrator's reality.

Electronic data has evolved over time to allow users to store all data sensitivity types. Data is most useful to users if it is available when needed. By stacking company data into disorganized piles within a File server infrastructure, data may be hard to come by when it is needed most. This is a problem that has existed since electronic data storage began, but the problem has become exacerbated as the amount of data that needs to be retained in the corporate world has grown. Another challenge that is occurring in most environments is the need to comply with stringent regulatory compliance requirements, which calls for data to be readily available and easily discoverable.

With Windows 2008 R2, Microsoft has introduced a new feature functionality that will begin to help administrators tackle this ever-growing problem. It is called File Classification Infrastructure (FCI) and its purpose is to assist in automatically classifying files in your environment to make them easier to manage and discover. Three methods exist to classify files:

- Automatic classification—This is rule driven and files are classified based on content or folder location

- Manual classification—Users can configure file properties that influence their classification
- Line of Business applications and IT scripts—by utilizing the FCI, API files can have their file properties configured automatically via applications and scripts

By creating file management policies, you can control the way files are classified and then, based on their classifications, tasks can be performed against the files. A good example of this occurs when data is considered stale. In many environments, data purge does not occur on a regular basis. As a result, stale data can accumulate and create unneeded file content that must be maintained. By utilizing policies, you can classify data, and then perform data management tasks such as expiring files on a routine basis. In the next sections, we will explore the concept of FCI in more depth and discuss what you need to do to deploy it successfully.

Planning for FCI

Like many things in IT, FCI is a technology better deployed with a good plan behind it. So before jumping in with both feet, it is a really good idea to come to an agreement as an organization as to what the FCI classification structure will look like. Group files into like categories sound easy, until you start to discuss within the organization what those classifications actually are.

Within a corporation, often times, a Document or Records Management policy already exists. These existing policies can form wonderful springboards when planning for an FCI deployment. Often, the policy will have each distinct file or record type called out along with the named classification and associated retention information document for each type. If you are lucky enough to work in an environment with a formalized and well-documented records management policy, your journey in deploying FCI will have a much more clearly laid-out path.

For those of you not quite as lucky, it is in your best interest to plan and design for the classifications infrastructure before you attempt to build it. Additionally, you will not only want to know how the files will be classified, but what types of actions are to be performed on the various classifications. It may be useful to create a matrix documenting the automated file classifications and the actions for each. Table 10.3 describes a fictional example. The next step is to map your plan to the functionality within FCI. We will discuss deploying FCI in the next section.

Table 10.3 File Classification Matrix Example

File Classification Information	Property Value	Associated Actions
Sensitivity Ratings		
Confidential	Yes or No	Backup and retain for 12 years Discoverable within 2 days Expires on disk after 1 year
Internal Only	Yes or No	Backup and retain for 3 years Discoverable within 2 days Expires on disk after 1 year
Public	Yes or No	Backup and retain for 3 years Discoverable within 1 day Expires on disk after 180 days
Personnel Content	Contains SS#, phone #, or home address Does not contain personal info	Move to Personnel file share No action
Business Impact	High	Discoverable within 1 day Expires on disk after 1 year
	Medium	Discoverable within 2 days Expires on disk after 1 year
	Low	Discoverable within 10 days Expires on disk after 180 days

Configuring FCI

To utilize FCI, the server must hold the File Services role. To install FCI open Server Manager, right-click the File Services role and select *Add Role Services*, as displayed in Figure 10.22. This will launch the *Add Role Services* wizard and allow you to select *File Server Resource Manager* from the list.

Once you have completed the installation wizard, you will then have the File Server Resource Manager console available to you on the Administrative Tools menu (see Figure 10.23). We will be reviewing Automatic Classification, and the configuration for each of the different components takes place from within this console.

The console contains a section called Classification Management. Within Classification Management, you have two subnodes: Classification Properties and Classification Rules. The Classification Properties section is where you will build out your classifications plan into Classification Property Definitions (see Figure 10.24). The *Create Classification Property Definition* screen will require you to name your property definition and

■ **FIGURE 10.22** Add Role Services.

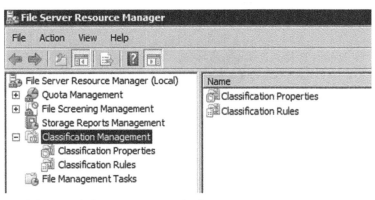

■ **FIGURE 10.23** File Server Resource Manager Console.

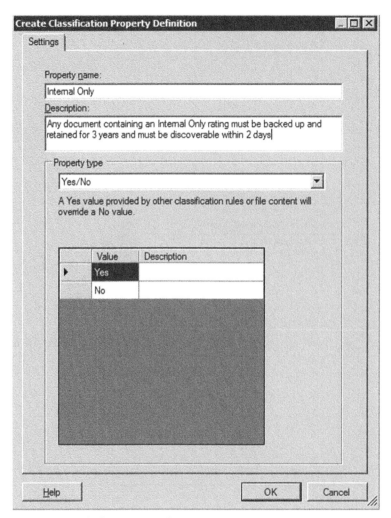

■ **FIGURE 10.24** Classification Property Definitions.

then identify the property type. You have quite a variety of choices to select from and will want to stick to your originally laid-out plan. Also, keep in mind that simplification of the classification structure you build will help to ease administrative burden down the road.

Once you have completed building your classification structure, the next step is to create rules. Classification Rules Definitions, displayed in Figure 10.25, are what will be used by the system to judge when to assign which property definitions to the various files you scan.

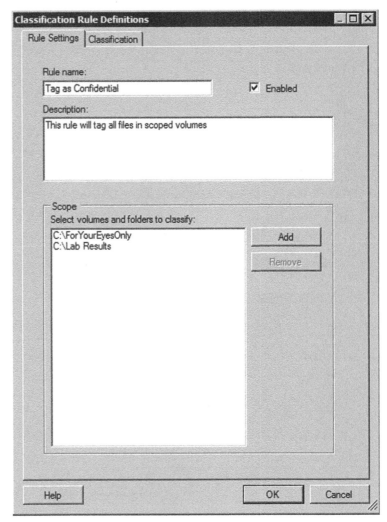

■ **FIGURE 10.25** Classification Rules Definitions.

Each rule must contain the directories which are to be classified, and the classification mechanism. The choices for classification mechanism are Folder Classification and Content Classifier. The Folder Classification allows you to specify folder information to be used as the match criteria to tag a file with a particular property. The Content Classifier allows for a more detailed match and can search file content in order to match. Regardless of the selected classification mechanism, you utilize the Advanced option on the Classifications tab to specify the parameters or values used to match (see Figure 10.26).

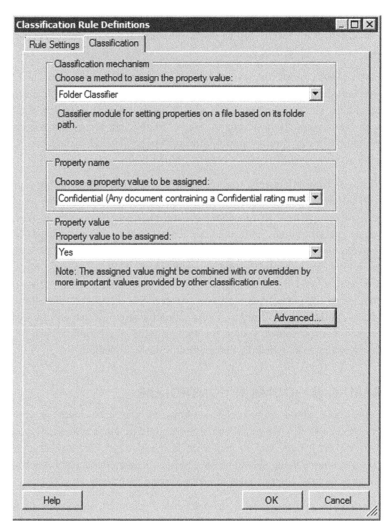

■ FIGURE 10.26 Classification Mechanism and Property Settings.

Managing FCI

Ok, now that you have built your Classification Properties and Classification Rules, do not sit back and wait for magic to happen. We have a few more steps to go before the system will start to work for you. First, we must send the rules you have just created out into your file structure to start scanning and tagging documents. You have two choices of how to accomplish this: One method is to run a manual scan for all rules on demand and the second method and preferred choice is to schedule scans to run on a recurring basis. After performing an on-demand scan, a statistical report of the results will be displayed. A portion of a sample report is displayed in Figure 10.27.

If you choose to schedule the scan, you will be asked to configure a standard scheduling window with your desired parameters for the scheduled execution. The schedule screen is part of the File Server Resource Manager options and is displayed in Figure 10.28. Scheduled scan reports are stored in the *%systemdrive%\StorageReports\Scheduled* directory by default.

Now you have effectively sent rules out into the file system to tag files with different classifications. Congratz! But ask yourself, what have you really accomplished? At this point, you have a whole pile of tagged files, but you have not really performed any actions on them besides categorization. So, the next step in working with FCI is to decide what to do with these classified files. In the File Server Resource Manager console, there is a section labeled *File Management Tasks*. File Expiration and Custom are the two file management tasks actions available. File Expiration allows you to configure a directory as a destination for any files that are deemed expired. Custom allows you, as the administrator, to create your own file management tasks which fit the needs of your organization.

READ-ONLY DOMAIN CONTROLLER

Let us talk about branch offices. Most of you have them in your environments. If your environment is centralized administratively, you probably find them hard to deal with in many ways. One key struggle revolves around being able to provide local authentication capability while still maintaining centralized administration and security.

For users to gain access to the network-based resources, authentication of the computer and user accounts must occur. In an environment that has deployed Microsoft AD DS, authentication is the responsibility of Domain Controllers (DCs). They each house a locally stored writable copy of the directory content, and through replication, they share changes among themselves.

Most branch offices of significant size place an administrator between a rock and a hard place. For instance, if a branch office were to become isolated from the rest of the corporate network, chances are that local productivity within the site will be dramatically impacted. So, the motivation exists to ensure that local authentication is available by placing a DC locally in the site.

Size By File Group

■ Image Files; 0.00 MB; (66.67 %)
■ Text Files; 0.00 MB; (33.33 %)

Size by File Group		
File Group	**Total size on Disk**	**Files**
Image Files	0.00 MB	2
Text Files	0.00 MB	1

To top of the current report

Size by Property		
Property	**Total size on Disk**	**Files**
Confidential	0.00 MB	3

To top of the current report

Statistics for files by 'Confidential'					
File name	**Folder**				
	Value	**Rule**	**Last accessed**	**Last modified**	**Owner**
Design1.bmp	c:\ForYourEyesOnly\New Designs				
	Yes	Tag as Confidential	2/9/2010 11:30:54 PM	2/9/2010 11:30:54 PM	SMEEKERS\NAlpern
Design2.bmp	c:\ForYourEyesOnly\New Designs				
	Yes	Tag as Confidential	2/9/2010 11:31:01 PM	2/9/2010 11:31:01 PM	SMEEKERS\NAlpern
Notes.txt	c:\ForYourEyesOnly\New Designs				
	Yes	Tag as Confidential	2/9/2010 11:31:11 PM	2/9/2010 11:31:11 PM	SMEEKERS\NAlpern

■ **FIGURE 10.27** Sample Scan Report.

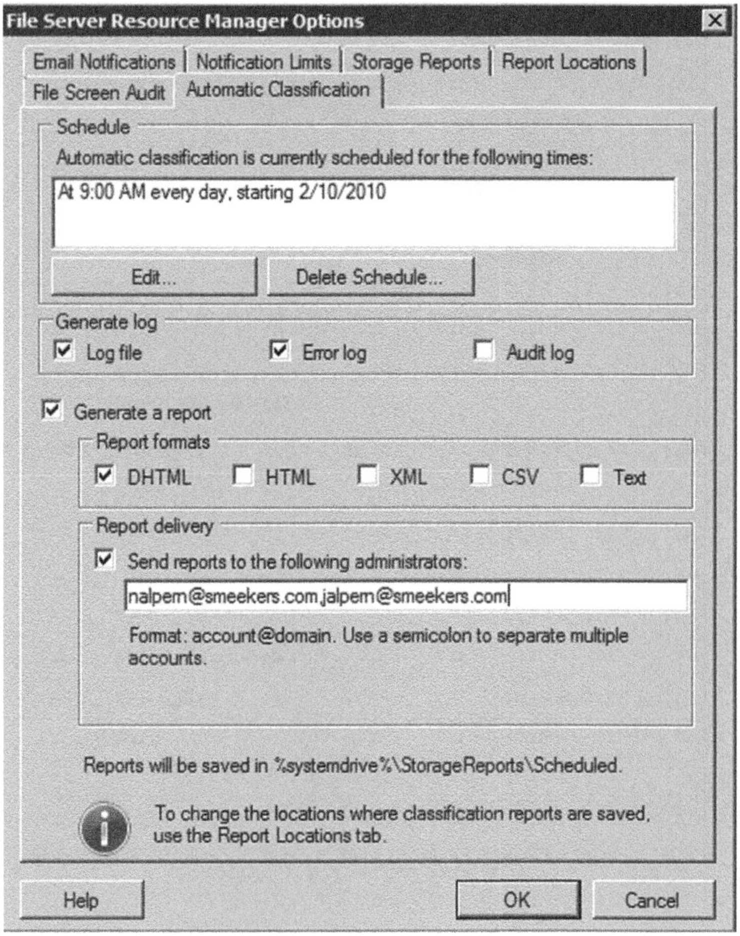

■ **FIGURE 10.28** Automatic Classification Schedule Creation.

Traditionally, all DCs house password information for domain accounts and are used to validate log-on attempts to the domain and access to network resources. To allow for continued autonomy of a branch office facility, an administrator will often deploy a DC into the local site. This ensures that if the network connectivity back to the centralized environment were to fail, the site can still function independently to a certain extent.

If the branch office does not have full-time administrative staff, placing a DC in the local facility can present security risks and concerns as well as create additional administrative overhead. One of the largest risks presented has to do with the accessibility of a key network asset. If the local

DC were to be stolen or compromised, the attacker would have all of the domain accounts and passwords at their disposal to attack.

Onto the scene enters the Read-Only Domain Controller (RODC). With the release of Windows 2008, Microsoft introduced the concept of the RODC. RODCs make it less of a security risk to place DCs in a branch office scenario since they are not writable copies of the directory. Many of the features of the RODCs allow administrators to customize the behavior of the RODC depending on the needs of the particular branch.

When administration is centralized, often one of the challenges associated with using RODCs is deploying them. Without administrative staff in branch offices, it is often the job of a centralized admin to get out to the branches to perform maintenance and build tasks. With Windows Server, you can choose to deploy RODCs in two stages. The first stage requires Domain Admin permissions and is performed from Active Directory Users and Computers. To stage the computer account in AD, you must right-click on the DCs OU and select *Pre-create Read-only Domain Controller account . . .* , as seen in Figure 10.29. This will launch the AD DS Installation Wizard and will allow you to complete the first stage of deploying a new RODC.

Figure 10.30 displays the portion of the Installation Wizard which allows you to specify the administrative account or group in the organization that is authorized to complete the RODC installation. The user account specified does not have to be a Domain Admins member, and often times, local administrative staff who work in the branch offices are ideal candidates for this task. The second stage of installing the new RODC will be handled by the specified account. Essentially, as part of the prestaging process, the account is granted rights to execute dcpromo.exe on the target RODC and complete the AD Installation Wizard. Additionally, the same selected account will be granted local administrative permissions on the RODC once installation is complete.

NETWORK POLICY AND ACCESS SERVICES

When providing your user base with remote access mechanisms, the foremost focus tends to be on authentication. The concern is that unauthorized users will gain access to the internal network and cause some damage or theft. While this is a valid concern and a real security threat to every environment allowing remote access today, there is another often overlooked security threat looming nearby.

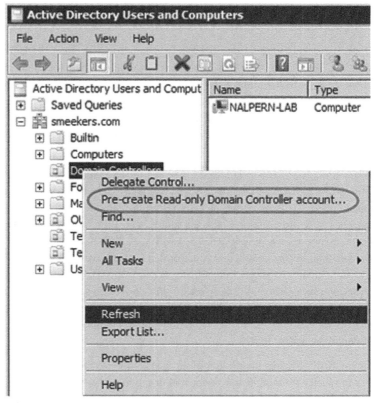

■ **FIGURE 10.29** RODC Prestaging Wizard.

While user authentication gets all the attention, a security concept that often falls through the cracks is device access. This is a focus not on *who* is access the network, but from *what device* are they accessing the network. The reason this is important is because without validating the client that is being used to dial into the remote access mechanism, there is not a way to protect the network from the security state that the client might be in.

Most VPN software is a load and go process. Even though many VPN providers allow for the configuration of additional security measures within their VPN software, such as computer certificates, not many customers actually deploy them. With focus commonly on the user, it is often that two-factor authentication is deployed, but machine authentication is often an afterthought.

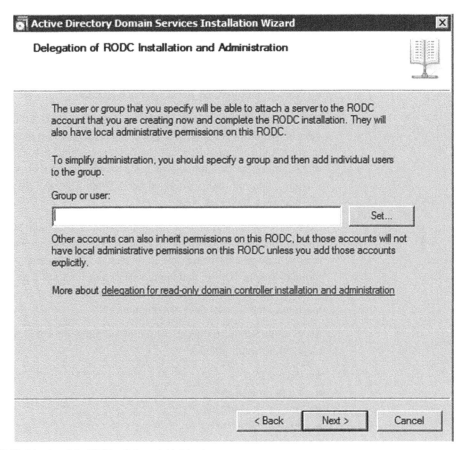

■ **FIGURE 10.30** Delegation of the RODC Installation and Administration.

So with publically downloadable VPN software in one hand and the Internet facing VPN URLs in the other, users are often able to connect to the company Intranet through VPN tunnels from machines that are not a part of the domain environment. Since these rogue machines are not a part of your domain environment, they do not fall under any type of centralized management policies. Therefore, their patch state is unknown, their antivirus software is a mystery and whether or not they are crawling with Trojans and worms is a mystery. Yet, you are allowing these machines connectivity into your Intranet environment each and every day.

To assist administrators with addressing the issue of these intruding rogue workstations, with the release of Windows 2008, Microsoft introduced the

Network Policy and Access Services role. This role includes the following components, all wrapped up in a single role:

- Network Access Protection (NAP)
- Network Policy Server (NPS)
- Routing and Remote Access Service (RRAS)

NPS and RRAS are not new to Windows and have been around since the days of Windows NT 4.0. NPS is the Windows 2008 rebranded name for Internet Authentication Services (IAS), representing Microsoft's rendition of Remote Authentication Dial-In User Service (RADIUS). While RRAS, was just plain old RAS with Windows NT 4.0. The new kid on the block for Windows 2008 was NAP.

NAP allows administrators to decide the required minimum health state of a client machine before it is allowed to complete its connection to the internal network. By being able to dictate acceptable compliance settings through System Health Validators (SHV) and then utilizing those SHVs to create health policies, administrators now have the authority to block machines identified as "out of compliance."

SHVs allow administrators to configure the following characteristics to be included in health policies:

- Firewall
- Virus Protection
- Antivirus up-to-date
- Spyware protection
- Antispyware up-to-date
- Automatic updating
- Security update protection

Health policies are utilized as part of network policies within Network Policy and Access Services to allow or deny access to the network, therefore, a machine that was not running the most recently Critical security updates, or had out-of-date antivirus software, could be denied access into the overall network. With the release of Windows Server 2008 R2, Microsoft has updated both NPS and NAP with new feature functionality described in the next sections.

NPS

The principal change in NPS with the release of Windows Server 2008 R2 is the introduction of templates. When configuring an NPS system that may house many RADIUS configuration settings, administration and management of the multiple settings and shared secrets can become an administrative challenge. With the addition of templates in Windows 2008 R2, administrators can now configure settings and then save them to template form to be exported for use on other NPS services, or even to be used locally as base templates in the creation and configuration of new RADIUS settings.

The templates are available in three distinct flavors:

- Shared secret
- RADIUS Clients
- Remote RADIUS Servers

Shared secret templates can be used in conjunction with the other two templates. So, for instance, while creating a Remote RADIUS Server Template, you can select to utilize a previously created Shared Secret template, as depicted in Figure 10.31.

Additionally, when you are ready to utilize the Remote Server template, you can do so locally, or you can choose to export the settings and import them into another server for use. Ideally, you should only ever have to configure RADIUS Proxy targets a single time.

In addition to the new NPS templates, Microsoft has also taken measures to enhance accounting with NPS in Windows 2008 R2. With the introduction of a new accounting configuration wizard, you can now easily set up and configure NPS logging. You can choose between Microsoft SQL logging, text logging, or even run both, as shown in Figure 10.32.

NAP

Deploying a NAP infrastructure requires multiple critical design decisions to be made. These decisions include both policy settings for enforcement scenarios which will indicate how and when clients are checked for compliance status, and also the selection of functioning mode the policies will enact once a machine is deemed out of compliance.

There are five different policy enforcement scenarios available:

- IPsec enforcement—utilizes health certificates to control host access on a per-connection level, so machines that are out of compliance are denied connectivity to requested resources
- 802.1X enforcement—works with supported wireless access points to place noncompliant machines into an isolated network environment
- VPN enforcement—does not allow access into the internal network environment, or only provides for limited access for noncompliant machines

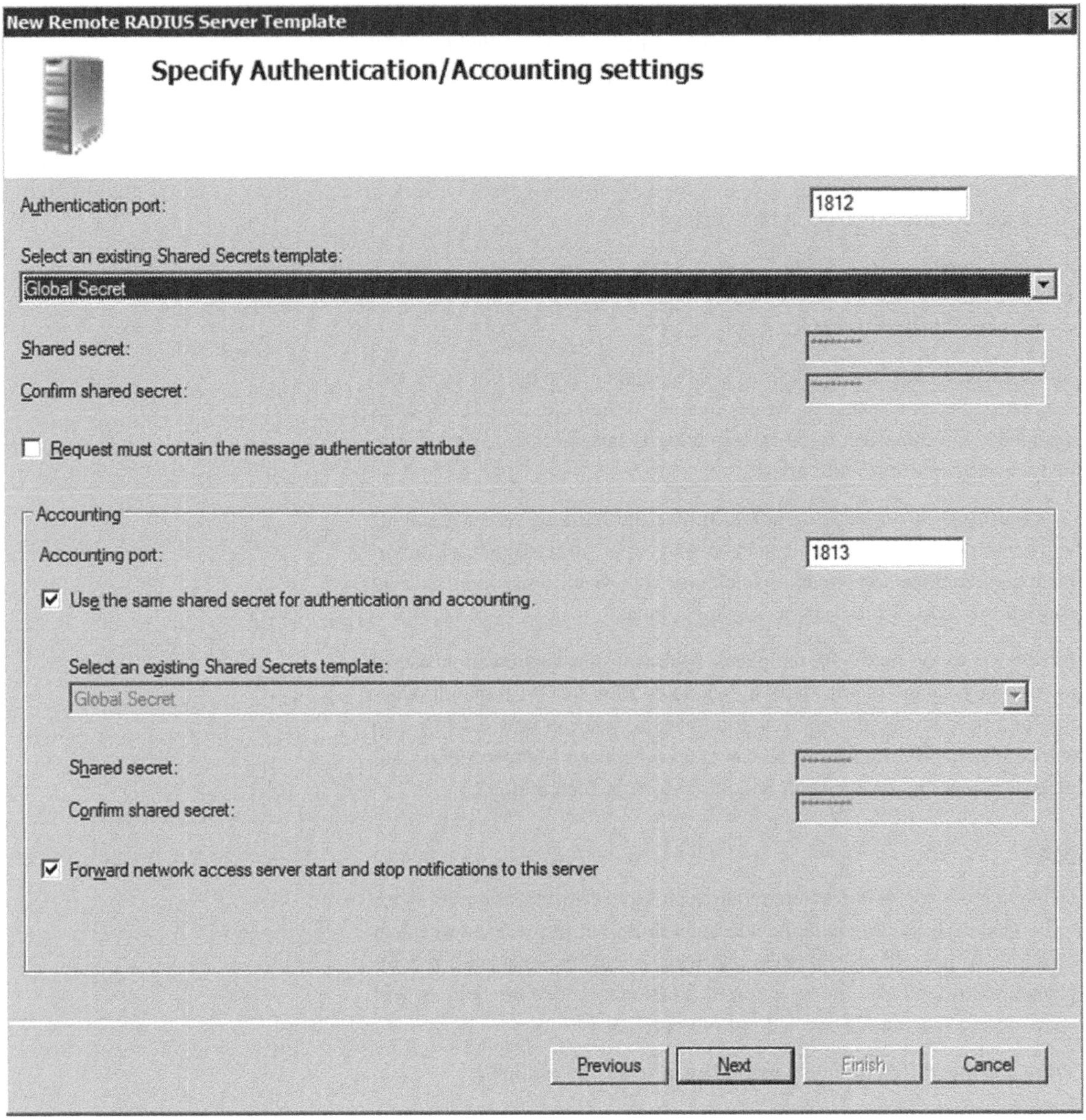

■ FIGURE 10.31 Remote Server Template
Utilizing Shared Secret Template.

- DHCP enforcement—enforces limited access by issuing restricted network IP addresses to machines that are noncompliant, does not function on machines with static IP addresses
- No enforcement—remediation actions can be taken on noncompliance machines, but limited access is not enforced

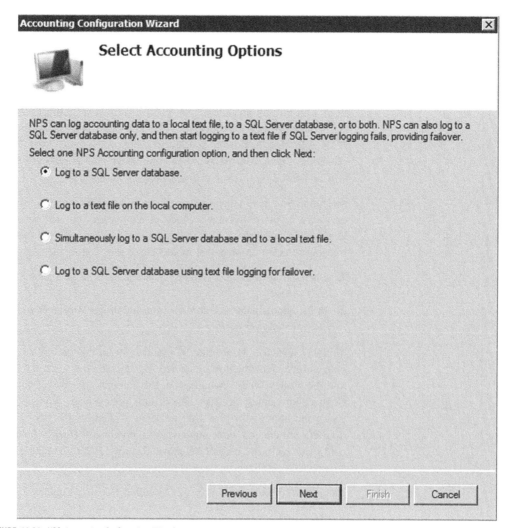

Accounting Configuration Wizard ☒

Select Accounting Options

NPS can log accounting data to a local text file, to a SQL Server database, or to both. NPS can also log to a SQL Server database only, and then start logging to a text file if SQL Server logging fails, providing failover.

Select one NPS Accounting configuration option, and then click Next:

◉ Log to a SQL Server database.

○ Log to a text file on the local computer.

○ Simultaneously log to a SQL Server database and to a local text file.

○ Log to a SQL Server database using text file logging for failover.

[Previous] [Next] [Finish] [Cancel]

■ **FIGURE 10.32** NPS Accounting Configuration Wizard.

Deciding which method to use is primarily based on your NAP deployment goals. For instance, if it is your goal to protect your internal network from remote access users, then selecting VPN enforcement is a logical choice, whereas attempting to accomplish the same goal with DHCP enforcement is not possible. On the other hand, if restricting your users is out of the question, then going with the No enforcement option still allows you to identify machines that do not match your configured health policies and perform remediation without negatively impacting the user's working day.

To begin the deployment of NAP, you must install the NAP role on a Windows 2008 R2 server by utilizing Server Manager. Once the role has been successfully installed, the server is effectively functioning as a NAP Health Policy Server (HPS). The NAP HPS is a server running the NAP role that has been configured with your selected enforcement scenarios. All of your policies and compliance configuration information will be housed on this server role in the environment.

Assuming you have taken the time to execute planning steps, you should be aware of the enforcement mode of choice for your enterprise. Once you have installed the NAP HPS, the next step is to configure the policies for your selected enforcement mode. To do this, follow these steps:

1. Open *Server Manager | Roles | Network Policy and Access Services | NPS (Local)*.
2. In the details pane, select NAP from the dropdown menu and then select *Configure NAP*.

This will launch a wizard that will guide you through policy creation for your enforcement method of choice. By default, the wizard will create multiple policy types, including: Health Policies, Network Policies, and Connection Request Policies. These three policy types work together to create the policy structure used to deem a client connection worthy or not. Wizard-created noncompliant and compliant Health Policies are configured with the default Windows Security Health Validator and are automatically utilized by the wizard-created Network Policies.

Three NAP enforcement modes exist within Network Policies:

- Reporting Mode—allows for data collection to occur, however, users are not impacted, no restrictions are enforced; configured as "Allow full network access" from within the Network Policy.
- Deferred Enforcement—grants noncompliant machines network access for a limited time; configured as "Allow full network access for a limited time" from within the Network Policy.

Full Enforcement—restricts noncompliance computers to access a restricted network to obtain remediation through updates; configured as "Allow limited access" from within the Network Policy.

The Network Policies created through the *Configure NAP* wizard include a noncompliant network policy that is configured to allow for limited access, and a compliant network policy that allows for full network access. Additionally, Connection Request Policies are created to allow the traffic type to connect to the system and be validated.

Since the wizard is not aware of what compliance or noncompliance configurations should be set to in your organization, once the wizard has created the policies, you may find it necessary to go back and adjust some of the settings, particularly on the Health Policy-selected SHV. To do this, open *Server Manager*, navigate to *Roles | Network Policy and Access Services | NPS (Local) | Network Access Protection | System Health Validators | Windows Security Health Validator | Settings* and either select the configuration you wish to modify or select *New* to create an additional configuration.

The Windows 2008 release of NAP SHVs was limited and constituted a one-stop shop per server for SHV configuration settings. So, for an installed instance of NAP, you could only have a single corresponding instance of a particular SHV on the server. So, essentially for each of the different health scenarios that you were required to support, you needed to have a separate NAP server to allow for the different SHV configurations. This created a situation where even in small environments, the deployment footprint for NAP could be very high.

To address the total cost of ownership and deployment concerns that existed with the Windows 2008 iteration of NAP, Microsoft adjusted NAP in Windows 2008 R2 to allow for the creation of multiple SHVs on a single NAP server instance. Any third-party vendor SHVs would need to be created by the vendor to support the new multiple SHV functionality before they can be used in this fashion. So, by being able to establish different health requirements, administrators are now able to set up different configuration models for different types of clients, reduce their NAP footprint and still retain central access control to their networks.

The manual high-level steps to multiple configurations within a single NAP deployment are as follows:

1. Configure the appropriate SHVs.
2. Configure multiple health policies and select the appropriate SHV (displayed in Figure 10.33).
3. Configure multiple network policies and select the appropriate health policy for each.

Utilizing the *Configure NAP*, wizard performs policy creation steps automatically based on your responses in the wizard; however, adjustments to the SHVs may still be a required postwizard task, depending on the complexity of your deployment.

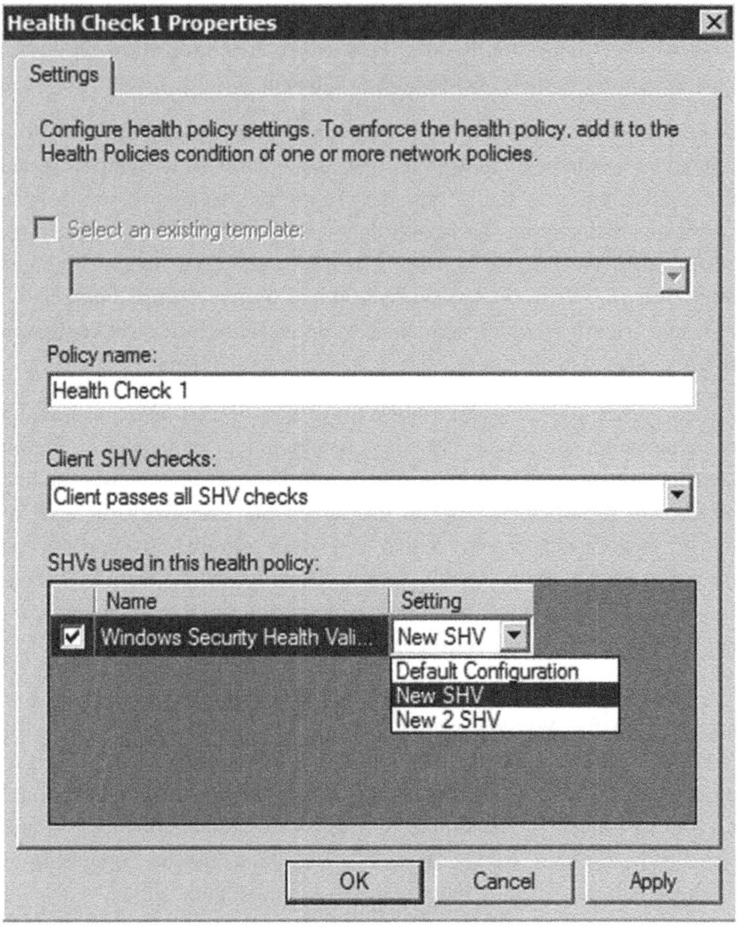

FIGURE 10.33 Health Policy Displaying Multiple SHVs to Choose from.

Once the NAP HPS configuration is completed, the next step in the NAP deployment is to you must ensure to identify and configure NAP Enforcement Points. NAP Enforcement Points are the connectivity points into your network that must be configured to utilize the NAP HPS settings, such as DHCP Servers, VPN solutions, including Microsoft NPS, and Wireless Access Points.

For instance, if you have chosen to utilize your VPN access mechanism as a validate check point for client health, you must configure that VPN solution to integrate with NAP. This allows the VPN solution to collect information about the connecting client and transmit it to the NAP HPS for policy processing. Once a response is received from the NAP HPS server, the VPN system will have the information it needs to properly respond to the client. If the client is considered compliant, access will be granted, and if the client is noncompliant, either limited network access or full network access for a limited time will be granted.

ACTIVE DIRECTORY RECYCLE BIN

Just imagine it: a new systems administrator begins working in your environment. You show him where the bathrooms are and where the break room is, you give him a run-down of the AD environment, and finally equip him with a shiny new laptop and matching administrative account. He works in your environment for a while, and seems to be adjusting well, and within no time, he does have a good understanding of what is required to keep the place running smoothly. After a time, you decide it is probably safe to take a short vacation, and to allow him to completely manage all systems while you are gone, you grant his administrative account membership in the Domain Admins group. Effectively, you have just handed over keys to the castle, displaying your trust and belief in this new member of the team.

Then, the inevitable occurs. You are 2 days into your relaxing vacation, having a drink on the beach, and your cell phone rings. On the other end is a very panicky admin, who is none other than the new member of the team. He explains to you how he created a new user account, but spelled the user's name wrong. In his attempt to delete the misspelled account, he inadvertently deleted a handful of active user accounts, and now he is calling you to resolve the crisis and determine what to do.

In the not so distant old school days of AD, your instructions to the distressed administrator would have involved digging out backups and performing authoritative restores of the deleted directory objects. Problems with this included the fact that your restoration potential was only as good as the time of your last backup. So, if by some chance, backups had not been performed for quite some time, you stood the chance of restoring the directory to a much older copy in order to recover the deleted items.

On the other hand, if backups are too cumbersome to attempt to utilize or if backups are not available for use, another possible recovery option may include performing a reanimation of newly formed Tombstone objects. Tombstone objects are created as a part of the normal deletion process in AD. In order to allow other DCs to be notified that an object has been deleted from the directory, the fact that the object deletion has occurred must somehow be replicated to all AD DCs. Since the absence of an object cannot be propagated, a Tombstone is created that represents the deleted item and it is assigned lifetime value. By default, Tombstone objects in Windows 2003 and Windows 2008 domains are assigned a lifetime value that allows them to remain in the directory structure for 180 days. Once the lifetime threshold is reached, the physical Tombstone object is removed from the DCs completely.

The process of reinstating the Tombstone object before the lifetime of an object has expired is referred to as Tombstone reanimation. When a Tombstone object is reanimated, unfortunately it only brings with it a shell of its original state. This is because when an object is deleted and a Tombstone object is created, the original object will have the majority of its attributes stripped to form the Tombstone. Therefore, the resulting Tombstone is only a shell of the former object, and attributes such as user group memberships would not be restored if a reanimation were to take place.

With the introduction of Windows Server 2008 R2, you now have the ability to enable a new feature called the Active Directory Recycle Bin. And yes, it is what it sounds like. Similar to the desktop Recycle Bin concept, once the feature has been enabled in AD, the administrators are given a second chance to restore an object that has been deleted from the AD. This allows you the ability to still save the day and recover from common administrative mistakes and blunders without as much effort. Utilizing the Active Directory Recycle Bin yields results faster than an authoritative restore and flaunts better end results than can be achieved with a Tombstone reanimation.

Enabling the Active Directory Recycle Bin

By utilizing the new Windows Server 2008 R2 Active Directory Recycle Bin feature, you can quickly and painlessly recover the deleted accounts with just a few clicks. In order to enable the capability, a few steps are required. First, the environment must be prepared for new Windows Server 2008 R2 DCs. The following commands must be executed:

- *Adprep/forestprep*—Schema extension
- *Adprep/domainprep/gpprep*—Creation of groups and the application of necessary permissions

Once you have completed the preparation tasks, you must ensure that all DCs are running Windows Server 2008 R2. Only if all legacy DCs have been removed are you able to make the final change required to enable the Active Directory Recycle Bin. The final task that must be performed is to raise the forest functional level to Windows Server 2008 R2. This change cannot be retracted.

As soon as all the prerequisites are in place, the AD PowerShell cmdlet *Enable-ADOptionalFeature* is utilized to enable the Active Directory Recycle Bin feature. Figure 10.34 is an example of the cmdlet in use:

Once you have enabled the Active Directory Recycle Bin, new object states and deletion behaviors are introduced. Now, when an object is deleted, instead of becoming a Tombstone object, it moves into a *logically delete* state and is placed into the Deleted Objects container. During the objects time as a logically deleted item, all of its attributes are retained and it can be completely recovered intact to its original state. By default, the logically deleted state will last for 180 days.

Once the lifetime of the logically deleted state object has expired, the object then moves to become a recycled object. Recycled objects behave very much like the original Tombstone objects in the iterations of

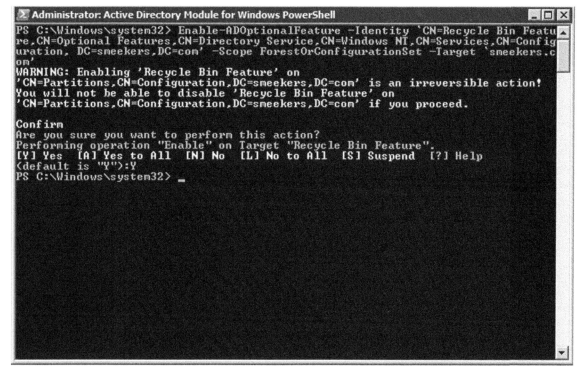

■ **FIGURE 10.34** Enabling the Active Directory Recycle Bin.

Windows Server 2003 and 2008. The objects are stripped of the majority of their attributes and a default lifetime timer of 180 days is applied. Once this timer counts down, the object is then physically removed from the directory.

Restoring deleted Active Directory objects

So, someone has executed AD administrative hari-kari and accidently deleted a chunk of the live AD. So, how do you fix this? If you had the Active Directory Recycle Bin enabled, help is just a few AD PowerShell cmdlets away.

The Recycle Bin will not display in your standard Active Directory the Users and Computers interface. If you want to take a peek at it and what is in it, one easy access mechanism is through ldap.exe. Ldap.exe allows you to bind to the AD and visually be able to see the Recycle Bin. See Figure 10.35 for what this looks like.

One way to restore an object from the Active Directory Recycle Bin is from within ldap.exe. By expanding the Recycle Bin and selecting an object listed, you can manually initiate a restore; however, a much easier method that we will explore here is to initiate a restore utilizing Active Directory PowerShell cmdlets.

The two key PowerShell cmdlets that you will use to restore objects from the Active Directory Recycle Bin are *Get-ADObject* and *Restore-*

■ **FIGURE 10.35** Viewing the Active Directory Recycle Bin with ldap.exe.

ADObject. The first command allows you to select or *Get* the object or objects you wish to restore, and the second command instructs the restore to occur. Let us start by looking at *Get-ADObject*. This cmdlet is used with PowerShell to search and select any AD object. By default, the command will not include deleted items and must be specifically told to also search the Active Directory Recycle Bin with the use of switch. The command to search AD for a particular item and include the Recycle Bin in the search scope may look like this:

> *Get-ADObject -Filter {String} –IncludeDeletedObjects*

The filter string can include anything that you know about the object, such as the display name. To execute the *Get-ADObject* cmdlet utilizing the display name of the object, you could execute the following:

> *Get-ADObject -Filter {displayname -eq "Justin Alpern"}*
> *-IncludeDeletedObjects*

See Figure 10.36 to see the returned results.

In this case, since you already know that the object you are looking for exists within the Recycle Bin, you can choose to scope the AD search to the Recycle Bin hierarchy. For example:

> *Get-ADObject –SearchBase "CN = Deleted Objects, DC = smeekers,*
> *DC = com" –ldapFilter "(objectClass = *)" -IncludeDeletedObjects*

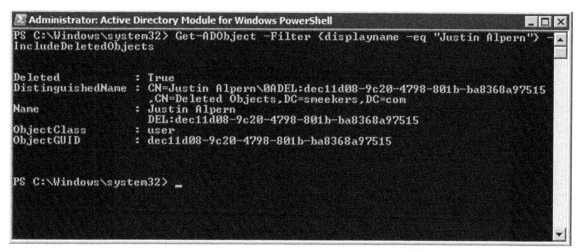

■ **FIGURE 10.36** Get-ADObject with Display Name Filter.

In this example, we have added an LDAP filter for objectClass. By supplying an * all object classes will be returned. Always remember that if you want the search to return items contained in the Recycle Bin, you must specify the *–IncludeDeletedObjects* switch.

So, once you have composed the *Get-ADObject* command syntax that returns the object, you wish to restore you can then pipe the results straight into a *Restore-ADObject*, for example:

> *Get-ADObject -Filter {displayname -eq "Justin Alpern"}*
> *–IncludeDeletedObjects | Restore-ADObject*

Notice in Figure 10.37 that this command has resulted in an error. If you examine the error, you will see that the error is generated because the parent object of the user object of "Justin Alpern" no longer exists in AD. You must validate that the target restore location for the object still exists in AD before attempting a restore. If the parent object of the deleted object no longer exists in AD, you cannot recover the object. However, if the original parent object still resides in the Recycle Bin, then it can also be restored, which would in turn allow for the child object to be restored as well.

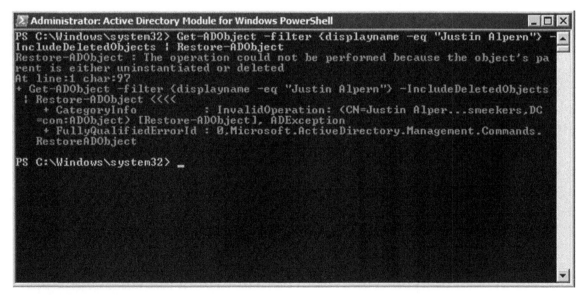

■ **FIGURE 10.37** Restore-ADObject Error.

DIRECTACCESS

Imagine if you could be anywhere on the planet, connected to the Internet and still have no hassle access to all of your corporate assets. I am sure many of you are thinking, "I already have that! I VPN in, and...". Well, to be more specific, how about the same LAN style corporate access, but without the VPN hassle?

Well, with Windows 2008 R2, Microsoft released an amazing new feature called DirectAccess, and the name says it all. DirectAccess allows you and your users to gain access to the internal corporate resources in your environment from the Internet, without first connecting to a VPN, and without requiring user intervention to connect!

The benefit is apparent from a user's perspective. They have access to corporate resources such as Web pages, file shares, and applications from any Internet-connected location. It is a secure connection and the user experiences mimics being directly connected to the corporate environment, thus giving the user a seamless experience between being in the office and out of the office.

The benefits that may not be as apparent are the advantages DirectAccess bring into play for the administrative team. Administrators can utilize DirectAccess technology to their advantage in a number of ways. One way DirectAccess lessens the burden of the help desk is by reducing the learning curve associated with VPN access. When users are in the office they have one way of accessing resources. Put them out on the Internet, and now they have to battle with VPN connections before their resource access returns. Account lockout problems can occur, issues around client VPN software must be addressed, and of course, users have to be taught to utilize the software as well.

By deploying DirectAccess connections into corporate resources, look and act the same for a user regardless if they are on the Internet or connected directly to the Intranet. The maintenance and management of VPN software and infrastructure is something that can be scaled down as its usage lessens. Additionally, the Windows 7 and Windows 2008 R2 native DirectAccess feature set leaves your users with little to nothing to learn, since the connection is seamless.

Another benefit that DirectAccess brings to administrators relates to system maintenance. In most corporate environments, mobile users are a wild card. Since they only connect to the environment intermittently, keeping them patched and up to date with the latest policies can be tricky.

Normally, an administrator must rely on a user to either VPN into the corporate network or actually walk into a company facility and connect to the LAN. This can make the time between updates unpredictable and it can leave users' machines in a vulnerable state. By being able to access a user's machine whenever they are connected to the Internet, the story changes dramatically.

With DirectAccess, the user merely has to connect to the Internet from anywhere in the world. Once on the Internet, their computer will automatically connect to the corporate network, authenticate, and give them access to network resources while at the same time giving your network maintenance tools the ability to connect to them. By being able to patch and manage policies on machines that normally might not connect into the network for long durations at a time, you can be that much more efficient at keeping your corporate systems up to date. In the next sections, we will explore DirectAccess in more detail to see how you can choose to utilize it to secure and also enable your mobile user workforce.

DirectAccess infrastructure requirements

In order to deploy DirectAccess, you will need to take into consideration the infrastructure dependencies that exist with DirectAccess. The first key thing to be aware of with DirectAccess is that both IPv6 and IPsec play a critical role in the deployment. Regardless of the deployment model chosen, users on the Internet will only be able to gain access to servers on the Intranet capable of running IPv6.

IPSec is the protocol of choice in routing traffic securing across the Internet; however, once a client has connected into the DirectAccess servers and been granted Intranet access, IPSec encryption becomes an option within the LAN. It is recommended to continue IPSec within the internal network, but ultimately, it is the administrator's choice by design. Regardless of whether IPsec is in use, only the IPv6-capable servers on the Intranet will be accessible by DirectAccess users.

Other DirectAccess infrastructure requirements include:

- Active Directory Domain Services
- Group Policy
- At least one Windows 2008 Domain Controller
- DNS services that support DNS message exchanges over Intrasite Automatic Tunnel Addressing Protocol (ISATAP)
- A PKI infrastructure for IPSec certificate issuance

DirectAccess protocols

Multiple protocols are in use when a client is utilizing DirectAccess. At times, the connection circumstances will dictate which protocol is to be utilized, while at other times, the architecture design will indicate which protocol is more appropriate. The following protocols may be utilized as a part of DirectAccess encapsulation technology:

- *Intra-Site Automatic Tunnel Addressing Protocol*—A transition technology that provides for IPv6 unicast communications between IPv4/IPv6 hosts across an IPv4-only Intranet.
- *6to4*—Provides for unicast communications between IPv4/IPv6 hosts and IPv6-capable sites across the Internet
- *Teredo*—Provides for unicast communication between NAT'ed IPv4/IPv6 hosts across the Internet to IPv6 capable sites
- *IP-HTTPS*—Tunnels IPv6 within an HTTP over SSL connection, allowing for connectivity even while in restricted sites.
- *IPSec*—Tunnels IPv6 across IPv4 networks.

If a client connected to the Internet has been assigned a publically routable IP address, they will utilize the 6to4 protocol to attempt connection into the DirectAccess architecture. If the client is behind a NAT, then they will instead utilize the Teredo protocol to connect. If the client cannot use either 6to4 or Teredo, it will then attempt to connect with IP-HTTPS. However, something to keep in mind is that IP-HTTPS is a slower technology, and there is the potential impact on client performance.

Selecting a DirectAccess model

Before jumping headlong into a DirectAccess deployment, the first step an administrator must take is to determine the DirectAccess model they would like to employ. The level of security required across organizations will vary in stringency, and administrators have the choice to build a design that maps to the organization's specific security needs. Microsoft defines three DirectAccess models that can be evaluated to determine the architecture that is a best fit for your environment. The three main access models that we will discuss are:

- Full Intranet Access
- Selected Server Access
- End-to-End Access

In some environments, the thought of allowing access to internal protected company resources from the Internet seems daunting, while in others, the accessibility is readily welcomed. Regardless of the security stance of your organization, you can build a secure access model to meet your business need. All three of the access models follow some of the same security principles and contain the same infrastructure elements. Let us review the high-level similarities across the three access models first.

The first commonality is: to ensure that data transference is secure when traversing the Internet, DirectAccess utilizes a two-step IPsec Encapsulating Security Payload (ESP) tunnel to connect. The first connection made by the client regardless of the access model will always be an infrastructure tunnel. The Infrastructure tunnel enforces computer authentication.

Full Intranet Access

This deployment model is the most similar to what exists today in many companies with VPN solutions deployed. In the traditional VPN model, the user makes an initial connection to a server on the perimeter, and once authenticated, is typically able to browse the internal network without restriction. With DirectAccess configured in the Full Intranet Access model, the scenario is similar.

The first step in connection is always the infrastructure tunnel. Once the infrastructure tunnel is complete, the user will authenticate and establish an intranet tunnel. The intranet tunnel users both computer and user-based authentication and it is used to connect to the DirectAccess server on the perimeter. Once the intranet tunnel has been established to the DirectAccess server, the client can browse and access LAN-based resources as if they were directly connected.

The DirectAccess server is functioning as an IPSec gateway and all IPSec traffic from the Internet terminates at the DirectAccess server. Transmissions from the client to the internal applications are still sent with the IPv6 protocol, but without the IPSec encryption that was present from the client to the DirectAccess server. The DirectAccess server continues to encrypt and decrypt IPSec traffic between the client and the Intranet resources.

For environments with Windows 2003-based resources in the LAN, this is the best deployment model. Since Windows 2003 servers do support the use of IPv6, but not IPSec with IPv6, they will only be accessible while the DirectAccess server is functioning as an IPSec gateway. Any resources that are not able to support IPv6 will not be accessible without the deployment of a third-party translator and DNS gateway.

Full Intranet Access with Smart Card Authentication

The Full Intranet Access with Smart Card Authentication model represents the same architecture as the Full intranet Access model, just with the

addition of Smart Cards for an additional layer of user authentication protection. The DirectAccess server can be configured to enforce the user of
Smart Cards on the Intranet tunnel before allowing user access to
resources.

Selected Server Access

If your organization requires more selective access to internal resources for
external clients, then this is the deployment model for you. By utilizing the
Selected Server Access model, you enforce that client to utilize the IPSec
Encapsulating Security Payload (ESP). It enables peer-to-peer authentication utilizing computer credentials and allows the clients to validate the
identity of the server they are connecting to. This way the clients can determine if IPSec is required to connect to specific services on the Intranet.

In environments that contain the services of a sensitive nature, this model
allows you to single out specific targets for Intranet-based IPSec encryption while traffic to other services on the Intranet remains clear. All traffic
to and from the Internet is still secured by the IPsec gateway services
provided by the DirectAccess servers.

End-to-End Access

In the End-to-End Access model, resources on the Intranet are made
accessible to Internet users directly. End-to-End Access enforces IPsec
from the DirectAccess client and the Intranet resource in a point-to-point
fashion. IPSec peer authenticate using computer credentials should be
configured and ESP is recommended.

Overall, in this model, the DirectAccess servers get a break. Since all
tunneling is performed directly between the client on the Internet and
the resource on the Intranet, much of the overhead is offloaded onto the
endpoints instead of relying on the DirectAccess server for translation.
The DirectAccess server simply performs pass-through for the IPSec traffic and does not function as a gateway in this model.

SUMMARY

In this chapter, we reviewed many of the new security features included
with Windows Server 2008 R2. Microsoft has made a concerted effort to
build components into their product to assist administrators in securing
their environments. Many of the features we reviewed assist directly with
security and compliance, such as the new auditing components and the
FCI. While auditing has been around for quite some time, it has now been

enhanced and expanded upon while still allowing for centralized adminis-tration. FCI holds a lot of potential. In a world where document manage-ment and data retention are becoming more and more important to corporate customers, Microsoft has put a ready foot forward to attempt to assist administrators in hauling their burden in this arena.

We also looked at some enhancements to toolsets. Old favorites have been revised, such as in the case of NPS, and new favorites have gotten a bit of an update as well, such as with NAP. Many of the changes we reviewed focused on enhancing user and administrative connection experience. Retaining a secure model in access is important, and as we saw with our discussion on encryption technologies, such as BitLocker and EFS, Microsoft is making good with staying current on industry standard cryp-tography protocols. By responding to the needs of customers with highly stringent security requirements, they have enhanced their security-centric commitment and it shows.

Irrespective of whether the feature is an old favorite with new enhancements, such as with SCW, or a new feature with a lot of potential and excitement around it, like DirectAccess, all of the components discussed in this chapter have an exciting future ahead. Administrators are being forced to handle more complex security requirements as time goes on, and by taking advantage of many of the new built-in security features for Windows 2008 R2, they can better arm themselves to tackle the problems of tomorrow.

By ensuring that administrators have the right tools at their disposal to deploy and administrate while still maintaining security and efficiency, Microsoft has made a concerted effort to enable the IT workforce of today. By reducing the administrative overhead and working to create a seamless user working environment, but without losing focus on security as a key design element, Microsoft hits a homerun. The release of Windows Server 2008 R2 goes to show that they are taking strides and making an effort that are leaps and bounds in the right direction.

PowerShell V2 feature focus

In this section of the book, we will introduce you to PowerShell and its many powerful features. If you are already familiar with PowerShell, then you will benefit from the overview of its many uses and its great new features. If you are new to PowerShell, do not despair; we will go over its powerful features and how they can help make your job easier and more productive. PowerShell will make administration a lot easier with its many features.

INTRODUCTION TO POWERSHELL

To start at the very beginning, we answer the most basic question, "What is PowerShell?" PowerShell is a command-based shell and scripting language built on the .NET framework with incredible power and versatility designed especially for system administration. The latest version as of this writing is version 2.0 and it was officially released on October 28, 2009. We say shell and scripting language because both components can be used separately. At its fundamental level, it is a command-based shell in a console-like interface that will allow you to simply issue it commands and call its powerful scripting language to accomplish what tasks you need it to do. In this interactive use, you directly issue commands to the console and it performs the desired tasks. The other powerful part of PowerShell that takes full advantage of the underlying scripting language is the ability to run longer or complex instructions from a script. This allows you to automate some of the tasks you might need to perform. The final piece which is brand new to version 2.0 is the ability to run commands on one or more computers from a single computer running PowerShell. These abilities together should allow you to tackle almost any job without problem.

Another aspect of PowerShell you need to become familiar with is its command syntax. The commands PowerShell uses are called cmdlets. It is through these simple instructions that you will be performing all the common system administration tasks. cmdlets all share a similar syntax composed of a verb and a noun in a verb-noun format. As an example, we will use one of the most helpful commands, get-help. The get-help cmdlet is an easy example. Typing *Get-help* followed by the subject or command you want to get help about will get you more information about it. It will either give you the help you need or give you a list of subjects so that you can narrow it down to which one you need (Table 11.1).

You will get a chance to try some cmdlets of your own later on in this chapter, but for now, it is enough that you simply see what they look like if you have not before.

As you can see, the main goal of Windows PowerShell is to give the administrator more control over the system and make it easier to perform the required tasks. It increases the administrator's bag of tools by adding automation and remoting and their associated advantages. Imagine only having to write a command once and then being able to run it multiple times on different machines. This eliminates the need to run the same thing over and over by simply having PowerShell let you run it multiple times. It also eliminates some of the human error aspects since you only need to write it once and therefore only check it once. In this chapter, we will cover many of the new commands for Windows Server 2008 R2 and try to give you a feel for them and what they are supposed to do.

What is new in PowerShell V2

Version 2.0 of Windows PowerShell was officially released on October 28, 2009 after much anticipation by the PowerShell community. It introduces a large amount of new features that were not available before. It stays true to its purpose of making system administration easier by adding remoting, debugging tools and other things to the administrator's new shiny toolkit.

Of all the new features in Windows PowerShell version 2.0, the one feature that seems to elicit cheers and get the most attention is the new remote management or remoting feature. PowerShell supports interactive remoting where you connect directly and issue commands, fan-in (1 pc

Table 11.1 Getting Help Is Easy

cmdlet	Description
Get-Help about	Will list all the subjects that start with about
Get-Help about_scripts	Will get the specific help file about_scripts
Get-Help *about*	Will give you a list of all the subjects that have "about" anywhere in them

to many) and fan out (many pcs to 1). It allows the administrator to run scripts on one or many remote computers with a single command. Gone are the days of tediously going to different computers and running the same script on each of them one at a time. Gone are the days of taking your preferred script and copying it from machine to machine. Now, all you have to do is establish a session to the other computer or computers you want to run the script on and then issue the commands. From running a single cmdlet to a whole script, it is that simple. PowerShell 2.0 does have to be installed on the computers you are running the scripts on, the originating one and the target ones.

Another new feature sorely lacking from the earlier versions of PowerShell is the ability to run background jobs. This new ability of PowerShell version 2.0 to run background jobs allows you to asynchronously run other jobs or processes in the background while you continue to work on your session. You issue the command for the background job and immediately get the prompt back so that you can continue to work while the background job executes. These background jobs can be run on your local machine or on a remote computer.

Windows PowerShell 2.0 has also included new script debugging capabilities. Included now is the built-in capability to debug your scripts. It allows you to set breakpoints, step through code, monitor variable values, and more. It also allows you to decide what actions to take when the break point is hit. These capabilities give you the tools necessary to debug all your scripts with relative ease.

Another new feature is that of eventing. Eventing is the new capability of PowerShell to handle and react to events. It now includes an infrastructure that not only can listen for system and application events and act based on them. In addition, you can now create your own events which allow you to set up a chain of actions based on what your scripts do.

The new version also comes with a large number of new cmdlets. PowerShell version 2.0 introduces a little over 100 new cmdlets with numerous capabilities. All these cmdlets range from all the new functionalities mentioned earlier to powerful logging tools and mail-sending cmdlets.

PowerShell 2.0 also supports script internalization. This allows PowerShell to display messages in multiple languages. In addition to the regular get-help command and man command at the command line, PowerShell includes online help via a parameter to the get-help command. Using get-help, the command to get help on and then the online parameter opens a browser for you with the command help in Microsoft TechNet.

Another new feature is the support of Modules. A module is a package that includes Windows PowerShell commands like cmdlets, providers, aliases, and variables. PowerShell now lets you create these modules and organize your commands so that you can share them with others. PowerShell version 2.0 has also included a lot of advanced functions. These functions behave just like cmdlets but they are fully written in the Windows PowerShell scripting language as opposed to C#.

Another new feature that PowerShell 2.0 has brought is the new Integrated Scripting Environment or ISE. The PowerShell ISE lets you run commands and scripts in an integrated development environment (IDE). It allows you to edit and debug your scripts with many options to figure out what is wrong and where it is going wrong like most graphical interfaces. It makes writing cmdlets easier with multiline editing and line and column numbers. It includes color coding like most graphical interfaces which makes it very easy for the user to write and execute their own commands by immediately showing them if they have made any syntax errors. It has several panes or windows to make it easier to see what is going on. One pane to write your command(s), one to show your scripts, and one to show you the output or results of your commands or scripts. In essence, it makes it really easy to get started with PowerShell by giving the user the tools to create what they want quickly and easily.

INSTALLING POWERSHELL

The most important thing that needs to be done before PowerShell can be used is to make sure it is installed, and if it is not, you need to download and install it. If you have Windows 7 or Windows Server 2008 R2, then you do not have to do anything. They both include PowerShell 2.0. If you do not have Windows 7 or Windows Server 2008, however, then you will most likely need to download and install PowerShell yourself. Installing PowerShell is simple, but first, you will check to see if it is already there. By far, the easiest way to check is to open a run window. You do this by clicking on the start menu → run. This will bring up a dialogue box, now type *PowerShell* and hit enter. If a command window comes up, then you have PowerShell. Now, you check to see if you have the latest version. The easiest way is to run PowerShell, and then when the shell comes up, you type *Get-help about_Windows_PowerShell_2.0.*

If the command runs, then you have PowerShell version 2.0. If you do not have PowerShell at all or if you do not have the latest version, then you need to go and install it.

Before you install it, you need to make sure that the minimum system requirements are met. WinRM 2.0 and Windows PowerShell 2.0 can be installed on the following operating systems:

- Windows Server 2003 Service Pack 2
- Windows Server 2008 Service Pack 2
- Windows XP with Service Pack 3
- Windows Vista Service Pack 1 or later

In addition, Windows PowerShell requires the .NET framework with service Pack 1 to function, so that needs to be installed as well.

The recommended steps are as follows:

1. Uninstall previous versions of Windows PowerShell from your computer.
2. Uninstall previous versions of WinRM from your computer.
3. Download and install the latest version of PowerShell 2.0 from http://support.microsoft.com/kb/968929

Once you have downloaded and installed the latest version of PowerShell, you are ready to move on with the rest of this chapter. Of course, if you already have PowerShell version 2.0, then you do not have to do anything.

INTRODUCTION TO POWERSHELL SCRIPTING

The mere mention of the word "scripting" sends many brave administrators running for the hills. Brave souls immediately pick up the phone and call their programmer friend. It does not have to be this way. PowerShell scripting is easy to grasp. In addition, PowerShell has easy help available for anything you need to use. I am not talking about online help, but built in, though it does have an online help option now in version 2.0 as well. Once you have PowerShell installed on your system, just open and run it. A window that looks a lot like a dos window should pop up. Now, you will type in a command. The way you issue commands to PowerShell is to type in a command and then hit enter. A commandlet or cmdlet is basically a windows PowerShell command. cmdlets are what allow you to accomplish what you want with PowerShell. All cmdlets follow a specific naming convention of "verb-noun" which makes them easier to learn and use.

The most important cmdlet in PowerShell is get-help. This cmdlet alone can get you the tools you need to get out of any bind. You can type *Get-help* followed by any PowerShell cmdlet to get some meaningful information about them. An alternative to the get-help cmdlet is the man command. It behaves just like the get-help cmdlet but will pause the screen for you and display a page at a time instead of displaying all the information at once.

To make sure you are ready to execute cmdlets, run scripts, and import modules in PowerShell, you want to make sure that your execution policy will let you run the cmdlets that you need. By default, the execution policy is set to restricted. You need to set it to RemoteSigned at the very least. RemoteSigned will allow you to run any script you write as well as any downloaded script that has been signed by a trusted publisher. The way you check your execution policy using the Get-ExecutionPolicy cmdlet is as follows:

Startup PowerShell as administrator. You will need to have administrator rights to change the execution policy.
Type *Get-ExecutionPolicy*. This command should return your current execution policy which will, by default, be Restricted. Your goal is to change it to RemoteSigned.
Type *Set-ExecutionPolicy RemoteSigned*. When the cmdlet runs, it will give you a warning that you are changing the Execution Policy and a confirmation dialogue (see Figure 11.1). The default is Yes, so just hit enter. Voila, you have just changed your execution policy to RemoteSigned. You can verify this by typing *Get-ExecutionPolicy* at the PowerShell prompt. Your new execution policy should show up as RemoteSigned if you did everything properly and this means that you are ready to proceed.

PowerShell lets you write cmdlets one line at a time and hit enter just like a command line shell, but one of the main advantages is the ability to write scripts. Throughout these sections, you will see several steps illustrating how something is done. Everything is done in a step-by-step manner simply for illustration purposes. All these things could have been done by writing them in a text file, naming the file with a .ps1 extension, and simply calling the file. The file would be treated as if you were typing all the cmdlets in at

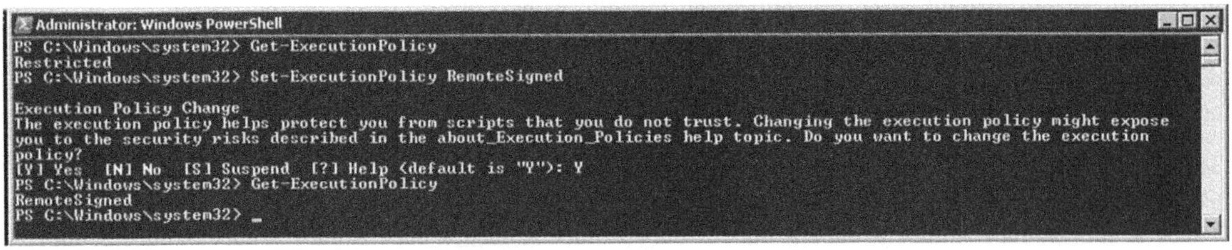

■ **FIGURE 11.1** Changing Policy from Restricted to RemoteSigned.

the prompt. This is one of the biggest advantages of PowerShell. You write it once and then can use it multiple times whenever you need it. This eliminates the human error inherent in mindless repetition as well as making it easier to share solutions with other administrators.

WINDOWS SERVER 2008 R2 POWERSHELL CMDLETS

The main focus of this chapter is to introduce you to a numerous amount of PowerShell cmdlets and how they fit into the more common tasks that they are needed for. By familiarizing yourself with these new cmdlets and their functions, you lay the groundwork for you to pick and choose the ones that are helpful and can make your life easier. As you go through the sections of the book and read about all the different cmdlets, feel free to read the help or test them out yourself. You will learn a lot more about them by using them than simply reading about them.

Active Directory cmdlets

The PowerShell Active Directory module introduces over 70 cmdlets to provide full support for almost any Active Directory function an administrator might require. But before you can use this newfound power, you either have to import the module or use the Active Directory Module for PowerShell. The easy path is to use the AD Module for PowerShell, but some people like to do things the challenging way. To get the Active Directory cmdlets in your active PowerShell window, type in *Import-Module Active Directory*. You can then check to see if it was imported properly by typing *Get-Help* *ADA**. If the get-help cmdlet returns some Active Directory commands, then you can be sure that the Module was installed (see Figure 11.2). Table 11.2 lists some Active Directory User focus cmdlets.

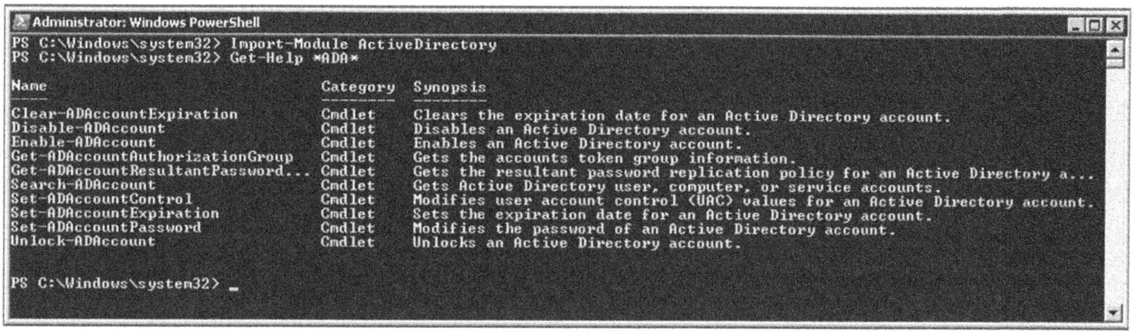

```
Administrator: Windows PowerShell
PS C:\Windows\system32> Import-Module ActiveDirectory
PS C:\Windows\system32> Get-Help *ADA*

Name                              Category    Synopsis
----                              --------    --------
Clear-ADAccountExpiration         Cmdlet      Clears the expiration date for an Active Directory account.
Disable-ADAccount                 Cmdlet      Disables an Active Directory account.
Enable-ADAccount                  Cmdlet      Enables an Active Directory account.
Get-ADAccountAuthorizationGroup   Cmdlet      Gets the accounts token group information.
Get-ADAccountResultantPassword... Cmdlet      Gets the resultant password replication policy for an Active Directory a...
Search-ADAccount                  Cmdlet      Gets Active Directory user, computer, or service accounts.
Set-ADAccountControl              Cmdlet      Modifies user account control (UAC) values for an Active Directory account.
Set-ADAccountExpiration           Cmdlet      Sets the expiration date for an Active Directory account.
Set-ADAccountPassword             Cmdlet      Modifies the password of an Active Directory account.
Unlock-ADAccount                  Cmdlet      Unlocks an Active Directory account.

PS C:\Windows\system32> _
```

■ **FIGURE 11.2** Importing the Active Directory module.

Table 11.2 Active Directory User Focus cmdlets

cmdlet Name	Description
New-ADUser	This cmdlet creates a new Active Directory User. Requires only a name and will populate the rest of the fields with default values for you
Set-ADUser	This cmdlet sets/modifies the properties of the specified ADUser
Get-ADUser	This cmdlet gets an object representing the ADUser
Remove-ADUser	This cmdlet removes/deletes the specified ADUser

If you actually want to list all the Active Directory cmdlets, then at the PowerShell prompt, type *Get-Command *AD** and hit *enter*. We must warn you that there are a lot of them. Now that the power is within your grasp, you must learn to use it properly, or else great destruction and loss of job could ensue. As soon as people hear you have the power, requests start coming in for you. The first cry for help comes from accounting. "Help brave superhero! We need you to create a new user account in AD for us" is the call for help. An e-mail arrives right afterward with all the details. The message reads, "Dear Superhero," we need a new AD User account for a new employee named Justin Michaels. You keep in mind the first initial last name naming convention that the company adheres to and quickly start on the task. You type *New-ADUser –Name "Justin Michaels" –SamAccountName "JMichaels"* and hit enter. This will create a basic user with the name of the User object as Justin Michael and the SamAccountName as JMichaels. The only mandatory field in the New-ADUser cmdlet is the –Name flag. If you leave that out, then you will get a prompt asking for it. If you only provide the –Name field and leave the SamAccountName out, the SamAccountName will be populated with the –Name value by default. This is because you need to have a SamAccountName for an Active Directory User to exist. When the cmdlet executes, it will have created a new Active Directory User for you. If a user with the same SamAccountName already existed, you would have gotten an error similar to how you get an error when trying to duplicate a user in the Active Directory Users and Computers GUI, and would have had to create him with a SamAccountName of JMichaels02 or as what the company naming convention dictated. You can check that the account you created exists by using *Get-ADUser "JMichaels"* and hitting the enter key (see Figure 11.3). This created a very basic account with almost nothing populated.

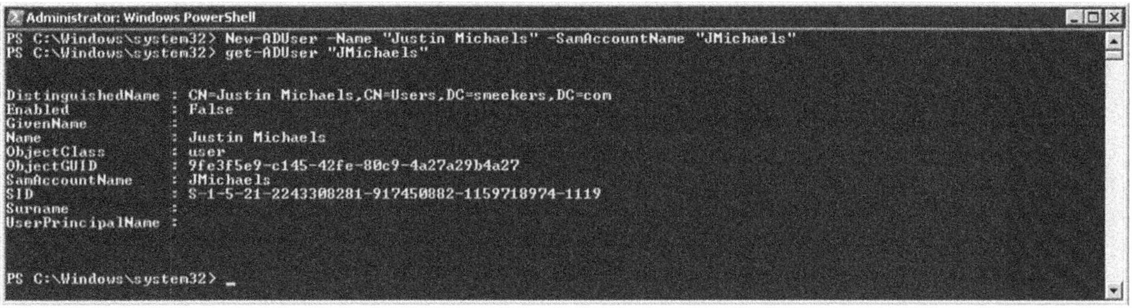

■ **FIGURE 11.3** ADUser creation.

You could also have created the user from a template. This would allow you to have a large amount of values already set consistent with the company policy and only change the necessary ones for the user. In the previous example of Justin Michaels, the account has all the default values for password expiration, change at next log on, etc. With a template, you would be able to specify universal properties for all new users as long as you create them all from the same template. Imagine you have a ADUser you created and populated completely with all the default values for any new account. When the time comes to create a new account, all you would have to do is to use the –Instance flag to specify the new user. Assume that you decided to create user "Justin Michaels" from the "New Guy" template, this is what you would do.

$templateAccountHolder = Get-ADUser –Identity "Nguy"

New-ADUser –Name "Justin Michaels" –SamAccountName "JMichaels" –Identity "JMichaels"

This would create the new user Justin Michaels using Nguy as a template. In essence, you are taking all his set properties and changing the ones you want for the new user you are creating. Once you have finished creating his account, you realize you did not specify his e-mail, and that Nguy@SuperTechs.com, the default one from the template, does not really work. It is time to use your skills again. You type *Set-ADUser –Identity "JMichaels" –EmailAddress "JMichaels@SuperTechs.com* and hit enter. When the cmdlet executes, you will have updated or set the e-mail for that user to the desired value. After clearly overcoming your first task, you check your inbox for the next one and click on it as soon as it arrives. A message comes in with a simple, yet sad request. You are to delete the account for the user Jason Todd with identity Jtodd. According to the message, he is no longer with the company, and therefore his name

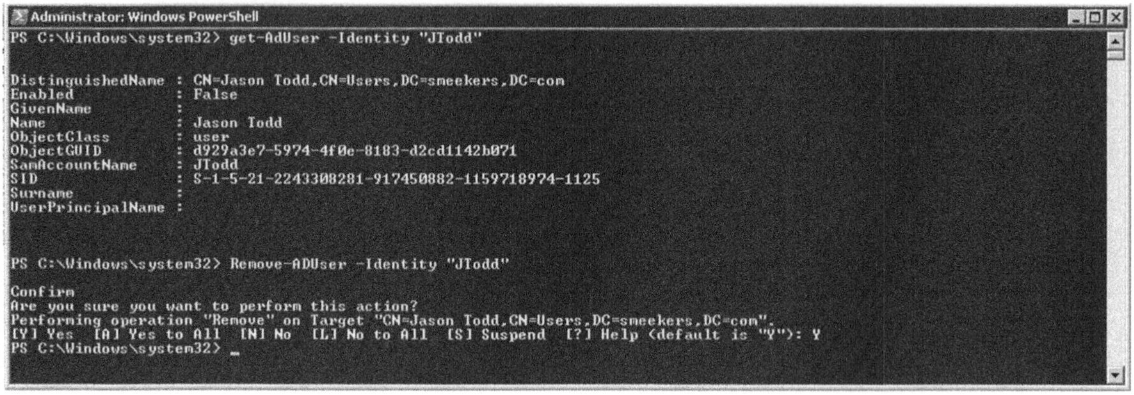

■ **FIGURE 11.4** Remove-ADUser example.

must be removed from Active Directory. You put your skills to use again and type *Remove-ADUser -Identity JTodd* and hit *enter*. You hit *Y* to confirm his deletion and then his name will cease to exist (see Figure 11.4).

You have now touched on the basics of the AdUser operations in AD. The full potential of these cmdlets is astonishing to say the least. But with the knowledge of these basic blocks, you can accomplish great things. Always keep in mind that when a cmdlet asks for the identity of a user, you will need to specify one of a few specific things. For identity, you can use the Distinguished Name (DN), the Global Unique Identifier (GUID), Security Identifier (SID), or the Security Accounts Manager (SAM) Account Name. All these fields have flags that correspond to their names like the –SAMAccountName flag.

Table 11.3 lists Active Directory group focus cmdlets.

Table 11.3 Active Directory Group Focus cmdlets

cmdlet	Description
New-ADGroup	This cmdlet creates a New Active Directory Group. Requires the name and group scope fields to create the group
Set-ADGroup	This cmdlet is used to set/modify existing properties of the ADGroup
Get-ADGroup	This cmdlet gets an object representing the specified ADGroup
Remove-ADGroup	This cmdlet removes/deletes the specified ADGroup

Your skills still need to grow in the area of Active Directory Groups. The next task that comes in proves to be the perfect testing ground. The new task being delegated to you is to create a new distribution group for all the users of special talents like yourself. You type *New-ADGroup –SAMAccountName "Supers" –GroupCategory 0 –GroupScope 0* and hit *enter*. The cmdlet will execute and create a new group for you with all the default values, except for the ones you specified. The –GroupCategory flag is what determines if the group is a security group or a distribution group. A value of 0 is set as a distribution group, while a 1 is set as a security group. The default value is 1, security group, if the flag is left off. The –GroupScope flag 0 corresponds to domain-local, while 1 is global and 2 is universal. You could have simply typed *New-AdGroup* and hit enter and it would have worked as well. It would then have prompted you for a Name and a group scope. It would be fast and easy, but some of the default·values are not what you want. The Name would then be used as the SAMAccountName as well, and you would have had to go back and modify the group and change it to a distribution group since that is what you wanted. To do this, you would have needed to use the Set-ADGroup cmdlet by typing *Set-ADGroup Supers –GroupCategory 0* and then hit enter. Another way you can create a new Active Directory Group is by using a different group as a template. Assume that you have a security group called "AM Shift" that has everything set perfectly the way you need it. Now, you have the need to create a new group called "PM Shift" but want to use the same settings and properties of the AM Shift group. This would save you all the trouble of reconfiguring the new group to match the already existing one, or even worse, you are not even exactly sure what all the properties are. You just know that you need another group just like that one. This is the perfect example of why you would use the first one as a template. This process is almost identical to what you did with the ADUser you created from a template. You start by declaring a variable and assigning the template group to it and then using the –Instance flag with the New-ADGroup cmdlet to accept the variable. This creates a new group based on the instance of the old group with all the properties of the old group, except for anything you add.

$groupUsedAsTemplate = Get-ADGroup –Identity "AM Shift"

New-ADGroup –Name "PM Shift" –Instance $groupUsedAsTemplate –GroupScope 0

You will also need to specify the –GroupScope of the new group you are creating or it will prompt you for it.

You can check the properties of any of the groups you created by using *Get-ADGroup Supers* (see Figure 11.5).

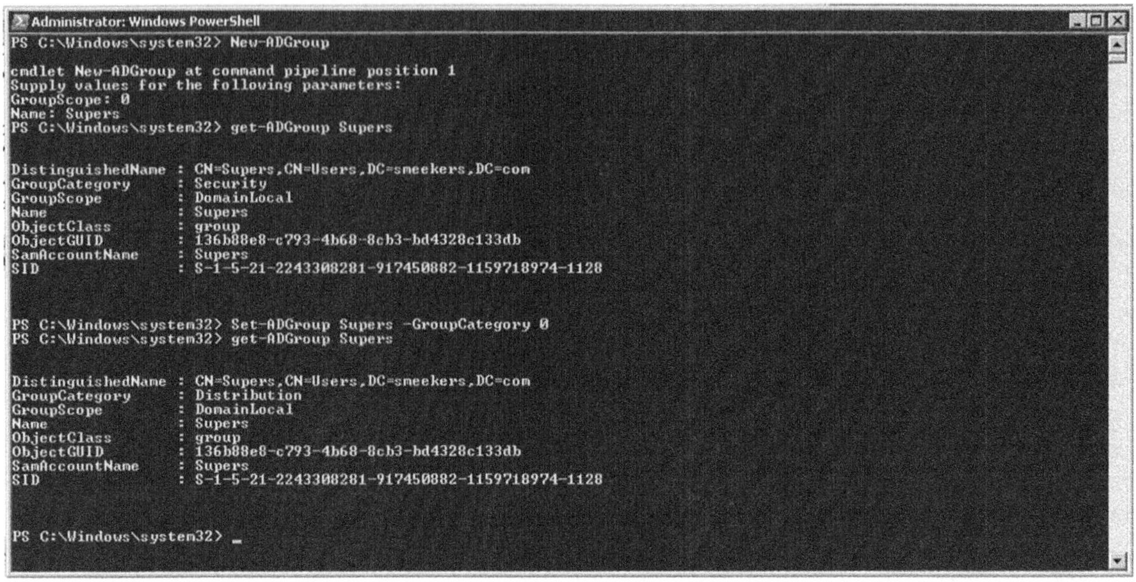

■ FIGURE 11.5 Default New Group and changing it from a security to a distribution group.

As you get more familiar with the cmdlets, you can see that groups are very similar to users in how you create them, get them, and modify/set them. So, it will come as no surprise to you that to remove them is just as simple. If you wanted to remove the group you just created, you would type *Remove-ADGroup Supers*. Once you hit enter, you will get the confirmation screen and then it is done.

Now that you have created the group, you need to move on to the next part of your task and add the users on the list to the Supers Group you just created. You will be using the Add-ADGroupMember cmdlet to accomplish your task. This cmdlet and some other Active Directory group member focus cmdlets are described in Table 11.4. Typing *Add-ADGroupMember* is enough since PowerShell will prompt you for the mandatory values it

Table 11.4 Active Directory Group Member Focus cmdlets

cmdlet	Description
Add-ADGroupMember	This cmdlet adds a user to specified AD Group
Get-ADGroupMember	This cmdlet gets the members of an AD Group
Remove-ADGroupMember	This cmdlet removes a user from a specified AD Group

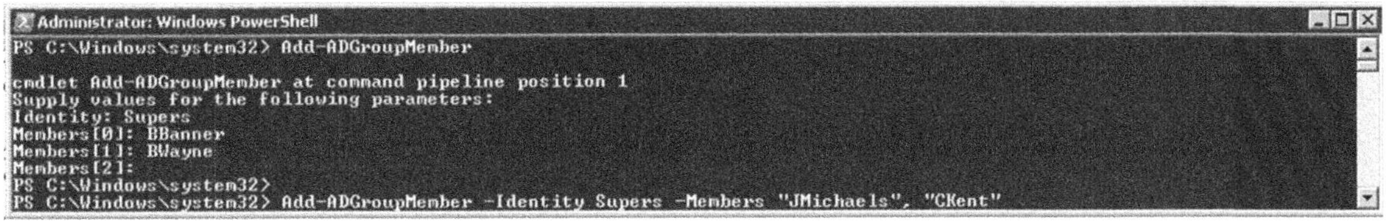

■ **FIGURE 11.6** Adding AD Users to the Supers Group both ways.

needs (see Figure 11.6). But since it is better to learn the common flags for when you are writing your own PowerShell scripts and need to automate as much as possible, you will *type Add-ADGroupMember –Identity Supers –Members "JMichaels," "CKent"* (see Figure 11.6).

Once you have added the AD Users to the group with the Add-ADGroupMember cmdlet, you check to see that they made it in properly by typing *Get-ADGroupMember Supers* and hitting enter (see Figure 11.7).

You finish adding all the members on the list to the group and start to relax thinking you are done when an updated request is sent to you. Apparently, one of the names in the original list should not be added to the group. His name is going to be cleared with the rest of the members before he is added, since apparently he is very volatile. You have already finished adding all the names though, so the only thing you can do is delete him from the group. You

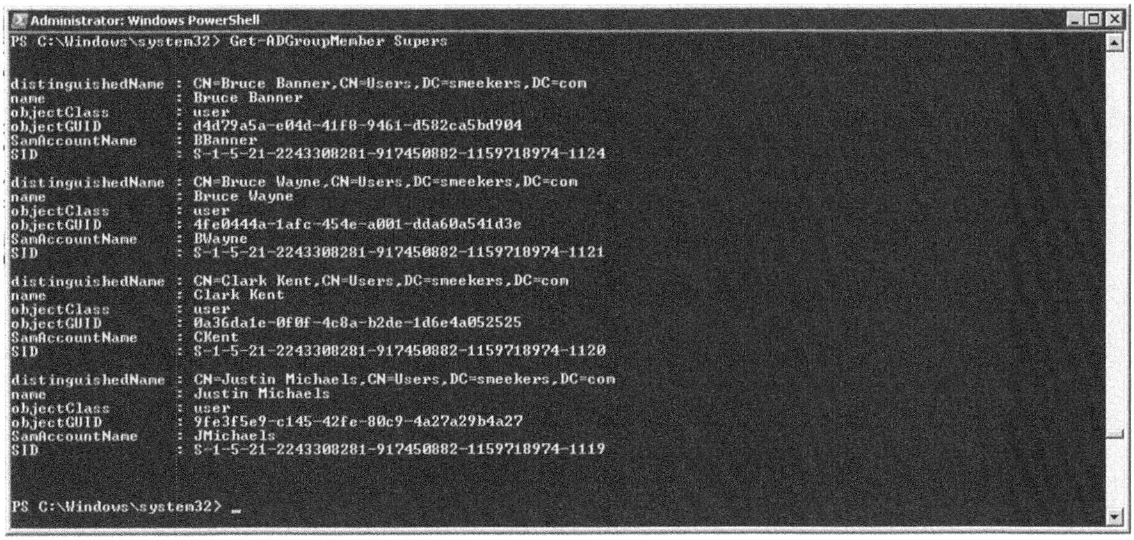

■ **FIGURE 11.7** Listing the Group Members.

type *Remove-ADGroupMember –Identity "Supers" –Member "BBanner"* and hit enter. A confirmation pops up and you hit enter. The named member is no longer a part of the group. You reply to the request that you are finished and get a heart-felt "thanks, you saved us."

You are taking a breather when your next task comes in. Clicking it you see that now that they are identifying these gifted individuals, they are going to need a way to apply GPOs to them as well as administer them separately from the rest of the users. You are tasked with creating an Active Directory Organizational Unit for them. Table 11.5 lists some Active Directory Organizational Units focus cmdlets.

Creating an Active Directory Organizational Unit is simple for someone with your powers. Just like a new AD User or AD Group, you can start one from scratch with as many default parameters or specific parameters as you want or you can base the creation on an already existing one using the –Instance flag. You start by typing *New-ADOrganizationalUnit –Name "VeteranSupers" –ManagedBy "CKent"* and hit enter. When the cmdlet executes, a new OU will exist. OUs do not have as many parameters as AD Groups or AD Users but they have one parameter that is worth mentioning, the one set by the –ProtectFromAccidentalDeletion flag. If this is set to True, then you cannot delete the OU by normal means without first setting the parameter to False. So, assume that the OU you created was not supposed to be protected from accidental deletion, but by default it is and you did not specify otherwise. You need to change the parameter with the Set-ADOrganizationalUnit cmdlet. The tricky part is that to set or get an OU, you need to know its DN; its regular name will not work. Trying any set or getting an OU using its name as its –Identity will fail. So, you need to get a list that would include the OU you need and get its DN from there. We know what you are thinking. Instead of going through all this, why not just

Table 11.5 Active Directory Organizational Units Focus cmdlets

cmdlet	Description
New-ADOrganizationalUnit	This cmdlet creates a new Active Directory Organizational Unit (OU). You must specify a Name at the bare minimum
Set-ADOrganizationalUnit	This cmdlet sets/modifies an AD OU
Get-ADOrganizationalUnit	This cmdlet gets an object representing an AD OU
Remove-ADOrganizationalUnit	This cmdlet removes/deletes an AD OU

delete it and create the OU again, this time with the flag specified as false? It won't let you because the flag is set to true. The name, however, lets you look for the OU with a –Filter. You type *Get-ADOrganizationalUnit –Filter "Name –Like 'VeteranSuper'" | FT Name, Distinguished Name* and hit enter. You see the DN and can now use that to call the *Set-ADOrganizationalUnit cmdlet*. Your DN will be different since you are going to have different AD environments, so for the italic part, just replace with your specific value. You *type Set-ADOrganizationUnit –Identity "OU=VeteranSuper, DC=smeekers,DC=com" –ProtectFromAccidentalDeletion $false* and hit enter. When the cmdlet executes, the property will be updated and VeteranSuper OU will no longer be safe from deletion, accidental, or otherwise (see Figure 11.8). You decide to test it and type *Remove-ADOrganizationUnit –Identity "OU=VeteranSuper,DC=smeekers,DC=com"* and hit enter.

Once the cmdlet executes, the OU is gone. You create the OU again, this time with the deletion protection absent. The request has a list of users that needs to be moved into the OU. You decide to get started right away.

You look at the list and it contains both users and groups. You smirk and get down to work right away. To add the requested users and groups to the OU, you will be using the Move-ADObject cmdlet. This cmdlet is described in Table 11.6. You start by moving a user on the list to the VeteranSuper OU. You need to get the Identity of the user, so you start

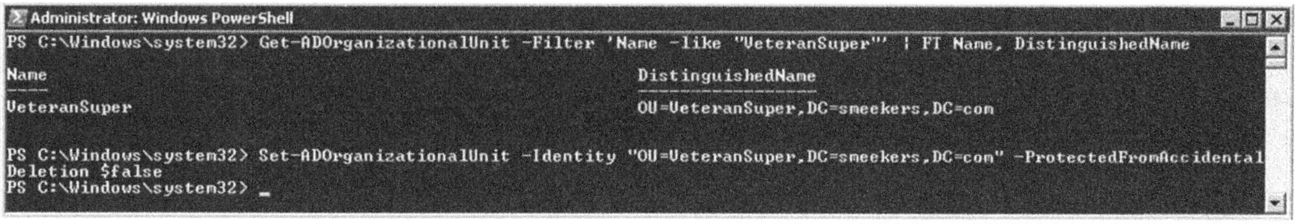

FIGURE 11.8 Getting the Identity and setting a property of an OU.

Table 11.6 cmdlet Used to Move Any Active Directory Object	
cmdlet	**Description**
Move-ADObject	This cmdlet moves an Active Directory Object specified by its DN or GUID to a specified location

by using the Get-ADUser cmdlet to show the DN and GUID, since you can use either as an identity. If you still have the DN of the OU handy from earlier, you won't need to retrieve it again. If you need to get this DN again, use the Get-AdOrganizationalUnit cmdlet as you did before. Once you have both Identities, you type *Move-ADObject -Identity "CN=Bruce Wayne, CN=Users, DC=smeekers, DC=com" –TargetPath "OU=VeteranSuper,DC=smeekers,DC=com"* and hit *enter* (see Figure 11.9).

When the cmdlet completes, user BWayne will be part of the VeteranSuper OU. You continue moving some of the other users and then have to move a group. You use the same cmdlet, only this time you use the DN of the group. You *Type Move-ADObject –Identity "CN=Supers, CN=Users,DC=smeekers,DC=com" –TargetPath "OU=VeteranSuper, DC=smeekers,DC=com"* and hit enter. When the cmdlet completes, the Supers Group will also be part of the VeteranSuper OU (see Figure 11.10). You finish all the moving you need to and reply that the task is complete.

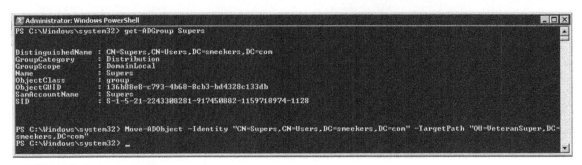

■ **FIGURE 11.9** Moving an Active Directory User to an OU.

■ **FIGURE 11.10** Moving an Active Directory Group to an OU.

The day is almost done and you are about to hang up your cape when a final request comes in. The user Justin Michaels needs his password changed.

Password operations are a very common request, and they require one cmdlet for setting or resetting (see Table 11.7). The main difference is that if you use the –Reset flag, then you do not have to worry about the old password. You type Set-ADAccountPassword –Identity "JMichaels" –Reset – NewPassword (Convert-To-SecureString –AsPlainText "JMichaels@1" – Force) and hit enter. His password has been reset to the company-dictated reset. You then set his user account so that he has to change it next time he logs in by using the SetADUser cmdlet as follows: *Set-ADUser "JMichael" –ChangePasswordAtLogon $true*. The last request of the day is done.

AppLocker cmdlets

This section will cover the AppLocker cmdlets that can be used to manage AppLocker policies in Windows Server 2008 R2. AppLocker is a new Windows 7 and Windows Server 2008 R2 feature that helps the administrator control how users can access and use files. AppLocker is described more in detail in Chapter 10. This chapter will address how the cmdlets can work to accomplish the same administrative tasks without having to go through the Group Policy Management Editor or the local computer security policy. Before you do anything with any AppLocker cmdlets, even use the get-help cmdlet on them, you must import the AppLocker module. You need to be running Windows 7 or Windows Server 2008 R2 to be able to import the AppLocker module.

The steps needed to import the module are as follows:

1. Startup PowerShell
2. Type *Import-Module AppLocker*

After the cmdlet has finished running, you can check to see if it worked by calling the get-help cmdlet on the AppLocker cmdlets, since if the import is not performed, PowerShell will not be able to find help on them. Type

---

Table 11.7 cmdlet for Setting and Resetting Passwords

cmdlet	Description
Set-ADAccountPassword	This cmdlet is used to set or reset an account password. Setting involves knowing the old password while resetting does not

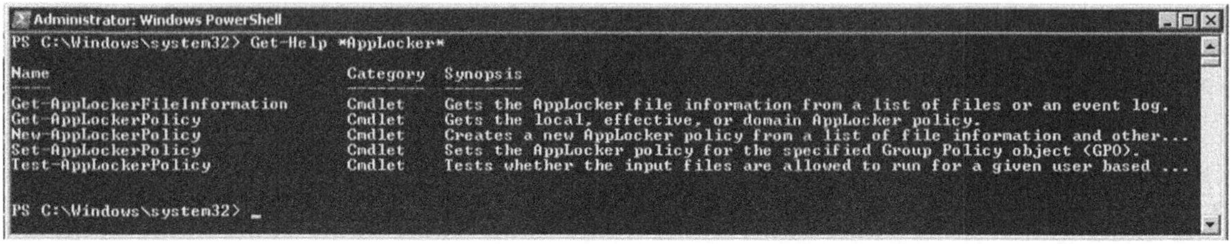

■ **FIGURE 11.11** The AppLocker cmdlets.

*Get-Help *AppLocker** and hit enter. You should now see a list of the five AppLocker cmdlets (see Figure 11.11).

If this did not work and you get an error, then make sure you are running Windows 7 or Windows Server 2008 R2. In addition, you need to make sure you have administrator rights and scripting enabled. If not, refer the Get-ExecutionPolicy directions in the Introduction to PowerShell Scripting earlier in this chapter on how to set your Execution Policy to allow the scripts to run.

The five AppLocker commands that should appear on your screen are described in Table 11.8.

These cmdlets are very straightforward in their use on a basic level but allow some very interesting complexities and applications as well.

As the name implies, the Get-AppLockerFileInformation cmdlet allows you to get the AppLocker file information from a list of files or an event log. For example, you could get all the AppLocker information for all the executable files and scripts in a specific directory. You could also be more specific and get the AppLocker information for a specific script or executable by simply typing *Get-AppLockerFileInformation filename*. You will

Table 11.8 Windows AppLocker cmdlets

cmdlet Name	Description
New-AppLockerPolicy	This cmdlet creates a new AppLocker policy. It can be created with default values or specific values determined during creation
Get-AppLockerFileInformation	This cmdlet gets the AppLockerFile information for the specified targets
Get-AppLockerPolicy	This cmdlet gets the specified AppLockerPolicy from the local computer or a specific GPO
Set-AppLockerPolicy	This cmdlet sets the AppLockerPolicy for a desired target Group Policy Object
Test-AppLockerPolicy	This cmdlet tests a target against a specific AppLocker policy to determine what execution rights it has

get multiple files for your example. Type *Get-AppLockerFileInformation –Directory C:\Windows\System32\ -FileType script* and hit *enter*, and you will see how the AppLocker File information is returned. The cmdlet you used is asking for the AppLocker File information for all the scripts in the Windows\System32\ directory. In the output, you can see the file and some of its information, which can include the file path, the publisher, and the file hash (see Figure 11.12).

This information might not seem very useful to you, but it is important when you use the rest of the cmdlets that require AppLocker File information. For some of them, you will need to pipe on the AppLocker File information, like the New-AppLockerPolicy cmdlet.

The New-AppLockerPolicy cmdlet is used to create new AppLocker rules for a group or user. It requires a list of file information to automatically generate these new rules for you. Let us say you have a directory where you do not want any new .exe files to have the ability to execute, except for the ones that are already there. That way, any new files that are added later can be checked for safety before they are allowed to run. In this example, you will create a new AppLocker Policy to only allow the existing script files in the Windows\System32\ directory to be allowed to run. You will need to use the Get-FileInformation cmdlet to get all the script files currently there and then pass them to the New-AppLockerPolicy cmdlet via the "|" or pipe.

The cmdlet you type is *get-AppLockerFileInformation –Directory C:\Windows\System32\ -FileType script | New-AppLockerPolicy –User Everyone XML > ScriptRestrictionPolicy.XML*. This first gets all the AppLocker file information for all the scripts in the specified directory, it then uses this to create a new AppLocker Policy file for all the users and writes the policy to the ScriptRestrictionPolicy.XML as you specified.

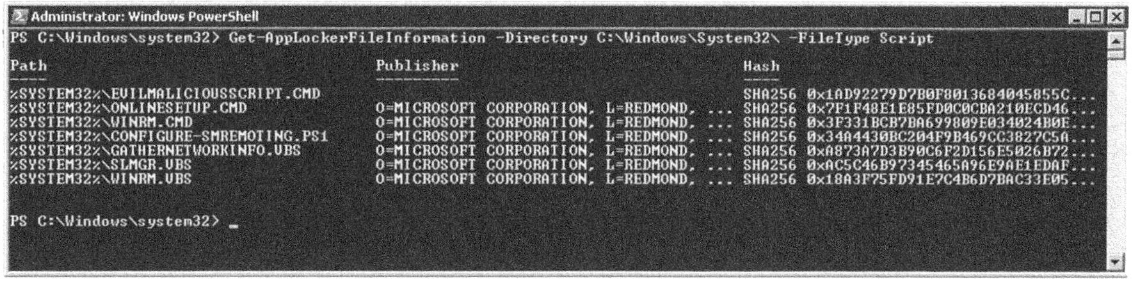

■ FIGURE 11.12 File Information for the Scripts in the System32 folder.

It will use a default rule type of publisher and then hash, since you did not specify one of your own. If you were to open the newly created ScriptRestrictionPolicy.XML in a text editor, you would be able to see that it contains xml entries for all the files that were returned by the get-AppLockerFileInformation –Directory C:\Windows\System32\ -FileType script cmdlet (see Figure 11.13). If you were to push this policy, only then those scripts would have permission to run by default and others would not be allowed unless you added them to the policy. You could have just as easily created a policy that would allow none to run, except for a specific file as well by simply removing the –Directory and –FileType flags like this *Get-AppLockerFileInformation* **fileToAllow** | *New-AppLockerPolicy –User Everyone XML > YourNewPolicyName.XML*.

The next cmdlet, Test-AppLockerPolicy cmdlet is a very useful straight-forward tool. It lets the administrator check the AppLocker Policy in a few different ways. You can check if users in a group are allowed to run an application, you can check if a list of applications can be run by a group of users and you can check to see which files a specific user is not allowed to execute. You are going to use the Test-AppLockerPolicy cmdlet to see how the policies you created earlier would impact the existing files and new files before you push the AppLocker Policies. You can test the ScriptRestrictionPolicy you created before that was supposed to create a policy for the existing scripts. You pick one of the scripts to test with the Test-AppLockerPolicy cmdlet (see Figure 11.13). You pick the first one, WINRM.CMD, and type *Test-AppLockerPolicy –XMLPolicy.\ ScriptRestrictionPolicy.XML –Path C:\Windows\System32\WINRM.CMD* to see if the policy will allow it like it is supposed to, and you see that it does (see Figure 11.14).

You now check to see that the policy is also restricting new scripts as it is sup-posed to by creating a new file and calling it "EvilMaliciousScript.CMD." You then test it to see if it can be run by typing *Test-AppLockerPolicy –*

■ **FIGURE 11.13** Scripts that will be allowed to run with the New Policy.

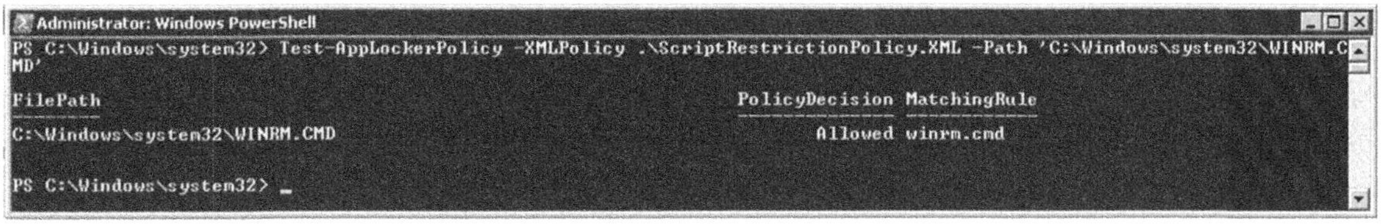

■ **FIGURE 11.14** Testing the Policy.

XMLPolicy.\ScriptRestrictionPolicy.XML   –Path   C:\Windows\System32\ EvilMaliciousScript.CMD and hitting *enter*. The result shows you that your policy is working. It is restricting it because it is not the one specified in your XML policy file (see Figure 11.15).

Now that you understand how to test AppLocker policies, you move on to another helpful cmdlet called the Get-AppLockerPolicy cmdlet. This cmdlet gets the AppLocker policy from either a specific GPO or from the effective AppLocker policy on the computer. To get the effective AppLockerPolicy on your local computer, you simply type *Get-AppLockerPolicy –Effective* and hit enter. In this way, you can also get a local or domain AppLockerPolicy with their corresponding flags of *– local* or *–domain* or even specify a specific GPO to get the policy from using the Lightweight Directory Access Protocol (LDAP) path of the GPO and the *–ldap* flag. Get-AppLockerPolicy can either return an AppLockerPolicy object or an XML-formatted string. So, if you wanted to write the local policy to an XML file, you simply add another flag to the command like this *Get-AppLockerPolicy –Local –XML > Local. XML*. This will then write the AppLockerPolicy to the file you specified Local.XML.

The final piece in the puzzle is the Set-AppLockerPolicy cmdlet. The Set-AppLockerPolicy lets the administrator set an AppLockerPolicy for a specific Group Policy Object (GPO). You either need to furnish an LDAP path or it will default to the local GPO. So, once you have an AppLockerPolicy that you have tested and are sure you want to push, you can use the

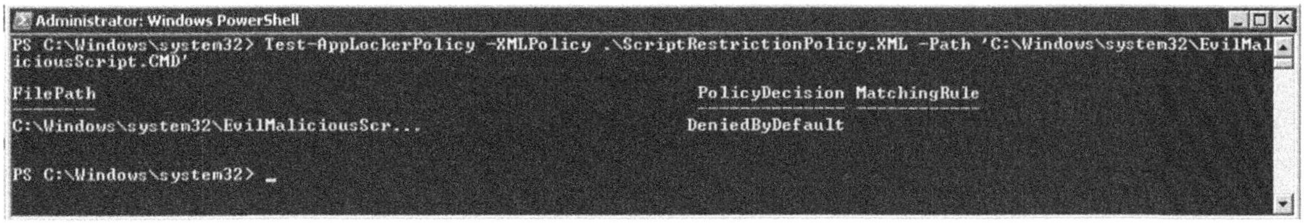

■ **FIGURE 11.15** Restricting New Scripts.

Set-AppLockerPolicy cmdlet to do so. So, assuming you were ready to set the local AppLockerPolicy to the ScriptRestrictionPolicy.XML AppLocker Policy you created earlier with the New-AppLockerPolicy cmdlet, you would simply type *Set-AppLockerPolicy –XMLPolicy C:\Windows\ System32\ScriptRestrictionPolicy.XML* and be done with it. One flag of interest is the *–Merge* flag. If the Merge flag is included, then the new AppLocker Policy you are setting is merged with the old one. If the –Merge flag is not there, then the old AppLockerPolicy is replaced with the new one you are setting. Going back to your ScriptRestrictionPolicy, you could create new AppLocker policies for any new scripts you wanted to allow to run and then use Set-AppLockerPolicy cmdlet with the –Merge flag to add them to the existing local AppLockerPolicy.

Failover Cluster cmdlets

To use the Failover Cluster cmdlets and their features, you will need to install them. They are not installed by default. To install the Failover Cluster cmdlets, you need to do the following tasks:

1. Start Server Manager
2. Click on *Features*, this will bring up the Features Wizard
3. Click on Add Features in the right Features panel
4. Check the *Failover Clustering checkbox*
5. Click *Install*

You have now installed the Failover Clustering feature. The next step is to make all the cmdlets available to you in PowerShell. To do this, you follow these steps:

1. Click *Start*
2. Click *Administrative Tools*
3. Click on *PowerShell Modules*, making sure you run it as an Administrator.

A PowerShell window will then open and start importing the modules you will need. To verify that it worked, you can type *Get-Command –Module FailOverClusters* and hit enter. If you did everything properly, you will see the cmdlet list for FailOverClusters.

When you work with Failover Clusters, there are a lot of different things that can happen or need to be done. You will try to illustrate how PowerShell can be used in performing some of the more important tasks as an alternative to using the Failover Manager Snapin for Server Manager.

Let us say that as an administrator it is your job to configure a new Failover Cluster. The first thing you would need to do is to test the cluster to make sure it is a valid candidate for a Failover Cluster. First, you need to connect all the hardware and then test it. You would type *Test-Cluster* (see Table 11.9) at the PowerShell Prompt and hit *enter*. This cmdlet will run all the validation tests on the cluster. Since you do not specify a cluster by name, it will run them on the local cluster. This cmdlet will not test an online disk that is being used as part of a Failover Cluster already. If you need to test one, then you need to offline it and then test it. Once the cluster has been tested, then you know it is ok to use for a Failover Cluster and can move on to the next step of actually creating the cluster. You create the cluster with the New-Cluster cmdlet. At the PowerShell prompt, you type *New-Cluster –Name NewCluster –Node node1, node2*, and hit *enter* to create a cluster named NewCluster with two nodes and default values for IP addressing. Next, you need to create the clustered file folder and specify the storage volume that it will use much in the same way as if you were using the High-Availability Wizard in Server Manager. You use the Add-ClusteredFileServerRole cmdlet to accomplish this. You can type *Add-ClusteredFileServerRole –Storage "Cluster Disk 2"* and hit *enter* where the *–Storage* flag corresponds to the cluster disk resource you want to use. You are almost done configuring your new Failover Cluster. The last part is to decide if you want to add more disks to the cluster. If you want to add more disks to the cluster, you first check to see which disks are available with the Get-ClusterAvailableDisk cmdlet by typing *Get-ClusterAvailableDisk* and then enter. This will then give you a list of the disks available to be added. If you decide you want to add them, you then type *Get-ClusterAvailableDisk | Add-ClusterDisk* and hit enter. This will look for available disks and then add them to the cluster. You now have a basic Failover Cluster.

Another task that might be required of you is the administration of the nodes on the Failover Cluster. PowerShell has some handy cmdlets to make this job easy as well (see Table 11.10). You are busy working and

Table 11.9 cmdlets Used in Creating a New Failover Cluster

cmdlet	Description
Test-Cluster	This cmdlet runs validation tests for Failover Cluster setup
New-Cluster	This cmdlet creates a new Failover Cluster
Add-ClusteredFileServerRole	This cmdlet creates a clustered file server
Get-ClusteredAvailableDisk	This cmdlet shows the available disks valid for failover not yet being used
Add-ClusteredDisk	This cmdlet adds a disk to the Failover Cluster

Table 11.10 Some Useful ClusterNode cmdlets

cmdlet	Description
Get-ClusterNode	This cmdlet gets information about the nodes in a Failover Cluster
Add-ClusterNode	This cmdlet adds a node to a Failover Cluster
Stop-ClusterNode	This cmdlet stops service for a node of a Failover Cluster
Start-ClusterNode	This cmdlet starts failover service in a Failover Cluster for a node
Suspend-ClusterNode	This cmdlet Pauses a node in a Failover Cluster
Resume-ClusterNode	This cmdlet Resumes a paused node in the Failover Cluster

someone high up wants you to know if all the nodes are up. You simply need to check if all the nodes that are supposed to be running are actually online. The Get-ClusterNode cmdlet is what you would use for this task. Typing *Get-ClusterNode –Cluster* **NameOfTheCluster** will give you a list of all the nodes in the cluster you specify along with their status allowing you to easily see if they are online or not. After you finish checking the nodes and assure the party concerned that all the nodes are up, you get another request. You are asked to add a new node, node4 to an existing cluster named MainClusterA. Using PowerShell, you would type *Add-ClusterNode –Cluster MainClusterA –Name node4*. The *–Cluster* flag specifies which cluster to add the node to and the *–Name* flag corresponds to the name of the node to add. You finish that request and start to check e-mail. Another request has hit your inbox. Once you start administering nodes, you might find yourself having to stop and start the cluster service on some nodes or even just pausing it for some time and then resuming it. PowerShell can help you do these things as well. For stopping and starting the cluster service, you will need to use the Stop-ClusterNode and Start-ClusterNode cmdlets, respectively. The new request you just received is asking you to stop the cluster service in node3 so that some routine inspection or troubleshooting can be performed on it. You type *Stop-ClusterNode node3 –Cluster MainClusterA* and hit enter. When the cmdlet runs, you will get a confirmation that the node is offline. When you stop a node, you do have to keep in mind that the number of nodes cannot drop below quorum or the system will not let you do it since this would jeopardize everything. You reply to the request that node3 is offline and that they can start their maintenance. The maintenance is performed on node3 and tests are run and everything checks out. You are now tasked with starting up the Cluster service back on it. No reason to worry at all. You type *Start-ClusterNode node3 –Cluster MainClusterA* and hit enter. You reply that node3 is backup and ready to go. Before you have even finished sending the message, another request comes in. You are asked to pause node4 because software updates need to be applied to it. They do not want you to stop the node since they guarantee the updates will be fast and they do not want to bring the node offline. Everything that needs to be stopped or moved has been done. They just need you to pause the node for them, so they can continue. You type *Suspend-ClusterNode node4 –Cluster MainClusterA* and hit enter. When the cmdlet runs, you see that the node status is "paused." After you pause the node, you inform them and wait for them to give you the green light to unpause the node. Eventually, you are given the green light to resume activity on the node and you type *Resume-ClusterNode node4 –Cluster MainClusterA* in PowerShell and hit enter. Check whether the status has the node back to "Up" and move on to your next task. You have handled yourself well and touched upon the basics on node management at the same time. You decide to take lunch and pat yourself on the back for doing so well.

You come back from lunch feeling energized and ready for the rest of the day. Just after you have sat down, you notice requests in your inbox. You are being asked to check on a disk in the cluster and make sure it is in maintenance mode, Disk 4. (The cmdlets for this task are described in Table 11.11.) A maintenance tool will be run on it later today and they need it to be in maintenance mode or it could trigger failover, which would be bad. You sit down and type *Get-ClusterResource* and hit *enter*. A list comes up with all the cluster resources and you see that the name of the disk is actually Cluster Disk 4. You notice that Cluster Disk 4 is shown online, but that is not enough for you, you need to see if it is in maintenance mode, if it has been suspended from active duty. To see if it is in maintenance mode, you have a choice and can use either the Get-ClusterResource cmdlet on Cluster Disk 4 or Get-ClusterResource, together with Get-ClusterParameter, for a more detailed overview of the disk. You decide to try both for kicks. After typing *Get-ClusterResource "Cluster Disk 4" –Cluster MainClusterA* and hitting enter, you are able to see in the list that the disk is not in maintenance mode since it says false. You double-check and *type Get-ClusterResource "Cluster Disk 4" –Cluster MainClusterA | Get-ClusterParameter* and hit enter. You notice

Table 11.11 Useful Cluster Resource cmdlets

cmdlet	Description
Get-ClusterResource	This cmdlet gets information about one or more resources on a Failover Cluster
Suspend-ClusterResource	This cmdlet turns on maintenance for a disk or cluster-shared volume
Resume-ClusterResource	This cmdlet turns off maintenance for a disk or cluster-shared volume

that maintenance mode is not on since it has a value of 0. You need to suspend the disk yourself, so you type *Suspend-ClusterResource "Cluster Disk 4" –Cluster MainClusterA* and hit enter. After the cmdlet executes, you notice that the display shows that the disk is still online, but it is in maintenance mode. You reply to the request and confirm that the disk is now in maintenance mode and ready for the necessary programs to be run. Once the programs are run, someone will need to take the disk out of maintenance mode, so it can go back to being fully productive. This someone will most likely be you and you will gladly type *Resume-ClusterResource "Cluster Disk 4" –Cluster MainClusterA* hit enter and be done with this request. You will notice that after the cmdlet is run, the disk will still show as being online but no longer in maintenance mode.

Just when you thought you were done, in comes a very different request. Your next task is to move a group of applications and services known as a Resource Group from one node, node3 to a different node, node6, so that node3 can be readied for maintenance. The first thing you do is type *Get-ClusterNode node3 –Cluster MainClusterA | Get-ClusterGroup* and hit enter. This brings up all the services and applications that are owned by node3. You notice that the display shows a resource group called "KittenCaboodle." You realize that you will need to stop this resource group first if you are to move it to node6. You type *Stop-ClusterGroup Kitten Caboodle –Cluster MainClusterA* and hit enter. Once the cmdlet runs, you can see that the resource group will show up as offline. Now that the Kitten Caboodle is offline, you need to move it. Next, you type *Move-ClusterGroup KittenCaboodle –Cluster MainClusterA –Node node6* and hit enter. The *–Node* flag specifies the destination node to move the resource group to. Now, all you need to do is bring it back online. You type *Start-ClusterGroup KittenCaboodle –Cluster MainClusterA* hit enter and watch the display. Once the cmdlet executes, you will notice that the Kitten Caboodle resource group will be back online and in node6, which means you are done. All you have to do now is wonder if they are going to make you move it back after the maintenance in node3 is done.

As you can see, using cmdlets to accomplish the same jobs as some of the Server Manager wizards for Failover Clusters is not difficult once you familiarize yourself with the capabilities of the PowerShell Failover cmdlets. You dabbled in configuring a Failover Cluster, performing some cluster node operations, monitoring some cluster disks, and moving a resource group from one node to another. The advantage of PowerShell is that once you become comfortable with it, you will find that your administrative job will become easier as you write scripts once and then have them there for the next time you need. You are also able to run them on multiple machines instead of going through the wizard on each individual machine.

Group Policy cmdlets

The Group Policy cmdlets in PowerShell follow in the footsteps of all the other cmdlets in raw power. They let you do almost anything you could normally do with the Group Policy Management Console (GPMC) using cmdlets. But just like many of the other new features in PowerShell 2.0, the cmdlets are not available from the start. To use the Group Policy cmdlets, you will have to import the corresponding module. First, make sure you are running Windows 2008 Server R2 on a domain controller or on a member server that has the GPMC installed. Startup PowerShell and type *Import-Module GroupPolicy*. Once the cmdlet completes, you can make sure it worked by typing Get-Help *GPO*. If the import worked, you should see a list with some of the Group Policy cmdlets (see Figure 11.16).

Once you know that the import cmdlet worked, you can move on. Tables 11.12–11.16 list cmdlets used for creating, getting, setting, and deleting things, as well as various utility cmdlets.

There are a large number of PowerShell cmdlets that are there simply to support Group Policies. The purpose behind them is to let you automate many of the tasks that are normally performed with the GPMC by giving you the cmdlets that duplicate the features of the console. The large number of cmdlets for Group Policies are divided into four kinds of cmdlets dictated by what their purpose is. The first group of cmdlets is used for

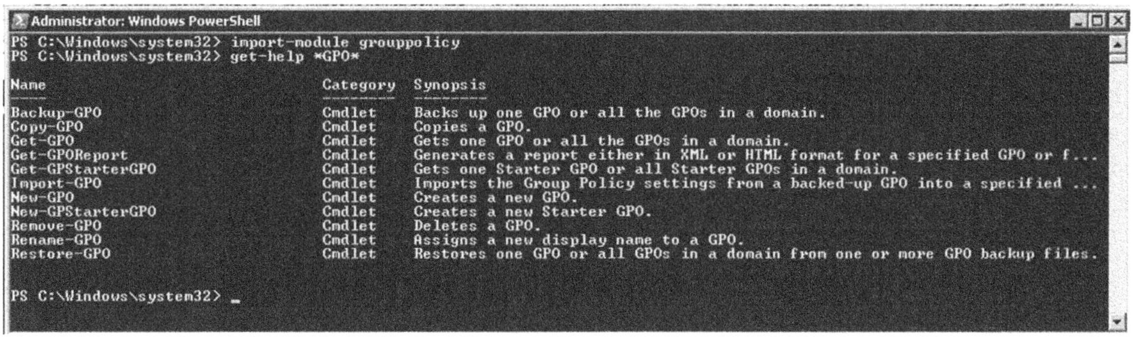

■ FIGURE 11.16 Some of the Group Policy cmdlets.

Table 11.12 Group Policy cmdlets That Create Things, the Constructors

cmdlet Name	Description
New-GPO	This cmdlet creates a new Group Policy Object (GPO)
New-GPStarterGPO	This cmdlet creates a new Starter GPO
New-GPLink	This cmdlet creates a new link between the GPO and a valid specified target with the specified values

Table 11.13 Group Policy cmdlets That Get Things, the Getters

cmdlet Name	Description
Get-GPInheritance	This cmdlet gets the inheritance information for a specified target
Get-GPO	This cmdlet gets a target GPO or all the GPOs in a domain with the –All flag
Get-GPOReport	This cmdlet gets a report for a specified GPO(s)
Get-GPPermissions	This cmdlet gets the specified permissions for a specific GPO
Get-GPPrefRegistryValue	This cmdlet gets a registry preference item for a specific GPO
Get-GPRegistryValue	This cmdlet gets a registry-based policy setting for a specific GPO
Get-GPResultantSetofPolicy	This cmdlet gets the ResultantSetofPolicy (RSoP) for a specified target. Target can be a computer, a user, or both
Get-GPStarterGPO	This cmdlet gets the specified starter GPO in the domain or all the starter GPOs in the domain

Table 11.14 Group Policy cmdlets That Set Things, the Setters

cmdlet Name	Description
Set-GPInheritance	This cmdlet sets the inheritance for a target domain or OU by setting it the –IsBlocked flag to Yes or No
Set-GPLink	This cmdlet sets the properties of a GPO link by setting the –Enforced, -LinkEnabled, and/or –Order flags
Set-GPPermissions	This cmdlet sets the permissions level for a security principal for one target GPO or all the GPOs in the domain. Permission levels must be set to a higher level or they will not be changed unless the –Replace flag is used.
Set-GPPrefRegistryValue	This cmdlet sets a registry preference item under a computer or user configuration in a GPO
Set-GPRegistryValue	This cmdlet sets one or more registry-based settings under a computer or user configuration in a GPO

GPO maintenance; the second group of cmdlets is used to associate GPOs with targeted AD sites, domains, or organizational Units (OUs) the third; group is used to set permissions and inheritance; and the final set of cmdlets is used for registry operations involving GPOs.

Table 11.15 Group Policy cmdlets That Remove Things, the Deleters

cmdlet Name	Description
Remove-GPLink	This cmdlet removes the link from a specific GPO to a specified target
Remove-GPO	This cmdlet removes a GPO
Remove-GPPrefRegistryValue	This cmdlet removes one or more registry preference items from either the computer or user configuration in a GPO
Remove-GPRegistryValue	This cmdlet removes one or more registry-based policy settings from either the computer or user configuration in a GPO

Table 11.16 Miscellaneous Group Policy cmdlets, the Utility cmdlets

cmdlet Name	Description
Backup-GPO	This cmdlet backs up a GPO or all the GPOs in the domain to a specified location that must already exist
Copy-GPO	This cmdlet copies a GPO. Will not create a GPO copy with the same name in a domain
Import-GPO	This cmdlet imports the GPO settings from a GPO backup to a specified GPO. The specified GPO does not have to exist and will be created from the backup if the –CreateIfNeeded flag is used
Rename-GPO	This cmdlet renames a GPO only changing its display name
Restore-GPO	This cmdlet restores a GPO or all the GPOs in the domain from backup files. The GPO(s) must exist for them to be restored

The group of GPO maintenance cmdlets are typically used for the backup, creation, removal, and import of GPOs. The first thing you will do is create a test GPO so that you can familiarize yourself with the cmdlets. Startup PowerShell and make sure you imported the Group Policy module. Type *New-GPO myPSGPO –Comment "My First Official PowerShell GPO."* When the cmdlet has finished executing, you will have a list with all the attributes for your newly created GPO. Now, you have a disposable GPO, you can use the rest of the cmdlets on if you please and not have to worry about. You can now try to create a backup of this GPO with the Backup-GPO cmdlet. Type *Backup-GPO –Name myPSGPO –Path C:\windows\GPOBackups*. Keep in mind that the path has to point to a directory that already exists, it will not create it for you. You might want to substitute that path with one of your own or create a directory to make that path valid. You should also be aware that as an alternative to the –name flag to specify the GPO, you can use the –GUID flag and give it the globally unique identifier. This is used when there is a possibility of more than one GPO with the same name. Once the cmdlet completes, you will once again see a status screen. Now, let us say that the prized GPO that you created gets zapped one day. You remember that you backed it up one day when you were preparing for a day just like this. All you have to do now is restore it. There is a cmdlet for that as well. You will now restore from the backup you created using the Import-GPO cmdlet. At the PowerShell prompt, you type *Import-GPO –BackUpGPOName myPSGPO –TargetName myPSGPO –createifneeded –path c:\Windows\System32\GPOBackups* and hit enter. When the cmdlet runs, you will see that the GPO will be back. The –createifneeded flag is what makes it a true restore, because without this flag, a new GPO would not be created from the old one and the cmdlet would just serve to restore the old settings from the backup GPO to the target GPO. You could also use the Restore-GPO cmdlet to accomplish the same thing, the main difference is that Restore-GPO allows a mass restore by using the –all flag, but for the restore cmdlet to work, the target GPOs must still exist, while the Import-GPO does not care as long as you use the –createifneeded flag. Now, assume that a lot of time goes by and you outgrow the GPO you created. Since then, you have grown much and created much better GPOs and no longer need myPSGPO. This is where the Remove-GPO cmdlet comes in. It allows you to quite simply remove or delete a GPO. When you are ready to delete myPSGPO, you type *Remove-GPO –Name myPSGPO*.

The second group of Group Policy cmdlets is used for Group Policy link maintenance. They allow the administrator to create links, remove links, and change the properties on existing links. The link maintenance Group Policy cmdlets are very powerful and straightforward. It should come as no surprise that to create a new link, you use the New-GPLink cmdlet. You will need the LDAP name of the target site, domain, or OU you are linking to. If you wanted to link the GPO myPSGPO you created earlier to one of your OUs, you would type *New-GPLink –name myPSGPO –Target "LDAP name of the target" –LinkEnabled Yes.* When you hit enter, a new link from your GPO would be created to the desired OU. Just as when you create links with the GPMC, you can specify the link order if you want it enforced and if you want the link enabled with the –Enforced –LinkEnabled and –Order flags. The –Enforced and –LinkEnabled flags takes a Yes or No, while the –Order takes an integer. Once you create a link, you might eventually decide to remove it. If this does happen, then you will need the Remove-GPLink cmdlet. To remove the link from myPSGPO, you type *Remove-GPLink –Name "myPSGPO" –Target "LDAP name of the target"* and hit enter. The link has now been removed. Let us say that instead of removing it, though, you wanted to change its properties. You decided that you wanted to make the link enforced, something that you did not do when you originally created the link. This is where the Set-GPLink cmdlet comes in handy. Assuming you wanted to change the link you had set up earlier instead of removing it, you would type *Set-GPLink –Name myPSGPO –Target "LDAP name of the target" –Enforced Yes.*

The next set of Group Policy cmdlets you will find useful are the ones that deal with permissions and inheritance. Let us say you want to check the permissions on a GPO. The Get-GPPermissions cmdlet is the answer. To illustrate how this works, you will use it on the GPO myPSGPO you created earlier. At the PowerShell prompt, type in *get-GPPermissions –Name myPSGPO –ALL* and hit enter. When the command executes, you will see a list of all the permissions for the GPO (see Figure 11.17).

Now, assume that you want to change some of the permissions for the GPO. You will need to use the Set-GPPermissions cmdlet to accomplish this. The Set-GPPermissions cmdlet is your all-purpose permission tweak and permission set cmdlet. By default, it will not replace an existing permission with a lower permission level unless you use the –Replace flag. You notice that in your GPO, any "Authenticated User" can apply a GPO. You want to change that so that the only thing they can do is read it. You type *Set-GPPermissions –Name myPSGPO –TargetName "Authenticated Users" –TargetType Group –PermissionLevel GpoRead*

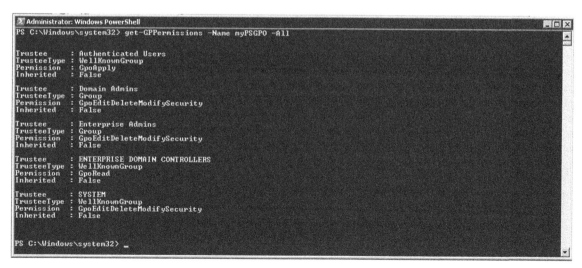

■ **FIGURE 11.17** Permissions list for PSGPO.

–Replace and hit enter. You need to use the –Replace flag since you are actually lowering the permission level. You can now check your GPO again with *Get-GPPermissions –name myPSGPO –TargetName "Authenticated Users" –TargetType Group* and see that the permission level has been changed from GpoApply to GpoRead (see Figure 11.18).

The Inheritance cmdlets, like the Permissions cmdlets, accomplish all they need with just two cmdlets. The Get-GPInheritance cmdlet is used to get the GP Inheritance information for a domain or OU, while the Set-GPInheritance is used to modify the existing Inheritance rule and either stop or allow inheritance in a domain or OU. Let us say you wanted to find out the GP Inheritance information for a specific OU. At the PowerShell prompt, you would type *Get-GpInheritance –Target "LDAP name of the OU"* and hit enter. The cmdlet would execute and return information, letting you know if inheritance is blocked or not as well as the number of GPO links and Inherited GPO links. If you decided you wanted to change the inheritance rule for an existing OU and block inheritance, then at the PowerShell prompt, you would type *Set-GPInheritance –Target "LDAP name of the OU" –IsBlocked Yes and* hit enter. This would then block inheritance for that OU, except for Enforced rules.

The final set of Group Policy cmdlets is used to make registry operations. The Get-GPRegistryValue and Get-GPPrefRegistryValue are the information getters, Set-GPRegistryValue and Set-GPPrefRegistryValue are the modifiers, and RemoveGPRegistryValue and Remove-GPPrefRegistryValue are deletion cmdlets. Their use and syntax are very straightforward.

Server Manager cmdlets

The Server Manager cmdlets are there to help the administrator with any action the Server Manager would normally allow them to perform (see Table 11.17).

■ **FIGURE 11.18** Permissions have been changed.

Table 11.17 Server Manager cmdlets

cmdlet Name	Description
Add-WindowsFeature	This cmdlet is used to install features
Get-WindowsFeature	This cmdlet is used to get the list of features available. The installed features will show an [X] by them and the ones that are not installed will show []
Remove-WindowsFeature	This cmdlet is used to remove an installed feature

With the PowerShell Server Manager cmdlets, you can add, check, and remove roles, roles services, and features from servers in your environment. Before you can have access to these cmdlets, you have to import the Server Manager module via the import-module cmdlet. Follow these steps to import the Server Manager Module:

1. Startup PowerShell
2. Type *import-module ServerManager*
3. Once the cmdlet completes, you can check that you have access to the Server Manager cmdlets by typing *get-help *windowsfeature**. Remember that the * are the wildcards and this will return all cmdlets with windowsfeature anywhere in them. A list of three cmdlets should then be listed for you as shown (see Figure 11.19), which will include Add-WindowsFeature, Get-WindowsFeature, and Remove-WindowsFeature.

These cmdlets are very straightforward in their use and purpose as can be determined by their names. Add-WindowsFeature is the one the administrator will be using to add the roles, role services, and features; Get-WindowsFeature is the one that will be used to get the information about them, and Remove-WindowsFeature to remove them directly. The syntax is just as straightforward. Assume that you wanted to install the telnet client on your server. Instead of starting up Server Manager and using the wizard, you can do it directly with PowerShell. The first thing you need is the

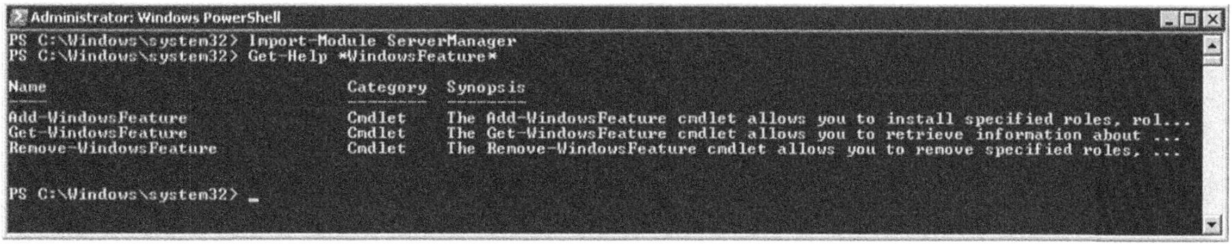

■ **FIGURE 11.19** The Server Manager cmdlets.

name of the feature you want to install. Sometimes, you will not know the exact name that Server Manager uses and will need to look it up. This is done with the Get-WindowsFeature cmdlet. Typing *Get-WindowsFeature* at the prompt will return a list with all the potential features with a column showing their display name in Server Manager and a column showing their name. The Display name column will also have an [X] next to any feature already installed. This way if you need to, you can check to see if the feature you want is already installed. The name column is what will be needed for the cmdlet to run properly. In this case, the name of the telnet client is telnet-client. Looking at the Display name column, you will see that it is not installed by default (see Figure 11.20). With this name, you can now call the Add-WindowsFeature cmdlet by typing Add-WindowsFeature telnet-client and then hitting enter. You will then get the prompt back. Now, you try the Get-WindowsFeature cmdlet again. You can type it without an argument like you did the first time, or you can specify that you want to see the telnet client feature specifically by giving it the name and typing Get-WindowsFeature telnet-client. You will now be able to see that the telnet client has an [X] before it, showing that it has been installed (see Figure 11.21).

■ **FIGURE 11.20** Telnet-Client is not installed.

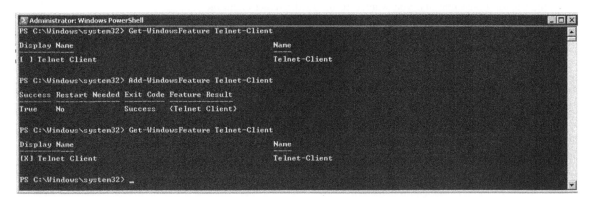

■ **FIGURE 11.21** Telnet-Client is installed.

The Remove-WindowsFeature cmdlet is the cmdlet you will be using to remove modules, as the name implies. Following the previous example, let us say you now want to remove the telnet client. Since you already know the name of the feature you want to remove, you do not need to look it up, but if you do not know the name, you could just look it up with Get-WindowsFeature as described earlier. The next step is to issue the cmdlet by typing Remove-WindowsFeature telnet-client and hit enter. PowerShell will process the cmdlet and then return a summary describing if the removal was successful, if a restart is needed, and a reminder of what feature was removed (see Figure 11.22).

So, the question is, when would you use these features? Imagine you are the lucky administrator tasked with building up a Web server farm consisting of 15 new servers which all require IIS to be installed. Instead of trudging your way through each server one at a time and utilizing the Server Manager GUI to perform the installs, you would instead be able to create and utilize a repeatable PowerShell cmdlet or a sequence of cmdlets. Even if you decided to log on to each server and execute the cmdlets instead of utilizing the GUI, you would save a hefty amount of time in performing the installations. Now, add to this the equation the fact that you can use PowerShell's new remoting features or even just write it once and have it available on the network, and you can see the reason why you would use it.

Windows Server Backup cmdlets

The Windows Server Backup cmdlets are the family of cmdlets that help the administrator manage his backups, just as the name implies. Before

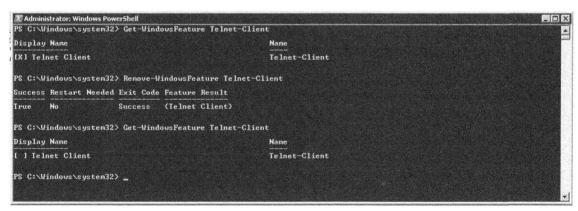

■ **FIGURE 11.22** Removing Telnet-Client cmdlet results.

these cmdlets can be used, you once again need to import the snap-in that contains all these cmdlets. Importing these cmdlets is not as straightforward as some of the other modules. First, you need to install the Windows Server Backup Tools and then, you need to import the PowerShell snap-in. To enable the Windows Server Backup cmdlets, you first install the Windows Server Backup Tools using Server Manager as follows:

1. Click *Start*
2. Click *Administrative Tools*
3. Click *Server Manager*
4. Server Manager will run, click on Features on the left panel
5. This will bring up the features panel on the right side
6. Click Add Features on the right panel
7. This will open the Add Features wizard and expand Windows Server Backup Features
8. Check the checkbox for *Windows Server Backup*
9. Check the checkbox for *Command-line Tools*
10. Click *Install*
11. Once the installation is complete, you have the backup tools and are almost done. Now, you need to import the Windows Server Backup cmdlet snap-in as follows:
12. Startup PowerShell
13. Type *add-pssnapin windows.serverbackup* and hit enter

The windows server backup cmdlets snap-in should now be available. You can verify whether it has been imported properly by typing the *get-pssnapin* cmdlet, which will list all the snap-ins, and check to make sure that the windows.serverbackup snap-in is listed (see Figure 11.23).

Once this is done, you are ready to start with the Server Backup cmdlets. You divide the cmdlets into five categories: the cmdlets that create, the cmdlets that get, the cmdlets that set, the cmdlets that remove, and the miscellaneous cmdlets (see Tables 11.18–11.22).

The Windows Server Backup PowerShell cmdlets give you access to all the tools you need to create your own backups, specify when they need to run, and specify what to backup and where to put it. Let us say you walk into work one day, and after passing through all the metal detectors and security checkpoints, you arrive at your desk. On it, you see a curious manila folder with the words TOP SECRET in red. You open it and pull out some yellow-lined paper with strange, illegible writing. You quickly take out your decoder ring and you are able to read the first few lines, "I need you to set up a Backup Policy" it says, followed by more and more specifics. You decide that the first thing you will need to do is create a

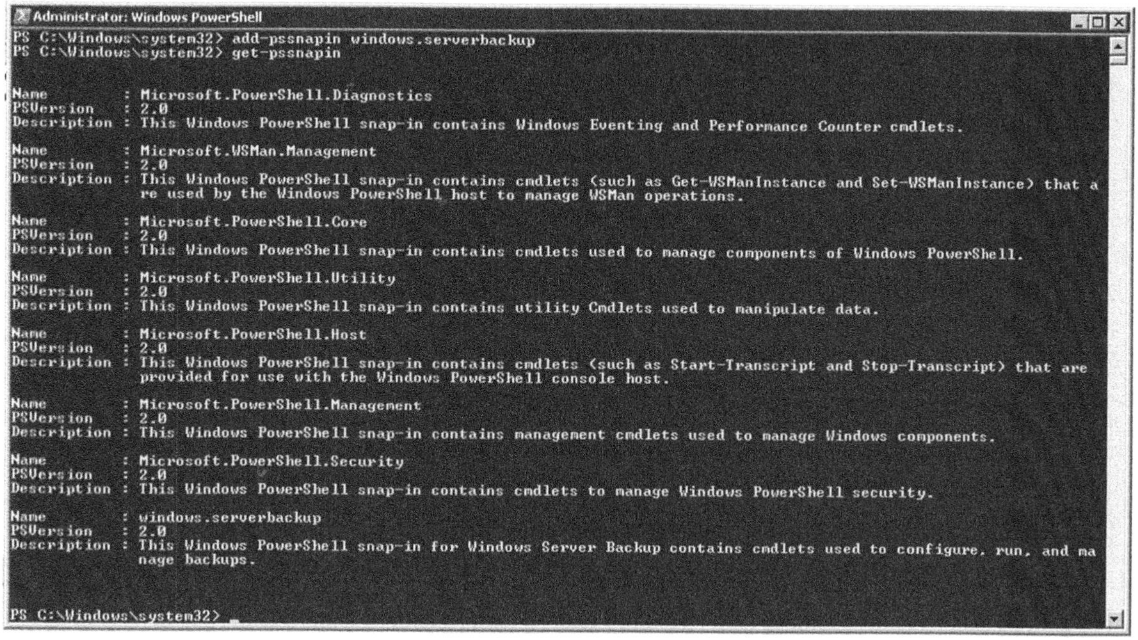

FIGURE 11.23 Windows.serverbackup is in the snap-in list.

Table 11.18 Windows Backup cmdlets That Create Objects, the Constructors

cmdlet Name	Description
New-WBPolicy	This cmdlet is used to create a new empty WBPolicy object. This is the object that will govern all your backup rules once you set it. You will need to populate it with all the specifications and properties you want it to have
New-WBFileSpec	This cmdlet is used to create a new WBFileSpec object. This object specifies a rule about what to include or exclude in a WBPolicy when the backup is run
New-WBBackupTarget	This cmdlet is used to create a new WBBackupTarget object. This object specifies where the backups are to be stored

WBPolicy object. You type *$secretPolicy = New-WBPolicy* at the prompt and hit enter. When the cmdlet completes, you will have created a new empty WBPolicy object in the $secretPolicy variable. It is this object that you will use to set up your backups. You want to make sure that your policy will create backups that can be used for bare metal recoveries if needed. You type *Add-WBBareMetalRecovery –Policy $secretPolicy* and hit enter. This adds the bare metal recovery setting to the policy you created. Using the Add-WBBareMetalRecovery cmdlet on a policy not only

Table 11.19 Windows Backup cmdlets That Get Items, the Getters

cmdlet Name	Description
Get-WBBackupSet	This cmdlet gets an object that represents a list of all the backups created for the location you specify
Get-WBBackupTarget	This cmdlet gets an object representing the backup target location for the specified policy
Get-WBBareMetalRecovery	This cmdlet gets a value that represents if the policy specified has the bare metal recovery option enabled. If this is enabled, then backups created by the policy can be used for bare metal recovery
Get-WBDisk	This cmdlet gets a list of disks that are available for the computer
Get-WBFileSpec	This cmdlet gets a list of the WBFileSpec objects that have been associated with the specified policy
Get-WBJob	This cmdlet gets the currently running WBJob object which represents a backup job
Get-WBPolicy	This cmdlet gets the policy that is currently set as the backup policy for the computer
Get-WBSchedule	This cmdlet gets the backup schedule for the specified policy. Giving it no parameter will default to the current active backup policy
Get-WBSummary	This cmdlet gets the history of backups performed
Get-WBSystemState	This cmdlet gets a value that represents if the policy specified has the system state recovery option enabled. If this is enabled, then backups created by the policy can be used for system state recovery
Get-WBVolume	This cmdlet gets a list of volumes determined by the parameters you give it
Get-WBVssBackupOptions	This cmdlet gets a value of either VssFullbackup or VssCopyBackup depending on the setting of the policy specified

Table 11.20 Windows Backup cmdlets That Set or Modify Items, the Setters

cmdlet Name	Description
Set-WBPolicy	This cmdlet sets the specified policy as the active policy to be used for backups
Set-WBSchedule	This cmdlet sets the time or times to create daily backups for the specified policy
Set-WBVssBackupOptions	This cmdlet sets the value specifying if the backups created by this policy are going to be VssFullbackups or VssCopyBackups

Table 11.21 Windows Backup cmdlets That Remove or Delete Items

cmdlet Name	Description
Remove-WBBackupTarget	This cmdlet removes a specified WBBackupTarget from a specified policy
Remove-WBBareMetalRecovery	This cmdlet removes the bare metal recovery capability from the specified policy. Backups created by the policy after this cmdlet is run will not be able to be used to make a bare metal recovery
Remove-WBFileSpec	This cmdlet removes a specified WBFileSpec from a specified policy
Remove-WBPolicy	This cmdlet removes the currently set backup policy if no policy is specified. If a policy is specified it removes it as long as it is the currently set backup policy
Remove-WBSystemState	This cmdlet removes the system state recovery option from the specified policy. Backups created by the policy will no longer be able to be used to make system state recoveries
Remove-WBVolume	This cmdlet removes a specified volume from a specified policy

adds the bare metal recovery setting to the policy but also adds the system state recovery setting without having to run the Add-WBSystemState cmdlet. So, now the policy can create backups which can be used for bare metal or system state recoveries as well as full server recovery. Decoding a few more lines, you read that the backups must be full VSS backups. *You put the decoder ring down and type Set-WBVssBackupOptions –Policy $secretPolicy –VssFullBackup and hit enter.* Now that you have taken care of that, you will also need to decide where you are going to back up to. You will need to set up a backup target object. Because you might not be aware of all the disks you could back up to in your server, you will check to see what is available by typing *Get-WBDisk* and hitting enter. When the cmdlet executes, you see a list of all the disks on the system (see Figure 11.24).

You then specify a backup location using the New-WBBackupTarget cmdlet by specifying the disk you want to backup to. In this case, you decide that to back up everything to a volume, set aside just for backups, you will be backing up to volume D:. *You type $secretDriveBackupLocation = New-WBBackupTarget –VolumePath D:* and hit enter. This has now created a WBBackupTarget object for you in the $secretDriveBackupLocation variable. You still need to do a few more things before you are ready because your policy is still empty. You have a backup policy and a backup target; you need to decide what exactly needs to be backed up. You check your top-secret mission objectives with your decoder ring and find that you need to back up all the files in a directory called C:\ForYourEyesOnly. Easy enough, you realize you need to create a WBFileSpec object to specify what to backup and what to exclude if anything. You will name the WBFileSpec object $secretFileSpec to be consistent and type *$secretFileSpec = New-WBFileSpec –FileSpec C:\ForYourEyesOnly* and hit enter. The C:\ForYourEyesOnly directory contents and all its subfolders have been marked for backup with this WBFileSpec. If you want to exclude some of the files in the directory, you would use the –Exclude flag. Reading in,

Table 11.22 Miscellaneous Windows Backup cmdlets

cmdlet Name	Description
Start-WBBackup	This cmdlet starts a backup operation using the specified policy

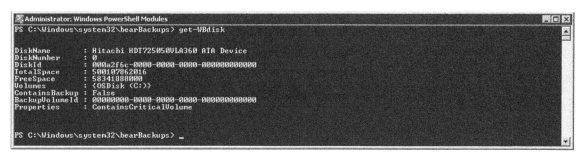

■ **FIGURE 11.24** A single disk on the system.

you notice that you need to exclude any files that have the word medals at the beginning. You create another WBFileSpec object by typing *$noMedalsFileSpec = New-WBFileSpec –FileSpec C:\ForYourEyesOnly *medals*.* -Exclude* and hit enter. You pick up your decoder ring and read through the instructions but they seem to stop suddenly. "Typical," you mumble to yourself. You once again open your desk drawer and take out the special pen that was handed to you for just an occasion. You quickly scribble with the pen over the next section of the instructions and wait for them to appear. You are to set the backup process to run at a secret time of your choosing. It can be anytime as long as you do not tell anyone. You decide to schedule it at 11 pm during the off-peak hours. You will set the WB schedule straight into the secret policy with the SetWBSchedule cmdlet by typing *Set-WBSchedule –Policy $secretPolicy –Schedule 23:00* and hitting enter. The time for the –Schedule flag must be written in HH:MM format. If you need to include more than one time to make backups, at then you can separate them with a comma. Once the cmdlet executes, you will see a confirmation that will show the next time the backup will run according to schedule, you set on that policy. You now have all the basic pieces and just need to put them together. First, you add all the WBFileSpec objects you created to the policy, otherwise it will not know what to backup and what to exclude. You type *Add-WBFileSpec –Policy $secretPolicy $secretFileSpec, $noMedalsFileSpec* and hit enter. This will add both of your specifications to the policy. If you had any more specifications, you would just create them and add them the same way. You can check the specifications on the policy by typing *Get-WBFileSpec –Policy $secretPolicy* and hit enter. This will list the specifications you have added so far (see Figure 11.25).

You continue by adding the BackupTarget object you created earlier to the policy. You type *Add-WBBackupTarget –Policy $secretPolicy –Target $secretDriveBackupLocation* and hit enter, suppressing the urge to look around the room in a paranoid way. When the cmdlet executes, the display will show you a list of properties as confirmation. You are pretty much

■ **FIGURE 11.25** Listing of the WBFileSpec
Objects in the $secretPolicy Policy.

done. You can put away the decoder ring and special pen and get ready to burn the directions in the garbage can. All that is left to do is set the policy you created as the backup policy. This time you disable the smoke detector before you set the garbage can contents on fire and sit down to finish. You type *Set-WBPolicy –Policy $secretPolicy* and hit enter. You wait for the cmdlet to execute and then you pick up your phone, dial your boss's extension, and as soon as he picks up, you whisper "The eagle has landed" and hang up. You sit back down amid the strange stares from your coworkers and wish you had a normal boss. The steps for creating a complete policy using PowerShell are very straightforward. Here are the steps needed.

1. Create the policy object with the New-WBPolicy cmdlet.
2. Create all the specifications about what to backup and what to exclude with a WBFileSpec object for each one using New-WBFileSpec cmdlet.
3. Add the WBFileSpec objects you created to the policy using the Add-WBFileSpec cmdlet.
4. Create a WBBackupTarget object to indicate where to backup to using the New-WBBackupTarget cmdlet.
5. Add the WBBackupTarget object you created to your policy using the Add-WBBackupTarget cmdlet.
6. The final step is to take the policy you created, which now has all the information you specified, and set it as the active backup policy using the Set-WBPolicy cmdlet.

Using the PowerShell Windows Backup cmdlets is easy and straightforward. You can accomplish everything with a few intuitive easy-to-remember cmdlets. Keep in mind the pattern that there are only three kinds of objects to create in the reference of Windows Backups. There are Policies, BackupTargets, and FileSpecs. All the other cmdlets are there to manipulate these objects or to actually run the backups themselves. You can force a backup to run at anytime using the Start-WBBackup cmdlet and you can make it run with a policy that you just created without setting it as the backup policy. This is useful for one-time backup runs with a specific policy instead of the standard backup policy that is set in place.

SUMMARY

In this chapter, you were introduced to the new version of PowerShell and given a brief description of its new features. After reading this chapter, you should have a good understanding of the PowerShell cmdlets that are often used with Windows Server 2008 R2. The early parts of the chapter introduced you to the installation and requirements of PowerShell version 2.0 as well as to how easy it is to get help with cmdlets from inside PowerShell. The section on Active Directory cmdlets walked you through some of the more popular Active Directory tasks. You performed some Active Directory User tasks. You created a new user using the New-ADUser cmdlet. You were introduced to two different creation steps, from scratch and from a template using the –Instance flag. You got the user information, modified some of it, and finally deleted the user using the get-ADUser, the set-ADUser, and remove-ADUser cmdlets, respectively. You also performed some group-based tasks where you created a new group using the New-ADGroup cmdlet. You created one from scratch and one from another group using the –Instance flag. You got the group information using the Get-ADGroup cmdlet and set some of the properties like changing it from a security group to a distribution group using the Set-ADGroup cmdlet with the –GroupCategory flag. You also learned how to add users to the groups with the Add-ADgroupMember cmdlet. You also learned how to delete a group as well using Remove-ADgroup. You then moved on to Active Directory Organizational Units. You created an OU using New-ADOrganizationalUnit. You changed some of the properties on the OU and got its Identity with the Get-ADOrganizationalUnit cmdlet. You also touched upon how to delete the OU with the Remove-ADOrganizationalUnit cmdlet as well as how to add groups and users to the OU using the Move-ADObject cmdlet.

The next section covered the AppLocker cmdlets and how they help the administrator manage AppLocker policies. You used the New-AppLockerPolicy cmdlet to create your own AppLocker Policy. You then tested the properties of the policy you created with the Test-AppLockerPolicy cmdlet and then you applied it as the local policy using the Set-AppLockerPolicy cmdlet. You also tried an example to see if the AppLocker policy would block a new malicious file.

The next section introduced you to the installation of the Failover cmdlets as well as the required Server Manager setup for Failover support. You then ran through some basic Failover Cluster administrative tasks like creating a new cluster. You tested the cluster first to see if it was adequate for a Failover Cluster using the Test-Cluster cmdlet. You then created the cluster with the New-Cluster cmdlet. You then added a role to the cluster, looked for available disks, and added one using the Add-ClusteredDisk cmdlet. You then ran through some of the tasks dealing with the nodes in a Failover Cluster. You checked their status with the Get-ClusterNode cmdlet and added a new node to the cluster with the Add-ClusterNode cmdlet. You also stopped and started a node with the Stop-ClusterNode and

Start-ClusterNode cmdlets as well as paused and resumed a node with the Suspend-ClusterNode and Resume-ClusterNode cmdlets. The next administrative tasks you performed involved Failover Cluster resources, disks. You got the disk information and then turned maintenance on for a disk using the Suspend-ClusterResource cmdlet. You then turned maintenance off for the disk using the Resume-ClusterResource cmdlet. You then did some ClusterGroup operations. You stopped a cluster group, moved it, and restarted it using the appropriate cmdlets.

The next section you tackled was the section dealing with all the new Group Policy cmdlets. You saw how to create a new GPO using the New-GPO cmdlet. You then modified some of its properties and deleted it. You then restored it using the Import-GPO cmdlet along with the –CreateIfNeededFlag. You then did some muscle flexing with GPO links using the appropriate cmdlets. You created a new Group Policy link using the New-GPLink cmdlet. You then enabled it using the Set-GPLink cmdlet and the –LinkEnabled flag. Last, you removed the link using the Remove-GPLink cmdlet. You then moved on to Group Policy Inheritance and Permissions. You blocked inheritance on a GPO using the –IsBlocked flag along with the Set-GPInheritance cmdlet. You changed some of the permissions on a GPO using the Set-GPPermissions cmdlet.

Next, we moved on to the Server Manager cmdlets and performed some examples of adding and taking away features using the Add-WindowsFeature and Get-WindowsFeature cmdlets. You used Get-WindowsFeature to see what features were available and what features were installed. You then installed and removed the telnet client and saw how PowerShell showed the differences in state using an X inside a [].

Last, we covered the Windows Backup cmdlets and went through some of the important administrative tasks involving Windows Backups. You created a new Windows Backup Policy using the New-WBPolicy cmdlet. You then added all the properties you wanted it to have like the capability to create backups that can be used for bare metal recovery. You then set the backup location for the policy. You then created some Windows Backup File Spec objects to control what was going to be backed up from where and what was to be excluded. Finally, you set the policy you created as the active Windows Backup Policy and set up its schedule to run.

After going through all these tasks, you should have a good grasp of just how powerful PowerShell is; how it can do almost anything in Windows Server 2008 R2 from the command line that an administrator can do using a wizard or interface. You should be able to see that because of its wide base of capabilities from Active Directory and Group Policy functions to Windows Backup scheduling, it is the perfect tool for automation. You can write a single script that can do a task that needs to be done on several machines and save yourself the time of going to each machine and going through the wizard or GUI to accomplish the task. With this knowledge, you can design and run scripts and cmdlets custom-tailored to your environment that will increase your productivity and efficiency. You will be more productive since once you write a script, it will always be there if you need it again and can be run again with one command. You will not have to go through the GUI another time. It will increase your efficiency since if you only write it once and make sure it works, then it should be error-free from then on.

12

Windows Server 2008 R2 monitoring and troubleshooting

As a Windows administrator, it is critical that you understand how to properly monitor your Windows servers for errors and warnings that may indicate problems. Additionally, you need to understand how to ensure that your Windows servers are performing optimally. You also need to know how to use the various tools available to troubleshoot problems with the operating system and applications. In this chapter, we will explore the various tools and features available in Windows Server 2008 R2 to ensure that your systems are proactively monitored for problems. We will also explore tools that will help you troubleshoot problems when they occur.

PERFORMANCE MONITORING

As a Windows administrator, it is important that you monitor the performance of your servers. Performance monitoring should be done proactively and used to create baseline performance statistics for your servers. By establishing baselines for "normal" performance, you can locate performance issues more quickly by looking for deviations from the baselines established over time. Some performance statistics do have best practice results that have been established by Microsoft product groups; however, this does not negate the need for you to establish your own baselines.

Understanding Performance Monitor

Windows Server 2008 R2 includes the Performance Monitor utility to help administrators easily gather and analyze performance data. Using Performance Monitor, you can monitor and capture data from various counters provided by the operating system. Before using Performance Monitor, you should understand the following terms:

■ *Performance counters*—Counters are the various components and objects that can be monitored using Performance Monitor. These are installed either as part of the operating system or by an application running on the server. Counters are also added when new roles are added. Examples of counters include % of Processor Time, Memory—Available Bytes, Logical Disk—% Free Disk Space.

■ *Instances*—Instances allow you to view data more granularly from a specific counter. For example, you may want to use the Processor "% of Processor Time" counter to view processor utilization. You can use the instances option to limit viewing the utilization of processors 1 and 3 only or of all the processors in the server.

In the following exercise, we will go through the process of using Performance Monitor to view performance data in real time and start collecting data to establish a baseline for some key performance indicators.

Performance Monitor is located under the Diagnostics node in Server Manager. To open Performance Monitor, perform the following:

1. Open *Server Manager*.
2. Expand the node *Diagnostics | Performance | Monitoring Tools*.
3. Select the node *Performance Monitor* (see Figure 12.1).

To monitor performance of a specific Windows component, you simply need to add it to the Performance Monitor main window. This is done by clicking the *Add* button at the top of the Performance Monitor window. This button is represented by a green plus sign as seen in Figure 12.2.

After clicking the *Add* button, the Add Counters window will appear (see Figure 12.3).

In this window, you can select the counters and instances you want to monitor. If you need a brief description of a counter, you can select the *Show Description* option. Table 12.1 lists some of the common objects and a brief description of what each object's counters captures:

NOTES FROM THE FIELD

Performance Monitoring management server

Performance Monitor can not only monitor the local server, but also has the ability to connect to remote servers and workstations to collect performance information from them as well. You may find it beneficial to set up a management server to centrally collect performance data from a set of servers opposed to running Performance Monitor on each system individually.

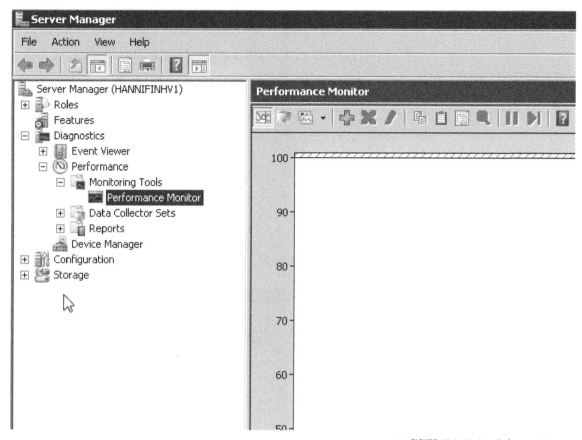

■ **FIGURE 12.1** Windows Performance Monitor.

Now that you have an understanding of Performance Monitor, let us take a look at adding counters to be display performance information:

1. Within the Performance Monitor window, click the *Add* button to open the Add Counters window.
2. Select a counter you wish to monitor, such as the % Processor Time counter. Select the instances; in this case, we wish to monitor all the processors in the system so select *All Instances*. Then click *Add*. This will move the counter to the Added Counters pane as seen in Figure 12.4.
3. Click *OK*. You will see a line graph with lines representing the percentage of utilization for each processor in the system (see Figure 12.5).

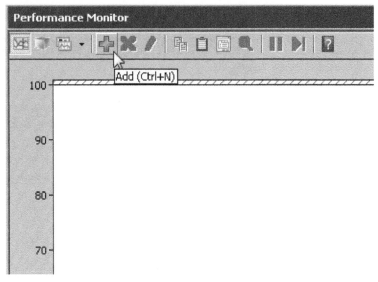

■ FIGURE 12.2 Add Performance counters.

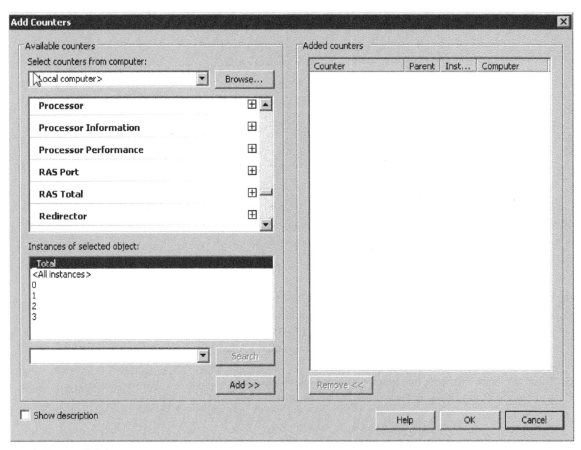

■ FIGURE 12.3 Add Performance counters.

Table 12.1 Common Performance Objects

Object	Description
Logical disk	Logical disk counters gather performance data related to logical disk drives (C:, D:, etc). These counters include % of Free Space, % Disk Read Time, % Disk Write Time, Average Disk Queue Length, and Free Megabytes. You will especially want to establish thresholds for free disk space counters to ensure you don't run out of free space on your server disk drives.
Memory	Memory counters allow you to monitor everything from available free megabytes to number or pages per second. Memory is often the number one bottleneck on servers so you should pay special attention to these counters. Since Windows servers page certain memory information to disk, you will want to ensure that excessive paging does not occur by monitoring Pages Per Second. You additionally will want to monitor available megabytes and committed bytes.
Processor	The processor performance counters monitor various aspects of processor performance. Though modern day processors are very fast, some processor intense applications such as SQL Server, can still see bottlenecks caused by poor processor performance. You will specifically want to monitor % of Processor Time. If you see a processor flat lined at 100% utilization, you know your server is very unresponsive and need to action immediately.
Physical Disk	Physical disk counters are used to measure the performance of the physical disk drive. Common counters include % Disk Read Time, % Disk Write Time, and Average Disk Queue Length.
Network Interface	Network Interface counters allow you to measure the performance of server network adapters including bytes sent or received per second, Current bandwidth, Packet Outbound Errors, and Packet Receive Errors. These counters can be helpful in monitoring utilization of the network adapter and troubleshooting adapter connectivity issues.

You can optionally change how you view the graph, using the change graph button (see Figure 12.6). You can choose between a line, histogram bar, or a table displaying values.

Later in this chapter, we will explore using Data Collector Sets to capture performance data over a period of time.

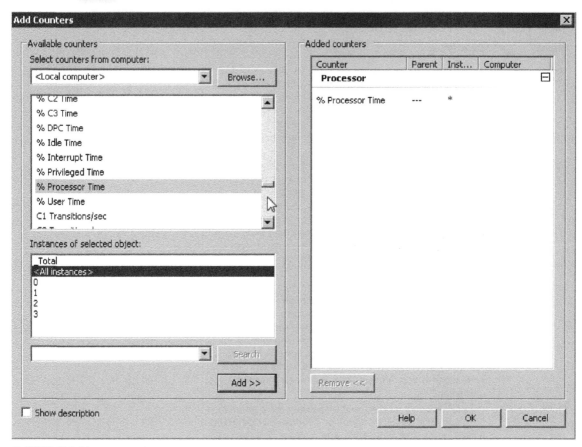

■ **FIGURE 12.4** Select counter to view.

NOTES FROM THE FIELD

Where is the reliability monitor?

You may remember that Windows Server 2008 R1 included the Reliability Monitor that continuously monitored your system for reliability. This included critical system errors and configuration changes such as installing new applications. You will notice that the Reliability Monitor is no longer available in Server Manager in Windows Server 2008 R2. The monitor still exists and is disabled by default. To enable the reliability monitor, you will need to change the registry key HKEY_LOCAL_MACHINE\SOFTWRE \Microsoft\Reliability Analysis\WMI. Set WMIEnable equal to "1." You will then need to ensure that the RacTask scheduled task is set to run. You can then access the reliability monitor from the Windows Action Center.

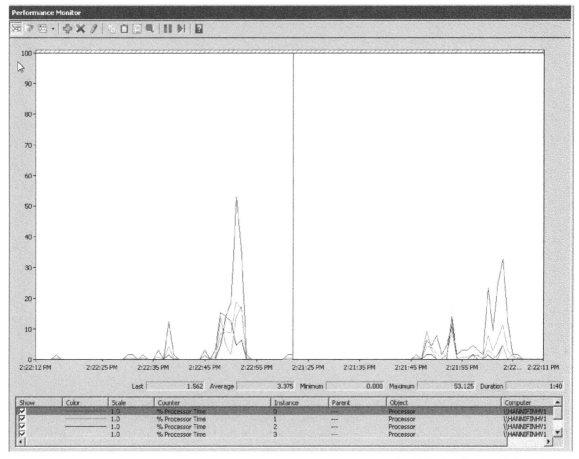

USING TASK MANAGER AND RESOURCE MONITOR

Windows Server 2008 R2 provides two utilities that allow you to quickly look at key performance statistics. Additionally, Task Manager allows you to manage open applications and processes including the ability to set a weighted priority on specified processes.

Task Manager

Task Manager provides a quick way to view important performance information, open applications and processes, and a list of users currently logged on to the server. Task Manager is broken down into the following six tabs:

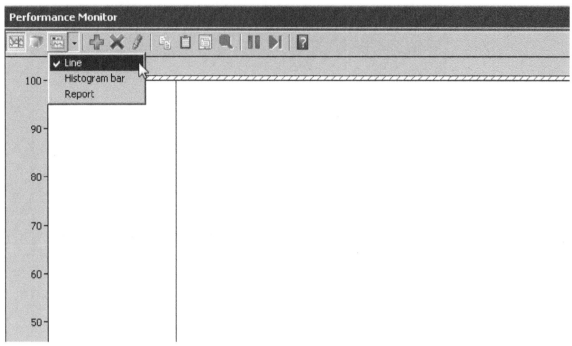

■ **FIGURE 12.6** Change performances graph type.

- *Applications*—The Applications tab lists all the currently running applications. If an application becomes unresponsive, you can select an application and click the End Task button to force the application to close.
- *Processes*—The Processes tab lists all the currently running processes for the user. By selecting the option "Show processes from all users," a full list of processes running for all the currently logged-on users will be displayed. You can use this tab to force unresponsive processes to close. Additionally, you can select a process and give it a higher or lower priority compared to other processes. In most cases, you will not need to set process priority but it may be helpful when performing troubleshooting or placing a particular line of business application higher on the priority list than a backup process. You can also use the Processes tab to set processor affinity for processes. This allows you to set certain processes to run on defined processors of the system. This gives an administrator the ability to manually split up the work load between processors. In most cases, this is unnecessary as Windows does a great job of balancing processing requests between processors.

- *Services*—The Services tab lists all the currently running Windows Services. From this tab, you can view all the current services on the server. You can also use this tab to stop and restart Windows Services.
- *Performance*—The Performance tab displays key performance statistics from a high level. You can see current processor utilization, used and available memory, and current uptime of the system.
- *Networking*—The Networking tab can be used to monitor the utilization of network adapters installed in the server. This can be beneficial to reviewing whether a specific network adapter is being overutilized. This tab is also beneficial to verifying that you have properly set up multipathing for network adapters connected to iSCSI networks. You should see traffic flowing evenly over both iSCSI network adapters.
- *Users*—The Users tab displays all the users who are currently logged on to the system. You can use this tab to send a pop-up message to a given users session, or force a logoff of a selected user.

Task Manager is one of the most heavily used tools for quick troubleshooting of Windows performance problems. Its ability to provide a high-level view of performance and ease of access makes this tool a valuable asset to Windows administrators. To access Task Manager, simply right click on the Windows task bar and select the option *Start Task Manager*. This will launch the main Task Manager window as seen in Figure 12.7.

Resource Monitor

The Resource Monitor (see Figure 12.8) is another useful utility included as part of the Windows Server 2008 R2 operating system. Resource Monitor is similar to Task Manager in that it provides high-level performance information including a list of running processes and the processor and memory resources they are consuming. However, Resource Monitor will also provide information about how many disk reads and writes a process is requesting per second as well as the number of bytes sent to and received from the network. You can also use Resource Monitor to suspend and resume processes if necessary. This can be useful if you want to temporarily put a process in a wait state instead of completely ending it.

Both Resource Monitor and Task Manager are valuable tools to provide you a high-level overview of key performance statistics and can help you locate any applications or services that may be causing performance problems. Additionally, you can take actions such as closing offending applications and the processes that support them.

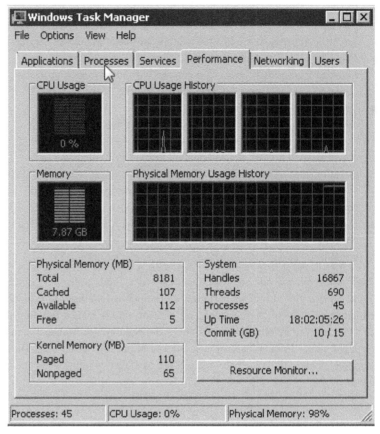

■ FIGURE 12.7 Task Manager.

EVENT VIEWER

The Windows Event Viewer could arguably be the most valuable tool available to troubleshoot Windows problems. The Event Viewer allows you to view the Windows Event Logs. Windows Event Logs have been part of the Windows operating system for years and provide detailed information related to proactive warnings of potential problems, and critical error events that may be caused by an operating system problem or an application crashing. Additionally, the Windows Event Logs collect security-related events such as network logons, users accessing audited files, and incorrect password attempts. Windows includes three main logs included as part of the operating system. The event viewer will allow you to view and search these logs:

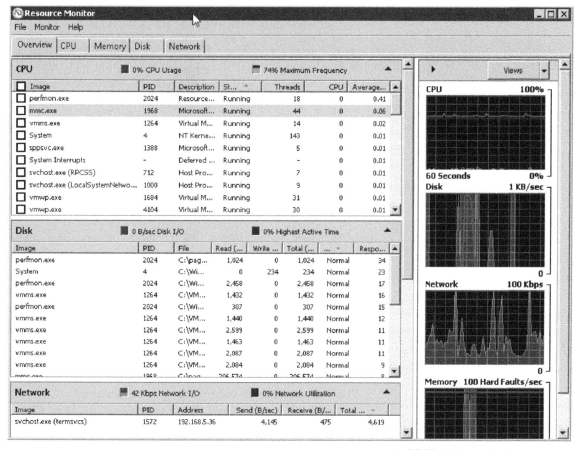

■ **FIGURE 12.8** Resource Monitor.

- *System*—The System log contains events related to the overall server operating system. These can include everything from informational events informing you that a service stopped or started to error information related to operating system crashes.
- *Application*—The Application log contains events related to applications running on the server. If a particular application experiences problems, it may write error events to the application log. Many third-party applications utilize the Application event log to log errors for applications developed for Windows.
- *Security*—The Security log contains events related to failed or successful security events that have occurred on the system. For example, if Bob logs on to the network, the authenticating domain controller will write an event to its security event log, stating that Bob

has been successfully authenticated. If auditing is turned on, any audit-related events, such as object access, are added to the Security log.

Windows also uses a Setup event log and a Forwarded Events log. The Setup log contains events related to installing/removing applications and services. Using this log, you can easily track new applications or services added to the server. The Forwarded Events log contains events from other servers that have been forwarded. Windows Server 2008 R2 allows you to configure servers to forward events to another server's event log, giving you as the administrator the ability to centrally view and search events. Events from remote servers show up in the Forwarded Events log on the central server.

Configuring event-based tasks

Windows Server 2008 R2 allows you to configure an automated task to take place based upon the occurrence of a specific event being written to the event log. For example, you could set up a task to restart a windows service when an event was logged that the given service was stopped. Let us look at setting up an event-based task:

1. First we need to trigger the event causing it to be written to the event log. In our exercise, let us stop the Windows service—DHCP Client. The service can be stopped by opening *Server Manager*, expanding the *Configuration* node, and clicking on *Services*. Locate the service *DHCP Client*. Right click the service and choose *Stop*.
2. Expand the *Diagnostics | Event Viewer | Windows Logs* node. Then select the *Application* log.
3. Locate the newly created event indicating that the DHCP Client service stopped (see Figure 12.9).
4. Right click on the event, and select *Attach Task to this Event*. This will launch the Create Basic Task Wizard.
5. Enter a name and description for the task (see Figure 12.10). Then click *Next*.
6. Verify the event information. Then click *Next*.
7. Select the option *Start a program*. Then click *Next*.
8. Enter the command to start the service (see Figure 12.11). Then click *Next*.
   - ❑ Program/script—Net
   - ❑ Add Arguments—Start DHCP
9. Verify the settings, and then click *Finish*.

Now start the DHCP Client Service, and then stop it again. You should see the service immediately restart.

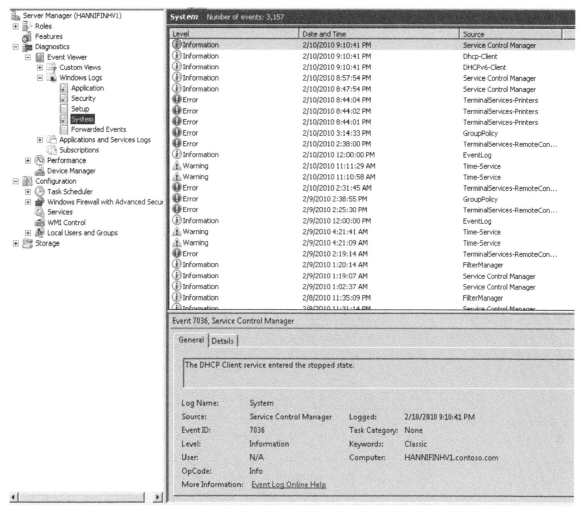

Setting up event log forwarding

We will now take a look at setting up a Windows server to forward event logs to a central log collection server. In this exercise, we will forward critical, error, and warning events logged to the system log from labclusnode1 to labdc1. To set up forwarding, perform the following:

1. Open *Server Manager* on LABDC1 (Central Log Collection Server).
2. Expand the node *Diagnostics | Event Viewer* and then select the *Subscriptions* node.

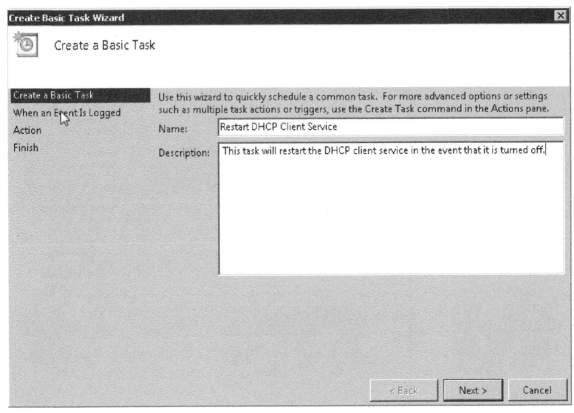

3. When prompted to enable the Windows Event Collector Service, click *Yes* (see Figure 12.12). This service is required to collect remote logs and store them on the central log collection server.

4. We now need to create a new subscription to the logs on the remote server (LABCLUSNODE1). This can be initiated from the collector server or the remote server. In this exercise, we will initiate log collection from the central log server. To create a subscription, right click the *Subscriptions* node. Then select the option *Create Subscription*. This will open the *Subscription Properties* window.

5. Enter a meaningful name and description for the subscription.

6. Select the destination log where you want collected events saved—typically, this will be the Forwarded Events log.

7. Select the subscription type and source computers (see Figure 12.13). As mentioned, in this exercise we will use the option *Collector*

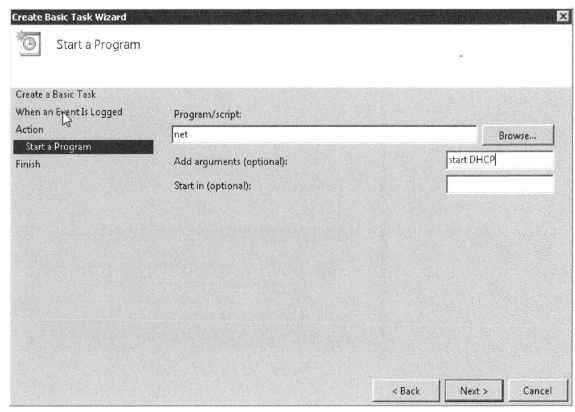

■ **FIGURE 12.11** Task command to restart service.

Initiated. Click the *Select Computers…* button to add the remote source computer you wish to collect logs from and add the server *LABCLUSNODE1*.

8. You now need to set up a filter to collect only the critical, warning, and error events from the System log. Click *Select Events* to launch the Query Filter window.

9. Select the options for *Critical*, *Warning*, and *Error*. Then select the *System* log, as seen in Figure 12.14.

10. Click *Advanced* to configure the account we will use to collect events. This account will need read permissions to the logs on the remote server. Click *User and Password* and enter the username and password with permissions to read the event logs from the source server (LABCLUSNODE1) as seen in Figure 12.15. Then click *OK*.

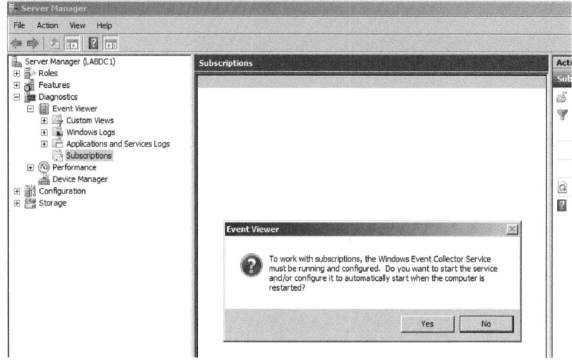

■ **FIGURE 12.12** Enabling Windows Event Collector Service.

11. Click *OK* to return to the Subscription Properties window.

12. Verify whether all information is correct, and then click *OK*.

You will now see the subscription listed under the Subscriptions node on the central log server (LABDC1). As the defined events are logged to the remote server, the subscription will collect the events from the remote server (LABCLUSNODE1) and forward them to LABDC1 where they will be logged to the Forwarded Events log.

Applications and Services Logs

The Applications and Services Logs were first introduced in Windows Server 2008 R1 (RTM) and contain events from individual applications, roles, and features. The Applications and Services logs are broken down into four subcategories to more easily debug and troubleshoot issues. The four subcategories are

■ *Admin*—Admin logs contain events about warnings or errors in the given application or service. Events in the admin logs will contain

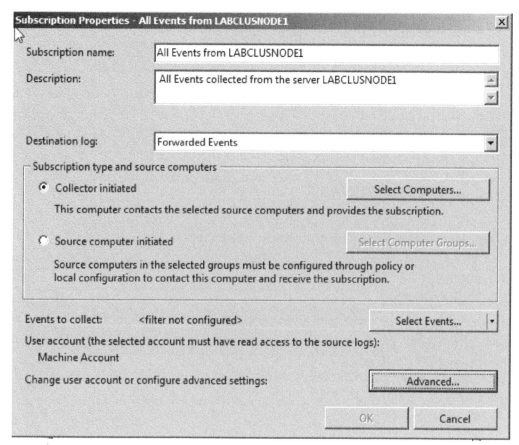

FIGURE 12.13 Select source computers.

detailed information about an error or warning in clear and easy to understand terms as well as information on how to resolve the issue.

- *Operational*—Operational logs provide error and warning events as well as informational events that can be used to further diagnose a problem.
- *Analytic*—Analytic logs provide detailed diagnostic information related to an error or warning. Analytic logs can be somewhat hard to understand and interpret but may be necessary when troubleshooting complex issues.
- *Debug*—The Debug logs provide very detailed diagnostic data that is typically not readable by an administrator. The Debug log is typically used by a developer, or Microsoft PSS support services to troubleshoot issues.

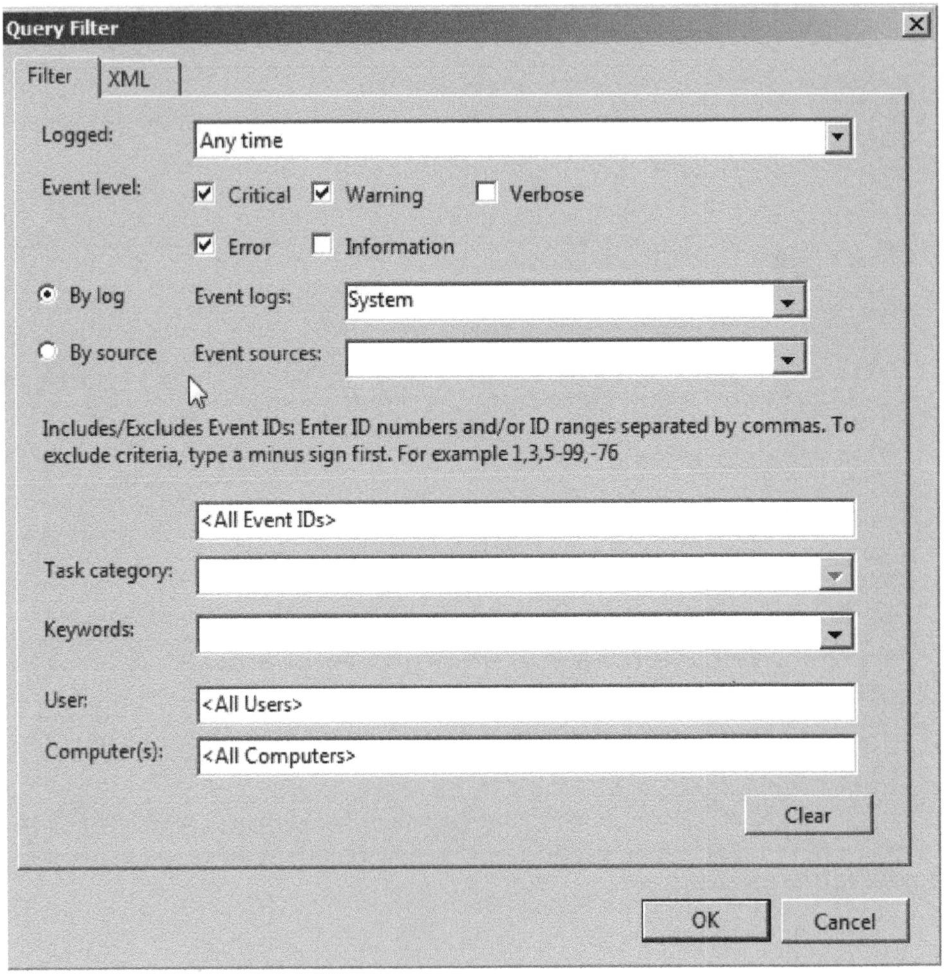

FIGURE 12.14 Subscription Events filter.

DATA COLLECTOR SETS

Data Collector Sets are groups of performance counters, event logs, and system information that can be used to collect multiple data sets on-demand or over a period of time. For example, you can set up a Data Collector Set to collect processor utilization, and available memory over a 10-min period. Typically, a report will be generated providing detailed information regarding the data collected and recommended fixes to performance issues. Data Collector Sets are broken down into two categories:

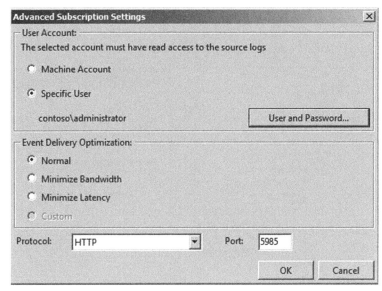

■ **FIGURE 12.15** Advanced Subscription Settings.

- *User Defined*—User-Defined Data Collector Sets are created and configured by an administrator. These are custom sets that contain counters, event logs, and trace information defined by the administrator.
- *System*—System Data Collector Sets are automatically created and defined by the operating system, applications, and components. By default, two data collector sets are created during the initial install of Windows Server 2008 R2. These are Systems Diagnostics and Systems Performance, as seen in Figure 12.16. These Data Collector sets gather core operating system information.

After a Data Collector Set is created, it is ready to be run. The Data Collector Set can be run manually or scheduled. During the run process, the collector will gather data based upon its defined settings. After the data collection has run, a report will be generated under the reports node. The report will contain results of the data collection process as any detected performance problems and information on how to correct the problems.

Running a System Data Collector Set

Let us take a look at running one of the System Data Collector Sets and reviewing the results created in the report:

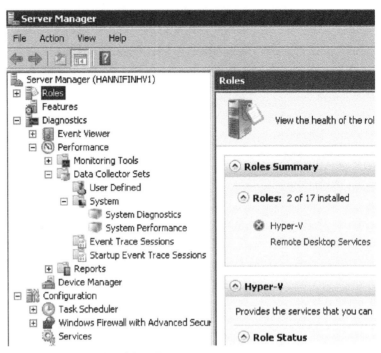

■ **FIGURE 12.16** System Data Collector Sets.

1. Open *Server Manager*.
2. Expand the node *Diagnostics | Performance | Data Collector Sets | System*.
3. Right click the *System Performance* Data Collector Set and choose the option *Start*. This will start the data collection process. While the process is running, you will see a green arrow icon on the Data Collector Set (see Figure 12.17).
4. When the Data Collector Set is complete, you will see a new report generated under the Reports node as seen in Figure 12.18.
5. You can now review the report containing the performance data collected. This report can be reviewed in the report console or sent to a printer.

Creating a custom Data Collector Set

Now that you have run Data Collector Set, we will go through the process of creating a new custom Data Collector Set. To create a custom Data Collector Set, perform the following:

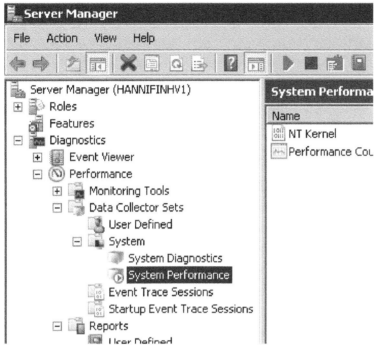

■ **FIGURE 12.17** Data Collector Set running.

1. Open *Server Manager*.
2. Expand the node *Diagnostics | Performance | Data Collector Sets*.
3. Right click *User Defined* and choose *New | Data Collector Set*. This will launch the New Data Collector Set wizard.
4. Enter a descriptive name for the Data Collector Set, choose the option *Create Manually*, and then click *Next*.
5. You now need to select what types of data you want to collect. In this example, we will select *Performance counter* and *System configuration information*. Then click *Next*.
6. Add the *% of Processor Time* counter as seen in Figure 12.19. We will keep the default sample interval of 15 s. This means that the data collector set will take a measurement of processor utilization every 15 s. Click *Next* to continue.
7. The Data Collector Set will use registry keys to determine system configuration information. You can add keys in the Registry Keys window, as seen in Figure 12.20. Then click *Finish*.

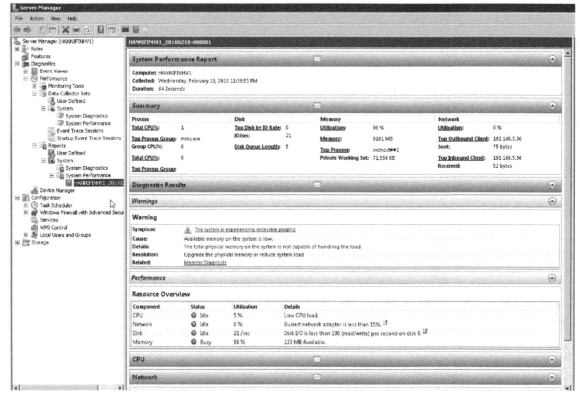

■ **FIGURE 12.18** Data Collector Set report.

You can now run the data collector, using the same steps used to run the System Data Collector Sets in the previous exercise.

WINDOWS MEMORY DIAGNOSTIC

Windows Server 2008 R2 includes a built-in tool for diagnosing memory errors in the server's RAM memory. If Windows detects an error, it will automatically launch the memory diagnostics tool, as seen in Figure 12.21. You can also manually run the tool from *Start | All Programs | Windows Memory Diagnostic*.

SYSTEM CENTER OPERATIONS MANAGER 2007 R2

If you need to manage and monitor a large number of servers, you may want to consider Microsoft's flagship server monitoring product,

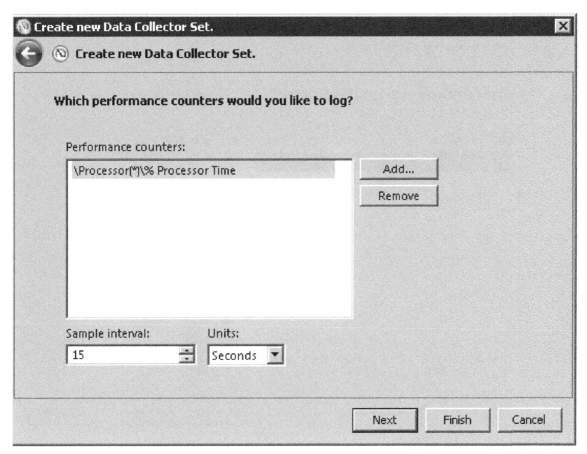

■ **FIGURE 12.19** Data Collector Set performance counters.

System Center Operations Manager (SCOM) 2007 R2. SCOM is an enterprise class systems and network monitoring solution allowing you to monitor key events and performance information. In the event that a server or application becomes unhealthy whether a server goes offline or a processor is overutilized, SCOM can be configured to send you notifications via e-mail, SMS text, or IM and even take corrective actions such as restart services or run scripts. If you need to monitor a large number of servers proactively, you will want to consider deploying SCOM.

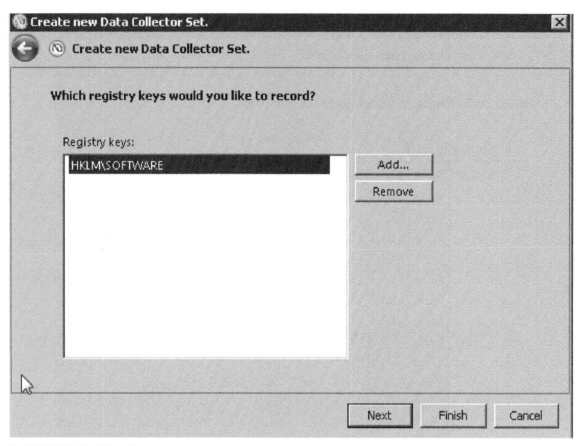

■ **FIGURE 12.20** Data Collector Set system
configuration Registry keys.

SUMMARY

In this chapter, we explored the tools necessary to ensure that your
Windows servers are performing efficiently to support your network infrastructure and applications. We discussed using tools such as Performance
Monitor and Data Collector sets to proactively create performance
baselines that can be used to ensure that Windows servers are performing
optimally. This chapter also covered using event logs to look for root
causes of problems as well as setting up a central logging server where

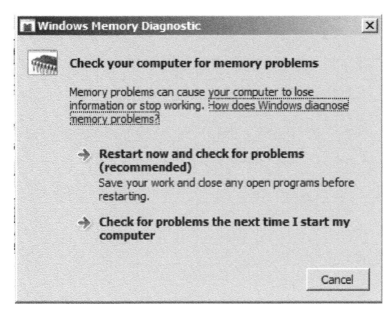

■ **FIGURE 12.21** Windows Memory Diagnostic tool.

events from remote servers can be sent for monitoring and review. We concluded this chapter by briefly discussing how System Center Operations Manager 2007 R2 can be used to proactively monitor your Windows Server 2008 R2 servers.

Windows Server 2008 R2 and Windows 7

Windows Server 2008 R2 includes several features and services that allow the server operating system to work in tandem with Windows 7, the client operating system. Features such as BranchCache and DirectAccess require Windows Server 2008 R2-based servers, and Windows 7 clients. Due to this requirement, you may want to consider deploying Windows 7 along with, or shortly after, your Windows Server 2008 R2 deployment.

In this chapter, we will discuss features that leverage both the Windows Server 2008 R2 and Windows 7 operating systems. We will explore how to plan for and deploy BranchCache within your network. We will also discuss planning and deploying DirectAccess to provide remote VPNless connectivity for Windows 7 clients.

OVERVIEW OF BRANCHCACHE

As previously mentioned in this book, BranchCache is a new feature available in Windows Server 2008 R2 and Windows 7. BranchCache provides a better end-user experience for users opening files across a Wide Area Network (WAN) by caching a copy in the branch office after the document or intranet Web site is opened for the first time. The cached copy can be stored on a branch office server running Windows Server 2008 R2 (hosted mode) or a Windows 7 client (distributed mode). When a second client attempts to open the same file, it is opened from the cached copy as opposed to attempting to access the file over the WAN. Figure 13.1 depicts what a typical BranchCache deployment might look like.

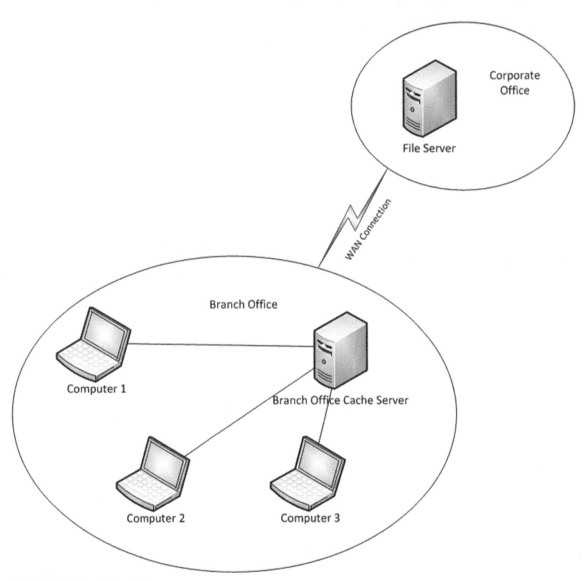

■ **FIGURE 13.1** Example BranchCache deployment.

By deploying BranchCache, you can not only improve the end-user experience, but also decrease traffic load on your WAN circuits. However it is important to remember that to take advantage of BranchCache, you need to deploy both Windows Server 2008 R2 servers (for hosted mode) and Windows 7 clients (for client access and distributed mode).

> **NOTES FROM THE FIELD**
>
> **BranchCache used for read access only**
> BranchCache is used for reading a file or Web site only. Write operations require the client to perform the write process back to the original source across the WAN.

PLANNING TO DEPLOY BRANCHCACHE

Prior to installing BranchCache on your network, you need to properly design and plan for your deployment. As with all features, you should properly test the deployment in a lab to verify your design and configurations. In this section, we will discuss things you need to consider when planning to deploy BranchCache within your organization.

Deployment options

BranchCache can be deployed in the following modes:

- *Hosted Mode*—BranchCache Hosted mode uses a Windows Server 2008 R2 server located in the BranchOffice to store the cache. When Windows 7 clients access a cached copy of a file or Web site, they access it on the branch office server with BranchCache installed. Hosted mode is recommended for larger branch offices, and offices that have a considerable amount of mobile users.
- *Distributed Mode*—BranchCache Distributed mode uses Windows 7 clients to host the branch office cache. When a Windows 7 client accesses a cached copy of a file, it pulls it from the cache of a peer Windows 7 computer. This does not require a Windows server in the branch office but if a computer with a cached copy of a file is offline, the other branch office computers must pull a new copy from the original source across the WAN. Distributed mode is recommended only for offices with less than 15 users and preferably with mostly desktop workstations. Figure 13.2 depicts how distributed mode works in Windows 7.

> **NOTES FROM THE FIELD**
>
> **BranchCache Distributed Mode security**
> Even though BranchCache deployed in Distributed mode uses a peer-to-peer configuration, file security is still enforced. When using distributed mode, the local cache is encrypted and can be accessed only by users that have been given access to the specific files.

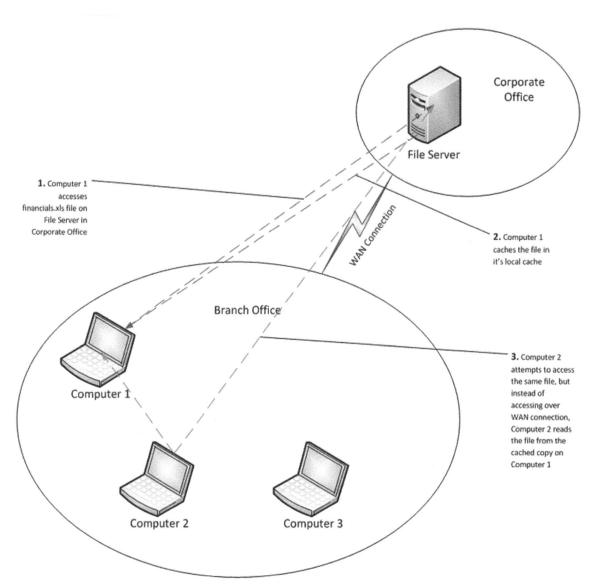

1. Computer 1 accesses financials.xls file on File Server in Corporate Office

2. Computer 1 caches the file in it's local cache

3. Computer 2 attempts to access the same file, but instead of accessing over WAN connection, Computer 2 reads the file from the cached copy on Computer 1

■ **FIGURE 13.2** BranchCache using distributed mode.

When deploying BranchCache, you will need to select the mode that best fits your branch office locations. You must choose a mode for each office; however, you can mix modes between branch offices. For example, a larger office with 100 users can have a hosted mode deployment, while a smaller office of 10 users can use distributed mode.

Prerequisites

The use of BranchCache requires that client and servers meet certain minimum operating system requirements. The main operating system requirements are outlined here.

Hosted BranchCache mode—When using hosted BranchCache mode, the branch office cache server must be running Windows Server 2008 R2 Enterprise, Windows Server 2008 R2 Itanium, or Windows Server 2008 R2 Datacenter editions.

Distributed BranchCache mode—Distributed mode requires that all clients, which also host the cached copy of files, be running Windows 7 Enterprise or Windows 7 Ultimate.

Client computers—Client computers must be running Windows 7 Enterprise or Windows 7 Ultimate to take advantage of BranchCache.

Additionally, any Web server that you wish to be cached in branch offices requires that the BranchCache feature be installed. For source servers that you wish to allow files to be cached in branch offices, you will need to install the BranchCache for Network Files role.

BranchCache certificates

When deploying BranchCache using hosted mode, each branch server hosting the cache will need a certificate from an internal Public Key Infrastructure (PKI) or third-party certificate provider.

NOTES FROM THE FIELD

BranchCache and WAN accelerators

BranchCache cannot be used across WAN connections that are using WAN acceleration appliances. These devices are configured to compress and optimize data performance across a WAN. If your network uses any of these devices, you will more than likely not be able to set up and use BranchCache.

Designing a BranchCache deployment

There are several aspects to designing a BranchCache deployment. You need to consider things such as

- Number of workstations in branch offices. In larger branch offices, you may need to use multiple servers to cache content for performance reasons. The number of workstations may impact on your decision to deploy a hosted deployment or a distributed deployment.

- Are branch office users mobile or stationary? If you have a highly mobile workforce, it may not be efficient to deploy BranchCache in a distributed fashion.
- Are workstations running Windows 7? If you still have workstations on your network running Windows XP, they will not take advantage of BranchCache features.
- Does the branch office have servers deployed? If there are no servers in the branch office you will need to deploy them if you plan to use a hosted mode configuration.
- If using a distributed deployment, how much disk space is available on workstations? If your workstations in the branch office do not have adequate disk space available, they will not be able to cache files properly.
- If using hosted deployment, you will need to deploy a certificate authority to obtain a third-party certificate.

You will need to properly document and test your design before rolling into production. As with all deployments, proper testing needs to be performed before making modifications to your production environment. The figures given earlier in this section depict what a typical BranchCache design might look like. You will want to create similar drawings of your deployment as part of your design process.

DEPLOYING BRANCHCACHE

After you have properly designed your BranchCache solution, you will be ready to test your design. In this section, we will explore the process of setting up and testing BranchCache. In this lab, we will be using a central file server (LABFS1) and a hosted mode cache server (LABBC1).

First we need to set up the file server to support BranchCache features. On LABFS1, perform the following:

1. Open *ServerManager*.
2. Select the *Roles* node then click the link *Add Roles*.
3. Click *Next* to start the Add Roles Wizard.
4. Select the *File Services* role. Then click *Next*.
5. On the File Services summary page, click *Next*.
6. Select the role services *File Server* and *BranchCache for network files* (see Figure 13.3). Then click *Next*.
7. Verify the settings on the confirmation page, and then click *Install*.
8. After the installation finishes, click *Close*.

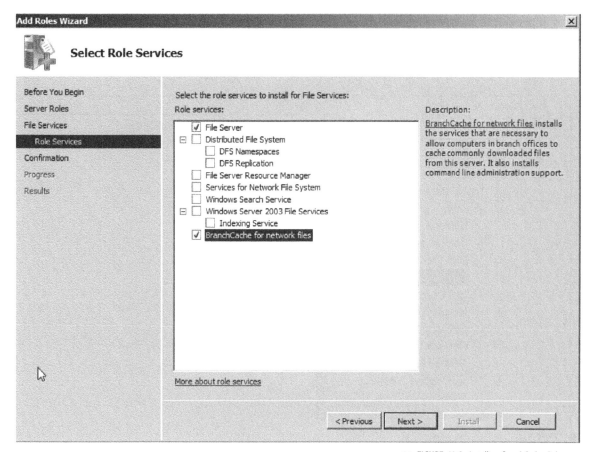

■ **FIGURE 13.3** Installing BranchCache Role Service.

Note that BranchCache does not add an administrative node to the Server Manager interface.

After adding the role service, you will need to configure hash publication. This can be done by creating an Active Directory group policy or by modifying the local group policy on the file server. In this exercise, we will configure hash publications, using the local policy on the file server. To configure hash publication, perform the following:

1. Open the Local Group Policy Editor by opening *Start | Run*. Then type *gpedit.msc* and click *OK*.
2. Expand the nodes *Computer Configuration | Administrative Templates, Network, Lanman Server*.

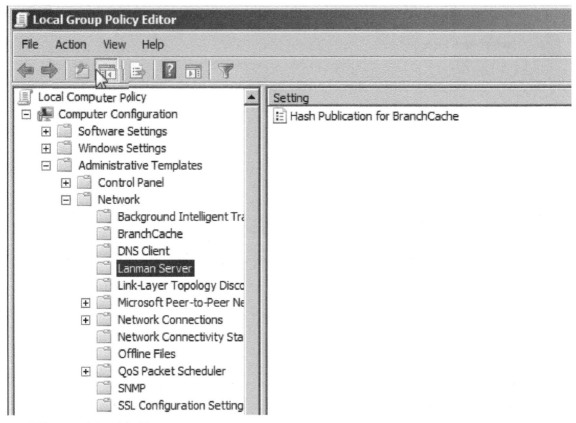

■ **FIGURE 13.4** Local Group Policy Editor.

3. Select the node *Lanman Server* as seen in Figure 13.4.
4. Open the policy object *Hash Publication for BranchCache* from the middle pane.
5. Select the option to *Enable* the policy. Then select the option to *Allow hash publication for all shared folders* (see Figure 13.5). Then click *OK*.

After enabling hash publication, you will need to enable BranchCache on shared folder that you wish to be cached in the branch office. Perform the following to enable BranchCache on a shared folder:

1. Open the Share and Storage Management console from *Start | Administrative Tools | Share and Storage Management*.
2. Right click on the shared folder you want to enable BranchCache and choose *Properties*. This will open the shared folder properties window as seen in Figure 13.6.

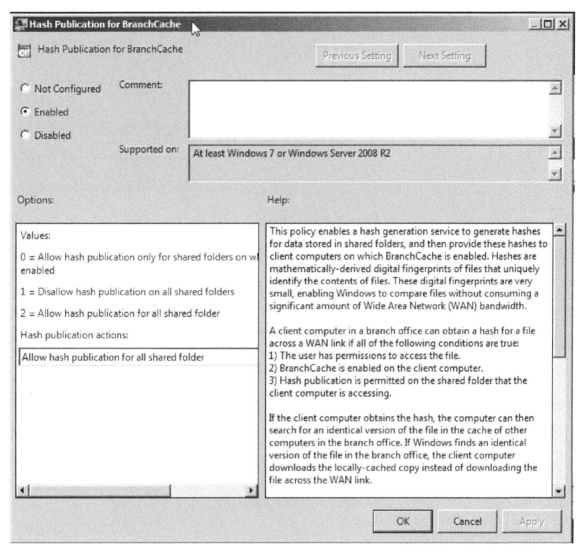

FIGURE 13.5 Enable Hash Publication.

3. Click *Advanced* to open the Advanced window. Then click the *Caching* tab as seen in Figure 13.7.

4. Select the option *Enable BranchCache*. Then click *OK*.

5. Click *OK* to close the shared folder properties window.

After enabling shared folders for BranchCache, you need to enable the branch office hosted cache server for BranchCache. The first step to

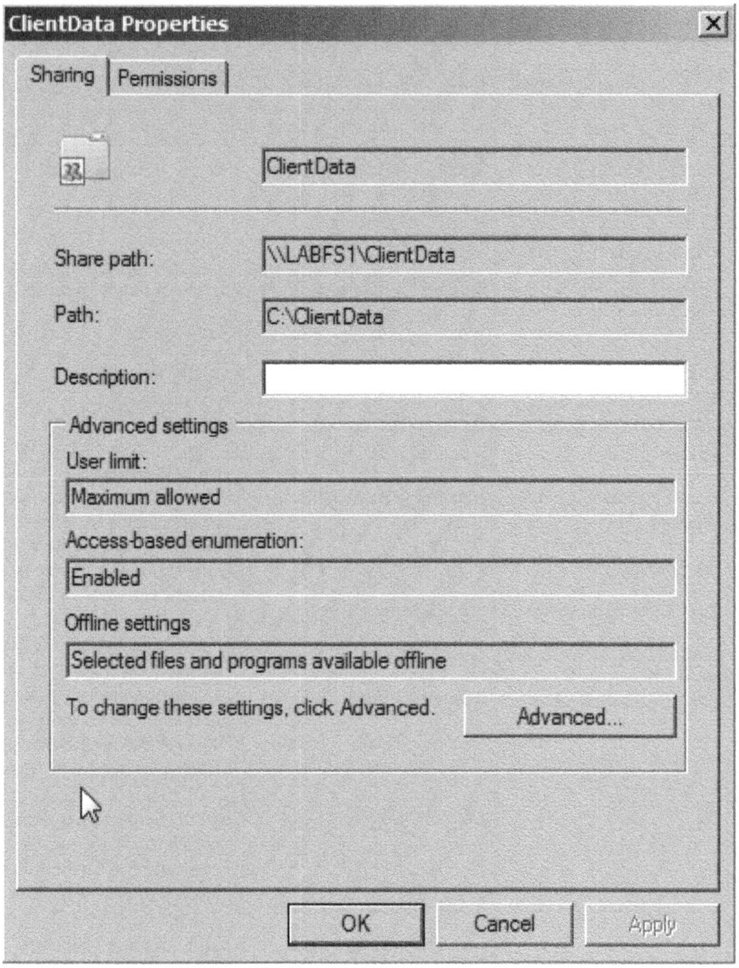

FIGURE 13.6 Shared Folder Properties.

perform this is to install the BranchCache feature. This is done by performing the following:

1. Open *Server Manager*.
2. Select the *Features* node. Then click the *Add Features* link in the middle pane.
3. Select the *BranchCache* feature as seen in Figure 13.8. Then click *Next*.
4. Verify settings on the confirmation page. Then click *Install*.
5. When the installation is complete, click *Close*.

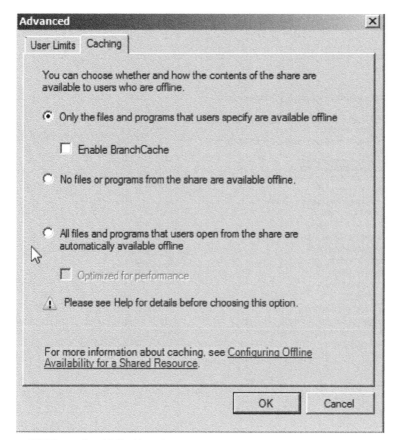

■ **FIGURE 13.7** Shared Folder Advanced settings.

After adding the BranchCache feature, you will need to enable the hosted cache mode and open correct firewall ports to allow this server to host cached files. This process is done via a command prompt, using the netsh command. Perform the following to enable hosted cache mode:

1. Open a command prompt from *Start | All Programs | Accessories | Command Prompt.*
2. Type the command: `netsh branchcache set service mode=HOSTEDSERVER`. Then hit *Enter.*

You should see several success confirmations as seen in Figure 13.9. After verifying whether the hosted cache has been enabled, close the command prompt.

One of the final steps to setting up BranchCache in hosted mode is to configure certificates on the branch office server hosting the cache. In our

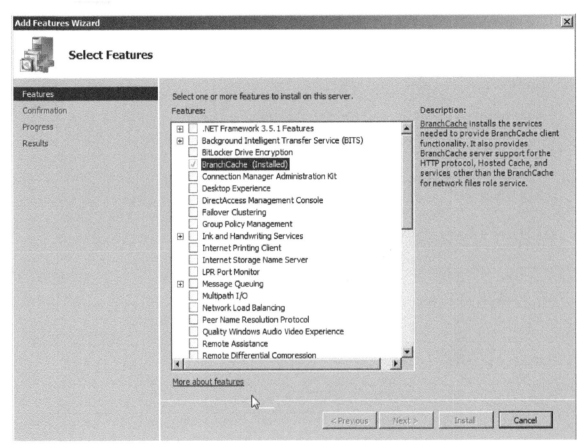

■ **FIGURE 13.8** Adding the BranchCache
Feature.

exercise, we will assume that a certificate authority has already been
deployed on the network. The first procedure we need to complete is to
configure the Web server certificate template and enable autoenrollment
on the hosted cache server, using the following steps:

1. Log on to the server with Active Directory Certificate Services
   installed and open *Server Manager*.
2. Select the node *Roles | Active Directory Certificate Services |*
   Templates.
3. Locate and right click the *Web Server* template in the middle pane.
   Then choose *Duplicate* (see Figure 13.10).
4. Choose the option *Windows Server 2003 Enterprise* as the version.
   Then click *OK*. The *Properties of New Template* window will open.

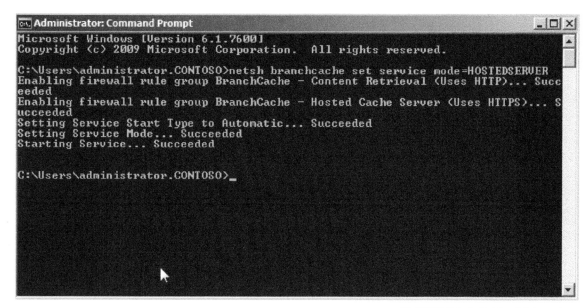

5. On the General tab, give the new template enter a meaningful name as seen in Figure 13.11.
6. Select the *Subject Name* tab and then select the option *Build from this Active Directory Information*.
7. Select the option *Fully Distinguished Name* from the drop-down menu (see Figure 13.12).
8. Select the *Security* tab. Add the hosted cache server name as seen in Figure 13.13.
9. Select the option to allow *Enroll* and *AutoEnroll* for the hosted cache server (see Figure 13.14). Then click *OK*.
10. In the left pane of the Server Manager window, expand the node of the certificate authority and select the *Certificate Templates* node (see Figure 13.15).
11. Right click the *Certificate Templates* node and choose the option *New | Certificate Template to Issue*.
12. Select the newly created template as seen in Figure 13.16. Then click *OK*.

After creating the new template, you will need to configure your domain for autoenrollment. If you have already deployed Active Directory Certificate Services for other PKI-dependent applications, you may have

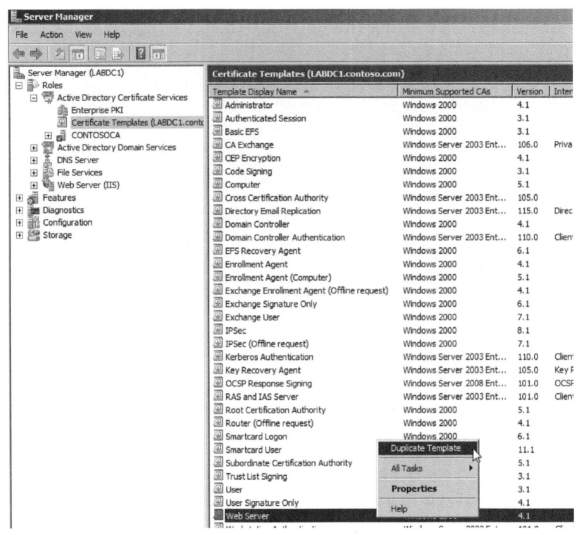

■ FIGURE 13.10 Duplicate Web Server template.

already enabled this setting. If not, it can be done by performing the following:

1. Log on to a domain controller and open *Group Policy Management* from *Start | Administrative Tools | Group Policy Management*.
2. Expand the nodes *Forest | Domains | <your domain name>* (see Figure 13.17).

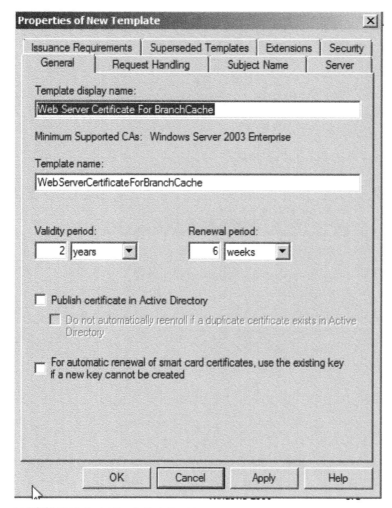

FIGURE 13.11 Naming New Certificate Template.

3. Right click the *Default Domain* policy and select *Edit*.
4. Select the node *Computer Configuration | Policies | Windows Settings | Security Settings | Public Key Policies*.
5. Open the policy object *Certificate Services Client—AutoEnrollment* as seen in Figure 13.18.
6. Select the option *Enabled*. Then select both *Renew expired certificates, updating pending certificates, and remove revoked certificates* and *Update certificates that use certificate templates* options (see Figure 13.19). Then click *OK*.

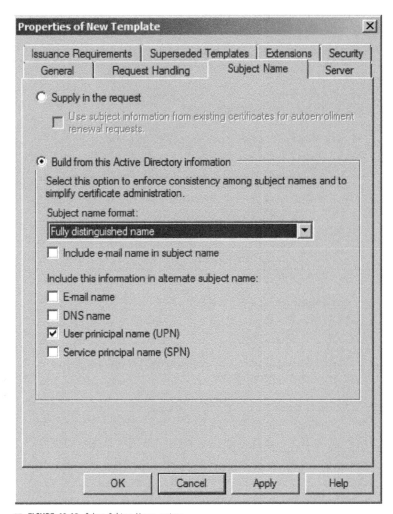

■ **FIGURE 13.12** Select Subject Name options.

7. You can now force autoenrollment to occur on the hosted cache server by logging onto that server and running gpupdate from a command prompt.

After configuring certificates for the hosted cache server, you need to link the certificate to BranchCache. This is done by obtaining the SHA-1 hash from the server's certificate and then using the netsh command to link the certificate. To complete this process, perform the following:

1. Open a new mmc console by opening a new dialog from *Start | Run*. Then type mmc in the run prompt and click *OK* (see Figure 13.20).

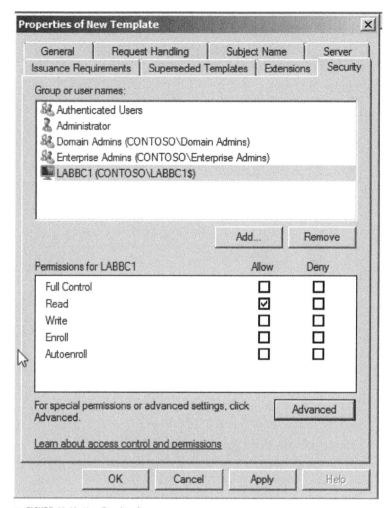

■ **FIGURE 13.13** New Template Security settings.

2. From the new mmc console, go to *File | Add/Remove Snap-in....*
3. Add the *Certificates* snap-in from the options as seen in Figure 13.21.
4. When prompted whether you would like to manage certificates for user, computer, or service, select the *Computer* option and then choose *Local Computer*.
5. From the MMC console, expand the nodes *Certificates | Personal | Certificates*. Then open the server certificate as seen in Figure 13.22.
6. Select the *Details* tab in the Certificate window.

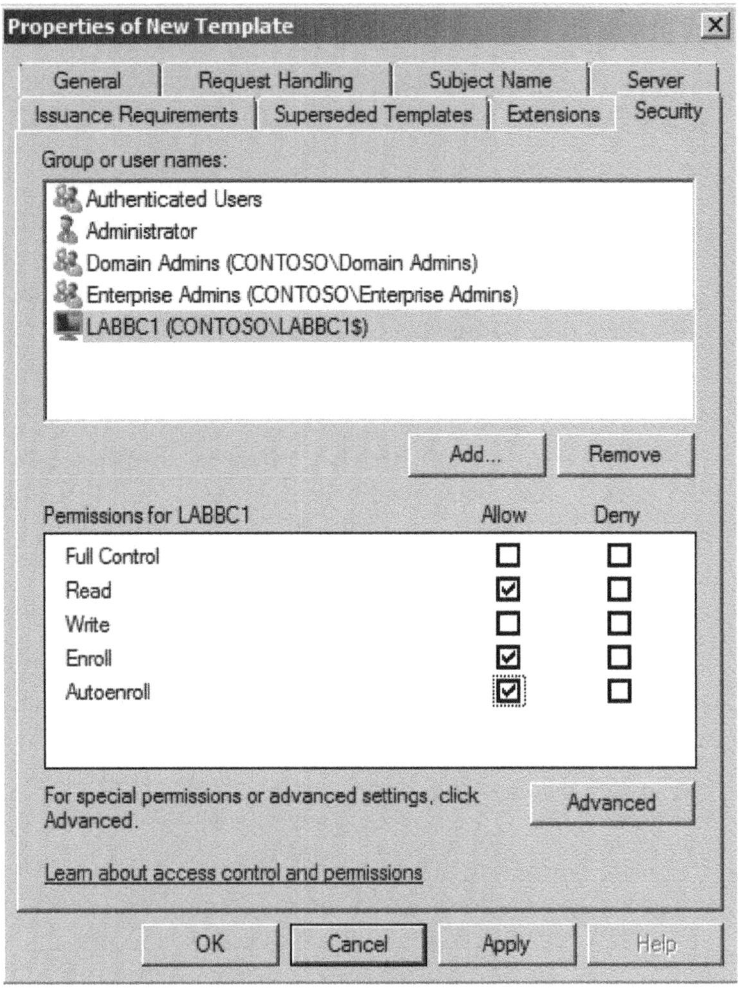

■ **FIGURE 13.14** Allow Enroll and AutoEnroll for the Hosted Cache Server.

7. Scroll through the fields in the details view and select the *Thumbprint* field as seen in Figure 13.23.
8. Copy the SHA-1 hash by selecting the hex-formatted number and using the Ctrl-C keystroke.
9. Open Notepad and paste the SHA-1 hash to verify whether it has been copied correctly (see Figure 13.24). Correct the formatting of the hash by removing all the spaces creating one long hexadecimal number. This is the number we will need to link the certificate to BranchCache.

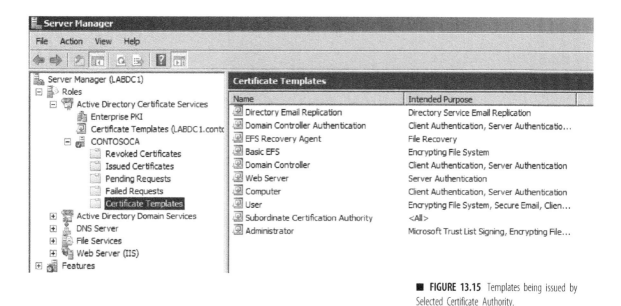

■ FIGURE 13.15 Templates being issued by Selected Certificate Authority.

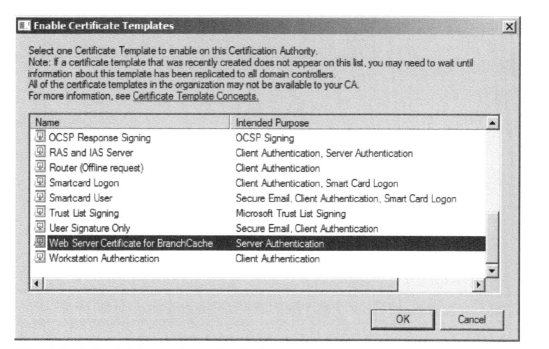

■ FIGURE 13.16 Allow Certificate Authority to Issue Certificates From New Template.

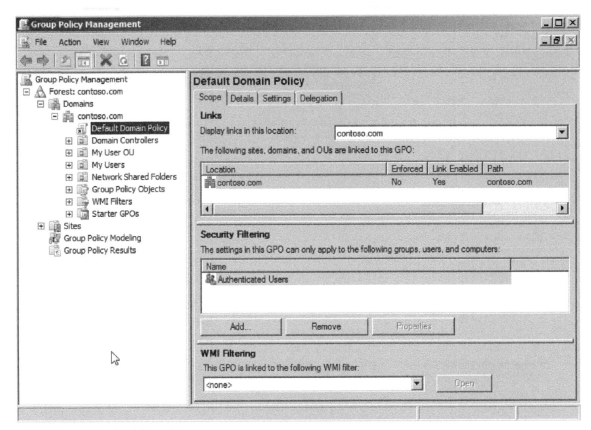

■ **FIGURE 13.17** Editing Default Domain Policy.

10. Open a command prompt on the hosted cache server and enter the following command netsh command which includes the SHA-1 hash we copied from Step 9. `netsh http add sslcert ipport=0.0.0.0:443 certhash=e8d749b788e9229c72bc672160499ccd265ae0ba appid={d673f5ee-a714-454d-8de2-494e4c1bd8f8}`.

You have now successfully completed the process of setting up the BranchCache hosted cache server. As clients begin caching files locally, they will be saved in the cache of this server. Now, you only need to configure client computers to use the hosted branch cache. This can be done on a Windows 7 client by using the netsh command: `netsh branchcache set service mode=HOSTEDCLIENT`. You can additionally update multiple Windows 7 clients to use the hosted cache by deploying a GPO which can perform the same functions.

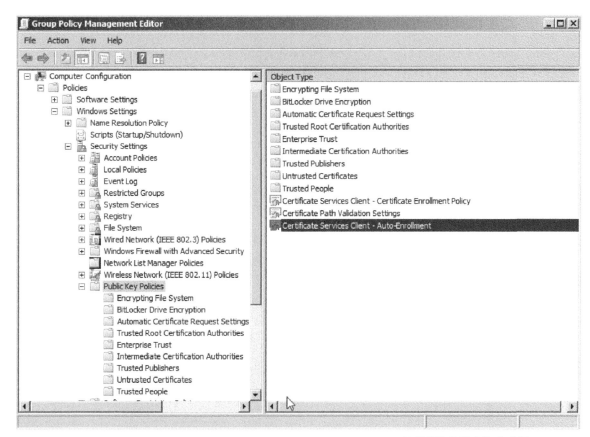

■ **FIGURE 13.18** Public Key Policies.

OVERVIEW OF DIRECTACCESS

DirectAccess, one of the most anticipated features of Windows Server 2008 R2, is Microsoft's new remote connectivity solution for Windows networks. DirectAccess allows companies to provide secure remote access to their corporate network without the need for Virtual Private Networks (VPN) connections. Connections are made from Windows 7 workstations and use IPSec security to create a DirectAccess tunnel between the workstation and the Windows Server 2008 R2 DirectAccess server located on the corporate network. Not only can workstations access the corporate network using DirectAccess, but management servers such as antivirus and patch management can also connect push updates to workstations that are connected via DirectAccess. This helps ensure that mobile users continue to get regular updates even when they are not physically in the

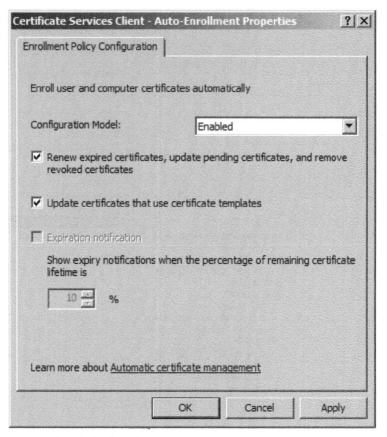

■ **FIGURE 13.19** AutoEnrollment Properties.

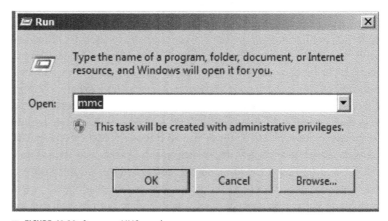

■ **FIGURE 13.20** Open new MMC console.

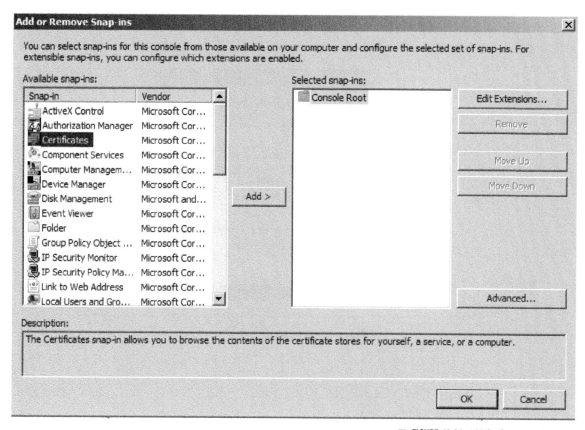

FIGURE 13.21 Add Certificates snap-in.

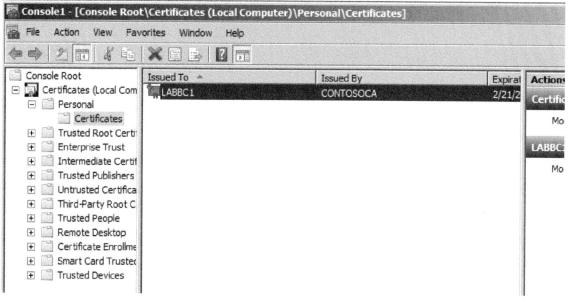

FIGURE 13.22 Certificates MMC console.

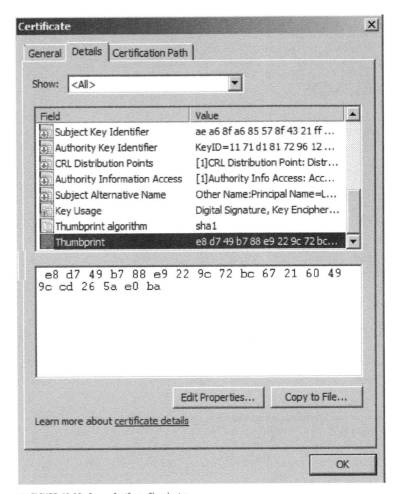

■ **FIGURE 13.23** Server Certificate Thumbprint.

office. DirectAccess requires both Windows Server 2008 R2 to be deployed for DirectAccess services and Windows 7 clients. Windows Vista, XP, and earlier clients cannot use DirectAccess services. Figure 13.25 provides a high-level overview of how DirectAccess works.

PLANNING TO DEPLOY DIRECTACCESS

DirectAccess is an exciting remote connectivity feature that many administrators may want to implement on their networks; however, it can be a complicated deployment without proper planning.

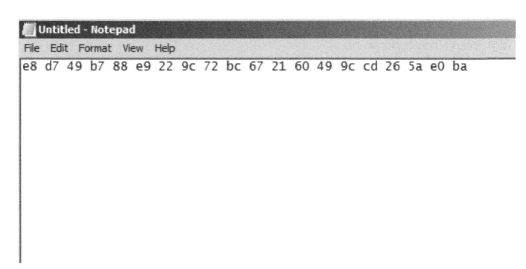

■ **FIGURE 13.24** SHA-1 Hash.

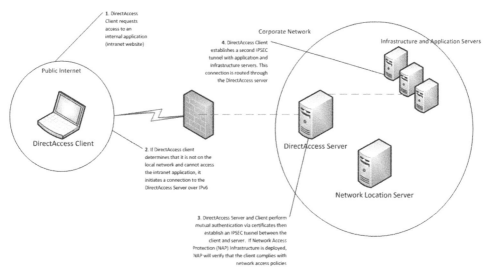

■ **FIGURE 13.25** DirectAccess overview.

DirectAccess Requirements

To deploy DirectAccess, you will need to ensure that your servers and network meet the minimum requirements outlined in Table 13.1.

IPv6 transition technologies defined

Some of the key IPv4 to IPv6 transition technologies used by DirectAccess are defined below:

Table 13.1 DirectAccess Requirements

Requirement	Description
IPv6 and IPv6 to IPv4 translation technologies	DirectAccess has a fundamental dependency on IPv6. Since most organizations, including Internet Service Providers (ISPs), have not yet replaced their IPv4 infrastructure with IPv6, IPv6 translation and transition technologies such as 6to4, Teredo, IP-HTTPS, and ISATAP are required to provide remote connectivity using DirectAccess.
Windows Server 2008 R2 (DirectAccess Server and Network location server)	You will need at least one Windows Server 2008 R2 server to host the DirectAccess Server and Network location server roles. This server must be running Windows Server 2008 R2 or later, have at least two network adapters with consecutive IPv4 addresses (not behind a NAT firewall).
Windows 7 (DirectAccess Client)	Windows 7 Ultimate, Enterprise, or Windows Server 2008 R2 are the only supported clients for DirectAccess. Windows Vista, XP, and earlier will not be able to use DirectAccess services.
Public Key Infrastructure	Active Directory Certificate Services, or another supported PKI service is required to issue certificates that will be used for authentication.
Active Directory	DirectAccess requires an Active Directory domain with at least one domain controller running Windows Server 2008 R1 (RTM) or Windows Server 2008 R2 that is also acting as a global catalog server. The DC must also have IPv6 enabled. Additionally, DNS services must be set up that support DNS over Intra-Site Automatic Tunnel Addressing Protocol (ISATAP). ISATAP can be enabled on Windows Server 2008 R2 DNS servers.

- *Teredo*—Teredo is a standards-based protocol that provides IPv6 connections for IPv4-based computers that are behind an IPv4-based NAT. Teredo is a key technology allowing organizations to make IPv6 connections without changing IP addressing of computers on their internal private subnets.
- *6to4*—6to4 is a standards-based protocol that allows computers with public IPv4 addresses make IPv6-based connections over the IPv4-based Internet. 6to4 is a key technology allowing organizations to begin transitioning to IPv6 while the Internet at large continues to be based on IPv4.
- *IP-HTTPS*—IP-HTTPS is a Microsoft technology that allows Windows 7 and Windows Server 2008 R2 computers behind a firewall establish IPv6 connectivity over an IPv4 network by creating an IPv4-based tunnel in which IPv6 packets can travel.
- *ISATAP*—ISATAP is a standards-based technology that provides IPv6 connectivity across an IPv4-based internal network.

NOTES FROM THE FIELD

DirectAccess connectivity to IPv4 applications

Even though DirectAccess uses IPv6 transition technologies to allow clients to connect over IPv4 networks, you should understand that DirectAccess clients only use IPv6 traffic meaning that DirectAccess clients cannot connect to applications on the local intranet that use IPv4 only. For example, Microsoft Office Communications Server (OCS) 2007 R2 uses IPv4 only thus clients cannot connect to OCS over a DirectAccess connection. You can, however, provide connectivity to IPv4 applications using a IPv4-IPv6 translator device.

Understanding the DirectAccess Server and Network Location Server

Two core server role services must be deployed as part of your DirectAccess solution. These services provide connectivity for your DirectAccess clients. You will need at least one server acting as a DirectAccess and Network Location Server. You may choose to break out the Network Location Server on its own hardware, depending on your security and connectivity requirements. We will now describe DirectAccess role and Network Location Server in more detail.

- *DirectAccess Server*—The DirectAccess server is the primary connection point for DirectAccess clients. This server acts as the gateway for DirectAccess connectivity. As previously stated, the DirectAccess server has at least two network adapters. One adapter must be assigned two consecutive public IP addresses and connected to the Internet without going through NAT services. The second interface is connected to the private Intranet in which you want remote computers to connect.
- *Network Location Server*—Client workstation computers used the Network Location Server to determine whether they are located on the internal network or on a remote connection. The Network Location Server is an IIS-based Web server that hosts a network location URL that is accessed over HTTPS. This server is crucial for any DirectAccess deployment, but especially on networks with branch offices. Computers on the local network must be able to access the location URL to determine whether they are on the internal corporate network, or trying to connect remotely.

Designing your DirectAccess deployment

After you understand the key requirements for deploying DirectAccess, you will need to properly design your environment and create a deployment plan as well as test the deployment in a lab. There are a few key decision points you will need to make during your design, including whether to allow full network access for DirectAccess clients or limit which servers they connect to on the network. Your design may also vary depending on whether you have fully or partially deployed an IPv6-based infrastructure on your network. In our design discussion, we will assume that your network is still IPv4 based.

NOTES FROM THE FIELD

Deploying DirectAccess on an IPv4 network

When you set up the DirectAccess server, it will automatically check to see whether the network is IPv4 or IPv6 based and will modify its configuration accordingly. For example, if an IPv4 network is detected, the DirectAccess setup wizard will automatically configure ISATAP routing on the DirectAccess server.

Determining which access model to deploy

As part of your core design, you need to determine which resources you will allow to be accessed via DirectAccess connections. There are three main access types you can use for your deployment:

- *Selected Server Access*—Selected Server Access allows an administrator to configure which IPv6-based resources and applications that a DirectAccess client can access on the network. For example, you may want to prevent DirectAccess connections to more sensitive applications that should be accessed only when physically connected to the corporate network.
- *Full Intranet Access*—Full Intranet Access means that clients can connect to any IPv6-based application on your corporate network. This type of connectivity is similar to that provided by traditional VPN services.
- *End-to-End Access*—The end-to-end solution provides an even more secure option for DirectAccess connectivity by ensuring that client connectivity uses peer authentication over IPSec and encryption occurs not only over the Internet, but also over the Intranet. This ensures the highest level of security and data protection. It should be noted, however, that using this option will prevent access to IPv4-based applications, even when using an IPv4 to IPv6 translator device.

Planning for network firewall configuration

More than likely, you will have a network firewall in front of your DirectAccess server. You will need to ensure that specific ports and protocols are allowed to pass through the firewall to the DirectAccess server. The following IPv4-based traffic must be allowed to pass through your firewall to the DirectAccess server:

- *UDP Port 3544*—You will need to open UDP port 3544 inbound and outbound to and from the DirectAccess server for Teredo to function properly.
- *TCP Port 443*—You will need to allow TCP port 443 inbound and outbound to and from the DirectAccess server. TCP 443 is used to create IP-HTTPS-based connections between the DirectAccess server and client.
- *Protocol 41*—You will need to allow Protocol 41-based traffic to and from the DirectAccess server. Protocol 41 allows 6to4 technologies to work properly between the client and server.
- *ICMPv6 Echo Requests*—DirectAccess clients use ICMPv6 echo requests to ensure that the DirectAccess server is online. Clients also use ICMPv6 Echo to contact application servers on the network. You will need to be sure to allow ICMPv6 echo requests to all computers on the network that should be accessible via DirectAccess.

Designing your DirectAccess server layout

As part of your DirectAccess deployment, you will need to design and document the placement and configuration of the servers used in your deployment. If you already have a Windows-based network, you may already have Windows-based Active Directory, Certificate, and Web servers available on your network. These can be used and simply added to your DirectAccess design. They may, however, require some configuration changes or operating system upgrades to fulfill deployment requirements. You will want to properly document your design and create a visual representation, using a tool such as Microsoft Visio. Figure 13.26 provides an example of what a server layout design might look like for a DirectAccess deployment.

After you have successfully planned for DirectAccess, you will need to begin testing your deployment plan in a lab environment. After proper lab testing and remediation, you can begin preparing for a pilot deployment for production testing.

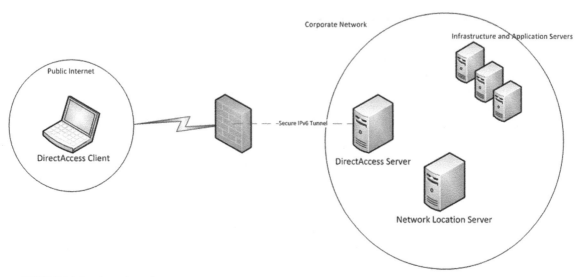

■ **FIGURE 13.26** DirectAccess design diagram.

DEPLOYING DIRECTACCESS

We will now go through setting up DirectAccess services using a single DirectAccess server for connectivity. We will be performing the following in this exercise to set up DirectAccess:

- Create A Certificate Template for computer autoenrollment
- Remove ISATAP from DNS global block list on corporate DNS Servers
- Create a CRL distribution point on the DirectAccess server
- Set up DirectAccess and Network Location Server on DirectAccess server

In our exercise, we will assume that you already have Windows Server 2008 R2 Active Directory Domain Services and Active Directory Certificate Services deployed on your corporate network. We will also assume that you have plugged one network adapter of the DirectAccess server into corporate local area network and one adapter into the network providing connectivity to the public Internet. We will also assume that certificate autoenrollment has already been enabled for your domain. The following sections will now take you through setting up DirectAccess.

Creating a certificate template for computer autoenrollment

Perform the following steps to create a new certificate template to be used for autoenrollment of network computers:

1. Log on to the server with Active Directory Certificate Services installed and open *Server Manager*.
2. Select the node *Roles | Active Directory Certificate Services | Templates*.
3. Locate and right-click the *Web Server* template in the middle pane. Then choose *Duplicate* (see Figure 13.27).
4. Choose the option *Windows Server 2008 Enterprise* as the version. Then click *OK*. The *Properties of New Template* window will open.
5. On the General tab, give the new template enter a meaningful name such as *Windows Server 2008 Web Server For AutoEnrollment*.
6. Select the *Security* tab.
7. Select *Authenticated Users* and choose the security options to enable for *Enroll* and *AutoEnroll*.
8. Add the group *Domain Computers* and also select the security setting to *Enroll* and *Autoenroll* (see Figure 13.28).
9. Select the *Request Handling* tab and choose the option *All private key to be exported* (see Figure 13.29). Then click *OK*.
10. In the left pane of the Server Manager window, expand the node of the certificate authority and select the *Certificate Templates* node (see Figure 13.30).
11. Right click the *Certificate Templates* node and choose the option *New | Certificate Template to Issue*.
12. Select the newly created template. Then click *OK*.

Removing ISATAP from DNS global block list

ISATAP can be removed from the DNS global block list by using the dnscmd command line utility. To remove ISATAP from the DNS global block list, log on to a Windows Server 2008 R2 DNS server and open a command prompt. Then enter the following command:

```
dnscmd/config/globalqueryblocklist wpad
```

After running dnscmd, you can close the command prompt and log off the DNS server.

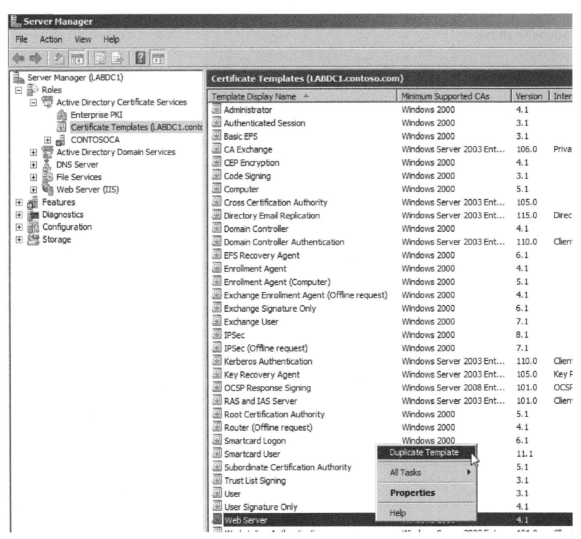

■ **FIGURE 13.27** Duplicate Web Server
Template.

Creating a certificate revocation list (CRL) distribution point on the DirectAccess server

In this section, we will configure a location on the DirectAccess server to store the CRL for clients connecting to the server. We will make this CRL web enabled by creating an IIS Web site on the DirectAccess server. We will then configure the Certificate Authority to publish the CRL to the

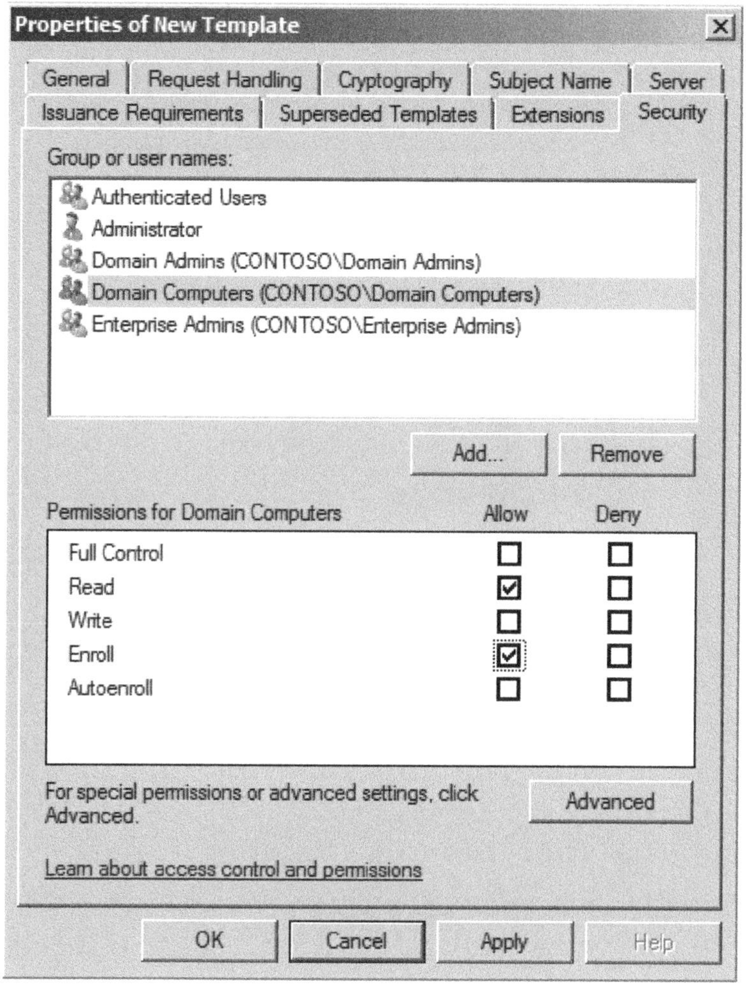

■ **FIGURE 13.28** Enable Enrollment using the Certificate Template.

DirectAccess server via a shared folder. To accomplish the above tasks, perform the following:

1. Log on to the DirectAccess server (LABDA1) and create a new folder on the root of C: named CRL (see Figure 13.31).
2. Add the Web server role by opening *Server Manager*.
3. Then select the *Roles* node and click the *Add Roles* link in the middle pane.
4. Click *Next* to begin the *Add Roles Wizard*.

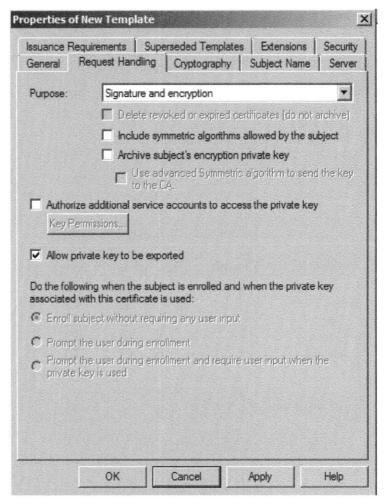

■ **FIGURE 13.29** Allow certificate private keys to be exported.

5. Select the *Web Server (IIS)* role as seen in Figure 13.32. Then click *Next*.
6. On the Introduction page click *Next*.
7. Accept the default role services and click *Next*.
8. Verify settings on the Confirmation Page. Then click *Install*.
9. When the installation is complete, click *Close* to close the Add Roles Wizard.

To create a Web site which will be used for web CRL distribution, perform the following:

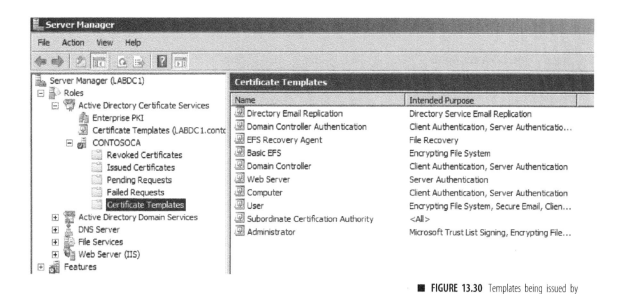

FIGURE 13.30 Templates being issued by selected Certificate Authority.

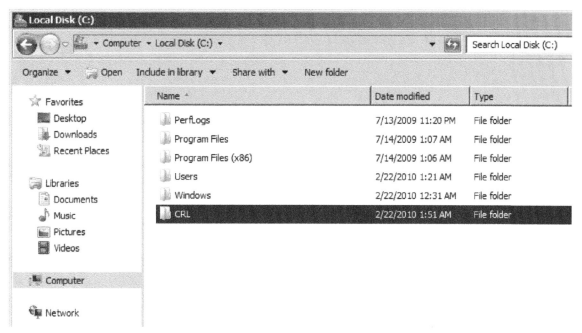

FIGURE 13.31 New folder to store CRL information.

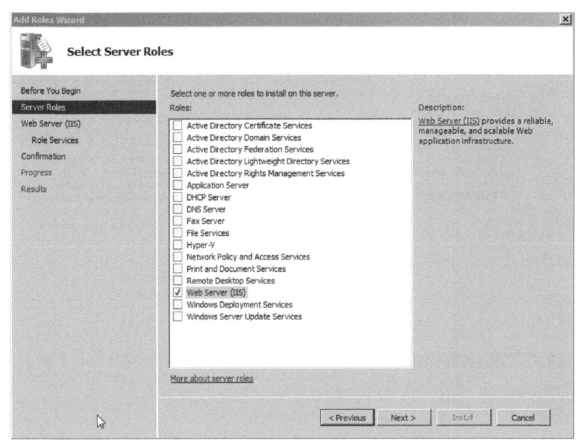

■ **FIGURE 13.32** Select Web Server Role.

1. Open *Server Manager* and expand the *Roles | Web Server (IIS)* nodes.
2. Select the newly added *Internet Information Services (IIS) Manager* node.
3. In the middle pane, expand the *Sites* node to reveal the *Default Website*.
4. Select the *Default Website* and then click the *Basic Settings* link in the right pane.
5. Change the *Physical path* to point to the CRL folder that you previously created (see Figure 13.33). Then click *OK*.
6. In the middle pane, double-click the *Directory Browsing* option. Then click the *Enable* link in the right actions pane as seen in Figure 13.34.
7. Close *Server Manager*.

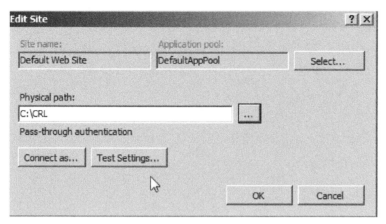

■ **FIGURE 13.33** Set Web Site home folder to CRL path.

■ **FIGURE 13.34** Allowing Directory Browsing of CRL Web Site.

We now need to share the CRL folder and give the Certificate Authority permission to access it. Perform the following steps to set up the CRL shared folder:

1. Browse to the CRL folder you previously created at the root of C:\. Right-click the CRL folder and choose *Properties*.
2. Select the *Sharing* tab and click the *Advanced Sharing* button as seen in Figure 13.35.

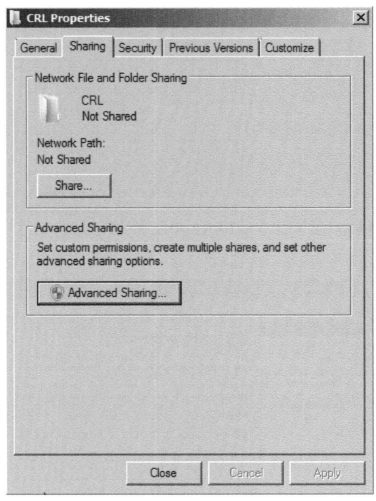

■ **FIGURE 13.35** Sharing Properties.

3. Click the *Share this folder* checkbox in the Advanced Sharing window. Then click the *Permissions* button (see Figure 13.36).
4. Click the *Add* button. Then click *Object Types*.
5. From the *Object Types* window, select *Computers* as seen in Figure 13.37. Then click *OK*.
6. Enter the name of the Certificate Authority computer and click *OK*.
7. Allow the CA computer *Full Control* permissions. Then click *OK*.
8. Click *OK* on the Advanced Sharing window and click *Close* on the Properties window.

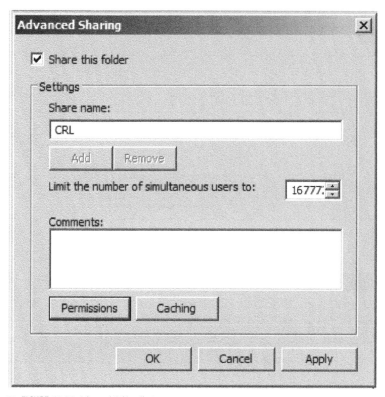

■ FIGURE 13.36 Advanced Folder Sharing.

You now need to enable the server as a CRL distribution point and publish the CRL to the distribution point. Perform the following to complete these tasks:

1. Log on to the Certificate Authority and Open *Server Manager*.
2. Expand the nodes *Roles | Active Directory Certificate Services*.
3. Right click the node representing the Certificate Authority, and select *Properties* (see Figure 13.38).
4. Select the *Extensions* tab in the CA Properties window.
5. Click *Add* to add a new CRL distribution point.
6. Enter the URL you wish to use for the CRL located on the DirectAccess server.
7. Select the variable *<CAName>* and click *Insert*.
8. Select the variable *<CRLNameSuffic>* and click *Insert*.
9. Select the variable *<DeltaCRLAllowed>* as seen in Figure 13.39. Then click *Insert*.

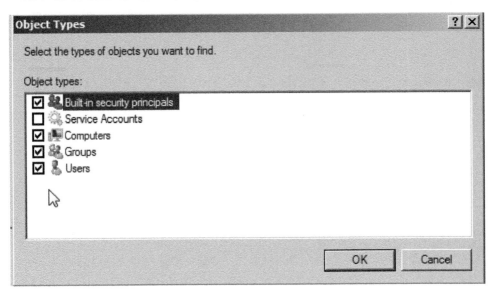

■ **FIGURE 13.37** Enable selection of the computer Object Type.

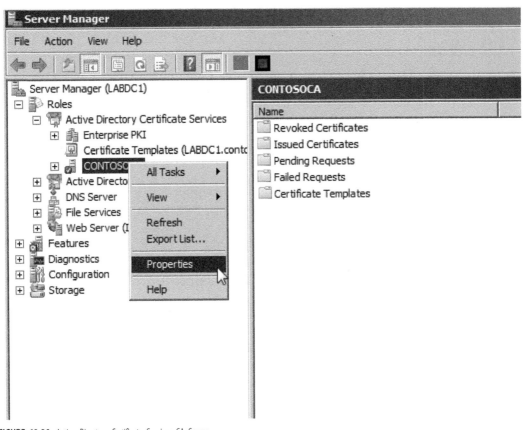

■ **FIGURE 13.38** Active Directory Certificate Services CA Server.

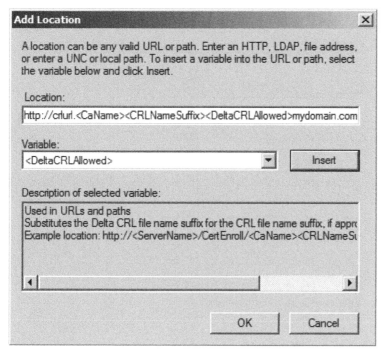

Add Location

A location can be any valid URL or path. Enter an HTTP, LDAP, file address, or enter a UNC or local path. To insert a variable into the URL or path, select the variable below and click Insert.

Location:

`http://crlurl.<CaName><CRLNameSuffix><DeltaCRLAllowed>mydomain.com`

Variable:

`<DeltaCRLAllowed>`   Insert

Description of selected variable:

Used in URLs and paths
Substitutes the Delta CRL file name suffix for the CRL file name suffix, if appr(
Example location: http://<ServerName>/CertEnroll/<CaName><CRLNameSu

OK   Cancel

■ **FIGURE 13.39** Add CRL Location.

10. Go to the end of the long URL string created in the Location field and enter a *.crl* at the end of the string. Then click *OK*.
11. Select the options *Include CRLs. Clients use this to find Delta CRL locations* and *Include in the CDP extension of issued certificates*.
12. Click the *Add* button.
13. In the Location text box, enter*locationofDAServer\CRL* (see Figure 13.40).
14. Select the variable *<CAName>* and click *Insert*.
15. Select the variable *<CRLNameSuffix>* and click *Insert*.
16. Select the variable *<DeltaCRLAllowed>* and click *Insert*.
17. Again add *.crl* to the end of the newly created location string as seen in Figure 13.41.
18. Select the option *Publish CRLs to this Location*.
19. Select the option *Publish Delta CRLs to this Location* (see Figure 13.42) and click *OK*.

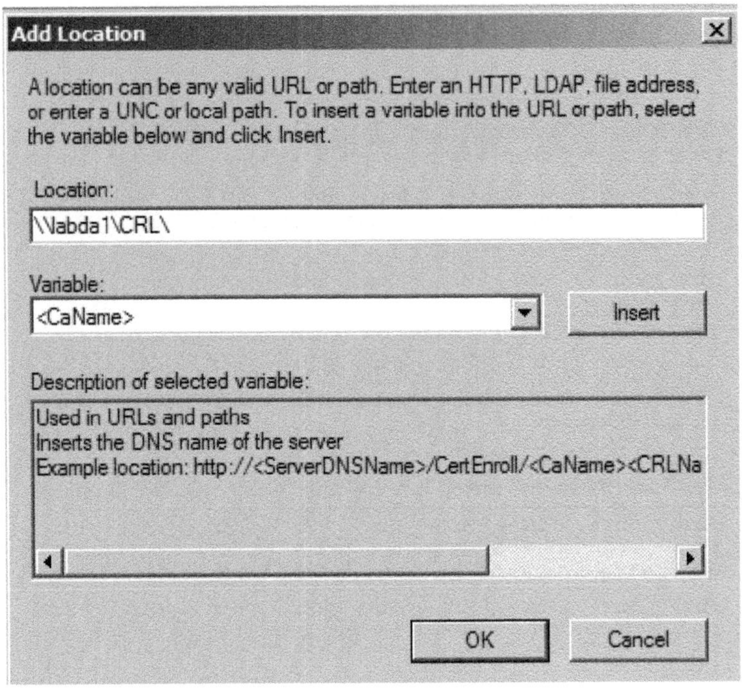

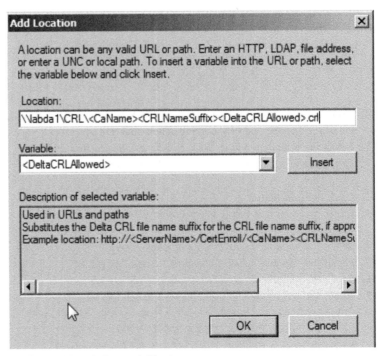

FIGURE 13.40 Location of CRL shared folder.

FIGURE 13.41 Newly Constructed CRL string.

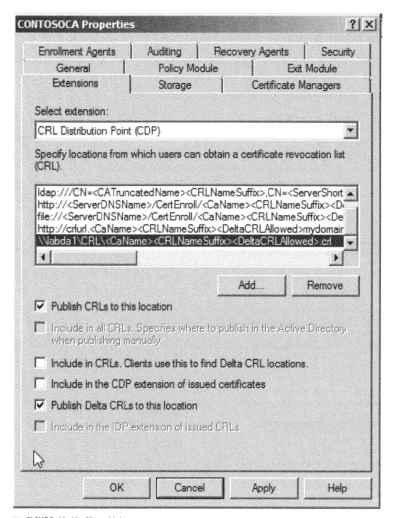

FIGURE 13.42 CRL publishing options.

20. When prompted to restart Active Directory Certificate Services, click *Yes*.
21. Expand the Certificate Authority node within Server Manager.
22. Right click on the *Revoked Certificates* node and select *All Tasks | Publish*.
23. Choose the option *New CRL* and click *OK*. This will publish the full CRL to the path, making it accessible via file share and the default Web site on the DirectAccess server.

Installing and configuring DirectAccess and network location server

You are now ready to install the DirectAccess and Network Location Server role services on the DirectAccess server. Perform the following steps to complete these tasks:

1. Open *Server Manager*.
2. Select the *Features* node and click *Add Features* link in the middle pane. This will launch the Add Features Wizard.
3. Select the *DirectAccess Management Console* feature (see Figure 13.43). If prompted to add the *Group Policy Management* feature, select *Add Required Features*. Then click *Next*.

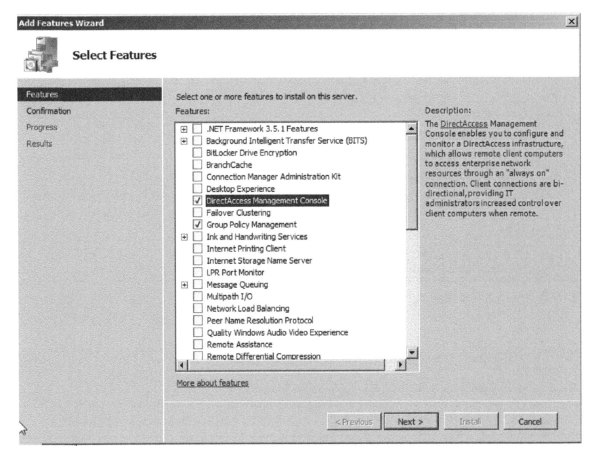

■ **FIGURE 13.43** Add DirectAccess Management Console Feature.

4. Click *Install* to install the selected features.
5. When the installation is complete, click *Close* to close the Add Features Wizard.
6. Open the DirectAccess Management Console from *Start | Administrative Tools | DirectAccess Management.*
7. Select the *Setup* node. You should notice a warning message indicating that the firewall is not configured to allow ICMPv6 Echo requests needed for Teredo. You will need to enable this on the local firewall and then access the management interface again.
8. Once you have enabled ICMPv6-Echo requests, the DirectAccess Management console setup node should display the configuration window as seen in Figure 13.44.
9. Click the *Edit* button under Step 1—Remote Clients.

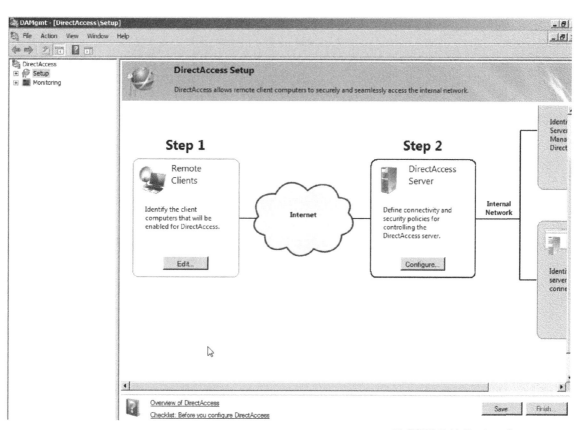

■ **FIGURE 13.44** DirectAccess Setup.

10. Add the Active Directory groups that contain computers you wish to allow to use DirectAccess. Then click *Finish*. You can create custom groups to limit DirectAccess usage only to computers you add to those groups.

11. Next click the *Configure* button under Step 2—DirectAccess server.

12. Designate which adapter will be connected externally facing the Internet. This is the adapter that inbound connections will connect to. Next designate the adapter to be used for communications to the internal local area network (See Figure 13.45). This is the adapter that the DirectAccess server will pass traffic from the outside to, so that it can access internal resources. After selecting adapters, click *Next*.

13. You now need to select the certificates that the DirectAccess server will use to provide connectivity (See Figure 13.46). You will need to select both the certificate of the certificate authority, and the local machine certificate used to secure DirectAccess communications. After selecting certificates, click *Finish* to complete Step 2.

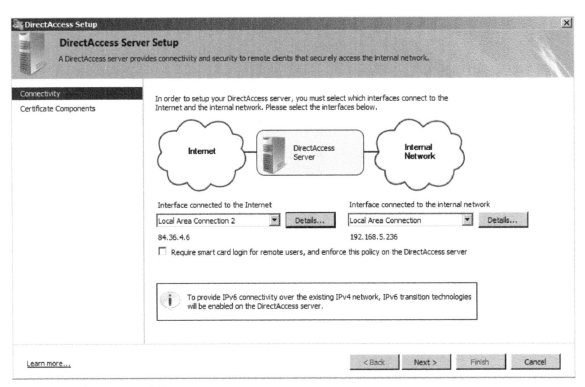

■ **FIGURE 13.45** DirectAccess Network Adapter configuration.

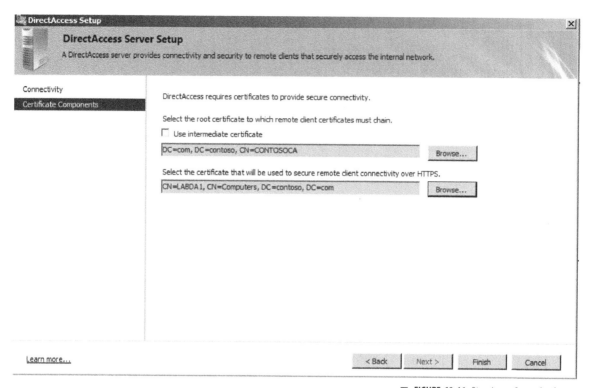

■ **FIGURE 13.46** DirectAccess Server Certificate selection.

14. Click the *Configure* for Step 3—Infrastructure Servers. The first option you need to configure is the location server. In our example, we installed the location server on the same server as DirectAccess. If the location server is collocated on the DirectAccess server, select the option *Network Location server is running on the DirectAccess server* and then select the certificate used to secure communications for the Network Location Server (See Figure 13.47). After selecting the Network Location Server click *Next*.

15. On the next screen, specify the DNS servers and domain controllers to be used by the DirectAccess server. After specifying DNS and DCs, click *Next*.

16. You can optionally specify the IP address or IP prefix of servers that can manage clients connected via DirectAccess. For example, you could enter the IP addresses of antivirus management servers and software deployment servers here. This will allow those servers

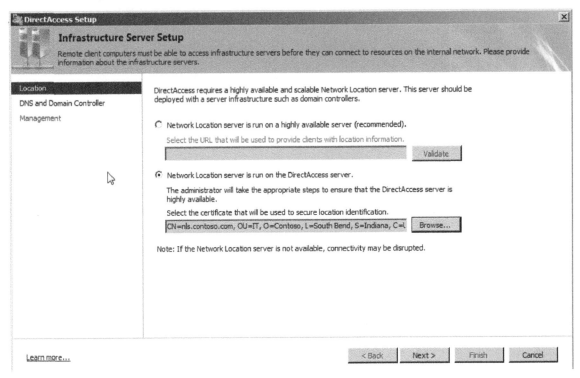

■ FIGURE 13.47 Network Location Server Certificate selection.

to initiate communications to DirectAccess connected clients. After entering the IP or IP prefix of management servers, click *Finish*.

17. Finally, you need to specify any application servers that you want to allow DirectAccess clients to connect to. Click *Configure* under Step 4—Application Servers.

18. If you want to provide end-to-end authentication, select that option and choose the domain groups that contain computers that DirectAccess clients should be able to access. If you do not need to provide full end-to-end authentication then select the option *Require no additional end-to-end authentication*. Then click *Finish*.

19. Now that you have completed all four configuration steps, click the *Finish* button on the main DirectAccess configuration page. You will be prompted with a DirectAccess review page. Verify all DirectAccess settings and click *Apply* as seen in Figure 13.48.

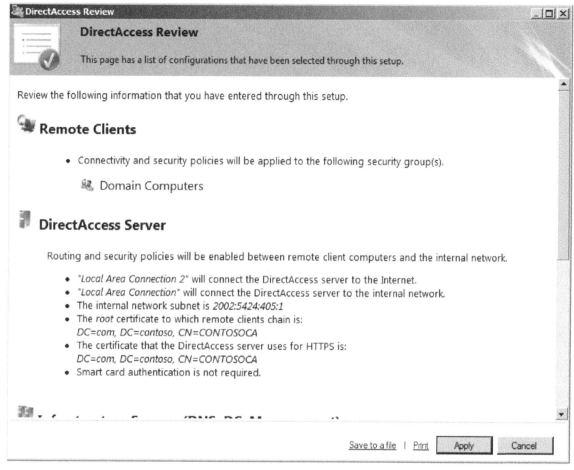

■ **FIGURE 13.48** Review DirectAccess configuration settings.

SUMMARY

In this chapter, we explored the new technologies included in Windows Server 2008 R2 and Windows 7 that allow the two operating systems together to provide better experiences for end users, including the ability to cache files locally in branch offices giving users quicker access when reading files. We also explored the DirectAccess feature giving users an always connected feature to provide them access to internal corporate applications and services, without the need to open a VPN connection.

14

Windows Server 2008 R2 delta changes

In this chapter, we will review the Windows Server 2008 R2 delta changes. The changes in this chapter are those that occurred between Windows Server 2008 R1 (RTM) and Windows Server 2008 R2 releases. If you have experience administering Windows Server 2008, this chapter will help you quickly gain an understanding of new enhancements offered in the R2 release. If you prefer reading individual chapters related to each of these features, the changes are also included in each feature's respective chapter. You may also find this chapter useful to review the new features that were previously introduced in earlier chapters of this book.

NETWORKING CHANGES

Windows Server 2008 R2 includes several new networking features to provide a better end-user experience and increase the security of your network. Two of the biggest network changes include the new services DirectAccess and BranchCache. We will introduce you to both of these services and additionally, network enhancements in this section.

DirectAccess

DirectAccess is a new feature introduced in Windows Server 2008 R2 and Windows 7. DirectAccess provides end users with constant, secure connectivity to the corporate network anytime an Internet connection is available and without the need for traditional VPN client software installed. This connection not only gives end users easy access to the company network but also provides systems such as configuration management and software distribution servers access to the PC. This is a Win-Win feature for end users and IT departments alike. DirectAccess is accomplished by creating a secure tunnel between the Windows 7 workstation and the Windows Server 2008 R2 network. We will be taking an in-depth look at DirectAccess in Chapter 13 as part of the Windows Server 2008 R2 and Windows 7 "Better Together" story.

BranchCache

BranchCache is a new feature in Windows Server 2008 R2 that allows branch offices to cache files from file servers and intranet Web sites locally to a branch office. With BranchCache enabled, the first time a file is accessed, it is copied across the Wide Area Network (WAN) and opened on the local computer. A cached copy is then saved on a server designated as the local cache or another client computer. The next time a computer tries to access the remote file, it is accessed via the branch office cache location instead of pulling the file across the WAN a second time. Figure 14.1 depicts a graphical overview of how hosted BranchCache works. BranchCache requires Windows Server 2008 R2 servers and Windows 7 clients. BranchCache is covered in-depth in Chapter 13.

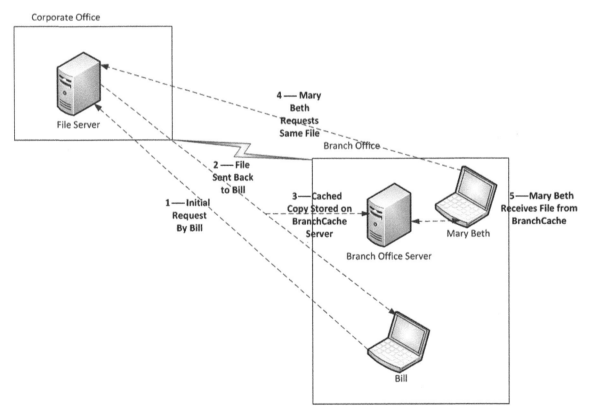

■ **FIGURE 14.1** Windows Server 2008 R2 BranchCache.

VPN Reconnect

VPN Reconnect is a feature that allows Windows 7 clients to automatically reconnect a dropped VPN connection due to intermittent loss of Internet connectivity. For example, you may be connected to an airport wireless network with multiple wireless access points. Typically moving from one access point to another could intermittently drop your Internet connection. This would result in you having to reconnect your VPN client, including reentering your username and password. A Windows 7 client using VPN Reconnect would automatically reestablish the VPN connection without you having to reenter your username and password. VPN Reconnect requires a Windows 7 clients and VPN connectivity via Windows Server 2008 R2 Routing and Remote Access Services.

DNS cache locking

Windows Server 2008 R2 introduces several new features to enhance the security of DNS. Included in these features is DNS cache locking. This feature allows an administrator to configure how often cached DNS entries are updated. When a Windows DNS server performs a recursive query, it caches a copy of the result locally. This allows future queries to be updated via cache instead of requiring the DNS server to perform the same query again. One of the risks of using this technology is the possibility of cache poisoning. This is where malicious DNS entries are brought into a DNS server's cache, which could redirect clients to malicious Web sites. DNS cache locking can help combat this risk by allowing the administrator to set a percentage of the time to live of the record, as the amount of time required before the cached copy can be updated. For example, the DNS administrator could set the cache locking to 80% of the time to live. This would mean that cached DNS records could not be updated until 80% of the time of live had passed. This is a global change per DNS server, meaning it cannot be set per zone or record. You can update the DNS cache locking percentage using the registry key HKEY_LOCAL_MACHINE\SYSTEM\CurrentControlSet\Services\DNS\Paramenters. A restart of the DNS service is required for any changes to take effect.

DNS Security Extensions

DNS Security Extensions (DNSSEC) is a new standards-based technology to help increase DNS security by using public key/private key technology to sign DNS records. A DNS server performing a recursive query of signed DNS zones will also receive a public key from the authoritative DNSSEC-enabled DNS server. The DNS server performing the query can use the public key to verify the validity of the results being returned. DNSSEC is supported by Windows Server 2008 R2 servers and Windows 7 clients.

Firewall profiles per network connection

Windows Server 2008 R1 and Windows Vista introduced the concept of Network Location. The Windows firewall could have different settings for different network types. For example, while connected to the domain network, the server could have more ports opened and less strict firewall rules than when connected to a public network such as the Internet. Servers with multiple network adapters connected to multiple networks could only use one profile, so the least restrictive profile would have to be used. Windows Server 2008 R2 resolves this issue by allowing administrators to configure individual firewall profiles for each network connection. This prevents you from having to lower firewall security for public networks while allowing all necessary connectivity for trusted networks.

ACTIVE DIRECTORY CHANGES

Active Directory (AD) was first introduced with the release of Windows 2000 Server. Most of the core functionalities have remained the same through Windows Server 2003, Windows Server 2008, and now Windows Server 2008 R2. However, with each release, Microsoft has made some performance improvements and added new features. In this section, we will take a look at some of the new AD features in Windows Server 2008 R2. Let us take a look at some of these new enhancements.

Active Directory Recycle Bin

AD now includes an undelete option known as the Recycle Bin. The AD Recycle Bin acts a lot like the Windows recycle bin we are all very familiar with. The AD Recycle Bin stores objects for 180 days (by default) after they are deleted from AD. This allows for easy full fidelity recovery of deleted AD objects using PowerShell commands. The one main requirement to use this feature is that your AD forest be in Windows Server 2008 R2 native mode, and all domain controllers in the domain need to be running Windows Server 2008 R2.

Offline domain join

Offline domain join is a new feature in Windows Server 2008 R2 and Windows 7 that allows you to join a computer to an AD domain without having connectivity to a domain controller. The offline domain join is a three-step process described subsequently:

1. The *djoin* command line tool is run on a Windows 7 or Windows Server 2008 R2 computer that is joined to the domain. The djoin/ provision option is used to provision a computer account for the computer for which you want to perform an offline domain join. This generates a file to be used by the computer that will be joining the domain.
2. The file is copied to the computer that will be joining the domain via offline domain join. The *djoin* command is run with the /requestODJ parameter. This will copy the offline domain join file to the Windows directory and instruct the computer to join the domain on boot.
3. Boot the computer when connected to the network hosting the AD domain. The domain join process will automatically join the computer to the domain.

The offline domain join process can be very useful when you are automatically deploying a large number of computers, or if you want to give someone the ability to join a computer to the domain, without them needing special privileges in AD. The following will walk you through the process to perform an offline domain join.

In this process, we will be using two computers. LABDC1 will be the domain controller hosting the contoso.com domain. Srv1 will join the LABDC1 domain using the offline domain join process.

1. Log on to the domain controller (LABDC1).
2. Open a command prompt and enter the command `djoin/provision/ domain contoso.com/machine Srv1/SaveFile C:\djoinprovision. txt` (see Figure 14.2). This command is telling the computer to run the djoin provisioning process for the contoso.com domain. Create a djoin file for the server Srv1 and save it as C:\djoinprovision.txt. After running the command, you should receive confirmation that the offline domain join file was created successfully.
3. You now need to copy the file to the computer you want to join to the domain. You can use any method you prefer to copy the file. We just need to have it on the machine that we want to join to the domain.
4. Log on to the server we want to join to the domain (Srv1). Check the computer properties to ensure that the computer is a member of a workgroup and not joined to the domain (See Figure 14.3).
5. Open a command prompt and run the command `djoin/requestODJ/ loadfile C:\djoinprovision.txt/Windowspath C:\Windows` (see Figure 14.4). This command is telling the computer that on next boot,

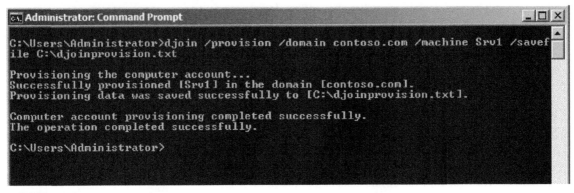

■ FIGURE 14.2 Provision computer and create offline domain join file.

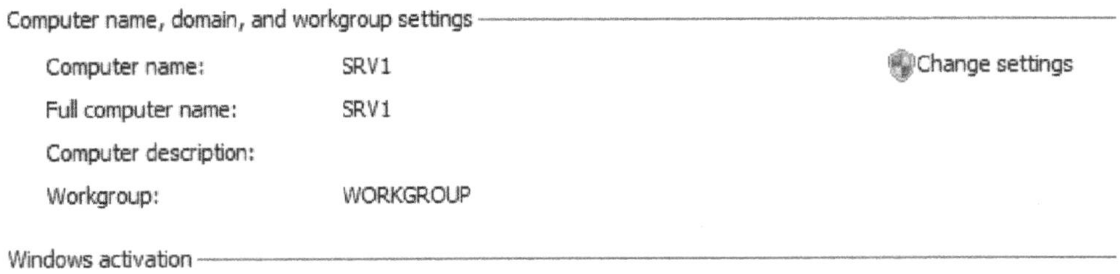

Computer name, domain, and workgroup settings		
Computer name:	SRV1	Change settings
Full computer name:	SRV1	
Computer description:		
Workgroup:	WORKGROUP	

Windows activation

■ FIGURE 14.3 Computer Properties.

it should join the domain using the information provided in the file C:\djoinprovision.txt. You should see a success message and a notice stating you must reboot the computer to enable it to complete the offline domain join process.

6. You can now power down or reboot the computer as you normally do after joining a computer to a domain. At this point, the computer is joined to the domain and needs to reboot for changes to take effect on the local machine.

7. Log on to the computer and view computer properties to verify it was indeed joined to the domain (see Figure 14.5).

Active Directory Best Practices Analyzer

AD now includes a best practices analyzer (BPA). BPAs for other Microsoft products have been around for several years. The most popular of these is the Exchange Server BPA. BPAs do exactly as their name

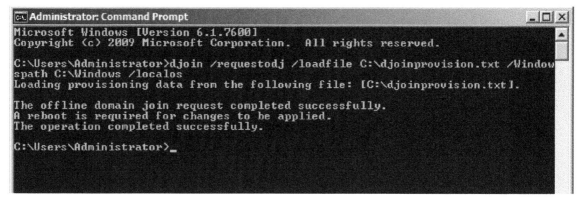

■ **FIGURE 14.4** Perform offline domain join process.

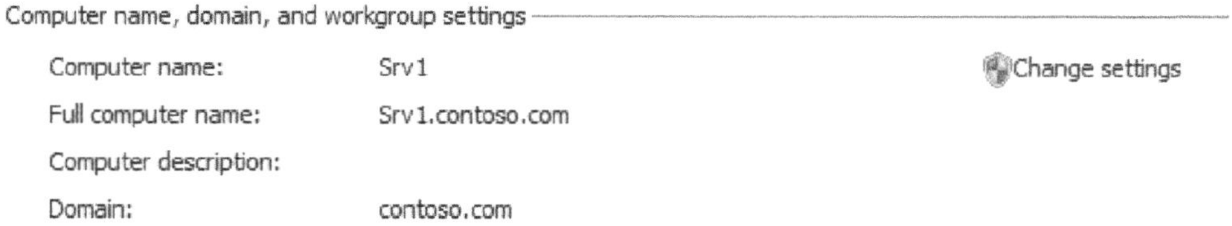

Computer name, domain, and workgroup settings ───

    Computer name: Srv1   Change settings

    Full computer name: Srv1.contoso.com

    Computer description:

    Domain: contoso.com

■ **FIGURE 14.5** Computer Joined to Domain.

implies. The BPA will scan your servers and analyze software configurations. It will then compare those configurations to a list of best practices provided by the Microsoft product group responsible for that particular piece of software. As an AD administrator, you should run the AD BPA not only after deploying AD but also on a regular basis postinstallation or when significant configuration changes have been made to your environment. Let us explore the AD BPA in more detail.

1. The AD BPA is automatically installed with the Active Directory Domain Services Role. You can access the BPA by selecting the AD node in Server Manager, then scrolling down to the BPA as seen in Figure 14.6.
2. To run the BPA, click the *Scan this Role* link. This will start a scan of the AD domain services on the server.
3. After the scan completes, results of the scan will be displayed inside the BPA window. You can immediately see any noncompliant configuration settings or warnings under the noncompliant tab. You

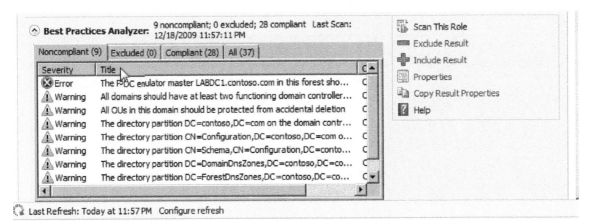

■ FIGURE 14.6 Active Directory Best Practices Analyzer.

can also click on any alert to see full details of the issue and how to resolve it (see Figure 14.7).

4. You can click the *Compliant* tab if you want to see the rules that were run in which the system was in compliance with best practices configurations.

5. The BPA can be rerun at any time from Server Manager. Run this tool and remediate any issues on a regular basis to ensure that your AD domain remains highly reliable and healthy.

Active Directory Web Services

Windows Server 2008 R2 AD includes Web services that provide remote management capabilities for AD. The AD Web services are primarily built to allow administrators to remotely administer AD using PowerShell. This allows you to send PowerShell commands to a remote domain controller from your local PC or other management server. Additionally, the AD Web services provide a way for developers to write applications that use the Web services to interact with AD.

Managed Service Accounts

Many applications and network services require the use of service accounts. These accounts are typically dedicated to a specific application and have passwords set to never expire. This ensures no accidental service disruption due to a password expiring. This, however, poses a security problem, especially for organizations which must comply with various

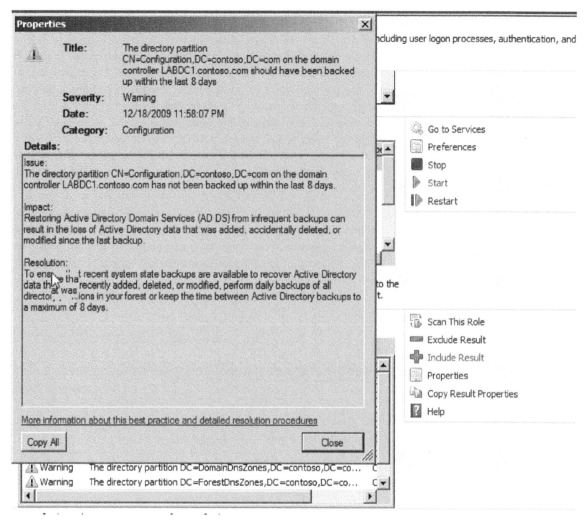

including user logon processes, authentication, and

Properties

⚠ **Title:** The directory partition CN=Configuration,DC=contoso,DC=com on the domain controller LABDC1.contoso.com should have been backed up within the last 8 days

Severity: Warning

Date: 12/18/2009 11:58:07 PM

Category: Configuration

Details:

Issue:
The directory partition CN=Configuration,DC=contoso,DC=com on the domain controller LABDC1.contoso.com has not been backed up within the last 8 days.

Impact:
Restoring Active Directory Domain Services (AD DS) from infrequent backups can result in the loss of Active Directory data that was added, accidentally deleted, or modified since the last backup.

Resolution:
To ensure that recent system state backups are available to recover Active Directory data that was recently added, deleted, or modified, perform daily backups of all directory partitions in your forest or keep the time between Active Directory backups to a maximum of 8 days.

More information about this best practice and detailed resolution procedures

Copy All   Close

- Go to Services
- Preferences
- Stop
- Start
- Restart

to the t.

- Scan This Role
- Exclude Result
- Include Result
- Properties
- Copy Result Properties
- Help

⚠ Warning   The directory partition DC=DomainDnsZones,DC=contoso,DC=co...
⚠ Warning   The directory partition DC=ForestDnsZones,DC=contoso,DC=co...

■ **FIGURE 14.7** Active Directory BPA warning.

government regulations. Microsoft has addressed this issue with a new feature known as Managed Service Accounts. Managed service accounts allows the AD to automatically manage the passwords and Service Principal Names (SPNs). AD will automatically manage and change the password on a regular basis and ensure that the service using the account gets the password update. A managed service account is created using the New-ADServiceAccount PowerShell cmdlet.

Active Directory Administrative Center

The new Active Directory Administrative Center (see Figure 14.8) provides a way for administrators to perform regular management tasks via an easy-to-use interface built on top of PowerShell. This means that as an administrator, you can use the GUI interface to perform a task and the GUI then makes a call to a PowerShell script or cmdlet to complete the requested task. Most of the same functions you perform in Active Directory Users and Computers (ADUC) can be performed in the new Active Directory Administrative Center rich GUI interface. Whether you are a new or seasoned Windows administrator, you will want to check out the new AD Admin Center.

ADAC provides enhanced features such as the ability to manage multiple domains from a single pane of glass, a comprehensive search, and an integrated password reset tool. You may choose to use this tool over ADUC for many of the common day-to-day administrative tasks for AD, such as resetting passwords or creating new user accounts. ADAC is accessed from the Administrative Tools folder in the Start Menu.

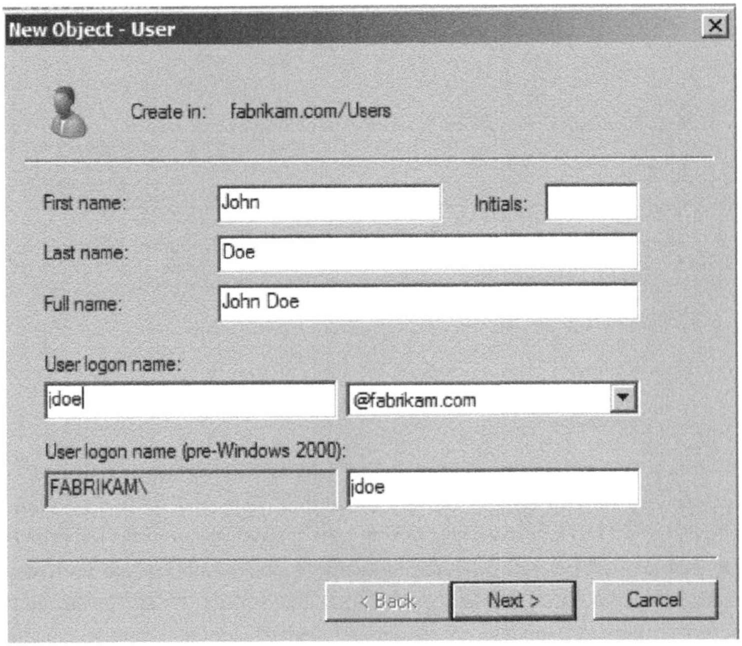

■ **FIGURE 14.8** Active Directory Administrative Center.

Active Directory Module for PowerShell

Windows Server 2008 R2 is the first Microsoft server operating system to include PowerShell as part of the standard OS installation. To go along with the built-in PowerShell functionality, Windows Server 2008 R2 includes a series of cmdlets to administer AD via PowerShell. Using the AD Module for PowerShell, you can use PowerShell to administer users, computers, groups, domains, and domain controllers.

The AD Module for PowerShell allows you to perform many of the core AD tasks from the PowerShell command line. By using PowerShell, you can easily automate common tasks or save scripts for future use. PowerShell also allows you to more easily update hundreds or thousands of accounts with a few simple commands. The following types of tasks can be performed within PowerShell with the AD Module loaded:

- User and Computer Account Administration
- Create and Administer Groups
- Create and Administer Managed Service Accounts
- Create and Administer Organizational Units
- Create and Administer Password Policies
- Manage the Forest or Domain
- Manage Domain Controllers
- Search for and Modify Objects in the Domain

Whether you are a "command line junkie" or new to PowerShell, the new module for AD could easily become one of your primary administrative tools. It could end up saving your hours of time by automating updates and streamlining the process to update mass numbers of objects. You can access the AD Module for PowerShell from the Administrative Tools folder in the Start Menu. The AD Module for PowerShell will be covered in-depth in Chapter 11.

Read-only SYSVOL for Read-Only Domain Controllers

In Windows Server 2008 R1 (RTM), the SYSVOL folder was writable on Read-Only Domain Controllers (RODC). Windows Server 2008 R2 now makes the SYSVOL folder read-only on RODCs.

FILE AND PRINT SERVICES CHANGES

Windows Server 2008 R2 introduces some new features and enhancements for file and print services. These new features provide better security, stability, and end-user experience. In this section, we will explore some of these new features and how you might use them on your network.

Read-only DFSR Replicas

Windows Server 2008 R2 allows administrators to set DFS Replication (DFSR)-based replicated folders to read-only. Using this feature, you can set up a central share with read-write access and provide read-only replicas to remote servers. This can allow administrators to easily publish files to various geographic locations, but ensure that remote users are only viewing files and cannot make updates to the remote copies.

File Classification Infrastructure

File classification is a new feature included in Windows Server 2008 R2. File Classification Infrastructure (FCI) allows administrators to classify files based upon folder or file type. Using these classification capabilities, administrators can then run reports or set retention policies on the file classes. Additionally, Windows Server 2008 R2 can automatically move files to an archive location after their retention periods have expired. This feature is added by installing the Windows Server 2008 R2 role service. For more info on setting up and managing FCI, see Chapter 10.

Print driver isolation

Windows Server 2008 R2 introduces a new print server reliability feature. Print driver isolation ensures that print driver functions run within their own processes. Prior to Windows Server 2008 R2, the driver functions and Windows print spooler ran in the same Windows process. If a poorly developed print driver crashed, it could bring down the entire print spooler service, resulting in the entire print server being unavailable. Using print driver isolation, an unreliable print driver no longer has any impact on the print spooler's process. This ensures that the print server remains online in the event an unreliable print driver fails.

Network scanner management

The new distribute scan management features in Windows Server 2008 R2 provide management and workflow features for network-based scanners. Using scan management, you can administer network scanners across your network from a single-pane-of-glass interface. Additionally, you can setup network scanners to perform workflow functions for scan jobs. For example, a user could log on to a network scanner and scan a legal document. The network scanner could then send the document to a scan management server, which could then route the document to a file server or SharePoint document library automatically.

INTERNET INFORMATION SERVER CHANGES

With the release of Windows Server 2008 R2, Microsoft has included a dot release of Internet Information Server (IIS) bringing the version to 7.5. IIS 7.5 on Windows Server 2008 R2 includes new administrative and security enhancements to further evolve and secure the popular Web server.

Request Filtering Module

The Request Filtering Module is introduced as an add-on extension for IIS 7.0 to allow administrators to block Web requests deemed harmful. Request filtering provides additional security to IIS by limiting the types of requests and commands that can be sent to IIS via the Web browser. IIS 7.5 now includes the module as a standard part of the Web server role.

Best Practices Analyzer

IIS 7.5 now includes a BPA. You should run the BPA after initial configuration and on a regular basis thereafter to ensure that your IIS deployment is healthy and optimally configured. We will look at the IIS BPA in greater detail later in this chapter.

PowerShell module

As with most roles in Windows Server 2008 R2, IIS 7.5 includes a PowerShell module allowing administrators to perform most administrative functions from the PowerShell command line. Administrators can use PowerShell to quickly perform IIS administrative tasks as well as automate the configuration of IIS for fast and standardized deployment of IIS Web servers.

Support for managed service accounts

You learned in Chapter 4 that Windows Server 2008 R2 AD allows administrators to create managed service accounts. Managed service accounts allow administrators to change the password of a service account without having to update each service using that particular account. IIS 7.5 application pools provide support for managed service accounts. For example, an IIS application pool could be running under the account IIS_Service. For security purposes, an administrator needs to change the password on this account. The administrator simply has to change the password of the AD account. Once the password has been changed, the IIS application pool will automatically update the password field to reflect the new password without administrator interaction.

Hostable Web core

The IIS engine itself can be hosted by other systems and applications. This gives developers the ability to include Web server functionality within their applications without having to write their own server. By using APIs they can leverage IIS directly inside their application code.

.NET support on server core installs

Windows Server 2008 R1 allowed IIS to be installed on a core install but did not support .NET. Windows Server 2008 R2 and IIS 7.5 now support the use of .NET in IIS Web applications running on a server core install of the operating system. .NET Framework versions 2.0, 3.0, 3.5.1, and 4.0 are supported.

HYPER-V CHANGES

Windows Server 2008 R2 includes several new enhancements to Hyper-V virtualization services. These enhancements include Live Migration, hot addition and removal of virtual disks, new processor features, and support for jumbo frames on virtual machines (VMs).

Live Migration

Windows Server 2008 R2 includes a much-welcomed feature to enhance the process of moving VMs from one Hyper-V host to another. Windows Server 2008 R1 includes a feature known as Quick Migration, which suspends VMs and quickly transfers them to another host. This process does, however, cause a brief outage to any VMs being moved. When using quick migration to move a VM, some applications on that VM may time-out and need to be restarted due to their sensitivity to network or machine disruptions.

Live Migration allows Hyper-V to overcome these limitations when moving VMs by removing the need for them to be temporarily suspended, thus removing downtime for applications running on the VM being moved. Live Migration uses a process to transfer memory pages from the current host to the destination host and then simply transfers ownership of the VM's virtual disks to the destination host. The Live Migration process is depicted in Figure 14.9.

Live Migration allows administrators to add easily, on the fly, new hosts to a Hyper-V cluster and instantly increase resources needed for VM workloads. Live Migration can also be used to allow administrators to service hosts during normal business hours without impacting business

Hyper-V Fail-Over Cluster

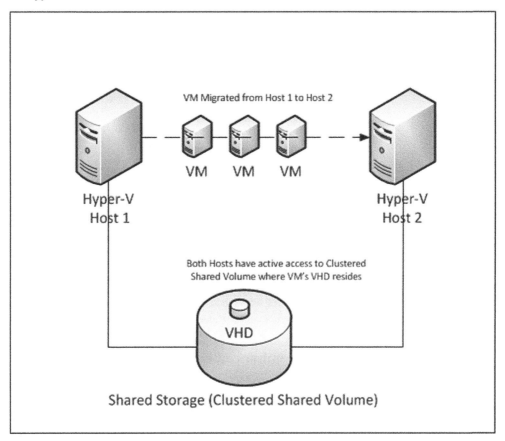

■ FIGURE 14.9 Hyper-V Live Migration Process.

services and applications. For example, an administrator might want to add additional memory to a Hyper-V host. He could use Live Migration to move any active VMs from the host to another host in the cluster. He could then turn off the host to add additional memory. After adding memory, the administrator could use Live Migration to move the VM workloads back to the host.

Live Migration requires that Hyper-V be deployed on a Windows Server 2008 R2 Failover Cluster. Additionally, Live Migration requires a dedicated network adapter on each Hyper-V host for migration traffic. It is also recommended that processors on all hosts are from the same manufacturer and of the same processor family. This ensures that all processor features can be used.

NOTES FROM THE FIELD

Live Migration and Hyper-V processor compatibility mode

Though it is recommended that all hosts in a Hyper-V cluster have the same processors, Windows Server 2008 R2 Hyper-V includes a new feature known as processor compatibility mode. Processor compatibility mode allows you to include computers with various processor types in a Hyper-V cluster. Processor compatibility mode turns off the features of newer processors so that all processors in the cluster use the same features as the processor with the least number of features. This allows you to add older hosts to Hyper-V clusters and will also cause newer hosts to run with a reduced set of processor features.

Processor enhancements

Windows Server 2008 R2 Hyper-V includes several new processor enhancements, including support for 32 processor cores per physical host. Hyper-V can also take advantage of Windows Server 2008 R2 Core Parking features. Hyper-V moves VM CPU loads to the fewest required number of processor cores and allows Windows to suspend the cores not being used. As workloads require more CPU resources, the cores are no longer suspended and Hyper-V moves VM workloads to those cores.

Storage enhancements

Windows Server 2008 R2 Hyper-V adds new storage features that allow administrators to easily add and remove VM storage. Hyper-V now allows administrators to add or remove virtual and physical storage hot, while the VM is still running. This feature allows administrators to easily reconfigure VM storage without requiring downtime. For example, assume that a production SQL server needs additional storage space for more databases. As the administrator, you can add a new virtual disk drive to store new databases without taking the server offline.

REMOTE DESKTOP SERVICES (FORMERLY KNOWN AS TERMINAL SERVICES) CHANGES

With the release of Windows Server 2008 R2, Terminal Services has been renamed Remote Desktop Services. If you have experience administering Terminal server in previous operating systems, you should be aware of the new Windows Server 2008 R2 names of various Terminal Server technologies. Table 14.1 lists the old versus new name for common Remote Desktop Services and admin tools.

Table 14.1 Common Remote Desktop Services and Admin Tools

Windows Server 2008 and Prior Name	Windows Server 2008 R2 Name
Terminal Services	Remote Desktop Services
Terminal Services Manager	Remote Desktop Services Manager
Terminal Server	Remote Desktop Session Host
Terminal Services Configuration	Remote Desktop Session Host Configuration
Terminal Services Licensing	Remote Desktop Licensing
Terminal Services Licensing Manager	Remote Desktop Licensing Manager
Terminal Services Gateway	Remote Desktop Gateway
Terminal Services Gateway Manager	Remote Desktop Gateway Manager
Terminal Services Session Broker	Remote Desktop Connection Broker
Terminal Services RemoteApp Manager	RemoteApp Manager
Terminal Services Web Access	Remote Desktop Web Access

Along with a new name, Microsoft has also added several new features to further enhance Remote Desktop Services. In this section, we will explore some of the feature changes to the various components of Remote Desktop Services.

Remote Desktop Session Host

The Remote Desktop Session Host role includes several new features to provide a better administrative experience as well as increased security for Remote Desktop Services deployments. Changes to Remote Desktop Session Host include:

- *Client Experience Configuration*—You can now centrally manage Remote Desktop audio/video redirection and Windows Aero interface options for Remote Desktop clients. These client experience features can be configured when adding the Remote Desktop Session host role.
- *Roaming User Profile Cache Management*—Larger Remote Desktop Services deployments may have hundreds or even thousands of users logging into Remote Desktop Servers. It is common to see cached copies of profiles using a lot of storage space on Remote Desktop Servers. To help control the disk space usage of cached profiles, a GPO can be applied to Remote Desktop Servers placing a quota on the

amount of disk space that can be used by cached profiles. If the quota is reached, the server will delete the profiles of users with the oldest last logon until the profile cache falls below the quota.

■ *Remote Desktop IP Virtualization*—Remote Desktop IP Virtualization allows administrators to create a pool of IP addresses allowing each remote desktop session to have a unique IP address. This feature is useful for applications that may require each instance to have a unique IP or when troubleshooting and you need to track the IP of a particular session on a remote desktop server.

■ *Enhanced CPU Scheduling*—Remote Desktop Services now includes a processor scheduling feature known as Fair Share Scheduling. This feature distributes CPU resources evenly across each Remote Desktop Session ensuring that one user session does not impact the performance of another user session. This scheduling is done automatically by the remote desktop server and does not require configuration.

Remote Desktop Virtualization Host

The Remote Desktop Virtualization Host is a new role included with Windows Server 2008 R2 Remote Desktop Services and provides a fully featured Virtual Desktop Infrastructure (VDI) solution for Windows. Remote Desktop Virtualization Host services allow administrators to set up pools of Hyper-V VMs that can be logged onto by users. Users can be assigned unique machines or assigned the next available machine in the pool. This gives users fully featured desktop computers accessible via a remote connection.

RemoteApp and desktop connection

Windows Server 2008 R2 further extends the features of RemoteApp to VDI-based virtual desktops. Windows Server 2008 R1 allows administrators to use RemoteApp to make access to Terminal Services-based applications seamless to end users. Users can launch an application shortcut from their local computer or terminal, and that application appears to launch locally instead of displaying a remote desktop session to the terminal server.

Windows Server 2008 R2, in conjunction with Windows 7, publishes available RemoteApp applications and Desktop Virtualization Host-based VMs to the Start Menu of Windows 7 clients. This allows end users to easily access applications and virtual desktops they have access to by simply opening them from the Start Menu on their local computer.

Remote Desktop Connection Broker

The Remote Desktop Connection Broker in Windows Server 2008 R2 now extends the broker capabilities to virtual desktops in a Remote Desktop Virtualization Host. As with previous versions of the sessions broker, the Remote Desktop Connection Broker provides load balancing and ensures that users reconnect to existing sessions after a disconnect. The Remote Desktop Connection Broker connects users to the new RemoteApp and Desktop Connection feature.

Remote Desktop Gateway

The Remote Desktop Gateway feature includes several new enhancements over the previous Terminal Services Gateway. The new Remote Desktop Gateway includes the following new features:

- Gateway level idle and session timeouts
- Logon and system messages
- Pluggable authentication
- Network Access Protection (NAP) remediation

Gateway level idle and session timeouts

This feature allows administrators to configure idle and session timeouts on the gateway itself. By setting these timeouts, administrators can ensure that unused sessions are disconnected and active users are forced to periodically reconnect.

Logon and system messages

Administrators can now configure special message windows to be displayed to users when connecting to a Remote Desktop Services Gateway. System messages can be used to provide active users with important notifications such as information regarding system outages. The Logon message can be used to provide users with important notifications every time they logon. These can be useful to advertise new applications or services available via the gateway.

Pluggable authentication

Pluggable authentication allows developers to write custom authentication modules for Remote Desktop Gateways. This can be used to further enhance Remote Desktop Gateway services by providing such features as Two-Token authentication.

Network Access Protection Remediation

NAP Remediation features allow computers connecting via a Remote Desktop Gateway remediate any noncompliant security settings prior to connecting to the network. This ensures that even computers connecting via Remote Desktop Gateways comply with corporate NAP policies.

Remote Desktop Web Access

Remote Desktop Web Access was first introduced in Windows Server 2008 R1 as Terminal Server Web Access providing users with a portal to view and connect to available RemoteApp-based applications within a Web browser. The new Remote Desktop Web Access feature includes the following enhancements over Terminal Service Web Access:

- Security trimmed RemoteApp filtering
- Forms-based authentication (FBA)
- Public and private computer options
- Single sign-on

Security trimmed RemoteApp filtering

Windows Server 2008 R1 Terminal Services Web Access displays any RemoteApp Web applications available on the system to all end users. This allows users to see RemoteApps even if they do not have access to them. Windows Server 2008 R2 Remote Desktop Web Access now security trims the interface so that users only see RemoteApp shortcuts they have access to.

Forms-based authentication

Remote Desktop Web access now offers the ability to provide FBA. This provides a more user-friendly logon page that users may be used to from other applications such as Outlook Web Access (OWA) in Microsoft Exchange.

Public and private computer options

Users can now specify what type of computer they are connecting from when logging into Remote Desktop Web Access. This provides more strict security settings when logging in from a public computer such as a kiosk.

Single sign-on

When using Terminal Server Web Access in Windows Server 2008 R1, users were prompted twice to logon to RemoteApps via the Web interface. They would be prompted once to access the Web access server and a second time when launching the application. Remote Desktop Web Access provides single sign-on so that users only need to initially logon to the Web access site. Credentials are then passed to the RemoteApp automatically.

Remote Desktop client experience

Several new features have been added to further enhance the Remote Desktop experience for Windows 7 client computers. Windows 7 clients connecting to a Windows Server 2008 R2 server gain these additional features:

- *Multiple Monitor Support*—Remote Desktop Services now support multiple monitors for Windows 7 clients. This allows RemoteApps to take advantage of multiple monitors in the same manner as if they were running as applications on the local computer.
- *A/V Playback*—Remote Desktop Services now redirects Windows Media Player-based A/V content to the client computer where it is played locally using that client computer's memory and CPU to view the content locally.
- *Windows 7 Aero*—Remote Desktop Sessions support Windows 7 Aero features when the connecting client is a Windows 7 computer.

Remote Desktop Services PowerShell module and Best Practices Analyzer

Remote Desktop Services now comes with more management features and options, including a PowerShell module and BPA. Using PowerShell, administrators can perform most Remote Desktop Services administration via a PowerShell command prompt.

The BPA helps administrators verify whether their Remote Desktop Services configuration is following best practices and that there are no misconfigurations that could negatively impact the deployment.

HIGH AVAILABILITY AND RECOVERY CHANGES

Windows Server 2008 R2 includes several features to further enhance high availability and backup services. These include new features such as PowerShell support for clustering and the ability to backup individual files and folders with Windows Backup.

Failover Cluster PowerShell support

Failover Clusters can now be set up and administered using PowerShell 2.0. This not only includes the new cmdlets for Failover Clustering but also the ability to remotely send commands to cluster services via PowerShell 2.0. With the added support for PowerShell, the cluster.exe command line utility is being deemphasized and may not be available in future releases of Windows.

Cluster shared volumes

Failover Clustering supports the use of Cluster shared volumes (CSV). These are volumes that can be accessed by multiple nodes of the cluster at the same time. This brings new benefits to Hyper-V deployments by providing Live Migration and a reduced number of LUNs required. Earlier in this chapter, we discussed how Live Migration allows you to move VMs between two hosts in a Failover Cluster with no downtime. CSV are what make this process possible.

Since previous versions of Windows could only have one host actively accessing the LUN, a fail-over would cause all VMs stored on a LUN to fail-over. Prior to Windows Server 2008 R2, Microsoft recommended that each VM in a Failover Cluster be assigned its own LUN to ensure that a single VM could fail-over. For many deployments, this resulted in a lot of LUNs being assigned to each Hyper-V host. Windows Server 2008 R2 removes this restriction using CSV allowing both hosts to access the volume and at the same time enabling a single VM on a LUN to fail-over without requiring over VMs on that same LUN to do the same.

Improved cluster validation

Windows Server 2008 introduced the Cluster Validation Wizard. By using this wizard, administrators could easily verify and set up a cluster ensuring it was in a supported configuration. If the cluster passed the validation wizard, it was considered to be in a correct configuration. Windows Server 2008 R2 adds additional tests to further ensure that a cluster can be validated using the Cluster Validation Wizard.

Support for additional cluster aware services

The Remote Desktop Connection Broker and DFSR can both be configured on a Failover Cluster to provide high availability and redundancy to these services.

Ability to backup individual files and folders

Windows Server 2008 R1 (RTM) backup did not have the ability to select individual files and folders to be backed up. This was a feature offered in previous versions of Windows such as Windows Server 2003. Windows Server 2008 R1, however, only provided the ability to backup a full volume. Windows Server 2008 R2 has brought back the feature to allow administrators to selectively choose which files and folders to include in a backup set.

SECURITY CHANGES

Windows Server 2008 R2 introduces new features to help ensure your network is more secure and protected. These new features include additions to existing services and entirely new applications and roles. In this section, we will discuss some of the security enhancements offered by the R2 release of Windows Server 2008.

DNSSEC support

As previously mentioned in this chapter, Windows Server 2008 R2 provides support for the standards-based DNSSEC. This technology is not proprietary to Microsoft and is being adopted by many DNS solution providers. DNSSEC helps ensure that DNS zones are more secure by offering public/private key signing of zones to help prevent man-in-the-middle attacks.

AppLocker

AppLocker is a new feature available in Windows Server 2008 R2 and Windows 7 to restrict which applications and scripts users can install on the system. AppLocker allows administrators to create rules based upon the file version, file name, publisher, and other attributes of the application. Using AppLocker, administrators can decrease the chances of malicious applications being installed and executed on the systems they manage.

Changes to Network Access Protection

Windows Server 2008 R2 NAP now allows administrators to implement multiple System Health Validators (SHVs). This allows different SHVs to be applied to different network policies. For example, an administrator could configure an SHV that requires that computers have all current windows updates and antivirus software to be installed. This SHV could then be applied to computers connected to the corporate network. The administrator could then configure a second SHV to require only antivirus software be installed and apply it to a network policy for computers connecting remotely such as via VPN.

Windows Server 2008 R2 also includes the ability to create Network Policy Server (NPS) templates. Administrators can now configure NPS settings and save them as a template. The template can then be used to deploy NPS policies without having to recreate all settings each time a new policy is needed.

Managed Service Accounts

It is a well-known best practice that account passwords should be changed on a regular basis. For years, administrators have struggled with performing password changes on service accounts because changing a password usually meant making configuration changes to the service itself. For example, by changing a password on a service account for an IIS Application Pool, the administrator would then need to logon to the Web server, open IIS Manager, and change the password settings of each application pool in which that password had been set. This not only caused huge administrative overhead, but sometimes resulted in forgotten app pools and Web applications experiencing service disruptions. As mentioned earlier in this chapter, Windows Server 2008 R2 now provides the ability to set up Managed Service Accounts. Managed service accounts allow an administrator to change a service account password without impacting services such as IIS application pools. If an administrator changes the managed service account password, the IIS application pool will automatically update its configuration with the new password.

New security auditing features

Microsoft has further expanded auditing capabilities in Windows Server 2008 R2. These include:

- Global object access auditing
- Reason for access reporting
- New audit categories can be enabled via GPO

Global object access auditing

In Windows Server 2008 R2, an administrator can globally audit object access to the file system or registry. This allows you to globally monitor access to the changes effected to the system no matter what settings are configured at the file and folder level.

Reason for access reporting

This feature allows you to review why a particular account was allowed or denied access to an object. For example, if a user was a member of a group that gave them access to a particular file, Reason for Access Reporting would indicate that this access was given because the user was a member of the group.

POWERSHELL CHANGES

Windows Server 2008 R2 includes the new PowerShell 2.0, providing new features, including remote management capabilities. Administrators can now send PowerShell commands to a server from a remote workstation or other server. Additionally, Windows Server 2008 R2 includes an expanded set of cmdlets to manage Windows Servers. In this section, we will take a look at some of the new features of PowerShell 2.0 on Windows Server 2008 R2.

Integrated scripting environment and debugger

Windows Server 2008 R2 includes the new integrated scripting environment (ISE) and fully functional debugger. The ISE is a GUI interface that provides script writers an easy way to create, edit, and validate PowerShell scripts. Using the ISE, you can also run the new debugger to perform common debug tasks such as the ability to step through code and add break points. If you write PowerShell scripts, you may want to familiarize yourself with the new ISE and debugger environments.

Background jobs

PowerShell now allows you to run commands in the background. This allows you to continue to work in the shell while a command is running. For example, you could issue a PowerShell command that could change a setting on 1000 AD accounts. Due to the number of accounts being updated, the command may take several minutes to complete. PowerShell will now allow you to continue issuing other PowerShell commands while the process to update the AD accounts completes.

Transactions

PowerShell now allows you to create transactions that can run a batch of scripts or commands as a single process, giving you the ability to commit or rollback mass changes. This is much like the behavior of SQL transactions.

Cmdlets for server administration

Windows Server 2008 R2 includes a large number of cmdlets for administering Windows Servers. In fact, an administrator can perform most administrative functions on a Windows Server 2008 R2 server using PowerShell 2.0. Providers and cmdlets have been written for most server roles, giving administrators the ability to automate common tasks and rapidly make configuration changes to hundreds or thousands of servers at once.

NOTES FROM THE FIELD

ServerManageCmd and PowerShell

ServerManagerCmd was introduced in Windows Server 2008 R1 (RTM) as a powerful command line utility to perform many common administrative tasks. Most of the ServerManagerCmd commands are now available in PowerShell 2.0 on Windows Server 2008 R2. With this in mind, Microsoft is deemphasizing the use of ServerManagerCmd and the utility may not be included in future releases of the operating system.

SUMMARY

In this chapter, we discussed the major changes released between Windows Server 2008 R1 (RTM) and Windows Server 2008 R2. This chapter provides current Windows Server 2008 administrators with a quick guide for identifying the new features and changes in Windows Server 2008 R2 from the previous operating system release. This chapter also provides reference to previous chapters allowing you to easily find content related to a new feature now available in R2.

Index

Note: Page numbers followed by *f* indicate figures and followed by *t* indicate tables.

Printed and bound by CPI Group (UK) Ltd, Croydon, CR0 4YY

03/10/2024

01040343-0004